Communications in Computer and Information Science 527

More information about this series at http://www.springer.com/series/7899

Gabriela Celani · David Moreno Sperling
Juarez Moara Santos Franco (Eds.)

Computer-Aided Architectural Design

The Next City - New Technologies and the Future of the Built Environment

16th International Conference, CAAD Futures 2015
São Paulo, Brazil, July 8–10, 2015
Selected Papers

Springer

Editors
Gabriela Celani
University of Campinas
Campinas, São Paulo
Brazil

David Moreno Sperling
University of São Paulo
São Carlos, São Paulo
Brazil

Juarez Moara Santos Franco
University of Campinas
Campinas, São Paulo
Brazil

ISSN 1865-0929   ISSN 1865-0937 (electronic)
Communications in Computer and Information Science
ISBN 978-3-662-47385-6   ISBN 978-3-662-47386-3 (eBook)
DOI 10.1007/978-3-662-47386-3

Library of Congress Control Number: 2015940732

Springer Heidelberg New York Dordrecht London

Printed on acid-free paper

Springer-Verlag GmbH Berlin Heidelberg is part of Springer Science+Business Media
(www.springer.com)

Preface

Since 1985, the Computer-Aided Architectural Design Foundation has fostered high-level discussions on the search for excellence in the built environment through the use of new technologies with an exploratory and critical perspective. In 2015, the 16th CAAD Futures Conference was held, for the first time, in South America, in the lively megalopolis of Sao Paulo, Brazil. In order to establish a connection to local issues, the theme of the conference was "The next city." The city of Sao Paulo was torn down and almost completely rebuilt twice, from the mid-1800s to the mid-1900s, evolving from a city built of rammed earth to a city built of bricks and then from a city built of bricks to a city built of concrete. In the 21st century, with the widespread use of digital technologies both in the design and production of buildings, cities are changing even faster, in terms of layout, materials, shapes, textures, production methods and, above all, in terms of the information that is now embedded in built systems.

Among the 200 abstracts received in the first phase, only 33 were selected for this book, after three tough evaluation stages. Each paper was reviewed by at least three different experts from an international committee of more than 80 highly experienced researchers. The authors come from 17 different countries. Among the papers, six come from Latin-American institutions, which have been usually under-represented in CAAD Futures; 34 other papers were selected for publication in the electronic proceedings and in Cumincad (cumincad.scix.net), where this book's abstracts are also displayed.

The papers in this book have been organized under the following topics: (1) modeling, analyzing, and simulating the city, (2) sustainability and performance of the built environment, (3) automated and parametric design, (4) building information modeling (BIM), (5) fabrication and materiality, and (6) shape studies. The first topic includes papers describing different uses of computation applied to the study of the urban environment. The second represents one of the most important current issues in the study and design of the built environment. The third topic, automated and parametric design, is an established field of research that is finally becoming more available to practitioners. Fabrication has been a hot topic in CAAD conferences, and is becoming ever more popular. This new way of designing and making buildings will soon start affecting the way cities look. Finally, shape studies are an established and respected field in design computing that is traditionally discussed in CAAD conferences.

The papers in this book cover three aspects of design computing: its origins, new research frontiers, and applications in practice. In a similar way, the conference keynote lectures were grouped into "CAAD in History," with Arivaldo Leão de Amorim (Brazil) and João Magalhães Rocha (Portugal), "CAAD in Research," with Axel Kilian (Germany/USA) and Jane Burry (UK/Australia), and "CAAD in Practice," with Milos Dimcic (Serbia/Germany) and Caroline Bos (The Netherlands).

The editors are very grateful to Professors Bauke de Vries and Tom Kvan, CAAD Futures' presidents, for their constant support throughout the entire process of evaluating papers for this book and preparing the conference. We also thank all the scientific committee members for their competent reviews and helpful comments to the authors, which resulted in the highest academic standard of the papers selected. Finally, the conference would not have been possible without the sponsorship of the following Brazilian public research foundations: the National Council for Scientific and Technological Development (CNPq), the Coordination for the Improvement of Higher Education Personnel (CAPES), and the Sao Paulo State Research Foundation (FAPESP, process number 2014/07186-5).

Hosting the CAAD Futures Conference was a great honor – we hope you enjoy reading this great selection of papers!

July 2015

Gabriela Celani
David Moreno Sperling
Juarez Moara Santos Franco

Organization

Scientific Committee

Bauke de Vries   Eindhoven University of Technology, The Netherlands
Tom Kvan   University of Melbourne, Australia
Mark Gross   The University of Colorado, USA

Organizing Committee

Gabriela Celani (Chair)   University of Campinas, Brazil
David Moreno Sperling   University of São Paulo, Brazil
   (Co-chair)
Juarez Moara Santos Franco   University of Campinas, Brazil
Jarryer de Martino   University of Campinas, Brazil
Maycon Sedrez   University of Campinas, Brazil
Elza Miyasaka   University of São Paulo, Brazil

Advisory Board

Arivaldo Leao Amorim   Federal University of Bahia, Brazil
Regina Coeli Ruschel   University of Campinas, Brazil

Homo Faber Exhibition Committee

David Moreno Sperling   University of São Paulo, Brazil
   (Chair)
Pablo C. Herrera   Peruvian University of Applied Sciences, Peru
Rodrigo Scheeren   University of São Paulo, Brazil
Rafael O. Sampaio   University of São Paulo, Brazil
Rafael G. de Almeida   University of São Paulo, Brazil

Workshops

Pedro Veloso (coordination)   Carnegie Mellon University, USA

Support at the School of the City

Ana Carolina Tonetti   School of the City
Ligia Velloso Nobre   School of the City

Support at Mackenzie Presbyterian University

Wilson Florio   Mackenzie Presbyterian University, Brazil

Program Committee

A. Benjamin Spaeth   Xi'an Jiaotong Liverpool University, China
Adriana Granero   Universidad de Buenos Aires, Argentina
Aleksander Asanowicz   Bialystok University of Technology, Poland
Alfredo Stipech   Universidad Nacional del Litoral, Argentina
Anand Bhatt   ABA-NET, India
Andrew Li   Athlone Research, Japan
Anetta K.-Walczak   Lodz University of Technology, Poland
Anja Pratschke   University of São Paulo, Brazil
AnnaLisa Meyboom   University of British Columbia, Canada
Arivaldo Amorim   Federal University of Bahia, Brazil
Arthur Lara   University of São Paulo, Brazil
Athanassios Economou   Georgia Institute of Technology, USA
Axel Kilian   Princeton University, USA
Bauke de Vries   Eindhoven University of Technology, The Netherlands
Bige Tuncer   Singapore University of Technology and Design,
                                  Singapore
Birgül Çolakoğlu   Yıldız Technical University, Turkey
Bob Martens   Vienna University of Technology, Austria
Branko Kolarevic   University of Calgary, Canada
Charles Vincent   Mackenzie Presbyterian University, Brazil
Chengyu Sun   Tongji University, China
Chengzhi Peng   The University of Sheffield, UK
Christian Tonn   Kubit GmbH, Germany
Christiane M. Herr   Xi'an Jiaotong-Liverpool University, China
Daniel Cardoso   Federal University of Ceará, Brazil
David Moreno Sperling   University of São Paulo, Brazil
Dirk Donath   Bauhaus University Weimar, Germany
Edison Pratini   University of Brasilia, Brazil
Eduardo Hamuy   University of Chile, Chile
Eduardo S. Nardelli   Mackenzie Presbyterian University, Brazil
Emine Mine Thompson   Northumbria University, UK
Emrah Türkyılmaz   Istanbul Kultur University, Turkey
Fabio Duarte   Catholic University of Paraná, Brazil
Frank Petzold   Technical University of Munich, Germany
Gabriela Celani   University of Campinas, Brazil
Gerhard Schmitt   ETH Zürich, Switzerland
Gideon Aschwanden   ETH Zürich, Singapore
Gilberto Corso Pereira   Federal University of Bahia, Brazil
Giuseppe Pellitteri   Università di Palermo, Italy
Gulen Cagdas   Istanbul Technical University, Turkey

Guohua Ji	Nanjing University, China
Hartmut Seichter	University of Applied Sciences Schmalkalden, Germany
Henri Achten	Czech Technical University in Prague, Czech Republic
Henriette Bier	Delft University of Technology, The Netherlands
Hyoung-June Park	University of Hawaii at Manoa, USA
Ih-Cheng Lai	Tamkang University, Taiwan
Jakob Beetz	Eindhoven University of Technology, The Netherlands
Jeremy Ham	Deakin University, Australia
Jie He	Tianjin University, China
Joachim B. Kieferle	Hochschule RheinMain, Germany
Johan Verbeke	University of Leuven, Belgium
John Gero	University of North Carolina, Charlotte/George Mason University, USA
Jos van Leeuwen	The Hague University of Applied Sciences, The Netherlands
Luís Romão	Lisbon University, Portugal
Luiz Amorim	Federal University of Pernambuco, Brazil
Marc Aurel Schnabel	Chinese University of Hong Kong, SAR China
Marcelo Bernal	Technical University Federico Santa María, Chile
Marcelo Giacaglia	University of São Paulo, Brazil
Marcelo Tramontano	University of São Paulo, Brazil
Michael Mullins	Aalborg University, Denmark
Mike Knight	University of Liverpool, UK
Mine Ozkar	Istanbul Technical University, Turkey
Nancy Diniz	Rensselaer Polytechnic Institute/CASE, USA
Ning Gu	The University of Newcastle, Australia
Oliver Neumann	University of British Columbia, Canada
Oliver Tessmann	KTH Stockholm, Sweden/TU Darmstadt, Germany
Pablo C. Herrera	Peruvian University of Applied Sciences, Peru
Pedro Soza	University of Chile, Chile
Pedro Veloso	Carnegie Mellon University, USA
Rabee Reffat	Assiut University, Egypt
Regiane Pupo	Federal University of Santa Catarina, Brazil
Regina Ruschel	University of Campinas, Brazil
Rodrigo G. Alvarado	Bío-Bío University, Chile
Sherif Abdelmohsen	American University in Cairo, Egypt
Sigrid Brell-Cokcan	Association for Robots in Architecture, Austria
Sotirios Kotsopoulos	Massachusetts Institute of Technology, USA
Stefan Krakhofer	City University of Hong Kong, SAR China
Sule Tasli Pektas	Bilkent University, Turkey
Sylvain Kubicki	Public Research Centre Henri Tudor, Luxembourg
Taysheng Jeng	National Cheng Kung University, Taiwan
Thomas Grasl	SWAP Architects, Austria
Thomas Kvan	University of Melbourne, Australia
Thorsten Loemker	ZAYED University Dubai, United Arab Emirates

Tomohiro Fukuda	Osaka University, Japan
Tuba Kocaturk	University of Liverpool, UK
Volker Koch	Karlsruhe Institute of Technology, Germany
Volker Mueller	Bentley Systems, USA
Werner Lonsing	Independent Researcher, Germany
Wilson Florio	Mackenzie Presbyterian University, Brazil
Yeonjoo Oh	Samsung Construction, Republic of Korea

Sponsors

National Council for Scientific and Technological Development CNPq, Brazil

Coordination for the Improvement of Higher Education Personnel CAPES, Brazil

Sao Paulo State Research Foundation FAPESP, Brazil

Contents

Automated and Parametric Design

Building Information Modelling (BIM)

Fabrication and Materiality

Shape Studies

Modeling, Analyzing
and Simulating the City

The Next City and Complex Adaptive Systems

Justyna Karakiewicz[✉], Mark Burry, and Thomas Kvan

University of Melbourne, Melbourne, VIC, Australia
{Justynak,Mark.burry,tkvan}@unimelb.edu.au

Abstract. Urban futures are typically conceptualized as starting anew; an urban future is usually represented as a quest for an ideal state, replacing the status quo with visionary statement about 'better' futures. Repeatedly, propositions reinvent the way we live, work and play. The major urban innovations for the changing cityscape from the last 100 years, however, have opportunistically taken advantage of unprecedented technical developments in infrastructure rather than be drawn from architectural inventions in their right, such as telecommunications, services, utilities, point-to-point rapid transit including the elevator. Howard's Garden City therefore presaged the suburb, just as Le Corbusier et al. proposed the erasure of significant sections of inner city Barcelona and Paris to replace them with the newly contrived towers; the city reformed as the significantly more mobile and dense 'Ville Radieuse'. More recently Masdar emerged from virgin sand and Milton Keynes from pristine pasture, serving as counterpoints to the paradigm of erasure and rebuild. Despite all these advances in technology and science, little has changed in the paradigm of urban form; the choices we have today are largely restricted to the suburban house or the apartment in the tower. Should the "next city" offer an alternative vision for the future, and what new design processes are required to realize the next city?

Keywords: Urban futures · Complex adaptive systems · Parametric urbanism

1 Introduction

Urban futures are typically conceptualized as starting anew. As Socrates observed: *"...artists will not start work on the city nor will draw up the laws unless given a clean canvas, or have cleaned it themselves."* Classically, an urban future is represented as a quest for an ideal state, replacing the status quo with visionary ideas about better futures, and often the outcome is a place of suspended evolution, a stasis of time and place that seeks to freeze change at a perfect moment, as Dostoevsky described St. Petersburg when he wrote of it as an *"abstract and intentional city"*. As he noted, *"there are intentional and unintentional cities"* with the inference that it is in the latter that a citizen finds satisfaction [1].

Repeatedly, urban propositions reinvent the way we live, work and play. It might be argued, however, that the major urban innovations from the last 100 years have opportunistically taken advantage of unprecedented technical developments in infrastructure rather than be drawn from architectural inventions in their own right. Principal drivers

© Springer-Verlag Berlin Heidelberg 2015
G. Celani et al. (Eds.): CAAD Futures 2015, CCIS 527, pp. 3–20, 2015.
DOI: 10.1007/978-3-662-47386-3_1

for the changing cityscape include telecommunications, services, utilities, point-to-point rapid transit, and the invention of the elevator.

Ebenezer Howard's ideas for the newly minted 'Garden City' therefore presaged the suburb just as Le Corbusier et al. proposed the erasure of significant sections of inner city Paris or Barcelona in order to replace them with the newly contrived towers; the city reformed as the significantly more mobile and dense 'Ville Radieuse'. Significant new cities such as Masdar have emerged from virgin sand and Milton Keynes from pristine pasture serve as counterpoints to the dominant paradigm of erasure and rebuild.

Despite all advances in technology and science, little has changed in the paradigm of urban form; the choices we have today are still largely binary, the suburban house or the apartment in the tower. Should the "next city" offer another vision for the future, and what new design processes are required to bring the next city into being? Will we have to once again erase what we already have to rectify our past mistakes or could we try softer approach, something similar to acupuncture? How do we start and how might technology help us to create anew?

2 Urban Acupuncture

Over 100 years ago American architect and planner, Daniel Burnham, directed construction of the 1893 World's Columbian Exhibition which inspired the City Beautiful Movement. He also proclaimed:

> 'Make no little plans. They have no magic to stir men's blood. Make big plans; aim high in hope and work' [2].

Just as Haussmann had intervened in Paris 40 years earlier (1853–1870), Burnham was looking for the healthy new city with wide avenues and boulevards, parks and squares in order to improve the quality of urban life. Both Burnham and Haussmann encountered considerable opposition yet today the concept of discrete interventions that trigger large changes within the urban structure is often the preferred strategy for city mayors around the world, either as point attractors or as pathways cutting across the fabric. This strategy is often referred to as an acupuncture technique that in theory should be performed quickly and cheaply without the need for political drivers. In the reality leaders such as mayors and city architects are the ones who are needed to make the acupuncture succeed.

2.1 Acupuncture in Rome

Although not named as such, an early example of the urban acupuncture strategy can be found in the 16th century with the work of Pope Sixtus V and architect Dominico Fontana. In 1585, when Cardinal Montalto became Pope as Sixtus V, he acted immediately to transform Rome from a dilapidated, disorderly city into a vibrant and elegant city, a fitting capital for Christendom.

By 1585 a substantial part of Rome was in ruins [3]. The former capital of the Roman Empire was deserted, even with its many monumental architectural structures and churches. While he was on the throne for fewer than 5 years, Sixtus V put in place an organisational structure for the city that continues to influence the way Rome functions and grows. Figure 1. Together with Fontana, Sixtus V reinvented the city. From being static, Rome was conceived as a network of urban spaces as nodes articulated by obelisks that had been brought from Egypt during the Roman expansion a few centuries earlier. Edmund Bacon described the intervention as

> "not manipulation of mass but articulation of experience along an axis of movement through space" [4].

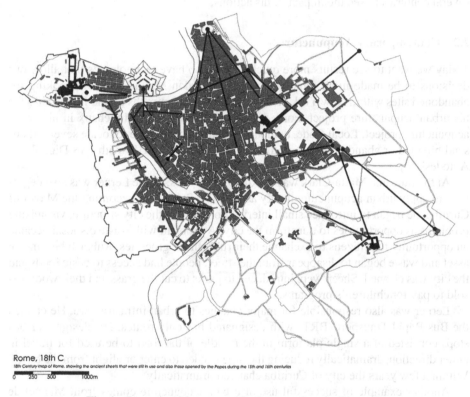

Rome, 18th C
18th Century map of Rome, showing the ancient streets that were still in use and also those opened by the Popes during the 15th and 16th centuries
0   250   500   1000m

Fig. 1. Rome in 18th century after interventions by Sixtus V

The obelisks were placed in strategic positions: next to the city gate, in front of churches and at other key points. Straight roads connected these points and allowed for clear visual axes that, in turn, promoted movement. Pilgrims could readily orientate themselves knowing that the obelisks would direct them towards the churches they wanted to visit. In all, seven major churches were connected this way. Pedestrian movement encouraged economic activity and people started to build houses and businesses along these routes.

The flow of pilgrims became a generator of urban form. From 1585 to 1590 Sixtus V managed to place only a few obelisks but his strategy was followed over subsequent centuries. One of the obelisks that Sixtus V ordered was the Flaminio obelisk, brought to Rome by Emperor Augusto in Piazza Popolo, the main northern entrance to the city. The obelisk was sited in 1589 outside Saint Peter's basilica, initiating a period of reconstruction by Bernini between 1656 and 1667 although the final shape of the piazza was not completed until Valadier reconstructed it in 1834.

In this example, we observe that Sixtus V created a lever point in the urban development. Holland [5] defines lever point as *"points at which small effort can produce a desired, directed effect. A little change makes a big difference and a small shift a big change"*. The obelisks achieved the desired end, the reconstruction and revitalisation of Rome. Sixtus V identified the points at which to intervene within the system but it took several centuries to see the impact of his actions.

2.2   Contemporary Acupuncture

Today we want to see results more quickly. We also have technologies that allow our decisions to be made more rapidly too. When Gordon Matta-Clark was looking for abandoned sites within New York in 1970s, it took him 3 months to find fifteen sites for his urban acupuncture project. Forty years later, Nicholas de Monchaux in his urban acupuncture project, Local Code, demonstrated that he was able to locate several thousand blighted or abandoned sites within few minutes, using GIS with JAS Digital and Autodesk [6].

At the time that Matta-Clark was looking for the sites, Jaime Lerner was also beginning to apply urban acupuncture theory as well [7]. Soon after becoming the Mayor of Curitiba, he began to introduce small interventions within the city structure, visualising problems as opportunities to transform the city. A problem with waste disposal became an opportunity for citizens to exchange their rubbish for groceries. Rubbish became an asset and waste began to disappear from the street; people had access to basic foods and the city was cleaned. Sheep were introduced to parks to cut the grass and their wool was sold to pay for children's programs.

Lerner was also responsible for major changes to urban infrastructure. He created the Bus Rapid Transport (BRT) with designated bus-only routes. His designs for bus stops consisted of a single platform in the middle of the road to be used for travel in either direction, dramatically reducing the time needed to enter or alight from the buses. Within a few years the city of Curitiba changed dramatically.

Another example of successful use of urban acupuncture comes from Manuel de Sola Morales. His interpretation of urban acupuncture comes a little bit closer to real acupuncture. The basic concept is in *"understanding city in terms of relation between space and time, rather than seeing it as finished design"* [8]. Just as needles are used in acupuncture to relieve stress in the body, he believes that urban acupuncture interventions relieve stress in the environment.

The metaphor of urban acupuncture continues to be used around the world. In most examples these are not small changes like needles but the metaphor is useful to describe substantial changes brought about by strategic intervention in urban systems. Sixtus V's insertion of obelisks in Rome was a clear example of needles, literally and metaphorically, but the beneficial consequences were observable only after a considerable period, perhaps hundreds of years. The interventions by Lerner, Casagrande and Sola-Morales demonstrate that positive change is possible in a comparatively short time span. These examples illustrate that for urban acupuncture to have an impact on city structure, the intervention has to trigger more than one change within the surrounding area, prompting the system in which it sits to reconfigure itself.

This is therefore more than acupuncture for which its main focus is on making sure that the system is able to operate without stress or disturbance. Acupuncture promotes a healthier city but rarely creates anything that is actually new. In this respect, the obelisks in Rome were slightly different: as 'attractors' they initiated slow but fundamental changes to the urban structure as lever points initiating growth and changed Rome from a dilapidated city to a thriving metropolis. It allowed Rome to undergo what in system theory is called 'change of regime'.

3 Urban Acupuncture and Complex Adaptive Systems

As described above, the power of Sixtus V's interventions lay in his ability to find lever points acting as attractors within the city, points at which to intervene in a system to obtain a magnified consequential effect. In the case of Rome, the points were sited adjacent to major churches in Rome. The obelisks were landmarks, visible at a distance, allowing pilgrims to Rome to identify destination points. In turn, they encouraged pedestrian travel and thus the creation of straight roads from one point to another. Movement between these points enabled businesses to appear along the way. People started to build new buildings and new public spaces were created. Rome as we know it today is result of these small intervention created by Sixtus V more than 400 years ago. The effects of the lever points that Sixtus V acted upon in Rome can now understood using Complex Adaptive Systems (CAS) theory.

Holland [9] suggests that cities and ecosystems share certain characteristics that allow us to conceptualise cities as CAS, which we understand as systems lacking in centralised control, never settling into permanent structures and constantly adapting to the new environment [10]. The application of CAS in the way we analyse and conceptualise cities has created a major shift in the way we think about cities. We now acknowledge that the static models that we have been using are no longer adequate. Even though we describe cities as CAS (or urban ecologies), we still have very little understanding about interactions and feedback systems between ecosystem dynamics and human intervention [11, 12]. We lack a clear understand of the models we should use for cities. Can we use models derived from nature or do we need to search for very different kinds of model?

As referred above, the concept of urban acupuncture can help us to promote a healthier city but, without a leveraged change, the city under our investigation will still operate as the same system - it will need many years or even centuries to reconfigure itself to something new. We are now aware that the existing systems for city operation are not adequate and need to change. The challenge then is how we can create positive change when we are unable to describe the future definitively.

Using traditional urban models we have thought that we could predict outcomes if we make certain decisions. We were confident that we were able to model the present with precision and therefore we were in a good position to predict the future [13]. In this our actions were governed by a cognitive and rational paradigm where inputs produce connected, predictable changes in outputs. CAS theory is now increasingly engaged to understand the social systems including cities [14]. In describing complex and unstable systems, CAS models do not predict the future definitively, instead they enable us to explore a variety of potentialities. In 1999, Epstein [15] argued that complex modelling is generative by definition and therefore it is not a technique for creating fully-fledged definitive models with strong predictive capabilities, but rather a strategy for generating possible model structures and showing their consequences.

4   Approaches to Urban Modelling

Parametric modelling has moved from the fringes to more mainstream in many architectural schools over the past 20 years. In many ways parametric modelling is proving to be very useful in allowing us to move from traditional paradigms of form following function and traditional form-prioritised modelling in urban design and planning to one of engaging with conflicting multi-criteria design parameters that require trading-off as part of the quest for optimal outcome, especially performance. Parametric modelling is deployed to search for design approaches beyond urban form to improve the lives of its citizens, addressing non-formal design facets such as improved air circulation, reduced pollution at the street level, more pleasant shadow patterns created by buildings, greatly reduced heat island effects, energy harvesting [16]. But these methods still rely on 'controlling' individual design parameters towards achieving the desirable effects through the manipulation of independent data (often through a two-dimensional spread sheet).

Although this approach has allowed architects to propose more relevant formal solutions and outcomes in recent decades, and to improve the urban environment by adding these new structures, such a form-oriented approach still is disposed to favour our preconceptions and is informed by a rather narrow understanding of the world around us. Agent-Based Modelling, however, can help us explore the potential not only to develop a broader understanding of the world around and the needs of the future cities' stakeholders – its citizens, but also give us opportunity to visualise things that will not be possible using just parametric modelling alone.

4.1   The City Modeled as a Complex System

Our understanding of interactions, feedback loops, learning processes and emergence phenomena are still relatively poor, and our actions in policy making, land use, planning and urban design risk being far less successful as a result. Although good progress has been achieved in modelling multi-agent human and ecological systems, there is still a lack of modelling that integrates human, ecological and urban systems [17, 18]. Complex Adaptive Systems (CAS) theory and agent-based modelling applied from a more bottom-up approach may be able to help us to redefine a wholly multi-disciplinary, theoretical framework for studying, analysing and conceptualizing the future more sustainable next city.

In applying CAS we understand systems that are open, non-linear, and unpredictable with emergent properties, thereby recognizing city behaviour as an emergent phenomenon [19, 20]. This in turn will enable us to maintain *"characteristics of the system that support the ecosystem and human function, i.e., resilience"* [9]. Instead of achieving a specific condition of fixed parameters including density, functional mix, population, heights, etc. We might understand cities more completely and build their performative attributes into the design rather than by tailoring their urban design through prescriptive regulation.

This is very different approach to ones we have been using. Most of our problems today are result of our assumption that systems under our investigation are stable. This led us to concept of static models close to equilibrium. CAS theory believes that systems under our investigation are not linear and they are far from equilibrium. Models are therefore unlikely to be able to predict the present or the future. At this point we come to one of the biggest obstacles. Our minds still demand that we must validate everything in order to determine some sort of certainty or truth. We are afraid of uncertainty and we are still uncomfortable in taking risk, forgetting that it is the certainty that often paralyses and prevents us from innovating. We are trained to test our theories against data; we do this often by specifying casual structures in which independent variables are used to explain dependent variables.

A further challenge with application of CAS is that:

"nonlinear relationship among variables – a hallmark of CAS – can go undetected if only traditional statistical methods are used" [21].

Critical information can easily be lost when values of parameters are averaged, or certain elements are dismissed, based on the assumption that they have no impact on system behaviour. In reality, however, it may be the case that the elements we eliminate from the model conceal temporal phenomena that are otherwise critical to overall system behaviour. Furthermore, many if not most of the situations contain more than we are able to test.

The question we address in the following section of this paper is: can CAS theory help us to attain a greater understanding of the present and allow us to identify the 'urban acupuncture' lever points that could initiate sufficient disturbance in an urban system and lead to regime shift?

5 A Case Study in Venice

In 2011, the first author led a design studio based on an urban analysis of Venice, Italy, with a focus on parametric modelling and applied CAS theory. Students were requested first to analyse Venice not by applying typical planning and urban design analysis but rather through using the concept of CAS as a framework for discovery. Students were asked to describe the morphological changes of the city structure in Venice both graphically and in text so as to trace possible reasons for today's crisis. The focus here was related primarily to the morphological changes of the city structure three centuries.

In the model of Cycle of Adaptive Change (Fig. 2) the process of distraction and reorganization, which often are neglected in favour of growth or conservation, are taken into account and embedded in the overall dynamic cycle.

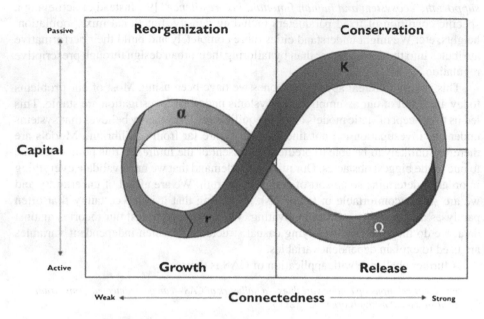

Fig. 2. Cycle of Adaptive Change (source Hollings 1986)

This dynamic cycle consists of four phases: growth, conservation, collapse/release and reorganization [23]. The growth phase is described as a period of rapid accumulation of resources (capital), competition and sizing opportunities, combined with high but decreasing resilience. In the conservation phase, growth is slowing down and resources are stored to be used for system maintenance. This phase is characterized by stability and certainty, which leads to reduced flexibility and lower resilience. In the next phase of creative destruction, chaotic collapse and the release of accumulated capital occur; certainty is replaced by uncertainty and resilience is increasing. The fourth phase of reorganization is characterised by extreme uncertainty when innovation and resilience are very high. In this model, our default desire for certainty is being questioned. It is clear from the model that certainty is not advantageous and can be paralysing; conversely, uncertainty can lead us to creativity and innovation.

Figure 3, developed in this class by Pablo Montero, describes sequential changes in the development of Venice using the Cycle of Adaptive Change as a model [22]. The figure traces changes from the early beginnings of Venice in the eighth century, illustrating the regime shifts of Venice and how complexity leads into adaptive cycles in which the city state transforms from a state of near collapse into thriving power. In this example we can see how in moments of high uncertainty, Venice has innovated and reconfigured to a different form, exhibiting a regime shift. This was not a certain process and required constant innovation, including reconfiguration of the lagoon.

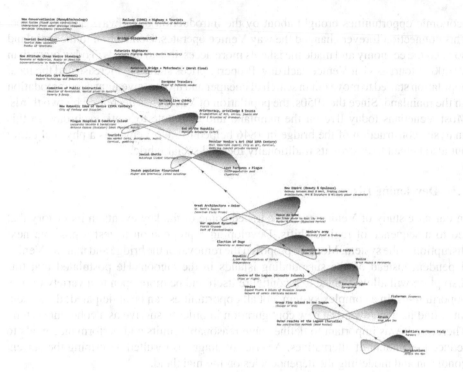

Fig. 3. The Adaptive Cycle of Venice (source: Montero 2011)

We can observe similar phenomena in many cities around the world. Sometimes major disruptions to the system are necessary in order for a system to reconfigure itself and thrive again. We can also observe this frequently whereby we are otherwise disinclined to try and meddle with the status quo through a fear of change and what could be dramatic negative consequences. As Peter Allen and Paul Torrens write:

> "A society that does not accept the reality of risk but only the satisfaction of blame will bring early fossilisation on itself. Exploring, innovating and experimenting will always present some risk, but without them there will be no learning, no contextual adaptation of learned procedures" [24].

Recognising this, we are also very much aware of the fact that today's problems often spring from yesterday's solutions. While we may believe that we have managed to fix a problem, short-term solutions give us short-term improvement but they do not necessary eliminate underlying problems, addressing the symptoms rather than the cause. In our case study of Venice, tracing reasons for the current crisis generates an extensive list of possible causes. Therefore instead of looking at all possible current problems, we decided to focus on what was the last major disruption, or lever point, that led to a regime shift.

As Fig. 3 shows, it was the building of the bridge to connect Venice to the mainland that can be considered as the next lever point that led to major regime shift in Venice history. The bridge was constructed in 1846 in order to allow Venice to partake of the economic opportunities brought about by the introduction of railways across Europe. This connection forever changed the way Venice operates. Connection to the mainland boosted the economy and made the islands more accessible to tourists. Today more than 60,000 of tourists visit Venice each day. Property prices started to increase and the local population started to move out in search of cheaper and more convenient accommodation on the mainland. Since the 1950s, the population of Venice has decreased by two thirds. Most Venetians today live on the mainland and commute to work each day. In this analysis, construction of the bridge in 1846 helped to save Venice as a physical entity but also helped to destroy its traditionally focused social fabric.

5.1 Developing Disruptions

In our case study of Venice, we have traced some of the key events in its history that led to a sequence of regime shifts. Developing a proposition to test a possible next disruption to the system, Montero proposed the removal of the bridge and making Venice dependent instead on the surrounding islands in the lagoon. He postulated that this disruption will allow Venice to reconfigure itself and be more open to a variety of new opportunities. In a complex system, not all opportunities can be anticipated; the system must find its way towards a new configuration in order to survive as a coherent system. Therefore it was important to define some reasonable limits and performance goals to reduce the amount of alternatives. A series of diagrams resulted describing the current condition and modelling the dependencies on the mainland.

Assumptions were made on possible incremental changes; these included relocating the existing Venetian population from the mainland to new developments in the lagoon, estimating quantities of food, water and other essential products necessary for maintaining reasonable lifestyles in the lagoon - including an estimation of the quantity of goods that could be produced in the lagoon and the amount that would otherwise need to be imported. Based on this data a series of diagrams were proposed and tests conducted in order to identify new networks, new interactions and new interdependencies.

The starting point was to understand existing connections and functions of existing islands as well as their areas of influence. Figure 4 illustrates existing connections in between the islands and the mainland. Red and yellow dots represent islands well connected by vaporetti (water buses) and water taxis. Green dots represent isolated islands that are not connected by public transport.

There are four clusters of these disconnected islands: one in the north of the lagoon, two to the south, and the largest cluster, included disconnected islands of Sant Angelo della Polvere, San Giorgio in Alga, Tresse, San Secondo, Campalto, Tessera, Carbonera and Buel del Lovo, lying parallel to the mainland acting as a buffer separating the mainland and lagoon. At the first stage, Montero intervened in the buffer zone only (Fig. 5) and used the function of human brain as a metaphor which, in order to develop (learn something new), rearranges the way it is interconnected by creating new synapses. In each there is a small gap, the synaptic cleft, and brain pathways are strengthened through repeated use. With this metaphor, connections in Venice are enhanced as disconnected islands increase their participation and influence. The influence of each island arises from their functional contribution that can be enhanced by adding functions and facilities

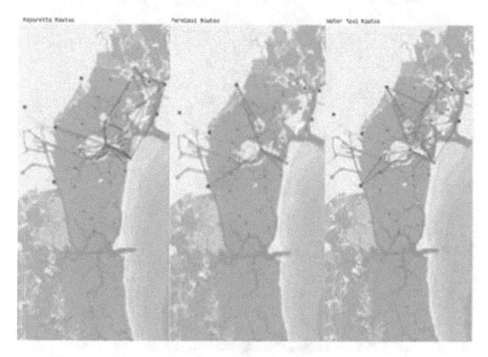

Fig. 4. Connections between islands and the mainland (source: Montero 2011)

missing from the Lagoon but available on the mainland. Thus the next step was to inventory functions to identify those needed to allow Venice to function without reliance on the mainland, and to locate them such that the system could perform more efficiently than previously (Fig. 5).

Using Rhino™ with a Grasshopper™ plug-in, Montero developed models in which functions and connections were established based on the proximity of the islands of the lagoon and their areas of possible influence. This established relationships between components and the opportunity to observe their response to variations of data input thus allowing for further adjustments to the models and playing through the incremental changes emanating from the regime shift of severing the connection to the mainland [21, 25].

In this analysis, it was identified that the existing islands within the lagoon did not provide sufficient area to accommodate all the residential population and the related services, food and goods production to make Venice interdependent. Therefore extra islands needed to be developed as they have been previously in Venetian history and their positions, areas of influence and corresponding new networks were explored. Figures 6, 7 and 8 illustrate how the system for creation of the new islands was carried out using Grasshopper™ scripting. Flocking rules were applied to explore locations and relationships as defined by these rules, with system components able to adapt, change their functions or behaviour patterns. The concept of flocking rules was derived from C. W. Raynold:

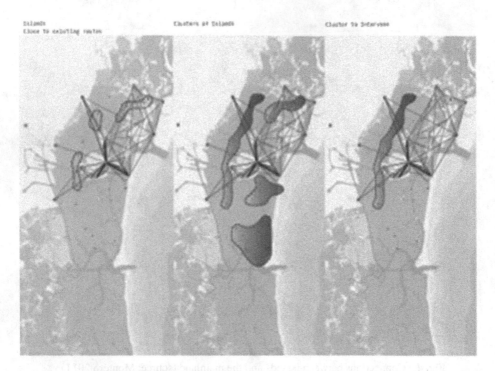

Fig. 5. Choosing the area to intervene (source: Montero 2011)

"Basic flocking systems define asset of desired relationships between elements in a flock such as ideal distance between elements and preferred position relative to other elements and keeping that rule and distance by readjusting their proximity continuously" [26].

Obviously flocking rules have limitations in this situation since new islands will need to fix their locations and cease flocking. As an exploratory tool, however, the approach allowed for their locations and proximity of functions, populations and frequency of transport to be modified and readjusted during testing (Fig. 8).

It was also proposed that an alternative approach could engender punctuated novelty [19] by encouraging the processes of creation for some new islands, new networks, new flows, and new hybrids. It is possible that punctuated novelty could result in a regime shift and therefore precipitate incremental novelty including the elimination of the bridge. Is creative destruction more effective than punctuated novelty? While a speculation, through the analysis in Fig. 9 we can postulate that Venice in the current situation is trapped in a conservation phase that has artificially extended and the only way to move out of this phase is by creative destruction.

CAS can be influenced by internal and external constraints guided by particular laws and frameworks [27]. As noted by Wootton:

"Cities will essentially evolve from state to state as a result of changing behaviour patterns of agents. Cities as a whole evolve by changing in size and prosperity, and clear cycles in wealth and condition of cities can be observed over many years" [28].

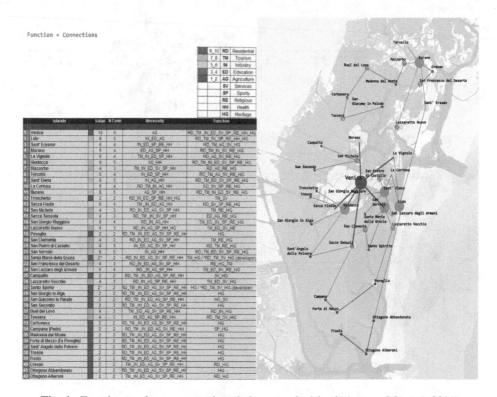

Fig. 6. Functions and new connections in between the islands (source: Montero 2011)

However, creative destruction is necessary occasionally in order to introduce a lever point that will lead to more rapid regime shift instead of allowing the system to artificially extend the conservation phase. In the case of Venice, the increase in residential population, necessary to serve ever increasing numbers of tourists in the past century has been achieved by expansion to mainland, particularly Mestre. This could be compared to any other city expansion through development of new suburbs and peripheries. With CAS this can be treated as an external transformation, difficult to control and, most of the time, it leads to unsustainable urban form. The alternative could be reuse of land inside the city creating an internal evolution. In Venice the historical areas cannot be easily densified. Land is no longer affordable for the local population and the quality of life poor.

An alternative approach needs to be found in order to keep the population in closer proximity to the city centre with similar if not better living conditions than offered by the short commute to the mainland. By removing the bridge and cutting connection to the mainland, densification of the lagoon remains the only option. This needs to be supported with adequate transport facilities and new urban morphologies that could offer better quality of life. Facilitating population growth within the lagoon, supported by new functions being constantly added and readjusted, will allow for internal transformation. In some ways this internal transformation can only happen if the bridge does not exist any longer. If the bridge remains in place as a link to the mainland the possibility of the

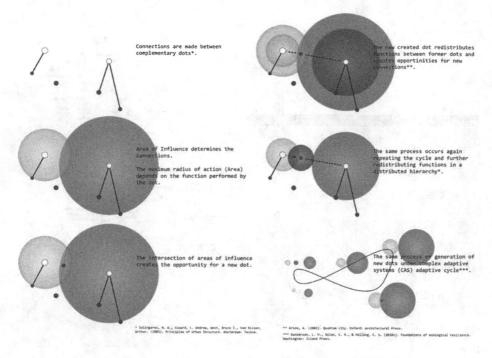

Fig. 7. Creation of new islands (source: Montero 2011)

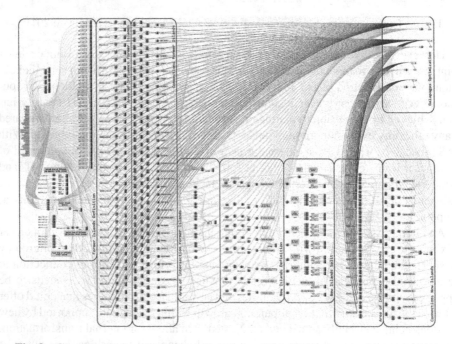

Fig. 8. Creation of new islands using Grasshopper™ scripting (source: Montero 2011)

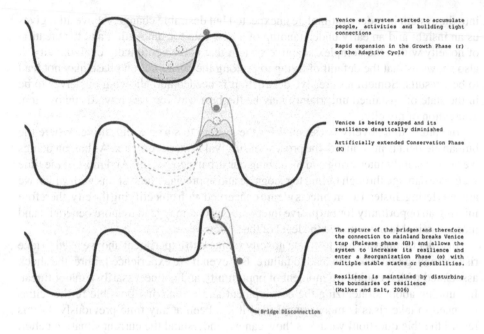

Fig. 9. Reinterpretation of resilience diagram (source: Montero 2011)

lagoon going through the regime shift will be minimal. Creation of the new islands will probably never happen, because the need for them may never crystalize; we can therefore reasonably assume that Venice will seek to survive again by prolonging the conservation phase.

6 Discussion

Applying CAS theory to the approach we are taking to envisage future cities has led to major changes in the way we perceive, analyse and respond to the world around us. This has required us to stop focusing as architects solely on isolated parts of urban development challenges and become increasingly involved in multidisciplinary practice.

Our understanding of the role of CAS theory in urban contexts is still developing, however, and often we have to reduce the situation to simple systems tailored both to our limited understanding and the limitations of the digital tools available to us. As a result urban designers also tend to stay away from testing possible major disturbances and instead we restrict ourselves to testing what we already know. Testing what we already know can still offer up unpredictable outcomes and surprises, which can allow us to learn more about the limitations of existing practices. Most often it allows us to at least commence the shift to a different paradigm [29]. A clear path to regime shift or system reorganization is still missing.

Our Venice case study that trialled the application of CAS theory not only helps us to understand resilience of our cities but also helps provide us with some guidance of where and how to introduce what might ultimately prove to be a well-judged disturbance into the system in order to stimulate unexpected but desirable change. Above all it gives us an insight and an early understanding of a new role for innovation and the creation of novelty within the complex adaptive system that is the continually evolving city. It also shows us that the default of trying to prolong the conservation phase may not lead to best results. Sometimes creative destruction is needed and allowing ourselves to be in the state of sustained uncertainty may be the best way forward towards innovation, or creation of novelty.

In nature, this novelty is essential for the system to survive and thrive. Where the human element is introduced, the process of survival is more complex. As human beings we are constantly interfering and disturbing our urban ecosystem. And most of the time we create damage through failing to recognise and appreciate the systems with which we are interfering. Instead as architects we are concerned with objectifying the city, therefore missing an opportunity for purposive interventions that may lead to more beneficial and more sustainable outcomes at the level of the system.

In order to innovate and to create novelty we need to experiment and we need to take risks knowing that risks can lead to failure. But even if we experience failure, the shock associated with it could be a moment of opportunity and not necessarily a major threat. In thinking about strategizing the development and visualizing possible further cities the need to take risks is more crucial than it has been at any time previously. In this regard the 'big question' we ask is 'how can we understand the current situation better, and what alternative methods can we use to improve our knowledge?' The knowledge gained from complex adaptive system models is difficult to validate, since it is based on uncertainty but, as we know, the knowledge gained from old models such as traditional parsimonious models (which were easy to validate) have turned out to be less than useful. Although CAS does not provide us with knowledge that can be validated, we can at least examine opportunities previously unimaginable.

In this paper, the case study of Rome was used to describe how small interventions into the urban structure not only helped to regenerate Rome, but also completely changed the way we perceive our cities, from controlled objects to something that exhibits emergent properties derived from movements, flows, and actions and interactions between its citizens. By conceptualising the city as a system of dynamic processes, Sixtus V intervened with relatively small insertions that allowed for dramatic changes and the reconfiguration of the whole city structure. We can argue, therefore, that Pope Sixtus V made Rome more resilient to decline as a city. The change was very slow and the city itself has not changed that much: more an evolution than revolution. It took years, centuries in fact, for us to appreciate how these small disturbances influenced and positively changed the whole of the system.

The second case study of Venice modelled the islands along CAS theory, illustrating how repeated introductions of disturbances over centuries allowed Venice to make regime shifts and change from a state of recession to one of economic power. Venetian resilience has been based on its great ability to reconfigure itself constantly into something new. Could this have been achieved only by the introduction of a major disturbance? Or could we achieve the same goals with small but much more highly targeted disturbances?

7   Conclusion

In this paper we have demonstrated that our early experiments in applying CAS theory already show positive potential as a novel approach to considering alternative designs for cities of the future but we recognise that this approach introduces yet another problem when dealing with improving the resilience of our cities. As Allen and Torrens [30] postulated:

> "... our previous academic goals of seeking 'objective knowledge and absolute truth' have to be relinquished. However, what it is that we should seek in its place is not clear, nor is the nature of the new relationship between Science and Society that we should expect".

Our research encourages us to analyse cities as complex adaptive systems with trans-continental boundaries and to seek lever points for change. The focus is to develop our capacity to understand the consequences of induced change through the agency of CAS theory; generating such questions as will changes to the urban design paradigm take effect and be lasting or will it be a mere perturbation, looking less towards forecasting and increasingly more towards helping us understand the world around us and promote a debate [31]. Underlying this is the question of extent and intent: should we be seeking to assist an urban system remain in its existing stage of development (the *status quo*), or go to work on testing the introduction of disturbances that promote regime shift, leading to differentiation, the addition of punctuations and potentially unscripted bene-ficial effects. *"[I]t is because systems can evolve and transform themselves that we can have hopes and dreams for better things"* [32].

References

1. Dostoevsky, F.: Notes from Underground. Epoch, St. Petersburg (1864)
2. Burnham, D.H.: Architect, Planner of Cities, vol. 2, p. 147. Houghton Mifflin (Burnham, D.H. (1907) quoted in: C. Moore (1921))
3. McBrien, R.P.: Lives of the Pope. HarperCollins, London (2000)
4. Bacon, E.: Design of Cities. Penguin, London (1976)
5. Holland, J.: Biology's gift to complex world. Sci. Exploring Life Inspiring Innov. 22(9), 36–43 (2008)
6. Monchaux, N. et al.: Local code: the critical use of geographic information systems in parametric urban design. In: Proceedings of ACADIA Life in: Formation, New York, NY (2010)
7. Lerner, J.: Urban Acupuncture. Island Press, Washington, DC (2014)
8. Casagrande, M.: Cross-over architecture and third generation City. Epifanio 9 (2008)
9. Holland, J.: Hidden Order: How Adaptation Builds Complexity. Addison-Wesley, Redwood City (1996)
10. Lansing, S.J.: Complex Adaptive Systems. Annu. Rev. Anthropol. 32, 183–204 (2003)
11. McDonnell, M., Pickett, S. (eds.): Human as Components of Ecosystems: The Ecology of Subtle Human Effects and Populated Areas. Springer, New York (1993)
12. Alberti, M., Marzluff, J.M., Shulenberger, E., Bradley, G., Ryan, C., Zumbrunnen, C.: Integrating humans into ecology: opportunities and challenges for studying urban ecosystems. Bioscience 53(12), 1169–1179 (2003)

13. Hwang, S.W.: The implications of the nonlinear paradigm for integrated environmental design and planning. J. Plan. Lit. **11**, 167–180 (1996)
14. Innes, J.E., Booher, D.: Consensus building and complex adaptive systems. J. Am. Plan. Assoc. **65**(4), 412–423 (1999)
15. Epstein, J.M.: Agent-based computational model and generative social science. Complexity **4**, 41–60 (1999)
16. Karakiewicz, J.: Air quality, social space and urban form: a case study of mong kok railway station. In: Proceedings from Conference on Technology and Sustainability in the Built Environment. King Saud University Press, Riyadh (2010)
17. Wooldridge, M.: An Introduction to MultiAgent Systems. Wiley, Chichester (2002)
18. Salamon, T.: Design of Agent-Based Models. Bruckner Publishing, Repin (2011)
19. Gunderson, L.H., Holling, C.S. (eds.): Panarchy: Understanding Transformations in Human and Natural Systems. Island Press, Washington, DC (2002)
20. Portugali, J.: Self-Organization and the City. Springer, Berlin (2000)
21. Burton, S.: Chaos, self-organization, and psychology. Am. Psychol. **49**, 5–14 (1994)
22. Hollings, C.S.: Surprise for science, resilience for ecosystem, and incentives for people. Ecol. Appl. **6**, 733–735 (1996)
23. Hollings, C.S.: Resilience of ecosystems; local surprise and global change. In: Clark, W.C., Munn, R.E. (eds.) Sustainable Development of the Biosphere, pp. 292–317. Cambridge University Press, Cambridge (1986)
24. Allen, P.M., Torrens, P.M.: Knowledge and complexity. Futures **37**(7), 581–584 (2005)
25. Schnabel, M., Karakiewicz, J.: Rethinking parameters in urban design. Int. J. Archit. Comput. **5**(1), 84–98 (2007)
26. Clarke, C., Anzalone, P.: Architectural applications of complex adaptive systems. In: Klinger, K. (ed.) ACADIA 22 Connecting – Crossroads of Digital Discourse, pp. 324 – 335. Ball State University, Indianapolis, (2003)
27. Manesh, S.V., Massimo, T.: Sustainable urban morphology emergence via complex adaptive system analysis: sustainable design in existing context. Procedia Eng. **21**, 89–97 (2011)
28. Wootton, B.: Cities as complex adaptive systems (2004) http://www.generation5.org/content/2004/complexCities.asp
29. Gonzales, J.: Rethinking the galapagos island as complex social-ecological system: implication for conservation and management. Ecol. Soc. **13**(2), 13 (2008)
30. Allen, P.M., Torrens, P.: Knowledge and Complexity (introduction) in Futures 37, pp. 581–584 (2005) www.sciencedirect.com
31. Batty, M., Torrens, P.: Modelling Prediction in a Complex World in Futures 37, pp. 745–766 (2005) www.sciencedirect.com
32. Allen, P.M., Strathern, M.: Models, Knowledge Creation and Their Llimits in Futures 37, pp. 729–744 (2005) www.sciencedirect.com

A Platform for Urban Analytics and Semantic Data Integration in City Planning

Achilleas Psyllidis[✉], Alessandro Bozzon, Stefano Bocconi,
and Christiaan Titos Bolivar

Delft University of Technology, Delft, The Netherlands
{A.Psyllidis,A.Bozzon,S.Bocconi,C.TitosBolivar}@tudelft.nl

Abstract. This paper presents a novel web-based platform that supports the analysis, integration, and visualization of large-scale and heterogeneous urban data, with application to city planning and decision-making. Motivated by the non-scalable character of conventional urban analytics methods, as well as by the interoperability challenges present in contemporary data silos, the illustrated system – coined SocialGlass – leverages the combined potential of diverse urban data sources. These include sensor and social media streams (Twitter, Instagram, Foursquare), publicly available municipal records, and resources from knowledge repositories. Through data science, semantic integration, and crowdsourcing techniques the platform enables the mapping of demographic information, human movement patterns, place popularity, traffic conditions, as well as citizens' and visitors' opinions and preferences about specific venues in a city. The paper further demonstrates an implemented prototype of the platform and its deployment in real-world use cases for monitoring, analyzing, and assessing city-scale events.

Keywords: Urban analytics · Semantic integration · Crowdsourcing · Ontologies · SocialGlass · Urban computing · Smart cities

1 Introduction

The growing urban populations pose broad challenges to contemporary cities that span across domains as diverse as transportation, energy, and environment while also affect everyday human activities. Such challenges impact the quality of life in urban environments [1]. The rising complexity of the aforementioned domains is nowadays coupled with an increasing amount of data that reflect each urban system's performance as well as pertinent activities. Performance-related data mostly stem from distributed sensor resources across the city, which monitor each system's operations in real time. In addition, human-generated data produced through smart devices and social media platforms constitute an increasingly important source of information, especially with regard to human activities in cities. Yet, these data sources are currently insufficiently leveraged or used by planning authorities [2, 3].

In particular, city-related organizations create and operate on datasets based on each sector's specific purposes and problems at hand. This results into disparate data silos

© Springer-Verlag Berlin Heidelberg 2015
G. Celani et al. (Eds.): CAAD Futures 2015, CCIS 527, pp. 21–36, 2015.
DOI: 10.1007/978-3-662-47386-3_2

linked to a single urban system, that are further characterized by diverse data models and schemas for storage purposes. Any correlation of information among different sectors is currently performed in a manual fashion, hence requiring great amounts of time and effort. Constrained by the interoperability barrier across the urban data silos, city planners accordingly tend to approach each urban system individually, while also employ a limited amount of the available data sources in their planning approaches [4]. Thereby, the emerging challenge lies in providing new methods and tools that support and extend the current urban planning processes, by further allowing for interoperable data sharing and reuse from diverse sources.

To address this challenge, the paper introduces SocialGlass, a novel web-based platform that supports the analysis, integration, and interactive visualization of large-scale and heterogeneous urban data, with application to urban planning and decision-making. SocialGlass systematically combines publicly available municipal records together with social media streams (Twitter, Instagram, and Foursquare in particular) and resources from knowledge repositories. To achieve this, it employs data science methods (e.g. anomaly detection analysis), semantic integration techniques (e.g. ontology-based data models), and crowdsourcing (e.g. sentiment analysis, reality sensing and verification). The presented framework pays special attention to the analysis and integration of content retrieved from social media. To further allow for the integration of heterogeneous urban data and for the extraction of semantically enriched content, an innovative domain ontology has been developed. Using well-studied techniques in knowledge representation [5, 6], it defines named relationships that link both the different urban systems together and the data generated within them, in a machine-processable way. Yet, as the system makes use of extensive human-generated data, crowdsourcing and reality verification are employed as part of the semantic enrichment process to tackle the relative bias, inherent to such pieces of information.

The aim of the presented platform is to provide a system and tools for efficient interpretation and understanding of urban dynamics, by embracing and harnessing the combined potential of heterogeneous city data sources. The contributions of this work are mainly three.

1. A novel web-based system for urban planners and other city stakeholders that blends state-of-the-art methods and tools for sensor and social media content analysis, user modeling, semantic data integration, crowdsourcing, and visual data exploration (see Sect. 4).
2. An example implementation of Semantic Web technologies, aimed at rich data description and integration. Owing to an innovative ontology for planning and management, the system enables mapping, and semantic enrichment of urban data from diverse city sectors (e.g. transport, energy, waste, water etc.), in a machine-processable way (see Sect. 4.2).
3. An empirical validation of the approach and the system. The paper describes how a fully functioning prototype[1] of the web-based platform has been used to support

---

[1] A live instance of which is available at the following link: http://social-glass.org with demonstrations for each use case mentioned in Sect. 5.

several real-world case studies. The latter exemplify the framework's conceptual properties and its potential value as a solution to urban analytics and management, with application to city-scale event monitoring and assessment (see Sect. 5).

The rest of the paper is structured as follows: In Sect. 2 the state-of-the-art and background context, as well as the related work are described. Section 3 presents the proposed method. Section 4 illustrates the system architecture. In Sect. 5 the paper presents the deployment of the web-based software system and its application to real-world case studies. Ultimately, Sect. 6 summarizes the conclusions and discusses future lines of research.

2 Background and Related Work

2.1 Urban Computing

The work illustrated in this paper adopts concepts and methodologies from the emerging field of urban computing. Fueled by the increasing proliferation of sensor and actuator mechanisms embedded in diverse systems across cities, as well as by the growing amount of data generated in these systems, urban computing aims to enhance and extend the current approaches to studying the dynamics of cities [1, 7, 8]. It specifically acts at the intersection of cities and urban data. Often also referred to as urban informatics [9], this interdisciplinary field exploits the potential of diverse data sources ranging from sensor networks to mobile devices and social media platforms. To address the contemporary challenges of complex urban environments, urban computing employs data science methods, information retrieval techniques, data integration, analysis, and visualization technologies. The latter are merged with tools and methods utilized in urban planning and social science with regard to urban contexts. To this end, the proposed framework aims to contribute to the field of urban computing, by providing a system and tools for better investigating and understanding the dynamics of cities through heterogeneous social urban data.

2.2 Related Work

Despite the fact that the field of urban computing is presently at a nascent stage, there is already a plethora of projects with purposes relevant to those presented in this paper. The projects described in the following paragraphs are related to this work either in terms of the methods and tools they use or in terms of the goals they set and, therefore, serve as appropriate cases for comparison.

Based on the rapid proliferation of Location-Based Social Networks (LBSNs) the Livehoods Project by Cranshaw et al. [10] introduces a clustering model in order to study the social dynamics of a city. Their approach is grounded on spectral clustering algorithms applied to a large-scale dataset of Foursquare check-ins, in an attempt to overcome the limitations of the traditional methods used in urban analyses, such as surveys and field observations. Based on people's movement and activity patterns revealed by the data stream, the authors achieved to map distinct neighborhoods – coined livehoods – within the wider urban fabric of the studied city. In most cases, the extracted livehoods showed a different organization compared to the one defined by municipal boundaries. Even though this project makes use of an interesting approach and method (i.e. spectral clustering algorithms) to studying urban dynamics, it is solely based on a data stream from one single source (i.e. Foursquare). Thereby, it is confined by the inherent limitations of this particular source (e.g. demographic representativeness, cultural bias, data veracity etc.), which is also a shortcoming of traditional urban analysis methods.

Similarly, Noulas et al. [11] model geographic areas and human activity within cities, by means of venue categories and based on a large-scale Foursquare dataset derived from geo-referenced Twitter messages. A spectral clustering algorithm is again being used for identifying citizen profiles and different activity areas in the city. As is the case with the Livehoods project, Noulas et al. considered a single data source to achieve the project goals, thus falling short on similar limitations. Further, the paper did not investigate user modeling in depth, meaning that it did not explicitly describe whether a particular activity is related to a resident, a local visitor or a foreign tourist. Besides, the work of Noulas et al. limits semantic annotations to the venue categories and social activities the geo-coordinates refer to. Similar shortcomings to the two aforementioned projects are observed in the work of Del Bimbo et al. and their LiveCities application [12], as well as in the CityBeat project by Xia et al. [13].

The projects described above demonstrate partial similarities to the methods used in our work. The purposes, however, are substantially different, as the web-based platform illustrated here aims to facilitate and enhance current urban planning and decision-making processes. In this regard, the LIVE Singapore! project by Kloeckl et al. [14] closely relates to this paper's proposal. It introduces an open platform for the collection, combination, and distribution of large-scale real-time urban data streams. An interesting feature of the aforementioned work lies in the correlation and integration of heterogeneous data sources for richer insights about city dynamics. Yet, at the stage presented in the publication, the authors mainly utilized data streams from sensors and call detail records (CDR). Human-generated data from social media networks were not investigated. In this paper, a novel and comprehensive framework for better understanding cities through heterogeneous social data is demonstrated. In addition, the developed web-based platform provides new methods and tools to create, integrate, analyze, and valorize urban data sources for the benefit of urban planning and decision-making.

3   Method

The demonstrated urban platform enables the (simultaneous) mapping of demographic information, human movement patterns, place popularity, traffic conditions, as well as citizens' and visitors' opinions and preferences with regard to specific venues in the city. To this extent, it leverages on content retrieved from social media (Twitter, Instagram, and Foursquare), mobile phone data, and spatial statistics and demographics retrieved from open municipal records. SocialGlass is also capable of incorporating dynamic sensor streams, either from already existing sensor resources or newly distributed sensor networks (DSNs). The implementation of these features relies on various methods and techniques applied to different modules, clustered in larger components, that respectively cater for data ingestion and analysis, semantic integration, as well as exploration and visualization (Fig. 1).

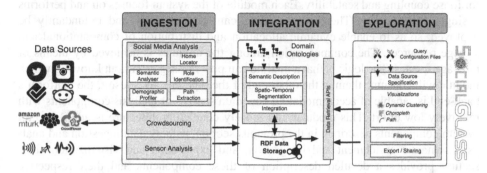

Fig. 1. Pipeline and system architecture of SocialGlass

The data ingestion and analysis component refers to the acquisition, cleansing, and processing of social and sensor data. In the proposed system, the active involvement of citizens is also possible in this process through a crowdsourcing sub-module that will further be described in the following section. To this end, data science methods, including information retrieval and social media analysis techniques, are employed for tackling issues pertinent to anomaly detection and data veracity. In addition, human computation techniques play a highly beneficial role when it comes to the efficient interpretation of personally, contextually, or culturally biased analyses of raw data [15]. This is particularly crucial for social web data, as their content is often unstructured in terms of machine readability and processing.

The semantic enrichment and integration component simplifies the interconnections amongst the different data providers. It specifically caters for interoperability issues across usage domains and their respective data sources, in an attempt to overcome the barriers set by the multiple data silos across city agencies. To achieve this, a knowledge representation model has been developed, based on a novel ontology that formally represents urban systems, the relations among them, and the corresponding data sources. The concepts of the aforementioned ontology are aligned with classes and properties from multiple external ontologies and controlled vocabularies [16]. This is for ensuring the interrelation among city sectors and further for facilitating the data integration process.

Finally, SocialGlass offers a web-based user interface for data exploration, interactive information visualization, comparison, and urban analytics. Through these components the different city stakeholders can gain insights about spatial and temporal parameters of the studied urban context. Data exploration takes place in a map-based web environment, on top of which city-related information is visualized in a layered fashion. The visualization types in use vary from dynamic point clusters to intensity heat maps, activity-related paths, and choropleths in combination with auxiliary spatio-temporal graphs.

4   System Architecture

To address the several scalability challenges posed by the diversity, quantity, and speed of social and sensor data sources, the platform adopts a modular architecture, optimized for loose coupling and scalability. Each module of the system focuses on and performs a single functionality. Thereby, a module can independently and redundantly be deployed, so as to enable dynamic allocation and distribution of computational and storage resources. The communication among the modules is achieved by means of message queues. The logic is that a module can post messages without knowing which module will consume them at the other end of the pipeline. As a result, the platform's back-end is capable of accommodating new data sources or analysis components with relatively low effort. This modular and loosely coupled architecture is applied to all system components described in the previous section, namely data ingestion and analysis, semantic enrichment and integration, and exploration and visualization. This section provides a detailed description of these components and their respective modules.

4.1   Data Ingestion and Analysis Component

The data ingestion and analysis component is further subdivided into three sub-systems, respectively devoted to social media analysis, crowdsourcing, and sensor analysis. Their functionalities are described in the following sections.

4.1.1   Social Media Analysis Sub-system

The Social Media Analysis (SMA) sub-system is devoted to the generation of information about a given urban environment, based on content created by users of popular social media platforms, such as Twitter, Instagram, and Foursquare. These platforms are particularly selected for their open-source APIs (Application Programming Interfaces). The modules constituting the SMA sub-system provide insights about citizens' activities, points of interest, as well as their spatial and temporal relationships. Each of these modules is briefly described below.

Point-of-Interest Mapper. This module maps geo-referenced micro-posts to urban Points of Interest (POIs). In the current implementation, this is achieved through the "check-in intent" Foursquare API[2], which selects the most popular venues amongst the ones that are in the proximity of a specific user's post. Because of the POI mapper, it is possible to enable the spatiotemporal analysis of an urban area according to a place's functionality (e.g. museum, educational institute, restaurant etc.). In the current implementation, POIs can also be specified independently. This is particularly interesting in the case of city-scale events that define their own POIs (such as in the examples described later in Sect. 5.2).

---

[2] https://developer.foursquare.com/docs/venues/search.

Semantic Analyzer. The content of the aforementioned micro-posts is processed through the semantic analyzer module, in order to extract entities (e.g. the name of a location) from its textual structure. These are further connected to entities in DBPedia[3]. In this way, it is possible to associate social media users, urban areas, and temporal intervals with the entities mentioned in the related posts, so as to create topics profiles. Entity extraction relies on DBPedia Spotlight, which features annotation functionalities in several languages.

Demographic Profiler. Given social media users observed in an urban area of interest, this module estimates their gender and age. This is achieved by means of a state-of-the-art face detection and analysis component (Face ++)[4], in combination with a dictionary-based gender recognition module (Genderize)[5].

Home Locator. This module estimates the home location of social media users owing to a recursive grid search, based on the geo-location of their micro-posts. The search finds the actual place where the user posts more often and uses that location as an approximation of the user's home location. Once identifying the coordinates of the estimated home location, the module makes use of a reverse geocoding service (Geonames)[6] to identify the user's city and country of origin.

User-Role Identifier. Particularly functional to urban analytics is the characterization of the types of people in a city. This module classifies people according to their home city – based on input from the home locator – in relation to the analyzed urban context. The system classifies people into residents (home location and analyzed urban context are the same), commuters (home location and analyzed urban context are different, but belong to the same country), and foreign tourists (home location and analyzed urban context are different and belong to different countries).

Path Extractor. This module constructs paths by examining all geo-referenced posts of a person in a fixed time period. Paths are formed through the coordinate concatenation of subsequent posts. Each point in the path is mapped to a known venue, based on input from the POI mapper module.

4.1.2 The Crowdsourcing Sub-system

To cater for issues of data sparseness, veracity, and sense making, the platform incorporates a crowdsourcing sub-system. This further allows for pro-active interaction with individuals and groups (drawn from social media or human computation platforms) for data creation, cleansing, and interpretation purposes. The crowdsourcing system can operate in two modes: (a) a Social Sensing mode, which has the ability to contact social media users in order to request services, such as on-demand data creation, cleansing,

---

[3] http://dbpedia.org/.
[4] http://www.faceplusplus.com/.
[5] http://genderize.io/.
[6] http://www.geonames.org/.

and linkage; and (b) a Human Computation mode to engage with anonymous crowd from human computation platforms, such as CrowdFlower and Amazon Mechanical Turk[7]. Examples of operations enabled by the crowdsourcing system may include: on-demand sensing of urban environment phenomena (e.g. rainfall, temperature variation etc.); disambiguation of textual and visual content with respect to sentiments; and verification of relatedness and appropriateness of images in relation to an observed event or a targeted group of people.

4.1.3 The Sensor Analysis Sub-system

Besides crowdsourcing, which relies on the participation of citizens who act as human sensors, SocialGlass also accommodates modules for analyzing data streams stemming from sensor devices distributed across the urban fabric. The latter may refer to already existing sensor resources and/or newly embedded DSNs. The combination of both human-generated data and information from sensor resources can cater for data sparseness and reality verification issues. Several experiments have already been conducted in this regard, while currently working on their integration in the system.

4.2 Semantic Enrichment and Integration Component

When combining heterogeneous data from complex urban environments it is common to encounter syntactic and semantic discrepancies, mainly due to spatial, temporal, and/or thematic diversities in the studied datasets. The use of different data models and schemas in the data repositories across city agencies further strengthens the aforementioned diversities. Therefore, discordant, incompatible with each other, and cumbersome data silos are created. The goal of the semantic enrichment and integration component is to specifically tackle this issue. By structuring and encoding municipal records, sensor and social media inputs from the ingestion component, it provides a coherent representation framework that simplifies their usage and unlocks their combined value. This is of particular importance to the city planning process, which can largely benefit from the simultaneous combination of heterogeneous urban information.

To achieve this goal, a novel ontology[8] (OSMoSys – OntoPolis Semantic Modeling System) was developed that describes the different urban systems (e.g. energy, waste, water, transport etc.), the respective data sources (e.g. spatial statistics, sensor data, social data etc.), the city technology enablers (e.g. interoperability types, connectivity, computational resources), and defines the relations among them. It also formally represents the different urban sectors/agencies and includes broader concepts that allow data mapping from different departments. The ontology reuses terms and concepts from various European and American standards and roadmaps on smart cities, as well as from relevant external ontologies and controlled vocabularies. The former namely refer to the Publicly Available Specifications (PAS) on Smart Cities [17] and Smart City Concept Model [18], the Smart Cities Readiness Guide [19], and the Operational

---

[7] Respectively, http://www.crowdflower.com and https://www.mturk.com/.

[8] A running instance of OSMoSys is available at: http://www.hyperbody.nl/demo/osmosys.

Implementation Plans of the European Innovation Partnership on Smart Cities and Communities [20]. In addition, it reuses terms from the following vocabularies: *dc*; *dct*; *foaf*; *gml*; *schema*; *skos*; *vann*, and external ontologies: *DUL*; *CityGML*; *dbpedia-owl*; *OTN* (Ontology of Transportation Networks); *SSN* (Semantic Sensor Network ontology); *OWL-Time*.

To further provide city stakeholders with straightforward access to the above-described ontology, a web ontology browser (WOB) was developed [21]. The latter offers a web-based user interface (UI) for navigating through the complete taxonomic hierarchy of classes and properties (relations), without requiring computational skills in ontology development environments or relevant software. The UI layout of the WOB is organized in three panes, providing different navigation possibilities and views of the ontology (Fig. 2). The upper-left pane lists the different ontology entities in groups of classes, object, data, and annotation properties, individuals, and data types. It also contains an option for returning back to the general overview. When any of the previous entity groups is selected, a complete index of the corresponding concepts in alphabetical order appears on the lower-left pane of the UI. Further, the main pane accommodates the full semantics, descriptions, and annotations of each selected entity, as well as its relations to other classes, and links to external vocabularies. The user can interactively browse the different entities and explore relations, either through the side-pane indexes or by directly clicking on any term included in the main pane.

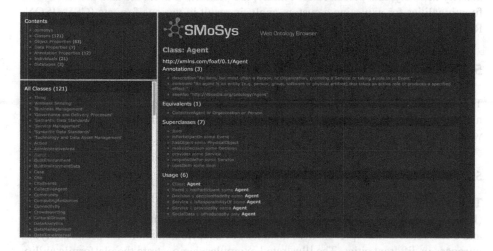

Fig. 2. Instance of the OSMoSys Web Ontology Browser user interface

The ontology was developed in OWL 2 (Web Ontology Language) and built with the Protégé 4.3.0[9] ontology development platform. The WOB is largely based on OWLDoc, as well as JavaScript and HTML5.

---

[9] http://protege.stanford.edu/.

4.3   Data Exploration and Visualization Component

The data exploration and visualization component uses the APIs of the semantic enrichment and integration cluster to provide interfaces for urban analytics. Interactive data exploration tools allow users to ponder on the collected and linked data and to extract insights about the spatiotemporal analysis of a specific urban environment. To facilitate exploration, the platform's user interface enables the creation of an arbitrary number of layers that can be initiated, deactivated, and organized in a customizable order. Each layer visualizes a partition of the retrieved information and is characterized by (a) the data source, (b) the visualization type, and (c) the filtering method. Owing to the semantic enrichment and integration component, it is possible to specify custom queries, spanning across multiple data sources. In relation to the visualization type, the platform's current implementation offers the following set of map-based data visualizations:

- Dynamic Point Clusters;
- Choropleth maps;
- Activity Paths;
- Data graphs depicting the people's roles, age, gender, popularity of POIs and venue categories, temporal distribution of micro-posts, semantics, and spatial statistics.

Once retrieved, data can be filtered according to the time span, the POI category, the activity intensity, and person roles. Finally, the platform's users are also provided with functionalities for exporting a custom analysis result in various formats (CSV, JSON, RDF) and save each exploration status for sharing or further reuse purposes.

5   Empirical Validation

This section indicates how the above-described components and modules were implemented in a working prototype of the SocialGlass platform. It, further, provides real-world examples, in which the system was empirically tested.

5.1   Platform Deployment

The implementation of SocialGlass consists of a fully working web-based user interface (UI), grounded on the previously described architectural components. Figures 3, 4, 5 and 6 showcase some representative instances of data visualizations for urban analytics purposes in different cities. The illustrated examples demonstrate the platform's ability to effectively combine content retrieved from social media platforms (Twitter, Instagram, Foursquare) with mobile phone data, and municipal records about spatial statistics and demographics, within a specific urban context. Each stakeholder (e.g. urban planner) is enabled to make customized combinations, so as to approach and gain insights about a specific urban situation from different angles.

Through a pop-up menu the user first specifies the data source s/he is interested in (Fig. 3). The available options include social media data (Twitter and Instagram) and statistical records. Custom queries fusing multiple data sources together are also made possible through the semantic enrichment and integration component. As the platform

Fig. 3. Dropdown menu with various data visualization options

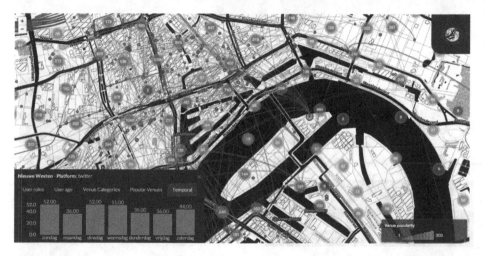

Fig. 4. Dynamic point clusters of Twitter micro-posts, in combination with path patterns of foreign tourists and their temporal variations in the city of Rotterdam

follows a layer-based visualization approach, users are further provided with various choices for visualizing and analyzing the selected data source, through a dropdown menu. The offered choices are listed below.

Dynamic Point Clusters. Available in the social media data sources, this visualization type displays geo-located objects (e.g. Twitter micro posts), POIs, and sensor records. Objects are dynamically clustered according to their spatial proximity to a certain location. Zooming modifies the cluster granularity, following the map's different Levels of Detail (LODs), thus giving an overview on the number of objects in a specific area (Fig. 4).

Fig. 5. Heat map of activity intensity during the Amsterdam Light Festival from 9 pm till 12 am

Fig. 6. Choropleth map visualizing the most popular venue categories and the corresponding activity intensity in each administrative district of Amsterdam, based on Instagram posts

Heat Maps. These graphical data representations of social media streams illustrate the frequency of objects, such as sensor measurements and/or micro posts, in a gradient, color-coded fashion. A timeline slider allows users to interactively analyze the real- or recent-time data streams in different time intervals (Fig. 5).

Choropleth Maps. This visualization option builds upon the urban space partitions of the underlying data source. For each partition it can show: (a) a color, representing a specific category (e.g. venue category, user roles, gender or age distribution, crime rates etc.); or (b) a color shade, in proportion to the measured variable. In other words, it depicts in real or recent time the social activity intensity in different administrative districts of a city (Fig. 6).

Path Patterns. A path pattern utilizes 3D arc projections connecting locations, typically POIs, which denote the paths taken by different people who traverse the city. The thickness and color of the arc represent the popularity of a specific path among the considered groups of people (Fig. 4).

By clicking on an area (choropleth maps – Fig. 6), point or a path (Fig. 4), a pop-up window appears in the lower left side of the UI. This further contains additional information about the selected area or path, such as: (a) the distribution of people according to their role (inhabitants, commuters, and foreign tourists), age, and gender; (b) the popularity of POIs and venue categories; (c) temporal distribution of micro posts over the days of the week; (d) semantic profiles of the people posting from the selected area; and (e) other static data from publicly available data sources (e.g. crime rate, income distribution etc.).

5.2   Real-World Use Cases

SocialGlass is designed for facilitating urban planners and city managers in understanding and making decisions about different urban phenomena. In this regard, city-scale events dynamically change ordinary activities in cities, by having a particular impact on a variety of urban aspects, such as mobility flows and occupancy levels in specific public spaces. This makes them interesting cases for empirically testing and validating the platform, in providing stakeholders with real-time (or near real-time) urban analytics pertinent to the events. In this context, SocialGlass has successfully been deployed for monitoring and assessing three city-scale events, in different cities and for diverse time periods. These namely refer to the (a) Milano Design Week 2014, (b) Amsterdam Light Festival 2015, and (c) Como Summer Holiday Season 2014.

Geographically limited to the city of Milan, the *Milano Design Week* (MDW) 2014 featured multiple events attended by half a million visitors in half a thousand venues that serve as temporary exhibition centers. The MDW case covers the largest urban area of the three presented examples, yet the deployment period is the shortest, as it refers to a ten-day monitoring in total, specifically from April 4, 2014 to April 14, 2014. The platform has been used for a twofold purpose: on one hand, to distill demographics and user profiles of attendees, so as to enable a venue recommendation system; on the other hand, to activate social media users for crowd sensing and data cleansing purposes.

The second deployment of the platform was for the purposes of the *Amsterdam Light Festival* (ALF) 2015. The latter refers to an art-related city-scale event, with a duration period from November 27, 2014 to January 18, 2015. The festival's organizers were interested in assessing the success of the event, while pulling demographic and mobility profiles of attendees to inform their planning decisions for the upcoming edition.

In both of the above-mentioned cases, instances of the platform were deployed focusing on the place and time period that each of the events took place. Social media data from Twitter (a total of ~15 K unique users, and 28,619,856 tweets) and Instagram (a total of ~80 K users, and 17,049,803 posts), pertinent to the events, were collected (before, during, and after their end) and were further integrated with municipal records and statistics gathered from the events' organizers. The system harvested information about the popularity of the festivals and the corresponding opinions of visitors. In this regard, special attention was paid to sentiment analysis (opinion miner module) and human computation components (image description). To further validate the results, the platform's urban analytics were compared with the observations collected from the events' official applications.

Finally, the *Como Summer Holiday Season* 2014 is a summer-long event organized by the municipality of Como in Italy. In this regard, it covers the longest deployment period of the three cases, but the surveyed urban area is the smallest in terms of scale. The goals of this use case were (a) to monitor for a long period of time the urban fabric of a mid-sized city, and (b) to validate the figures obtained from social media data against data produced by the main Italian mobile telecommunications provider. The work included the analysis and linking of more than 8,000,000 phone calls (incoming or outgoing), 6,000,000 of SMSs, ~42,000 tweets, ~4,500 twitter users and more than 22,000 unique hashtags. While exemplifying the potential of an approach based on heterogeneous data, the *Como Summer Holiday Season* served as a relevant testbed for the integration and analytical nature of the initiative.

6   Conclusions and Future Work

This paper introduced SocialGlass, a novel web-based system that supports the analysis, modeling, semantic integration, crowdsourcing, and interactive visual exploration of large-scale and heterogeneous urban data. The presented platform enhances the processes of urban planning and decision-making, by providing state-of-the-art tools and methods to better understand the dynamics of cities from various perspectives. The analysis and planning approach described in this paper is essentially data-driven. To that end, the paper showed how to efficiently incorporate dynamic data streams (real- or recent time) from sensors and social media platforms, in combination with (semi-)static datasets from the municipality. Contrary to conventional urban analytics, which are solely based on slowly updated and non-scalable census records and demographics, the presented platform provided a holistic framework for addressing diverse aspects of urban environments, by deploying a fully scalable city analytics framework.

The system's modular architecture allows new components and data sources to easily be incorporated in the back-end structure. Further, the developed ontology tackles the syntactic and semantic discrepancies among urban data of different nature and, thus, offers a new approach in bridging the interoperability barriers set by the existing data silos. Besides, the crowdsourcing components give citizens the opportunity to actively contribute to the system, while the map-based UI and its layered data visualization possibilities allow stakeholders to simultaneously explore various urban variables, according to their needs. Finally, the deployment of the platform in real-world cases showed its potential value as a solution for city-scale event monitoring and assessment, as well as for helping stakeholders in dynamically rearranging their plans and decisions.

As part of future work, the plan is to further develop the sensor analysis modules to better accommodate data streams from sensor devices across the urban fabric. In addition, mechanisms for deriving more detailed and accurate views of activities within cities from social media, as well as more advanced data search components are currently in progress. In this regard, the system seeks to break new ground in the emerging field of urban computing and, hopefully, aims at better support for planning.

Acknowledgements. This research is funded by the Greek State Scholarships Foundation I.K.Y. (by the resources of the Educational Program "Education and Lifelong Learning", the European Social Fund (ESF), and the EU National Strategic Reference Framework (NSRF) of 2007–2013). It is further funded by a scholarship of the Alexander S. Onassis Foundation. It is also financially supported by the Foundation for Education and European Culture (IPEP) and the A. G. Leventis Foundation.

References

1. Zheng, Y., Carpa, L., Wolfson, O., Yang, H.: Urban computing: concepts, methodologies and applications. ACM Trans. Intell. Syst. Technol. (ACM TIST) **5**(3), 1–55 (2014)
2. Ciuccarelli, P., Lupi, G., Simeone, L.: Visualizing the Data City: Social Media as a Source of Knowledge for Urban Planning and Management. Springer, Heidelberg (2014)
3. Vaccari, A., Liu, L., Biderman, A., Ratti, C., Pereira, F., Oliveirinha, J., Gerber, A.: A holistic framework for the study of urban traces and the profiling of urban processes and dynamics. In: 12th International IEEE Conference on Intelligent Transportation Systems, IEEE Press, New York, pp. 273–278 (2009)
4. Métral, C., Falquet, G., Cutting-Decelle, A.F.: Towards semantically enriched 3d city models: an ontology-based approach. In: Kolbe, T.H., Zhang, H., Zlatanova, S. (eds.) GeoWeb Conference Academic Track – Cityscapes, vol. XXXVIII-3-4/C3, pp. 40–45. The International Archives of the Photogrammetry, Remote Sensing and Spatial Information Sciences (ISPRS Archives), Vancouver, Canada (2009)
5. Domingue, J., Fensel, D., Hendler, J.A. (eds.): Handbook of Semantic Web Technologies. Springer, Heidelberg (2011)
6. Euzenat, J., Shvaiko, P.: Ontology Matching, 2nd edn. Springer, Heidelberg (2013)
7. Kindberg, T., Chalmers, M., Paulos, E.: Guest Editor's Introduction: Urban Computing. Pervasive Computing, vol. 6(3), pp. 18–20. IEEE Press, New York (2007)
8. Kostakos, V., O'Neill, E.: Cityware: urban computing to bridge online and real-world social networks. In: Foth, M. (ed.) Handbook of Research on Urban Informatics: The Practice and Promise of the Real-Time City, Information Science Reference, pp. 196–205. Hershey, New York (2009)
9. Foth, M., Jaz, H.-J., Satchell, C.: Urban informatics. In: Conference on Computer Supported Cooperative Work (CCSCW), ACM, pp. 1–8 (2011)
10. Cranshaw, J., Schwartz, R., Hong J.I., Sadeh, N.: The livehoods project: utilizing social media to understand the dynamics of a city. In: Sixth International AAAI Conference on Weblogs and Social Media (ICWSM), AAAI, pp. 58–65 (2012)
11. Noulas, A., Scellato, S., Mascolo, C., Pontil, M.: Exploiting semantic annotations for clustering geographic areas and users in location-based social networks. In: Workshop on the Social Mobile Web at ICWSM 2011, AAAI, pp. 570–573 (2011)

12. Del Bimbo, A., Ferracani, A., Pezzatini, D., D'Amato, F., Sereni, M.: Livecities: revealing the pulse of cities by location-based social networks venues and users analysis. In: 23rd International Conference on World Wide Web (WWW), ACM, pp. 163–166 (2014)

13. Xia, C., Schwartz, R., Xie, K., Krebs, A., Langdon, A., Ting, J., Naaman, M.: Citybeat: real-time social media visualization of hyper-local city data. In: 23rd International Conference on World Wide Web (WWW), ACM, pp. 167–170 (2014)

14. Kloeckl, K., Senn, O., Ratti, C.: Enabling the real-time city: LIVE Singapore! J. Urban Technol. 19(2), 89–112 (2012)

15. Bozzon, A., Fraternali, P., Galli, L., Karam, R.: Modeling crowdsourcing scenarios in socially-enabled human computation applications. J. Data Semant. 3, 169–188 (2014)

16. Psyllidis, A., Biloria, N.: Ontopolis: a semantic participatory platform for performance assessment and augmentation of urban environments. In: 10th IEEE International Conference on Intelligent Environments 2014 (IE 2014), IEEE Press, New York, pp. 140–147 (2014)

17. British Standards Institution (BSI): Smart cities – vocabulary. BSI Standards, London (2014)

18. British Standards Institution (BSI): Smart City concept model – guide to establishing a model for data interoperability. BSI Standards, London (2014)

19. Smart Cities Council: Smart Cities Readiness Guide: The Planning Manual for Building Tomorrow's Cities Today. Smart Cities Council, Redmond (2014)

20. European innovation partnership on smart cities and communities (EIP-SCC): operational implementation plan. EIP-SCC, Brussels (2014)

21. Psyllidis, A.: OSMoSys: a web interface for graph-based rdf data visualization and ontology browsing. In: Cimiano, P., Frasincar, F., Houben, G.-J., Schwabe, D. (eds.) 15th International Conference on Web Engineering (ICWE 2015). LNCS. Springer, Heidelberg (2015, in press)

Distributed and Heterogeneous Data Analysis for Smart Urban Planning

Eduardo A. Oliveira(✉), Michael Kirley, Tom Kvan, Justyna Karakiewicz, and Carlos Vaz

University of Melbourne, Melbourne, VIC, Australia
{eduardo.oliveira,mkirley,tkvan,justynak,
carlos.vaz}@unimelb.edu.au

Abstract. Over the past decade, 'smart' cities have capitalized on new technologies and insights to transform their systems, operations and services. The rationale behind the use of these technologies is that an evidence-based, analytical approach to decision-making will lead to more robust and sustainable outcomes. However, harvesting high-quality data from the dense network of sensors embedded in the urban infrastructure, and combining this data with social network data, poses many challenges. In this paper, we investigate the use of an intelligent middleware – Device Nimbus – to support data capture and analysis techniques to inform urban planning and design. We report results from a 'Living Campus' experiment at the University of Melbourne, Australia focused on a public learning space case study. Local perspectives, collected via crowd sourcing, are combined with distributed and heterogeneous environmental sensor data. Our analysis shows that Device Nimbus' data integration and intelligent modules provide high-quality support for decision-making and planning.

Keywords: Smart city · Smart campus · Middleware · Data fusion · Urban design · Urban planning

1 Introduction

The concept of a 'smart' society encapsulating the use of Information and Communication Technologies (ICT) to help manage systems, operations and service delivery is now widely accepted [1, 3, 4, 7]. ICT can be found at many levels, ranging from the collection of data from ordinary daily tasks (e.g. traffic monitoring), to informing managerial tasks that involve decision-making based on the monitored data (e.g. electricity and water management; education and health; climate change monitoring).

Typically, each of the smart systems and sensors has specific requirements, processes and outputs. In practice, current ICT solutions targeting a smarter society are focused on the collection of sensor information from different sources – a type of command and control systems for monitoring urban environments. These systems collect data through sensors (e.g. traffic sensors) or through people (e.g. using mobile devices), store and process the data, in order to extract useful information to aid planning and decision-making. However, most of the data found over the ICT (e.g. social

© Springer-Verlag Berlin Heidelberg 2015
G. Celani et al. (Eds.): CAAD Futures 2015, CCIS 527, pp. 37–54, 2015.
DOI: 10.1007/978-3-662-47386-3_3

networks, websites, smartphones and sensors) has an 'unstructured' format, residing not in structured databases but in a variety of files (e.g. in documents, presentations, calendars, e-mails, social media posts etc.). In this context, the construction and use of complex systems for monitoring, controlling and supporting decision-making in cities involves a large number of independent, autonomous, heterogeneous and interacting sub-systems [1].

A great deal of analysis based around smart cities has been geared towards planning and design. Architects, planners, and urban designers typically require access to spatial and temporal data, which considers how people perceive, behave and interact with their environment. However, the data collection and analysis is rarely pitched at the micro scale – typically it is not based on small public spaces, walkways/lanes, and interactions between small groups of people. Consequently, such analysis does not support urban designers and planners when proposing small interventions, such as: (i) modifying pedestrian thoroughfares to improve mobility; (ii) altering public spaces to improve citizens' engagement and communication; (iii) making adjustments to outdoor learning environments.

In this paper, we investigate urban-scale mobile sensing, using the Device Nimbus intelligent middleware [3]. Middleware refers to the software that is common to multiple applications and builds on the network transport services to enable ready development of new applications and network services [2]. Key features of the Device Nimbus middleware include: data collection and integration modules that are used when harvesting heterogeneous data, analytics modules, and visualization of the operational processes. As part of a 'Living Campus' experiment at the University of Melbourne, we use crowdsourcing techniques to collect social media data, which is combined with environmental sensor data and Device Nimbus' analytical modules in an attempt to paint a coherent picture of user behaviour in a case study area. We argue that the middleware provides a robust and flexible framework to inform planning and design.

This remainder of the paper is organized as follows: Sect. 2 briefly describes smart cites and the role of digital technologies to inform urban design. Section 3 provides a comprehensive review of existing software platforms for cities and small urban areas – university campuses – in the context of middleware and technologies. Section 4 introduces a high level overview of the Device Nimbus architecture and details the first phase of the implementation of Device Nimbus. Section 5 discusses a preliminary case study used to demonstrate the efficacy of the middleware. Section 6 provides conclusions and highlights future work opportunities.

2   Background: Smart Cities and Urban Planning

The term 'smart city' emerged in the late 1980s as a means to visualize urban context. However, the term has many different meanings [4–7]. A smart city is often thought of as the utilization of networked infrastructure to improve both economic and political efficiency and to enable social, cultural, and urban development [6]. Here, the infrastructure term indicates business services, housing, leisure, lifestyle services, and ICT (mobile and fixed phones, computer networks, e-commerce, and Internet services) [8].

Harrison and colleagues [9] suggest that a smart city is a city that connects the physical, the ICT, the social, and the business infrastructures to leverage the collective intelligence of the city. Toppeta [10] believes that a smart city is a place where ICT and Web 2.0 technology are combined with other administrative, design and planning efforts to speed up bureaucratic processes and help to identify new, innovative solutions to city management complexity, improving sustainability and livability. Coe et al. [11] extend this idea to include both social and relational capital in urban development.

When designing and managing urban space in the 21st century, it is important to understand both the social and spatial implications of new lifestyles, attitudes to sustainability, and models of future life patterns [12–14]. In his recent book, Michael Batty [15] attempts to describe and explain complex urban systems using theoretical inspirations from complexity and network science using concepts of flows and networks. He suggests that by building spatial databases of urban performance, and analyzing the patterns within these databases using simulation, it should be possible to provide service planners and government authorities with timely information to guide the planning process. Obviously, the collection and processing of data streams encapsulated by smart cities plays an important role in such analysis. Large global technology providers are consistently investing in ICT solutions to meet the demand of these smart environments. Unfortunately, many of these solutions are closed, preventing the development of solutions provided by local market platforms.

Given the brief discussions above, it is clear that the capture of heterogeneous streams of data and new analytic tools can potentially be used to guide the design of innovative urban form and the re-imaging of existing urban environments. Crowdsourcing or 'participatory sensing' is an emerging data collection technique that allows individuals to engage in this process. Such techniques allow individuals to interact in new, more efficient and meaningful ways. However, solving the problem of data fusion, both from the ubiquitous environmental sensors deployed in many urban spaces and mobile smart devices is a significant challenge. In addition, the development of appropriate data mining and analysis modules must be addressed.

3 Middleware: A Review

In this section, we present a critical review of the literature describing middleware implementations. We start by describing middleware and platforms for collecting, integrating and analyzing data. We focus the discussion on literature encapsulating smart cites, urban growth and the planning of smart urban spaces. We follow this with a more specific discussion of middleware appropriate for 'smart university campuses,' which forms the basis of our case study investigation in Sect. 5.

3.1 Middleware Platforms for Smart Cites

Nimbit [16], Etherios [17] and ThingSpeak [18] are middleware platforms that were developed to connect people, sensors and software to the cloud (and to each other). Nimbit provides web services that can process time and geo-stamped data that trigger calculations, statistics, alerts and more. Etherios is a machine-to-machine (M2 M) platform-as-a-service that can manage many different connected devices via one user interface. ThingSpeak is an open source 'Internet of Things' (IoT) application that has an open Application Programming Interface (API), used to store and retrieve data from device assets via a Local Area Network (LAN) or via HTTP over the Internet.

The WSO2 [19] is a middleware platform that is 100 % open source. WSO2 not only uses an open-source license, but also follows an open development process. The WSO2 platform consists of over 25 products, covering all major categories from data integration and API management to identity and mobility mechanisms.

Although other initiatives such as Magic Broker [20, 21], SOFIA [22] and Xively [23] provide part of their infrastructure as free and open source software, they describe system architectures limited to a subset of smart environment concepts, focused on creating interacting objects ecosystems (sensors, devices, appliances and embedded systems). However, the middleware examples are not concerned with the simultaneous collection of different data streams (e.g., electricity, traffic, water consumption), or with closed or proprietary wearable solutions. In addition, experimental middleware that have been released releases have typically been custom-tailored solutions, where components or subsystems have not been modelled as interchangeable parts, nor were they conceived to be integrated with other subsystems.

Different from many middleware solutions, Anthopoulos et al. [24] proposed a software architecture based on the analysis of different initiatives already implemented - AOL Cities, Digital City of Trikala, Digital City of Kyoto [25], Digital City of Amsterdam [26] and Base Copenhagen [27]. Anthopoulos et al. highlights that the construction of a smart city must forecast legacy systems integration to the new infrastructure, migration and reuse of existing data, simplification of urban processes through participatory performance, resource utilization optimization, systems interoperability, and providing tools for monitoring, management and analysis.

3.2 Middleware Platforms for University Campuses

University campuses represent an urban space that in many circumstances reflects what is happening on a larger scale across a city. University campuses just like cities are complex and dynamic. Both have buildings interconnected by circulation networks, allowing flow of people and things. Both also have public spaces where people can interact. Obviously, university campus and cities have many differences, according to their purpose, scale and socio-economic factors.

It is quite complicated (if not impossible) to define primary purpose of a city. SA city's function can be defined as a matrix of different roles, according to different knowledge fields (and context). In contrast, a university campus has a very clear main purpose, which can be defined as being an environment for learning and research. The campus should be able to adapt or create new infrastructure according to changing pedagogies and technologies, providing to the campus community an environment suitable for learning and research.

With the recent development of ICT, smart campuses are been constructed to benefit the faculty and students, to manage available resources and to enhance user experience with proactive recommendation/suggestion (services) [28]. Context-awareness has been introduced to provide proactive services for faculty and students on campus. Context-awareness, in this domain, may be thought of as the ability to define what is relevant at any given time. The use of context allows systems to filter and disseminate useful information and adapt its services to the particular needs of the student/staff, providing them proactive recommendations/suggestions [29].

According to Yu et al. [28], a smart campus ranges from a smart classroom, which incorporates ICT in the teaching process within a classroom, to an intelligent campus that provides many proactive services in a campus-wide environment. Kenney [30] believes that students can learn wherever they have opportunity for interaction, and every part of a campus must be considered a learning environment, anything less is a missed opportunity. Based on information such as location, activity and user profiles, the university campus can provide proactive services, based on social contexts (e.g., the proximity and the communication history). Elements surrounding the student and faculty/staff that are of interest are: their location, the devices used by them, their activities, date time, among others [31]. For instance, where a campus is located and the site climate can be considered important factors that may guide decisions.

A university campus is also a social environment, where students have many social interactions with other students (and academics/researchers). However, little research has been conducted on specific social aspects, e.g., supporting social interactions [28], in this domain. From an ICT perspective, in many studies focused on smart campuses, proactive services are not taken into account.

In the prototype presented by Stephen et al. [32], a reconfigurable context-sensitive middleware was designed to achieve collaborative learning. As part of the middleware design, individuals were equipped with a PDA to recognize situation and the system provides different services to users based on their current situations to enhance the collaboration among students and teachers. With the evolution of pervasive computing, a number of smart campus prototypes [33–35] have been developed to provide services for users situated in a smart space. Talal et al. [33] proposed a solution to efficiently integrate services in a campus with the use of smart cards. The ETHOC system, presented by Michael et al. [34], focuses on the integration of virtual and physical elements in the campus environment, like virtual counterparts of printed document using a variety of devices, such as mobile phones or PDAs.

Numerous researchers [35–37] have focused on exploiting the development of friendship network structures based on mobile phone data. The social contexts, such as call logs, text message, location, proximity and time are taken into account. The Location Base Services (LBS) are triggered when users enter or leave the range. A crucial aspect of the LBS, is to accurately detect the locations of users. Currently, many positioning technologies such as the GPS, NFC and Beacons are available [38, 39] and can be explored on campus.

4   Device Nimbus

Developing an integrated computing framework to efficiently manage heterogeneous and distributed social-environmental data, with a particular focus in an urban planning context, is a non-trivial challenge. A recently introduce intelligent middleware – Device Nimbus [3] – can be used to meet this challenge.

4.1 High-Level Overview

In this sub-section, we present a high-level overview of the Device Nimbus architecture.[1] The middleware, conceptually presented in Fig. 1, provides a mechanism to integrate mobile devices, social networks and physical sensors. The overarching goal is to provide an architecture enabling general interoperability. Specifically, the role of the platform is to track devices, systems and sensors that can provide relevant information to users in smart environments.

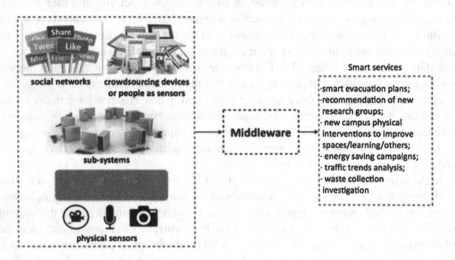

Fig. 1. A conceptual view of 'middleware' that can be used to combine distributed and heterogeneous data to help deliver smart services.

From a functional viewpoint, the context-aware system can be represented as a layered middleware consisting of sensors, raw data retrieval, pre-processing, storage or management, and an application layer. This approach allows for the identification of common concepts in both context-aware and prediction computing frameworks. The key blocks (or components) of the Device Nimbus middleware are presented in Fig. 2. These blocks are: (i) *Data Collectors*: the part of the middleware that is responsible for collecting data from different devices and sensors; (ii) *Data Integration*: the part of the middleware that is responsible for persistence and data integration; (iii) *Intelligent Modules*: the part of the middleware that is responsible for data mining and data analysis at a micro scale.

---

[1] More technical details can be found in [3].

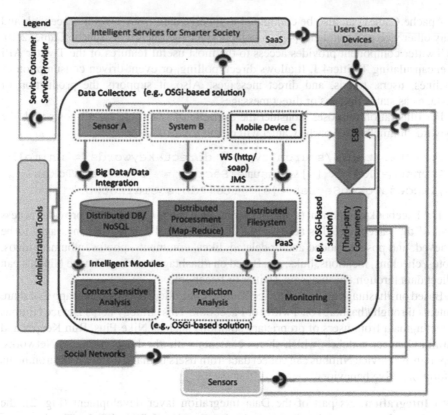

Fig. 2. The high-level view of the Device Nimbus architecture [3]

4.2 Implementation: Minimum Viable Product

In this sub-section, we describe the implementation steps necessary to deploy an instance of the Device Nimbus middleware in the nominated domain. Here, we adopt a standard software engineering methodology and detail the minimum viable product (or phased prototype). Figures 1 and 2 illustrate the conceptual view and the high-level architecture respectively.

Data Collectors. As part of the Data Collectors layer development (Fig. 2), the Apache Camel [40] routine engine (with a lightweight embedded ESB) was integrated with Device Nimbus. The middleware currently has the capacity to receive data from six different physical sensors (noise, temperature, humidity, luminosity, NFC and PIR). Apache Camel is a messaging technology glue with routing, chosen because of the ease at which it can be deployed. It joins together messaging start and end points, allowing for the transferring of messages from different sources to different destinations. Based on the architecture (Fig. 2), the ServiceMix Kernel was converted into an Apache Camel route container. The Apache ServiceMix Kernel is a small OSGi based runtime which provides a lightweight container onto which various bundles can be deployed.

Apache Camel can also be configured to receive data from Twitter, Facebook and many other web environments [41]. Available since the release of Apache Camel 2.10, the Twitter component provides access to the most useful features of the Twitter API by encapsulating Twitter4 J. It allows direct, polling, or event-driven consumption of timelines, users, trends, and direct messages. Also, it supports the production of messages as status updates or direct messages.

For illustration purposes, consider the example of searching for all posts with the keyword "unimelblc". Apache Camel will create routes as:

```
from("twitter://search?type = direct&keywords = unimelbl
c&consumerKey = [s]&consumerSecret = [s]&accessToken = [
s]&accessTokenSecret = [s]").to("db:socialnetwork");
```

The Facebook component (available in release Apache Camel 2.12), provides access to all of the Facebook APIs accessible using Facebook4 J. It allows messages to be retrieved, and posts to added and/or deleted, likes, comments, photos, albums, videos, photos, checkins, locations, links, etc. Based on #hashtags tracking, Device Nimbus can collect data through #hashtags on Twitter or Facebook.

Based on #hashtags tracking, Device Nimbus can collect data from any app that share contents through #hashtags on Twitter or Facebook. This strategy helps Device Nimbus collecting data from users of proprietary solutions such as Nike Plus, Run Keeper and Garmin Connect watches, which shares contents with #hashtags in Social Networks. Importantly, Device Nimbus can collect data from users in many different environments (a form of active behavior).

Data Integration. As part of the Data Integration layer development (Fig. 2), the NOSQL database can receive data from the Apache Camel. Two different databases are being used: (i) a general database that contains data collected from a variety of sensors and devices, routed from Apache Camel; (ii) a contextual database, which contains data analytics from different users. The intelligent modules (implemented using intelligent agents) are responsible for updating the contextual database using either the general database or previous analysis results already stored in the database. Apache Camel is responsible for updating the general database. The rational behind the use of a contextual database is to improve performance when providing feedback to users.

Intelligent Modules. As part of the Intelligent Modules development (Fig. 2), a knowledge base (rule-based system) was developed using JBoss Drools [42].

It is important to note the distinction between the concepts of *contextual element* and *context*. A contextual element is any piece of data or information that can be used to characterize an entity in a given domain. The context of an interaction between an agent and an application, in order to execute some task, is the set of instantiated contextual elements that are necessary to support the task at hand [29]. Here, the knowledge base was designed/developed in the context of learning spaces located on the University of Melbourne campus (see the case study in the following section). The specific contextual elements used in our implementation where: (i) New posts in Twitter using #unimelblc hashtags; (ii) Significant changes in weather (temperature, humidity); (iii) Holidays and special dates; (iv) New NFC input; (v) New PIR input.

The contextual intelligent module is also responsible for monitoring user behavior via the updating of the contextual database, based on users profile, behavior and routines. Here, we use JBoss Drools, to process any new data. Feedback provided to users is triggered from the contextual database. In our Device Nimbus implementation, the knowledge based was integrated with the middleware. Given the encapsulated rules, the intelligent module has the ability to identify patterns within/between the data collected from a variety of sources and integrated into the general database. As a representative example, Fig. 3 details a rule designed to identify the mode/type of conversation (scenario of interest) between individuals in the case study area.

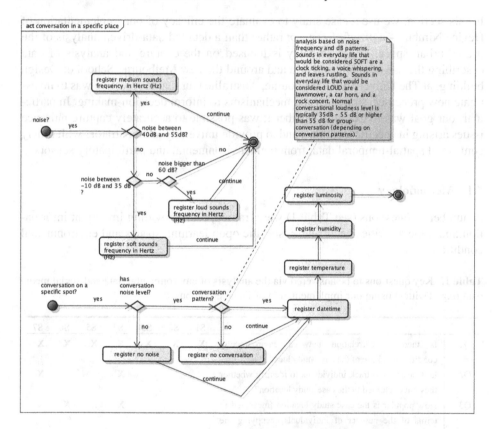

Fig. 3. An example of a rule (from the knowledge base), designed to identify if people are having conversation in a specific location based on sensor data input.

The contextual intelligent module is also responsible for monitoring user behavior via the updating of the contextual database, based on users profile, behavior and routines. Here, we use JBoss Drools, to process any new data. Feedback provided to users is triggered from the contextual database.

Deployment. Our implementation of the Device Nimbus middleware is running on the Cloud, hosted via the National eResearch Collaboration Tools and Resources project (NeCTAR).[2] It should be noted that the data collection sub-systems and design of the core infrastructure with extensible features and integrated visual environments for data management and monitoring was not implemented in this minimal viable product phase. The predictive module is currently under development.

5 Case Study: The Use of Public Space on Campus

In this section, we use a case study to evaluate the efficacy of our implementation of Device Nimbus – a *proof-of-concept* rather than a detailed data-driven analysis of the use of urban space. The case study is focused on the capture and analysis of data describing the use of public space in and around the new Melbourne School of Design building, at The University of Melbourne, Australia. Our major objective was to investigate new processes, strategies and mechanisms to inform decision-making. In particular, our goal was to examine whether it was possible to accurately capture nuisance issues arising in specific locations, and to provide university administrators with timely contextual spatial-temporal data, from both environmental and participatory sensors.

5.1 Methodology

A number of questions (see Table 1) were framed, each providing important information about the activities occurring in specific open learning spaces and environmental conditions.

Table 1. Key questions to be answered via the analysis of environmental data and social media data (e.g. Twitter) using our implementation of Device Nimbus.

		S1	S2	S3	S4	S5	S6	S7
Q1	Is there a correlation between environmental conditions and use of the case study location?	X	X	X	X	X	X	X
Q2	Is it possible to track individuals to identify whether they have returned to the case study location?				X			X
Q3	How popular is the case study location (measured in terms of the number of individuals occupying the location)?				X	X	X	X
Q4	Can noise levels be used to indicate how the case study location is being used?					X	X	
Q5	Are individuals (or groups) occupying/visiting the nominated locations?				X	X	X	X
Q6	Do individuals use the #hashtag to post relevant messages							X

---

[2] https://www.nectar.org.au.

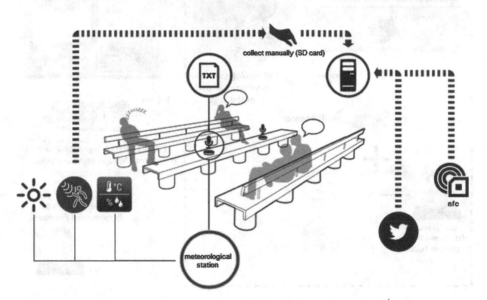

Fig. 4. **(Top)** The case study area – open public learning areas on the university campus. **(Bottom)** A schematic representation of the benches within the case study area, including the environmental and participatory sensors.

Data collection was limited to one location – an open public learning area consisting of large outdoor benches distributed along the perimeter of the Melbourne School of Design building (see Fig. 4). The case study area was signed-posted informing students and staff (and visitors) that they were entering a 'test area' and that data was being collected.

Data collection consisted of two components: environmental physical sensor data and crowdsourced data. The environmental sensor data was collected via a small meteorological station using six different sensors: humidity (S1), temperature (S2), luminosity (S3), NFC sensor (S4), noise (S5) and Passive Infrared Sensor PIR (S6) (see Figs. 4 and 5). The Arduino microphone was calibrated with SPLnFFT iPhone App [43]. With this strategy, the unit value used with the microphone was considered in dB. The crowdsourced data was primarily based on Twitter data (S7).[3] A special #unimelblc hashtag was defined and advertised to students/visitors in the case study area. Significantly, any individual could use the tag to share tweets. Volunteer participants were asked to share their GPS location when posting using the #unimelblc hashtag. A NFC Tag was used to share the experiment website and to collect data from users, such as smartphone type, date, time and the location that the user tapped the tag. This data allowed us to determine whether an individual returned to the case study area.

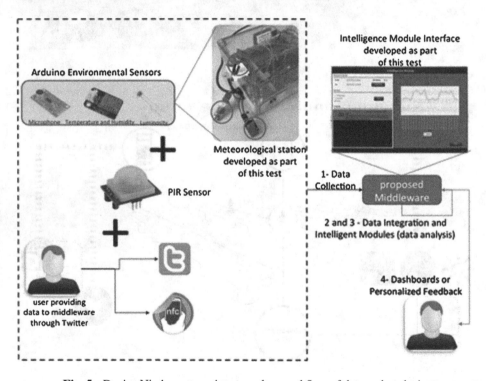

Fig. 5. Device Nimbus sensor inputs and general flow of data and analysis.

The test data was collected over a three-week period. Each weekday, the data from the noise, PIR and NFC sensors was collected spanning a 5 h period. The noise sensors were adjusted to collect data only after the PIR or NFC sensor was activated. After activation, noise data was collected every 10 s. The environmental data was collected every 30 min from 07:00 h to 22:00 h and was added to the Device Nimbus database. The Twitter specially defined #hashtag was monitored over 24 h per day (automatically)

---

[3] Facebook data was removed from the initial series of tests to simplify the analysis in the case study.

during the tests period. The database was updated by the Apache Camel every time that a new #hashtag was found. It is important to note that no personal data was collected as part of the case study tests.

As part of the evaluation of our Device Nimbus implementation, a series of small tests were carried out to evaluate the ability of the middleware to integrated data into the knowledge base using the Intelligent Modules (as described in Sect. 4.2). Here, we limit the analysis to an example machine learning implementation focused on context-awareness. The specific contextual elements considers included:

- New posts in Twitter using predefined hashtags
- Changes in weather conditions
- University holidays and special dates
- New inputs in NFC and PIR sensors

5.2 Analysis

In the first step of our analysis, the focus was on the integration and analysis of environmental data with other sensors. In order to answer question Q1 (Table 1), an interface was developed as part of this experiment (Fig. 5). The system interface uses graphical representations for the collected and integrated environmental and Twitter data in both the general and contextual database, in order to support pattern recognition. To analyze the integrated data, 17 different rules were created and added to the intelligent module as knowledge base in the JBoss Drools.

The JBoss Drools implementation within the intelligent module was able to handle a large number of facts (java objects) in the working memory (facts should match with Drools rules to trigger events), and the contextual knowledge base provided personalized outputs and dashboards for the different locations, based on identified patterns. With this simple experiment, the Device Nimbus implementation was able to identify that: (i) when the weather was too hot or cold, or when it was raining, people avoided the outdoor spaces; (ii) the benches around the perimeter of the architecture building was generally used by individuals, during the lunch time period, while the lawn areas (close by) were shared by groups of people and during the whole day; (iii) the addition of new benches in the case study area results in a modification in usage patterns.

In the second step of our analysis, we have examined whether the Device Nimbus implementation was able to combine/integrate Twitter data with environmental sensor data in order to answer the questions Q1, Q2, Q3 and Q5.

The tracked Twitter messages in Device Nimbus were always read using the same format:

```
#user#USERNAME#messagecontent#CONTENT#HASHTAG#locat
ion#LOCATIONNAME#timezone#TIMEZONE
```

An example analysis of a small tracked message:

```
#user#oliveiraeduardo#text#It's a beautiful day at
Uni.#unimelblc#location#MSD Building#timezone#null
```

shows that it is possible to extract useful information such as: (i) the main locations occupied by the students (visitors) when on campus; (ii) determine whether the same individuals visited different locations when on campus; (iii) identify the date and time of all Twitter post; (iv) determine the 'destination of choice' for specific individuals when on campus, and (v) an indication as to the population/crowd size at the case study location – whether the location was empty or crowded at a specific date and time. Importantly, the intelligent module of Device Nimbus was able to split and analyse Twitter posts in order to help answer questions Q1, Q2, Q3 and Q5 based on an individuals' use of specific hashtags. We were able to determine how often individuals frequented the open learning space.

To test the ability of Device Nimbus to track #hashtags, each time a user tapped a NFC tag, a message was posted on Twitter. We observed that the Twitter sample streaming data used by Device Nimbus was not able to reliably track users – only 31 % of the shared tweets were based on NFC posts. Device Nimbus found an additional 38 % of posts came from individuals who did not use the NFC. If we consider that possibility that additional posts may been published by individuals who did not use a NFC tag, then a large volume of data may have been lost. This can in part be attributed to the fact that Device Nimbus was using the sample streaming (limited) channel of Twitter, which provided millions of messages to Device Nimbus. These messages were subsequently filtered using JBoss Drools. Only messages with special #unimelblc were recorded in general database. An alternative approach to improve data collection from Twitter would be to use Firehose, a more complete streaming channel (note: permission is required from Twitter to access the stream).

Despite the fact that all the individuals' hashtags were not tracked successfully, the intelligent module of Device Nimbus was able to analyze Twitter posts in order to answer questions Q2, Q3, Q5. It is interesting to note that the Twitter analysis did not provide a reliable framework to describe the routine/behavior patterns of unique individuals.

For every tracked individual post in Twitter, the intelligent module was responsible for updating the contextual database of Device Nimbus. This updating process consolidate Twitter post information, including the locations where the posting was done, the date and time of the posting as well as the contents of the messages. Given the small number of participants in the tests, it is not possible to paint a coherent picture of student (and visitor) behavior. In future work, it will be interesting to increase the scale the tests to include more individuals and locations.

The content analysis of Twitter tracked messages suggests that: (i) individuals/groups of people were studying for an exam/test (5 posts); (ii) the area surround the Melbourne School of Design building was a positive place to study (3 posts); (iii) one post also contained a photo and a link to Instagram. This analysis, when merged with other data sources, provides valuable information for planners and designers – specifically when considering the introduction of interventions/changes to the learning environment. Unfortunately, Device Nimbus' intelligent module was not able to semantically understand what people were saying about locations by interpreting texts (thus, not answering Q6). However, additional natural language processing analysis will be the focus of further work.

In the third step of our analysis, we move away from the social media data and focus on analyzing the environmental sensor data. In particular, our goal was to determine whether the intelligent module was able to identify individuals' presence in the case study area based on noise inputs. Over 4 h of noise data (recorded as dB variations in a text file) were collected and analyzed by the intelligent module (based knowledge of rules) of Device Nimbus. To validate the collected noise input with the actual presence of individuals in the designated locations, observations (over a 1 h period) were conducted daily. Based on the recorded conversations patterns in the noise data, as shown in Fig. 6, it was not possible to provide a definite answer to the question of noise levels and conversation format in groups. Even collecting noise data after the activation of the PIR or NFC sensors by real individuals, the Arduino microphone did not provide reliable data inputs. Significantly, Q4 can only be answered satisfactorily by merging the PIR, the noise sensor, the NFC data and the Twitter data together.

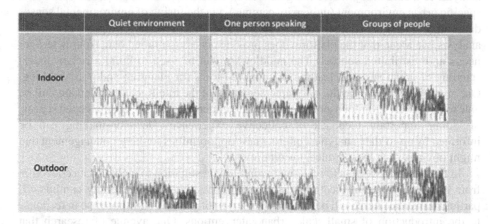

Fig. 6. Noise patterns observed after analyzing the collected data in the case study area.

Identifying conversations (mode/style and participants) is a significant challenge. In future investigations, more powerful microphones should be used as part of the data collection so that more reliable and robust analysis of noise patterns can occur.

The integration of the NFC data and Twitter helped us provide a more accurate answer to Q3. However, the acceptance and use of NFC technology was low and, as discussed before, Twitter hashtags could not be tracked by the Twitter public stream channel. In the future, different sensors, such as iBeacons (Bluetooth devices) and GPS values should be used as a way of collecting more reliable data detailing user locations.

In the final step of our analysis, the robustness of the middleware, measured in terms its ability to handle large volumes of data was examined. The volume of data generated via both the participatory and environmental sensors (environmental data collected every 30 min, Twitter monitored 24 h and noise collected when NFC or PIR detected people in the locations every 10 s) was non-trivial. Significantly, the ESB and the data integration module performed as expected (based on benchmarking). No problems were identified during the data collection phases or when using the integration modules in this first controlled tests. The middleware performed without errors or exceptions during all the tests.

6 Conclusion

The convergence of ubiquitous computing and mobile devices within a smart urban environment suggests that an evidence-based approach can be used to inform planning decisions. In this paper, we have examined the use of Device Nimbus, an open source middleware package, in this domain. Device Nimbus' middleware includes key blocks (or components) for data collection from heterogeneous sensors and devices; data retrieval; pre-processing; storage or management, and an application layer.

To illustrate the efficacy of the Device Nimbus middleware, we have limited our analysis to a case study where the goal was to document the use of public space in a specific urban environment (university campus), via the fusing of environmental sensor data and crowdsourced data from smart phones and devices. Based on a proof of concept analysis, we argue that the platform does provide access to unified data from heterogeneous and distributed sources. The middleware can be used to build a richer understanding of urban systems, leading to improved tools for planning and policymaking. Our analysis suggests that the full implementation of the intelligent middleware will be able to effectively monitor users' routines and to understand the use of small open spaces, providing important feedback of collective experience. Decision-making can be informed by up-to-date analytics, offering new opportunities for better management that might obviate, or at least reduce, uncertainty.

In future work, we plan to scale-up our initial investigation to include data collection from a diverse range of locations distributed across the main university campus. Of particular instance here, will be the documentation of patterns and space use in response to the introduction of small-scale urban interventions. One avenue of research that requires further investigation will be to explore the effective use of collaborative outdoor learning environments. It might also be interesting to investigate the use of mobile augmented reality within this domain.

Acknowledgements. Eduardo A. Oliveira and Carlos Vaz would like to thank National Council for Scientific and Technological Development (CNPq) – Brazil, for supporting their postdoc position (scholarship provided under reports n° BEX 9213/13-9 and n° BEX 11523-13-1).

References

1. Oliveira, E.A., Kirley, M., Vanz, E., Gama, K.: hSpy: An intelligent framework for context and predictive analysis for smarter health devices (2014)
2. Sun, X.H., Blatecky, A.R.: Middleware: the key to next generation computing. J. Parallel Distrib. Comput. **64**(6), 689–691 (2004)
3. Oliveira, E.A., Michael, K., Jorge, C.B.F.: Device nimbus: an intelligent middleware for smarter services for health and fitness. Int. J. Distrib. Sens. Netw. Article ID: 454626. Provisional PDF (2015)

4. Chourabi, H., Nam, T., Walker, S., Gil-Garcia, J.R., Mellouli, S., Nahon, K., Pardo, T.A., Scholl, H.J.: Understanding smart cities: an integrative framework. In: 2012 45th Hawaii International Conference on System Science (HICSS), IEEE, pp. 2289–2297 (2012)
5. Boulton, A., Brunn, S.D., Devriendt, L.: 18 Cyberinfrastructures and smart world cities: physical, human and soft infrastructures. International Handbook of Globalization and World Cities, 198 (2011)
6. Hollands, R.G.: Will the real smart city please stand up? intelligent, progressive or entrepreneurial? City 12(3), 303–320 (2008)
7. Batty, M., Axhausen, K.W., Giannotti, F., Pozdnoukhov, A., Bazzani, A., Wachowicz, M., Portugali, Y.: Smart cities of the future. Eur. Phys. J.-Spec. Top. 214(1), 481–518 (2012)
8. Caragliu, A., Del Bo, C., Nijkamp, P.: Smart cities in Europe. J. Urban Technol. 18(2), 65–82 (2011)
9. Harrison, C., Eckman, B., Hamilton, R., Hartswick, P., Kalagnanam, J., Paraszczak, J., Williams, P.: Foundations for smarter cities. IBM J. Res. Dev. 54(4), 1–16 (2010)
10. Toppeta, D.: The smart city vision: how innovation and ICT can build smart, livable, sustainable cities. The Innovation Knowledge Foundation (2014). http://www.inta-aivn.org/images/cc/Urbanism/background%20documents/Toppeta_Report_005_2010.pdf
11. Coe, A., Paquet, G., Roy, J.: E-governance and smart communities a social learning challenge. Soc. Sci. Comput. Rev. 19(1), 80–93 (2001)
12. Saelens, B.E., Sallis, J.F., Frank, L.D.: Environmental correlates of walking and cycling: findings from the transportation, urban design, and planning literatures. Ann. Behav. Med. 25(2), 80–91 (2003)
13. Thompson, C.W.: Urban open space in the 21st century. Landscape Urban Plan. 60(2), 59–72 (2002)
14. Force, U.T.: Towards an urban renaissance: final report of the urban task force chaired by Lord Rogers of Riverside, The Department of the Environment. Transport, and Regions (DoE), London (2002)
15. Batty, M.: The New Science of Cities. MIT Press, Cambridge (2013)
16. Nimbits. http://www.nimbits.com
17. Etherios. http://www.idigi.com
18. ThingSpeak. http://www.thingspeak.com
19. WSO2. http://www.wso2.com
20. Blackstock, M., Kaviani, N., Lea, R., Friday, A.: MAGIC broker 2: an open and extensible platform for the internet of things. In: Internet of Things (IOT), IEEE, pp. 1–8, (2010)
21. Erbad, A., Blackstock, M., Friday, A., Lea, R., Al-Muhtadi, J.: Magic broker: a middleware toolkit for interactive public displays. In: Sixth Annual IEEE International Conference on Pervasive Computing and Communications, PerCom 2008, IEEE, pp. 509–514 (2008)
22. Filipponi, L., Vitaletti, A., Landi, G., Memeo, V., Laura, G., Pucci, P.: Smart city: an event driven architecture for monitoring public spaces with heterogeneous sensors. In: 2010 Fourth International Conference on Sensor Technologies and Applications (SENSORCOMM), IEEE, pp. 281–286 (2010)
23. Xively. https://xively.com/
24. Anthopoulos, L., Fitsilis, P.: From digital to ubiquitous cities: defining a common architecture for urban development. In: 2010 Sixth International Conference on Intelligent Environments (IE), IEEE, pp. 301–306 (2010)
25. Ishida, T.: Digital city kyoto. Commun. ACM 45(7), 76–81 (2002)
26. Lieshout, V.: Configuring the digital city of Amsterdam. N. Media Technol. 3(1), 27–52 (2001)

27. Van Bastelaer, B.: Digital cities and transferability of results. In: 4th EDC Conference on Digital Cities, Salzburg, pp. 61–70 (1998)
28. Yu, Z., Liang, Y., Xu, B., Yang, Y., Guo, B.: Towards a smart campus with mobile social networking. In: 2011 International Conference on Internet of Things (iThings/CPSCom), and 4th International Conference on Cyber, Physical and Social Computing, IEEE, pp. 162–169 (2011)
29. Vieira dos Santos, V., Salgado, C.B.: CEManTIKA: a domain-independent framework for designing context sensitive systems (2008)
30. Kenney, D.R., Dumont, R., Kenney, G.: Mission and Place: Strengthening Learning and Community Through Campus Design. Greenwood Publishing Group, Westport (2005)
31. Oliveira, E.A., Tedesco, P.: I-collaboration: um modelo de colaboração inteligente personalizada para ambientes de EAD. Revista Brasileira de Informática na Educação. **18**(1), 17–31 (2010)
32. Yau, S.S., Gupta, S.K., Karim, F., Ahamed, S.I., Wang, Y., Wang, B.: Smart classroom: enhancing collaborative learning using pervasive computing technology. In: ASEE 2003 Annual Conference and Exposition, pp. 13633–13642. Sn (2003)
33. Halawani, T., Mohandes, M.: Smart card for smart campus: KFUPM case study. In: Proceedings of the 2003 10th IEEE International Conference on Electronics, Circuits and Systems. ICECS 2003, vol. 3, IEEE, pp. 1252–1255 (2003)
34. Rohs, M., Bohn, J.: Entry points into a smart campus environment-overview of the ETHOC system. In: Proceedings 23rd International Conference on Distributed Computing Systems Workshops 2003, IEEE, pp. 260–266 (2003)
35. Eagle, N., Pentland, A.S., Lazer, D.: Inferring friendship network structure by using mobile phone data. Proc. Natl. Acad. Sci. **106**(36), 15274–15278 (2009)
36. Mirisaee, S.H., Noorzadeh, S., Sami, A., Sameni, R.: Mining friendship from cell-phone switch data. In: 2010 3rd International Conference on Human-Centric Computing (HumanCom), IEEE, pp. 1–5 (2010)
37. Ankolekar, A., Szabo, G., Luon, Y., Huberman, B.A., Wilkinson, D., Wu, F.: Friendlee: a mobile application for your social life. In: Proceedings of the 11th International Conference on Human-Computer Interaction with Mobile Devices and Services, p. 27. ACM (2009)
38. Estimote Beacons. http://estimote.com/#jump-to-products
39. Li, K.A., Sohn, T.Y., Huang, S., Griswold, W.G.: Peopletones: a system for the detection and notification of buddy proximity on mobile phones. In: Proceedings of the 6th International Conference on Mobile Systems, Applications, and Services, pp. 160–173. ACM (2008)
40. Apache Camel. http://camel.apache.org/
41. Apache Camel Components. http://camel.apache.org/components.html
42. JBoss Drools. http://www.drools.org/
43. SPLnFFT. https://itunes.apple.com/au/app/splnfft-noise-meter/id355396114?mt=8

Tangible Mixed Reality On-Site: Interactive Augmented Visualisations from Architectural Working Models in Urban Design

Gerhard Schubert[✉], David Schattel, Marcus Tönnis, Gudrun Klinker, and Frank Petzold

Technische Universität München, Munich, Germany
{schubert,petzold}@tum.de,
david_schattel@gmx.de, {toennis,klinker}@in.tum.de

Abstract. The consequences of architectural planning and design decisions made in the early design phases are hard to foresee. While professionals are used to reading plans and understanding architectural models, most laypeople are not familiar with their abstractions. This can lead to misinterpretations and misunderstandings between the different participants in the design process, especially in complex building situations, and decisions can be made or rejected that can have far-reaching consequences for the remainder of the project.

In this paper we describe the concept and prototypical implementation of a decision-support system for the early design and discussion stages of urban design projects that aims to address precisely this problem. The setup directly connects physical volumetric models and hand-drawn sketches with an interactive, mixed-reality visualization presented on a tablet or mobile phone, making it possible to see an interactive real-time view of an architectural design within the context of the actual site. In addition, the system is able to incorporate interactive simulations conducted on the model and presented in the AR-view.

Keywords: Early design stages · Urban design · HCI · Tangible interfaces · Immersive environment · Simulations

1 Problem

During the early design phases presentations and discussions between architects and clients usually involve sketches, paper and models. While designers are used to working intuitively with these tools, laypeople are not used to reading plans or scale models and find it difficult to relate these abstract representations to the real world. Many people, therefore, find it hard to assess the impact of design decisions at this stage for the later result.

An alternative means of presentation is the use of perspective drawings and visualisations that show how an architectural design will look in a real scenario or the actual context. With the availability of affordable and ever more powerful computers, hand-drawn perspectives have mostly been replaced by digital visualisations, initially in the form of individual rendered images and more recently in the form of immersive and

© Springer-Verlag Berlin Heidelberg 2015
G. Celani et al. (Eds.): CAAD Futures 2015, CCIS 527, pp. 55–74, 2015.
DOI: 10.1007/978-3-662-47386-3_4

interactive environments such as Augmented Reality or Virtual Reality presentations. A key problem in this context is the fact that sufficiently detailed computer models take time to construct and are therefore costly to produce. In addition, in the early design phases, the design idea is typically in a state of flux with many unknowns. At this stage such presentation methods are therefore only really suitable for presenting and choosing between pre-prepared versions and variants. While these offer a certain degree of choice, new ideas that arise during discussions with the users and clients cannot be visualised on the spot. These methods do not, therefore, support a true exchange and collaborative exploration of ideas.

With the increasing complexity and size of modern building tasks comes a concomitant rise in the amount of information that informs a design project. To stay on top of this, digital analyses and simulations are increasingly being used to verify the feasibility of design decisions. The information that needs to be communicated increases along with the complexity of their internal interrelationships. As these become harder to understand, the more reliant we will become on using digital media to present, communicate and discuss ideas.

The fundamental problem therefore can be traced to a discrepancy between the different presentational media. Hand-drawn sketches and models make it possible to work interactively and to explore and discuss ideas in real time, but they contain a reduced set of information. Digital models make it possible to present complex analyses and simulations but, due to inadequate interfaces on the one hand and their complex preparation requirements on the other, are only partially suitable for interactive use. We are not, therefore, exploiting the full potential of digital tools.

2   Approach

Given the problem of this discrepancy between established design tools and digital presentation media, we need to find new approaches that make it possible to also communicate complex interdependencies to the viewer in a comprehensible way. In addition, we need to progress beyond the current rigid methods to facilitate a direct and intuitive way of working with the design idea. Only then will it be possible to directly develop and interactively present design ideas for all participants whether experts or laypeople. In this paper we describe a method for interactively presenting architectural ideas in an AR context using established design tools such as hand sketches and models. This approach gives rise to a totally new interactive presentation and discussion platform that bridges the gap between established design methods and mixed-reality architectural presentation techniques. The primary objectives are to find a simple, intuitive and direct means of input and to simultaneously make it possible to see the presentation of the design changes in real time in an immersive context and a real environment. To achieve this, the test platform creates a direct connection between physical volumetric models and hand-sketches, and an interactive, mixed-reality visualisation presented on a tablet or mobile phone. This makes it possible to see an interactive view of architectural design ideas at the actual building site.

Over the past few years as part of the research project "CDP /Collaborative Design Platform", we have developed a concept and a prototype for a design platform based on an analysis of the design process and the identification of the key requirements of a design tool [1–3]. A central feature of this self-developed and self-built hardware and software setup is the seamless coupling of established design tools, such as a working model and hand-drawn sketches, with interactive, digitally computed analyses and simulations, and interactive presentation methods. This seamless, real-time connection between the physical working model and hand-drawn sketches eliminates the need for complex modelling activities: changes in the physical models (position, shape) or in the hand-drawn sketches are digitally reconstructed in real time and interactively displayed in a mixed-reality view. While the architect can design using familiar tools and methods, the observer has an entirely new mode of viewing. Different ideas and scenarios can be tested spontaneously and new ideas can be developed and viewed directly in three dimensions on site. This not only promotes dialogue and design exploration between professionals, but also helps non-professionals participate as they see the results simultaneously presented virtually but within in a tangible environment. The client is involved more directly in the process and can contribute own ideas and changes, and then see these presented on the fly in 3D on the real building site.

The ability to also present interactive analyses and simulations, both in the model as well as in the AR-view, makes it possible to provide additional information for decision-making and augments the physical tools with digital data. This makes it possible to assess the further implications of an architectural design decision directly on site by providing additional objective parameters for consideration. As such, decisions are not made purely on the basis of subjective criteria but are backed up by real-time analyses and simulations, such as overshadowing, energy efficiency calculations, or noise impact simulations presented interactively within the actual context. This information, which would normally only be available at a later stage in the design process, can therefore be accessed much earlier, and can inform design decisions and creative deliberations in the early design phases by providing objective data to support decision-making. Design participants and decision makers can therefore make more informed decisions in the early design and planning stages.

2.1 User Scenario

Using the setup described above, we can describe a typical use case for this concept as follows. The design task is the development of a master plan for an urban design project. The client and developer meet with the architects and representatives from the local planning authority on site to discuss a number of aspects ranging from cost minimisation to factors such as the shadows the buildings cast and the build up of traffic noise. Instead of poring over 2D printouts of plans and an accompanying model, the participants have several tablets and a multi-touch environment with automatic real-time 3D object recognition.

The multi-touch table shows the as yet unbuilt site plan of the building site, on top of which lie physical blocks of styrofoam (XPS: extruded polystyrene foam) cut to size to show an initial design for the arrangement of the urban blocks. The table display shows the results of a noise impact simulation, with critical areas highlighted. On the tablets, the users can also see the design proposal as an augmented reality visualisation superimposed onto the real environment. Here too, the viewer can see the results of the noise impact simulation.

The lead architect explains the design idea to all present making use of the model and simulations. As he describes specific aspects, he alters the arrangement, adding, removing or shifting blocks around the model to illustrate how he or she arrived at the current design. The digital simulation adapts immediately to reflect the different situations. The arrangement of the physical blocks is reflected in the display on the tablets, and the noise impact simulations is re-calculated and displayed both within the model as well as on the tablets (Fig. 1).

Fig. 1. Using an AR app, users can experience the design scenario immersively and view it in the context of its real surroundings. The scenario itself is modelled using a physical model and hand-sketching on a multi-touch table and then computed for display in real time on a mobile device. Simulations can be displayed in the app, adding an additional layer of digital information to the modelled scene and providing additional objective information for more informed decision-making.

When the architect is finished, the client responds with questions of his own regarding the placement of certain buildings and suggests a position for the company's high-rise headquarters. He takes a new larger block of Styrofoam, trims it to size and places it at the corresponding location. The building volume is immediately recalculated and redisplayed in the AR-view on the tablets. The perspective view of the simulation shows that the height of the new building impacts on its neighbours. The overshadowing simulation also shows in numbers that the potential solar gain of the neighbouring buildings would fall by around 40 % annually. The combination of the view in perspective, backed up by the numerical analysis of the design implications convinces the client that this option brings disadvantages, and the group then discuss among themselves how the different interests could be reconciled.

2.2 Related Work

In 2013, Chi et al. [4] presented "Research trends and opportunities of augmented reality applications in architecture, engineering, and construction". Two aspects of this paper are relevant in our context: on the one side these are digitally-supported design tools. On the other side it discusses tools for Augmented Reality presentation using virtual geometries on site.

Augmenting additional information such as simulations and analyses directly in a physical model can be seen in URP [5] and the project "Tangible 3D tabletops" [6]. Projects that employ purely virtual models include "The Augmented Round Table" [7] and the project by Seichter and Schnabel [8]. Using a Head-Mounted Display, a virtual scene of a digital tabletop model can be viewed and edited by several different users as a means of improving communication and collaboration. Another approach in this vein is sketchand + [9] in which a real, physical model of the surroundings serves as the basis for the scene. Using a Head-Mounted Display in combination with markers located in the real model where the design is to be inserted, virtual design variants can be viewed directly within the scene. By switching different markers, one can compare different design variants within the physical model. The projects mentioned here offer the possibility of examining and discussing urban designs in a model view but do not show it within its real context. Välkkynen et al. [10] presented a project that aims to address this. The paper describes a concept for a "Mixed Reality Tools to Support Citizen Participation in Urban Planning" comprising a system that "includes a tangible tabletop interface combined with 3D printing and on-location AR visualizations" [10]. Using 3D printed tokens, insertions such as noise-protection barriers can be placed within an interactive map. The AR app shows a mixed-reality view of the building site. The authors hope to incorporate a feedback function such as the possibility to make comments and to include questionnaires in a future development of the project. While the authors describe a concept, they do no elaborate on the approaches and description of its technical realization. The inclusion of the models as 3D printed objects in the creative process is also disruptive to the designer's flow of thinking between visualising and analysis.

In 2009 Wagner et al. [11] showed an approach for supporting social collaboration processes in an urban design context. As part of the project "Urban Planning in the MR-Tent", an interactive environment was developed in prototypical form for use in public participation procedures. The on-site setup included a multi-touch table and two large projection screens that showed a superimposed live image of the building site. Tokens placed on the table represented objects in the mixed-reality scene and could be positioned and controlled. The tokens were linked via so-called content cards with the virtual objects (3D volumes, simulations or similar), making it possible to communicate flexibly with them. This approach does make it possible to flexibly re-assign the purpose of the tokens, but the system still requires pre-defined elements. The "Urban Sketcher" [12] project is also worth mentioning in this context. The tool is a mixed reality application for improving communications between project participants in the urban planning phases. Urban Sketcher makes it possible to sketch interactively within a mixed reality view directly on the building site. The physical setup in both projects uses a wired webcam and the projection method limits freedom of movement and only allows the scene to be seen from a single viewpoint.

The project by Allen et al. [13] is interesting from the public participation viewpoint. Using a mobile AR app, different design variants can be viewed on site. The interface provides a means of assessing different variants. However, these have to be modelled in advance and anchored within the system, and it is not possible to make changes to them while viewing. As such it is not suitable for use in creative thinking and design processes.

Wang et al. [14] have investigated on-site information systems for activities at the construction site and for discussing rationales. Among others aspects, the authors describe a requirement for interdependency between different roles of participating individuals and the need for a link between paper, whether digital or traditional, and the physical situation. Their work focuses more on on-site project progress monitoring and controlling than on real-time design. With their proposed setup, markers also need to be added to the environment.

Kwon et al. [15] investigated the development of a defect management system that provides on-site visualisation on tablet devices. Their system requires the users to place fiducial markers in the environment to facilitate registration of the visual content. Registration with the markers needs to be undertaken manually and it seems that there is no network interconnection to disseminate data online.

Zollmann et al. [16] built a tool for construction sites to support monitoring and documentation by incorporating aerial snapshots. Their work focuses primarily on data capturing and 3D reconstruction. It investigates dedicated visualisation techniques for information on the progress of the built structure. Aerial photos are taken with a drone and are transmitted to a 3D reconstruction client which then provides a 3D model of the differently timed states of the construction process for on-site visualisation. The on-site visualisation can then be used for surveying tasks, such as measuring the dimensions and sizes of objects and for annotating information.

The work by Sørensen [17] aims to improve communication of construction and maintenance plans for large-scale buildings and uses on-site AR in the form of AR binoculars with built-in position and orientation trackers. The system is portable but not meant for completely free movement. Because the position is fixed at any one time, the system need only continuously measure orientation. The system provides robust precision data and therefore reduces accuracy problems for distant objects.

3   System Setup

To realise our proposed concept, we use a combination of hardware and software. Both aspects need to be considered in order to build an integrated system. The system setup consists of two linked areas – the Collaborative Design Platform (CDP) (Fig. 2, left) and the on-site AR application (Fig. 2, right):

- **Collaborative Design platform** (Sect. 4): The first component of the system setup is an interactive design environment in the form of a real-time interface between established design tools, such as a working model and hand sketches, and digital tools, such as analyses and simulations [1, 2]. The context of this example is the early design phases of an urban design project at a scale of 1:500.

- **On-site AR application** (Sect. 5): The second component of the project described in this paper is the mobile Augmented Reality application [18]. The application is a bipolar network protocol operating in real time with the design environment. This link makes it possible to use mobile devices to view the design scenario as it stands in the physical model as a mixed-reality view in the context of the actual environment.

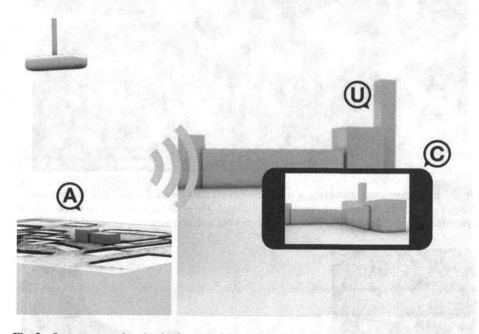

Fig. 2. System setup showing both parts of the system: the design-platform (left) and the on-site AR application (right). A network protocol links the physical model placed on a display of the design environment (A) with the display on the mobile device (C) in real time. The real environment (U) is augmented with the design model, providing the viewer looking at – or rather "through" – the mobile device with an immersive view of the design proposal on location in its actual context.

The real-time link-up between these two parts of the system makes it is possible to offer an entirely new form of interactive presentation. The following section describes each of the system components in greater detail.

4   CDP /Collaborative Design Platform

The technological basis of the Collaborative Design Platform (CDP) is a large-format multi-touch table with real-time 3D object recognition [19]. This system obviates the needs for markers in the physical model, making it possible to flexibly and freely alter the model as desired and to have these changes reflected immediately in the digital reconstruction (Fig. 3).

Fig. 3. Interactive simulations (e.g. a wind simulation) are produced in real time in response to changes made to the three-dimensional physical model. The system requires no markers, making it possible to model flexibly and freely when exploring a design idea.

Fig. 4. An additional vertically mounted touch screen makes it possible to sketch interactively in the perspective view.

An additional vertical touch screen serves as an info panel and can be used to sketch interactively into the perspective scene of the design scenario [20, 21]. The physical model and digital sketch are seamlessly linked. If the physical model is altered, the virtual scene, including any hand-sketches, analyses and simulations, updates to match it. This makes it possible to work very flexibly with different kinds of tools and information.

The software setup uses a plugin-oriented software architecture that comprises two components:

- The middleware, programmed in C++, which serves as the basis for processing the system-relevant basic functions such as 3D object reconstruction, tracking, data basis, output on the different screens, recording of data including versioning, and so on. Semantic GIS data served as the basic underlying plan for the map, providing not only geographical position data but also additional information of use for the analyses and simulation. The positioning in the coordinate system is on the basis of worldwide referenced spatial data.
- The second component comprises the plugins, written in C#. This principle enables different design-support tools, such as digitally computed analyses and simulations, to be attached flexibly to the middleware for use in the system. It also allows the system to be extended to meet specific needs so that it can be tailored to different building tasks and their respective requirements.

This setup makes it possible to develop new modules for calculating overshadowing or wind simulation and to incorporate these flexibly into the system. All of these respond to the data transmitted from the design environment with the arrangement of the physical model on the multi-touch table, adapting interactively and in real time to the new situation, and therefore to the momentary expression of the idea of the designer.

To be able to effectively compare different variants, the software prototype for the design platform supports versioning, making it possible to recall different prior states of the design. The software uses GIT as its concurrent versioning system. The geometric data of the reconstructed physical working model is stored as .ifc files. Different variants are shown as a timeline in a tree structure and each separate state is marked with a timestamp and screenshot as versioning attributes (Fig. 5).

The flexible concept of the platform also makes it possible to extend the scenario as required. The interaction method is achieved using a flexibly deployable TCP/UDP-protocol that makes it possible to establish a two-way platform ⇔ device connection [22] (Fig. 6).

In this way, the digitized design geometries based on the physical models and sketches are provided for further applications, such as the in this paper described AR-application. In addition to the reconstructed models and sketches, the geometry of the surrounded buildings, as well, as the semantic data based on the underlying GIS-model, are also provided via the protocol.

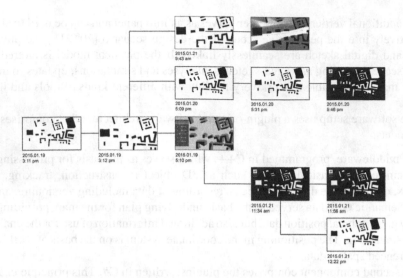

Fig. 5. Screenshot of the design platform. Different versions in a tree structure sorted by time.

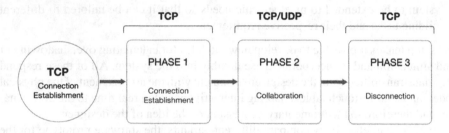

Fig. 6. Overview of the connection phases [22]

5   On-Site AR Application

As part of the sub-project described in this paper, the Collaborative Design Platform (CDP) has been extended with a concept for and prototypical implementation of an interactive AR app. The AR app makes it possible to interactively view an architectural design elaborated in the form of a physical model as a virtual representation in its real intended context (Fig. 7).

To implement the concept, it needs to fulfil the following requirements:

- Use a physical model or hand-drawn sketch as input device
- Transfer of data provided by the design platform in real time
- Ability to recall previously saved design variants
- Ability to track in the AR app without using markers
- Presentation of simulation data to assist decision-makers

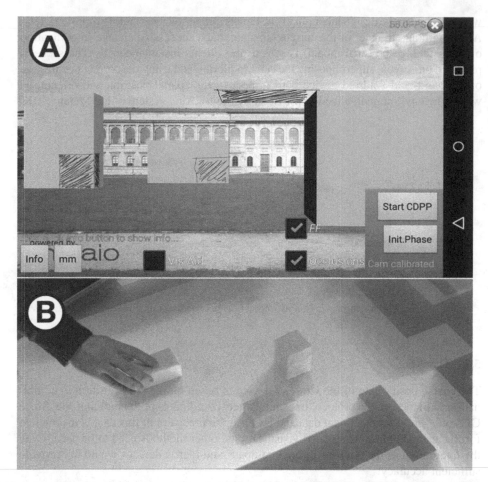

Fig. 7. Screenshot of the mobile application (A): The reconstructed geometry of the physical objects on the multi-touch table (B) is shown directly in its actual environment as a mixed-reality view on a mobile device (A).

5.1 On-Site Setup

The on-site visualisation tool is implemented as an Android application that acts as a new client connecting to the server. The connection can use either WiFi or a mobile network. The user selects an architectural sketch to show from a menu list and can choose from previous versions and variants of a design, or apply a real time visualisation of the physical model on the design platform plus any hand sketches augmented onto the physical working models. After selecting the desired scenario, the camera of the hand-held device is activated and the camera picture is shown on the screen.

On logging in to the server, the protocol transports building data (reconstructed from the physical working models as well as from the GIS data) and data about any currently existing hand sketches augmented to the physical models (see Fig. 4). Since the Android application uses another rendering system (Metaio SDK [23] instead of OpenSG [24], which is used in the design laboratory), the data is converted to be handled appropriately. After login and transfer of the current lab state, each successive change (modification of the sketch or physical model) is sent to the clients instantaneously. The scene is rendered on-screen, superimposing the camera picture and using the correct perspective of the hand-held Android device with respect to the spatial position and orientation within the environment, a facility provided by the tracking system of the Metaio SDK.

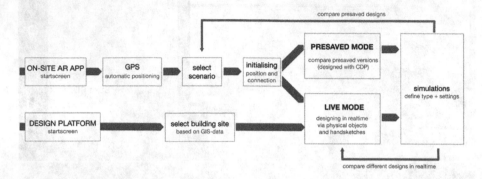

Fig. 8. Information flow interaction between system and user

5.2   Tracking

The coarse positioning of the viewer's device is based on the GPS-position in combination with the, via the protocol transmitted geo-coordinates of the building site. Since GPS only provides positional data and because the precision of this data is insufficient for the accurate placement of AR visualisations, other methods need to be used. Even the integration of the device's in-built compass and inertia devices would not provide sufficient accuracy.

The AR rendering system therefore relies on optical feature tracking. After assessing different available solutions, the Metaio SDK was selected. It provides facilities for two methods of initialisation and subsequent tracking.

To initialise the estimation of the correct pose (position and orientation), a line model of a neighbouring building (or another arbitrary object) is required which can be mapped to the edges found in the camera picture of the Android device. This replaces the need to place additional markers in the environment. The line model is shown on the screen of the hand-held device and the user must move the device so that the line approximately aligns with its physical counterpart in the vicinity. The line model can be scaled and rotated via touch gestures so that it aligns with the real building. Once the alignment is sufficiently near to the actual situation, the system automatically snaps the line model to the detected edges of the physical building and starts tracking (Fig. 9).

Tracking is then handled using natural features found in the camera picture. The Metaio SDK stores these feature points internally and generates a 3D world map that remains active even if one turns around so that none of the initial features are visible in the camera view. To tracking the system requires features that can be detected and stored.

Fig. 9. Initialisation phase: the line model is matched to the features that are found in the camera picture.

A white wall, for instance, would not provide any natural features and tracking would have no reference points to follow. While tracking is operating, the system calculates the position and orientation of the hand-held device and feeds this data into the rendering system so that the architectural sketches are superimposed and correctly aligned to the camera picture (Fig. 10). To define the area where the features should be created and tracked, a surface model of the environment needs to be provided. Assuming that the geolocation of the line model is known, a future version of the application could return the estimated position and orientation of the device, in turn giving the table user visual feedback on the outdoor user's location and viewing direction on the digital map on the multi-touch table. This would allow collaborators to have a better understanding of what they are discussing during a session.

Fig. 10. Due to the image feature tracking, it is possible to walk through the scenario. As long as the tracked element is in sight, the object are displayed on real position.

5.3   Occlusion Handling

As the virtual content is simply rendered on top of the camera image, occlusions can be incorrect when a physical structure is nearer to the viewer than the computer-generated sketch. The virtual sketch then incorrectly overlays the physical object.

The surface model of the environment, based on the data of the surrounded buildings provided via the TCP/UDP protocol, can be used to remedy this occlusion problem. This surface model is invisibly added to scene rendering and prevents the parts of the sketch that would not be seen from being rendered (Fig. 11).

Fig. 11. Screenshot of the app showing occlusion-handling activated and deactivated

Occlusion problems can, however, still arise with physical objects that are not part of the surface model. For example, the surface model typically includes building struc-tures but not trees, bushes or passing cars and pedestrians. These cannot be rendered into or out of the scene.

Ongoing research in the fields of computer vision and rendering is, however, in the process of trying to identify the distance of objects from the viewer, and can already provide a degree of full occlusion handling. As yet, these aspects have not been inte-grated in the demonstration prototype.

5.4   Simulations

As hand-held devices have a touch panel and motion sensing, they provide a means for the user to interact with the scene. One example of such interaction exploits the potential to add simulations to the scene by simulating the passage of the sun. The user could activate a computer-generated sun that illuminates the scene with a correctly placed light source. The user can then see how the sun illuminates the planned building. The incident sunlight simulation can respond to the respective geolocation, orientation and time of day. A fast forward mode allows the user to gain an impression of sunlight incidence over the course of a day (Fig. 12).

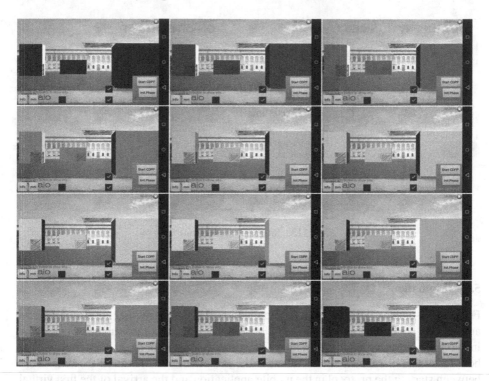

Fig. 12. Screenshot of the sun-simulation: course of a day.

5.5 Implementation

The prototype was developed for Android smartphones and tablets. The main part, including the interactive GUI, is therefore written in Java, while all the network communication with the design-platform runs using native C++ routines, to facilitate the ease of maintenance of the protocol that also runs at the table. The natively running part of the application asynchronously communicates all events received from the architects working on the model to the user interface without interrupting real-time rendering. Java Native Interface JNI bridges between Java and C++ code.

An event triggered by an action at the table is transmitted as a message via the provided protocol (see Sect. 4). Messages that transport data on buildings or sketches contain lists of three-dimensional vertices and how they are interconnected. The mobile application receives these lists and uses them to generate a file in a format that can be interpreted by the rendering engine. Rotations and translations of existing buildings are simply applied to the respective virtual object.

To achieve maximum flexibility, the application was tested with and adapted for display on devices of different sizes from 4.7" to 12.2" and on different OS versions from Android 4.1.2 to 4.4.2.

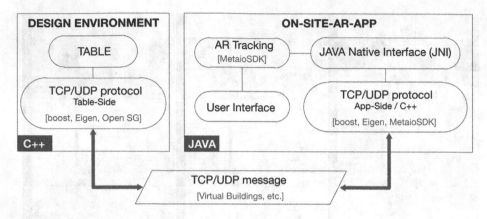

Fig. 13. Software architecture

5.6 Evaluation

For the real-time experience of an AR application it is important that all virtual objects and actions – undertaken by the design-platform-user – are available in the virtual scene in real time. To ascertain how fast the connection between both peers is established and how fast data messages are transmitted to the AR client, we measured the time taken between starting the protocol in the mobile application and the arrival of the first virtual object sent by the table (see Fig. 14). The peer connection is always established via a virtual private network (VPN). The time taken, based on an average of 20 measurements, was 122 ms using a Wireless LAN connection and 1807 ms using a mobile network connection (see Fig. 15). To measure how long it takes for a single message to be sent from one peer to another, it would be necessary to synchronize times between the multi-touch-framework and the mobile device. Nevertheless, the measurements show that a real-time AR experience is possible using network managed virtual buildings.

Test conducted with different numbers and sizes of virtual buildings showed that a single model of about 200,000 triangles can be displayed at a frame rate of 25 frames per second (FPS). The more buildings that are loaded into the virtual scene, the less detail they should exhibit. Even with 50 buildings displayed at once, the system can still render 1000 triangles per building model at a frame rate of about 25 FPS.

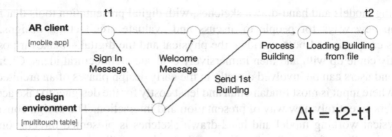

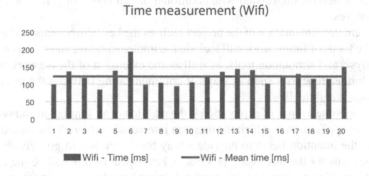

Fig. 14. Protocol time from connection establishment to first received object

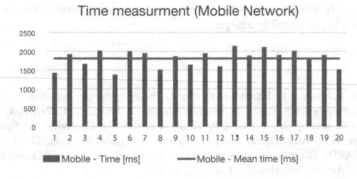

Fig. 15. Time Δt from protocol connection establishment (t1) to displaying the first virtual building (t2)

6   Summary and Outlook

The concept outlined in this paper, as well as its prototypical implementation, clearly demonstrate the possibilities of using digital presentation and design exploration tools in a creative context. While augmented techniques are already being used in many areas of digital life, here it is the real-time coupling of established working methods, such as working models and hand-drawn sketches, with digital presentation tools that really opens up new ways for people to discuss and evaluate architectural designs. The seamless connection of both worlds – the physical and the digital – makes it possible to directly come up with and then immersively evaluate architectural ideas. Clients as well as end users can be involved directly in the early design phases of an architectural project where input is most fundamental and least costly for the designer to take account of. It offers an entirely new way of presentation and interaction. The design consisting of a physical working model and hand-drawn sketches is presented directly on site. The incorporation of interactive analyses and simulations likewise makes it possible to assess the impact of a design on the environment more objectively. They enhance the personal subjective impression with additional digital levels of perception such as shading analyses.

The current implementation of the project realises the key components of the project concept. The focus of future work will include the implementation and incorporation of further analysis and simulation tools, as well as the extension of the network protocol to include further functions such as ways of communicating between the participants (e.g. video-calls and the like).

Another possible avenue of exploration is the addition of an annotation and sketching tool to the AR application in which the user can interact directly with the mixed-reality application, the intention being to provide a way for the viewer to give feedback and make suggestions for the discussion process. A key aspect of this will be the bringing together of the different sketches and feedback input into the same virtual model. An aim of future projects is also to better incorporate the real existing buildings in the AR view, specifically aspects such as the projection of simulation results onto them, such as overshadowing or visibility analyses.

References

1. Schubert, G., Artinger, E., Petzold, F., Klinker, G.: Bridging the gap - a (collaborative) design platform for early design stages. In: Zupančič-Strojan, T., Juvančič, M., Verovšek, Š., Jutraž, A. (eds.) Respecting fragile places. Proceedings of the 29th Conference on Education in Computer Aided Architectural Design in Europe, Ljubljana, Slovenia, 21–24 September 2011, eCAADe, Education and Research in Computer Aided Architectural Design in Europe; Faculty of Architecture, Brussels, Ljubljana, pp. 187–193 (2011)
2. Schubert, G., Artinger, E., Petzold, F., Klinker, G.: Tangible tools for architectural design: seamless integration into the architectural workflow. In: Taron, J.M. (ed.) Integration Through Computation. Proceedings of the ACADIA 2011. Association for Computer Aided Design in Architecture, Stoughton, WI, pp. 252–259 (2011)
3. Schubert, G.: Interaktionsformen für das digitale Entwerfen. Konzeption und Umsetzung einer rechnergestützten Entwurfsplattform für die städtebaulichen Phasen in der Architektur. Dissertation, Technische Universität München (2014)
4. Chi, H.-L., Kang, S.-C., Wang, X.: Research trends and opportunities of augmented reality applications in architecture, engineering, and construction. Autom. Constr. **33**, 116–122 (2013)
5. Underkoffler, J., Ishii, H.: Urp: a luminous-tangible workbench for urban planning and design. CHI **99**, 386–393 (1999)

6. Dalsgaard, P., Halskov, K.: Tangible 3D tabletops: combining tangible tabletop interaction and 3D projection. In: Malmborg, L., Pederson, T. (eds.) NordiCHI 2012. Making Sense Through Design. Proceedings of the 7th Nordic Conference on Human-Computer Interaction, Copenhagen, Denmark, pp. 14–17 (2012)

7. Broll, W., Stoerring, M., Mottram, C.: The augmented round table - a new interface to urban planning and architectural design. In: Rauterberg et al. (ed.) Human-Computer Interaction - Interact'03, pp. 1103–1104 (2003)

8. Seichter, H., Schnabel, M.A.: Digital and tangible sensation: an augmented reality urban design studio. In: Lee, H.S., Choi, J.W. (eds.) CAADRIA 2004. Proceedings of the 9th International Conference on Computer-Aided Architectural Design Research in Asia, Yonsei University Press, Seoul, pp. 193–202 (2004)

9. Seichter, H.: Sketchand+ a collaborative augmented reality sketching application. In: Choutgrajank, A. (ed.) CAADRIA 2003. Proceedings of the 8th International Conference on Computer-Aided Architectural Design Research in Asia. CAADRIA, Bangkok, Thailand, pp. 18–20 October 2003, Master of Science Program in Computer-Aided Architectural Design, Faculty of Architecture, Rangsit University, Thailand, pp. 209–222 (2003)

10. Välkkynen, P., Siltanen, S., Väätänen, A., Oksman, V., Honkamaa, P., Ylikauppila, M.: Developing mixed reality tools to support citizen participation in urban planning. In: ExS 2.0: Exploring Urban Spaces in the Web 2.0 Era, Munich, Germany (2013)

11. Wagner, I., Basile, M., Ehrenstrasser, L., Maquil, V., Terrin, J.-J., Wagner, M.: Supporting community engagement in the city: urban planning in the MR-tent. In: Carroll, J.M. (ed.) C & T'09. Proceedings of the 4th International Conference on Communities and Technologies, University Park, Pennsylvania, USA, 25–27 June 2009, ACM Press, New York, pp. 185–194 (2009)

12. Sareika, M., Schmalstieg, D.: Urban sketcher: mixed reality on site for urban planning and architecture. In: ISMAR 2007, 6th IEEE and ACM International Symposium on Mixed and Augmented Reality. IEEE, Piscataway (2007)

13. Allen, M., Regenbrecht, H., Abbott, M.: Smart-phone augmented reality for public participation in urban planning. In: Paris, C., Colineau, N., Farrell, V., Farrell, G., Huang, W. (eds.) Proceedings of the 23rd Australian Computer-Human Interaction Conference (OzCHI 2011). Held at the Australian National University, Canberra in cooperation with the ACM SIGCHI, pp. 11–20, 28 Nov–2 Dec 2011

14. Wang, X., Truijens, M., Hou, L., Wang, Y., Zhou, Y.: Integrating augmented reality with building information modeling: onsite construction process controlling for liquefied natural gas industry. Autom. Constr. 40, 96–105 (2014)

15. Kwon, O.-S., Park, C.-S., Lim, C.-R.: A defect management system for reinforced concrete work utilizing BIM, image-matching and augmented reality. Autom. Constr. 46, 74–81 (2014)

16. Zollmann, S., Hoppe, C., Kluckner, S., Poglitsch, C., Bischof, H., Reitmayr, G.: Augmented reality for construction site monitoring and documentation. Proc. IEEE 102, 137–154 (2014)

17. Sørensen, S.S.: Augmented reality for improved communication of construction and maintenance plans in nuclear power plants. In: Yoshikawa, H., Zhang, Z. (eds.) Progress of Nuclear Safety for Symbiosis and Sustainability. Advanced Digital Instrumentation, Control and Information Systems for Nuclear Power Plants, pp. 269–274. Springer, Japan (2014)

18. Schattel, D.: On-site mobile augmented reality by means of network managed architectural design content. Master's Thesis, Technische Universität München (2014)

19. Schubert, G., Riedel, S., Petzold, F.: Seamfully connected: real working models as tangible interfaces for architectural design. In: Zhang, J., Sun, C. (eds.) CAAD Futures 2013. CCIS, vol. 369, pp. 210–221. Springer, Heidelberg (2013)

20. Schubert, G., Artinger, E., Yanev, V., Petzold, F., Klinker, G.: 3D virtuality sketching: interactive 3D-sketching based on real models in a virtual scen. In: Cabrinha, M., Johnson, J.K., Steinfeld, K. (eds.) Proceedings of the 32nd Annual Conference of the Association for Computer Aided Design in Architecture (ACADIA), Synthetic Digital Technologies. Annual Conference of the Association for Computer Aided Design in Architecture (ACADIA), San Francisco, 18–21 Oktober, pp. 409–418. The Printing House Inc., WI, ACADIA, San Francisco (2012)
21. Yanev, V.: 3D virtuality sketching: a freehand sketch tool for conceptual urban design in architecture. Master's Thesis, Technische Universität München (2012)
22. Goldschwendt, T.: The collaborative design platform protocol - design and implementation of a protocol for networked virtual environments and cave peer development. Bachelor's Thesis, Ludwig-Maximilians-Universität München (2013)
23. Metaio GmbH: Metaio |SDK overview. http://www.metaio.com/sdk/ (2015). Accessed 2 Feb 2015
24. OpenSG. http://www.opensg.org (2015). Accessed 2 Feb 2015

Development of High-Definition Virtual Reality for Historical Architectural and Urban Digital Reconstruction: A Case Study of Azuchi Castle and Old Castle Town in 1581

Tomohiro Fukuda[1(✉)], Hirokazu Ban[2], Katsuhito Yagi[3], and Junro Nishiie[2]

[1] Osaka University, Suita, Japan
fukuda@see.eng.osaka-u.ac.jp
[2] Omihachiman City Government, Omihachiman, Japan
{048200,390100}@city.omihachiman.lg.jp
[3] Toppan Printing Co., Ltd., Tokyo, Japan
katsuhito.yagi@toppan.co.jp

Abstract. This study shows fundamental data for constructing a high-definition VR application under the theme of a three-dimensional visualization to restore past architecture and cities. It is difficult for widespread architectural and urban objects to be rendered in real-time. Thus, in this study, techniques for improving the level of detail (LOD) and representation of natural objects were studied. A digital reconstruction project of Azuchi Castle and old castle town was targeted as a case study. Finally, a VR application with specifications of seven million polygons, texture of 1.87 billion pixels, and 1920 × 1080 screen resolution, was successfully developed that could run on a PC. For the developed VR applications, both qualitative evaluation by experts and quantitative evaluation by end users was performed.

Keywords: Cultural heritage · Digital reconstruction · Virtual reality · Visualization · 3D modeling · Presentation

1 Introduction

3-dimensional (3D) visualization makes it possible for people to experience and understand 3D virtual space of defunct architecture and city intuitively. 3D visualization using a computer, in the 3DCG (3-Dimensional Computer Graphics) field, began with the pre-rendering technique to create a CG still image, which requires a certain amount of time [1]. In recent years, with the advance of computer technology, real-time rendering technique referred to as Virtual Reality (VR) has become common even in the use of personal computers [2]. VR gives a designer and an end-user the ability to interact with a 3D Virtual Environment (VE). Therefore, the VR use in architectural and urban fields, has been demonstrated value in the functions of walk-through, comparison of design alternatives, and dynamic simulation, etc. in real time.

© Springer-Verlag Berlin Heidelberg 2015
G. Celani et al. (Eds.): CAAD Futures 2015, CCIS 527, pp. 75–89, 2015.
DOI: 10.1007/978-3-662-47386-3_5

When VR in architectural and urban field runs, the number of defining objects tends to be large, and all the objects from a small scale to a huge scale should be handled at the same virtual environment become a problem to perform real-time rendering of high accuracy and realism. Therefore, various element techniques such as game engine techniques with texture mapping instead of geometry, the culling technique to render only the objects contained inside the viewing frustum, and the Level of Detail (LOD) technique to change the 3D models and textures of different detail levels which depend on the distance from the VR virtual camera, have been developed to reduce the rendering load [3–5]. Previous studies on constructing a VR application by applying such techniques in architecture and urban fields have been reported, covering areas such as the future simulation of architecture and urban spaces at the design stage [6, 7], digital archiving of existing architecture and townscapes [8], digital reconstruction of past architecture and ancient cities [9–11], and architectural education [12]. However, studies to construct a finely detailed realistic VR application applying these techniques using recent advances in the PC environment have not been reported. Work on the creation of higher quality VR applications in the architectural and urban fields is expected to be more widely published and should be discussed in the digital age.

Therefore, this study aimed to illustrate the fundamental data to construct a high-definition VR application. The VR restoration of Azuchi Castle and its old castle town which consists of wide-area architectural and city objects was targeted as a case study because the authors have been involved in this collaborative project between local government, research scientists and VR creators. The paper is organized as follows. After developing the VR application of Azuchi Castle in Sect. 2, both qualitative and quantitative investigations were conducted for validation in Sects. 3 and 4. The final Sect. 5 is a conclusion.

2 Development of High-Definition Virtual Reality Application

2.1 Target and Process of Developing Virtual Reality

Azuchi Castle was built by Oda Nobunaga who was one of the most powerful samurai of Japan in the late 16th century. It is situated on the shores of Lake Biwa, in Omi Province (currently, Omihachiman city, Shiga Prefecture, Japan). The keep tower was approximately 40 m high and was located at the top of Mt. Azuchi which is approximately 110 m high. The buildings and stone walls of Azuchi Castle were built over the whole area of Mt. Azuchi. A castle town was built at the foot of Mt. Azuchi. After Nobunaga's death in the Honnoji Incident in 1582, Azuchi Castle was destroyed and left for a long time. In recent years, an archaeological dig of Azuchi Castle has been carried. It started in 1989 and went on for 20 years. It elucidated some historical facts, and some stone steps and stone walls were physically restored. However, complete physical reconstruction has been a major challenge because it is difficult to discover the evidence necessary to fully elucidate the historical facts, so academic historical elucidation has not been completely finished yet. Also, economic issues will affect the physical reconstruction once the academically historical elucidation is finished. The old castle town has been modernized. A VR digital restoration project of Azuchi Castle and its old castle town in 1581 was conducted. The elements of the digital restoration are roughly divided into terrain, the keep tower, the buildings except the keep tower and stone walls of Azuchi Castle, and the old castle town.

The VR reconstruction procedure and major software used was follows: (1) Survey and planning, (2) Scenario scripting, (3) Data collection and analysis, (4) Texture generation (Adobe Photoshop), (5) 3D data modeling (Autodesk 3ds Max), (6) Programming and visual effects (Microsoft Visual Studio), (7) BGM, sound effect and narration, (8) Integration and final adjustment. In the 3D data modeling stage, in recent years, the development and supply of BIM (Building Information Modeling) software has advanced. However, data compatibility problems with BIM and VR software have been reported [13]. In this study, 3DCG software with higher data compatibility with VR software was used.

2.2 Materials for the VR Reconstruction

To carry out the digital restoration of Azuchi Castle, the authors used record books [14, 15], excavation reports by Shiga prefecture and Omihachiman city government, and illustrations showing the state of the castle in the late 16th century. More detailed information follows.

The keep tower of Azuchi Castle was created on the basis of the restoration plan by Dr. Naito Akira [16, 17]. During the restoration process, in addition to the documents, reference was made to both the fifth and sixth floors of the physical keep tower model which was restored to its full scale, and another one-twentieth scale physical keep tower model, under the supervision of Dr. Naito Akira.

A few buildings such as Honmaru palace and Hideyoshi House were created based on a one-fortieth scale model and drawings. Other facilities such as turrets and gates were deduced from excavation reports, from existing castles of the same era (Kanazawa Castle and Hikone Castle etc.), and from the architectural style of that time.

For the creation of the old castle town, based on the old maps in the Meiji period (1868–1912) which was before modernization began, the roads, temples and shrines which existed during the founding period of Azuchi Castle in 1581 were deduced. Also, the layout of the houses and people's lifestyles in the old castle town were deduced from materials of the same period, such as *Rakuchurakugaizu* from the late 16th century.

A digital elevation model (DEM) to represents terrain surfaces as a triangulated irregular network (TIN) was created over a 65 km square range that included Lake Biwa. As regards the resolution of the terrain, a 5 km square in the center part which included Mt. Azuchi and the old castle town was created with a grid resolution of 1 m using a one-thousandth scale topographical map, and another area was created with a grid resolution of 30 m using the ASTER Global Digital Elevation Model.

2.3 Level of Detail

In order to represent a high-definition VR, the 3D modeling of detailed elaboration polygons, and high-resolution texture generation are necessary. In contrast, these features are generally disadvantageous for real-time rendering. Therefore, LOD technique has been applied in this study. The application of LOD for the roof tiles of the keep tower and terrain texture mapping was described below.

For the architectural components of the keep tower model, roof tiles are major elements to represent an architectural facade. The roof of a castle building such as Azuchi Castle generally consists of flat tiles and round tiles with *sori* (warpage/camber line) curve shapes. In contrast, the data amount increased when the roof tile objects were repeatedly presented in the roof image. Therefore, the object to be displayed was changed depending on the distance of the VR virtual camera from the center of gravity of the keep tower as a threshold of the LOD technique which determines the active child model from all the various models to represent the roof tile objects. When the distance was from 0 m to 50 m, both the flat tile model (74,000 polygons) and round tile model (168,000 polygons) were rendered (see Fig. 1). When the distance was from 50 m to 100 m, the round tile model was linearly faded out in proportion to increase in distance from the VR virtual camera. When the distance was 100 m beyond, only the flat tile model was rendered.

Fig. 1. Keep tower model of Azuchi Castle with roof tiles

For real-time rendering, the texture data amount must not use too much video RAM (VRAM). To represent a terrain with wide range efficiently, the texture material of the terrain is generally mapped repeatedly. In contrast, when the terrain model is viewed from the sky, this repetitive representation of the terrain texture becomes apparent. A problem with representation of reality will appear. Then, if the texture is not mapped repeatedly, it is necessary to reduce the texture size. As a result, it is impossible to obtain sufficient resolution when viewing the terrain textures close up. In order to solve this conflict, the terrain texture to be displayed was changed depending on the distance of the VR virtual camera from the terrain model as a threshold of the LOD technique which determines the active child texture from all the textures to represent the terrain texture. When the distance was from 0 m to 20 m, terrain textures were not rendered repeatedly (see Fig. 2 left). When the distance was 20 m beyond, terrain textures were rendered repeatedly (see Fig. 2 right).

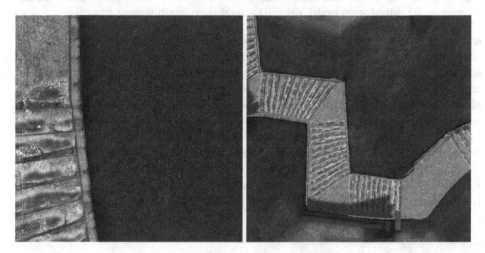

Fig. 2. Texture mapping to terrain (left: distance from VR virtual camera to terrain was less than 20 m, right: 20 m beyond)

2.4   Representation of Natural Objects

Curved surfaces are present in many natural objects, as compared to artificial objects. In addition, the repeating texture pattern is difficult to contain. These features are generally disadvantageous for real-time rendering [18, 19]. Then, a representation technique for natural objects such as stone walls, shade and shadow, water surface, settlement disposition etc. was developed.

For representation of the stone walls, some of the stone walls that exist in Azuchi Castle were used as a texture material. When viewing the stone wall of the base of the keep in close proximity it is necessary to enhance the representation of reality. Thus, 3D polygons of the stone wall were created (see Fig. 3). At the end of the stone wall, different texture materials abut. A mismatch of texture patterns is likely to occur. Therefore, the texture pattern of the stone wall was mapped to match.

For representation of lighting, two techniques were investigated. First, in order to represent natural shading, the IBL (Image Based Lighting) technique was applied to a wide area and four time zones, namely morning, afternoon, evening and night. For the

Fig. 3. Stone wall model (left: texture mapping to a normal flat polygon, middle: texture mapping to 3D natural stone model, right: 3D natural stone model without texture)

texture material of the sky, HDR (High Dynamic Range Imaging) was created by combining more than 600 photographs taken at different time periods from the same spot. Each scene was rendered using the texture material as a lighting source. For representation of shadows, the shadow data generated by the shadow mapping technique was blended with texture materials. Second, beams of sunlight shining using a volume metric lighting technique penetrated into the top floor of the keep tower. The light intensity was controlled to soften the degree of penetration of the sunlight in response to the angle between the VR virtual camera and the sun's rays.

In order to express the reflection of a water surface, the texture of a mirrored image which was produced by an off-screen rendering technique, and a normal map created from the height map of waves generated in real time, were blended (see Fig. 4).

Fig. 4. Reflection of water surface (left: daytime, right: evening view)

To represent the settlements in the old castle town, it was inefficient to make and place more than 1000 houses one by one. Therefore, objects such as houses, gardens and roads were created, and the objects were placed at random using procedural modeling techniques (see Fig. 5). Then some objects were adjusted to form a natural arrangement by manual operation. To express the liveliness of the castle town, smoke rising from houses in the old castle town was expressed. In detail, by applying the particles technique, billboard objects executed by texture mapping of various smoke types were faded out while rotating. By controlling the orientation, speed and rendering number of the objects, the representation of smoke with motion and randomness could be achieved.

Fig. 5. Representation of the old castle town (morning view)

2.5 Developed High-Definition VR Application

Finally, high-definition VR application of Azuchi castle and its old town which was comprised of a consolidated 3D virtual space was developed based on excavations and research materials described in Sects. 2.3 and 2.4. This VR application was comprised of both short movie and manual modes. In the short movie mode, 15-minute captured movie of VR walk/fly-through is set against the backdrop of Azuchi Castle in 1581 (see Fig. 6). In the manual mode, the controller facilitates free movement within the virtual Azuchi Castle seamlessly. Viewers can feel the perspective of characters such as Oda Nobunaga who was the leader of a samurai.

Table 1 shows the specification of the developed application which consists of approximately 7.86 million polygons and 1.87 billion texture pixels, and total 7 GB data volume but can keep 1920 × 1080 resolution and 30–60 fps.

Table 1. Specification of the developed VR application.

3D model	Number of polygons	7.86 million
	Number of vertices	6 million
Texture	Number of textures	1000
	Number of texture pixels	1.87 billion
	Data amount	3 GB
	VRAM use when running VR application	6.27 GB
Total system	Data amount	7 GB
	Frame rate	30-60 fps

Fig. 6. Main shots of the VR short movie

Table 2. Evaluation items (partial revisions from the previous research [20]).

Factor	Element	Evaluation items	Evaluation contents
3D modeling	Shape	Outline	Outline is smooth.
		Surface	Surface is finely expressed.
		Detail	3D model is created in detail.
		Extensiveness	3D model is created on a large scale.
Rendering	Lighting	Light source	Light source is set closer to reality.
		Color shade	Both ambient light and indirect light are expressed.
	Shade and shadow	Shade	Curved surface is smooth.
		Shadow	Realistic shadows are expressed.
	Material	Color	Realistic colors are expressed.
		Pattern	Textures are expressed.
		Texture	Metals, mirrors, glass, etc. are expressed.
	Depth	Focus	Distant blur is expressed.
		Haze	Distant haze is expressed.
	Scene	Natural scene	Clouds, fog, trees, waves and water etc. are expressed.
	Image quality	Color	Image is expressed in full color.
		Aliasing	Jaggies and moire do not exist. Resolution is high.
Expressing	Image synthesis	Color	Differences in color, shadow and focus of the synthesized image are small.
		Outline	Outline of the synthesized image is smooth.
		Composition	Scale and composition of the synthesized image are accurate.
	Staffage	Staffage	Staffage (person, car, etc.) are represented.
		Scale	Comparable object is represented.
		Perspective	Objects are represented as perspective drawings.
	Garnish	Time	Time, season, weather, date, are represented.
		Motion	
		Effect	Water flow and wave swell are expressed. Central object is sharply defined. Light is well used. Texture mapping is not monotonic.
	Output	Condition	Output system is ideal.
		Dimension	Image size is large.
		Effect	Output appears three-dimensional.

3 Validation of Qualitative Method

3.1 Methodology

In the qualitative investigation, after VR experts observed typical VR scenes, they responded to the three categories questionnaires about modeling, rendering and impression. The subjects were three of the VR creators (30 s male, 30 s female and 20 s female) who could understand the expression level of VR technology. By referring to the evaluation items which were partial revisions from the previous research [20], the subjects responded with their first impressions, and described the pros and cons of the representative VR scene briefly. Four typical VR scenes were selected: a VR scene which included all of Azuchi Castle, the old Castle Town and terrain (hereinafter "Full view"), a VR scene at whose center was the keep tower (hereinafter "Keep tower view"), a VR scene that looked at the old castle town against a background of Mt. Azuchi (hereinafter "Castle town view") and a VR scene that looked up at the keep tower from the main road (hereinafter "Main road view"). There were three time zones, except for the Main road view; morning, daytime and evening. There were four time zones for the Main road view; morning, daytime, evening and night. Table 2 shows the evaluation items. Table 3 shows the PC specifications and display resolution of equipment used in the experiment.

Table 3. PC specifications and display resolution used in the experiment

PC specifications	PC model	HP Z820 Workstation
	OS	Windows7 Professional 64-bit
	CPU	Intel Xeon E5-2643 v23.5 GHz
	Main memory	64 GB
	Graphics board	NVIDIA Quadro K6000(VRAM: 12 GB)
Display resolution	Display resolution	1920 × 1080

3.2   Result and Discussion

Table 4 shows VR screenshots from the four viewpoints and the main comments by three subjects. A summary is given below.

Full view: Positive judgments, such as an integrated set of VR images was realized amounted to eight. In contrast, there were four negative judgments, such as the green texture rendered in Mt. Azuchi was unnatural.

Keep tower view: Positive judgments, such as the Azuchi Castle model was represented in detail, amounted to eight. In contrast, negative judgments, such as a part of the daytime scene showed inconsistency between shade and shadow, amounted to eight. Shade and shadows should be calculated integrally based on the physical quantity of light and material properties. In fact, using the pre-rendering method of 3DCG, possible photo-realistic representation by the global illumination technique has been realized. On the other hand, in the real-time, wide area rendering techniques targeted in this study, it is still hard to apply the global illumination technique owing to the large computing capacity required. In this study, as described in Sect. 2.4, the shade data obtained by the IBL technique and the shadow data obtained by the shadow mapping technique had to be defined separately, and inconsistency between shade and shadow was observed.

Castle town view: Positive judgments, such as the modeling quality of the houses was high, amounted to four. In contrast, negative judgments, such as the liveliness of the castle town could not be observed, amounted to 13. Vario-items such as people,

Table 4. Evaluation result

Full view	Keep tower view	Castle town view	Main road view
Positive (N=8) - Azuchi Castle and its surrounding landscape were expressed in detail. - In the daytime scene, the green of fields and hills was beautifully expressed using shallow color and deep color. - In the morning and evening scenes, representation and color shades of the fog and reflections of the water surface were well-balanced and appeared beautiful. **Negative** (N=4) - The green color texture of Mt. Azuchi was felt to be unnatural, like a physical model, because most of the surface of the mountain seemed to use the same texture.	**Positive** (N=8) - Azuchi Castle was realistic in overall detail such as stone walls. - 3D modeling of the keep tower and the distant view, the integrity of 3D model and shadow, and the reflection of the lake were expressed in high quality. - By ensuring consistency between the 3D model and its shadow, VR representation brought especially a feeling of unity in the case of long shots, such as a view overlooking the keep tower from a distance. **Negative** (N=8) - Since the placement of trees and buildings was too orderly, unnaturalness, as in a physical model, was felt. - In the daytime scene, consistency between the shade and shadow of buildings and trees was not realized.	**Positive** (N=4) - Each house was well modeled. - A sequence of houses was well-represented, and looked like a castle town. **Negative** (N=13) - Placements of buildings and trees were unnatural. In particular, the landscape in which the same buildings appeared was particularly unnatural. - Liveliness of the castle town was not felt. - Roughness of the 3D model close to the VR virtual camera was noticeable. - Representation of water's edge of the lake and rivers was unnatural. - A feeling of strangeness was created because shadow was rendered too clearly.	**Positive** (N=7) - For stairs by rubblework, each step was well reproduced to ensure the consistency of texture mapping. - Since roof tiles were reproduced in detail, reality was felt. - Lanterns in the night scene were very impressive and beautiful. **Negative** (N=3) - Some inconsistencies between the sky and lighting were observed. - In the daytime scene, texture resolution was low in one portion of the stone walls.

small animals and store curtains etc. need to be placed in the old castle town to add liveliness. However, they were placed manually, which entailed much labor and expense. Study on automatic placement, etc. is required and a system to place them automatically is necessary.

Main road view: Positive judgments, such as roof tiles and stone walls were expressed realistically, amounted to seven. In contrast, negative judgments, such as the consistency of the sky and lighting were insufficient, amounted to three. To remedy this issue of inadequate consistency and to realize a highly realistic VR representation, real photos were used as textures of the sky and wall stones. In contrast, buildings such as the keep tower and turrets were calculated using CG on the computer as it no photos existed. The inadequate consistency resulted from these reasons.

4 Quantitative Investigation

4.1 Methodology

In the quantitative investigation, after a number of end-users viewed both short movie and manual modes, they responded to the evaluation of the developed VR application. Therefore, a symposium to experience the developed VR application was held over two days in March and May 2014 in the music hall named Bungei Seminariyo. At the symposium, after screening the developed short movie of 15 min, a panel discussion lasting about 1 h took place (see Fig. 7). In the panel discussion, using the VR manual mode, while exploring the 3D virtual environment of Azuchi Castle and its castle town, experts commentated on history, architecture etc. of the time. In addition, a few audience members came up on the stage, and experienced the developed VR from the first-person point of view. After the symposium, the audience answered a questionnaire about the developed VR application and the high-definition VR experience of Azuchi Castle and its old town as they were in the past. The questionnaire items were answered using a Likert five-point agree/disagree scale with the responses: "Strongly Agree", "Agree", "Neither agree nor disagree", "Disagree" and "Strongly Disagree".

Fig. 7. Symposium to experience the developed VR application (left: panel discussion, right: VR experience by end-users)

4.2 Result and Discussion

There were 286 subjects. According to gender, 68 % were male and 32 % were female. According to age group, 8 % were in their 20 s or below, 8 % were in their 30 s, 11 % were in their 40 s, 19 % were in their 50 s, 40 % were in their 60 s, and 14 % were in their 70 s and above. Figure 8 shows the result. In the evaluation of the developed VR application, "Very good" and "Good" of respondents accounted for 88 % of responses. And, for the high-definition VR experience of the old Azuchi Castle and its castle town, "Very interesting" or "Interesting" of respondents accounted for 89 %. From these figures, we can say that the developed VR application received a very positive evaluation by end users in a wide age range.

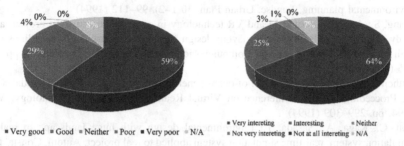

Fig. 8. Result of Quantitative investigation (left: on the developed VR application, right: high-definition VR experience)

5 Conclusion

In this study, in order to construct a high-definition VR application, a digital reconstruction project of Azuchi Castle and its old town was targeted as a case study. To solve the problem which occurs when a wide-area and accurate architectural and urban objects are rendered in real-time, techniques of LOD and natural object representation were studied. Finally, a VR application with seven million polygons, and that had a texture of 1.87 billion pixels, and a 1920 × 1080 screen resolution, was developed running on a PC. For the developed VR applications, both qualitative evaluation by experts and quantitative evaluation by end users was performed. The contributions of this research are as follows:

- In order to perform 3D-VR real-time rendering with high resolution, accuracy and realism for the VR reconstruction project of Azuchi Castle and its old town, both LOD and representation techniques of natural objects and phenomena such as stone walls, light and shadow, reflections of water surface, settlement of the castle town and smoke were developed, and the VR application was constructed by integrating them.
- Through the qualitative evaluation performed by VR creators, the developed VR obtained a certain number of positive judgments. Problems to be solved such as shade and shadow, and lively representation of the castle town were also clarified. In the quantitative evaluation by end users, about 90 % of the end users in a wide age range evaluated the developed VR positively.

As mentioned above, valid creation techniques for constructing a high-precision VR application were illustrated in this study.

Acknowledgements. We thank all the participants for their generous assistance in conducting Azuchi Castle VR project and experiment.

References

1. Lange, E.: Integration of computerized visual simulation and visual assessment in environmental planning. Landsc. Urban Plan. **30**(1–2), 99–112 (1994)
2. Wang, S.: Application of BIM and VR technology in complex construction project: a case study of iceberg 3d BIM structure layout design for an ocean park. In: Proceedings of the 15th International Conference on Computer Aided Architectural Design Futures, pp. 245–255 (2013)
3. Astheimer, P., Pöhe, M.-L.: Level-of-detail generation and its application in virtual reality. In: Proceedings of the Conference on Virtual Reality Software and Technology, VRST 1994, pp. 299–309 (1994)
4. Lou, C., Kaga, A., Sasada, T.: Environmental design with huge landscape in real-time simulation system: real-time simulation system applied to real project. Autom. Constr. **12**(5), 481–485 (2003)
5. Pelosi, A.: Obstacles of utilising real-time 3D visualisation in architectural representations and documentation. In: Proceedings of the 15th International Conference on Computer Aided Architectural Design Research in Asia, pp. 391–400 (2010)
6. Dorta, T., Perez, E.: Immersive drafted virtual reality a new approach for ideation within virtual reality. In: Proceedings of the 25th Annual Conference of the Association for Computer-Aided Design in Architecture, pp. 304–316 (2006)
7. Shen, Z., Kawakami, M.: An online visualization tool for internet-based local townscape design. Comput. Environ. Urban Syst. **34**(2), 104–116 (2010)
8. Hirayu, H., Ojika, T., Kijima, R.: Constructing the historic villages of shirakawa-go in virtual reality. IEEE Multimedia **7**(2), 61–64 (2000)
9. Liu, Y.T.: Virtual chang-an: towards a better simulation for a disappeared city. In: The 2007 International Conference on Digital Applications in Cultural Heritage (DACH 2007), pp. 509–529 (2007)
10. Chevrier, C., Perrin, J.P.: Generation of architectural parametric components: cultural heritage 3D modelling. CAAD Futures **2009**, 105–118 (2009)
11. Boeykens, S.: Using 3D design software, BIM and game engines for architectural historical reconstruction. In: Proceedings of the 14th International Conference on Computer Aided Architectural Design Futures (CAAD Futures 2011), pp. 493–509 (2011)
12. Schnabel, M.A., Kvan, T.: Spatial understanding in immersive virtual environments. Int. J. Archit. Comput. **1**(4), 435–448 (2003)
13. Fukuda, T., Taguchi, M.: Data pipeline from BIM to energy simulator and virtual reality for upgrading interoperability. In: Proceedings of the First International Conference on Civil and Building Engineering Informatics (ICCBEI 2013), pp. 403–409 (2013)
14. Ota, G., Kuwata, T.: Shincho koki [The chronicle of Oda Nobunaga in Japanese], Shinjinbutsuoraisha (1997)
15. Luis, F., Matsuda, K., Kawasaki, M.: Frois Nihonshi [The history of Japan by Luis Frois in Japanese], 2, Chuokoron-Shinsha (2000)
16. Naito, A.: Azuchi-jo no kenkyu [The research of Azuchi Castle in Japanese], Kokka 987 (1976)
17. Naito, A.: Azuchi-jo no kenkyu [The research of Azuchi Castle in Japanese], Kokka 988 (1976)

18. Fukuda, T., Sakata, K., Yeo, W., Kaga, A.: Development and evaluation of a close-range view representation method of natural elements in a real-time simulation for environmental design. In: Proceedings of the 24th eCAADe (Education and Research in Computer Aided Architectural Design in Europe), pp. 58–65 (2006)
19. Rafi, A., Paul, A., Noraishah, S., Nazri, M.: Techniques on heritage preservation using lighting computation virtual environment. CAAD Futures **2009**, 95–104 (2009)
20. Sakakibara, K., Miyake, R., Tsukamoto, N., Ban, K.: A study on image quality evaluation of visual simulation for planning/design. J. Civ. Eng. Inf. Process. Syst. **4**, 9–16 (1995)

Sustainability and Performance
of the Built Space

Interrogating Interactive and Responsive Architecture: The Quest of a Technological Solution Looking for an Architectural Problem

Sara Costa Maia[✉] and AnnaLisa Meyboom

University of British Columbia, Vancouver, BC, Canada
sara.maia@alumni.ubc.ca, ameyboom@sala.ubc.ca

Abstract. Interactive Architecture and Responsive Architecture are provocative fields of investigation and have potentially disruptive and far reaching effects for architecture. However it can be argued that these fields haven't been developed as a direct response to previously identified architectural demands. Instead, they have risen as consequence of new technology availability, with ad hoc discussions in the context of the built environment. In order to test this hypothesis, 229 publications were examined and narrowed down to 77 papers and 41 design projects, which were systematically analyzed. The primary objective of this investigation is to understand Interactive Architecture's development with regard to justification. This understanding provides us with the basis to speculate on the possibly expanding introduction of extraneous technological solutions to the discipline of architecture. The research findings indicate a mismatch between theoretical discourse and projects being developed in those fields. They also describe the current state of Interactive Architecture research.

Keywords: Interactive architecture · Responsive architecture · Literature analysis · Design projects analysis

1 Introduction

It can be argued that Interactive Architecture (IA) and Responsive Architecture (RA) are a typical case in the history of modern technology development: they are a *solution* looking for a *problem*. The increasing economic and technological feasibility of Ubiquitous Computing propels an idea brought about by cybernetics several decades ago, namely the conception of architectural spaces that are able to sense their environment and respond accordingly, in a dynamic feedback system [1].

We suggest that RA and IA have not been fundamentally developed as a direct response to previously identified architectural problems and demands. They were rather a consequence of new technology availability, with ad hoc discussion in the context of the built environment. Nonetheless, RA and IA are enthusiastically regarded by their potential applications and have been raising the interest of researchers around the world and across different fields.

© Springer-Verlag Berlin Heidelberg 2015
G. Celani et al. (Eds.): CAAD Futures 2015, CCIS 527, pp. 93–112, 2015.
DOI: 10.1007/978-3-662-47386-3_6

We acknowledge that the evolution of Architecture through time has been closely related to available resources and technology. Kolarevic argues that the ongoing Digital Information Revolution has started to shape architecture's practices and products in an analogous way to the Industrial Revolution in late 19th and early 20th century [2]. However, it is our understanding that such a precedence of technology availability over an established demand in architecture has caused the fields of IA and RA to develop disjointedly and explore possibilities without a unifying agenda.

Up to this point, no framework has successfully coordinated IA/RA's research development. While this dispersed endeavor in IA/RA may have been beneficial for an exploratory examination of possibilities, it can also work as a barrier for thorough analytical studies, especially regarding the measurement of impacts, successes and fail-ures of the field concerning identified demands. Furthermore, it may contribute to the explanation of why integration of RA/IA in industry is still modest.

This research analyses the discourse behind the literature in support of IA and RA, identifying the main stated reasons for incorporation of the technology. Furthermore, this research also analyses built projects and identifies the main purpose behind their propositions. The primary objective of this investigation is to understand IA's and RA's development with regard to justification. This understanding provides us with the basis to speculate on IA/RA's further trajectories and on the possibly expanding introduction of extraneous technologies to the field of architecture.

Ultimately, this study contributes to the discussion on the accelerated introduction of new technologies in architecture which are dissociated from pre-existing needs and demands. It starts a description of their behavior and progress in search of their purpose, with a focus on RA and IA, highlighting how this process might be determinant in the architecture of tomorrow.

2   Background Research

2.1   Terminology

This study broadly defines RA and IA as architectural spaces empowered with compu-tational technology that are able to sense their context and behave accordingly.

Such computational technologies provide RA/IA systems with three distinct abili-ties, which are highly dependent on ongoing, interrelated and yet distinct technological developments. These abilities are: "reading" the environment and its use (through sensors); processing the data and formulating a response (through processors); and executing a response (through effectors). Between each of these operations there is a need for transfer of information (through wired or wireless communication).

The purposes of these systems vary, as well as the technologies adopted and the foci of exploration. For this reason, as well as the fact that it is an immature field of study, there is a "terminological inflation" [3] around the discussion that takes place in IA/RA publications. For example, along with the terms Responsive and Interactive Architecture, other similar domains refered to are: Intelligent Buildings, Automated Architecture, Architectronics, Reactive Architecture, Transactive Architecture, Smart Architecture, Smart Homes, Kinetic Architecture, Hybrid Spaces, Tangible Bits,

Ambient Intelligence, among others. These are by no means mutually exclusive domains. They not only overlap in large extent, as they often lack clear limit of scope.

Another main reason for such diversity and incongruence in terminology is the fact that IA domain falls on the border of different disciplines. For this reason, Yiannoudes proposes the understanding of such architectural structures as 'Marginal' objects [4], i.e. objects with no clear place, on the lines between categories.

This study selected the terms RA and IA exclusively for analysis, due to their apparent prominence. However, in a first instance, we don't assume these terms to be interchangeable. A responsive system is here defined as a system that responds to an environmental stimulus, according to its nature, intensity or other characteristics. It distinguishes itself from purely reactive systems – such as a motion detector light switch – by the ability to respond not only to a trigger stimulus but also to gradients and context.

Interactive systems differ from responsive systems in the ability of the system to learn and/or build upon previous interactions. Therefore, Interactive Architecture is the one in which the communication between the architectural components and the users is a dialogue with new messages being related to previous ones [5].

2.2 The Rise of Interactive and Responsive Architecture

It is argued that the development of IA originated from the introduction of cybernetics in architecture. A main proponent of this movement was Gordon Pask, who claimed that "architects design systems, not just buildings" [6]. With cybernetics, architecture is considered as part of a dynamic feedback system with users [1], an idea that greatly assisted in defining IA.

Also in 1969, Andrew Rabeneck wrote in Architectural Design magazine about the use of cybernetic devices in automated architecture [1]. Rabeneck advocated for building technologies that were flexible, an agenda that was gaining particular strength in the period. This argument resonated with the post-modern concern that individuals have diverse and ever-changing needs which are not as universal as previously thought.

In 1971, Charles Eastman published his Adaptive-Conditional Architecture model [7], which reinforced the proposal that *feedback could be used to control an architecture that self-adjusts to fit the needs of users* [1]. The concept of adaptability to users' continuously changing needs was therefore the first purpose explicitly justified by IA potentialities.

The term responsive architecture was first used by Nicholas Negroponte, in the sense here described, also around the same period [8]. He proposed an architecture where the inhabitants could articulate their own spaces by interacting with a computing empowered architecture. This view sustains a different justification for RA, more focused on the agency of inhabitants, as also supported by Pask.

Remarkably, a full exploration of these concepts introduced in the literature could not be immediately realized in built projects. Speculation soon revealed itself to be a very strong front in IA/RA development, which also brought depth to the purposes and implications of the field. With the Archigram group, speculative projects of the time, such as the Fun Palace by Cedric Price or the New Babylon by Constant Nieuwenhuys, became icons of IA.

However, since the 90's, due to widespread technological accessibility, the most relevant research in the field turned largely practical. Kas Oosterhuis, for instance, opposes speculative approaches to IA, advocating that research should be *based on immediate practical possibilities* [9].

Regarding format, several published works in the recent years, arguably a large majority, are project reports that present IA prototypes and describe their behavior, e.g. [41, 62, 68]. Several built architectures, prototypes and installations have also emerged during the past decade. The current focus of theoretical discourse, as well as of the design research mentioned above, varies widely. Schnädelbach notes that IA seems to range *from designs for media facades to eco buildings, from responsive art installations to stage design* [10].

Furthermore, researchers like Jaskiewicz alert that the notion of IA is being commonly oversimplified to fit projects that can be executed with current inexpensive technology. The term is thus *being used to refer to buildings and built spaces which are capable of simple responsive adaptations and spatial customizations* [11].

In fact, it makes sense that in order to fulfill the requirement of adaptation to (unforeseen) changing conditions, IA needs to reason, learn and adapt; and to be an active part of the ecology it is inserted into. To this point, this has not been achieved. Therefore, IA does not exist yet in a format to satisfy its initial justification. RA, on the other hand, as described in this paper, can be considered a simpler system which is currently attainable.

This paper will present a systematic analysis of the available literature concerning RA and IA, in order to examine how the incorporation of the new technologies is justified in discourse. Built projects are also analyzed and confronted with the findings from the literature analysis.

3   Related Work

Several papers have cited a wealth of reasons why RA/IA development is useful to architecture, often offering their own contributions. However no previous work has methodically studied the uses and reasons for RA/IA.

The only work found to conduct a similar exploration was developed by Joshua D. Lee [12]. His research was focused on the concept of Adaptable Architecture, including four specific terms in his search: "adaptable," "kinetic," "responsive," and "transformable". Lee surveyed, among other things, the rationales that designers, architectural journalists and critics indicated for each term, in order to understand what people have meant when using these words. He presented these rationales in broad categories.

Lee also surveyed several projects, classifying them by type (i.e. architectural function). He didn't attempt to analyze the rationale of the projects, or to confront these with theoretical discourse. Despite the methodological similarity, Lee's work was exploratory and followed a grounded theory perspective. Contrarily, this study departed from defined hypotheses and was intended to understand specifically the rationales for RA/IA. Finally, Lee's work on Adaptable Architecture refers to a different range of projects and concepts, despite an interesting intersection concerning the term "responsive".

4   The Research Hypotheses

The hypotheses for this research were defined as follows.

H1. Theoretical justifications have not been determinant in the proposed applications of IA and RA design projects.

H2. Technological availability and accessibility are highly correlated with the proposed applications of IA/RA projects.

H3. There is a significant difference between IA and RA with regard to H1 and H2.

This study is also expected to generate a classification system to assist in the study of past and future project endeavors. Moreover, the classification system will provide a comprehensive description of the field.

5   Methodology

5.1   Literature Survey

The bibliographic list used in this paper's analysis was composed by searching in the Google Scholar index. Other indexes were also searched (e.g. Avery Index to Architectural Periodicals); however the number of returned results was significantly lower.

Google Scholar returned a total of 3,250 results to the search of the following line: "Responsive architecture" OR "Interactive architecture". Google Scholar only showed the first 1000 results, as this is the custom limit of the search engine. However, as the results are sorted by relevance, these 1000 results are expected to include the large majority of the papers pertinent to this study's scope.[1] A main limitation of this study refers to the comprehensiveness and accuracy of Google Scholar's search algorithms, which is beyond the control of the authors of this paper.

In a first filtering iteration, the following publications were removed from the 1000 titles collected: papers addressing computer and software architecture, papers about passive climate-responsive architecture (large quantity), and papers which are not in English language. This resulted in a total of 239 publications, 229 (95.8 %) of which the authors of this study had direct access to.

A second filtering iteration looked more closely to each publication. Only publications which explicitly approached IA or RA, with the adoption of one of these terms exactly, were retained. Several papers were excluded for making one quick reference to either of the terms, without further development. We found several examples of publications where the terms IA and RA were present only in the references section. Although these often related directly to the research problem, they were not included in the review, because they did not provide IA/RA specific justifications.

---

[1] This was empirically observed during the analysis of the returned results. As we approached the end of the 1000 results list, few papers were in English language and, after some point, none would relate to the study's scope.

The second filtering iteration also excluded publications that were not peer-reviewed. Although this made the bibliography more consistent, it caused the removal of books and articles published in the Architectural Design Journal. Therefore, another limitation of this study is that it focuses only in peer-reviewed publications for analysis. Nonetheless, a few most important books will be commented when relevant.

The final bibliographic list counted with 59 conference papers and 18 journal articles, in a total of 77 publications.

5.2 Project Survey

The design projects reviewed in this research are of two natures: (1) built architectural projects, or (2) works officially exhibited to the public as installations. The first medium to find such projects were the publications themselves surveyed as described in Sect. 5.1. Main books and publications about RA and IA were also searched for projects.

While the literature search strived to be comprehensive and provide a descriptive analysis of the whole population of such publications, the projects search did not have such pretention. One of the reasons is that while specific parameters could be defined for literature, these could not be rigidly drawn for projects. The lack of a comprehensive index for such projects posed the largest complication. Additionally, the lack of stated labels, i.e. RA and IA, prevented us from selecting only projects originally intended to address these fields specifically. As a result, projects like ADA, which are repeatedly cited in RA/IA literature, were included in our study despite the fact that official notes and academic publications from ADA's authors would not refer to the project as RA or IA. Finally, while the justifications for IA and RA are typically made explicit in the literature, allowing us to reference exact citations, this was not possible with projects. Their official descriptions were often vague or nonexistent. Therefore the issues being addressed by each project were in large part inferred by the authors of this study.

Given the extensive search for projects conducted by this research, we expect that our sample is qualitatively representative of what is being made under the umbrella of RA and IA. Yet, the reader must bear in mind the limitations presented at this stage of the process.

5.3 Data Analysis

Both literature and projects were analyzed individually. For each literature entry, the authors of this study filled a series of data fields in a spreadsheet, including: authors' institution of origin; authors' field of origin; year; vehicle of publication; research design/method; references; definition of RA/IA; clear justifications; and unclear justifications. For projects, the fields included: type of building; program; location; sensors, processors and effectors used; system and user classification; and justifications.

"Justifications" was an open field, generating individual entries. Justifications that were very similar in content were merged together, creating sufficiently comprehensive categories, as will be later described.

This process is subjective and therefore prone to different interpretations. Because of this fact, it was important that the data collected was presented with the most detail possible, at the scale of the individual entry, so that this research's findings can be tested and replicated by any other researchers interested in this study.

Therefore, the data concerning the main question of this paper, i.e. justification of IA and RA, will be presented in data visualization figures. All the findings will also be presented in simple descriptive statistics. Finally, all the findings will be tested against the hypotheses.

6 Results and Discussion

6.1 Definition of Categories

The first stage of analyzing the rationales for RA/IA in the literature and in design projects consisted of grouping together individual justifications, thus creating categories. The list of categories itself is an exhaustive description of the breadth of rationales existent in the field.

Figure 1 presents the list of categories for both literature and design projects. It also organizes all categories in relation to 11 macro categories derived from the lists. The macro categories show the categories that are closely related to each other with regard to the issues they address. They also allow the list of literature categories and the list of project categories to relate to one another, despite the fact the each list composes different sets of categories.

The macro categories also compensate for the apparent inflation of individual categories too closely related. For instance, the number of literature categories (4) for the macro category of "Sustainability and environmental conservation" point towards the relevance of this topic in literature, instead of suggesting the existence of several discrete and unrelated topics. Similarly, the number of categories in "people-environment relationship" suggests beforehand the relevance of perceptual issues to the design projects surveyed.

It is important to note that certain issues discussed in the literature could not be assessed in the projects. For example the category "New paradigms" could not be evaluated. Certainly several project, if not all, challenge existing paradigms and make use of new views on architectural design; however to classify such issues would compose an overly speculative task.

"General" was also not addressed in the projects' analysis. The reason for such is that the projects are specific in their approach by their nature.

The following sub-sections will present the frequency of all these categories in the groups of literature and project design, as well as describe and discuss their overall behavior.

6.2 Literature on RA and IA

The literature surveyed is distributed in time as show in Fig. 2. The total numbers of RA publications (n = 38) and IA publications (n = 39) were remarkably balanced.

MACRO CATEGORIES	LITERATURE CATEGORIES	PROJECT CATEGORIES
Servicing	1 - Assistance/support in performing activities 2 - Improve comfort/quality of living of inabitants	1 - Assistance/support in performing activities
User-centered architecture	3 - Adapt to changing needs of inhabitants 4 - Adapt to different uses and activities / Increase flexibility of architectural spaces 5 - Adapt to different people / Maximize person-environment fit	2 - flexibility
Sustainability and Environmental conservation	6 - Sustainability (ample) 7 - Adapt to changing environmental conditions / Improve environmental performance 8 - Minimize use of resources / Rationalization 9 - Energy eficiency	3 - Improve environmental performance
Functional and spatial performance	10 - Spatial efficiency 11 - Deliver intended functionality/ performance under varying conditions 12 - Improve performance (unspecific)	4 - Spatial organization of people and activities 5 - New functionalities
Negotiation	13 - Find best-fit formal solutions to both user activities and environmental changes 14 - Mediate the environment	
Social support	15 - Adapt to changing social conditions 16 - Faciliate social connections	6 - Architecture to reflect collective social conditions 7 - Faciliate social connections 8 - Expand the individual's sphere of influence in public
People-environment relationship	17 - Promote connection or engagement with environment 18 - New kinds of interactions between people and environment 19 - New sensory/spatial/aesthetical experiences	9 - sensory/aesthetic/artistic 10 - New meanings 11 - architecture's connection with the surrounding landscape 12 - Architecture as sentient/emotive entity 13 - Entertainment 14 - visibility / surveillance / exposure
Technocentric architecture	20 - Fulfillment of possibilities/demands posed by technology 21 - Architecture as an interface for digital information and virtual embodiment	15 - Architecture as an interface for digital information and virtual embodiment
Agency	22 - Inhabitant participation in construction/behaviour of environment 23 - Expand human capabilities	17 - Inhabitant participation in construction/behaviour of environment
New paradigms	24 - Continuity to parametric modelling qualities 25 - Paradigmatic shift towards performative architecture and others 26 - Paradigmatic shift towards ecologic integration	
General	27 - Potentially solve several contemporary problems (open)	

Fig. 1. Categories and macro categories for literature and design projects

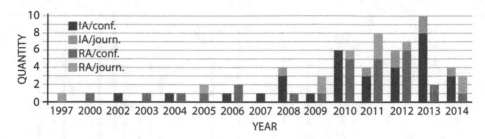

Fig. 2. Frequency distribution of RA and IA publications in time

These publications were originated from 56 unique institutions, the main institutions being: RMIT University (n = 8), TU Delft (n = 7) and National Cheng Kung University (n = 4). A total of 12 papers came from outside the field of architecture, i.e. the authors didn't have architectural background nor did they represent architecture schools.

Some publications, e.g. [67], describe IA broadly, in terms of a built environment which reacts to the user or other contextual inputs. In other instances, the same authors refer to RA in one paper and IA in others, but don't differentiate between them; e.g. [61, 62]. Other papers are more specific and differentiate IA as a multi-loop system, a "conversation"; e.g. [63]. This shows that despite the terminological inflation, some of these most popular terms are still not used consistently.

One characteristic that stands out among these publications refers to the kind of research. 41.6 % of all the publications (n = 32) were strictly a form of project report. Their logic follows the architectural projects tradition of documenting formation process and final products. However, they are not typically concerned with providing rigorous performance results of such projects against their original assumptions. Only 5.2 % of the publications (n = 4) presented experimental research designs.

Another concerning observations refers to the fact that authors don't typically build upon IA's or RA's own theoretical literature; only for definitions and for a conceptual contextualization of the field. Theoretical works and frameworks exist, but they often don't communicate with each other nor are applied to more practical researches outside their original institutions. Only 5.2 % of the publications (n = 4) were considered to build upon IA's or RA's own theoretical literature.

Finally, when analyzing frequency distribution of RA and IA publications in time, it is important to note that the two most influential publications in the field, according to Google Scholar, are not part of the graph. "Interactive architecture", a book by Michael Fox and Miles Kemp, published in 2009, is the most cited publication with 124 citations. It is followed by the book "Responsive Environments: Architecture, Art and Design", by Lucy Bullivant, published in 2006 and counting with 98 citations.

Fox and Kemp justifies IA concerning its ability to *create spaces that can meet changing needs with respect to evolving individual, social, and environmental demands* [5]. They also highlight a transition in architecture from a mechanical to a biological paradigm. Bullivant is less direct in her approach to RA, observing its value as *mediating devices for a new social statement* [13]. She focuses on the experiential, social and artistic possibilities offered by responsive environments.

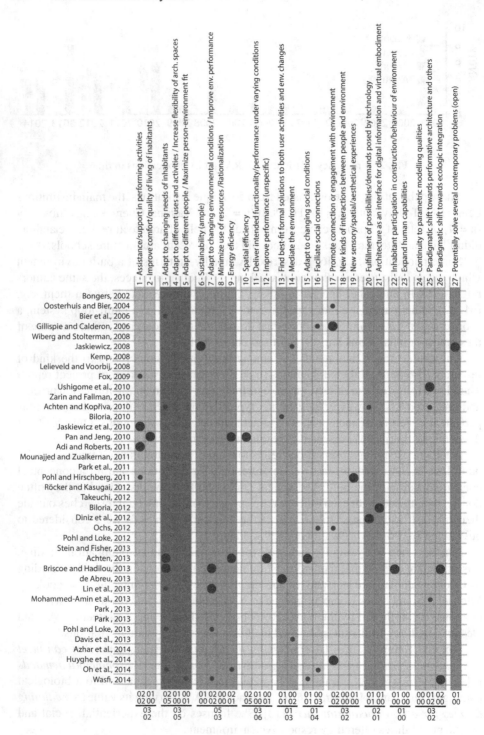

Fig. 3. Matrix of justifications found in the publications addressing IA

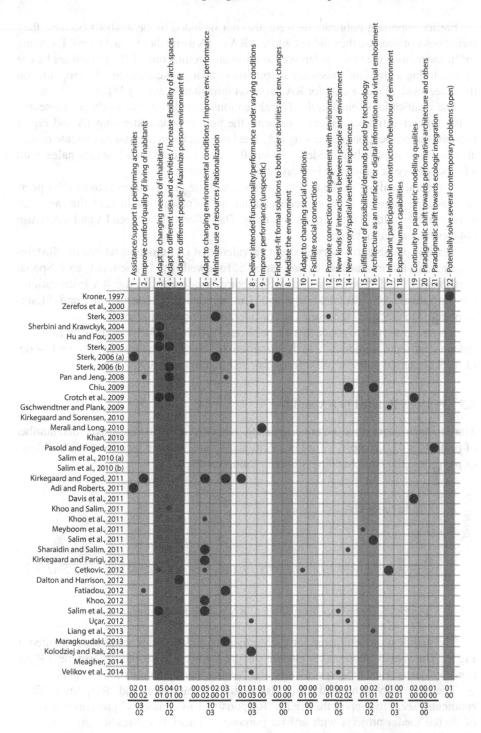

Fig. 4. Matrix of justifications found in the publications addressing RA

Earlier important publications were also not included in the analysis because they were books or because they did not address RA or IA using these exact terms. Eastman, for instance, uses the term "Adaptive Conditional Architecture" [7]. He justifies its use by remarking a building's need for adaptation to changing conditions. Negroponte, on the other hand, makes a case for RA based on inhabitants' agency [8].

The justifications found in the 77 publications included in this study are presented in the following figures. Figure 3 presents the publications addressing IA and Fig. 4 presents the publications addressing RA. The large circles in the figures indicate rationales that were explicitly provided. The small circles indicate less clear rationales, with a higher degree of subjective interpretation.

A general analysis of the figures suggests that the justifications provided by peer-reviewed literature are not overly concentrated in few categories. Instead, they are scattered over a breadth of different perspectives. The difference between IA and RA is also not too evident on first sight.

Yet, it is possible to observe a slight prevalence of IA rationales related to "Sustainability and Environmental Conservation", followed by "Functional and Spatial Performance" and "User-Centered Architecture" categories. In the RA justifications, the prevalence of "Sustainability and Environmental Conservation" and "User-Centered Architecture" categories is considerably more pronounced.

It is also important to notice that the publications from outside the field of architecture did not contribute significantly to the distribution described on those figures. Only 4 out of the 12 external publications offered any justification for IA/RA at all.

6.3 Projects Related to RA and IA

The design projects surveyed are distributed in time as show in Fig. 5. The total number of projects is 41. Of these, 22 are installations, 11 are building façades, 5 are buildings or pavilions, and 6 are building's interior components.

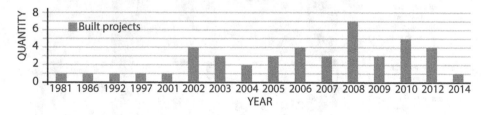

Fig. 5. Frequency distribution of RA and IA design projects in time

The justifications estimated for each project included in this study are presented in Fig. 6. The visualization makes evident the prevalence of "People-Environment Relationship" categories; most specifically, the "sensory/aesthetic/artistic" category.

The previously mentioned books "Interactive Architecture" and "Responsive Environments" seem to support this trend. "Responsive Environments" presents a majority of digital media projects with artistic purposes. "Interactive Architecture" excluded digital media projects from their review. Yet, its section with the largest number of built

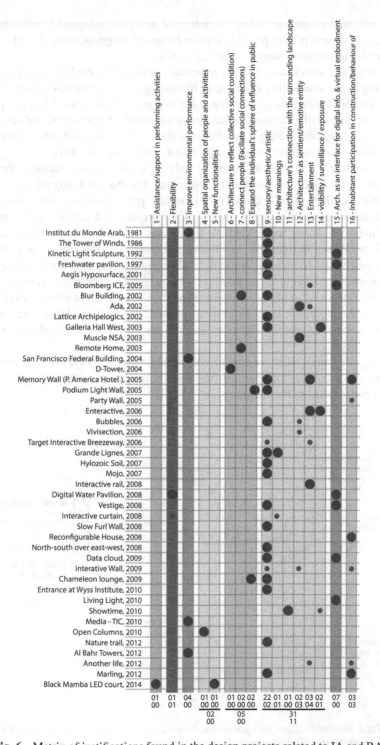

Fig. 6. Matrix of justifications found in the design projects related to IA and RA

projects reviewed is the one titled "sociological and psychological implications". If excluding component prototypes, this section brings 18 projects, more than the double of the remaining sections summed together (n = 7).

This trend was anticipated and our hypothesis attempts to explain such prevalence by referring to the availability of low-cost technology that favors this sort of effect. In order to test this hypothesis, we analyzed the types of effectors used in each project. Effectors are potentially the most expensive components of interactive and responsive systems, especially considering a building's scale. Additionally, different categories of justifications require different sets of components, including actuators.

We found that 19 projects made use of only light emitters as effectors. Four more projects used light, media and/or sound as outcomes. These are not only widely available technologies, as they mainly allow for addressing perceptual purposes. One project explicitly uses cheap components from toys. 19 projects use actuators of some sort, however mainly in small scale. Medium size actuators (less economically accessible) are used in kinetic façades for environmental purposes, therefore not addressing primarily perceptual intentions. Building scale actuators are only used in one of the projects, namely the Digital Water Pavilion. This project is perhaps more closely related to prevalent categories in literature justification than the prevalent categories of design projects. Furthermore, the large majority of projects can be considered either reactive or simple responsive systems. The exact proportions were not computed due to a large uncertainty factor.

Although this analysis is not conclusive, we believe it supports our hypothesis that RA/IA projects are influenced more strongly by technological accessibility than by the rationales put forward in the literature.

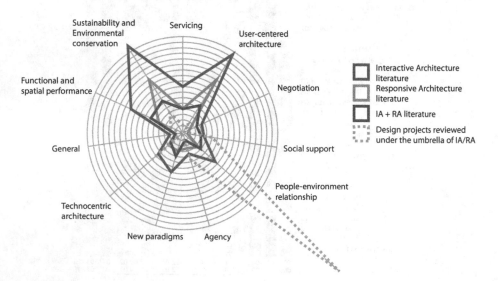

Fig. 7. Total number of times that justifications were counted in each macro category for RA literature, IA literature and design projects.

6.4 A Comparative Analysis

In order to make clear the distinctions between the different groups analyzed, a new graph was created. Figure 7 presents the total number of times that justifications were counted in each macro category. Main (explicit) justifications were assigned a weight value of 1 (one), while peripheral (implicit) justifications were assigned a weight of 0.5 (half).

The graph shows a relatively even distribution of IA literature, the "sustainability" and "user-centered" prevalence in both RA and overall literature, and the striking prevalence of "people-environment relationship" justifications in design projects.

These finding support our hypothesis that theoretical justifications have not been determinant in the proposed applications of IA and RA design projects. However they do not support our hypothesis that there is a significant difference between IA and RA with regard to the previous hypotheses.

7 Conclusion(s)

The adoption of new technologies is an important aspect of architectural history. It is possible that such importance is becoming more relevant and evident given the fast pace of technological development in the last few decades. In this paper, we have argued that technology availability exists prior to established demands and robust theoretical basis within the fields of IA and RA.

We found in our review that justifications in the literature commonly try to match available technology with existing issues and demands in architecture. However, the ad hoc rationale of IA and RA has done little to connect their built exemplars to real word problems and demands. Almost 20 years ago, Kroner addressed several specific demands and endeavors that could potentially benefit from IA/RA capabilities [48]. However, despite the decades old academic investment on IA/RA, they don't. So what is keeping IA from addressing these immediate demands?

The current hype on smart environments has also not assisted significantly in RA/IA uptake by the industry. It seems that such hype is satisfied by add-on ambient intelligence systems, thus not justifying the active (and expensive) participation of spatial forms, which persistently remain static. The popularity of interactive art has also mostly remained restricted to installations; when applied to buildings, it hardly challenges the solidity of architecture as it is, typically composing façade displays.

It is possible that despite the persuasive range of justifications found in literature, these potential applications are simply largely disconnected from actual demands due to the architects' approach to the field. Other reasons could be that technology is still lagging behind architects' intentions or that the accelerated development of computing technologies is creating their own demands at the expense of addressing existing problems.

This research paper has only started to tackle these questions. In our extensive literature review, we observe that outstanding research gaps in the field have been systematically neglected. There are no performance studies that support IA's claim to improve user experience of architecture or to optimize spatial organization, among many other justifications. Most importantly, there are very limited efforts put towards addressing specific current demands in architecture and generating evidences regarding the adequacy of specific strategies towards specific problems. The lack of such supporting information might be a key reason as to why IA is still largely limited to speculative discourses, even decades after its concept was popularized.

References

1. Sterk, T.: Responsive architecture: user-centered interactions within the hybridized model of control. In: Proceedings of the Game Set and Match II, On Computer Games, Advanced Geometries, and Digital Technologies, Netherlands, Episode Publishers, pp. 494–501 (2006a)
2. Kolarevic, B.: Architecture in the Digital Age: Design and Manufacturing. Taylor & Francis, New York (2005)
3. Glanville, R.: An intelligent architecture. Convergence: Int. J. Res. N. Media Technol. 7(2), 12–24 (2001)
4. Yiannoudes, S.: Kinetic digitally-driven architectural structures as marginal objects–a conceptual framework. FOOTPRINT 4(6), 41–54 (2010)
5. Fox, M., Kemp, M.: Interactive Architecture. Princeton Architectural Press, New york (2009)
6. Pask, G.: Architectural relevance of cybernetics. In: Architectural Design, September, pp. 494–496 (1969)
7. Eastman, C.: Adaptive-conditional architecture. In: Proceedings of the Design Research Society's Conference Manchester 1971, Academy Editions, London, pp. 51–57 (1971)
8. Negroponte, N.: Soft Architecture Machines. MIT press, Cambridge, MA (1975)
9. Oosterhuis, K.: Hyperbodies: Towards an E-motive Architecture. Birkhauser Publishers, Basel, Switzerland (2003)
10. Schnädelbach, H.: Adaptive architecture: a conceptual framework. In: Proceedings of Media City (2010)
11. Jaskiewicz, T.: DYNAMIC DESIGN MATTER[S]. In: Proceedings of the First International Conference on Critical Digital: What Matters(s)?, Harvard University Graduate School of Design, Cambridge (USA) (2008)
12. Lee, J.D.: Adaptable, kinetic, responsive, and transformable architecture: an alternative approach to sustainable design. Doctoral dissertation, University of Texas (2012)
13. Bullivant, L.: Responsive Environments: Architecture, Art and Design. V&A Publications, London (2006)
14. Achten, H.: Buildings with an attitude. In: Proceedings of the 31st eCAADe Conference, vol. 2, Delft University of Technology, Netherlands (2013)
15. Achten, H., Kopřiva, M.: A design methodological framework for interactive architecture. In: Proceedings of the 28th eCAADe Conference, pp. 169–177 (2010)
16. Adi, M.N., Roberts, D.J.: The use of online virtual environments to assess the appeal of interactive elements within buildings, IEEE, pp. 189–196 (2011a)
17. Adi, M.N., Roberts, D.J.: Using VR to assess the impact of seemingly life like and intelligent architecture on people's ability to follow instructions from a teacher. In: 2011 IEEE International Symposium on VR Innovation (ISVRI), IEEE, pp. 25–31 (2011b)
18. Azhar, M., Malik, F.R., Sajjad, M., Irfan, M., Gu, B.W., Park, W.J., Baik, S.W.: VIP-emulator: to design interactive architecture for adaptive mixed reality space. In: Proceedings of the International Conference Data Mining, Civil and Mechanical Engineering (ICDMCME 2014), International Institute of Engineers, Indonesia (2014)

19. Bier, H., de Bodt, K., Galle, J.: SC: prototypes for interactive architecture. In: Zha, H., Pan, Z., Thwaites, H., Addison, A.C., Forte, M. (eds.) VSMM 2006. LNCS, vol. 4270, pp. 21–28. Springer, Heidelberg (2006)
20. Biloria, N.: Interactive environments: a multi-disciplinary approach towards developing real-time performative spaces. In: Yang, H.S., Malaka, R., Hoshino, J., Han, J.H. (eds.) ICEC 2010. LNCS, vol. 6243, pp. 254–261. Springer, Heidelberg (2010)
21. Biloria, N.: Interactive morphologies: an investigation into integrated nodal networks and embedded computation processes for developing real-time responsive spatial systems. Front. Archit. Res. 1(3), 259–271 (2012). doi:10.1016/j.foar.2012.07.003
22. Bongers, B.: Interactivating spaces. In: Proceedings of Symposium on Systems Research in the Arts, Informatics and Cybernetics (2002)
23. Briscoe, D., Hadilou, A.: Collective intelligence: an analytical simulation of social interaction with architectural system. In: Conference on Computer-Aided Architectural Design Research in Asia (CAADRIA 2013), pp. 375–384 (2013)
24. Cetkovic, A.: Unconscious perception in a responsive architectural environment. In: Proceedings of MutaMorphosis Conference (2012)
25. Chiu, H.: Research on hybrid tectonic methodologies for responsive architecture. In: CAADRIA 2009 (2009)
26. Crotch, J., Mantho, R., Horner, M.: SPACE MAKING –Between the virtual and the physical. Int. J. Archit. Comput. 03(07), 403–414 (2009)
27. Dalton, C., Harrison, J.D.: Conceptualisation of an intelligent salutogenic room environment. In: Breedon, P. (ed.) Smart Design, pp. 87–95. Springer, London (2012)
28. Davis, D., Salim, F.D., Burry, J.: Designing responsive architecture: mediating analogue and digital modelling in studio. In: Proceedings of the Computer-Aided Architectural Design Research in Asia (CAADRIA), pp. 155–164 (2011)
29. Davis, F., Roseway, A., Carroll, E., Czerwinski, M.: Actuating mood: design of the textile mirror. In: Proceedings of the 7th International Conference on Tangible, Embedded and Embodied Interaction, pp. 99–106 (2013)
30. De Abreu, S.C.: Permeability regimes between man and interactive spaces. In: Proceedings of the 31st eCAADe Conference, vol. 1, Faculty of Architecture, Delft University of Technology, Delft, The Netherlands, 18–20 September 2013, pp. 449-457 (2013)
31. Diniz, N.V., Duarte, C.A., Guimarães, N.M.: Mapping interaction onto media façades. In: Proceedings of the 2012 International Symposium on Pervasive Displays, ACM (2012)
32. Fortiadou, A.: Responsive architecture and software: a prototype simulation software for responsive constructions. In: eWork and eBusiness in Architecture, Engineering and Construction. CRC Press, Boca Raton (2012)
33. Fox, M.: Flockwall: a full-scale spatial environment with discrete collaborative modules. In: ACADIA 09: reForm()–Building a Better Tomorrow, pp. 90–97 (2009)
34. Gillispie, D., Calderon, C.: A framework towards designing responsive public information systems. In: Proceedings of the 3rd International Conference of the Arab Society for Computer Aided Architectural Design, Alexandria, Egypt, pp. 767–782 (2007)
35. Gschwendtner, G., Plank, C.M.: From an architecture of sign to an architecture of consciousness. In: Proceedings of Architecture and Phenomenology, Second International Conference, Kyoto Seika University (2009)
36. Hu, C., Fox, M.: Starting from the micro: a pedagogical approach to designing interactive architecture. In: Smart Architecture: Integration of Digital and Building Technologies, Savannah, Georgia (2005)

37. Huyghe, J., Wouters, N., Geerts, D., Vande Moere, A.: LocaLudo: card-based workshop for interactive architecture. In: CHI 2014 Extended Abstracts on Human Factors in Computing Systems, ACM Press, New York, pp. 1975–1980 (2014)
38. Jaskiewicz, T., Aprile, W.A., van der Helm, A.: Creative approach to the design and prototyping of experimental smart spaces, case studies from the interactive environments minor. In: Balandin, S., Dunaytsev, R., Koucheryavy, Y. (eds.) ruSMART 2010. LNCS, vol. 6294, pp. 135–147. Springer, Heidelberg (2010)
39. Kemp, R.M.: Interactive interfaces in architecture: the new spatial integration of information, gesture and cognitive control. In: Proceedings from ACADIA 08: Silicon + Skin–Biological Processes and Computation, pp. 422–429 (2008)
40. Khan, O.: Open columns: a carbon dioxide (CO2) responsive architecture. In: CHI 2010 Extended Abstracts on Human Factors in Computing Systems, ACM (2010)
41. Khoo, C.K.: Sensory morphing skins. In: Proceedings of the 30th eCAADe, Czech Republic (2012)
42. Khoo, C.K., Salim, F., Burry, J.: Designing architectural morphing skins with elastic modular systems. Int. J. Archit. Comput. 9(4), 397–420 (2011)
43. Khoo, C.K., Salim, F.D.: Designing elastic transformable structures. In: Proceedings of the 16th International Conference on Computer-Aided Architectural Design Research in Asia, CAADRIA, Hong Kong, pp. 143–152 (2011)
44. Kirkegaard, P.H., Hans Isak Worre, F.: Development and evaluation of a responsive building envelope. In: Proceedings of Adaptive Architecture, London (2011)
45. Kirkegaard, P.H., Parigi, D.: On control strategies for responsive architectural structures. In: IASS-APCS 2012 Proceedings from Spatial Structures to Space Structures, Korea (2012)
46. Kirkegaard, P.H., Sorensen, J.D.: Robustness analysis of kinetic structures. In: Proceedings of the International Association for Shell and Spatial Structures (IASS) Symposium, Valencia (2009)
47. Kolodziej, P., Rak, J.: Responsive building envelope as a material system of autonomous agents. In: Conference on Computer-Aided Architectural Design Research in Asia (CAADRIA 2013), vol. 945, p. 954 (2013)
48. Kroner, W.M.: An intelligent and responsive architecture. Autom. Constr. 6(5), 381–393 (1997)
49. Lelieveld, C., Voorbij, L.: Dynamic material application for architectural purposes. Adv. Sci. Technol. 56, 595–600 (2008)
50. Liang, H.-N., Nancy, D., Man, K.L., Wan, K., Zhang, N., Lim, E.G.: Real-time environmental sensing-adaptive surfaces for architecture. In: 3rd International Conference on Ambient Computing, Applications, Services and Technologies, pp. 74–79 (2013)
51. Lin, H.C., Jeng, T., Chen, C.: Reimaging humane cities: interaction design, city sense, and smart living. Int. J. Affect. Eng. 12(2), 155–159 (2013)
52. Maragkoudaki, A.; No-mech kinetic responsive architecture: kinetic responsive architecture with no mechanical parts, IEEE, pp. 145–150 (2013)
53. Meagher, M.: Responsive architecture and the problem of obsolescence. Int. J. Archit. Res.: ArchNet-IJAR 8(3), 95–104 (2014)
54. Merali, R., Long, D.: Actuated responsive truss. Modular Robots: The State of the Art, 36 (2010)
55. Meyboom, A., Johnson, G., Wojtowicz, J.: Architectronics: towards a responsive environment. Int. J. Archit. Comput. 9(1), 77–98 (2011)
56. Mohammed-Amin, R.K., von Mammen, S., Boyd, J.E.: ARCS architectural chameleon skin. In: Proceedings of the 31st eCAADe Conference (2013)

57. Mounajjed, N., Zualkernan, I.A.: From simple pleasure to pleasurable skin: an interactive architectural screen. In: Proceedings of the 2011 Conference on Designing Pleasurable Products and Interfaces, ACM, p. 30 (2011)

58. Ochs, S.W.: Architectural sociability as a strategy to drive technology integrations into architectural structures and smart environments. Int. J. Archit. Comput. **10**(2), 301–318 (2012)

59. Oh, S., Patrick, V., Llach, D.C.: Typologies of architectural interaction: a social dimension. In: Proceedings of the Symposium on Simulation for Architecture & Urban Design, Society for Computer Simulation International, p. 7 (2014)

60. Oosterhuis, K., Bier, H.: Real time behavior in ONL-architecture. In: Proceedings of Conference on Construction Applications of Virtual Reality, Lisbon (2004)

61. Pan, C., Jeng, T.: Exploring sensing-based kinetic design for responsive architecture. In: Conference of Computer-Aided Architectural Design Research in Asia (CAADRIA). (2008)

62. Pan, C., Jeng, T.: A robotic and kinetic design for interactive architecture. In: Proceedings of SICE Annual Conference 2010, IEEE, pp. 1792–1796 (2010)

63. Park, J.W.: Interactive kinetic media facades: a pedagogical design system to support an integrated virtual-physical prototyping environment in the design process of media facades. J. Asian Archit. Build. Eng. **12**(2), 237–244 (2013)

64. Park, J.W., Huang, J., Terzidis, K.: A tectonic approach for integrating kinesis with a building in the design process of interactive skins. J. Asian Archit. Build. Eng. **10**(2), 305–312 (2011)

65. Pasold, A., Foged, I.: Performative responsive architecture powered by climate. In: Proceedings of the 30th Annual Conference of the Association for Computer Aided Design in Architecture (ACADIA) (2010)

66. Pohl, I.M., Loke, L.: Engaging the sense of touch in interactive architecture. In: Proceedings of the 24th Australian Computer-Human Interaction Conference, ACM (2012)

67. Pohl, I.M., Loke, L.: Touch toolkit: a method to convey touch-based design knowledge and skills, ACM Press, pp. 251–258 (2013). doi:10.1145/2540930.2540957

68. Pohl, I.M., Urs, H.: Sensitive surface. A reactive tangible surface. In: CAAD Futures 2011: Designing Together, ULg (2011)

69. Röcker, C., Kasugai, K.: Interactive architecture in domestic spaces. In: Wichert, R., Van Laerhoven, K., Gelissen, J. (eds.) Constructing Ambient Intelligence, vol. 277, pp. 12–18. Springer, Heidelberg (2012)

70. Salim, F.D., Burry, J.R., Peers, J., Underwood, J.: Augmented spatiality. Int. J. Archit. Comput. **10**(2), 275–300 (2012)

71. Salim, F.D., Mulder, H., Burry, J.: A system for form fostering. In: Proceedings of the 15th International Conference on Computer-Aided Architectural Design Research in Asia CAADRIA 2010 (2010)

72. Salim, F.D., Mulder, H., Burry, J.R.: Form fostering: a novel design approach for interacting with parametric models in the embodied virtuality. J. Inf. Technol. Constr. **16**, 135–150 (2011)

73. Salim, F.D., Mulder, H., Jaworski, P.: Demonstration of an open platform for tangible and social interactions with responsive models. In: ACADIA2010, pp. 227–233 (2010)

74. Sharaidin, M.K., Salim, F.D.: Affordable, performative, and responsive. In: Proceedings of the 16th International Conference on Computer-Aided Architectural Design Research in Asia, CAADRIA, Hong Kong, pp. 113–122 (2011)

75. Sherbini, K., Krawczyk, R.: Overview of intelligent architecture. In: 1st ASCAAD International Conference, e-Design in Architecture KFUPM, Dhahran (2004)

76. Stein, J., Fisher, S.: Ambient storytelling experiences and applications for interactive architecture. In: AMBIENT 2013, The Third International Conference on Ambient Computing, Applications, Services and Technologies, pp. 23–28 (2013)

77. Sterk, T.D.E.: Using actuated tensegrity structures to produce a responsive architecture. In: Proceedings of the Annual Conference of the Association for Computer-Aided Design in Architecture - ACADIA (2003)
78. Sterk, T.D.E.: Building upon Negroponte: a hybridized model of control suitable for responsive architecture. Autom. Constr. **14**(2), 225–232 (2005)
79. Sterk, T.: Shape control in responsive architectural structures–current reasons & challenges. In: Proceedings of the 4th World Conference on Structural Control and Monitoring, San Diego, CA, USA (2006b)
80. Takeuchi, Y.: Synthetic space: inhabiting binaries. In: CHI' 12 Extended Abstracts on Human Factors in Computing Systems, ACM pp. 251–260 (2012)
81. Uçar, B.: Constant redefinition of relations in responsive environments: unpredictability and boredom as generative impulses. In: Proceedings of the 15th Generative Art Conference GA2012 (2012)
82. Ushigome, Y., Niiyama, R., Nishimura, K., Tanikawa, T., Hirose, M.: Archi/e machina: interactive architecture based on tensegrity. In: 2010 16th International Conference on Virtual Systems and Multimedia (VSMM), IEEE, pp. 55–62 (2010)
83. Velikov, K., Thün, G., O'Malley, M., Simbuerger, W.: Nervous ether: soft aggregates, interactive skins. Leonardo **47**(4), 344–351 (2014)
84. Wasfi, A.: Architecture as a second nature. J. Sustain. Archit. Civ. Eng. **7**(2), 3–9 (2014)
85. Wiberg, M., Stolterman, E.: Environment interaction: character, challenges & implications for design. In: Proceedings of the 7th International Conference on Mobile and Ubiquitous Multimedia, ACM, pp. 15–22 (2008)
86. Yueh-Sung, W., Jia-Yih, C., Yu-Pin, M.A., Cheng-An, P., Tay-Sheng, J.: Eco-machine: a green robotic ecosystem for sustainable environments. In: Conference on Computer-Aided Architectural Design Research in Asia (CAADRIA 2013), vol. 925, p. 934 (2013)
87. Zarin, R., Fallman, D.: Ambient Interactive Architecture: Enriching Urban Spaces with Low-cost, Lightweight Interactive Lighting. In: Colour and Light in Architecture_First International Conference 2010 Proceedings (2010)
88. Zerefos, S.C., Kotsiopoulos, A.M., Pombortsis, A.: Responsive architecture: an integrated approach for the future. In: Proceedings of the Annual Conference of the Association for Computer-Aided Design in Architecture, ACADIA, p. 245 (2000)

A Model for Sustainable Site Layout Design of Social Housing with Pareto Genetic Algorithm: SSPM

Yazgı Badem Aksoy[✉], Gülen Çağdaş, and Özgün Balaban

Istanbul Technical University, Istanbul, Turkey
yazbadem@hotmail.com, cagdas@itu.edu.tr,
ozgunbalaban@gmail.com

Abstract. Nowadays as the aim to reduce the environmental impact of buildings becomes more apparent, a new architectural design approach is gaining momentum called sustainable architectural design. Sustainable architectural design process includes some regulations itself, which requires calculations, comparisons and consists of several possible conflicting objectives that need to be considered together. A successful green building design can be performed by the creation of alternative designs generated according to all the sustainability parameters and local regulations in conceptual design stage. As there are conflicting criteria's according to LEED and BREAM sustainable site parameters, local regulations and local climate conditions, an efficient decision support system can be developed by the help of Pareto based non-dominated genetic algorithm (NSGA-II) which is used for several possibly conflicting objectives that need to be considered together. In this paper, a model which aims to produce site layout alternatives according to sustainability criteria for cooperative apartment house complexes, will be mentioned.

Keywords: Sustainable site layout design · Multi objective genetic algorithm · LEED-BREEAM

1 Introduction

The development of computer technology has affected architectural design process efficiently. In architectural design, as a result of multidisciplinary researches, evolutionary computation is being used at least for 10–15 years [1]. In design industry, advanced computer aided design tools have an important impact on design process, but still early design stage and sustainable design are problematic issues, and need to be solved. Sustainable building design refers to a process that begins with selecting the site and optimizing economic and environmental performance throughout a building's life cycle. As Rivard [2] declared that in order to achieve a successful sustainable building, particular attention needs to be paid to the conceptual design stage when the most important decisions are taken, nevertheless it is the stage with least computer support. There are huge numbers of simulation programs used for sustainable design; but most of these simulation tools do not support conceptual designs appropriately.

G. Celani et al. (Eds.): CAAD Futures 2015, CCIS 527, pp. 113–133, 2015.
DOI: 10.1007/978-3-662-47386-3_7

In addition, these simulation tools typically cannot communicate among themselves and have time-consuming data inputs and complex interfaces [2].

On the other hand, green building rating systems and certification programs created by the developed countries play an efficient role in usage of green buildings. In this paper, LEED and BREEAM certification systems are going to be considered, as being the most representative building environment assessment schemes that are in use. Although these certification systems are used all over the world, the parameters are prepared according to America's and Britain's geographical, economic and cultural conditions, though other countries are experiencing difficulties during sustainable design process. As a result of this, green buildings should be designed also according to the climate of the region and local building construction regulations.

As it consists of several possible conflicting objectives that need to be considered together, sustainable building design process becomes more complicated than traditional building design. At that point, the reason of preferring multi-objective Pareto genetic algorithm in the model, which we will focus on this paper, will be better understood.

There are simultaneous optimization of several possibly conflicting objectives in multi-objective optimization problems that result in a set of non-dominated solutions. There does not exist a single solution that simultaneously optimizes each objective. In that case, there exists an infinite number of non-dominated solutions which are also known as Pareto optimal solutions. In sustainable design, maximum energy conservation and utilization of natural light can be given as an example of two conflicting objectives, so during sustainable design process Pareto genetic algorithm will be successful to generate design alternatives according to conflicting criteria.

To summarize, today some tools developed to assist designers during sustainable building design process, address more detailed design stages when important design decisions already have been taken in conceptual stage. As there are conflicting criteria's according to LEED and BREAM sustainable site parameters, local building codes and local climate conditions, an efficient decision support system can be developed by the help of Pareto genetic algorithm.

2 Literature Review

2.1 Simulation Models Used for Sustainable Architectural Design

Many simulation models have been developed to assist designers in green building design. GBTool [3] is a simulation model that evaluates buildings according to resource consumption and energy performance by using a rating system. ATHENA has been developed as a tool to assess the environmental performance of a building. It provides a convenient platform for simulating processes used in semiconductor industry, but it is limited with construction materials and installation [4, 5]. Radford and Gero [6] used multi objective design optimization to create a dynamic model that optimizes thermal load, daylight availability, construction cost and usable area performances.

All simulation models try to explore effective ways to assist designer in complicated design process, but especially during the early sustainable design process, there
are several limitations in practice. As indicated by Harputlugil and Yahiaoui [7] previous studies about sustainable building design have some problems during design
process. The program inputs are very detailed, scientifically there are wide ranges of
inputs and the data are not yet available in the early stages of design. Sustainable
building design criteria needs to be evaluated from the sketch phase, because the most
important decisions of sustainability are taken from the settlement of land. For these
reasons, it is clear that there is a need for better decision support system to support the
early stages of sustainable design.

2.2   Evolutionary Models Used for Sustainable Architectural Design

Evolution is a method of searching enormous number of alternatives to find the
solution and in between 1950s and the 1960s, it is used as an optimization tool for
engineering problems. The aim is to generate a population of alternative solutions using
natural selection operators and genetic algorithms [8].

Genetic algorithm is a population-based search technique inspired from the biological principles of natural selection and genetic recombination [9]. Genetic algorithms is a suitable tool for multi-objective optimization problems because it can
generate multiple Pareto optimal solutions in a single simulation run. NSGA is a
popular non-domination based genetic algorithm for multi-objective optimization [10].
It is a very effective algorithm but it has computational complexity, lack of elitism.
NSGAII was developed as a modification, which has a better sorting algorithm,
incorporates elitism and no sharing parameter needs to be chosen a priori. The NSGA-
II procedure has three features to find multiple Pareto-optimal solutions in a multi-
objective optimization problem: It uses an elitist principle and an explicit diversity
preserving mechanism, and also it emphasizes non-dominated solutions [11].

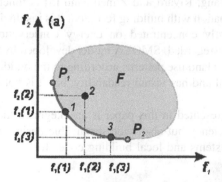

Fig. 1. Example of a bi-objective space (f_1, f_2) [12]

An example of a Pareto correlation is shown in Fig. 1. A minimization problem is
assumed. These criteria are expressed as computable functions $f_1(\mathbf{x}),\ldots, f_M(\mathbf{x})$ of the
decision variables, which are called objective functions. The Pareto front is the

boundary between the points P_1 and P_2 of the feasible set F. Solutions 1 and 3 are non-dominated Pareto optimal solutions. Solution 2 is not Pareto optimal as solution 1 because solution 1 has smaller values for both objectives [12].

In architectural design process, generally optimization algorithms have been used to automate the generation of design layouts. Especially in green building design process many efforts have been made to integrate multi objective optimization models and sustainable design. Wang, Zmeureanu and Rivard [5] optimized the building envelope using multi-objective genetic algorithm. Variables in the model include the parameters that are usually determined at the conceptual design stage and have critical impact on building performance. Life cycle analysis methodology is employed to evaluate design alternatives for both economic and environmental criteria. A multi-objective genetic algorithm is employed to find optimal solutions. They concentrate on building envelope because of its importance in environmental and economic performance of buildings. The multi-objective optimization model they used for building envelope design, can be used to locate the optimum or near optimum green building designs for given conditions [5].

In sustainable design, land use is another subject designers take care of. Zelinska, Church and Jankowski [13] present a new multi objective spatial optimization model-SMOLA which minimizes the conflicting objectives of open space development, infill and redevelopment, land use neighborhood compatibility and cost distance to already urbanized areas. They examine the applicability of spatial optimization as a generative modeling technique for sustainable land-use allocation. The model uses a density based design constraint developed by the authors. The constraint imposes a predefined level of consistent neighborhood development to promote contiguity and compactness of urban areas. The model is tested on a hypothetical example. Further, they demonstrate a real-world application of the model to land-use planning in Chelan, USA. The results indicate that spatial optimization is a promising method for generating land-use alternatives for further consideration in spatial decision-making [13].

These developed models are chosen for using evolutionary algorithms to solve different scaled design problems. The plan optimization model for green building design developed by Wang, Rivard and Zimeureanu [5] is functional for considering material and cost information with building form, but it is insufficient for early stages of design. Also it is mostly concentrated on energy conservation, site planning for building complexes is disregarded. SMOLA model developed by Zelinska, Church and Jankowski [13] generates land use patterns according to the building functions. For city scale the model is useful and has visual readability, but it is not convenient for small-scale problems.

The SSPM model presented in this paper is an integrated model that concentrates on not only energy efficiency but also wide sustainable design criteria; such as green building certification systems and local building codes for.

3   Sustainable Site Planning Model: SSPM

SSPM model is at the intersection of two different disciplines which are evolutionary algorithms and sustainable architectural design. The SSPM (Sustainable Site Planning Model) will generate site-planning alternatives for social housing on selected site, according to LEED and BREEAM certification systems sustainable site usage criteria, local building codes and local climate conditions which are accepted as sustainable design objectives.

NSGA-II-based optimization process is used to develop the SSPM model. In the NSGA-II-based optimization process, a novel chromosome representation and modified genetic operators are presented while a final selection decision-making process is developed to select the final solution from a set of Pareto optimal solutions. Processing 2.1 programming language is used as the evaluating software of SSPM model, for having advanced visual environment and the ability of working with Windows.

3.1 Algorithm of the SSPM Model

Step 1 Definition of the site:
  1a. Creation of site matrix in Excel,
  1b. Selecting climate type (a. Hot, b. Cold),
  1c. Input values for FSR (floor space ratio), FAR (floor area ratio) and maximum building height value,
  1d. Input percentage value of green area according to local building regulation,
  1e. Selecting direction of prevailing wind,
  1f. Selecting direction of view,
Step 2 Create and visualize the site by using Excel matrix data prepared by user before, with regular grid of d dimensions ($d = 1$ m),
Step 3 Production: Randomly generate initial population,
Step 4 Showing produced site individuals,
Step 5 Evaluation: Calculate the values of the n objectives for each solution in the current population. Then update the tentative set of non-dominated solutions;
Step 6 Give fitness scores to population according to fitness functions (1: successful, 0: unsuccessful) and do tournament selection;
Step 7 Do crossover operator between selected parents;
Step 8 Do mutation operator to new generation;
Step 9 Sorting new population according to Pareto efficiency (NSGA-II);
Step 10 Adding sorted individuals to new parents gene pool (2 N);
Step 11 Selecting N individuals from new parents' pool;
Step 12 Termination Test: If the user is not contended return to Step 6; if stopping condition is satisfied, end the algorithm.

Flowchart of the SSPM algorithm is shown in Fig. 2.

3.2 Site Definition Method

The first step of the model is definition of the site to the computer. Matrix definition technique in Excel is used to define the site with numbers. The defined digital site is used as a base to generate site planning alternatives on by SSPM. Excel program is chosen for providing quick and easy data input for matrix definition.

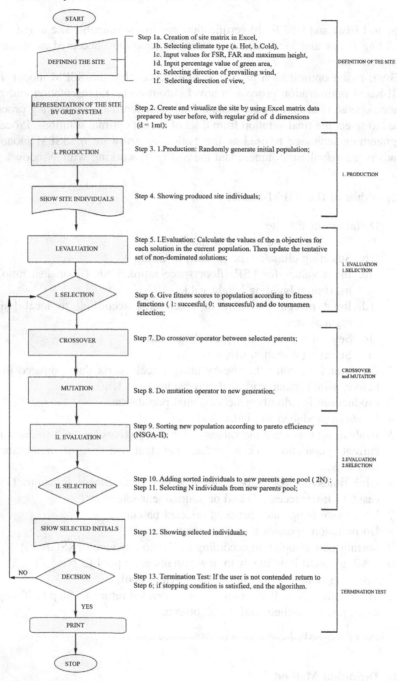

Step 1a. Creation of site matrix in Excel,
    1b. Selecting climate type (a. Hot, b.Cold),
    1c. Input values for FSR, FAR and maximum height,
    1d. Input percentage value of green area,
    1e. Selecting direction of prevailing wind,
    1f. Selecting direction of view,

Step 2. Create and visualize the site by using Excel matrix data prepared by user before, with regular grid of d dimensions (d = 1mt);

Step 3. 1.Production: Randomly generate initial population;

Step 4. Showing produced site individuals;

Step 5. I.Evaluation: Calculate the values of the n objectives for each solution in the current population. Then update the tentative set of non-dominated solutions;

Step 6. Give fitness scores to population according to fitness functions (1: succesful, 0: unsuccesful) and do tournamen selection;

Step 7. Do crossover operator between selected parents;

Step 8. Do mutation operator to new generation;

Step 9. Sorting new population according to pareto efficiency (NSGA-II);

Step 10. Adding sorted individuals to new parents gene pool (2N) ;
Step 11. Selecting N individuals from new parents pool;

Step 12. Showing selected individuals;

Step 13. Termination Test: If the user is not contended return to Step 6; if stopping condition is satisfied, end the algorithm.

Fig. 2. Flowchart of the SSPM model

The rows and columns of the matrix represent 1 unit = 1 m2 of the site. The x, y values of the site corner points and the center or corner points of existing elements are used to define the matrix. Each of the Excel cell is considered as a point in a coordinate system. R1C1 reference style in Excel is used to represent x and y axes to make data input apparent. The rectangular area which uses the values of maximum x and y coordinates of site corner points as its dimensions, is the boundary of the matrix. The cells inside the defined boundary are collared according to their functions so that visual presentation is provided. Each cell has functions shown below:

0   Empty cells outside the site boundary: They have no functions only used to define the boundaries of the site to the model. They are represented with white color.

1   Empty cells inside the site boundary: They can transform to different functions (housing, green, pedestrian road, vehicle road, car park, etc.). They are represented with beige color.

2   Existing reserved tree cells: Their positions are fixed, cannot be changed. Two neighbor rows placed around these cells are accepted as green cells and their positions are fixed too. They are represented with dark green color.

3   Empty cells without function after the production.

4   Vehicle road cells: They are generated by the model according to fitness functions. They are represented with grey color. If there is no reserved vehicle roads in the selected site, they won't take place in excel matrix and model.

5   Car park cells: They are generated by the model according to fitness functions. They are represented with dark grey color. If there is no reserved car parks in the selected site, they won't take place in excel matrix and model.

6   Pedestrian road cells: They are generated by the model according to fitness functions. They are represented with brown color. If there is no reserved pedestrian roads in the selected site, they won't take place in excel matrix and model.

7   Existing main vehicle road cells: They are outside the site boundary. They are represented with black color.

8   Reserved water cells: Their positions are fixed cannot be changed. Two neighbor rows placed around these cells are accepted as green cells and their positions are fixed too. They are represented with blue color.

9   Reserved green cells: Their positions are fixed cannot be changed. They are represented with light green color.

10 Used polluted area cells: They are priority areas for generating housing cells on. They are represented with yellow color.

11 Existing public transportation station cell: They are represented with the letter of "T". In large scale sites, being close to this cell has the priority.

12 Existing noise origin cells: They are represented with the letter of "N". In large scale sites, being far from this cell has the priority.

13 Underground cells because of the elevation difference: They are represented with slightly transparent grey.

    20. Garden cells: They show courtyard and backyard lengths. They are represented with green color.

    Up to 20: Housing unit cells: They don't appear in the excel matrix, they are generated by the model according to fitness functions. They are represented with red color.

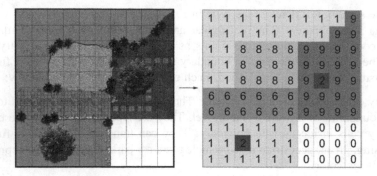

Fig. 3. Piece of land matrix defined in Excel

In Fig. 3, a piece of land matrix defined in Excel is given.

The selected site must be digitalized closed to the real terrain data without disregarding the topography and the natural formations, so that the site is presented in 3D grid with its slope data. User will divide the site into different zones according to its slope data. As a result of this, terracing high-leveled sites will be possible and environmentally sensitive solutions will be able to generate. The SSPM model will generated social housing cells according to this terraced site-zones.

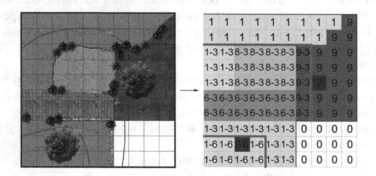

Fig. 4. Piece of terraced land matrix defined in Excel

As it is shown in Fig. 4, if an empty cell (presented with "1") are 3 m higher than the accepted zero-level elevation, the cell is presented with the numbers of 1–3. If it is 6 m higher than the zero-level elevation, it is presented with the numbers of 1–6. In addition, if a reserved tree cell (presented with "2") is 3 m higher than the zero-level elevation, it is presented with 2–3. In this way, the visual readability of each cell's elevation is provided.

3.3   User Interface

After definition of the site with an Excel matrix by user, the model will use this data to visualize the selected site. At this stage SSPM model needs more information about the site. User interface is used to input essential data about the selected site by user. User interface has seven values which will be determined by user (Fig. 5):

- Number of Building type: Model is able to produce "randomly, one type, two type, three type" building blocks. If user has fixed sizes building blocks, model uses same dimensions to do site planning.
- Climate type (a. Hot, b. Cold),
- FSR(floor space ratio), FAR(floor area ratio) and maximum building height value,
- Percentage value of green area according to local building regulation,
- Direction of prevailing wind,
- Direction of view.

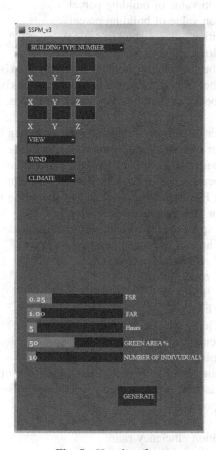

Fig. 5. User interface

Each cell in Excel matrix is used as a gene of genetic algorithm. After defining the site with existing elements and the user chooses climate type, the direction of sun, wind and view the model will start producing site layout alternatives according to the sustainable design parameters. This step is where the genetic algorithm takes place. The fitness functions of genetic algorithm are the sustainable architectural design parameters mentioned below. Pareto based non-dominated sortinggenetic algorithm (NSGA-II) evaluates each alternative according to priorities and ranks the each alternative to find the best sustainable site alternative.

3.4 SSPM Notation

sited: site data read from excel matrix.

sitev: virtual produced site.

siteheight: site matrix which shows height data.

site function: site matrix which shows function data.

parcelPosX: x position value of building parcel.

parcelPosY: y position value of building parcel.

buildingPosX: x position value of building block.

buildingPosY: y position value of building block.

buildingXDim: Number of cells of building block on X axis.

buildingYDim: Number of cells of building block on Y axis.

buildingZDim: Number of cells of building block on Z axis, which shows building height.

sidegardenX: Number of cells of side garden of a building block on X axis.

sidegardenY: Number of cells of side garden of a building block on Y axis.

backgardenX: Number of cells of back garden of a building block on X axis.

backgardenY: Number of cells of back garden of a building block on Y axis.

requiredFloorSpace: Floor space area calculated according to FSR.

totalFloorArea: Floor area calculated according to FAR.

filledm2: Total floor space area of produced building blocks.

filledm3: Total floor area of produced building blocks.

subtractm2: filledm2-requiredFloorSpace.

subtractm3: filledm3 total FloorArea.

fsr: floor space ratio (FSR).

far: floor area ratio (FAR).

hmax: maximum building height.

green: produced green are m^2.

crpoint: crossover point.

spaceCount: Total number of cells in the site, shows site m^2.

direction: direction data (1: north, 2: east, 3: south, 4: west).

score: Total fitness points.

mutationType: Type of mutation.

mutationRatio: Mutation efficiency ratio.

buildingViewScore: view score of a building.

buildingWindScore: wind score of a building.

siteViewScore: total view score of the site.

siteWindScore: total wind score of the site.

3.5   Evaluation System of the Model

The conflicting parameters will be evaluated according to their importance values by the model to find the optimal site planning with the help of Pareto genetic algorithm. The sustainable design parameters that are going to be used in the model coming from LEED and BREAM sustainable site parameters, local regulations and local climate conditions can be classified in three objective functions (Fig. 6):

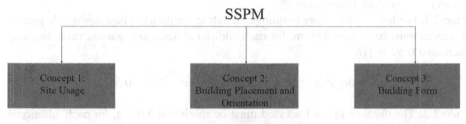

Fig. 6. Concepts of SSPM

Site usage: The placement of the building and its surroundings are determined at this stage. It is a need to focus on the existing ecological values on the site. Maximizing open area and reducing heat islands have priority.

Building Placement and Orientation: According to climate, wind and view direction housing units that are placed.

Building Form: According to climate and local regulation formulas (FAR-floor area ratio, FSR-floor space ratio and maximum height) buildings get form.

The conflicting parameters will be evaluated according to their importance values by the model to find the optimal sustainable site planning with the help of Pareto genetic algorithm.

Concept 1: Site Usage

The placement of the building and its surroundings are determined at this stage. It is a need to focus on the existing ecological values on the site. The fitness functions for sustainable site usage are listed below:

Rule 1.1: Conserve existing natural areas and restore damaged areas to provide habitat and promote biodiversity so all existing elements which are needed to be protected on the site such as trees, lakesmust be defined to the model [14].

In model, there won't be ant production on tree cells (2), water cells (8) and green area cells (9).

Rule 1.2: The approach limit to existing water supplies is 30 m and to wetlands is 15 m [14]. In model, there won't be any production on 30 cells near water supplies, they "0" value is given to these cells.

Rule 1.3: For reserved trees, 25 m^2 place must be provided.

Rule 1.4: The percentage of the open space must be more than 25 % of the value of open space given in the land use regulation [14].

Rule 1.5: If there is zoning but no open space requirement, provide open space equal to 20 % of the project's site area [14].

Rule 1.6: If there is no regulation, the open space area must be equal to building footprint [14]. Rule 1.7. Polluted areas on the site are preferential to be used as a building placement area [15].

Rule 1.8. If there is an on old building on the site, 50 % of outside area or 20 % of the site area must be used as open space [14].

Rule 1.9. If there is a noise source around, buildings must be placed 800.00 m away from the source [15].

Concept 2. Building Orientation

Rule 2.1. For low rise to 4 story buildings including the floors in basements side garden distances must be at least 5.00 m, for each additional floor, side garden value must be increased 0.50 m [16].

$$sidegardenX = 4 + [buildingZDim - 5)] \times 0.5 \tag{3.1}$$

Rule 2.2. The distance of the backyard must be minimum 5.00 m, for each additional floor backyard values must be increased 1.00 m [16].

$$backgardenY = 5 + [buildingZDim - 5)] \times 1 \tag{3.2}$$

In Fig. 7, building variables used in model is shown.

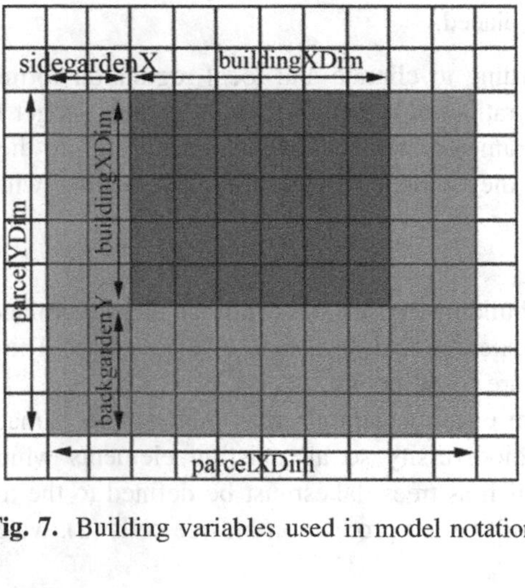

Fig. 7. Building variables used in model notation

Rule 2.3: In cold climate low wind scores, in hot climate high wind scores are important.

Rule 2.4: Orientation according to direction has the priority.

Concept 3: Building Form

Rule 3.1. The maximum building height value defined by the user must be considered [16].

Rule 3.2. Building floor space area must be lower than 600 m^2, [16].

$$buildingXDim \times buildingYDim \leq 600 \tag{3.3}$$

Rule 3.3. Building envelope width should be minimum 6.00 m from the front of the building and should not exceed 30.00 m [16].

$$6 \leq buildingXDim, buildingYDim \leq 30 \tag{3.4}$$

Rule 3.4: Floor space ratio (FSR) and floor area ratio (FAR) are two important preferential values that model uses during optimizing process. Floor space area of a building cannot exceed the %40 of the parcel [16].

$$fsr = \text{filledm}^2 / \text{spaceCount} \leq \%40 \tag{3.5}$$

$$far = \text{filledm}^3 / \text{spaceCount} \tag{3.6}$$

Rule 3.5. Building form has a huge impact on building energy performance. Compact forms must be chosen in cold climate to reduce the heat losses [17].

In cold climate maximum area minimum perimeter is preferred;

$$\sum_{i=0}^{allbuildings} = buildingXDim \times buildingYDim \div 2(buildingXDim + buildingYDim) \tag{3.7}$$

In hot climate minimum area maximum perimeter is preferred;

$$\sum_{i=0}^{allbuildings} = 2(buildingXDim + buildingYDim) \div buildingXDim \times buildingYDim \tag{3.8}$$

3.6 Fitness Scores of the Model

Model gives scores to randomly produced population according to five main fitness functions:

1. Fitness Score (fit1):
If the floor space area of an individual is equal to the value calculated according to FSR (floor space ratio), its score is 1; if not equal its score lays between 0-1.

$$0 \leq fit1 \leq 1 \text{ subtract}m^2 = \text{filledm}^2 - \text{requiredFloorArea} \tag{3.9}$$

If total building floor space area (*filledm*^{2}) exceeds the maximum floor space area value, the *subtractm*^{2} will be higher than "0" and the fit1 score of this individual will be;

$$\text{subtractm}^2 > 0 \quad fit1 = 1 - \left(\text{substactm}^2/600\right) \tag{3.10}$$

If total building floor space area ($filledm^2$) is under the maximum floor space area value, the $subtractm^2$ will be lower than "0" and the fit1 score of this individual will be;

$$\text{subtractm}^2 < 0 \quad fit1 = 1 + \left(\text{subtractm}^2/1000\right) \tag{3.11}$$

So that the individuals which exceeds the floor space area limit value, will have the lowest scores and their selection chance will decrease.

2. FitnessScore (fit2):
If the total floor area of an individual is equal to the value calculated according to FAR (floor area ratio), its score is 1; if not equal its score lays between 0 and 1.

$$0 \le fit2 \le 1 \quad \text{subtractm}^3 = \text{filledm}^3 - \text{totalFloorArea} \tag{3.12}$$

If total building floor area ($filledm^3$) is under the maximum floor area value, the $subtractm^3$ will be higher than "0" and the fit2score of this individual will be;

$$\text{subtractm}^3 > 0 \quad fit2 = 1 - \left(\text{subtractm}^3/1000\right) \tag{3.13}$$

If total building floor area ($filledm^3$) is under the maximum floor area value, the $farkm^3$ will be lower than "0" and the fit2 score of this individual will be;

$$\text{subtractm}^3 < 0 \quad fit2 = 1 + \left(\text{subtractm}^3/2000\right) \tag{3.14}$$

So that the individuals which exceeds the floor area limit value, will have the lowest scores and their selection chance will decrease.

3. Fitness Score (fit3):
It is calculated according to building block dimension. In cold climate maximum area minimum perimeter is preferred so fit 3 value is;

$$fit3 = (buildingXDim \times buildingYDim) \div 2(buildingXDim + buildingYDim) \tag{3.15}$$

In hot climate minimum area maximum perimeter is preferred so fit 3 value is;

$$fit3 = 2(buildingXDim + buildingYDim) \div (buildingXDim \times buildingYDim) \tag{3.16}$$

4. Fitness Score (fit4):
The wind score of a produced individual is calculated according to edge cell numbers which faces wind directly. In Fig. 8, the wind scores of each building blocks are; A: 10, B: 6, C: 7, D: 7. Building A and C, prevent building B and D from getting all the wind. The total wind score of an individual (produced site) is the total of the wind scores of each building blocks produced by the model. In cold climate, the site individual which has the highest total wind score takes "0" points and the site individual

which has the lowest wind score takes "1" points, others are sorted between 0 and 1 according to their total wind scores.

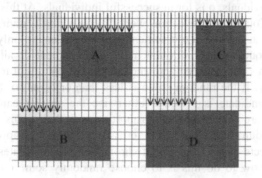

Fig. 8. Wind score calculation method

$$\sum_{i=0}^{buildingcountin} buildingWindScore = SiteWindScore \qquad (3.17)$$

5. Fitness Score (fit5):

The view score of a produced individual is calculated according to edge cell numbers which see view directly. In Fig. 9, the view scores of each building blocks are; A: 10, B: 6, C: 7, D: 7. Building A and C, block building B and D from seeing all the view. The total view score of an individual (produced site) is the total of the view scores of each building blocks produced by the model.

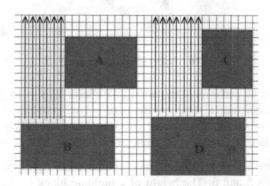

Fig. 9. View score calculation

$$\sum_{i=0}^{buildingcountin} buildingViewScore = siteViewScore \qquad (3.18)$$

3.7 Production and Selection System of the Model

The total fitness scores of the site individuals are normalized between 0 and 1; 1 is for most successful individuals, o is for unsuccessful individuals. At this stage tournament selection is done. Tournament selection works by selecting a number of individuals from the population at random, a tournament, and then selecting only the best of those individuals. The "tournament" isn't much of a tournament at all, it just involves generating a random value between zero and one and comparing it to a pre-determined selection probability. If the random value is less than or equal to the selection probability, the fitter candidate is selected, otherwise the weaker candidate is chosen. Chosen individuals are copied in direct proportion with their fitness scores, then they divided into two groups as parents. Next, crossover operator is applied between parents. Crossover selects genes from parent chromosomes and creates a new offspring. The simplest way how to do this is to choose randomly some crossover point and everything before this point copy from a first parent and then everything after a crossover point copy from the second parent. It is not possible to consider the most appropriate crossover point, so crossover point is randomly selected on y axis (Fig. 10).

Fig. 10. Selected crossover point

After a crossover is performed, mutation take place. This is to prevent falling all solutions in population into a local optimum of solved problem. Mutation changes randomly the new offspring. For binary encoding we can switch a few randomly chosen bits from 1 to 0 or from 0 to 1. There are 4 types of mutation in SSPM model;

a. Mutation between 1 and 4: Building block is moved to right, left, up and down.
b. Mutation between 5 and 6: The height of a building block is changed.
c. Mutation between 7 and 10: The edge dimensions of a building block is changed.
d. Mutation number 11, direction of a building block is changed.

Mutation ratio is a measure of the rate at which various types of mutations occur over time. Lower mutation ratio is preferred for not losing high scored strings. This procedure is repeated until the stopping condition (choosing Pareto optimal individual) is satisfied, then the algorithm ends.

3.8 Testing SSPM Model

The SSPM model was tested on a site in Kağıthane in İstanbul. The reason for choosing Kağıthane was twofold. First, urban regeneration in the residential areas of Kağıthane has recently been a central issue of consideration in Turkey. Second, the selected study area is a realistic example that has reserved water supplies, green areas and polluted areas to test sustainable social housing units. In Fig. 11 selected area is shown with existing elements. Polluted area, shown with yellow, it is preferential to be used as a building placement area. Reserved trees, green areas and water body will be protected and buildings will land with 30 m of water body.

Fig. 11. The visual display of the selected site

The input data coming from user interface are:

- Climate type: Temperate
- Direction of prevailing wind: East
- Direction of view: West
- Floor space ratio (FSR):0.25
- Floor area ratio (FAR): 1.2
- Open space ratio: %20
- Maximum building height value: 45.50 m

On the next step, the matrix of the site is created in Excel (Fig. 12). In the matrix, the Kağıthane River is shown by the number of "8" in blue, as reserved water supply. Existing green area near the river is shown by the number of "9" in green, as reserved green area. The number of "2" is for reserved trees on the site and the polluted areas used before is shown by the number of "10". There is difference in elevation on the site. The elevation of the river s accepted as 0.00, so as shown is Fig. 12, 3 m higher empty cells are shown as "1–3".

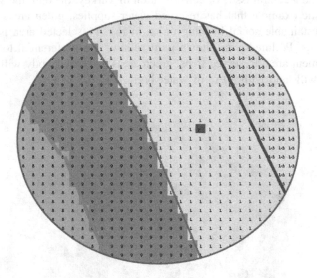

Fig. 12. A part of the excel matrix of the Kağıthane site

After defining the site to the model, by clicking "GENERATE" button, model starts to generate site individuals. In Fig. 13, random sized building blocks are placed on the site. Building blocks are colored in red, side gardens and backyards are colored in green. High-rise building blocks have larger gardens. All the blocks are directly positions to the view. The building blocks are minimum 30 m away from the Kağıthane River and they are also placed according to the reserved tree areas.

Four site individuals which can be accepted as best solutions for each generation are shown on the model interface. The rank point and all the scores of each individual are shown under the site individuals. Lower rank point is preferred. In Pareto correlation each individual are shown according to their scores. The value of FSR + FAR score is plotted on the y-axis and the total view score is plotted on the x-axis. The individuals which has higher view scores have the higher chance of selection. Non-dominated Pareto optimal individual has the rank value of "0", which means it has the higher FSR + FAR score and view score and it is not dominated by other any individual. This individual is placed at the left of the first row of the four individuals and it is protected till the model generates an individual which dominates it. Each generated individual on correlation is clickable, so that rank value and all the FSR, FAR, wind and view scores can be viewed by user. Until the user stops the generation, model generates populations and evaluates the new individuals according to their scores.

In Fig. 14, one type of fixed sized building blocks are used. The SSPM model decides how many to use each of them. The difference between garden dimensions can be seen, it is directly proportional to the building height.

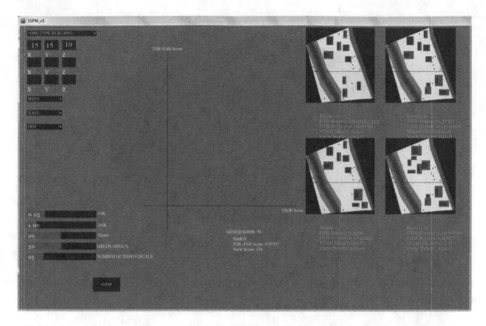

Fig. 13. Randomly generated individuals which have random edge and height dimensions

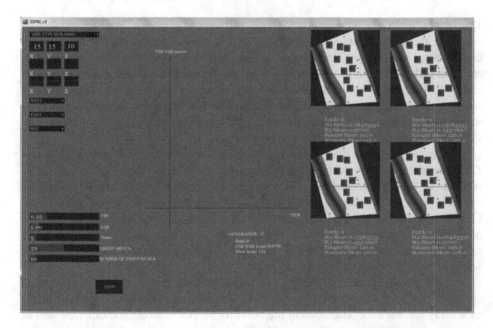

Fig. 14. One type of fixed sized buildings placement on the site

By clicking "STOP", generation process can be paused and produced individuals can be viewed detailed in 3D perspective. In Fig. 15, 3D view of the generated

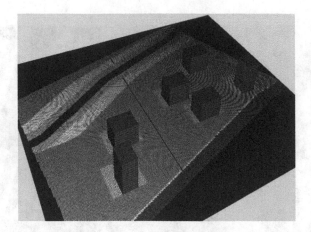

Fig. 15. 3D view of an individual

individuals can be seen. The direct proportion between garden distances and building height can be realized.

4   Conclusion

This study is in the intersection of two different disciplines that are evolutionary algorithms and sustainable design. The evolutionary algorithm that has been implemented for this project is based on the NSGA-II algorithm. It is proposed to combine cellular structures with a multi-objective genetic algorithm for using its search ability to find Pareto-optimal sustainable site planning solutions for social housing complexes by the help of Pareto correlation. The SSPM model is used for building scale and the layout of the site is detailed with roads, lakes, trees and buildings. The slope of the site and the buildings are presented in 3D space.

The green building plan optimization model developed by Wang, Rivard and Zimeureanu [5] is only focused on building envelope in early design stage and as sustainable design parameters, only energy conservation, maximum daylight and minimum cost are considered. Furthermore, the SMOLA model developed by Zelinska, Church and Jankowski [13] only generates land use patterns and it addresses the problem with optimization of such sustainability objectives like new development, redevelopment, land use compatibility, and accessibility. This model is only focused on sustainable large-scale land-use in 2D space.

A case study regarding the design of a social housing complex using the proposed approach has been carried out. The site is in Kağıthane in İstanbul. The focus of the case study has been the adaptation of the building blocks to local conditions, as well as the sustainable site usage parameters. The site layout alternatives that were generated by the SSPM model show a good adaptation to the site specific constraints and parameters, and good variation, within the limits that are imposed by the view, wind, FAR and FSR values. This approach would introduce an effective computational design tool for early design stage of sustainable design, which does not currently achieved by current technologies. For future work, by adding different fitness functions, the model can be used for different scaled projects, also in city scale, as a decision support system.

References

1. Bentley, P.J.: Aspects of evolutionary design by computers. In: Roy, R., Furuhashi, T., Chawdhry, P.K. (eds.) Advances in Soft Computing, pp. 99–118. Springer, London (1999). Department of Computer Science, University College, London
2. Rivard, H.: Computer assistance for sustainable building design. In: Smith, I.F.C. (ed.) Intelligent Computing in Engineering and Architecture, EG-ICE 2006, pp. 559–575. Springer, Berlin (2006)
3. Cole, R.J., Larsson, N.: GBTool user manual, Green Building Challenge (2002)
4. Trusty, W.B., Meil, J.K.: Introducing ATHENA™ v. 2.0: an LCA based decision support tool for assessing the environmental impact of the built environment. In: Proceedings of the eSim 2002, the Canadian Conference on Building Energy Simulation, Montréal, Canada (2002)
5. Wang, W., Zmeureanu, R., Rivard, H.: Applying multi objective genetic algorithms in green building design optimization. Build. Environ. 40(11), 1512–1525 (2005). Elsevier
6. Radford, A.D., Gero, J.S.: Design by Optimization in Architecture, Building and Construction. Van Nostrand Reinhold, New York (1987)
7. Harputlugil, G.U.: Analysis and simulation on energy performance based design. J. Megaron 6(1), 1–12 (2010)
8. Mitchell, M.: An introduction to genetic algorithms. A Bradford Book, The MIT Press, Cambridge, Massachusetts, pp. 7–12 (1996)
9. Goldberg, D.E.: Genetic Algorithms in Search, Optimization, and Machine Learning. Addison-Wesley, Reading (1989)
10. Deb, K.: Multi-Objective Optimization Using Evolutionary Algorithms. Wiley, Chichester (2001)
11. Deb, K., Pratap, A., Agarwal, S., Meyarivan, T.: A fast elitist multiobjective genetic algorithm: NSGA-II. IEEE Trans. Evol. Comput. 6(2), 182–197 (2002)
12. Lahanas, M., Baltas, D., Zamboglou, N.: A hybrid evolutionary algorithm for multiobjective anatomy based dose optimization in HDR brachytherapy. Phys. Med. Biol. 48(3), 399–415 (2003)
13. Zelinska, A.L., Church, R., Jankowski, P.: Sustainable urban land use allocation with spatial optimization. J. Geog. Inf. Sci. 22(6), 601–622 (2008)
14. USGBC: LEED for new construction & major renovations, v. 2.2, USA (2005)
15. BREEAM: BRE Environmental Assessment Method, UK (2008)
16. Istanbul Zoning Regulations, Turkey (2007)
17. TS825: Rules of thermal insulation in buildings, Turkish Standards Institute, Turkey (1999)

Algorithmic Design Tool for Integrating Renewable Energy Infrastructures in Buildings: Object Oriented Design for Energy Efficiency

Florin C. Popescu[✉]

Fraunhofer Institute for Open Communication Systems, Berlin, Germany
Florin.popescu@fokus.fraunhofer.de

Abstract. We present a tool which empowers 'green' design freedom for architects by presenting ever expanding choices in components and materials and automatizing their configuration and placement. Several time- and resource-consuming initial design iterations are eliminated by optimizing the energetic efficiency of the building in the original draft phase. The smart, efficient, energy producing building of the future can thereby offer increased cost and energy efficiency, security and comfort, without any compromise in style and form - on the contrary, the proposed tool stands to open up a novel palette of creative 'green' architectural design elements, which would effectively be co-designed by architects. The proposed algorithmic CAD design tool allows direct integration of renewable sources in the architectural design phase, taking into account local meteorological and solar radiation conditions. Furthermore locally optimized evolution and modification of renewable components integrated into the building's structure is possible, leveraging an increasingly wide range of possibilities in form, finish and renewable energy generation.

Keywords: Algorithmic and parametric design · Data analytics · Performance-based design · Smart buildings and smarts cities

1 Introduction

In this paper a prototype schema of representing and evolving architectural designs is presented in which basic cognitive science precepts of Object Oriented design or Constructive Object design, already long applied to other creative design processes (in engineering and computer science). This schema is mapped onto a deeper layer of abstraction than that of parametric design, even if by *parametric* we mean something already complex, such as evolving and computer-optimisable design. The need for this step-back is to *re*-present some concepts which are familiar along with others which belong to abstract mathematics, but with a strict aim of making a case for a completely new and highly automatized design process for the future architect.

Whereas much is made of the novelty of algorithmic design in architecture, it can be said of humans that architecture is and has always been algorithmic: a building is algorithmically equivalent to the instructions made by its designer to (re-)build it. This

© Springer-Verlag Berlin Heidelberg 2015
G. Celani et al. (Eds.): CAAD Futures 2015, CCIS 527, pp. 134–153, 2015.
DOI: 10.1007/978-3-662-47386-3_8

knowledge is learned and transmitted either explicitly or ad hoc, and includes instructions to find, select and modify primary construction materials (ultimately) found in nature. The act of building is thinking with one's hands. It is not just that the houses built by humans are more complex than temporary branch huts built by primates, or even more eye-pleasing than the creations of the feathered avian aesthetes of New Guinea: houses, man-made habitats are mobile and evolving machines, carefully optimized for energetic interaction with the surroundings, armed with levers and anchors and isolation that provide safety from fire and earthquakes and comfort from assault by sun, rain, wind and harmful organisms. Local and traditional cultures have slowly identified materials, shapes and construction methods highly optimized to specific habitats and ecosystems. Whereas monumental architecture is built to defy the logic of nature and impose the somewhat less straightforward logic of social organization, residential or utilitarian housing has traditionally been and in our view, should remain sustainable, economic and tuned to its environment. For this to occur, the engineer, artist and craftsman that are also embodied in the architect must work in close unison. Therefore we advocate an architecture which begins with imposing general constraints dictated by the environment and build from that level down to detailing and rendering, and easily include renewable energy sources, not as a retrofit addition but as an integral part of the structure. While this does not by force limit itself to solar energy, we limit ourselves to modeling this source of energy because it is the primary source of energy available in most habitats and new conversion techniques (not necessarily into electricity) are appearing on the market each year, while the amortized net cost of solar conversion is decreasing to the point where including it in architectural designs may become the norm rather than the exception.

It is not without coincidence that currently and industry wide shift towards support of Industry Foundation Classes, which is also an object oriented architecture for architectural CAD, is concurrent with our study. The difference between what we propose, which is aimed at software engineers working on updates to major CAD suites and IFC is that we emphasize a hierarchy which algorithmic and top-down – IFC is parametric, detail oriented and bottom-up, designed with a complete project in mind, especially the contracting phase. We're restricting ourselves to sketching a CAD tool to be used in the original concept/design phase mostly – the proposed architecture would blend in *on top* of IFC.

1.1 Paper Structure

The structure of the paper will be as follows:

- In Sect. 2 we will highlight the difference between algorithmic design parametric design, using parallels to information theory and engineering design, as well as provide some illustrative examples from architectural history.
- In Sect. 3 we will work to define a house in algorithmic terms.
- In Sect. 4 we will present a sample *class hierarchy* of houses called `HouseBuilder` and an abstract schema of components, operands, and operators, as well as present certain probability distributions over *random* house designs.

- In Sect. 5 we present results of a *digital heliodon* for solar radiance analysis of a building or group of buildings which is specific to a given location and its meteorological profile.
- In Sect. 6 we will present the basis for optimizing house designs which are tuned to local conditions and seasonal illumination patterns.
- In Sect. 7 we will outline future directions using more complex energy simulation environments, CAD environments, middleware and currently emerging *building information models*.

2   Algorithmic Design Versus Parametric Design

The two terms *algorithmic* and *parametric* appear to be synonymous. Indeed, with some effort we can expand the two categories until they are practically indistinguishable. We begin with describing the commonly known term *parametric CAD*. While all CAD files are essentially text-based instructions for building a 2D or 3D geometrical object, it follows that dimensions of graphic within these files can be scripted, and that these scripts (first popularized in applications such as AutoCAD, CATIA, etc.) are more powerful than simply assigning variable names to critical dimensions. Not just basic dimensions can be scripted parametrically but also interrelations among dimensions, e.g. a chamfer is an operation on edges, and when they modified, the position of the chamfer (even its radius) automatically adapts.

As the computer languages which CAD scripting extensions implement are fully enabled general computing languages such as LISP, BASIC, Python etc., they are Turing-compatible, meaning that whatever designs can exist, can described by any of them, and can construct them algorithmically. Therefore, in a strict sense, scripted CAD programs, widely known or marketed as parametric CAD, are potentially *algorithmic* CAD programs able to describe and generate any computable 3D geometries and elements thereof.

Rather than distinguish algorithmic CAD programs by what they *can* potentially achieve, we propose that the distinction lies in the intelligence of the tools available to the designer and the *organization of design workflow* which they embody. This means not just in maintaining geometric relationships among subcomponents, computing patterns or filling out details but use physics modeling and artificial intelligence to collaborate with the designer at every step: sketch, mockup, refinement, detailing. Let us consider a couple of specific examples in residential housing.

Terraced housing, though it began as luxury housing in Paris and London (the townhouse), became during the industrial revolution a convenient solution for developers who needed to build large housing districts at low cost and at a quality premium over tenement housing. Terraced housing is the simplest of algorithms: serial copy-paste. It is cost efficient as side walls (and structural loads) are shared, and energy efficient, as there is reduced head loss in the winter with a relatively simple repeated chimney heating arrangement. As the typical English urban-scape shows, it is essentially a long building that reuses the same design and building materials and can adapt gracefully to the landscape. Before the tenement design returned to dominate affordable urban housing, *terraces* fit all sorts of niches and budgets: the luxury component is mostly a matter of dimension, with ceiling heights and widths to suit different budgets. Inspired by a visit to Europe, American developer Samuel Gross built a peculiar modification of the terraced housing complex: the Alta Vista Terrace District (See Fig. 1). Chicago was then in the middle of an economic and housing boom – the same that would afford the building of the first skyscraper by Sullivan and the early luxury residential housing of his former employee Frank Lloyd Wright later to become 'organic' architecture. Gross realized that his clientele valued individualism too highly to accept the copy-paste anonymity of their neighbors' houses. He then commissioned molds and designs that could be reused, making every house structurally identical but leaving the façade unique, in any of the number of design styles then popular – except for one quirk: while all houses on the same side of the street are different but each has an identical twin on the opposite side. This type of algorithm would, if slightly modified, allows developer to build entire cities using the same components, many prefabricated, and offer appear to offer unique houses (and even non-repeating arrangements) of design but actually it is a mechanization of the design and building process itself: an assembly line construction site. This was to be the algorithm that generated the modern U.S. suburb during the post-war boom (modeled not on the townhouse but rather the wood-framed colonist house, with an atrophied front porch and a side 'car house', and with minor style variations among neighboring houses and arranged as leaves on tree-branch patterns of streets).

Another interesting example of architecture which we will use to frame our work in this paper is a renowned house in the CAADfuturehs host city of São Paulo: the residence of João Batista Vilanova Artigas (Fig. 2).[1] While for architects and visitors the modernist design, the immersion of the house in the surrounding flora and blurring of boundaries between interior and exterior perhaps inspire the most fascination, the civil engineer would first notice one peculiar aspect of the basic shape of the house: the roof is concave, not convex as in a traditional house. This brings to mind the question: assuming that the house is large enough that the living space is proportional to interior volume (independently of its shape), what is, from an energy flow perspective, the actual optimal form and orientation of a house, given its location, and given modern construction techniques, materials and active components such as photovoltaic panels? While that particular question is perhaps too complex to answer fully in this article, being dependent on multiple hard to model factors (e.g. the relative costs of insulation materials and photovoltaics), we shall lay out an extensible framework which will be able to tackle this question in a quantitatively precise fashion. In this article, however, many simplifying assumptions will be made to serve our main purpose which is illustrative. However, we have developed software (`houseBuilder` class hierarchy, segmented voxelization, digital heliodon) which can be used to size up the solar energy flow and photovoltaic generation potential of most of the residential housing currently built.

---

[1] Basic floor plans available at: http://www.archdaily.com.br/br/01-172411/classicos-da-arqui-tetura-segunda-residencia-do-arquiteto-vilanova-artigas/52c6ca8ae8e44e41f100005b,   CAD representation also online (see text).

Fig. 1. Alta Vista Terrace District, Chicago, USA

3   What Is a House?

The Artigas residence, as mentioned, arouses some basic questions from a cognitive and algorithmic point of view. A small child, looking at a small model of this house, would probably not recognize it as such, because its shape is too unusual. "Roofs look life roofs" in other words, we learn to categorize similar objects according to shape, purpose, location, etc.: any consistent attribute at all. Cognitively speaking, we do not instinctively define, but rather we recognize and associate, much like Gertrude Stein's famous ironic take on semantics. What we require, however, is a *generative* definition which can be used to write a program that can *build* any house, or roof, at all, but not a general descriptive geometry of polygons and solids (which is a legacy of how CAD tools developed, and in variable terms still carry the older legacy of computer graphics over the semantics of the purpose of the objects designed): we should limit this category and arrive at a reasonable compromise between generality (freedom) and practicality (tools tailored for a specific purpose).

A roof, we propose, is a series of surfaces which at, at their bottom end, arrive at a horizontal surface, at their top have no horizontal tangents, and is large enough for human habitation. This, as we will see, is not a just an entry in a hypothetical dictionary, or even a mathematical axiom, but a probability distribution coded into an actual program that can be used to generate any roof, or house, at all. The definition – actually a structure of inter-related definitions - will be *built* in such a way that, with a series of modifications, it can describe any (computable) shape at all, but it provides simple codes and parameterizations of the most common shapes of a particular category. Much in the sense of Shannon information, it assigns shorter codes to the most frequently occurring characters, but in spirit, it is closer to the more complex *Kolmogorov information* [1] approach to encoding, which rather than limiting itself to classes of parametric models, searchers for the language or algorithmic organization which most compactly describes a category of observations, objects or any other computable set. Contrasting Shannon and Kolmogorov definitions of entropy and information form, mathematically speaking, the heart of the difference between parametric and algorithmic encoding.

The Artigas house is remarkable in that is immersed in garden vegetation and well shadowed by nearby structures (which are tall buildings, not adjacent but nearby). The other aspect of the Artigas house which poses a vexing question, other than the inverted shape of the roof, is: what are the boundaries of a house? Is the description of a house just the description of the position of the materials used to build it and therefore the boundaries of the house: are they strictly those of the building materials, the walls, roof, columns, etc.? More than half of the roof area of the Artigas residence covers a floor space without side walls which it is arranged and used in such a way that it seems to be a living area integral to the house itself. The 'walls' are seemingly the vegetation of the garden area around the house. The strict definition of a house is found in local building, registry and real estate codes, since they regulate what portions of the structure may be described, sold and taxed as living space. For the purpose of our article, however, which is of universal scope, this is much too dependent on local conditions and to some degree arbitrary history of local legislation. Our definition will be broad enough to solve riddles such as that posed by the Artigas house but extensible, so that by minor modification it can incorporate any local regulation and code. See Fig. 5 for digital model representations of complete structure.

Our definition of a house is simply: the volume covered by a roof. If one makes a large umbrella and places a bed, chairs etc. under it, in other words uses it as a residence, even temporarily, it is a house. Its living volume is $V = h\pi r^2$ where h is the height of the umbrella at the edges. Of course, one habitually breaches the boundaries of this 'house' when lying on the beach without a second thought, but our geometric definition becomes directly apparent the moment the clouds bear rain. Also, the importance of walls becomes apparent when there is a gust of wind: it may be a house in a strict sense, but not a very good one (the structure is not resilient to environmental stress). A house is not just the shape of a structure but an object with a strict functionality, and while the functionality is not explicitly coded in our computer code, we always implicitly add (to any shape description of a house) the qualifier '*for the purpose of or suitable for habitation.*'

This qualifier allows us to solve other ambiguities which derive from our definition: the roof overhang. In order to shield exterior walls from rain and sun, roofs may overhang, but the area underneath the roof outside the wall is not suitable for habitation (it is too small) and therefore remains excluded from the house. However, let us present actual code and some results so as to move onto more practical, quantitative concerns.

4 Object Oriented Algorithmic Design: Sample Hierarchy

Object oriented (OOP) programming design in computer science is not a new computer programming language but simply a means of organizing code in existing (and new) computer languages such that applications are built using re-usable elements of code which are easy to understand for developers (not just those that wrote it), that it is extensible, modular and able to be developed in compact packages serving some general purpose (for example graphical user interfaces) [2]. Existing languages have been retro-fitted as object oriented (C to C++) while newer languages have been built as object oriented from the ground up, appropriating an ever expanding cornucopia of abstract abilities which computer science appropriated from set theory such as *coercive subtyping* and *dynamic polymorphism*. The computer language used in this paper is the computational language MATLAB (Mathworks, Cambridge MA, USA) but it can be implemented in any language. Let us present a concrete class hierarchy that allows us to describe and analyze the great majority of house designs in their most basic of thermodynamic behavior, interaction with the sun. Figure 3 shows the `houseBuilder` package /class hierarchy, represented using the abstract Universal Modeling Language (UML) designed in the open-source computer aided *software* design (CASD) application called *Dia* and implemented in MATLAB.

The class hierarchy begins with the abstract class `structuralElement` which is essentially a descriptive geometry primitive. Under the UML schema, every box corresponds to a *class* (essentially a set description), and every box in Fig. 2 has 3 sub-boxes describing some aspect of the UML schema: at the top is the class name (bold), in the middle are the class properties or *attributes*, and below are methods or *operations*. There is also actual code which implements these classes - not all the methods in our code are shown, many are utility functions, drawing and rendering routines or basic geometric calculations not essential to understanding the class hierarchy.

For the `structuralElement` class we have **components** which are properties (marked by a +) such as `+materialProperties` and **parameters** such as `position` and `scale`. Components refer to physical substructures of a given design (e.g. walls, roof, door etc.) whereas parameters are numbers (integers, scalars, matrices) which modulate operators, and by tuning which a design may be modified and optimized. Note that unlike almost all traditional CAD programs, all graphics elements are material descriptions and have material properties: there are no mere polygons as in computer graphics but rather objects such as `flatPolygonWall` objects having a nonzero thickness. Structural elements can be hierarchically organized in objects called `structuralElementAssembly` which *inherit* methods related to geometric operations from the base `structuralElement` class. This class represents more than parametric tree-like structures in modern CAD systems, because it is an algorithm rather than a parametrizable data structure. To reinforce this point, the basic operation is called `build` – it describes how the `children` substructures are combined in order to construct the object. One crucial aspect of this method is that it *only generates physically plausible structures*. In a `rowhouse` object, `build` would copy the basic house design and share walls given inputs such as a street description – it is not simply a list *house1, house2*, etc. where each element can be expanded in a menu. Object classes *inherit* from others further up the *object hierarchy* (this is what is meant by the arrow in Fig. 3), re-using operators, parameters and substructures already defined in the parent class - unless specifically over-ridden (i.e. redefined). Note that inheritance does not mean that a subclass is a subset (or even a superset) of the superclass it inherits from, and that the OOP framework does *not* guarantee that inheritance

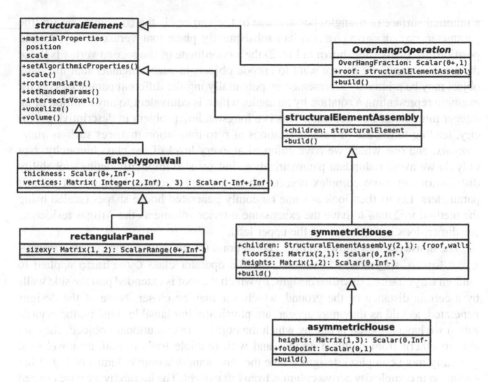

Fig. 2. *houseBuilder* package class diagram

imposes an evolution from simple to ever more complex elements. We attempt to build our hierarchies using *strict structural subtyping* and simple-to-complex inheritance. This aspect of design in computer science is as much art and craft as it is a logical process, since a large program is a structured organization of many such classes. In fact, it would be easier for a programmer to have `symmetricHouse` inherit from `asymmetricHouse`, since all one has to do is enforce a constraint on the wall heights on each side of the roof parallel to the fold and ensure that the fold is centered. All other methods re-use the same code. Note that in our example, `asymmetricHouse` inherits from `symmetricHouse` and changes the dimensionality of the parameter `heights` and adds a new parameter `foldpoint`. The actual code we used in `symmetricHouse` is actually applicable to the more general case (because it was indeed more convenient to write it this way) but it will be important at later stages in design optimization to enforce (or attempt to enforce) complex-from-simple inheritance. Also important is that parameters in our code are defined not as basic types (reals, integers, etc.) but have predefined dimensionality (or range of dimensions), left/right boundaries when they are intervals, and indications on whether these boundaries are included or not in the set that defines them. This type of definition is not native to most languages, including MATLAB (it appears in other specialized languages such as *Mathematica*). In `flatPolygonWall` the parameter `vertices` is 2 or more triples of non-infinite scalars. There are 2 rather than 3 triples necessary to construct a minimal surface (a triangle) because one of the vertices is the coordinate origin (the parameter `rototranslation` can subsequently place that vertex in any desired position). Actually (not shown in Fig. 2) the x coordinate of the second vertex is 0, for the same reason – we do not want to encode objects in such a manner that the same object may be arbitrarily represented by potentially infinite different parameters (as for example representing a rotation by an angle, which is equivalent to any addition of an integer multiple of 360 degrees). This is a longstanding problem in descriptive geometry, leading to the use of parametrizations of roto-translation matrices such as *quarternions*, and one which we have enforced at every level of the class hierarchy. Not only do we avoid redundant parametrization, but we also implicitly define probability distributions of more complex objects which use substructures having well defined parameters. Let us then look at some randomly generated house shapes (scaled using the method `volume` to have the exact same interior volume as the Artigas residence, see dimensions in the house on the upper left).

The houses shapes shown in Fig. 3 correspond (by column) to the classes `symmetricHouse`, `asymmetricHouse`, and the operator class `Overhang` applied to random `asymmetricHouse` designs, by which the roof is extended past the side walls by a certain distance or the ground, whichever may be closer. None of the designs generated, as odd as they may appear, are physically implausible. Finally, the organization we have imposed is one by which the objects are evolutionary objects, they are able to inherit from multiple designs and with multiple tools to entirely novel (and generally more complex) designs – note the randomness within columns of Fig. 3 but evolution in complexity across columns from left to right. The hierarchy we have created builds on prior work which has aimed at giving existing building models a shape grammar [3] (a semantic tagging of shape components) for the purpose of exporting models to building simulation models – but in this case we aim at having a 'grammar' which allows generation, evolution and optimization of design from the very first stage (concept, stage) to the last (retrofit).

The illustrative purpose of this paper needs no further complexity, but one can easily imagine further extensions to the class hierarchy such as shapes that result from the intersection of the house shapes shown (but naturally ones in which the build method specifies all necessary walls), methods which construct floors, staircases, chimneys etc. Suffice it to say that most house designs today are already contained in Fig. 3, which also shows unusual (but perfectly realizable) house designs, including inverted roofs. There is no judgment as to utilitarian or aesthetic value – just an illustriation of the generative capacity of the grammar used. However, importantly, only the basic shape of the roof, walls, cardinal orientation and geographical location of a house, determines already how much solar energy reaches the house. Further parameters, such as albedo and absorptivity of the materials influence how much of that energy is absorbed, reflected, refracted and converted (in case of photovoltaic arrays or solar pipes). Most important is: how much sunlight falls upon the various exterior surfaces, considering cloudiness and other obstructions, and of course the position and declination of the sun?

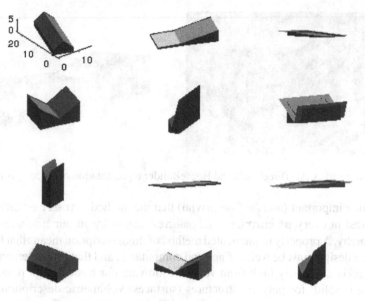

Fig. 3. Random housebuilder shapes

5 Digital Heliodon as an Analytic Tool

Among architectural CAD tools and thermodynamic modeling suites, many packages are available that perform the most complex of ray-tracing based rendering available (including multiple reflection/refraction among a path, and including multiple light sources – not just the sun but streetlights, etc.) however their main purpose is photo-realistic rendering: after rendering it is very difficult to decide which polygon belongs to what structure (semantic segmentation) and integrate the solar input over time (scripted analytics) and the rendering is optimized to compute a single viewpoint. One exception is the *Radiance* package for the *EnergyPlus* building energetics modeling suite, which does have an astronomic model of the sun and its illumination and keeps track of energy interactions. However, this level of detail is beyond that necessary to keep track of simple initial designs. Furthermore getting structured information from CAD programs into *EnergyPlus* is currently a laborious task. Therefore we have implemented our own voxel-based rendering [4] using a detailed astronomical model [5] using only shadows[2] (no reflections) and an estimate of diffuse/direct light in cloudy conditions as (1/6,0) of direct light intensity in very cloudy conditions linearly scaling to (1/6,1). This model is sufficient to account for solar energy interactions, and can be relatively quick compared to a rendering suite. A *heliodon* is a clock-like instrument which simulates the sun (astronomically but mechanically) shining upon a physical mock-up of a design. We do the same job digitally and assume that the solar profiling of a design is done early in the sketch phase so that simplifying the geometry does not lead to great loss of precision, given the uncertainty of later modifications.

---

[2] Implemented by Vincent Roy. Amanitides-Woo algorithm implemented by Jesus Mena-Chalco.

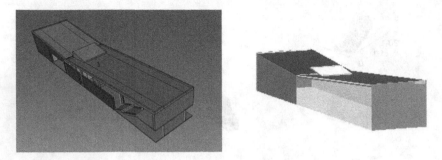

Fig. 4. Parametric CAD (FreeCAD) and HouseBuilder representation of the artigas residence

It is quite important (and far from trivial) that the method `intersectsVoxel` is implemented in every `structuralElementAssembly` in our `houseBuilder` class hierarchy. A properly implemented method of this description means that the actual interior of a design must be well defined and computable, and that finite element meshes can be quickly and easily built from voxels: following our basic design principle that everything is solid: for polygon structures (surfaces) volumetric descriptions are not obvious, although in cases in which the CAD program used adheres to true solid modeling, it is not difficult, apart from the algorithmic operation of defining a house interior not strictly as the enclosed space but covered space.

For the illustrative purposes of this study we limit our solar analysis to one house design in particular (the Artigas house design) and ask ourselves the hypothetical question: what if this design reached a certain level of fame such that many other people around the world wanted a replica (at least in spirit) of this house design. How would they place and orient it so that it would be most energy-efficient?

In Fig. 5 we see different representations of the Artigas residence: one rendered in the open-source parametric CAD application FreeCAD featuring the Arch package (see www.freecad.org and yorik.uncreated.net). FreeCAD/Arch provides fully parametric architectural design and export to Building Information Modeling compatible systems (Fig. 4).

Note that the difference between the two representations (the draft/algorithmic one on the right and the parametric CAD one on the right) is a matter of resolution fidelity. For the purposes of sunlight interaction, we have modeled the full walls of the house as completely opaque and the walls which are partially filled as translucent. In a hypothetical sketch phase, the final details are settled after the overall shape is chosen – although, clearly, an architect may prefer to design holistically, that is, details and overall shape together. Similar design tools may be based on full ray tracing and admit any level of geometric detail desired.

Finally, we have taken the original São Paulo location of the house and another colder climate (north Central Europe), both with a major axis tilted from E/W by 30 degrees as in the original, and simulated their interaction with the sun. To do so, we have simulated sunlight twice a season, for every 15 min during the (daylight) day, and calculated the direct component of incident light on the roof and the side walls of the house. Figure 6 shows the two averaged yearly shadow profiles at the 2 locations

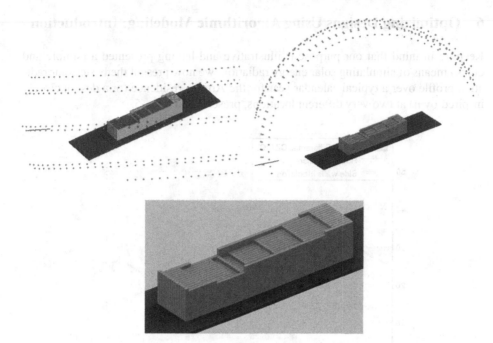

Fig. 5. Yearly averaged shadows computed by digital heliodon. Note voxelized representation of the target design (accuracy 50 cm). Top left: north central Europe. Top right and detail below: actual location. The red dots in the top figure represent the paths of the sun across the sky in different times of the year. The northern location has a significantly lower sunlight path and tends to illuminate the side walls (or the interior) far more than at the São Paulo location (Color figure online).

(and the ground around them). To account for seasonal changes in cloudiness, as well as the thermal load on the structure, we have built a digital model of cloudiness and min/max daily temperatures (source: www.weatherspark.com) throughout the year.

The average shadow (or illumination) profile is useful in several ways: it provides a direct view of the sunlit portions of the house and its surroundings, such that the space can be maximized. The original location favors morning light, and provides direct shade for a vertical sun, while the hypothetical northern location would accept a lot of interior light from its southern face. It is worth repeating that while one can perform ray tracing – based rendering and automate sunlight using usual polygon structures in most full featured CAD environments, the advantage of voxel methods are speed (there are less objects considered), direct solid modeling for further simulations of heat transfer, for which there are voxel-based methods, and the somewhat less obvious advantage that averaging sunlight across a variety of lighting scenarios is also a computational challenge (since shadows occur at higher geometric detail than the polygons used to construct the image).

6   Optimizing Designs Using Algorithmic Modeling: Introduction

Keeping in mind that our purpose is illustrative and having presented a (simple and quick) means of simulating solar energy radiation, we now present the basic solar radiation profile over a typical calendar year for the Artigas residence (or a design closely inspired by it) at two very different locations, presented in Sect. 5.

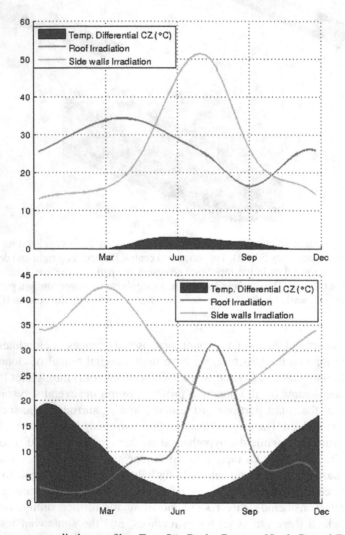

Fig. 6. Solar energy radiation profiles. Top: São Paulo. Bottom: North Central Europe. Green traces: incident side wall solar energy. Red traces: incident rooftop solar energy. (1 unit = direct solar radiation over 1 m² over 12 h). Blue region: difference between outside temperature and nearest point in the band of residential comfort zone (dependent on outside temperature, assuming constant humidity, as per cbe.berkeley.edu/comforttool). The incident radiation is calculated as sunlight available considering shadowing effects averaged over a typical day in the period shown, and scaled by the cloudiness % factor for that location and time of year (Color figure online).

We can observe a remarkable pattern: the same house performs in synchrony with completely different environments. In the southern hemisphere location (Fig. 5 bottom), which is much warmer, the side walls (which usually have a low albedo or are transparent/translucent) receive a peak of sunlight in the southern winter, well timed to warm the house in the brief period where this is needed, while providing a nearly constant rooftop energy which can be reflected/refracted away (as in current solar housing designs employing green or smart roofs). Alternatively one may convert a portion of it using solar panels (currently 25 % energy efficiency per surface area is achievable with Silicon photovoltaics, higher with newer multijunction devices [6]).

In the northern, considerably colder climate, the energy available to the exterior side walls is well correlated to the comfort zone temperature differential (apart from a slight lag in the cloudy early winter months). Whether or not this is sufficient for a solar house or passive house design is a matter of technical detail (reflectance of walls and roof, insulation materials and thickness, air flow and heat exchange and recovery, etc.). Note that both locations are quite cloudy, averaging approx. 80 % cloudiness throughout the year. The relatively less cloudy periods are southern winter for São Paulo and northern summer in North Central Europe – though a good part of the profiles shown are dependent on basic climate, the designer can, however, affect how the available energy is apportioned (absorbed, reflected or converted) and can modulate the yearly pattern of this mix by changing the house design.

The further north one situates a building, the more difficult it becomes to compensate for the seasonal variation and low elevation of the sun, however, it should be noted that the igloo is essentially a passive house design that functions in the most extreme and coldest of human habitats, all while having high albedo on the exterior. There are other practical concerns in habitat design than simply energy efficiency, not just in terms of interior comfort zone, but also items such as the living volume per inhabitant, wall thickness and natural light availability in the interior. The major outcome of an digital heliodon analysis is what maximal sun energy is available given a basic shape and where. This information can be used to choose material properties for the roof and walls, and whether and what type of solar energy conversion is required for surplus solar energy. A high longitude design may prefer well insulated large windows and dark exterior walls and sharply sloped roofs in order to absorb as much solar energy as possible during winter – a dry subtropical design may prefer to reflect or convert as much of the rooftop from a flatter roof.

Combining material from Sects. 4 and 5 we now have both a well-regulated parametrization, a genetic programming basis of evolvable designs, and an analytic means by which we could attempt to optimize house shapes for different zones. There are several obstacles to doing so. First, to state the obvious, a house shape is also an aesthetic and cultural choice (although we have seen that very different designs, the townhouse and the North American wood framed house, are perfectly acceptable to similar clients living in different cultures, depending on means of transportation, geography, history, etc.). The role of taste and preference in form and the context of urban design weigh very strongly and hard to gage in a computerized optimization process. Our presentation the last 2 sections were analyses of designs and sketches already in progress (or hypothetically in progress, as they are based on an existing building). Suffice it to say that we have a mechanism by which architectural concept sketches may be evaluated and optimized for energy efficiency.

The problem of meaningful efficiency optimization is two-fold:

(1) Is there enough detail in the simulation such that small changes in configuration have correct (and meaningfully different) changes in measured efficiency?
(2) Is the cost function we are minimizing by numerical means meaningful?

We will discuss these 2 questions in the following section, as they impact the path further work and are a very important topic of dialogue among computer scientists, engineers and architects. As a proof of concept, let us consider one simple and meaningful cost function which does not depend on other parameters and information than the shape, location and surroundings. We can try to optimize the correlation between primary heating (or cooling) demand as a function of orientation and albedo of the exterior walls and roof (allowing the 2 roof panels and each face of the exterior to have different light absorption properties). Note again that this is a *gedankenexperiment* and has little to do with the existing Artigas residence (whose orientation is determined by the street layout and orientation, and which is surrounded by vegetation on its open end and several high-rises in the vicinity). The question is rather, if we had an inverted roof design in 2 different conditions, would the optimal orientation differ greatly, from a solar energy interaction perspective?

For this reason, we propose a basic cost function (the correlation of heating demand and solar energy) of a design, calculated according to the following formula:

$$\max_\alpha \rho\left(\Delta(t),\ (1-\alpha)\cdot E(t)\right),\quad 0 < \alpha_j < 1 \tag{1}$$

Where $E(t)$ (a time-varying vector) is the total solar energy absorbed by the building at some time t and $\Delta(t)$ is the temperature difference from ambient temperature to the nearest point in the indoor comfort zone, while α is the distribution of albedo over the building's exterior, the dot product is defined as usual, and ρ is the linear (Pearson) correlation statistic (a *nonlinear* function of the 2 input vectors, despite its name). The simplifying assumptions made in our study are that humidity is relatively constant (it affects the comfort zone temperatures and the thermal mass of the building), that the building itself stores heat such that over a week or month long period the average daily temperatures are more important than highs and lows (because the building can store heat well enough to average out outside temperature variations over short periods). Note that this is a quadratic programming problem (written as a minimization of ρ^2), - which in low number of dimensions is relatively straightforward to solve. The motivation of this cost function that modulating albedo will only have $O(1)$ magnitude effects on total absorbed energy, and that storing energy for use in another season is still prohibitively expensive, such that a nearly constant demand or surplus of energy is most economically viable at present (Table 1).

Observe that the maximal correlation (alignment) between heating demand and absorbed solar radiation differs widely and sharply with changes in orientation. Furthermore the actual numerical solution tends to have many values on the acceptable constraint boundaries and the solution is highly sensitive to orientation. Mostly, though, roof panels optimally have high albedo and wall panels low albedo, thus photovoltaic panels are still an efficient addition since they recover otherwise reflected energy in the summer (not considering overall cost efficiency, of course).

Table 1. Results of albedo optimization for North Central Europe.

Orientation	ρ max	α roof panels					α wall panels		
0	0.58	1.00	1.00	1.00	1.00	1.00	0.00	0.00	0.00
30	0.55	1.00	1.00	0.98	1.00	1.00	0.00	0.00	0.00
60	0.44	1.00	1.00	1.00	1.00	1.00	0.00	0.00	0.00
90	0.79	1.00	1.00	0.00	0.00	0.32	1.00	1.00	0.00
120	0.86	1.00	1.00	0.00	0.00	0.00	0.24	1.00	1.00
150	0.65	1.00	0.81	1.00	0.00	0.00	0.00	1.00	1.00
180	0.74	0.95	1.00	0.34	1.00	0.02	1.00	0.01	1.00
210	0.52	1.00	1.00	0.00	0.00	0.00	1.00	0.99	1.00
240	0.36	1.00	1.00	1.00	0.00	0.00	1.00	1.00	1.00
270	0.74	1.00	1.00	1.00	1.00	0.00	0.93	0.00	1.00
300	0.68	1.00	1.00	1.00	1.00	0.00	0.00	0.00	0.99
330	0.65	1.00	1.00	0.01	1.00	1.00	0.00	0.00	0.01

7 Conclusions and Future Directions

The paper we have presented is first of all meant to provide direction for an automatized architectural design workflow not just for individual houses but for entire communities and housing developments (the HouseBuilder class hierarchy is easily included in a wider CommunityBuilder class hierarchy, and sketch-level 3D drafts can be exported to CAD tools, which then preserves and is consistent with the semantic and object information as part of the CAD program's in-built parametric design structure). We have used FreeCAD but a number of commercial alternatives are possible. In this sense the principal advantage of algorithmic design is scalability, in that it minimized duplicated efforts. The basic paradigm shown, the digital heliodon, is a compact enough tool that it can be added to CAD packages without adding a large and costly computational infrastructure of complex simulation tools. The analysis of solar interaction (including occlusions and cloudiness) can be generated for a design and a suggestion made as to the optimal albedo characteristics of main exterior components, which would narrow down the choices of exterior finish and still allow the architect wide freedom in choosing among these. By enforcing this organizational infrastructure of information – achievable no matter what computer language underlies a particular CAD program's script – we can 'close the loop' around workflows for houses or communities by iterating the configure-optimize-detail-evaluate cycle. Importantly, at each new cycle the designer imposes new constraints on the optimization, which may be orientation, material or shape constraints, until the design is satisfactory from all crucial aspects: cost, safety, ergonomic and lifestyle factors, aesthetic factors, and last but not least, energy efficiency. Modern house design increasingly features photovoltaic solar panels, but this article should serve to remind the designers that we do not obtain electrical energy for free – houses need solar irradiation for to make up for comfort zone differentials even in a subtropical climate (which is often a rainy climate). They store heat from the sun accumulated the day and slowly dissipate it at night. In northern latitudes the solar heating demand is even higher. Photovoltaics make sense if they are so configured that they recover energy the building would otherwise optimally reflect, in other words if they can form a cost-effective portion of the optimal seasonal profile of its *effective* albedo,[3] which should be well synchronized to seasonal changes in solar radiation.

In Sect. 6, we have introduced the question of simulation detail and its accuracy in gaging energy efficiency. First we must consider what types or errors are important in a simulation. In any simulation, there is a certain amount of random error: for example, the cloudiness and temperature profiles were averages over the past: future temperatures are likely to have deviances from these which are mostly random (on a day-to-day or year-to-year basis). Voxelization (like any volumetric integration scheme) has an inherent numerical error generally treated as random. These types of errors are less important, since they equally affect all changes in the design – remember that if we optimize designs it is the accuracy of the relative difference in efficiency of comparative designs that is as important as their average. The other kind of error is systematic error: for example the lack of consideration of occlusion of nearby buildings (note that with more effort and information we could have modeled that as well in the real-life scenario). On the topic of nearby conditions, note that in the design of individual houses this is a difficult topic no matter how high the realism of the simulation, conditions can change, with little predictability except that given by the building code. For example, it is possible that some of the high-rises currently around the Artigas residence were not planned at the time of its construction.

Nearby conditions are not limited to occlusions, which are relatively easy to model. Very important is the reflectance and the albedo of nearby conditions: high-albedo materials, with colors spectrally matched to the albedo of the particular photo-voltaic material (which in photo-voltaics is referenced to the color, rather than averaged over the color spectrum) with effects on the order of 50 % or more [7]. For example, crystalline Silicon devices receive a significant boost in effective albedo (and therefore efficiency) by having green, rather than red tiles nearby, because of its natural spectral albedo. Likewise, all materials (e.g. exterior walls) tend to absorb light from colors away from their dominant color. This means that a community of similar colored houses next to each other will not absorb as much solar heat as multi-chromatic (but not bright or

---

[3] By effective albedo we mean the ratio of energy reflected to that received by the building (the effective solar radiation) during a certain time period.

reflective) mix. The Artigas residence we have chosen to feature in this study is not only a stunning piece of architecture but has one particular advantage for a modern energy efficiency house, or those of the future, over a traditional roof, an advantage most likely hard to envisage at the time of its conception. The 'inverted' roof can feature one solar panel installed on one of its panels, and a spectrally matched high albedo finish on the opposite panel, which then boosts its energetic (and cost) efficiency. This 'trick' is simply not possible for the traditional convex roof, in which the two roof panels do not concentrate light but reflect it away from each other. Our paper did not concern itself with the design of a *solar house* or *passive house*, one which depends only on the sun for all its energy needs, since this is a matter of minute detail and other considerations (how many inhabitants, etc.). Similar computer-based simulations have been done since the 60s in hopes of building such a house, [8], it is only recently that information technology has progressed such that all the required information is easily accessible and the simulation programs (or CAD add-ins) can run on a standard personal computer. We performed basic simulations while at the same time proposing an object-oriented basis for evolutionary computing in an architectural context which is energy aware.

As mentioned, for scientists, engineers and architects alike, there are simulation tools which can currently capture and account with a significantly higher level of detail than shown in this paper and which we routinely use in our own research. A long history of academic research revolves around the U.S. Department of Energy's EnergyPlus simulation environment [9], which is specific to buildings and requires files in which the components are tagged according to its inbuilt semantics, and in which each component has well defined material properties. Other important aspects of energetic modeling there are other specialized programs. A thermodynamics model of the building is typically simulated using tools such as EnergyPlus and Radiance (for solar radiation), often created using graphical front ends to these tools. Occupancy models or those derived from measured data (e.g. records of past usage consumptions, sensor data) are typically built using statistical analysis tools (Matlab, Python, R, Excel, etc.) and can execute in any number of forms as created by such tools. Control systems for HVAC are simulated by dedicated 'flow-chart' type programs such as Modelica, Simulink, simul8 and ExtendSim. On top of these, depending on the application, there are finite-element solvers for wind conditions and optimal placement of wind turbines. All of these diverse numerical tools can be integrated using the open-source simulation middleware BCTVB (Building Controls Virtual Test Bed, http://simulationresearch.lbl.gov/bcvtb). Despite the numerical sophistication of the tools, it should be noted that a current area of research centers around understanding the reasons for an often reported discrepancy between the energy efficiency of the building as simulated *ex-ante* and that as measured *ex-post* once the building is commissioned and in use [10] – this analysis has mainly been performed for commercial buildings because monitoring data is more widely available, but simulations of residential buildings and houses are likely to encounter similar challenges. Since IT-progress has recently lowered basic costs on automation, it is relatively cheap and efficient for a home to have the same sophistication in controls and monitoring as a commercial building, using low-cost sensors and wireless signals and encryption for privacy.

While architects may not currently work with UML diagrams directly, they do so implicitly: First, the majority of the CAD software they use was written in object-oriented code in which teams of developers collaborate using UML or UML-like diagrams, and the functionality of the final product reflects this organization (e.g. the tool palettes, the entering/editing of measurements has a consistency deriving from it). Second, the Industry Foundation Classes are already UML models and the upcoming integration of UML into CAD suites is essentially a mapping of IFC onto the internal ontology/class hierarchy of the particular CAD suite. Finally, the emergence of graphical, hierarchical parametric models in Rhino and other suites, which are increasingly used by architects, prepares the ground for the use of UML-like diagrams. Algorithmic objects are not just hierarchical. That is because a given object might embody certain features from one object, certain others from another (called multiple inheritance), and define new ones of its own (e.g. think of a roulot or camper that has an extensible, triangular roof with photovoltaics–both a house and a vehicle, and a power generator). UML is a powerful method of expressing not just architectural but all kinds of algorithmic ideas, which are complex, and collaborative. Software designers use it today, but other practitioners might in the future. Sharing among project partners and colleagues is another feature of UML. Ideas can be shared and re-used, even algorithmic ones, designs can be repeated with different finishes, other additions, etc. The important issue is not UML or not UML, but rather that the creators of an algorithmic design would need to spend extra effort documenting its functionality and purpose so that other people can understand it. There are automation tools for software that do exactly that, generate.html documents by mining special comments and instructions in the design itself, written as the creator is doing the work (rather than ipso-facto, taxing memory and time).

Another pertinent question may arise as to the ultimate scalability of a numerical optimization procedure, especially as a design may have thousands of components even at the concept phase. It is true that optimization and the concept of optimality is a numerical one, and ultimately algorithms are programs: while architects are not expected to learn scientific programming languages (those are only used in this paper for convenience, the exact same function can be achieved in any number of other languages), they are natural mathematicians: they solve difficult geometrical problems routinely. So, much like spreadsheet programs, some means of expressing equations needs to be built in, even as these are simple algebraic relations, if/then statements and loops. Many architects already program in the internal scripting languages of CAD suites, and the syntax of algorithmic statements will be consistent with those. The building of optimality criteria in mathematical terms by architects is also a challenge to eventual implementation. Scientists and software engineers might find a solution by pre-programming modules such as 'energy efficiency', 'interior light', 'aspect ratio', etc. and allow the architect to modify weights given to each of these sub-criteria iteratively until a satisfactory design is found. The scalability of the optimization is a matter of computational effort (cloud resources can aid in this respect). The nature of organization in object-oriented design make scalability easier by identifying 'causal' parameters among the many free design parameters (an automatic procedure), which allows optimization over this smaller subset – the other parameters (the actual size and position of windows along a wall, for example) are then determined by the top-level causal parameters (the size of the wall itself).

Within the closed loop we have mentioned earlier there is another important development in IT and architectural CAD which might increase the use of building energy simulation models, namely the full development and cross-platform use of Building Information Models [11] which would allow not only energy accounting and simulation but overall cost evaluation and optimization including that of energy. The design of a house or community is but part of a wider 'tuning' loop with longer time periods, in which controls automation adapts for efficiency while the building is operational, and temporary retrofits which are efficiency ware. Despite the accelerated recent advances in information technology there is much work ahead to be done in order to understand, optimize and design attractive, affordable and energetically sustainable living communities and to integrate this analysis with architectural CAD tools.

References

1. Li, M., Vitanyi, P.: An Introduction to Kolmogorov Complexity and its Applications: Preface to the, 1st edn. Springer, New York (1997)
2. Coad, P., Yourdon, E.: Object Oriented Analysis, 2nd edn. Prentice Hall PTR, Englewood Cliffs (1990)
3. Hohmann, B., Havemann, S., Krispel, U., Fellner, D.: A GML shape grammar for semantically enriched 3D building models. Comput. Graph. 34(4), 322–334 (2010)
4. Amanatides, J., Woo, A.: A fast voxel traversal algorithm for ray tracing. In: Eurographics 87, pp. 3–10 (1987)
5. Reda, I., Andreas, A.: Solar position algorithm for solar radiation applications. Sol. Energy 76(5), 577–589 (2004)
6. Green, M.A., Emery, K., Hishikawa, Y., Warta, W., Dunlop, E.D.: Solar cell efficiency tables (Version 45). Prog. Photovolt. Res. Appl. 23(1), 1–9 (2015)
7. Andrews, R.W., Pearce, J.M.: The effect of spectral albedo on amorphous silicon and crystalline silicon solar photovoltaic device performance. Sol. Energy 91, 233–241 (2013)
8. Buchberg, H., Roulet, J.R.: Simulation and optimization of solar collection and storage for house heating. Sol. Energy 12(1), 31–50 (1968)
9. Fumo, N., Mago, P., Luck, R.: Methodology to estimate building energy consumption using EnergyPlus Benchmark Models. Energy Build. 42(12), 2331–2337 (2010)
10. Menezes, A.C., Cripps, A., Bouchlaghem, D., Buswell, R.: Predicted vs. actual energy gperformance of non-domestic buildings: Using post-occupancy evaluation data to reduce the performance gap. Appl. Energy 97, 355–364 (2012)
11. Schlueter, A., Thesseling, F.: Building information model based energy/exergy performance assessment in early design stages. Autom. Constr. 18(2), 153–163 (2009)

Pedestrian as Generator: Implementing a Stand-Alone Piezo Power Generating Device in the Urban Context

Elena Vanz[✉] and Justyna Karakiewicz[✉]

University of Melbourne, Melbourne, VIC, Australia
{elena.vanz,justynak}@unimelb.edu.au

Abstract. During the past decade the implementation of energy harvesting sensor technology, at micro scale, has occurred due to the rapid growth of low-powered device usage, such as mobile phones, laptops, and the development of LED lights significantly increasing in efficiency. Studies have demonstrated that the ability of this technology to harvest energy from the human body, such as footfalls, can be used in the generation of electricity. Piezoelectric sensor technology has been investigated for this purpose, due to its significant advancement in the efficiency and its application in a variety of designs. This research investigates how pedestrians can become generators of their own service, through the use of piezoelectric sensor technology, in the form of safety lighting. Proposed urban design scenarios explore the opportunity implementing a piezo power-generating device along high traffic pedestrians pathways in the City of Melbourne (Australia), evaluating real time and storage options, considering harvesting the energy during the day and using it at night time when needed.

Keywords: Piezoelectric sensor technology · Micro-scale distributed generation · Public space

1 Introduction

Energy harvesting technology, such as piezoelectric, challenges the role of the individual to no longer be a passive consumer. The term 'end-user' is then redundant in a scenario where the individual becomes producer of energy to be used for their own benefit. Considering this feedback loop model, the following paper explores how the individual can contribute in a novel way of experiencing public spaces by generating energy instead of consuming it.

Beginning introducing emergent technologies that harvest energy from kinetics, such as piezoelectric and electromagnetic, the first part discusses how the implementation of these technologies in urban spaces have affected the way in which energy infrastructure operate having the individual contributing in the generation of energy to be consumed for their own service(s). Thus, with these technologies, the infrastructure has shift from a linear to a feedback loop model where the user is also a producer. This idea is discussed presenting latest design experiments focusing on these technologies implementation in urban spaces, specifically considering harvesting force of pedestrians' footsteps.

G. Celani et al. (Eds.): CAAD Futures 2015, CCIS 527, pp. 154–171, 2015.
DOI: 10.1007/978-3-662-47386-3_9

In the second part the paper discusses an example of the proposed feedback loop tested through the construction and evaluation of urban design scenarios. The investigation is driven by the construction and evaluation of urban design scenarios considering the implementation of a piezo power-generating device along public stairways in the City of Melbourne powering LED lights for the benefit of pedestrians. Established the feasibility of safety lighting in real time, the proposed scenarios investigate the possibility of storing the energy harvested from footsteps during the day and using it at night only, when the service is mainly required. This evaluation demonstrates the validity of the proposed power-generating system, and the use of piezoelectric sensor technology following the established research aim. It also supports the value of investigating technology implementation not only considering energy output but also other conditions, such as context and service provided. The presented work is part of a PhD research developed within a multidisciplinary collaboration between universities and multiple industry partners such as ARUP Engineering, Johnson Matthew Catalysts (piezoproduct manufacturer in Germany) and Melbourne City Council, who expressed the interest of implementing the proposed design as a public installation in the studied urban sites.

2   From a Linear Model to a Feedback Loop in the Energy Infrastructure: The Individual Becomes the Producer as Well as the Consumer

A city has been always perceived as a major core of energy consumption, and the end-user of energy as a passive receiver of the service provided by the city's infrastructure. Over time, energy infrastructure has been developed as a linear model, focused on optimizing efficiency with two main goals: ensuring a 24/7 generation of power based on peak demand; and responding to the increment of demand by physically expanding the infrastructure itself [1]. The introduction of energy harvesting technologies has brought major shifts to this model and to the way the infrastructure has been implemented in

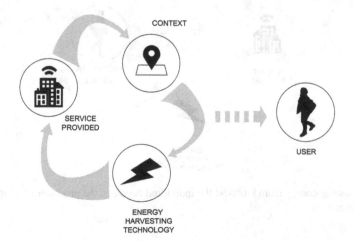

Fig. 1. Distributed generation as a linear model providing the service to the End-User

urban spaces [2, 3]. By definition, energy harvesting technology has the ability to capture ambient energy from the surrounding environment, providing a renewable source of power [4]. The implementation of these technologies in urban spaces has defined what is called a distributed generation model (DG), challenging the design of the infrastructure not only based on the amount of energy produced but also responding to specific urban "conditions" such as context, service and user demand (Fig. 1).

Along with energy harvesting technologies, the generation of power also shifted in scale, reaching an urban dimension, bringing with it a higher level of awareness of the user in both production and consumption of energy [5]. Energy infrastructure was then no longer perceived as a hidden underground system, but began reclaiming open spaces, liaising with buildings and public spaces, and establishing a closer relationship with the consumer [6]. Despite all this, users are still perceived as intermediaries within an energy infrastructure model that operates as a liner system [7]. Emergent energy harvesting technologies have, however, proven the benefit of capturing energy from kinetics - converting movement, often in the form of vibrations, into electrical power. These technologies are mainly known as piezoelectric, electromagnetic and electrostatic technologies, and operate at a small scale of energy generation (micro- to milliwatts) [8]. Harvesting energy from kinetics has led to experiments considering collecting energy from the human body, especially investigating how to capture force of footsteps [9]. Although these technologies were discovered in the late 1800 s [10], only recently have they been reconsidered because of the shift in scale of user power consumption due to the proliferation of low-powered technologies as well as the possibility they offer of providing an alternative to conventional batteries [11].

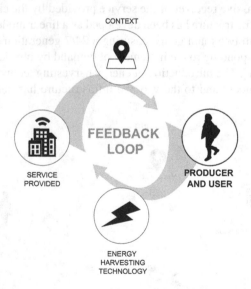

Fig. 2. Harvesting energy from kinetics: the individual becomes the producer of energy as well as the consumer

Thus, with these technologies the user is challenged to directly contribute to the generation of energy [12, 13]. The linear infrastructural model then shifted toward a feedback loop situation, where the individual becomes the producer of energy to be used for their own benefit (They are no longer an 'end-user') (Fig. 2). This shift in paradigm established the ground for design experimentations considering the implementation of these technologies in urban spaces. Most of all, this feedback loop model began to re-define the individual experience, challenging how the individual contribution to the production of energy might potentially be used for a collective service.

3   Harvesting Energy from the Human Body

Whereas some of the energy harvesting technologies introduced in cities, such as photo-voltaic panels and wind turbines, are usually considered to have a broader urban scale of impact, for instance capable of providing household power, the energy harvested by sensor technology coming from kinetics can be measured at a smaller scale, ranging between mill-watt to many watt levels of power, depending on the system. The micro scale implementation of energy harvesting sensor technology has been highly researched and evaluated during the past decade [4, 12] due to the rapid growth of use in low-powered devices such as mobile phones, laptops etc. as well as the development of LED lights, with their increasing efficiency providing a realistic substitute for the old 60-watt light bulb. Energy harvesting technology has also been used to power sensors such as Wireless-Sensor Nodes (WSN), used in communication; and monitoring sensors, usually used to provide data on environmental conditions such as temperature, humidity etc. or energy consumption [12]. Moreover, one of the major benefits relies on providing an alternative to conventional batteries, avoiding high costs related to maintenance as well as providing off-grid devices [4].

Energy harvesting technologies can be implemented to harvest kinetic energy from the human body providing electricity for low-powered devices (Fig. 3). Thus the indi-vidual has the potential to become a generator, acquiring control of the production of energy, because the way these technologies perform can be predicted by the user, and also providing the possibility of consuming the power for his or her own needs. As a consequence, in this scenario the term *end-user* has been made redundant within a model where the individual is both generator and consumer of the service (end-user no longer). The concept of *user as generator* revolutionizes the way the electricity infrastructure model is conceived, moving from a linear operational mode to a feedback loop design where the individual provides an off-grid micro-scale power supply. Most importantly, the user becomes aware of his or her action as well as of his or her ability to generate power.

Two main technologies, piezoelectric and electromagnetic, have been investigated to be implemented with the purpose of harvesting energy from the human body, espe-cially from the footstep. Both technologies perform along the same principle but differ in terms of operation as well as in their size and occupied space. Whereas the electro-magnetic technology captures energy using a rotary generation conversion, comprising multiple components such as coils and magnets [11], the piezoelectric effect is based on

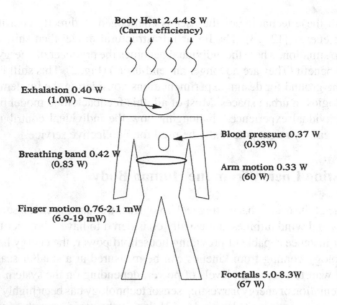

Fig. 3. Power from body-driven sources, T. Starner 1996

the capability of certain materials to generate alternating current (AC) from mechanical stress, when bent, squeezed, twisted or in vibration, which can then be converted into direct current (DC) [8]. During the last ten years, piezoelectric materials for sensor elements have advanced in efficiency and have been investigated with the purpose of energy harvesting, considering a variety of design applications [11]. Whereas electromagnetic systems have previously been considered the most efficient in terms of power output, when considering design applications, the small size of piezoelectric sensors and limited physical space occupied for the generation become desirable and relevant, especially in design applications.

This concept has been investigated in several design projects involving a multidisciplinary group of designers, architects and engineers. Most of the proposed ideas began by evaluating how to harness energy expended from human actions, considering reutilizing the wasted energy resulting from force of footstep which is currently dissipated in the surrounding environment, such as walking, running and even dancing [9]. For this reason, it has been proposed to integrate energy-harvesting technology within pavements in form of tiles or surfaces. In this way, designers aim to capture most of the force of footstep and release it in the form of power, which is then either stored or used in real time scenarios for lighting or low power devices.

3.1   Case Studies Investigating Design Applications of Piezoelectric and Electromagnetic Technologies

The following case studies bring together specific implementation of piezoelectric and electromagnetic technologies, focusing on harvesting the force of footstep. Walking is considered one of the most essential and energy-consuming activities, providing a valuable source of power generation [9]. During the past ten years, developments have been made in investigating the possibility of integrating a piezoelectric system within the shoe sole (generation of energy for individual use) [14–16] (Fig. 4) as well as considering implementation of both technologies (piezoelectric and electromagnetic) along pedestrians footpaths [17–20]. These last investigations unfold urban design scenarios where the individual energy production could be used collectively in urban spaces to inform a larger scale infrastructure system such as in the design project presented at MIT in 2007, the Crowd Farm [21]. The project became a provocation, a representation of an idea (concept) of pedestrians as generators (Fig. 5).

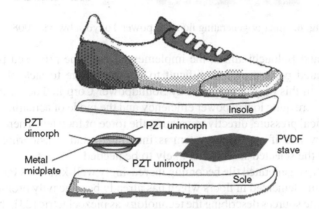

Fig. 4. Energy scavenging with shoe-mounted piezoelectrics

Fig. 5. Crowd Farm project, MIT 2007

The energy-generating floors implemented in the subway in Tokyo proposed by Sound power Corp, began to explore the possibility of strategically locating the technology within defined walkable areas and considering high pedestrian flow (Fig. 6). Rubber mats containing piezoelectric sensors were integrated along ticket gates, harvesting energy from the 4,000,000 people who move through the station daily [19].

Fig. 6. Energy-generating floors to power Tokyo subways, 2008

As Gilbert and Balouchi affirm, the implementation of the proposed piezoelectric system and related performance is difficult to document due to lack of information published [22]. In this project proposed by Soundpower Corp in Tokyo, it seems that the sensors used are quite low in power efficiency and the mode of actuating the element is through physical pressure, directly translating the force of footstep. There is no understanding of how and if a storage system is integrated, and considering the energy performance of the selected sensor, it is likely to be needed.

Another energy-generated tile becoming increasingly well-known is Pavegen (UK), a module to be implemented in floors which has already been heavily promoted around the world. Despite sources describing the technology as piezoelectric [23], the tile seems to be designed and to operate with an electromagnetic system. The tiles have been highly promoted due to the efficiency in power generation, with each tile harvesting 6 to 8 joules of energy per footstep. The system uses 5 % of the power to light the central luminaire for instant feedback to pedestrians; the other 95 % of the power can be stored in internal or external batteries or used instantly for external applications. In situations where no central light is required, the output is 100 % of the power (Christopher Bertacco, Pavegen). The tile has been studied by the researcher having the possibility of obtaining a module from the company as well as observing the layout of five tiles implemented in Federation Square, Melbourne (Australia) (Fig. 7). The design of the tile is based on a module dimensioning $600 \times 450 \times 68$ mm. The central core, around 200 mm in diameter,

Fig. 7. Pavegen tiles in Melbourne, Australia 2013

hosts the technology, leaving space around for the battery and any additional electronic equipment.

Mainly used in temporary installations, the Pavgen tile presents a valuable method of harvesting energy from footsteps using electromagnetic technology. In order to operate, the system needs quite a lot of force which must be specifically applied vertically within the area where the core is located. What the tiles proposed in Japon and Pavegen unfold is the possibility of using the small amount of power generated to inform and improve pedestrian mobility. However, it seems that the decisions made behind the placement of the tiles on site could be further investigated, along with the module developed, considering for instance mediating between technology spatial requirements and specific context.

3.2 Potentials of Investigating Urban Design Scenarios

The potentials of energy harvesting technologies from kinetics have yet to be explored investigating ways in which the individual can interact with the surrounding environment by producing energy instead of consuming it. The case studies presented above demonstrated initial design applications of energy harvesting technologies in urban spaces, but each seemed mainly to focus on a specific aspect of the overall design, such as "aesthetic" (Crowd Farm), or context of implementation (Tokyo), or energy output (Pavegen). These examples have begun investigating users' awareness of the production of energy and speculating on its use. However, the missed opportunity seems to be investigating the possible benefit of further investigating the relationships between all of these conditions in order to fully visualize and exploit the potentials user interaction with energy production in space. The opportunity relies on the understanding of possible urban design scale implementations considering the benefit of harvesting energy from pedestrian footfalls informing mobility.

MIT media lab is investigating the challenge of providing density in cities by exploring different design strategies that take advantage of the introduction of sensor technology to be used both as a tool for gathering real-time data (i.e. when considering air pollution, temperature etc.) and for facilitating (or increasing) the interaction between the individual and the space (i.e. pressure sensors, movement detection sensors and energy harvesting sensors), with the aim of reinventing a contemporary city for people. A future challenge would be how to develop and expand this network to also communicate with pedestrians and traffic lighting. MIT Media Lab is now in the phase of developing a new car prototype that incorporates "mechanical eyes" with the aim of detecting pedestrians' movement. The following step explored by the Lab will be also considering street lighting communication with both cars and pedestrians. The need to address pedestrians' mobility and the idea of a walkable city are fundamental if we are to design a city for people.

Energy harvesting technology from kinetics might provide a possible opportunity to further investigate this challenge, considering the contribution of pedestrians to the production of energy to be used as means of communication within a proposed network. Further research could potentially investigate how the implementation of these technologies within urban spaces has the potential to affect the pedestrians' experience providing micro-scale power generation as way of exchanging information for a more interactive and safe environment. The increasing efficiency of energy harvesting technology such as piezoelectric sensors, together with the proliferation of low-powered digital technologies that trigger the experience of users in space, is what motivated the following study.

4   Constructing Urban Design Scenarios

The construction of urban design scenarios investigating the possible implementation of energy harvesting technology from kinetics such as piezoelectric and electromagnetic began through a series of exercises developed as part of two master design studios: *Repowering Cities*: *Sydney Case Study*, at UTS (Sydney); and *Empowering Places: Melbourne and New York*, at the University of Melbourne in collaboration with Parsons, The New School for Design (NY). Both studios embraced the vision of introducing distributed generation within urban public spaces, specifically considering integrating small-scale demand-sited models of power production implementing energy harvesting technologies, as well as retrofitting existing structures belonging to the centralized infrastructure model, such as building substations. The projects mainly challenged the use of the energy generated by footsteps to inform pedestrians' mobility and experience in public spaces (Fig. 8).

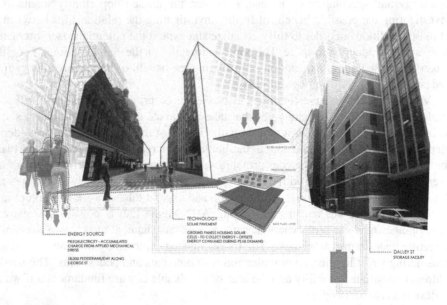

Fig. 8. Piezoelectric tiles applied along pedestrians' footpaths (students: Michael Pachin, Simon Gollan, Laura Cantali and Natalie Adams)

The studios presented a platform for the following:

- Exploring the notion of "productive urban spaces": implementing energy harvesting technology, specifically piezoelectric and electromagnetic, with the individual becoming producer of energy (from the linear to the feedback loop model);
- Challenging the use of small-scale power generation: it is not about the quantity of energy generated but about how to most efficiently use the power produced for a specific service and context;
- Investigating the production of power by individuals for a collective benefit in public spaces;
- Considering how the service produced might include a form of communication and improve pedestrians' mobility.

4.1   Reasons for Choosing Piezoelectric Sensor Technology

Energy harvesting technologies from kinetics provide the tool to allow the feedback loop model to operate having the user becoming the producer as well as the consumer. Then the challenge is to determine which technology to choose based on aspects such as the mode the individual uses to actuate the technology, the type of service provided and the context where this service is consumed. Thus it is crucial to consider that it is not about selecting the technology that generates the most power, but the one that most efficiently embraces all of these aspects. Although both electromagnetic and piezoelectric technologies have been researched and compared along the process, the main focus of the proposed work is to test the feedback loop model further investigating piezoelectric sensor technology. There are three main reasons driving this decision.

The first reason for this selection is that the electromagnetic effect has already been recently explored in the form of Pavegen technology, a successful tile that harvests energy from footfalls through an electromagnetic system which creates a current by moving a magnet inside a coil [18].

The second reason directly relates to the flexibility of the design and geometry of the piezoelectric technology, compared to the Pavegen electromagnetic technology. The Piezoelectric effect is the capability of certain material to generate alternating current (AC) from mechanical stress, when bent, squeeze, twisted or in vibration then to be converted into direct current (DC) [8]. The technology is used in the form of sensors that are small in scale, requiring fewer components to operate as well as less force applied to actuate them. These design features challenge a broader range of design applications, including the harvesting of different forces than footsteps, such as force of hand (also tested along the proposed research as part of prototype testing).

The third reason refers to the continuous Research and Development of the piezoelectric technology. During the last ten years, piezoelectric materials for sensors elements have been advanced in efficiency and have been investigated with the purpose of energy harvesting, considering a variety of design applications that use power generated from human motion [11].

4.2   Selecting "Examples" for Testing the Feedback Loop Model

In the proposed study the urban scenario is constructed using specific "examples" of each of the four proposed conditions defining the feedback loop model: type of force actuating the technology, type of technology, service provided and context. Whereas the researcher initially established the selection of piezoelectric sensor as energy technology harvesting force of footstep, safety lighting (as service provided) and public stairs (as context) began to be considered following the interest of Melbourne City Council in implementing the prototype along poorly lit pedestrians stairways, specifically located near major public transport hubs in Melbourne's Central Business District. Thus all of the four conditions used to test the feedback loop model were defined as the following: force of footstep was chosen as the mode of actuating the piezoelectric sensor technology, implemented along pedestrian stairways providing safety lighting (Fig. 9).

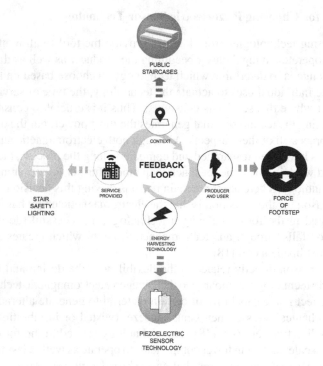

Fig. 9. Selected "examples" to test the feedback loop model

Having the force of footstep as a constant mode of technology actuation, the other three conditions (technology, service provided and context) were continuously investigated during the research process.

4.3   Observations on Stair Safety Lighting as Service Provided

At the end of 2012, an initial presentation of the power-generating device to private companies, including ARUP and IBM, and Melbourne City Council established an interest in the use of the proposed power device for two main design applications: (1) harvesting energy from footsteps: off-grid real time LED lighting system with the aim of increasing safety along pedestrians' footpaths; and (2) a pedestrian counting system (via electronic signals), providing data to inform the analysis of pedestrians' mobility. This provided an opportunity for investigating the implementation of the proposed power device finalized to a specific use and urban site, with a view to testing and assessing it with a public installation supported by Melbourne City Council, who provided expertise and funding.

The conversation with Melbourne City Council brought up a consideration of integrating the power-generating prototype along pedestrians' walkways for the purpose of stair safety lighting, beginning to recognize and evaluate the benefits of testing the power device within a defined area considering the applied force of footstep. Initial comments were made on the number and placement of the piezoelectric sensors along the tread considering the walkable area (where the user is most likely to step), as well as the number of LED lights needed to illuminate the path for safety purposes. The energy was thought to be produced by the pedestrian in real time at night having lights located along the steps. With the power device in place, another option was to add a storage device (a battery) to collect the energy harvested by footsteps during the day and use it at night to light a display. In this case, light is used not only for safety purposes but also as a means of communication.

Another aspect when thinking about the placement of the device (number of units and their distribution) was to consider multiple piezoelectric sensors along the stair tread and the possibility of actuating all of them by distributing the force of footstep along the whole tread (capturing most of the force of each footstep applied). However, when considering the integration along staircases, the opportunity to actuate the sensor technology using the whole tread surface is a valuable alternative to be explored and presented in the following paragraph discussing the urban design scenario.

This required staircases that represent ideal spatial conditions, channeling the person within a very well contained space. The benefit relies on multiple sensors operating at the same time, consequently producing more power. This implies the use of an additional mechanical device to be placed on the topside of the sensors, able to redirect the force how and where wanted based on where the footstep is applied. The number and placement of the sensors was then tested based on the existing dimension of the step on site. Sensors and related components were distributed along the tread, also considering the location of the LED lights and the space needed to run the electric wires. At this stage, various parameters came into play, such as length of the area to be considered, in order to calculate the possible number of sensors to be placed next to one another; the number of pedestrians who can step at the same time; and the number and location of LED lights.

Moreover, additional observations are made when designing the external surface of the stair tread in view of the direct contact with the user required (pedestrian footstep) and the outdoor location. The surface where the footstep is applied needs to be and feel safe. Because the actuation of the device placed on the step requires physical displacement of the tread (10 mm), additional studies investigated user comfort when stepping on the device, considering also the strength of the displacement mechanism required in order to support the weight applied. The selected material has to be strong enough to resist the continuous up and down movement and protect the overall electronic system underneath, considering all requirements need to be integrated in a public space. Moreover, materials have to be waterproof because they will be exposed to outdoor weather conditions.

Final comments were also related to the opportunity of designing a stair tread module. The proposed power device could be designed as a final product, in the form of a kit ready to be installed on site, retrofitting existing staircases. An option was to design the step as a box structure (void space) with tread that can be lifted (as a lid) to integrate the power device. If the technology was placed underneath the tread surface of the stair nosing profile, the location of lights becomes relevant, along with their number and orientation, keeping in mind the low visibility of LEDs. At the same time as piezoelectric sensor technology has been increasing in efficiency of power generation, LED lights have also become more efficient in their ability to output light with a relatively small amount of power. Considering this framework, where the two technologies are converging, it is clearly valuable at this moment in time to start experimenting. On the other hand, lighting is only one possible way of using the generated power; other possibilities valuable to investigate might include the use of the technology in pedestrian counter mode in order to visualize or map pedestrian flow; or as power source and data collection from environmental sensors.

5   Evaluating Urban Design Scenarios: The Implementation of the Power-Generating Device in Public Spaces

The following study discusses urban design scenarios evaluated considering the implementation of a power-generating device along specific pedestrians pathways in Melbourne Central Business District. Parallel research has been done developing the power-generating device through prototyping in scale 1:1, investigating sensor technology, electronic circuit, proposed mechanical devices for sensor actuation given the force of footstep applied, and a preliminary LED lighting system. Specific attention was given to exploring modes of piezoelectric sensor deformation, especially bending and vibration, using force of hand and a mechanical device to simulate the required action (force of footstep applied) in order to maximize voltage output (as force of pressure also tested by the researcher seemed not to be the most efficient applied force). In a second phase, the development of the device focused as well on investigating ergonomics - the comfort and safety of the pedestrian, specifically considering the action of stepping on the device; considering the displacement of the stair tread needed to actuate the sensors located underneath.

Having demonstrated the feasibility of implementing the power-generating device for the production of real time LED safety lighting, the following urban scenarios begin unfolding opportunities of storing the power generated by pedestrians' footsteps during the day when light is not needed and using it at night time, providing for instance additional use of the lighting for example as part of information display. This also means that during the day individuals are generating stored power by walking on the installed power device without necessarily being aware of their contribution to the production of energy. The engagement with the individual becomes relevant at night, when stepping on the power device actuates LED lights.

The scenarios were constructed considering implementing the device along two public staircases in Melbourne Central Business District, one located at the Southbank to Elizabeth Street underpass and the other one at the Degraves Place underpass, both areas characterized by high pedestrian volumes (Fig. 10).

Elizabeth St Underpass   Degraves Underpass

Fig. 10. Selected "examples" to test the feedback loop model

A tally counter was used to collect data on pedestrian traffic on site. Data were collected during a workday at three different times: morning, lunch and evening. Numbers were taken every 40 min, at intervals of 2 min (Fig. 11). A preliminary analysis of the data collected showed a higher amount of pedestrian movement during peak-hour time compare to the numbers gathered by City Council using infrared camera (data available from the City of Melbourne monitoring pedestrians website: http://www.pedestrian.melbourne.vic.gov.au/#date=10-11-2014&time=13). It was then possible to estimate the total number of pedestrians walking through the selected sites each day being around 30,000.

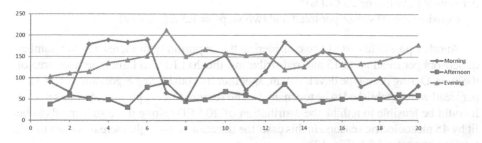

Fig. 11. Graph showing data on pedestrian traffic during peak hour time

Having established the sites and related pedestrians traffic, the proposed calculations consider the 20 LEDs and 30,000 steps as fixed parameters and the number of sensor per tread and the number of steps as variables. The scenarios presented below show a significant amount of the time lights could be powered at night time.

The first diagram in Fig. 12 shows the selected piezoelectric sensor (EG300 type) and the distribution of the sensors per tread considering a channel design proposed to be integrated along existing staircases. The section shows the two mechanisms included, one instigating the displacement of the tread harvesting the force of footstep, and the second converting that movement into a flipping actuation to make the sensor underneath in vibration. The LED light is thought to be positioned along the stair nosing profile of the tread. The plan view shows the layout of the sensors (position and number) along the two treads.

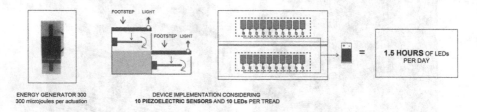

ENERGY GENERATOR 300
300 microjoules per actuation

DEVICE IMPLEMENTATION CONSIDERING
10 PIEZOELECTRIC SENSORS AND 10 LEDs PER TREAD

Fig. 12. Hypothetical scenario considering using EG 300 type of piezoelectric sensor

Considering that the selected piezoelectric sensor Energy Generator 300 is generating 300 µJ per actuation, and having determined it is sufficient to have 10 sensors (thus 10 LEDs) per tread, the 20 LEDs selected are distributed along two steps. The calculation is made as following:

Power of each LED = Current * Voltage
P = 1 mA * 1.6 V = 1.6mW
For 20 LEDs, it would be 20*1.6 = 32mW.
Energy consumed by 20 LEDs for 1 s = 32 mW* 1 s = 32 mJ.
From each sensor producing 300 µJ, the energy can be converted to power as
30,000 steps a day generates 9000 mJ
For 20 LEDs, 9000 mJ would ideally last for 3000 mJ/32mW = 281.25 s (5 min per day per sensor lighting the 20 LEDs)
Considering 10 sensor per tread and two steps = 1.5 h (per day)

Another possibility would be considering the opportunity of increasing the number of sensors per tread up to 15 and redistributing the 20 LEDs to light a broader area of the stair. During prototype development, specifically considering ergonomics, 10 LEDs per tread were established to be too many for the required safety purpose. For this reason it could be feasible to rethink the distribution of 20 LEDs along three stair treads to be lit by 45 piezoelectric sensors. In this case, the duration of the light increases even more, totaling just over 3.5 h (Fig. 13).

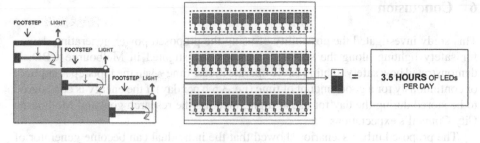

Fig. 13. Lighting output when using 15 sensors and 20 LEDs per star tread

This evaluation demonstrated the benefits and potentials of further developing the prototype considering the feasibility of this specific service provided and context. In fact, having demonstrated the feasibility of providing stair safety lighting in the specific sites Melbourne Central Business District (considering both real time and storage options), scenarios could then be further explored considering higher pedestrians traffic pathways such as in the example of the subway in Tokyo previously discussed. Considering the pedestrians traffic being 4 million pedestrians daily, having 10 sensors (EG300) along one stair tread actuated every step and storing the energy during the day, the power-generating system in place could potentially provide 200 LED lights continuously on for 10 h at night time (Fig. 14). In changing the proposed parameters multiple scenarios can be built, for instance considering a lower number of pedestrians, or higher number of sensor per tread, or higher number of steps etc.

	Number of footsteps per day	Energy output per piezo sensor	Number of piezo to be placed along stair treads [max 20 per tread]	Tot sensors energy output	Energy output per 1 LED	Number of LEDs	Tot hours of light
MELBOURNE	30,000	0.3mJ	20	180,000mJ	1.6V	20	1.5
TOKYO	4,000,000	0.3mJ	20	24,000,000mJ	1.6V	400	10

Fig. 14. Examples of urban scenarios considering pedestrians stair safety lighting

At this stage additional observations were made also when comparing the developed design scenarios integrating piezoelectric sensors with Pavegen technology (electromagnetic technology) considering the specific investigation of the feedback loop model. When considering the relationship between the four specific established conditions (force of footstep, technology, service provided and context), it could be argued that the proposed prototype is more efficient, not only in terms of the physical space required for the systems to operate, but also in terms of most efficient system to capture the force of footstep using the flexibility of the prototype design. This preliminary observation might also be reinforced when considering the economic aspect, which is not considered by this research.

6   Conclusion

This study investigated the possibility of using the proposed power-generating device for safety lighting along the specific stairways investigated in Melbourne CBD. It demonstrated how safety lighting could operate in real time when the footstep is applied, or continuously for a good amount of time (i.e. 3.5 h per day) if the energy is considered to be stored during the day for use at night, meeting the research goal and Melbourne City Council's expectations.

The proposed urban scenarios showed that the individual can become generator of their own service through the use of piezoelectric sensor technology directly contributing to the collective experience in public spaces. In providing this event, the users' experience is challenged to change or shift, because of the increase in users' awareness in both their active contribution to the production of energy and the consequent use of the power for a collective service, such as safety lighting, tested in the research. The individual becomes conscious of the possibility of generating power through their action (such as walking) as well as of the immediate use of that energy for their own, and the public's safety. Main findings also established the validity of piezoelectric sensor technology following the specific research aim (proof of concept). The research provided feedback on the use of new piezoelectric sensor prototypes, tested and evaluated in a novel mode considering a cantilever-based design specifically for harvesting force of footstep. Suggestions were also provided specifically to design an electronic circuit and LED lighting system for the piezoelectric sensor technology.

During this study the feedback loop model was tested with both generation and production of energy, considering the relationship with each of the other four main conditions: force of footstep, piezoelectric sensors, safety lighting and public staircases. Considering the findings and the value of further investigating force of footstep and piezoelectric sensor technology as energy harvesting, the research could be further developed exploring different services provided and contexts. The challenge is then to investigate what type of service(s) the public can benefit from and how the public can contribute to the production of that service using piezoelectric sensor technology. Future research is currently exploring opportunity of building a computer simulation model considering data collected by this research.

References

1. Mangelsdorf, W.: Metasystems of urban flow: buro happold's collaborations in the generation of new urban ecologies. Archit. Des. **83**(4), 94–99 (2013)
2. Alanne, K., Saari, A.: Distributed energy generation and sustainable development. Renew. Sustain. Energy Rev. **10**(6), 539–558 (2006)
3. Ghosn, R.: Energy as a spatial project. New Geogr. **02**, 7–10 (2009)
4. Priya, S., Inman, D.J.: Energy Harvesting Technologies, vol. 21. Springer, USA (2009)
5. Droege, P.: The Renewable City: A Comprehensive Guide to an Urban Revolution. Wiley-Academy, Chichester, UK (2006)
6. Stoll, K., Lloyd, S. (eds.): Infrastructure as Architecture : Designing Composite Networks. Jovis, Berlin (2010)

7. Mitchell, W.: Intelligent cities. UOC Pap. **5**, 1–12 (2007)
8. Kaźmierski, T.J., Beeby, S. (eds.): Energy Harvesting System: Principles, Modeling and Applications. Springer, New York (2011)
9. Starner, T.: Human-powered wearable computing. IBM Syst. J. **35**(3&4), 618–629 (1996)
10. Bouffard, F., Kirschen, D.S.: Centralised and distributed electricity systems. Energy Policy **36**(12), 4504–4508 (2008)
11. Erturk, A., Inman, D.J.: Piezoelectric Energy Harvesting. Wiley, Chichester (2011)
12. Sodano, H.A., Inman, D.J., Park, G.: A review of power harvesting from vibration using piezoelectric materials. Shock Vib. Dig. **36**(3), 197–205 (2004)
13. Shenck, N.S., Paradiso, J.A.: Energy scavenging with shoe-mounted piezoelectrics. IEEE Micro **21**(3), 30–42 (2001)
14. Shenck, N.S.: A demonstration of useful electric energy generation from piezoceramics in a shoe. Ph.D. Dissertation, Dept. of Electrical Engineering and Computer Science, Massachusetts Institute of Technology (1999)
15. Shenck, N.S., Paradiso, J.A.: Energy scavenging with shoe-mounted piezoelectrics. IEEE Micro **21**(3), 30–42 (2001)
16. Mateu, L., Moll, F.: Optimum piezoelectric bending beam structures for energy harvesting using shoe inserts. J. Intell. Mater. Syst. Struct. **16**(10), 835–845 (2005)
17. S.D. Club: Sustainable Dance Floor (2007)
18. Webster, G.: Green sidewalk makes electricity—one footstep at a time. CNN (2011)
19. Chapa, J.: Energy generating floors to power tokyo subways. Inhabitat (2013). http://inhabitat.com/tokyo-subway-stations-get-piezoelectric-floors/attachment/17513
20. Bischur, E., Schwesinger, N.: Energy Harvesting In Floors
21. Graham James, J.T.: MIT duo sees people-powered Crowd Farm. MIT News (2007)
22. Gilbert, J.M., Balouchi, F.: A vibrating cantilever footfall energy harvesting device. J. Intell. Mater. Syst. Struct. **25**(14), 1738–1745 (2014). doi:10.1177/1045389X14521880
23. Cramm, J., El-Sherif, A., Lee, J., Loughlin, J.: Investigating the feasibility of implementing pavegen energy: harvesting piezoelectric floor tiles in the new SUB (2011)

Dynamic Façades and Computation: Towards an Inclusive Categorization of High Performance Kinetic Façade Systems

Rodrigo Velasco[1,2(✉)], Aaron Paul Brakke[1], and Diego Chavarro[1]

[1] Universidad Piloto de Colombia, Programme of Architecture, Bogota, Colombia
{rodrigo-velasco,aaron-brake,diego-chavarro1}@unipiloto.edu.co
[2] Frontis3d Facade Systems, Bogota, Colombia
rodrigo@frontis3d.co

Abstract. This chapter provides a panorama of the current state of computationally controlled dynamic facades through a literature review and a survey of contemporary projects. This was completed with an underlyings interest in understanding how innovative design solutions with the capacity to 'react to' and/or 'interact with' the varying states of climatic conditions have been developed. An analysis of these projects was conducted, and led to the identification of tendencies, which were subsequently synthesized and articulated. While most classifications are limited to describing the *movement* or *structure* needed to achieve morphological transformation, an important recommendation is to also consider *control* as a determining factor. For this reason, the culmination of the investigation presented here is a proposal for a classification structure of dynamic facades, developed according to the functional modus operandi of each structure in terms of *movement* and *control*.

Keywords: Dynamic facades · Kinetic architecture · Computational control · High performance building envelopes

1 Introduction

In my view, there are two overarching factors driving building design today: the critical need for sustainable solutions, and the power of computation. The convergence of these two is leading to a new generation of adaptive technologies - Chuck Hoberman [1].

Research on dynamic enclosures has been of interest in the architectural academia for at least 40 years and general developments of such structures can be traced back to pre-historic nomadic settlements [2, 3]. However, the advent of widely available computational tools has meant a significant growth not only in research but also in the implementation of dynamic responsive facades. In the context of pervasive computing, the designer is aided in the planning, simulation, fabrication and control of dynamic processes. Exploration in this area continues to grow as the acquisition of related electronic equipment, including; micro-processors, sensors and actuators becomes more economically feasible. Moreover, the global environmental crisis necessitates

© Springer-Verlag Berlin Heidelberg 2015
G. Celani et al. (Eds.): CAAD Futures 2015, CCIS 527, pp. 172–191, 2015.
DOI: 10.1007/978-3-662-47386-3_10

innovation in the development of the building envelope in order to achieve higher energy efficient buildings. Studies of the C2ES: Center for Climate and Energy Solutions [4] state that optimized window design and specification in residential projects could lead to 10-50 % energy savings and a 10-40 % decrease in costs in commercial buildings through a reduction in lighting and HVAC. Dynamic façade systems seem to offer new grounds for hitherto unattainable high performance solutions.

The work presented in this chapter is situated in the above mentioned context and intends to contribute to a growing field of research by first discussing tendencies in both literature and practice. An evaluation of this work leads to the articulation of a new framework based on operational factors. This has been created with the objective of providing a new classification structure for kinetic envelopes that includes both *movement* and *control* as determining factors. This text provides a number of considerations that pertain to the possibilities and future challenges of designing dynamic facades.

2 Performance and Dynamic Facades

The analysis and critique of the building façade has consistently maintained noteworthy presence within architectural criticism. A significant transition has occurred in recent history as an increasing interest in the *performance* of the envelope has become the predominant criteria for this. Whereas late twentieth century theoreticians had placed attention on semiology and the formal issues of composition and representation, concern now presides in how *form* is *informed*. Branko Kolarevic and Ali Malkawi state: '*increasing emphasis on building performance - from the cultural and social context to building physics - is influencing building design, its processes and practices, by blurring the distinction between geometry and analysis, between appearance and performance*' [5].

Expanding research in building performance indicates that improving the capacity of the building envelope to mitigate external conditions with the needs of internal comfort is critical in diminishing the environmental impact of the high energy consumption (nearly 40 % of total energy consumption) attributed to buildings [6–9]. Significant advances have been made in the development of double skin façade systems, however the engineering goals of these solutions tends to veer towards average conditions (generally in order to mitigate seasonal swings in climatic conditions). Although double skin facades might be able to meet the standards of certifications such as BREAM or LEED, achieving zero emission architectural projects is nearly impossible following the traditional design process [10, 11]. The shift from static towards dynamic kinetic facades aims to cope with the fact that the natural environmental conditions are in a constant state of change. Adding to this, Michael Hensel has proposed a: '*reconceptualization of the relation between architectures and the environments they are set within on a spatial, material and temporal level*' [12]. To accomplish this, he proposes a consideration for: '*context and time-specific exterior-to-interior relations, the associated question of extended threshold conditions and the interaction with a dynamic environment*' (ibid).

In this paper we shall understand the term *dynamic* as *kinetic*, that is, we shall limit the scope of dynamic facades to those whose changing properties are due to the physical motion of the material elements constituting the system, and thus mechanical properties of the materials and/or systems will be considered. Our approach to the subject places emphasis on the different variables that affect the performance of dynamic facades. In our literature review, we found that the variables of control, computation and/or inner material were not adequately covered. However, in contrast with the scarcity of these topics in literature, we have found many recent research projects and built works that have been designed and implemented with a prioritization placed on the component of *control*.[1]

With the hope of providing the reader with a wide-ranging view of recent developments in dynamic facades, a description and interpretation of how various authors have written about the topic is provided. Eleven examples of kinetic facades are reviewed which serves to expand the panorama of how these structures should be classified. Our analysis of both literature and projects is then synthesized and a new classification of dynamic facades is proposed.

3 A Comparison of Existing Classifications of Dynamic Facades

The texts that aim to provide a look at the underpinnings of the recent developments of dynamic facades tend to utilize either *movement* or *structure* as the conceptual framework. Movement definitions include terms like rotation and translation to articulate the morphological output. Structural definition uses terms such as telescopic, scissor and folding plates among others to describe how the morphological transformation is achieved. Four texts have been analysed with the aim of deriving the common denominators between them.

The texts that approached the kinetic architecture via a morphological transformation through movement perspective were: *Designing Kinetics for Architectural Facades: State Change* by Jules Moloney and *move: Architecture in Motion – Dynamic Components and Elements* by Schumacher, Schaeffer and Vogt. On the other hand, the texts that are oriented towards understanding kinetic architecture via the structural definitions include "Morphological Principles of Kinetic Architectural Structures" by Stevenson and *New Proposals for Transformable Architecture, Engineering and Design* edited by Felix Escrig and Jose Sanchez. At present there are no definitive texts on the matter. However, the combination of these two angles as articulated in the aforementioned texts are an ample sample for this study. The following paragraphs of this text illustrate how the authors mentioned above have organized their discourse about the topic.

---

[1] From the perspective described, however, we would still be covering a potentially enormous spectrum, as the possible number of configurations would be exponentially increased in the system by the particular behaviour of its component elements in time. We have narrowed our consideration towards computationally controlled facades where we see fertile ground for contemporary designers. We have also tried to be selective about how the kinetic façade is used and have developed a preference for examples that look to address environmental performance.

3.1 Designing Kinetics for Architectural Facades: State Change (Moloney, 2011)

The first text from the movement-morphology category was found in the book, *Designing Kinetics for Architectural Facades: State change* [2]. In this text, a foundation is set for the exploration of kinetic facades through an introduction of philosophical constructs that deal with dynamic morphological patterning (transformation in time) and the analysis of practical precedents. The primary motivation of this text is to delineate the latent aesthetic potential of a kinetic building skin, hence movement is defined through a categorization of visual syntax (and the infinite moments created during the transition from one state to another) which are termed; wave, fold and field ([2], p. 146).

Based on the set of variables that would be needed for the development of kinetic facades, a diagram is created with the different variables that should be considered when designing a kinetic façade: tectonics, control and sampling. With regard to tectonics, the author refers to the morphological output created by dynamic facades. This section is subdivided into kinetic types (movement of parts) and the granularity (number of parts in relation to a whole). The basic movements are demarcated as translation, rotation and scaling which could be combined to allow for greater possibility. Though Moloney acknowledges that the definition of kinetics includes material deformation, he prefers to maintain an abstract level of engagement in which physical deformation is described geometrically. When writing about control systems, the author's primary concern is in pattern formations. Credit is given to the work developed by Michael Fox and Miles Kemp following that of William Zuk and Roger H. Clarke is cited as an example of a taxonomy of interactive architecture that contemplates the control systems; however, Moloney criticizes this framework for not more fully bearing in mind kinetic output and opts for a classification built upon the three orders of cybernetic theory ([2], p. 29–31).

In Moloney's taxonomy, reflexivity and spatial differentiation are the variables that are regulated by control mechanisms. By *reflexivity* the author refers to the behavior and potential reconfiguration of the control system. By *spatial differentiation*, reference is made to the control system in regards to an area of a façade (if it controls singular or multiple elements of the façade). With regard to the sampling plane, Moloney's concern is twofold: the data source and the density of samples ([2], p. 80–90).

While the text goes into depth about understanding morphological transformation, the emphasis on aesthetics via the topic of dynamic patterning occupies the focus of this discourse and consequently the concept of performance oriented control is relegated to this interest. Move: Architecture in Motion – Dynamic Components and Elements (Schumacher, Schaeffer and Vogt, 2010).

The second text reviewed from the movement-morphology category was developed by Schumacher, Schaeffer and Vogt in the book *Move: Architecture in Motion – Dynamic Components and Elements* [13]. This text approaches kinetics through a broader lens and lays a foundation for the consideration of movement in architectural structures. Movable structures, movable connections, movable actuators and measuring, control and regulating factors are the categories that are developed. The application and function of movement is explored by illustrating the possibilities that these structures could have and are filtered through several considerations, such as; the idea of function, conservation and generation of energy, and interaction. Another important area of attention found in this text is that of materiality. Taking into account these themes, we have organized our outline of the book into five categories: structures, connections, actuators, control and materials.

In the structural category, the authors provide an explanation from a functional perspective that outlines lessons from simple machines, such as; pulleys, levers and inclined planes. This leads into the consideration of connections, which depicts the use of rotation bearings, translation bearings and hinges. This text also explains another pragmatic, yet significant consideration of how movement can be generated. The authors explicate the capacities of an engine and subdivide this explanation into four groups: electromechanical, hydraulic, pneumatic and micro-actuators. When talking about control the authors refer to the changes that a structural system has when it interacts with the data received. This narrative is subdivided into control and regulation and sensors.

From our perspective, this text treats a number of variables that should be considered for the design and construction of kinetic architecture. In regards to control, the reader is exposed to a description of sensors and the difference between control and regulation is explained, yet key information related to the programming necessary for control is exempt. This absence is unfortunate since the gathering of data and explanation of whether the data is processed locally or centrally is relevant and essential for a deeper understanding of kinetic architecture (Fig. 1).

Fig. 1. Inferred classification extracted from the book *Designing Kinetics for Architectural Facades: State change* which illustrates the way to which tectonics, sampling and control are considered.

3.2 New Proposals for Transformable Architecture, Engineering and Design (Escrig and Sanchez, 2013)

The next two classifications are developed from a structural-morphological perspective. The first is gathered from the conference *New Proposals for Transformable Architecture, Engineering and Design*, chaired by Felix Escrig and Jose Sanchez [14]. As an attempt to extract and structure a taxonomy from the array of articles, we classified the content presented into five categories: scissors, telescopic, tensegrity and tension, rigid foldable and pneumatic.

Even though this book was not developed as a structural design taxonomy for kinetic facades and several structural systems have not been included (telescopic and scissor systems are discussed, yet other common structural systems developed throughout history, such as; diaphragm, pivoting, folding plates and hybrid pneumatic umbrella systems were not included), we consider this collection important to examine in our literature review. It expresses both significant examples from the past as well as contemporary tendencies being developed in kinetic structures around the world ([14], p. 22) (Fig. 2).

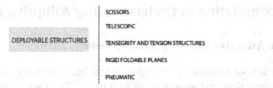

Fig. 2. Inferred classification extracted from the proceedings *New Proposals for Transformable Architecture, Engineering and Design* edited by Escrig and Sanchez.

3.3 Morphological Principles of Kinetic Architectural Structures (Stevenson, 2011)

The second classification from a structural-morphology perspective was extracted from the article *Morphological Principles of Kinetic Architectural Structures* [15]. The article uses historical research of kinetic building structures as an attempt to identify characteristics and typologies. Through a narrative that ruminates kinetic architecture, an evolution unfolds through a description that is oriented towards the formal characteristics and components needed for the development of kinetic facades. A diagram has been constructed to synthesize the physical transformation of building objects and tendencies in the structural configurations frequently used in kinetic architectural structures ([15], p. 12).

Physical transformation is treated by exposing a range of possibilities that includes everything from material shape transformation to the change of position (through rotation, displacement, etc.). Position in space and direction of transformation is developed in detail through the elaboration of a text that provides a description of the structures needed to give movement to facades objects.

The article places an emphasis on the formal outputs that kinetic buildings could have. Furthermore, this text highlights developments in kinetic architecture from a slightly different angle than the other texts reviewed. The amalgamation of structural systems (scissor, reciprocal, diaphragm, foldable rigid, foldable membranes, pneumatic etc.) are brought into focus through the physical transformation, direction of movement and position in space (Fig. 3).

Fig. 3. Inferred classification extracted from the article "Morphological Principles of Kinetic Architectural Structures" written by Stevenson

4   Use of Simulation in Understanding Adaptive Envelopes

4.1   Climate Adaptive Building Shells (Loonen, 2010)

The visualization of building performance has become very important in the design, planning, construction and operation of buildings. The text on dynamic facades developed by Roel Loonen called, *Climate Adaptive Building Shells. What can we simulate?* [16] provides an interesting look at what computational performance simulations can provide. This text highlights function (how an adaptive façade can respond to varying relevant physics), structure, (adaptive behaviour) and interaction (control).

Relevant physics refers to the optimization of electrical systems, air-flow, optical and thermal performance variables. Since this study emphasizes the simulation of environmental performance, the category that specifies the improvements in comfort produced by facades becomes an indispensable item in the kinetic façade design taxonomy. The adaptive behaviour section concentrates on the movement of facade elements and is subdivided into mechanical movement (displacement and rotation) and movement controlled by material properties. The main focus of the interaction (control) category is the interaction of the façade with the data received. This section is subdivided into; *open loop,* façades that respond to the data received and *closed loop*, facades that have the possibilities of feedback between the building and the environment.

The classification proposed is similar to the aforementioned example, both of which incorporate the variables of control (reflexivity) and adaptive behaviour (tectonic). However, Loonen introduces another notion; the possibility to simulate and design the control of dynamic facades which aim to optimize environmental performance, which is deemed a significant variable for contemporary practice (Fig. 4).

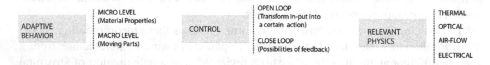

Fig. 4. Inferred classification extracted from the text by Loonen [16]

5   Case Studies

A review of projects is included to illustrate tendencies in built work (from the level of prototype to implementation). Several examples fit into the categories mentioned in the literature review. For example the Integrated Glare Control Blade System by Li, Schwartz, and Navvab and the Aldar Central Market by Hoberman both use translation. The Institute du Monde by Jean Nouvel relies upon an intricate system of in-plane rotation to achieve its effect, while the Adaptive Cellular Automata Façade by Marilena Skavara and the Responsive Sun-Shading System by Velasco use off-plane rotation. The façade system for Al Bahr Towers by Aedas uses a hybrid umbrella system with rigid folding planes. It may appear that the existing classifications that describe morphological transformation in terms of either movement or structure are sufficient. However, there are examples that are not so cleanly classified. Examples such as Bloom by Sung, HygroSkin by Menges or Spaceshift by Kretzer that exploit inner material properties for their transformation. One noteworthy observation is that a number of recent applications place emphasis on the nature to which the façade is controlled. This can be found in projects such as: Bioclimatic Responsive Skins BRS [17], Adaptive Solar Envelope ASE [18], Intelligent Building Skins IBS [19], Responsive Envelopes [20], and Advection Based Adaptive Building Envelopes ABABE [21]. The description of projects by contemporary designers illustrates an inclination to explain what data is obtained and how it is processed. Another observation is that the concern towards environmental performance is addressed in a majority of projects found.

Overall the reader is provided with unique and innovative examples that are the fruit of exploratory design processes. Though numerous other projects have been analysed, the projects included here are a small sample that serves to illustrate some of the tendencies found in contemporary projects. The brief comments given to each project should suffice as basic references to understand the basic notions of *movement* and *control*.

5.1 Façade for the Institute Du Monde Arabe, Paris, F (1987) Atelier Jean Nouvel

The Jean Nouvel designed Institute du Monde Arabe in Paris, France is perhaps the most well-known project illustrated in this chapter. Built in 1987, it is the oldest facade we analysed. This "In-plane Rotating" (diaphragm) with a local light sensitive direct control system was developed as a contemporary response towards the creation of the mashrabiya, an archetypal element of Arabic culture which has been used for centuries for solar protection as well as a way to provide privacy. The southern façade is composed of 30,000 steel diaphragms that are very similar to the shutter mechanism of a camera lens. Circle, square and hexagon shapes are formed when the lenses are in the closed state. The physical make of the system limits the opening ratio to roughly 50 % of the net opening area due to the two-layer system. Though this project continues to serve as an exemplary example of a kinetic façade, the high number of singular mechanical devices has proved problematic in the long-term due to the constant maintenance required. Currently the system is inoperable (Fig. 5).

 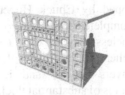 

Fig. 5. Diagram that shows how the apertures of the Façade for the Institute du Monde Arabe transition from open to closed states

5.2 Adaptive Cellular Automata Facade Trained by Artificial Neural Networks, UCL (2009-Project and Partial Prototype) Marilena Skavara

In terms of its mechanical movement, this is an 'Off Plane Rotating System with one Degree of Freedom' (a variation of the common louver). In terms of control it is 'Systems Based' and involves a complex system including the use of Cellular Automata, Genetic Algorithms and Artificial Neural Networks. The main problem this ANN tries to solve is "*to train the system to respond to different sun positions during the year, that is, different shadows, generating successful CA patterns that acquire specific starts*" ([22], p. 18). This is a problem with a predictable solution as the geometry of a sun's trajectory can be easily predicted with analogue tools (sun path diagram). In the case that this system is employed on a mobile structure, the façade would change its orientation or position constantly with data that could be constantly updated by employing a GPS system. Several issues should be addressed to make this a more viable solution. The first observation is that problem of solar access is not quantitatively defined, nor takes into account the changing geometry of the system regarding reflections. The use of Cellular Automata employed here only makes this solution a purely aesthetical composition. Though viewed as a negative factor in the prototype, the possibility of employing this type of system at a local urban level in which microclimates fluctuate due to physical obstructions might offer interesting results (Fig. 6).

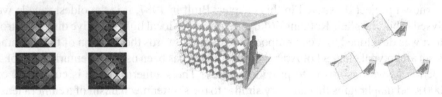

Fig. 6. Diagram of the movement generated in the adaptive cellular automata facade trained by artificial neural networks

5.3 Shading Roofs for the Aldar Central Market, Abu Dhabi, UAE (2006-2010) C. Hoberman for a Foster and Partners Project

This roof shading system developed by Chuck Hoberman Associates (Permea™ System) [23] and used in recently completed project by Foster and Partners uses a hybrid mechanical system, which nonetheless may be classified as 'In Plane Translation' (sliding panels). Compared with other sliding systems this one gives a very high ratio of aperture thanks to the seven layers that are sandwiched into each module. This, however, implies that the component is of substantial thickness. From the images found it can be implied that the modules are mechanically interconnected, which has advantages in terms of robustness by using less actuators, though it also means less flexibility. A variable panel assembly is herein disclosed which is comprised of a plurality of panels and a plurality of links where by rotating one or more links, the assembly shifts between a largely uncovered configuration to a covered configuration, where in the first configuration the panel profiles are essentially aligned, and in the second configuration the panel profiles are offset relative to one another. Further disclosed herein are methods to control the movement of the assembly, both manual and motorized.

Based on the description found in the patent application US7584777 [24], it could be deduced that this system is 'Reactive and Centrally Controlled' and continually responds to the environmental conditions found locally. Hoberman has been exploring solutions capable of increasing environmental performance for some time now. He states: *'One key strategy to achieve sustainable performance is for buildings to actively adapt and respond to changing climatic conditions.'* A promising strategy is for buildings to actively adapt and respond to changing climatic conditions. In the context of the façade, this strategy may be implemented by motorizing operable façade elements, so that, for example, shades can extend and retract automatically. Sensors can take environmental data (i.e., temperature, light intensity and wind flow), and, utilizing computational intelligence, the building can optimize its environmental profile in a responsive manner (Fig. 7).

Fig. 7. Diagrams of the planar kinetic system used in the Aldar Central Market

5.4 Vertical and Horizontal Integrated Glare Control Blade System (2011-Proposal) Mathew Schwartz, Robin Li, Mojtaba Navvab

This case study is a design proposal where the possibilities of simple translational movement are well employed by relating the differential position of two separated layers to the direction of solar rays. Two dispositions are possible in the translational possibilities in this system, vertical or horizontal, which are chosen according to specific requirements defined by location and orientation. The movement of the louvers can be characterized as 'Off Plane Translation' that is 'Centrally Controlled with the input being Direct', solely relying on the solar trajectory of the specific site and orientation to fulfil its purpose. As in the previous example, the mechanically interconnected components have advantages in terms of robustness by using less actuators, but which also implies less flexibility. Taking into account the simplicity of the system and its performance, this may be qualified as one of the most sensible proposals (Fig. 8).

5.5 A Responsive Sun-Shading System Supported by the Use of Fuzzy Logic (2014-Proposal) Velasco, Rodrigo - Frontis 3d

The design concept is relatively simple, a facade made out of independent plates with two functional sides (rotating with two degrees of freedom), one with PV energy concentrators, and the other exhibiting a highly reflective surface. If more light is

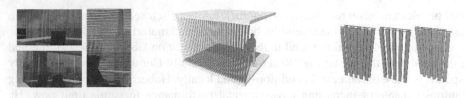

Fig. 8. Photos and diagrams of vertical and horizontal integrated glare control

required inside the covered space, the panels would reflect solar rays to the interior of the space by exposing the reflective side oriented in space as to reflect the solar rays towards selected interior areas, whereas if the opposite is true, the panels would track the sun exposing the PV side. Two more possible states are Closed (parallel to the façade plane and covering the gaps) and Open (perpendicular to the façade plane and allowing for maximum views).

The implementation of its control, however, is slightly more complex, as various factors are involved in the process, and it is not always straightforward to define when more or less light is required in the interior space. The implementation of its control uses fuzzy logic, taking into account 4 input ranges; namely, internal sensors, external sensors and the position of the sun, and user preferences. The approach of fuzzy logic was designed by the Fuzzy toolbox of Matlab. The lighting simulations carried out demonstrated the high performance of the proposed solution compared to conventional brise-soleil systems, both in terms of quantity and distribution (Fig. 9).

Fig. 9. Façade detail of a sun-shading system that has tracking (energy harvesting) and image that shows the small PV concentrators embedded in the panels

5.6 Façade's Shading System for the Al Bahr Towers, Abu Dhabi, UAE (2012) Aedas Architects

The curved cylindrical glass tower, is covered by a dynamic screen system that is composed of 'Hybrid In-Plane Translation /Out-of-Plane Rotation System' (Folding plates), where screens respond directly to insolation by opening when no direct sunlight is present and closing when the opposite is true. While possible that this is a reactive system, we are led to believe that the components of this façade are 'Directly and Centrally Controlled' as in the previous example. Even if relatively basic in terms of movement and control, this system seems functionally very adequate, giving 50 % of extra solar protection [25] while minimising the use of artificial lighting. Particularly important is its size (the height of the towers is 2,145 meters), which opens the way for introduction of dynamic façade systems at a large scale in practice. Part of the success in this kinetic system is the way to which this system revolves around a cylindrical form and the façade is transformed according to the radiation at each angle (Fig. 10).

  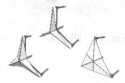

Fig. 10.   Diagram of the kinetic façade of the Al Bahr Towers designed by Aedas Architects

5.7   Bloom, San Diego, USA (2011-Installation) D. Sung et al.

Bloom, the dynamic installation using thermal bimetal plates (panels that are composed of two metals of different thermal expansion coefficients laminated together) demonstrates the potential of passive control. This structure moves according to 'Material Deformation according to Temperature' and is 'Locally Controlled by the Inner Properties of the Material'. The exploration involved in the creation of this prototype examines the potential of new material application. Professor Sung has posited that when: *'Reacting with outside temperatures, this smart material has the potential to develop self- actuating intake or exhaust for facades'* [26]. As interesting and promising as this type of proposal is, it also demonstrates that much more development is necessary. With 14,000 parts assembled into 414 components and very little control possible, functionally speaking, any other solution would outperform it (Fig. 11).

Fig. 11.   Diagram of the thermal bimetal panels used in the Bloom installation

5.8   HygroSkin-Meteorosensitive Pavilion, ICD (2013-Pavilion) A. Menges et al.

This example is similar to Bloom in that it relies on a material embedded control system (Movement by Material Deformation and Local Inner Material Control), which in this case reacts to humidity levels. This could be contrasted with the previous example as the behaviour of the system as composite configuration (veneers) allows for higher control than isotropic materials like metals (fibre direction, fibre percentage, etc.), but is still highly limited in terms of control, particularly when user subjective parameters are important (Fig. 12).

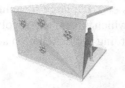
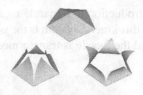

Fig. 12. Diagram of the veneer panels used in the HygroSkin-Meteosensitive Pavilion

5.9 Spaceshift Electroactive Polymer Façade, ETH (2010-Installation)
M. Kretzer et al.

Spaceshift [27] is another prototype installation, and even if no real control is implemented to achieve functional performance, this project opens new ground in terms movement possibilities. In this case Electro Active Polymers (EAP) are used to convert electricity into movement. This means that 'Movement is produced through Material Deformation through External Input (Electricity)', the result of the application of external power and 'Locally and Directly Controlled'. The components of each panel are built of three layers, in the middle a pre-stressed thin acrylic film is painted with conductive powder on both sides and protected with silicon layers on each face. As electricity is transmitted through the conductive coatings of the inner pre-stressed layer, the material expands to find a flat shape, otherwise it stays in its doubly curved pre-stressed shape. What is interesting in this example is the possibility of embedding actuators within the component material, yet having complete control of its behaviour. Several drawbacks are that the existing configurations are very unstable, fragile and the energy requirements may be considerable (Fig. 13).

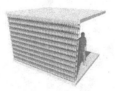
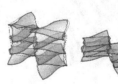

Fig. 13. Diagrams of the panels developed for Shapeshift project.

5.10 Façade for the Media-ICT Building, Barcelona, ES (2010), Vector Foiltec

This ETFE façade by Cloud9 in conjunction with the material and component providers Vector Foiltec is the latest of a series of projects that imply the movement of layered matching printed patterns by means of differential air pressures inside a cushion. The 'Movement is a Fluid External Input Material Deformation' which is 'Responsive and Centrally Controlled'. This system is equipped with sensors that continually calculate the immediate environmental changes, such as cloud cover that affect insolation. The drawback of this façade is its impossibility to react quickly to the ever changing environmental conditions as the inflation-deflation cycle might take an average of one hour (Fig. 14).

Fig. 14. Diagram showing how the transformable ETFE panels in Media-ICT project can allow for change that affects insolation.

5.11 Active Façade for Expo 2012, Yeosu, SK (2012) Soma Architects, Knippers-Helbig Eng.

This dynamic façade was developed for a pavilion that uses 'External Force to Produce Movement through Material Deformation' and is 'Directly and Centrally Controlled'. This final example, although quite basic in terms of mechanics, for the very same reason appears to offer robustness from the actuator side, and may offer advantages for the development of large sized components. Even if the movement seems to obey purely aesthetical desires as opposed to environmental performance requirements, the typology seems convenient from a functional viewpoint (Fig. 15).

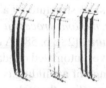

Fig. 15. Diagram that shows how the fins of Expo 2012 Pavilion can be compressed to generate material deformation.

6 A Look at Interactive Architecture: Bridging the Gap Between Texts About Kinetic Facades and the Case Studies

Our review of projects, both built and at the prototype stage, leads us to believe that control is one defining factor that should be more thoroughly considered in the design process. Though largely exempt from books on the subject, various articles have documented these projects. Though not aimed at the topic of facades, a text by Fox and Kemp [28] is oriented towards interactive architecture and one chapter treats this topic. Another text that looks at the idea kinetic facades via a study of adaptability in the shell of the building is that of Roel Loonen [29]. This work analyses the performance of the building envelope and posits techniques to improve building performance simulation which leads to suggestions in regard to the building skin.

Fig. 16. Classification extracted from the book *Interactive Architecture* by Fox and Kemp

6.1 Literature About the Control of Interactive Architectures (Fox and Kemp, 2009)

Interactive Architecture written by Michael Fox and Miles Kemp [28] emphasizes control and computation as the principal way to achieve kinetic architecture. It begins with an explanation of the importance of computation for kinetic architecture and ends with an analysis of case studies, which contextualizes the technologies used for the development of interactive architecture. A classification of kinetic systems is presented which names three typologies for organization: Embedded, Deployable and Dynamic Systems. Embedded systems are an integral part of the whole building, a system used to control the adaptability of the building to external conditions. When writing about deployable systems, a structural system is proposed that allows for the "deconstruction and reconstruction" of the whole building. Dynamic structures are smaller systems within the building that can be integrated with others in the building or also function autonomously.

Fox and Kemp promote the idea of embedded computation for the control of the physical structure of a building and call for systems that have: *'the ability to gather information, process it and use it to control the behaviour of the actual physical architecture'* ([28], p. 58). A classification of computation is developed around control being, active, automated or adaptive. Active control is a system that allows for the behavioural change of a building confronting external variables. These systems obtain the external information through sensors and generally have a decentralized control. Automated systems are systems that integrate computation with human interaction to control the performance of the building. The focal point of these systems is the development of interactive application for humans to control and change the performance of the building. Adaptive control is the third system explained as a system that learns how to adapt to external changes. These systems are programmed with algorithms that respond to external changes and have no need for human control. Though not explicitly written to address kinetic facades, the contribution of this book is significant as it includes computation as a design variable for control systems (Fig. 16).

7   Towards an Inclusive Classification that Considers Both Movement and Control

The advantage of this categorisation is the possibility of recombining factors in different ways as to create new theoretical possibilities for Dynamic façade systems. In this classification the primary factors will be two, *Movement and Control*. Each factor has been divided into subcategories that can be mixed in various ways. In the graph below, we see the proposed system, including eleven representative examples that have already been briefly introduced in this paper (Fig. 17).

7.1 Movement

Understanding movement factors as those defining the typological configuration of actuators, we have defined two main groups, and the first group represents the classical mechanical classification of movement and includes rotation, translation and hybrid modes. The second group considers movement as caused by material deformation and includes the particular factors that may cause such deformation (temperature, humidity or electricity).

7.1.1 Mechanism Based

This category contemplates all classical mechanisms made out of distinguishable invariable components acting together by means of dynamic connections to transmit movement. Here we classify them into three categories according to the type of movement allowed:

Rotation: Mechanisms allowing movement around a fixed axis. This can be further categorized according to the relative position of the façade plane, being in-plane when

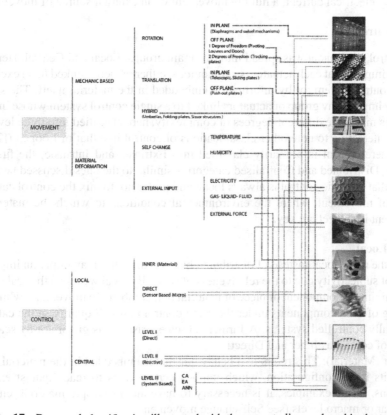

Fig. 17. Proposed classification illustrated with the case studies analyzed in the text

the movement is so (and the axis of movement perpendicular) and out of plane when the opposite is true.

Translation: Mechanisms allowing movement along an axis, which can also be categorized according to the relative position of the façade plane, being in-plane when the axis and movement are parallel, and out of plane when the opposite is true.

Hybrid: Mechanisms implying any combination of the above mentioned types. As each type of transformation will act in different ways, it would be unfeasible to further categorize the movement as in plane or out of plane.

7.1.2   Material Deformation

As opposed to the previous category, movement here is allowed by the physical characteristics of the components themselves and not exclusively by the connections. We have further categorized them according to the input provoking the action:

Self-Changing (Environmental conditions): Energy is normally available in the environmental conditions of the site and it is within the material itself where such energy is transformed into particular kinds of movement (See Local-Inner control). The energy sources may be related to differential humidity or temperature levels.

Direct External Input: In this case material deformation is provoked by an artificially controlled force, either on the surface of the material itself or externally, and may be caused by electrical current, a fluid in movement or an external source of movement.

7.2   Control

The control component was spread into two main groups, Local and Central. Here, the first one implies that each actuator is autonomous, either by being linked to an exclusive sensor-control system, or by information embedded in the material itself. The second category implies any group of actuators linked to a single control system whose internal processes may have different degrees of complexity, here classified into three levels. It may be interesting to note other classifications of control like that of Loonen ([29], p. 488), where control is primarily classified into Extrinsic and Intrinsic, the first one implying Distributed and Centralised categories similar to the ones discussed here. We assume that intrinsic control is always local, and prefer not to mix the control category to that of movement, where the environmental conditions to which the material or component is subject are key.

7.2.1   Local

We use the name local instead of distributed because the latter may imply an important degree of subjectivity due to the relativeness of scale. By local we mean the scale of the actual minimum component or piece of material that is subject to movement, whilst any grouping of such components under the same control unit will qualify in the category of centrally controlled systems. A further sub-categorisation is given not by scale but by type of control as Inner and Direct:

Inner (Material): This refers to a behaviour that is embedded in the material itself, that is, its inner configuration, which implies certain rules to react against external conditions. In the examples, it is necessary to have an anisotropic material, either at molecular or macro levels (see Self-change movement).

Direct (Sensor-Micro): This refers to artificial i.e. external control systems controlling the component, commonly a sensor, microprocessor and actuator within the actual component, and with no relation to other components or systems.

7.2.2 Central Control

Central control may refer to different scales, but always implies a number of components being directed by a single logical unit (processor). Normally, we would be talking of the scale of the room or space that the façade is covering (the case for illumination levels as division walls are not normally light transmitting). Three subcategories are proposed according to the complexity of the processes carried on within the logic unit or processor:

Level 1 (Direct): The lowest degree of complexity refers to a system where all the responses are straightforwardly pre-programmed in the logic unit, that is, without the need of external inputs (sensors), even if user overriding or regulation is possible.

Level 2 (Reactive): The second degree of complexity refers to sensor-based behaviour at its simplest level, that is, a deterministic (predictable) system built on the repetitive use of Boolean expressions to yield decisions at different levels.

Level 3 (System based): This last degree of complexity implies significant data processing inside the control component as to be able to solve complex problems by using exploration strategies with either multi-deterministic or stochastic processes normally implying heuristic methods. Although the possibilities of this type are multiple, they are represented in our chart by three particular bio-inspired computational processes: Cellular Automata, Evolutionary Algorithms and Artificial Neural Networks. A caveat shall be made here, for if the use of this degree of complexity is compulsory for most complex problem solving -particularly multi-objective optimization- the real-time implementation of such processes may be prohibitive with current available hardware.

8   Conclusions

At the moment the developments of dynamic (kinetic) facades, though diverse, are most commonly linked to movement definitions (rotation and translation) and classified as systems integrating those two definitions (Diaphragm systems, Pivoting systems, Telescopic systems, Scissor systems, Folding plate systems and Umbrella type systems among others). The review of case studies as well as the book *Interactive Architecture* leads us to believe that a more inclusive classification system for high performing dynamic facades should be considered. Here, instead of basing the understanding of dynamic facades on particular mechanical systems, we propose a more bottom-up classification that takes into account generic operational factors, not only mechanical ones, but also embrace other types of movement, and most importantly, include control factors, which we consider fundamental[2] in the design and operation of functionally oriented Dynamic facades.

---

[2] Following the logic of any artificial dynamic system as composed of sensor, control and actuator devices, in this study we would give most importance to the control component, firstly because ifs the are directly linked to computation, and secondly because is the least explored within the subject of kinetic facades.

Based on the literature review carried out in terms of research and developments in practice, we can attest that the field of dynamic façade systems for high performance environmental solutions is far from mature, yet growing steadily and will most likely continue to do so. There are two main reasons for such growth: On the one hand, the need for better performing environmental systems to help cope with the current environmental crisis, and on the other, the relatively recent advent and popularization of computational tools and electronic devices that allow for the design and control of dynamic systems. In this context, the proposed classification may help build and consolidate the understanding of dynamic façade systems. The recommendation for future research would include an in-depth analysis of built work, including interviews with the designers that focus on the decisions made regarding the computational design of control. This study should also include post-occupancy evaluation and assessment of performance to better aid the next generation of dynamic façade designers.

Acknowledgements. The authors wish to thank Nicolas Arias for the great effort in developing the diagrams that illustrate the functionality of the case study projects.

References

1. http://www.hoberman.com/insights.html
2. Moloney, J.: Designing Kinetics for Architectural Facades: State Change. Routledge, Abingdon, Oxon [England], New York (2011)
3. Kronenburg, R.: Flexible: Architecture that Responds to Change. Laurence King, London (2007)
4. http://www.c2es.org/technology/factsheet/BuildingEnvelope
5. Kolarevic, B., Malkawi, A.: Performative Architecture: Beyond Instrumentality. Spon Press of the Taylor & Francis Group, New York (2005)
6. Aksamija, A.: Sustainable Facades: Design Methods for High-performance Building Envelopes. Wiley, Hoboken (2013)
7. Vassigh, S., Chandler, J.R.: Building Systems Integration for Enhanced Environmental Performance. J. Ross Publishing, Fort Lauderdale (2011)
8. Keeler, M., Burke, B.: Fundamentals of Integrated Design for Sustainable Building. Wiley, New York (2009)
9. Yudelson, J., Meyer, U.: The World's Greenest Buildings: Promise versus Performance in Sustainable Design. Routledge/Taylor & Francis Group, New York (2013)
10. Maclay, W.: The New Net Zero: Leading-edge Design and Construction of Homes and Buildings for a Renewable Energy Future. Chelsea Green, White River Junction (2014)
11. Voss, K., Musall, E.: Net Zero Energy Buildings. Detail Green Books, GmbH: DETAIL, Munich (2013)
12. Hensel, M.: Performance-oriented Architecture: Rethinking Architectural Design and the Built Environment. Wiley, Print. AD Primer, London (2013)
13. Schumacher, M., Schaeffer, O., Vogt, M.: Move: Architecture in Motion – Dynamic Componenets and Elements. Birkhäuser, Berlin (2010)
14. Escrig, F., Sanchez, J.: New Proposals for Transformable Architecture, Engineering and Design. Starbooks, Seville (2013)
15. Stevenson, C.: Morphological principles of kinetic architectural structures. In: Adaptive Architecture Conference Proceedings, pp. 1–12 (2011)

16. Loonen, R.: Climate adaptive building shells: what can we simulate?. M.Sc. thesis, Technische Universiteit Eindhoven (2010)
17. Urquiza, R.: Parametric performative systems: designing a bioclimatic responsive skin. Int. J. Archit. Comput. **8**(3), 279–300 (2010)
18. Rossi, D., Nagy, Z., Schlueter, A.: Adaptive distributed robotics for environmental performance, occupant comfort and architectural expression. Int. J. Archit. Comput. **10**(3), 341–359 (2012)
19. El Sheik, M.: Intelligent building skins: parametric-based algorithm for kinetic facades design and daylighting performance integration. A thesis presented to the Faculty of the USC School of Architecture, University of Southern California (2011). http://digitallibrary.usc.edu
20. Thün, G., Velikov, K.: Responsive envelopes: bridging environmental response and human interaction. In: 8th Energy Forum Conference Proceedings, Advanced Building Skins, Bolzano, pp. 317–321 (2013)
21. Vollen, J.O., Winn, K.: Climate camouflage: advection based adaptive building envelopes. In: 8th Energy Forum Conference Proceedings, Advanced Building Skins, Bolzano, pp. 305–310 (2013)
22. Skavara, M.: Learning Emergence Adaptive Cellular Automata Façade Trained By Artificial Neural Networks, Graduation work at the MSc Adaptive Architecture & Computation. Bartlett, UCL London (2009)
23. http://www.adaptivebuildings.com/permea-surface.html
24. Hoberman, C., Davis, M.: Panel assemblies for variable shading and ventilation. Chuck Hoberman, assignee, Patent US7584777, 8 Sept 2009 Print
25. Cilento, K.: Al bahar towers responsive facade - Aedas" 05 Sep 2012. ArchDaily. http://www.archdaily.com/?p=270592 (2015). Accessed 13 April 2015
26. Sung, D.K.: Skin deep: making building skins breather with smart thermobimetals. In: 99th ACSA Annual Meeting Proceedings, Where Do You Stand, ACSA, pp. 145–52 (2011)
27. http://dl.dropbox.com/u/1325890/shapeshift_booklet.pdf
28. Fox, M., Kemp, M.: Interactive Architecture. Princeton Architectural Press, New York (2009)
29. Loonen, R., et al.: Climate Adaptive Building Shells: State-of-the-art and Future Challenges, Renewable and Sustainable Energy Reviews. Elsevier, Oxford (2013)

Automated and Parametric Design

The Future of the Architect's Employment

To Which Extent Can Architectural Design Be Computerised?

Gabriela Celani[✉], Maycon Sedrez, Daniel Lenz,
and Alessandra Macedo

University of Campinas, Campinas, Brazil
celani@fec.unicamp.br, {mayconsedrez,danieulenz,
alessandracelani}@gmail.com

Abstract. This paper was motivated by Frey and Osborne's [1] work about the probability of different occupations being computerised in the near future, titled "The Future of Employment". In their study, the architect's profession had a very low probability of being automated, which does not do justice to the past fifty years of research in the field of architectural design automation. After reviewing some concepts in economics and labor, and identifying three categories of tasks in regards to automation, we propose a new estimate, by looking independently at 30 architectural tasks. We also took into account the reported advances in the automation of these tasks through scientific research. We conclude that there is presently a change in skill requirements for architects, suggesting that we have to rethink architectural education, so architects will not need to compete against the computer in the near future.

Keywords: Computerisation · Design automation · Architectural profession · Architectural education

1 Introduction

Design automation has been discussed since the 1960's (e.g. [2–4]), but despite all efforts, computer implementations developed so far have not been able to completely automate the architectural design process. The automation of the construction process, on the other hand, has gained a lot of attention since the end of the 1990's [5, 6] and progress has been made very quickly in this field.

Work can be categorized as manual and cognitive, and as routine and non-routine [7]. Routine work is usually easier to automate. Abstract problem-solving, such as architectural design, is considered a cognitive, non-routine task, while tasks that require flexibility and physical adaptability, such as construction work, are considered manual, non-routine [1, 7]. Figure 1 shows a categorization of tasks and their likelihood of computerisation with some examples from [7], to which we added tasks related to the architectural and construction fields. With the recent advancements in computer technologies, particularly in terms of making sense of large amounts of information (big data), it is becoming possible to automate many non-routine tasks, both intellectual

© Springer-Verlag Berlin Heidelberg 2015
G. Celani et al. (Eds.): CAAD Futures 2015, CCIS 527, pp. 195–212, 2015.
DOI: 10.1007/978-3-662-47386-3_11

and manual, and some researchers estimate that 47 % of a US jobs will disappear in the next two decades due to computerisation [8].

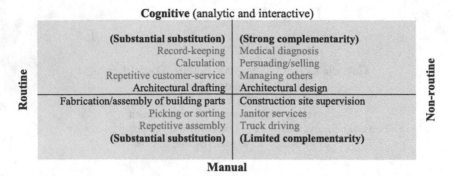

Fig. 1. Categories of tasks and their likelihood of computerisation: some examples in architecture and other fields (based on [7, 1])

According to Frey and Osborne [1] there are still some bottlenecks to automation, but beyond them "*it is largely already technologically possible to automate almost any task, provided that sufficient amounts of data are gathered for pattern recognition*" (p. 23). In a paper titled "The Future of Employment" they have assessed the probability of all professions of becoming computerised in the near future. The architectural profession received a mere 1.8 %, which obviously does not do justice to all the research and development in the field of formal methods in design seen in the past fifty years.

Motivated by Frey and Osborne [1], and drawing on the literature on labour studies on one hand, and on design automation on the other, this paper aims to discuss how computerisation will impact the architect's work. We start by defining some key concepts used in economy, such as technological unemployment, job polarization and the decoupling of productivity and employment. Each concept is followed by its application to the field of architecture. We then describe Frey and Osborne's [1] study about the susceptibility of jobs becoming computerised and we propose a new method for estimating the probability of computerisation of the architect's profession. Finally, we discuss the impacts of automation for architects and what can be done to prepare the present generation for the expected changes in the near future.

2 Key Concepts in Computerisation

In this session we review some important concepts that are frequently used in the literature about economics and labour, but are not so commonly discussed in the field of architecture. Our objective is to open the discussion to researchers from the field of economics and labour studies, by clarifying how these concepts apply to our field.

While **automation** is defined as "*the use of machines or computers instead of people to do a job, especially in a factory or office*" [9], **computerisation** is "*the use of* *computers to do something that used to be done by people or other machines before"* [9]. In other words, it is a form of automation that necessarily involves computers controlling some type of task. The first concerns about automation, appeared in the 19th century, when textile workers protested against the introduction of the automated loom, fearing it would lead to unemployment. The concept of "technological unemployment" was formalized in the 1930's [10], and defined as *"unemployment due to our discovery of means of economising the use of labour outrunning the pace at which we can find new uses for labour"* (p. 359). However, instead of leading to unemployment, the raise in textile productivity resulted in the creation of new industries, which ended up absorbing the workers who had been laid off. Since then, increase in productivity has always been accompanied by an increase in employment rates.

Similarly, when Computer-Aided Design (CAD) software was introduced in architecture offices, at the end of the 20th century, drafters were forced to learn a new skill, or were substituted by young architects or interns. There was effectively a reduction in the number of drafters, because the new system was more productive, but there was an increase in the number of jobs for architects, because IT also introduced new complexities in the design process.

Productivity is defined as *"the rate at which a country, company, etc. produces goods or services, usually judged in relation to the number of people and the time necessary to produce them"* [9]. By increasing productivity it is possible to increase profit. In architecture, a discipline that stands between art and technology, the term "productivity" often has a negative connotation, as illustrated by Benedikt [11]:

> *"The efficiencies that computers afford raise a critical question: who benefits from the increased productivity? I would venture that it is not the architect. I would venture that intense market competition between architects, focused on service for fee and the ability to control costs, has passed these productivity-won savings cleanly along to clients, and that architects have not, with these savings, bought one minute more of their own time to spend on the design or refinement of their buildings".*

Although definitions and ways to measure productivity in services vary, one simple way to express it in architecture offices is by ratio of output (total billings) to input (total compensation costs) [12]. Productivity has been a major goal of architects since the end of the 20th century, and a marketing strategy of CAD software. In the late 1990s, Autodesk's Architectural Desktop was developed specifically to *"dramatically increase"* architects' productivity, by introducing drafting automation. Goldberg [13] estimated as 30 % the amount of productivity gain that could be achieved with this software:

> *"How much productivity gain? Results of a recent study [...] compared times required to complete a set of typical tasks. Results indicated that an AutoCAD user with limited experience in Architectural Desktop could improve architectural design and drafting productivity by over thirty percent using the Architectural Desktop software" (p. 1).*

A recent survey in the Graphisoft's online forum, "ArchiCAD Talk", revealed that "productivity" is the most desired wish from users [14]. For Eastman et al. [15], *"an obvious current goal* [of BIM software] *is to automate the drawing production process as much as possible, since most initial design productivity benefits (and costs) will depend on the extent of automatic generation"* (p. 51). As a result, according to the

American Institute of Architects (AIA), more than half of the American architectural firms have report increased productivity in recent years [16].

Offshoring is another way of increasing profits. Companies in different fields move production to low-cost locations, such as India or China - either to their own specialised units or using outsourced services [17]. For Levy and Murnane [18] offshoring, as well as computerisation, happen typically to "*rule-like*" or "*moderate skilled*" jobs, i.e., jobs that can be easily "*scripted*". For Brynjolfsson and McAfee [8] offshoring is "*only a way station on the road to automation*". Jobs that can easily be codified can also be assigned to lower paid workers in other countries, but eventually they tend to be substituted by computers or robots.

Information technology and CAD software made it possible to offshore design and construction management services, especially by larger firms and for larger projects. For smaller projects, offshoring has been usually limited to CAD drafting, 3D modelling, and detailing [19], but BIM software is already automating these tasks.

Exporting architectural services to other countries, on the other hand, is a big source of income for developed countries such as the USA and the UK. In 2001 architectural activities and technical consultancy were the industry with the third largest service trade surplus in the UK, accounting for around 10 % of non-financial services employment and 16 % of the service trade surplus [20]. The use of IT in this sector is so intense that Architectural services are classified as IT-enabled services in the UK [17].

Autor, Levy and Murnane [7] have suggested that when computers are introduced in an industry, they "*simultaneously reduce labour input of routine cognitive and manual tasks and increase labour input of non-routine cognitive tasks*" (p. 1302). Computerisation has **created many other jobs** that did not exist a few decades ago, such as cell phone salesmen and internet installers [18] due to horizontal innovation (the introduction of new products and creation of new industries). New technologies have also created new jobs at the architecture office, from the IT technician to the computer rendering specialist.

According to Levy and Murnane [18], computers can only **substitute human skills** if (1) it is possible to represent the information to be processed in a form that can be processed by the machine and (2) the processing can be described as a set of deductive or inductive rules. When the rules are deductive, the automation is straightforward. If the rules are inductive, then the processing is much more complex, involving advanced artificial intelligence techniques, such as pattern recognition, neural networks or statistical models over large amounts of data. However, when one of the conditions above does not exist, computers can only **complement human skills**, but not substitute them completely. Moreover, the likeliness of automation also depends on the cost and availability of labor, which, in many cases, is still cheaper than technology.

The application of computers in architecture has a long history. Academic research on design automation has targeted parts of the design process that can be described by both **deductive and inductive rules**, including the early phases of design that require creative thinking. Advanced methods from the field of Artificial Intelligence have frequently been applied, such as evolutionary computation and neural networks. Most of these studies have aimed at complementing the architect's work, rather than completely substituting it. The results have been presented in conferences such as Formal Design Methods for CAD (1985–1997), Computational and Cognitive Models of

Creative Design (1989–2008), Artificial Intelligence in Design (1991–2002), Design and Decision Support Systems (1992–present), CAADRIA (1996–present), Agents in Design (2002–2002), Design Computing and Cognition (2004–present), Algorithmic Design for Architecture and Urban Design (2011–present) and Robotic Fabrication in Architecture, Art & Design (2012–present).

In architectural practice, however, computerisation has usually targeted **productivity**. Since the 1990s, companies have been created with the purpose of automating tasks to enhance CAD, and later BIM, productivity. The main tasks being automated are those that do not require creative intelligence, such as the generation of construction documents and schedules, MEP layouts, clash detection and digital fabrication drawings. This has resulted in an abrupt reduction in the number of technical drafters in most architecture offices on one hand, and in an increase in the number architects, confirming Autor, Levy and Murnane [7] proposition.

More recently, some prominent architecture offices have invested on hiring programmers and mathematicians to develop specific algorithms and tools that complement and enhance the conceptual, creative phases of the design process. Some examples are Arup's Advanced Geometry Unit, Foster and Partners' Specialist Modelling Group and Zaha Hadid's ZHA/CODE.

Bottlenecks are particular difficulties that are hard to overcome, due to technological limitations. Levy and Murnane [18] point to two main limitations to computerisation: the inability to represent information and the inability to articulate rules. For Frey and Osborne [1] the three main bottlenecks to automation are perception and manipulation, creative intelligence and social intelligence.

Architecture is a complex activity, which involves many different tasks, manual and cognitive, routine and non-routine, each one requiring different skills and experience levels, and involving different types of representation. For some of these tasks it is possible to define what Levy and Murnane [18] call "*rules that describe the processing*", because they do not involve creative intelligence or social intelligence. For other tasks, it is impossible to define deductive or even inductive rules to completely automate the process, but the computer has become indispensable to complement the architect's work.

Although the number of jobs keeps growing despite the raise in productivity, its distribution among pay levels has changed over time, which is referred to **job and polarization** [21]. Levy and Murnane [18] have studied the changes in "*Adult Occupational Distribution*" from 1969 to 1999. They [18] found what they called a "*hollowing out of the occupational distribution*", with the number of blue collar and administrative support workers, in the medium salary range, being reduced. During the same period, the number of both lower paid (service workers) and higher paid jobs (salesmen, technicians, professionals and managers) increased.

This change can be attributed to multiple factors, among which are computerisation and offshoring of medium wage jobs [18]. At the same time, computers have improved the efficiency of the decision-making of skilled workers at the upper income level [1]:

"The expansion in high-skill employment can be explained by the falling price of carrying out routine tasks by means of computers, which complements more abstract and creative services. [...] The result has been an increasingly polarised labour market, with growing employment in

high-income cognitive jobs and low-income manual occupations, accompanied by a hollowing-out of middle-income routine jobs" (p. 12).

We can say that job polarization is already happening to architecture offices. In the US, for example, the Bureau of Labor Statistics has predicted a strong decrease in the proportion of drafters from 2012 to 2022 (which was certainly due to the introduction of CAD and BIM software), while they believe the proportion of architects tends to increase (Table 1).

Table 1. Employment Projections in architectural offices in the US

Title	Employment (in thousands)		Employment change, 2012–2022		Job openings due to growth and replacement needs, 2012–2022 (in thousands)
	2012	2022	Number in thousands	Percent	
Architects	107.4	126	18.6	**17.3**	44.1
Architectural and civil drafters	87.9	88.5	0.7	**0.8**	12.4
Landscape architects	20.1	22.9	2.9	**14.3**	7.6

Source: Adapted from the table 1.2 Employment by detailed occupation, 2012 and projected 2022 of U.S. Bureau of Labor Statistics [22].

With the availability of more powerful and less expensive computers (as a result of Moore's Law) at the end of the 20th century, Brynjolfsson and McAfee [8] have proposed that productivity and employment rates started decoupling, due to *"the changing nature of technological progress"*. This has been called "the great decoupling". While productivity grew even more, the raise in employment slowed down. According to them, more and more occupations have been progressively automated since then, with the first substitutions typically happening in routine tasks, with less-skilled workers losing their jobs. They [8] cite Marc Andreessen, for whom there are now two categories of jobs, with obviously very different wages: *"people who tell computers what to do and people who are told by computers what to do"*. They [8] also affirm that the decoupling tends to accelerate as computers get even cheaper and computer technologies become even more powerful:

"[Computers] *can already drive cars, understand and produce natural human speech, write clean prose, and beat the best human Jeopardy! Players. Digital progress has surprised a lot of people, and we ain't seen anything yet. Brawny computers, brainy programmers, and big data are a potent combination, and they're nowhere near finished".*

The *"decoupling theory"* has been questioned by many critics, who say that the study used different indexes for comparing workers' salaries and economic output. They also state that higher productivity results in lower prices of goods and services, which means higher workers' purchase power [23]. But even those critics agree in two things: productivity is increasing, and to secure the most productive workers, firms raise their salaries, augmenting competition.

There is no comprehensive study, at least to our knowledge, about the impact of increasing productivity due to the progressive incorporation of computers in architecture employment. Even if specific data were available, it would still be very difficult to draw conclusions, since employment in the construction industry is volatile and strongly related to the highs and lows of world economy.

In a study about the **effect on technical innovation on the distribution of income**, Saint-Paul [24] takes into account many factors, such as market forces, institutional forces, immigration of unskilled workers, international trade and offshoring. According to him, the impact of a technological innovation on wages varies a lot but, in general, when all workers have the same skill level, it ends up raising their salaries. However, when labour is not homogeneous, with unskilled and skilled workers, and when the technical innovation raises the productivity of one group more than that of the other, then innovations may result in wage loss for the other group, because there is a greater demand of a specific type of workers. This is what the author [24] calls *"skill-biased technical change"*, a possible explanation for changes in wage distribution. Saint-Paul [24] attributes this type of inequality to the introduction of computer technologies:

> *"A key potential driving force has been the sharp progress in information technology, which picked up in the mid 1970s. Research has documented how computers and a number of other information and communication technologies (ICTs) are complementary with skilled labour and substitute for unskilled labour".*

In other words, technological innovation may replace less skilled workers and **increase the productivity** (and thus the wages) of more skilled workers. Acemoglu [25] had already documented the complementarities between high skills and new technologies, which, according to him, led to a high increase in skilled workers wages in relation to unskilled workers in the 1980s. However, this only happened after a short period of wage decrease, which is related to the cost of discovering and implementing the new technology.

Saint-Paul [24] also asserts that when the work done by lower skilled employee's complements that of higher skilled employees, and when investment on a new technology can substitute the lower skilled employees' work, then their wages tend to decrease. This is probably what happened to drafters, who used to be the less skilled workers in the architectural office, when CAD systems were introduced in architectural offices in the past decades. The capital previously spent to pay them was relocated to investments in computers and software.

Hemous and Olsen [21] also assert that throughout the professions, **wage inequality** has grown since the 1980s and automation has lead to the polarization of wage distribution. The consequences of that is employment in traditional middle-class jobs falling over the last few decades, wages of higher skilled workers raising and wages of unskilled workers decreasing, due, as Autor and Dorn [26] affirm, to the *"falling cost of automating routine, codifiable job tasks"* (p. 1553).

It is hard to relate those theories to the architect's wage, due to the lack of detailed data about salaries within the profession. Moreover, the impact of the 2008 crisis on the construction industry can mask the effects of technology in salary trends. But according to the Bureau of Labour Statistics [22], the projected increase in employment from 2012 to 2022 for drafters is just 1 %, while for architects is 17 %, well above the average growth rate for all occupations, which is 11 %. This may indicate that drafters' work tends to be absorbed by architects using automated drafting software. This trend can be illustrated by some chats in job search forums, such as Indeed [27]. Five years ago, in a thread titled *"Are CAD operator job opportunities growing or declining?"* [27], one participant wrote:

> *"Drafting has long been a dead end career. [...] In no way am I questioning the quality of architectural (or other) drafters. I'm only noting these positions have been marginalized in the last decade or so, and many companies on the whole have discovered the need no longer exists to employ a cad "drafter" (insert discipline) because the engineer/architect is fully capable of taking on those responsibilities".*

In architecture, we can guess that many lower paid jobs (such as drafters, secretaries, model-makers, etc.) in the architectural office will disappear, with their tasks being added to the scope of the architect's profession, as asserted by Kalay [28]:

> *"CAD tools make the production of contract documents more efficient and better coordinated. In a similar fashion, computer modelling has reduced the production costs associated with making physical models while increasing the options for their end use" (p. 376).*

New abilities will also be expected from architects. Still according to Kalay [28], the automation of the construction industry impacts the design process:

> *"The advent of computer-assisted construction technologies, and of computer-controlled buildings, promises to have as much of an impact on the architectural design process and its products as these earlier technological advances have had" (pp. 365–366).*

However, it is important to differentiate "building" from "architecture", as today many buildings are not designed by architects and the idea of what is architecture is also changing.

3 The Automation of Jobs

Motivated by Keynes's [10] concept of *"technological unemployment"* and by Brynjolfsson and McAfee's [8] claims that computer-controlled equipment could be a possible explanation for growing unemployment, Frey and Osborne [1] have proposed a methodology *"to estimate the probability of computerization"* of jobs in the near future. According to them, the relationship between technology and unemployment needs to be better qualified, looking at computer development in greater detail and considering the recent overcoming of leaps, which have changed the expectations about its applications.

The authors start by describing the disappearing of routine manufacturing jobs, due to the development of algorithms that can perform well-defined procedures, based on authors such as Charles et al. [29] and Jaimovich and Siu [29]. As a consequence, some of these workers had to move to lower-paid, manual task jobs, which are supposedly less susceptible to computer-automation, while there was also a new demand for highly paid cognitive skill jobs, due to the decreasing value of computers. This is what Goos and Manning [31] have called *"job polarization"*.

However, based on Brynjolfsson and McAfee [8], Frey and Osborne [1] assert that computer automation is no longer limited to routine tasks, due to the recent development of even more sophisticated algorithms. This will soon result, for example, in cars that can drive themselves around, something that would have been unthinkable ten years ago.

While Autor et al. [7] have asserted that only routine tasks (both manual and cognitive) could be automated by computers, Frey and Osborne [1] argue that this could also happen to some non-routine jobs, due to new developments in Machine Learning, Data Mining, Computer Vision, Computational Statistics, Artificial Intelligence in general and, above all, the availability of Big Data and the capacity to deal with it. For that purpose, they [1] propose to "*determine which problems engineers need to solve for specific occupations to be automated*".

In order to do that, the authors explain that they could not simply relate the appearance of innovations to employment and wage data because their study was "forward-looking". Therefore, they had to "speculate about technology that is only in the early stages of development", about which there is no data available, previewing the possible implementation of new technological developments in the near future.

The methodology used by Frey and Osborne [1] started with the definition of (virtually) all existing occupations, based on a data base provided by the US Department of Labour (O*NET). Next, they [1] ranked these occupations according to "*the mix of knowledge, skills and abilities they required*", and "*the variety of tasks they involved*". Then, they asked a group of Machine Learning researchers to categorize the occupations as fully automatable or not. They [1] also identified the main bottlenecks to computerisation, based again on a survey with specialists, who evaluated O*NET skill descriptions. Finally, they [1] developed a model based on Autor, Levy and Murnane [7] task model for ranking all jobs according to their susceptibility to computerisation, based on complex probabilistic methods, and taking into account many factor, such as the susceptibility to offshoring of each occupation, which was based on the literature.

The results were displayed in a table, with the probability of computerisation ranging from 0 to 1. Occupations such as Recreational Therapists, Emergency Management Directors and Mental Health and Substance Abuse Social Workers were the beginning of the list, with a mere 0,3 % probability of automation, and jobs such as Telemarketers, Library Technicians and Cargo and Freight Agents were at the end of the list, with a 99 % probability of automation. Most jobs related to Education, Community Services, Arts and Media, Management, Business, Healthcare, Computer Science, Engineering and Sciences had a low probability of computerisation. On the other hand, most professions related to Office and Administrative Support, Services, Sales, Production, Transportation, Construction and Extraction showed a high probability of becoming automated.

Based on their study, Frey and Osborne [1] inferred that the number of job positions will decrease in "*tasks that can be routinised by means of pattern recognition*". The three main bottlenecks to automation found were:

1. Perception and manipulation (finger dexterity, manual dexterity, the ability to work in cramped spaces and in awkward positions);
2. Creative intelligence (originality and artistic sensibility);

3. Social intelligence (social perceptiveness, negotiation, persuasion and the ability to assist and care for others).

With computer technologies, finger and manual dexterity are irrelevant to the architect's profession, given the possibility of generating drawings and geometric models digitally. Perception, on the other hand, – in special visual perception – is intimately related to the design activity. Arnheim [32] asserts that "*Perception involves problem solving [...] Most noteworthy is the awesome complexity of the cognitive processes that must be performed in order to make adequate perception possible*" (pp. 37–40).

Creative intelligence was defined by Dewey [33] as the opposite of "*routine mechanic*" activities. Finally, social intelligence was defined by Thorndike [34] as "*the ability to understand and manage men and women, boys and girls, to act wisely in human relations*". Both, creative and social intelligence, are very unlike to be completely computerised, but computers could help to manage some tasks.

3.1   The Probability of Computerisation of Architecture-Related Professions

Despite the "*perception and manipulation*" bottleneck, in Frey and Osborne's [1] study construction-related occupations, such as carpenters, glaziers, tile and marble setters, painters, brick masons, stonemasons, plasterers, floor sanders and construction labourers in general, were considered as having a high probability of automation, ranging from 70 % to 90 %. This is not surprising, because the recent literature shows many reports of research projects aiming at that objective, ranging from the use of automotive robots for laying down bricks or putting up structures (e.g. [35]) to large scale 3D-printers, which will be able to produce entire buildings based on virtual geometric models (e.g. [36]). Moreover, Frey and Osborne [1] asserts, "*prefabrication will allow a growing share of construction work to be performed under controlled conditions in factories, which partly eliminates task variability*" (p. 39), and will make automation possible to a great extent.

Architectural-related occupations supporting the design process, such as drafting and model-making, were also given relatively high computerisation probability levels. It is not surprising to see that model-making is considered 96 % computerisable, given the recent popularization of rapid-prototyping machines, with growing precision level and number of materials options [37]. The Civil Engineering Technicians occupation has a 75 % probability of computerisation, also very high. It is just somehow surprising to see that the probability of automation for the Architectural and Civil Drafters occupation is only 52 %, considering the orientation of CAD and BIM software towards productivity, as seen above, but it is still a relatively high probability.

In regards to design, however, they are less optimistic. Frey and Osborne [1] mention that it is possible, in principle, to automate some creative tasks, and that "*some approaches to creativity already exist in the literature*" (p. 26), but they affirm, based on Boden [38], that the main difficulty in this case is clearly stating the criteria for success. Autor [39] has also pointed out the difficulties in automating work that requires creativity and professional experience:

> "[...] we don't have computers substituting for people who are doing professional, technical, and managerial tasks - you know, things that require intuition, creativity, expertise, and a kind of a mixture of fluid intelligence with technical knowledge".

As a result, in Frey and Osborne [1] study, all professions that involve design, and thus required a high degree of creative intelligence, such as civil engineering, architecture, urban planning and interior design, were considered as having a very low probability of automation, ranging from 1,8 to 13 %, as shown in Table 2. These professions also require social intelligence, another bottleneck to computerisation, especially when meeting with clients to determine objectives and requirements for projects, and seeking new work. However, the authors' [1] predict *"strong complementarities between computers and labour in creative science and engineering occupations"*, and they say it is even possible that computers will fully substitute these occupations eventually.

Table 2. Rank of probability of computerisation for occupations related to Architecture and Urban Design, from 0 to 1, according to Frey and Osborne [1]

Probability to computerisation	Occupation
0.018	Architects, Except Landscape and Naval
0.019	Civil Engineers
0.022	Interior Designers
0.045	Landscape Architects
0.130	Urban and Regional Planners
0.520	Architectural and Civil Drafters
0.750	Civil Engineering Technicians
0.960	Model Makers, Wood

Although we understand that Frey and Osborne [1] estimates had complete substitution, not complementarities, in mind, the very low probability of automation of design-related professions is still rather surprising, if we consider the last fifty years of academic research in design automation [40, 41]. In particular, the Architects' category had an extremely low probability of automation (1, 8 %) in Frey and Osborne's [1] study.

4   Re-evaluating the Probability of Computerisation of Architectural Tasks

In this session, we propose a new methodology to evaluate to which extent the architect's occupation can be automated, firstly by looking at Autor, Levy and Murnane's [7], Autor and Dorn's [26] and Autor's [39] categories of tasks, according to the possibilities of computerisation, and then splitting the architect's work in a number of sub-tasks, in order to estimate each one's probability of being computerised.

4.1 Categories of Tasks and How Subject They Are to Computerisation

Autor, Levy and Murnane [7] have categorized four types of human tasks according to two main criteria: the work being routine or non-routine, and the work being manual or cognitive. According to them, routine tasks more automatable than non-routine tasks. Among the non-routine tasks, and "cognitive" tasks are more automatable than "manual" tasks. In a later work, Levy and Murnane [18] have proposed a fifth category, splitting the cognitive non-routine tasks into Expert Thinking and Complex Communication, actions that require different types of intelligence. The five categories are summarised below:

1. Non-routine cognitive:
a. Expert Thinking: Solving problems requiring *"pure pattern recognition"*, for which there are no rule-based solutions. However, they [18] assert that *"while computers cannot substitute for humans in these tasks, computers can complement human skills by making information more readily available"* (p. 14).
b. Complex Communication: Interacting with humans to get information, to explain things, or to persuade them. One of the examples given is an engineer describing why a new design for a DVD player is an advance over previous designs.
2. Routine Cognitive Tasks: Mental tasks that can be described by deductive or inductive rules. These are the first candidates for computerisation.
3. Routine Manual Tasks: Physical tasks that can be described by deductive or inductive rules. These tasks can also be computerised because they involve precise, repetitive movements.
4. Non-routine Manual Tasks: Physical tasks that cannot be described by rules and require optical recognition or tactile feedback, and thus cannot be computerised.

Levy and Murnane [18] explained the reason why some human tasks could be substituted by computers, while others could only be complemented by the machine. Computerisable tasks must be described by rules, either deductive or inductive. In the first case it is rather straightforward to automate the task. The second case involves information processing based on pattern recognition, and thus a lot of data and processing, which is becoming more viable nowadays. A third category of tasks requires what the authors [18] called *"pure pattern recognition"*. These cannot be described by inductive or deductive rules. Non computerisable tasks can happen both in "high skilled" and in "low skilled" work. Although the authors [18] considered that non-routine manual tasks were not automatable, ten years later we are already seeing evidences of automation of tasks such as car-driving [42].

In a more recent work, Autor and Dorn [26] have related their previous categories to lower, medium and high-skill for different occupations. Engineers were shown as an example of higher skill level with lowest routine index score. Architects were not mentioned in the study, but they would probably fall in a similar category.

4.2 The Architect's Sub-tasks

Frey and Osborn's [1] description of architects' occupation, based on the Bureau of Labour Statistics' classification, is very general: *"plan and design structures, such as*

private residences, office buildings, theatres, factories, and other structural property".
The definition of the architect's basic services by the American Institute of Architects
(AIA) [43], includes five separate phases: (1) schematic design, (2) design development, (3) construction documents, (4) bid/negotiation and (5) construction. Each of
them includes a number of services, totalling 14 sub-tasks. AIA also defines 48 supplemental architectural services [44]. However, many of these tasks or services are not
typically carried out by architects, because some of them overlap civil engineers',
mechanical engineers', landscape designers', interior designers', and urban planners'
tasks. All the bidding and construction administration, for example, are usually
developed by civil engineers or technicians. If we do not consider those, we are left
with 20 tasks that are typically carried out by architects. These, in turn, can still be
unfolded into sub-tasks, because they are composed by routine and non-routine parts.
For example, post occupancy evaluation has a data gathering part and an analytical
part, the first one being routine and the second one being non-routine. Similarly,
lighting design, architectural acoustics and energy analysis all have a calculation part,
which is very automatable, and a design part, which is hard to codify.

In order to take a deeper look into the probability of the architects' occupation
being automated, we have considered these 30 architectural sub-tasks, and placed them
in a table similar to that published by Autor, Levy and Murnane [7] but also including
Levy and Murnane's [18] new categories (Table 3). The placement of each task in the
table was based on evidences of computerisation of each task found in the literature.
Some examples of publications illustrating them are provided in the table. We can
notice that most of the tasks fell in the cognitive, rather than the manual, category. This
is due to the fact that most architectural tasks that were traditionally done manually,
such as drawing, drafting, rendering and model-making, can now be performed with
the help of the computer, and thus there is no clear distinction between manual and
cognitive tasks.

Our table shows that 40 % of the tasks analysed can be considered routine, thus
being candidates to substantial substitution by computerised systems. 60 % of the tasks
can be considered non-routine, but among these 20 % were considered to be codifiable
by inductive rules, thus being candidates to possible automation in the near future. We
ended up with 60 % of all the tasks being subject to complete computerisation. All the
other tasks were considered subject to being complemented by computer tools.

Although our estimates are much higher than Frey and Osborne's [1], we are
aware that they cannot be directly compared to theirs, since we have used a completely
different methodology. Moreover, rather than based on an extended survey with
architectural design professionals and design automation specialists, we based our
categorisation on our own knowledge. Besides, the existence of research on automation of a given architectural task cannot prove that it will effectively be used in
practice. Finally, even if we based our list of services on official documents from AIA,
an important architectural association, it still lacked some sub-tasks that are just
starting to appear motivated by new technologies, such as digital fabrication planning.
In this specific case, we know that the level of automation would be very high. But
even if our numbers are just an educated guess, they strongly point to the probability
of the architect's profession becoming automated in the near future being much higher
than 1.8 %.

Table 3. Categorisation of Architectural sub-tasks based on Autor, Levy and Murnane [7] and on Levy and Murnane [18] categories

Non-routine tasks (18) 60 %			Routine tasks (12) 40 %
Cognitive			
Complex Communication	Expert Thinking		Deductive rules
	True pattern recognition	Inductive rules (6) 20 %	
• Search for new clients • Present design proposals	• Determine project goals and requirements • Historic Preservation • Site Analysis/ Evaluation and Planning • Sustainable Building Design [47] • Outline material specifications • Develop details • Lighting Design • Space Planning [48]	• Study zoning requirements and restrictions • Make MEP, structural & architectural layouts • Architectural Acoustics design • Energy Analysis and Design • Post occupancy Evaluation (analysis) • Programming [49]	• Illustrate design concepts [50] • Estimate costs [51] • Produce detailed drawings [52] • Write specs for constr. details & materials [53] • Accessibility compliance [54] • Code compliance [55] • Acoustics (calculations) [56] • Energy Analysis (calculations) [57] • Lighting Design (calculations) [58] • Post occupancy Evaluation (data-gathering) [59] • Produce 3D models
Complementation			Substantial substitution
Manual tasks			
• Make conceptual hand drawings while conceptualising design • Visit construction site			• Make scale models
Complementation			Substantial substitution

5 Conclusions

In this paper we have described many key concepts in the field of labour computerisation from the architectural point of view. So far, computerisation has not diminished the number of architects job offer, but it has almost eliminated the drafter's profession. By taking a detailed look in the scope of the architect's work, we have suggested that the probability of computerisation of this profession in the near future is much higher than Frey and Osborne's [1] prediction. One difficulty that we faced was establishing the limits between tasks in which automation can be complete, completely substituting the architect, and tasks in which the computer can only complement and amplify the architect's work. For example, even advanced automated phone responding systems and bank teller machines have not completely eliminated phone attendants or bank clerks. They still exist, but just in a much smaller number.

Based on our proposed estimates of the computerisation of architectural tasks, we ask the following questions: should architects worry about the future of their employment? Are computerised designs better or worse than human-made designs? What can be done to avoid technological unemployment in the near future?

Moe [45] asserts that the *"'Change or Perish' approach to technology is euphorically embraced by software manufacturers, contractors, and subsequently the American Institute of Architects"* (p. 437). However, he [45] makes a distinction between buildings and architecture, and he believes that most new technologies in architecture have only been useful, on the one hand, for *"couture architects"* and, on the other, for *"capitalist-driven builders"*, resulting in big *"box stores, cheap hotels, and suburban houses faster for less and less"*. Not all buildings are designed by architects, and part of the public does not even think they are necessary.

The present state of computerisation of the architectural profession shows these two directions, both aiming at increasing profit: on the one hand the complete automation of standardised projects targeting the larger public, and on the other hand the automation of specific tasks to enhance the creative process in customized projects for very special – and rich – clients in an inevitably small niche market. The former aims at augmenting productivity and the later at producing a higher value added product being delivered. The former relies on commercial software that requires only training, and the later depends on high level interdisciplinary knowledge involving architecture, computer science, and mathematics. The former can potentially cause unemployment, since it only requires typing in simple parameters, while the later is a good opportunity for those who have a more comprehensive set of skills but will remain as a marginal share of the market.

Ideally, we could find something between these two directions, using automation to achieve good designs that are both accessible and customized. For this to happen, a greater number of architects must be proficient in design automation techniques.

As proposed by Brynjolfsson and McAfee [8], the only way to face automation in any profession is by reforming education and inventing the new products, services and industries that will create jobs. According to Moe [45], the *"introduction of technology in architecture has been technologically determined rather than socially constructed"* (p. 437). In order to aim at a *"socially constructed"*, rather than a *"technologically determined"* use of automation, in Moe's [45] terms, we need to *"reposition"* the computer in architectural profession away from the *"look no hands"* attitude, as suggested by Coates [46]. This kind of attitude was present in the early day of Computer-Aided Architectural Design, as stated by Coates [46]:

> *"The early pioneers of artificial intelligence [...] began to think about the epistemological importance of their new machine – the computer – almost as soon as it was invented. It was realised that the computer allowed a new way of thinking about knowledge and was not just a more powerful calculator or data processor. This led to seeing computers as creative tools for learning"* (p. 26).

From our point of view, the only way in which architects will be able to keep their jobs and allow automation to happen without losing control over the quality of the architecture that is produced, is by incorporating the needed technological knowledge in education. Architectural schools have consistently introduced software training and made agreements with software houses, but most initiatives of introducing any deeper computation knowledge into the curricula have been marginalized and accused of removing the artistic aspects of architecture. One possible way of doing this is by directing research towards the main bottlenecks, such as creative thinking.

We can conclude that the greatest impacts of computerisation on the architect's profession are the change in scope and the change in skill requirements. This points to the need to rethink architectural education in a way that architects will not be competing against computers (a competition they cannot win), but rather taking better advantage of it. Contrary to the view of Moe [45] that architecture aims only at profit, we believe that with technology we can make a shift in this trend.

Acknowledgements. The authors thank CNPq, the Brazilian National Council for Scientific and Technological Development, and the Sao Paulo State Research Foundation, FAPESP (process number 2012/10498-3) for supporting the present research.

References

1. Frey, C.B., Osborne, M.A.: The Future of Employment: How Susceptible Are Jobs to Computerisation? Accessed 17 September 2013, Oxford Martin School, Oxford (2013)
2. Negroponte, N.: The Architecture Machine: Towards a More Human Environment. MIT Press, Cambridge (1970)
3. Stiny, G. and Gips, J.: Shape grammars and the generative specification of painting and sculpture. In: Information Processing 71, pp. 1460–1465. North-Holland Publishing Company (1972)
4. Broadbent, G.: Methodology in the service of delight. In: EDRA4/1973, vol. 2, pp. 314–318 (1973)
5. Kolarevic, B.: Architecture in the Digital Age: Design and Manufacturing. Spon, London (2003)
6. Caneparo, L.: Digital Fabrication in Architecture, Engineering and construction. Springer, London (2014)
7. Autor, D.H., Levy, F., Murnane, R.J.: The skill content of recent technological change: an empirical exploration. Q. J. Econ. **118**(4), 1279–1333 (2003)
8. Brynjolfsson, E., McAfee, A.: Jobs, Productivity and the great decoupling, The New York Times, 11 December 2012 (2012)
9. Cambridge: Cambridge Dictionaries Online (2014)
10. Keynes, J.M.: Economic possibilities for our grandchildren. In: Keynes, J.M. (ed.) Essays in Persuasion Essays in Persuasion, pp. 358–373. W. W. Norton & Co., New York (1963). (orig. from 1930)
11. Benedikt, M.L.: Less for less yet: on architecture's value(s) in the marketplace. Harv. Des. Mag., Winter/Spring **7**, 10–14 (1999)
12. Harding, K.: Changing the productivity paradigm. Des. Intell. (2006)
13. Goldberg, H.E.: Making AutoCAD software better for architects. Autodesk White Paper (2008)
14. Graphisoft: ArchiCAD Talk (2013)
15. Eastman, C., Teicholz, P., Sacks, R., Liston, K.: BIM Handbook: A Guide to Building Information Modeling for Owners, Managers, Designers, Engineers and Contractors. Wiley, New York (2008)

16. Riskus, J.: Architecture Firm Billings Continue to Improve: More than Half of Firms Report Increased Productivity in Recent Years. The American Institute of Architects, New York (2013)

17. Abramovsky, L., Griffith, R., Sako, M.: Offshoring of business services and its impact on the UK economy, 28 November 2004. Advanced Institute Management (AIM) Research (2004)

18. Levy, F. Murnane, R.J.: How computerized work and globalization shape human skill demands, Mit Industrial Performance Center working paper series, Cambridge (2005)

19. Messner, J.I.: Offshoring of engineering services in the construction industry. In: Committee on the Offshoring of Engineering (ed.) The Offshoring of Engineering: Facts Unknowns and Potential Implications. The National Academies Press, Washington, DC (2008)

20. Sura, W.: Architecture, engineering and technical testing. In: Eurostat: Statistics in Focus, 42 (2008)

21. Hemous, D., Olsen, M.: The rise of the machines: automation, horizontal innovation and income inequality. Horizontal Innovation and Income Inequality, CEPR Discussion Paper n. DP10544. pp. 1–40 (2014)

22. U.S. Bureau of Labor Statistics. Employment Projections program, U.S. Department of Labor (2013). http://www.bls.gov/emp/ep_table_102.htm. Accessed on 26 January 2015

23. Boudreaux, D., Palagashvili, L.: The myth of the great wages 'decoupling'. Wall Street J. (2014)

24. Saint-Paul, G.: Innovation and Inequality: How Does Technical Progress Affect Workers? STU Student edition. Princeton University Press, Princeton (2008)

25. Acemoglu, D.: Why do new technologies complement skills? directed technical change and wage inequality. Q. J. Econ. 113(4), 1055–1089 (1998). The MIT Press

26. Autor, D.H., Dorn, D.: The growth of low-skill service jobs and the polarization of the US labour market. Am. Eco. Rev. 103(5), 1553–1597 (2013)

27. Indeed: One search, all jobs: Indeed forum (2010)

28. Kalay, Y.E.: The impact of information technology on design methods, products and practices. Des. Stud. 27(3), 357–380 (2006)

29. Charles, K.K., Hurst, E. Notowidigdo, M.J.: Manufacturing decline, housing booms, and non-employment. The National Bureau of Economic Research, NBER Working Paper No. 18949 (2013)

30. Jaimovich, N., Siu, H.E.: The trend is the cycle: job polarization and jobless recoveries. The National Bureau of Economic Research, NBER Working Paper No. 18334 (2012)

31. Goos, M., Manning, A.: Lousy and lovely jobs: the rising polarization of work in Britain. Rev. Econ. Stat. 89(1), 118–133 (2007)

32. Arnheim, R.: Visual Thinking. University of California Press, Oakland (1969)

33. Dewey, J., Moore, A.W., Brown, H.C., Mead, G.H., Bode, B.H., Stuart, H.W., Tufts, J.H., Kallen, H.M.: Creative Intelligence: Essays In The Pragmatic Attitude. Henry Holt and Company, New York (1917)

34. Thorndike, E.L.: Intelligence and its use. Harper's Mag. 140, 227–235 (1920)

35. Alexander, K.: Robotic bricklayers shake up construction. Archit. J. 12, 37 (2008)

36. Khoshnevis, B., Hwang, D., Yao, K., Yeh, Z.: Mega-scale fabrication using contour crafting. Int. J. Ind. Syst. Eng. 1(3), 301–320 (2006)

37. Wohlers, T.: Additive manufacturing advances: the fast-growing frontier includes metals and mainstream parts production. SME Mag. 55–63 (2012). Manufacturing and Engineering Magazine, April 2012

38. Boden, M.A.: The Creative Mind: Myths and Mechanisms. Routledge, New York (2003)

39. Autor, D.H.: David Autor on the future of work and Polanyi's paradox, EconTalk Episode with David Autor, Hosted by Russ Roberts, Podcast, 6 October 2014

40. Bayazit, N.: Investigating design: a review of forty years of design research. Des. Issues **20** (1), 16–29 (2004). Winter
41. Cross, N.: Forty years of design research. Des. Stud. **28**(1), 1–4 (2007)
42. Davies, A.: Google's self-driving car hits roads next month - without a wheel or pedals. Wired, 23 December 2014
43. AIA: Defining the architect's basic services (2007)
44. AIA: Supplemental architectural services (2014)
45. Moe, K.: The non-standard, un-automatic prehistory of standardization and automation in architecture. In: Bing, J., Veikos, C. (ed.) 95th ACSA Annual Meeting Proceedings, Fresh Air, ACSA Annual Meeting, pp. 435–442 (2007)
46. Coates, P.: Programming Architecture. Routledge, New York (2010)
47. Jalaei, F., Jrade, A.: An automated BIM model to conceptually design analyze, simulate, and assess sustainable building projects. J. Constr. Eng. **2014**, 1–21 (2014)
48. Bier, H., Jong, A., Hoorn, G., Brouwers, N., Huele, M., VAN? Maaren, H.: Virtual systems and multimedia. In: Revised Selected Papers, 13th VSMM International Conference, Brisbane, Australia (2007)
49. Akin, O.: SEED-PR: a framework for automated architectural programming. In: Knowledge Based Environmental Design Systems Symposium of the 7th International Conference on Systems Research, Informatics and Cybernetics, Baden-Baden, Germany (1994)
50. Mueller, V.: Concept design tool requirements: Developing a framework for concept design tool Specifications. In: Tidafi, T., Dorta, T. (eds.) Joining Languages, Cultures and Visions: CAADFutures 2009 (2009)
51. Abdelmohsen, S., Lee, J., Eastman, C.: Automotated cost analysis of concept design BIM models. In: Proceedings of the 14th International Conference on Computer Aided Architectural Design Futures, Computer Aided Architectural Design Futures 2011, Liege, Belgium, pp. 403–418 (2011)
52. Menges, A.: Instrumental geometry. In: Corser, R. (ed.) Fabricating Architecture: Selected Readings in Digital Design and Manufacturing. Princeton Architectural Press, New York (2010)
53. Ceton, G., Grant, R.: Transitioning object orientation into specifications workshop. In: 2009 AEC Ecobuild Conference, London. Construction Specifications Institute (2009)
54. Han, C.S., Kunz, J., Law, K.H.: Making automated building code checking a reality. Facility Manag. J. **1997**, 22–28 (1997)
55. Dimyadi, J., Amor, R.: Automated building code compliance checking - where is it at? In: Proceedings of the 19th CIB World Building Congress, Brisbane 2013: Construction and Society, 19th International CIB World Building Congress, Brisbane, Australia (2013)
56. Tsingos, N., Funkhouser, T., Ngan, A., Calbom, I.: Modeling acoustics in virtual environments using the uniform theory of diffraction. In: Proceedings of ACM SIGGRAPH 2001, SIGGRAPH 2001, Los Angeles (2001)
57. Bazjanac, V.: IFC BIM-based methodology for semi-automated building energy performance simulation. In: CIB-W78 25th International Conference on Information Technology in Construction, Santiago, Chile, 15–17 July 2008
58. Lima, G.F.M., Tavares, J., Peretta, I.S., Keiji, Y., Cardoso, A., Lamounier, E.: Optimization of lighting design using genetic algorithms. In: 9th IEEE/IAS International Conference on Industry Applications, São Paulo, Brazil (2010)
59. Li, C., Wu, S., Xu, R., Yang, F.: A project post-occupancy evaluation system and knowledge base model based on knowledge management. In: Xie, A., Huang, X. (eds.) Advances in Electrical Engineering and Automation. AISC, vol. 139, pp. 499–506. Springer, Heidelberg (2012)

Design Agency

Prototyping Multi-agent Systems in Architecture

David Jason Gerber(✉), Evangelos Pantazis, and Leandro Soriano Marcolino

University of Southern California, Los Angeles, CA, USA
{dgerber,epanatazi,sorianom}@usc.edu

Abstract. This paper presents research on the prototyping of multi-agent systems for architectural design. It proposes a design exploration methodology at the intersection of architecture, engineering, and computer science. The motivation of the work includes exploring bottom up generative methods coupled with optimizing performance criteria including for geometric complexity and objective functions for environmental, structural and fabrication parameters. The paper presents the development of a research framework and initial experiments to provide design solutions, which simultaneously satisfy complexly coupled and often contradicting objectives. The prototypical experiments and initial algorithms are described through a set of different design cases and agents within this framework; for the generation of façade panels for light control; for emergent design of shell structures; for actual construction of reciprocal frames; and for robotic fabrication. Initial results include multi-agent derived efficiencies for environmental and fabrication criteria and discussion of future steps for inclusion of human and structural factors.

Keywords: Generative design · Parametric design · Multi-Agent systems · Digital fabrication · Form finding · Reciprocal frames

1 Introduction

An important paradigm shift is occurring in the architecture, engineering and construction (AEC) industry, one of less reliance on the mass produced to that of the 'infinitely' computed and customized [32]. The shift is characterized through the change in dependency on fordist modes of production to that of the post-fordist manufacturing technologies and possibilities [15]. As serial production of similar building elements become less necessary for design, given mass customizable digital fabrication processes, the types of design inquiry, exploration and production become ever more inclusive of complexity. As data and analysis become more readily accessible to design process, a parallel and companion shift is also occurring; one of a growing interest by designers to utilize performance, fabrication and user related feedback as new types of 'design agencies'. Further effects of the shift computing and fabrication advances have brought to architecture, is that of our ability to model, simulate, and incorporate techniques and theories from biology and computer science, here the incorporation of multi-agent

© Springer-Verlag Berlin Heidelberg 2015
G. Celani et al. (Eds.): CAAD Futures 2015, CCIS 527, pp. 213–235, 2015.
DOI: 10.1007/978-3-662-47386-3_12

systems (MAS). In order to be able to design and build highly articulated and equally resource efficient structures our work seeks to harness the 'design agency' paradigm shift's key features.

The first feature can be characterized by burgeoning access to 'infinite' computing for generation, search, ranking and analysis of expansive solution spaces of designs. The second feature can be characterized by the ability to conceive design solutions with vastly more intricate and perhaps higher performing geometry which are no longer constrained by off the shelf elements and the fordist paradigm. Arguably these paradigmatic trends are in large part due to the rapid evolution of computational design tools such as associative parametric modeling [16], algorithmic and generative design methods [42], and finally rapid additive and robotic manufacturing. Together these features have provided architecture and the entire AEC with expanded design solution spaces and richer interdisciplinary collaboration and integration. In concert with increased integration and accuracy of design models, the increasing availability of computer aided manufacturing and digital fabrication in architecture continues to enhance the possibilities and economics for the production of highly articulated, performatively tuned building elements, systems, and assemblies. Computer Aided Design and Engineering (CAD/CAE) enable architects and engineers to integrate early in the design phase by improving upon model fidelity, ease of collaboration and furthermore provide solution space search and optimization approaches through the integration of simulation and computer science techniques [24]. In addition, the recent introduction of industrial robots into architectural design discourse and processes is marking a transition from job-specific to flexible, programmable and extensible robotic-fabrication processes resulting in additional novel forms of agency, both for geometric intricacy and for the informing of these forms performatively. With these contemporary design technologies – parametric modeling, multidisciplinary design optimization (MDO), agent based simulation, and robotic and rapid additive manufacturing – architecture is realizing the potential to harness and manage complexity through distributed design models rather than reducing via an over reliance on simplistic and deterministic models. The design complexity our research addresses includes the coupling of human, spatial, environmental, structural, material and emergent behaviors. This is achieved in large part within simulations used in design practice for evaluating different performance factors such as cost, environmental and structural efficiency, as well as social utility [44].

Our research presents an evolution of the work from parametric design and MDO through to Multi-Agent Systems (MAS) for use in architectural design. The research investigates the affordances and convergences between architectural form generation – parametric and generative, digital fabrication, and multi-objective optimization and search. It does so with an interest in complex geometry and complexly coupled objective functions for generating intricate and articulated performance for architecture. The primary objective of the work is to introduce and test a hypothesis that a MAS framework can lead to informed and improved design process and architectural outcomes without a reduction in terms of inputs used and their geometric outcomes. The inputs include user, environmental, structural, and fabrications parameters, constraints and objectives. Our vision is of an integrated approach for architectural design where multi-agent algorithms are combined with parametric models to coordinate and negotiate for improved design decion making. The paper presents a developing framework and series of experimental studies to benchmark and test the vision. We started by exploring and optimizing the design of building envelopes by aggregating the opinions of multiple agents through voting [27], and in this paper we further elaborate on the agent algorithms and fabrication of window panels and funicular shell structures. The sequence of experiments illustrate research tasks including framework definition, form finding, algorithm design, simulation, the future use of immersive virtual environments (IVE) for data capture and digital fabrication for one to one construction. Their combination serve as a proof of concept of the framework in its current form and lay the foundation for further research steps, which include performance evaluation, multi-objective optimization, and further refinement and development of multi-agent algorithms for design.

1.1 Design Research Contexts

Our work is focused on the architectural cases of shell structures and façade panels. These are chosen in order to measure impact upon indoor environmental and social conditions as well as for criteria of structural performance and fabrication due to the geometric complexity and structural logics shell structures engender.

Historically, empirical methods allowed for the calculation of funicular shells, while building techniques emerged and developed alongside in order to master the geometric complexity of such forms [12]. In the 20th century, digital technologies and new materials rendered such traditional techniques virtually obsolete. However, designers and engineers such as Felix Candela, Pier Luigi Nervi, Antoni Gaudi, Frei Otto, and Heinz Isler, Erwin Hauer provide precedent and inspiration for the framework. Through innovating physical and empirical testing and form finding methods these pioneers proved ability to build a wide variety of efficient and yet geometrically complex and multipurpose shell structures and panel systems [1, 26]. The contemporary advancements in computation and the capability to model and analyze complex non-Euclidean geometries has brought about the resurgence of interest in their methods and the related traditional techniques.

In our research, we explore not only computational design approaches for generating such structures and systems, but we also study actual fabrication through 3D printing and automated robotic construction. The other test case is that of non-structural building components and in particular geometries for tiling the envelope components for the purpose of enhancing environmental conditioning (i.e., generating window panels). Our interest in the second design context is in part predicated on the ability to measure human subjects and their behavior to indoor environmental factors through immersive virtual environments (IVEs), for gathering real world data to be used in our multi-agent system simulations.

The motivation of this research is in part a reaction to the disconnect between digital techniques and algorithms for designing with complexity that produces geometric performance, and that of analogue fabrication and materiality [21]. While there is research to integrate structural and environmental performance feedback through simulations [38] our work looks to advance this discourse through the development of multi-agent algorithms. Furthermore, new possibilities for rediscovering the potential of designing efficient shell structures by revisiting traditional structural techniques is becoming possible [37]. Along with the challenges of developing methods to work with complexity for articulating geometry our work also seeks optimizations in these structures and systems that minimize their environmental impact while incorporating the dynamics of human behavior and preferences. Finally the work looks to full scale prototyping as a means to provide further tangible value to architecture through demonstrating the links to fabrication and tectonics.

2 Literature Review

To provide background to the research an overview of contemporary computational tools and techniques for form finding, for performance evaluation, shell structures, as well as precedents and literature influential to our MAS framework is presented. Work related to the development of our framework including precedents from immersive virtual reality (IVE) and digital prototyping and robotic fabrication workflows are also highlighted and gaps are introduced.

2.1 Form Finding Tools and Techniques

The structurally efficient free-form design challenge lies in determining the 'right' structural shape that will resist loads within its surface without the need for extra structural systems. Of all traditional structural design parameters such as material choice, section profiles, node type, global geometry and support conditions, the global geometry predominantly dictates whether a curved surface will be stable, safe and stiff. Precedent work in the field includes the works of Gaudi, Nervi, Candela, Xenakis. Otto and contemporary work from Ochsendorf, Block, and Sasaki, to name but a few [1, 10, 33]. As just one example from these precedents Heinz Isler made extensive use and analysis of physical scale models, which were cast in plaster upside down, and then scaled to full size. Isler believed that physical models built physically ensure a more holistic simulation of the problem although they posed the ensuing challenges of accuracy and scalability of material and mass.

In part inspired by Gaudi's physical hanging chain models, work at MIT introduced the use of particle spring systems for simulating the behavior of hanging chain models digitally for finding structural forms composed of only axial forcers [11, 16]. Another critical precedent is the work of Daniel Piker who introduced an intuitive visual scripting tool, Kangaroo that enables digital form finding. Kangaroo, a non-linear "physics based" engine, is embedded directly within the Rhinoceros-Grasshopper computer-aided design (CAD) environment, enabling geometric forms to be shaped by material properties, applied forces and interacted with in real time. By embedding rapid iteration and simulation in the early-stage design process, Kangaroo allows for a faster feedback loop between modification of design and engineering analyses [31]. This is particularly useful for the design of structures involving large deformations of material from their rest state, such as tensile membranes, bent-timber grid shells and inflatable structures. Kangaroo can also be applied to the interactive optimization of geometric and aesthetic qualities that may not themselves be intrinsically physical.

Another research group lead by Philippe Block has developed a structural form finding software package -Rhinovault- that implements the Thrust Network Approach (TNA) to create and explore compression-only structures. It uses projective geometry, duality theory and linear optimization, and provides a graphical and intuitive method, for adopting the advantages of graphic statics, for three-dimensional problems [5]. Rhinovault, is based on relationships between form and forces expressed through diagrams that are linked through simple geometric constraints: a form diagram, representing the geometry of the structure, reaction forces and applied loads, and a force diagram, representing both global and local equilibrium of forces acting on and in the structure [43]. Rhinovault takes advantage of the relations between force equilibrium and three-dimensional forms and explicitly represents them by geometrically linking form and force diagram.

From these precedents we observe an evolution from physical simulation methods and historical form finding techniques to a series of contemporary form finding tools that implement contemporary mathematical models and digital simulations for computing and analyzing form. We note that in the case of TNA, linear optimization is used whereas in the case of Kangaroo the geometry optimization is non-linear. Moreover TNA's reduction of the problem into two dimensions offers a more efficient computational model for computing the force distribution.

2.2 Historical Building Techniques

Key characteristics of two precedent traditional building techniques, that of stereotomy and that of reciprocal frames, are described in brief in terms of how they can inform the agent behaviors as well as for their potential use in a robotic manufacturing context. Both techniques are of particular interest given the challenge they bring to the motivation for enhancing geometric and performative intricacy and complexity. Our research is in part motivated by these techniques which we conjecture within a MAS framework offer new possibilities for the conceptualization, materialization, and optimizations of shell structures and highly articulated building envelopes.

2.2.1 Reciprocal Frames

The reciprocal frame is a three-dimensional structure consisting of mutually supporting sloping beams placed in a closed circuit [23]. It is a structural system, formed by a number of short bars that are connected using friction only. Most importantly, the reciprocal frame can span many times the length of the individual bars [30]. The application of the reciprocity principle requires: (a) the presence of at least two elements allowing the generation of forced interactions; (b) that each element of the assembly supports and is supported by another one; and (c) that every supported element meets its support along the span and never at the vertices in order to avoid the generation of a space grid with pin joints. Structures that conform with the above requirements are called 'reciprocal' [34].

2.2.2   Stereotomy

Stereotomy is the technique of processing solids such as stone, to build vaulted architectural systems. The word stereotomy or 'cutting solids' appears in 1644 and per Jacques Curabelle represented the cultured abstraction of something handed down through the centuries as "the art of the geometrical line" [14]. By carefully examining the principles of the stereotomic discipline, stereotomy is regulated by three distinctive and invariant principles: (a) *Pre-figurative invariant*: the subdivision capacity in appropriate sections of a vaulted system; (b) *Technical/geometric invariant*: the capacity of geometric definition of an architectural system and the related structural components (ashlars) through its realization constraints (projective technique and cutting technique); and (c) *Static invariant*: the capacity of providing static balance of the architectural system through dry-stone jointing (graphic and mechanic static of rigid structures). According to these three principles, capable of being variously ordered, one can discriminate between general stone architectures and stereotomic ones [14].

Stereotomy and reciprocal frames represent two building techniques, which take advantage of local resources and material capacities. Their technical complexity led to near extinction in architecture after the introduction of fordist standardization and the dominance of concrete and steel. Recent research has shown that the application of robotic manufacturing and digital fabrication can be appropriated to offer an opportunity to reconsider them in a computational context [22]. Recent developments in digital fabrication processes allow for the generation and materialization of complex information driven geometries as is seen in the work of M. Burry, G. Epps, W. McGee and A. Menges to list a few [8, 20, 29, 41].

2.3   Multi-agent Systems for Integrated Design

Multi Agent Systems (MAS) and agent based modeling (ABM) techniques are becoming an avenue for exploring non-linear, emergent, and behavioral modeling in architecture. Exemplary real world problems where agent based approaches have been implemented involve open systems whose main characteristics are that the structure, often described through their network topology, is capable of dynamically changing and their components are not know in advance. De Loach, who introduced the Multi agent Systems Engineering (MaSE) methodology, uses a number of graphically based models to describe system goals, agent types and behaviors and argues that most of the current research related to intelligent agents has focused on the capabilities and structure of individual agents which is not sufficient enough for solving more complex, more realistic and large scale problems. He argues, in order to solve such problems, these agents must work cooperatively with other agents and in a heterogeneous environment [11]. Sycara suggests that if we assume a problem domain, that is particularly complex, large or unpredictable, such as architecture, then it can be reasonably addressed by developing a number of functionally specific and modular components (agents) that are programmed to solve a particular task [40].

Recent research in the field of Artificial Intelligence has tested a theoretical model, which suggests that voting across agents can provide a higher number of optimal solutions for complex design problems. This model has been applied in an architectural context with the aim to provide designers with higher ranking design alternatives in the early design stages [27]. Despite the extensive precedents on MAS in the fields of software engineering and computer science in general, the introduction of ABM and MAS in architectural design is albeit relatively recent and has mostly focused on generating complex self-organizing geometry through the implementation of a limited set of algorithms. The body of precedents include both researchers/research units and practitioner's whose work is predominantly based on Craig Reynolds' flocking algorithm [3, 15, 36, 39]. These precedents have mostly focused on the generative aspects of the simulations and not on the impacts of performance criteria nor the incorporation of human and real world data, gaps we highlight and anticipate addressing through our MAS framework.

These architectural precedents generally achieve the geometric complexity and aesthetic but remain arguably still in their infancy when compared to the advances we see in computer science. The applicability of ABMs in different stages of the architectural process have yet to be fully identified which highlights a noticeable gap, again that the majority of the precedent work has been limited by investigating only behavioral models based on variations of Reynold's algorithm. By contrast there is considerable work from engineering and construction researchers where ABMs and MASs have been applied to addresses logistics and negotiation driven optimizations [2]. Our work in part identifies a critical opportunity for architecture to utilize MAS affordances where behavioral design methodologies are not simplistically a negotiation of geometries but of geometry coupled with local and global performance objectives. The research perceives this as a significant shift from the direct and top-down invention of form or organization to intensive, intrinsic, bottom up, and collectively intelligent processes of formation, generation and rationalization that we conjecture can lead to higher performing solutions without a reduction of geometric intricacy and articulation [29].

2.4 Fabrication Aware Form Finding

Currently there are more than a million multi-functional robots in use and the number is rising. An obvious observation can be surmised, namely that the programmable and extensible character of robotics offers architects the opportunity to create evermore complex and yet economically viable projects. There are a number of significant precedent research teams who have influenced our methodology and design of the MAS framework [4, 29].

For example, Gramazio & Kohler investigate digital materiality and how robotic manufacturing can lead designers to shift from designing standardized forms to designing material processes intrinsically for the non-standard and therefore potentially higher performing [17]. Based on the assumption that architecture is mostly accumulation of material they implement industrial robots in order to precisely accumulate material where needed and thus weave form and function directly into building components. Their research includes a range of experiments at one to one scale with different materials and custom fabrication workflows.

Another example is Achim Menges who investigates how concepts from morphology and biology can be transferred into architecture with respect to design computation and robotic fabrication [29]. Matias del Campo explores autonomous tectonic systems without the need of indexical formwork. By setting up rule sets that trigger a specific response of a robotic system he investigates deposition of thermoplastic material behaviors that lead to the erection of spatial configurations more efficiently [15].

Our review also highlights a growing number of integrations of robotic manufacturing and design exploration methods being developed in architecture. This includes the development of interfaces and of research projects [6, 13]. Critical to our framework is the inclusion of the fabrication constraints and the sequence of the fabrication activities as a feedback loop to the MAS design as discussed in the following methodology and experimental design sections.

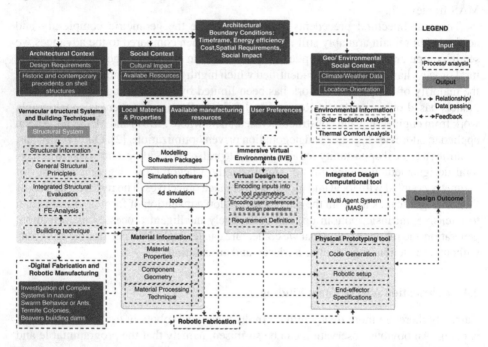

Fig. 1. Research framework diagram illustrating our integrated MAS approach. The diagram illustrates the inputs, processes, design context constraints and outputs.

3   Research Methodology

Our research methodology is based on a series of survey, theoretical, design experiment and analytical activities. It is also a continuation of existing research on the multi-objective nature of complexly coupled parameter problems. The research methodology is an evolution from parametric design, to MDO, and now towards the incorporation of MAS. At this point we are introducing and developing a framework and a set of experimental designs that operate as initial proof of concept. In this section we introduce our main hypothesis and our proposed MAS framework (see Fig. 1), while in Sect. 4 we present our initial algorithms for the agents within this frame work. Generated design outcomes and detailed results are presented in Sect. 5.

3.1 Multi-agent Framework

The research hypothesizes that geometric and multi-objective complexity can in fact lead to novel high performance design solutions through MAS enabled design generation, optimization, ranking and search. To further decompose our hypothesis, the challenge for contemporary architects is an issue of managing complexity and of equal importance, the inclusion of real world complexity rather than the prevalent use of reduced models. Instead of perpetuating reliance on reduced models and exaggerated margins of error in design, our goals is to prove that well formulated parameter design problems can be supported by MAS with follow on performative results.

Due to the complexity of the design problems, we argue that single agent solutions may not be enough, as the development of such a design agent that can handle all aspects of design seems to be inherently hard. Hence, we envision a system with multiple agents, each one responsible for a different aspect/objective of design. These agents could be completely decoupled, if the design "tasks" (i.e., aspects) are completely independent. However, the complexity of design seems to indicate that negotiation mechanisms are also necessary. While in this paper we present initial algorithms and results for some of these design agents (see Sects. 4 and 5), the development of the negotiation mechanisms is still a work in progress.

In a parallel research, however, we explore the potential of plurality voting (i.e., pick the option decided by the highest number of agents) when aggregating the opinions of multiple design agents [27, 28]. However, in [7] all agents are using heuristics for the same optimization problem, so it is still not clear if plurality would be the best option when agents are responsible for different design aspects. Other alternatives to voting would include argumentation (i.e., agents use a logic-based language to defend and/or refute arguments) [45]; or hierarchy-based rules, where an agent would be allowed to change the design of others that are bellow in the hierarchy (for example, the agent responsible for designing forms that can actually be constructed should have a higher priority).

Our proposed framework, however, goes beyond teams of agents that negotiate into solving complex design problems. We argue that dynamic data sets are also crucial. Designs exist in a physical world with complex interactions between the design model and the "real" world, and of course are used by actual people. Therefore, two types of information seem to be essential: (i) Environmental Analysis; (ii) User preferences. Each change in a design will also affect these data, besides their natural change (the light that illuminates a surface changes according to the season, a certain person may change her preference over time or according to a certain task that she must perform, etc.). Hence, we envision systems that not only use environmental analysis and user preferences data as input, but also that continually read such information and adapt according to the current information, in a continuous feedback loop.

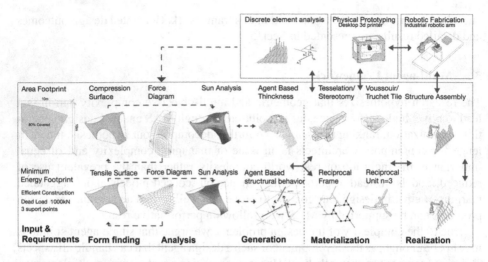

Fig. 2. Illustration of the MAS framework and detailed workflow for the shell and reciprocal frame design context. It includes the design context, form finding, analysis, constraints and rules, agent based results, physical prototyping through to robotic fabrication.

Finally, we also envision the construction of the designs proposed by the MAS system. Hence, such agents would also have to verify the constructability of the proposed designs. Note, however, that this can be easily incorporated in our framework by having a construction agent, and forcing the other agents to continuously negotiate with such agent in order to ensure constructability. We go beyond manual construction and consider automatic construction of the designs by robotic systems (as we will discuss in Sect. 3.2). In Fig. 1 we can see a high-level view of our proposed framework.

We are currently investigating the framework in the design of shells, façade panels and reciprocal frames (while in [27] we explore building envelope components), all the way from design in simulation through to actual construction. In Fig. 2 we can see one instantiation of our framework, focusing on designing and constructing shell structures. We test our hypothesis by applying our framework to experimental cases that measure the impacts of MAS for the structural, environmental and fabrication parameters. In Sect. 4 we introduce our initial algorithms for three design agents within our framework: one responsible for creating a window panel that regulates the amount of light that enters an environment, one responsible for emerging a geometric structure according to an environmental analysis, and one responsible for a generation and materialization of a perforated reciprocal frame structure.

3.2 Immersive Virtual Environments

Finally, we also anticipate using data from preferences of users. In order to obtain such information, our MAS framework includes the use of Immersive Virtual Environments (IVE) and technologies to effectively allow end-users to respond to design alternatives, and therefore provide another real world data stream and feedback loop through their evaluation. Researchers have proposed the need for the AEC industry to adopt the concept of User Centered Design (UCD) by involving users early on during the design phase [7] and have emphasized the need for accurate measurement of occupant behavior [19, 35]. By creating a better sense of realism through an IVE's one-to-one scale, architects and engineers can incorporate IVEs in their work processes as a tool to measure end-user behavior, understand the impact of design features on behavior, as well as receive constructive user feedback during the design phase. Previous research has suggested that these environments have the potential to provide a sense of presence found in physical mockups and make evaluation of numerous potential design alternatives in a timely and cost-efficient manner [18].

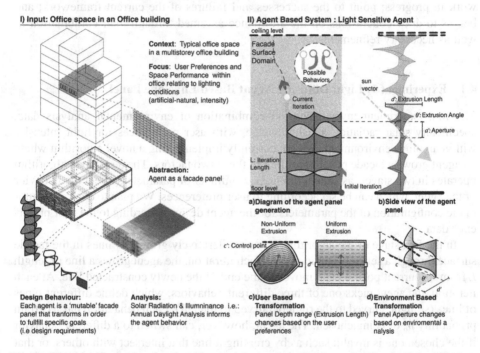

Fig. 3. Diagram illustrating the algorithm and design experiment context for the light diffusing panel agent.

We are working on the collection of end-users lighting preferences through an IVE system. Such information will be used to inform our MAS system during the design. For example, we can use it as a target for the agent responsible for the creation of the façade panel. More specifically, our agent has a set of probabilities of picking different behaviors while generating the panel described in Sect. 4.1. Hence, we can search for the best parametrization of these probabilities in order to generate a light profile as close to the user preference as possible. In order to create user profiles, participants have been recruited to measure their most preferred light settings in an office environment given a set of tasks and options. The integration of the IVE into the framework is used in the context of office environments with a direct relationship to building envelopes. So far the data used in the MAS is hypothetical as we are still aggregating the human profile data sets.

4 Experimental Designs

To demonstrate, test, measure and iterate upon the MAS framework a series of experimental designs are pursued. These include: (1) the development of an agent based system for the generation of light diffusing non-structural façade components that aggregate to form a building envelope; (2) the development of an agent based system for the generation of structural components that comprise a form found shell; and (3) the digital to physical prototyping of a one to one form found shell with agent based porosity. Through the synthesis of the experiments the research begins to; analyze the work in progress; point to the successes and failures of the current framework; and begins to draw conclusions on the affordance assumed through their combination as well as necessary refinements.

4.1 Experiment 1: Light Diffusing Agent Based Envelope Panel

The first experiment investigates the combination of environmental analysis data, specifically solar radiation and luminance, with user preferences for light intensity within an office environment. We are currently implementing a novel algorithm where an agent grows a façade panel according to these two factors. The developed algorithm operates in two stages, as shown in Fig. 3. A number of parameters affect the behavior of the agent, which can be set according to user preferences. We plan to derive an automatic configuration of the parameters for the agent design according to the user preference data.

In the first stage of the algorithm, an agent iteratively grows 2D lines in the façade surface through a series of iterations. At each iteration, the agent grows a line of length L from its current position and moves to the end of the newly constructed line. At each iteration, the agent picks one of three different behaviors, which define different types of lines (straight, curved to the right or curved to the left). Each behavior b has a certain probability p_b of being chosen. The agent, however, can switch to a different behavior if the chosen one is invalid such as by creating a line that intersect with others, or that goes beyond the limit of the panel. The agent starts in a corner of the surface and runs for a pre-determined number of iterations, the starting point and iterations are adjustable.

In the second phase, the lines are transformed into 3D surfaces (i.e., linear extrusion), finalizing the realization of the window 'brise soleil.' For the second phase, the user specifies d, the maximum extrusion length; and θ, the maximum extrusion angle. Hence, the lines are not only transformed into 3D surfaces according to a certain length, but also rotate. The actual extrusion length and angle of each line is given by $d' = d * w$; $\theta' = \theta * w$, where $0 \leq w \leq 1$ is a weight defined by the current sun radiation entering the panel in the position of the line. All these aspects affect how the sun light enters the room, changing the illumination inside.

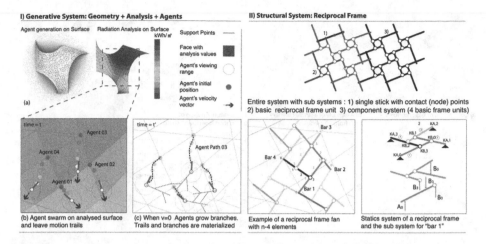

Fig. 4. (I) Diagram illustrating the geometry, analysis and agent behavior of our second experiment, (II) Constraints and behavior of the reciprocal principle configuration and the statics graph of a frame with 4 elements.

4.2 Experiment 2: Agent Based Thickness of Form Found Shells

In our second experiment, we develop a system of agents to generate structural thickness on zero thickness form found geometries. The objective is to achieve gradient permeability of the structure which allows for enhanced light condition below the structure while minimizing self-weight. Figure 4(a), (b) and (c) present our initial algorithm. The experiment uses Rhino Grasshopper and two form-finding plugins depending on the type of shell structure. Rhinovault is used for computing compression only surfaces, and Kangaroo for the calculation of tensile surfaces. The Ladybug environmental analysis plugin for Grasshopper is used to measure radiation analysis on and below the generated shells.

The generated geometries are first structurally and environmentally analyzed (Fig. 4(a)). We, then, uniformly distribute a set of agents on the surface. As shown in Fig. 4(b), the agents move while depositing material. The movement of each agent is governed by attraction and repulsion forces, which are weighted based on the environmental and structural analysis (force diagrams). Each agent has a local sensing radius, and it is attracted by its neighbors and the deposited material. Moreover, the agent is influenced by an attraction force towards the initial geometry, thus allowing a user to influence the final shape. Each agent is repelled by the sun radiation, forcing them to avoid areas with high solar radiation values. Therefore, the agents create a structure with openings in the areas of high solar-exposure, allowing the interior of the geometric structure to be well illuminated. The relative weights of these forces are specified by the user. Eventually the agents reach an equilibrium state, where their velocities (v) are close to 0.

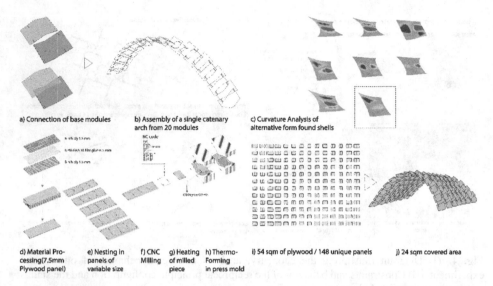

a) Connection of base modules   b) Assembly of a single catenary   c) Curvature Analysis of
                                     arch from 20 modules   alternative form found shells

d) Material Pro-   e) Nesting in   f) CNC   g) Heating   h) Thermo-   i) 54 sqm of plywood / 148 unique panels   j) 24 sqm covered area
cessing(7.5mm   panels of   Milling   of milled   Forming
Plywood panel)   variable size   piece   in press mold

Fig. 5. Diagram illustrating the structural notching (a, b), curvature analysis of the form found shells (c), fabrication process (d–h) and assembly logic of the NEW VIEW pavilion (i, j).

The algorithm, then, changes to a different phase, illustrated in Fig. 4(c). Each agent grows geometric "trees", by growing "branches" according to an L-system algorithm. This is executed for two reasons: first, to ensure that the final structure is connected; second, in our next step we plan to use these branches to create reciprocal frames structures (as illustrated in Fig. 4 (II)). We consider all agents' paths and branches in a voxelized 3D space. We implement a Marching Cube algorithm and consider each voxel where there is either a deposited material from an agent's path or part of an agent's branch as full (while other voxels are empty), thus generating the final surface [25]. With this final surface we will further explore, through the agents where the non-uniformity is a negotiation of structural efficiency, and the need for porosity based on the environmental conditioning, and user profile preference data.

A final step analyzes the method's success for moving from simulation into analogue physically prototyped shells using rapid 3D printing in SLA with light sensitive resin [9]. Here we implemented a two-step process: step one, the geometry is printed and evaluated using rapid 3D printing; and step two, a part of the geometry is discretized using a technique common in vault construction, Truchet Tiling. This is done in order to examine the construction and assembly process through scaled physical mock-ups.

4.3   Experiment 3: Reciprocal Frame Structure from Design to Production

In the third case study, illustrated diagrammatically in Fig. 5 the research focused on combining structural form finding with an environmentally informed MAS to perforate and articulate reciprocal panels. Our NEW VIEW pavilion experiment is fabricated from and with the design of a modular lightweight funicular shell constructed out of thermo-processed timber elements comprised of curved plywood [30]. The reciprocal element is treated uniquely as a notched panel as opposed to the normative reciprocal stick element. Custom scripts in Grasshopper Kangaroo are implemented for the form finding. The environmental sun radiation analysis was generated using Grasshopper and the ladybug plugin in conjunction with a custom Java (Eclipse and Processing) feedback loop for generating perforation patterns.

The perforation patterns are based on behavior of agents negotiating between environmental sun radiation analysis and formal and structural criteria. The sun radiation analysis (which was performed over a specific time period from 22nd of May to the 22nd of December) informs the trajectory of the agents. Twelve agents per panel are generated and swarm towards surface regions that are less exposed to the sun. Their motion path is inscribed on the panels at given intervals and a simple circular perforation pattern is applied on the panels while trying to maintain the structural integrity of the panel. One hundred parametrically defined and form found shell designs were generated from which ten were further design explored based on the constraints of the reciprocal structure and selected material (1 cm curved plywood). A single shell was chosen for final digital fabrication and the optimized environmental articulation. A single shell was chosen for final digital fabrication and the optimized environmental articulation.

5   Results

The results of the experiments to date include quantitative and qualitative observations and measures. As the development of the MAS framework is a work in progress of multiple thrusts the results include general observations for refinement as well as initial empirical data for implementation (environmental, fabrication, structural, and user preference) into the agent designs and algorithms.

We start by discussing Experiment 1, where an agent grows a façade panel. The experiment included running daily and annual radiation analysis of 30 different design outcomes of an office space over a specific time-period (9 pm–6 am) with parametrically varied glazing ratios (20–90 %) of the façade. We use the results of a 90 % glazing ratio window wall as a baseline, in order to compare it with parametrically designed paneling alternatives and then to results from our agent generated paneling alternatives. Specifically, across these three approaches normative, parametrically tiled, and agent driven generative tiles we measure and compare the following analyses: (a) daylight radiation (DLA) in Lux; (b) central daylight autonomy (CDA) as a percentage of area with light values above 300 lx; and (c) useful daylight illuminance (UDI) as percentage of area with light values between 300 and 800 lx. (See Fig. 6).

Figure 6 illustrates that for the same office space our algorithm was able to generate façade panels that provide 14 % more area of useful daylight illuminance (UDI) than the 90 % glazing ration baseline and 24 % more area when compared to the parametric alternative. It also demonstrates a slight decrease to the direct radiation. Hence, our method is at initial reading more energy efficient. Moreover, in comparison with the parametric alternatives, there is an 8 % increase of the area that has a Continuous Daylight Autonomy (CDA) for the tested time period (9:00 pm–17:00 am). As mentioned, the proposed approach includes gathering human data for light preferences, from 20 participants that experienced an office space environment through a virtual reality head mounted display (Oculus Rift) and the IVE.

The participants are being asked to adjust the lighting levels through either the blinds for altering the glazing ratio or turning more artificial lights on in order to perform a specific office related activity. As a next step the user preference information will be used to automatically adjust the parameters of our system, allowing a feedback loop that automatically adjusts the system according to the user and the current environment condition.

Annual Environmental Analyses for a time-period of 8:00-17:00

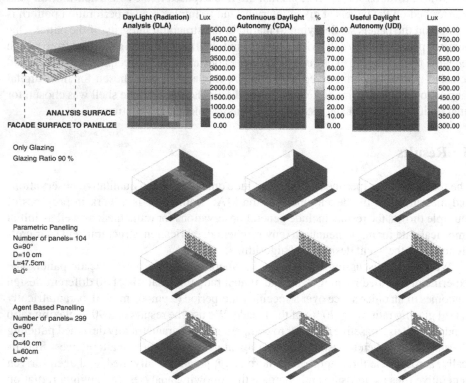

Fig. 6. Illustrates the three design approaches comparatively, normative 90 % glazing, to parametrically designed tiles, to that of agent driven generative tiling. The legend on the left describes the design parameters and their values; *G* is glazing ratio, *D* is depth of louver or panel, *L* is length, and θ is rotation angle of the panel or louver. The heat maps show DLA, CDA and UDI analyses for comparison.

We now discuss Experiment 2, where we generate shell structures. Our analysis of the experiment to date includes observations that by implementing a fabrication related discretization to the shell the agents' behavior can be informed by assembly related boundary conditions for each tile. Moreover, by physically simulating and integrating the assembly process, the research investigates how the assembly sequence and related constraints can inform the form finding process and be translated into agent behaviors. One important result to date is an observed limitation of the Marching Cubes algorithm, which is used for the voxelization.

The algorithm provides us with complex and "water-tight" geometries (see Figs. 7 and 8) that are suitable for rapid prototyping but are challenging to process with CAM software and hardware. However, we could effectively fabricate the surfaces by 3D printing using our proposed methodology, as shown in Fig. 11.

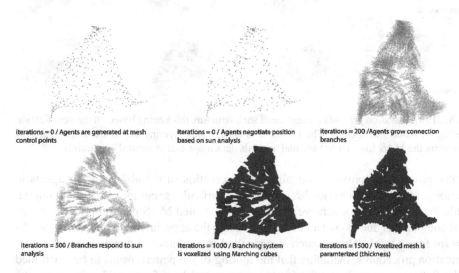

iterations = 0 / Agents are generated at mesh control points

iterations = 0 / Agents negotiate position based on sun analysis

iterations = 200 /Agents grow connection branches

iterations = 500 / Branches respond to sun analysis

iterations = 1000 / Branching system is voxelized using Marching cubes

iterations = 1500 / Voxelized mesh is paramterized (thickness)

Fig. 7. Illustration of six time steps of the shell MAS interaction where the agents exhibit the reaction to the environmental values, branching and resultant voxelization (i.e. "agent based thickness").

Experiment 3, the NEW VIEW pavilion, served as our initial experiment for developing the MAS design to construction approach. The computational results are the development of the algorithm as illustrated in Fig. 9. The fabrication results illustrated in Fig. 10 reflect upon the tectonic and a built set of architectural parameters and include the ability to environmentally, more efficiently shade an area 24 m^2 with 53 m^2 of material. In terms of architectural and constructability performance the free form funicular shell spanning 8 m, and with 2 support lines was discretized into 148 plywood components totaling 5.4 m^3 of plywood volumetrically. The reciprocal components, reconceived in a panel format were 1.1 cm thick and were thermo-formed for added structural performance. A workforce of 4 skilled people for 2 days was needed for the production of the material and fabrication of the components while 4 unskilled workers were required for the assembly of the pavilion in 2 days [30].

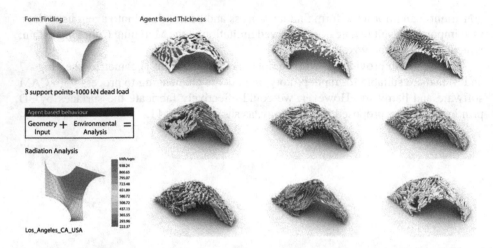

Fig. 8. The illustration presents a sequence of shell structure thickening based on the voxelization (i.e. "agent based thickness"). The resultant thickness and layering of voxels is generatively derived by the MAS from environmental analysis data maps and structural constraints.

The project also provides a qualitative observation of the ability of our agents to inscribe permeability for a complex surface for a particular geography and urban context. While the project did not achieve the fully implemented MAS patterning of the reciprocal components due to cost and time constraints the experiment proved out the workflow for future work. The research also resulted in a number of conclusions for future fabrication procedures, including that the routing of the pattern needs to be performed in the flat stage of each panel prior to pressure and heat forming. Furthermore, the building of the NEW VIEW pavilion highlighted that production related constraints could be implemented as an agent behavior, in addition to the agents' environmental behavior described in Fig. 9. Such an additional behavior would account for the critical issue of keeping the material in place when being processed. Specifically in order to avoid breaking the vacuum that holds the piece in place. Future agent behaviors will include avoiding adding perforations on the positions of the air outlets on the CNC table as well as near the edges and joints of the panels. The limitations of the experiment also include the observation that the generative perforation pattern did not prove feasible given the selected fabrication technique of using a 5 axis CNC milling machine, though were achieved and analyzed in simulation.

This was due to the fact that the perforations would distort the fixation of the piece on the cutting table and therefore made the process time consuming and approximately 3 times longer. Another observation is that the agent's path trajectory was informed only from environmental analysis and not synchronously negotiating (i.e., optimizing in a multi-objective fashion with the structural analysis). The form finding and MAS are being developed to work synchronously in future steps. Finally, though the sliding joint facilitated the assembly it proved to be insufficient for providing rigidity to the structure in and of itself.

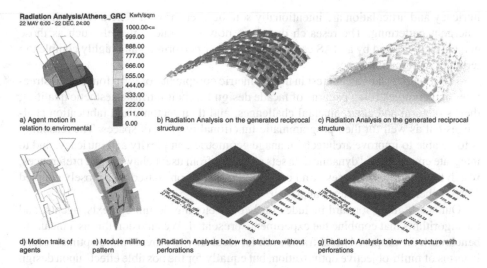

a) Agent motion in relation to enviromental

b) Radiation Analysis on the generated reciprocal structure

c) Radiation Analysis on the generated reciprocal structure

d) Motion trails of agents

e) Module milling pattern

f)Radiation Analysis below the structure without perforations

g) Radiation Analysis below the structure with perforations

Fig. 9. Diagram illustrating agent motion's path on a reciprocal panel in relation to the environmental radiation analysis (a) and the resulting path and perforation pattern on the panel (d, e) and the whole surface (c). The diagram also illustrates radiation analysis on the whole structure (b) and comparatively the radiation result at the ground of the covered area without the agent based perforations (e) and with it (g).

Fig. 10. Photographs of full vault, detailed joint of reciprocal panel and the final assembly of the NEW VIEW structure in situ on a rooftop in Athens Greece, May 2014.

However, sufficient rigidity is achieved when more than 2 arches were assembled together. The research to date has presented a series of preliminary steps taken towards further testing and proving that an MAS research framework can lead to efficiency in the design to production process as well as to enhance the performance characteristics of geometries that are generatively form found through a combination of environmental, geometric, structural, end user and fabrication objective functions.

6   Discussion and Future Work

The research goal is to improve design process and outcomes through an integrated and interdisciplinary MAS approach for architectural design problems. The research aims to provide architectural design teams, enhanced ability to explore forms where geometric intricacy and articulation are intentionally sought after through generative design and emergent patterning. The research questions how un-reduced models such as those generatively created by a MAS can in fact be higher performing and highly complex in terms of material outcomes.

The research takes an interest in the geometric complexity of form found shell structures and complex tiling patterns of façade design for their intrinsic aesthetic qualities, their structural and environmental challenges, and their tectonic and fabrication challenges but as well for their programmatic functionality of work spaces. The reasoning is to be able to improve architects' manage geometric complexity and intricacy, and to integrate emergent and dynamic data sets collected from user behaviors and preferences, which together provide a new kind of *'design agency'*; one based on a closely coupled MAS, cyber physical systems approach.

Our work going forward includes further developing design contexts, agents, and the algorithms that combine the experiments presented. We envision this as a means to benchmark the proposed MAS framework for its ability to provide more optimal results in terms of multi-objective optimization, but equally for the possible effects upon design all the way through to full-scale prototyping and fabrication. As a next step the team will continue; to analyze results of the existing agent designs and algorithms, assess validity and refine; to refine the agent models and combination of the algorithms by testing multiple negotiation and coordination methods; and, in parallel, to find the correct weighting factors and probability distribution functions for making the agents as accurate as possible for all the domains. In that regard, we are continuing to build up a repository of environmental, structural and fabrication analyses as well as user behaviors and preferences. These will in large part help to define the agent tendencies, which in turn enable a feedback between the real world users and simulation of numerous design alternatives, a requisite of design exploration. Future work includes the continued testing and acquiring of the constraints and behavioral definition of the robotics to develop agent behaviors for the fabrication, material, and automated constructions we have presented and envisage.

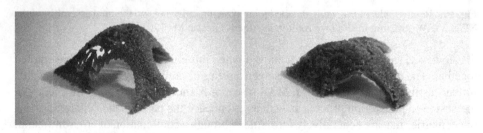

Fig. 11. Photographs of scaled 3D printed resin models representing the physicalized results from MAS.

Specifically, we are developing the framework to accommodate for the form-finding of shell surfaces, where the user will be able define the material and based on that choose either the TNA method for a compression or mesh relaxation for a tensile surface workflow. A stress strain analysis force diagram is being developed to affect the behavior and trajectory of structural agents that operate within the domain of the surface. Refinement of the environmental agent currently informed by the sun analysis will be further enhanced through the collection of user preferences collected through the IVEs. We will continue to test how these agents need to be designed to negotiate their positions in order to optimize light intensity and thermal comfort beneath the structures or inside the building as well as eventually for material embodied energy efficiency. Finally, an agent class will be further developed and implemented in order to cater for the production and robotic assembly constraints. In the subsequent combination of these agents, the MAS will continue to be refined to negotiate the position of the agent at each iteration based on the constraints of the fabrication technique and dimensions of the robot, the structural and environmental objectives, in conjunction with human preferences. At given intervals, all agents will examine the current state of the environment and negotiate to decide their next actions.

We are currently exploring plurality voting, but other negotiation mechanisms may be necessary when agents have different specializations, this is a crucial question and next step for our MAS framework. Work on developing the negotiation and optimization algorithms in close collaboration with our computer science and engineering colleagues will continue. We will add to our metrics of interest questions of accuracy, empirical multi-objective optimization results (as pareto fronts or otherwise), and comparative benchmark, as well as try to measure improvements in terms of design process through the metrics of design cycle latency, solution space size, ease of use and feasibility. Finally, we will continue to ambitiously fabricate the results, as a key motivator of the work is to continue to challenge the opportunities for research at the intersection of cyber (agent simulations), physical (material and robotic agency), and social (human agency) systems, for proving the affordances and limitation of our MAS framework.

Acknowledgements. The work has been supported by grants from Autodesk Inc. and the National Science foundation. This project is partly supported by the National Science Foundation funding under the contract 1231001. Any discussion, procedure, result, and conclusion discussed in this paper are the authors' views and do not reflect the views of the National Science Foundation. We would also like to acknowledge the contributions from Ye Tian, Arsalan Heydarian, and Joao P. Carneiro, Jingbo Yan, Yuze Liu and Rheseok Kim.

References

1. Adriaenssens, S., et al. (eds.): Shell Structures for Architecture: Form Finding and Optimization. Routledge, London (2014)
2. Anumba, C., Ren, Z., Ugwu, O.: Agents and Multi-Agent Systems in Construction. Routledge, London (2007)
3. Balmond, C., Smith, J., Brensing, C.: Informal. Prestel, Munich (2002)
4. Bhooshan, S., El Sayed, M.: Use of sub-division surfaces in architectural form-finding and procedural modeling. In: Proceedings of the 2011 Symposium on Simulation for Architecture and Urban Design. Society for Computer Simulation International, Boston, Massachusetts, pp. 60–67 (2011)
5. Block, P., Ochsendorf, J.: Thrust network analysis: a new methodology for three-dimensional equilibrium. Int. Assoc. Shell Spat. Struct. **155**, 167 (2007)

234 D.J. Gerber et al.

6. Braumann, J., Brell-Cokcan, S.: Parametric robot control: integrated CAD/CAM for architectural design. In: ACADIA 11 Integration through computation, Calgary/Banff, pp. 242–251 (2011)
7. Bullinger, H.-J., Bauer, W., Wenzel, G., Blach, R.: Towards user centred design (UCD) in architecture based on immersive virtual environments. Comput. Ind. **61**(4), 372–379 (2010)
8. Burry, J., Burry, M., Tamke, M., Thomsen, M.R., Ayres, P., Leon, A.P., Davis, D., Deleuran, A., Nielson, S., Riiber, J.: Process through practice: synthesizing a novel design and production ecology. In: ACADIA 12 Synthetic Digital Ecologies, San Francisco, pp. 127–138 (2012)
9. Chandru, V., Manohar, S., Prakash, C.E.: Voxel-based modeling for layered manufacturing: computer graphics and applications. IEEE **15**(6), 42–47 (1995)
10. Chilton, J., Isler, H.: The Engineer's Contribution to Contemporary Architecture, p. 168. Thomas Telford Publishing, London (2000)
11. DeLoach, S.A., Wood, M.F., Sparkman, C.H.: Multiagent systems engineering. Int. J. Softw. Eng. Knowl. Eng. **11**(03), 231–258 (2001)
12. Evans, R.: The Projective Cast: Architecture and its Three Geometries. MIT Press, MA (2000)
13. Scheurer, F., Schindler, C., Braach, M.: From design to production: three complex structures materialised in wood. In: 6th International Conference Generative Art, Milan (2005)
14. Fallacara, G.: Digital stereotomy and topological transformations: reasoning about shape building. In: Proceedings of Second International Congress Construction History, Queen's College, Cambridge, pp. 1075–1092 (2006)
15. Gerber, D.J.: Paradigms in Computing: Making, Machines, and Models for Design Agency in Architecture. Gerber, D.J., Ibanez, M. (eds.). eVolo, Los Angeles (2014)
16. Gerber, D.J.: The Parametric Affect: Computation, Innovation and Models for Design Exploration in Contemporary Architectural Practice. Graduate School of Design (GSD), Cambridge (2009)
17. Gramazio, F., Kohler, M.: Digital materiality in architecture, vol. 1, p. 111. Lars Müller Publishers, Baden (2008)
18. Heydarian, A., Carneiro, J.P., Gerber, D.J., Becerik-Gerber, B., Hayes, T., Wood, W.: Immersive virtual environments: experiments on impacting design and human building interaction. In: Proceedings of the 19th International Conference on Computer-Aided Architectural Design Research in Asia (CAADRIA), Rethinking Comprehensive Design: Speculative Counterculture, Kyoto, pp. 729–738 (2014)
19. Hoes, P., Hensen, J.L.M., Loomans, M.G.L.C., De Vries, B., Bourgeois, D.: User behavior in whole building simulation. Energy Build. **41**(3), 295–302 (2009)
20. Kaczynski, M.P., McGee, W., Pigram, D.: Robotically fabricated thin-shell vaulting: a method for the integration of multi-axis fabrication processes with algorithmic form-finding techniques. In: ACADIA 11: Integration through Computation, Banff, Alberta, pp. 114–121 (2011)
21. Kilian, A., Ochsendorf, J.: Particle spring systems for structural form Finding. J. Int. Assoc. Shell Spat. Struct. IASS **46**, 147 (2005)
22. Lachauer, L., Rippmann, M., Block, P.: Form finding to fabrication: a digital design process for masonry vaults. In: Proceedings of the International Association for Shell and Spatial Structures (IASS) Symposium (2010)
23. Larsen, O.P.: Reciprocal Frame Architecture. Elsevier, Oxford (2008)
24. Lin, S.-H.E., Gerber, D.J.: Designing-in performance: a framework for evolutionary energy performance feedback in early stage design. Autom. Constr. **38**, 59–73 (2014)
25. Lorensen, W.E., Cline, H.E.: Marching cubes: a high resolution 3D surface construction algorithm. In: ACM Siggraph Computer Graphics, ACM, pp. 163–169 (1987)

26. Maher, A., Burry, M.: The Parametric Bridge: connecting digital design techniques in architecture and engineering. In: ACADIA 03: Crossroads of Digital Discourse, Indianapolis, pp. 39–47 (2003)
27. Marcolino, L.S., Pantazis, E., Kolev, B., Price, S., Tian, Y., Gerber, D., Tambe, M.: Agents vote for the environment: designing energy-efficient architecture. In: AAAI Workshop on Computational Sustainability (AAAI 2015), Texas (2015)
28. Marcolino, L.S., Xu, H., Jiang, A.X., Tambe, M., Bowring, E.: Team formation in large action spaces. In: 17th International Workshop on Coordination, Organisations, Institutions and Norms (COIN 2014), Paris (2014)
29. Menges, A.: Morphospaces of Robotic fabrication. In: Brell-Cokcan, S., Braumann, J. (eds.) Robl Arch 2012, pp. 28–47. Springer, Vienna (2013)
30. Pantazis, E., Gerber, D.J.: Material swarm articulations - new view reciprocal frame canopy. In: Thompson, E.M. (ed.) 32nd eCaade: Fusion, Newcastle, pp. 463–473 (2014)
31. Piker, D.: Kangaroo: form finding with computational physics. Archit. Des. 83(2), 136–137 (2013)
32. Pine, B.J.: Mass Customization: the New Frontier in Business Competition. Harvard Business Press, Cambridge (1999)
33. Pottmann, H., Eigensatz, M., Vaxman, A., Wallner, J.: Architectural geometry. Comput. Graph. 47, 145–164 (2015)
34. Pugnale, A., Parigi, D., Kirkegaard, P.H., Sassone, M.: The principle of structural reciprocity: history, properties and design issues. In: IABSE-IASS Symposium- Taller, Longer, Lighter: Meeting Growing Demand with Limited Resource. Hemming Group Ltd., London (2011)
35. Reinhart, C.F.: Lightswitch-2002: a model for manual and automated control of electric lighting and blinds. Sol. Energy 77(1), 15–28 (2004)
36. Reynolds, C.W.: Flocks, herds and schools: a distributed behavioral model: ACM Siggraph. Comput. Graph. 21(4), 25–34 (1987)
37. Rippmann, M., Block, P.: Digital Stereotomy: Voussoir geometry for freeform masonry-like vaults informed by structural and fabrication constraints. In: Proceedings of the IABSE-IASS Symposium, London, vol. 9 (2011)
38. Rippmann, M., Lachauer, L., Block, P.: Interactive vault design. Int. J. Space Struct. 27(4), 219–230 (2012)
39. Schumacher, P.: Parametric order – architectural order via an agent based parametric semiology. In: Spyropoulos, T. (ed.) Adaptive Ecologies – Correlated Systems of Living. AA Publication, London (2012)
40. Sycara, K.P.: Multiagent systems. AI Mag. 19(2), 79–92 (1998)
41. Tachi, T., Epps, G.: Designing One-DOF mechanisms for architecture by rationalizing curved folding. In: Proceedings of the International Symposium on Algorithmic Design for Architecture and Urban Design (ALGODE), Tokyo (2011)
42. Terzidis, K.: Algorithmic architecture. Architectural Press, Oxford (2006)
43. Van Mele, T., Lachauer, L., Rippmann, M., Block, P.: Geometry-based understanding of structures. J. Int. Assoc. Shell Spat. Struct. 53(4), 285–295 (2012)
44. Weinstock, M., Stathopoulos, N.: Advanced simulation in design. Archit. Des. 76, 54–59 (2006)
45. Wooldridge, M.: An Introduction to Multiagent Systems, p. 453. Wiley, Glasgow (2009). 1 ed

ModRule: A User-Centric Mass Housing Design Platform

Tian Tian Lo[1(✉)], Marc Aurel Schnabel[2], and Yan Gao[3]

[1] The Chinese University of Hong Kong, Shatin, Hong Kong
skyduo@gmail.com
[2] Victoria University of Wellington, Wellington, New Zealand
marcaurel.schnabel@vuw.ac.nz
[3] University of Hong Kong, Pok Fu Lam, Hong Kong
yangao@hku.hk

Abstract. This paper presents a novel platform, ModRule, designed and developed to promote and facilitate collaboration between architects and future occupants during the design stage of mass housing buildings. Architects set the design-framework and parameters of the system, which allows the users to set their space requirements, budgets, etc., and define their desired way of living. The system utilizes gamification methodologies as a reference to promote incentives and user-friendliness for the layperson who has little or no architectural background. This enhanced integration of a both bottom-up approach (user-centric/player) with a top-down approach (architect-centric/game-maker) will greatly influence how architects design high rise living. By bridging the gap between the architect and the user, this development aims to instill a greater sense of belonging to people, as well as providing architects with a better understanding of how to give people more control over their living spaces. The paper also presents an evaluation of a design process that employed ModRule.

Keywords: Mass housing · Collaborative design · Participatory system

1 Introduction

Mass housing has constituted a major concern for city dwellers, especially with the increasing numbers of city dwellers, resulting in increases in population densities and limitations of urban land resources. It has, at different levels, become a major topic of discussion, politically as a form of nation building [18], economically in search of ways to provide affordable housing to the masses [16] and using housing as a form of investment [6], and socially to develop community bonds and identity [1].

Mass housing, as the name suggests, is intended for the masses. Participation in building design can come in many forms [27]. Most of the time, urban planners have invited government officials, and even the public community, to be involved in the projects to provide better knowledge of the locals [17]. In the context of housing, there are cases [30], such as Okohaus by Frei Otto, NEXT21 by 13 architects owned by the Osaka Gas Corporation, La Meme, and Zilvervloot by Lucien Kroll, that demonstrate the possibilities of participation of the occupants. However,

© Springer-Verlag Berlin Heidelberg 2015
G. Celani et al. (Eds.): CAAD Futures 2015, CCIS 527, pp. 236–254, 2015.
DOI: 10.1007/978-3-662-47386-3_13

the main industry is still in such a top-down state that the occupants do not have much input in the design process. In conventional design of high-rise mass housing, developers will plan based on their experience and market analysis. They will then proceed with their design based on their visualization and realize it in a profitable and cost-effective manner. In order to provide efficient and affordable housing, modular systems and fabrication techniques are adopted. Developers and architects even developed standards to further enhance the efficiency and fitness of housing products. This has not only suppressed creativity and opportunities for innovation in the housing industry, it has also changed the notion of the home in modern living.

While housing design is being simplified to increase efficiency, family structures have become more complex. For example, the typical 'two parents, two children' family has become much less common [4]. This results in many mass housing designs not reacting effectively to multi-facetted social needs, 'forcing' these people to live in identical units designed and prefabricated for efficiency and affordability. Using old China housing as a comparison, these old houses are designed for gatherings of family members or even entire families. Now, mass housing is just stacked container boxes to 'house' families. Modernism and advancement of construction techniques have also unified design typology so much so that it is currently quite difficult to distinguish the identity of each mass housing building, even in different countries. Architects have been trying to elucidate the desires of people [31] and translate them into design: however, the outcome has largely remained the same.

With the advancement of computer-aided, -generated, and -supported architectural design, novel possibilities have emerged to allow the user to participate in mass housing architectural design. User-centric design processes [11], such as the 'Barcode housing system' [32] are such early attempts. However, their full potential has not been exploited in order to allow full participation and individual design variations of the occupants. At present, most of the computational methods address only a fully parameterized design, i.e., they are mainly generated by a top-down approach and are controlled by architects without, or with only little, involvement of the users. It has been a well-established praxis to offer a housing design that highly engages occupants. These were generated by using non-digital methods [2], and subsequently mostly do not exist in large scale mass housing. Currently, sophisticated computational systems can aid architects in their choices of designs, while at the same time allowing for customized mass production of housing that is economically viable [13].

Design tools, such as Rhino-Python™ script, Grasshopper, and Autodesk Revit™ that focus on Building Information Modelling (BIM) could aid architects in providing alternative and better solutions for housing design. The abovementioned design constraints and issues can be re-examined to liberate architects in the process. By adopting open-source systems and open-collaborative design strategies, this research examines the need to develop a platform for a bottom-up design approach that allows for mass-customization, and maintains efficiency and cost-effectiveness in the housing industry.

2   Open Design in Mass Housing

In product development, open source, as a philosophy, promotes universal access via free licenses to a product's design or blueprint, and universal redistribution, including allowing subsequent improvements to be made to it by anyone [15]. Opening the source code enables diversified customization to further develop the original products to break through the limitations of the initial creators of the source codes, i.e., collective intelligence for innovation and development. Open source has been nurturing the IT industry for developing programs. Consequently, different virtual communities have formed around the source code.

Open Source Architectural (OSA) is an emerging paradigm describing new procedures for the design, construction, and operation of buildings, infrastructure, and spaces. Drawing from references as diverse as Open Source Culture, avant-garde architectural theory, science fiction, language theory, etc., it describes an inclusive approach to spatial design, a collaborative use of design software, and transparent operation throughout the course of a building's and city's life cycle [35].

In the architectural field, the ideas and the approaches of Open Source Design have been borrowed for years. However, it could not yet produce a new practice of architecture due to the complexity of the architectural industry, including but not limited to design, procurement, construction, and numerous other intertwined issues. The recent Wiki-house could only deal with the simplest house solutions, without truly exploiting the power of collective design with participation of the end users for collective housing, i.e., the type of architecture that requires negotiation between multiple users, the designer, and the stake holders.

Open building is an approach for building design that was promoted by John Habraken (1961) and was recognized internationally during the 1960s to constitute a new wave in the architectural field. The idea of a bottom-up design approach is not new. Specifically, Habraken proposed two main domains of action - the action of the community and that of the inhabitants. Without the individual inhabitant, the result is usually uniform and brutal, which can be seen in most mass housing projects currently. On the other hand, the community, which in this case involves the designers, is necessary as well. Without design control, the spontaneous result will be chaotic and disturbing. Achieving a coherent balance between individual participation and top-down design manipulation is challenging, as it involves all parties during the building process, which is ideally led by the building makers, i.e., the architects.

Building design can be divided into three levels of decision-making: the tissue, the support, and the infill. They are separate, yet dependent on each other. The town fabric (tissue level) constitutes a higher level than the buildings, positioned within the town fabric. Buildings can be altered or replaced, while the town fabric remains consistent. The buildings, in turn, can be divided into the base buildings (support level) and the fit-out (infill level). The higher level (support) accommodates and limits the lower level (infill), which in turn determines its requirements towards the higher level [9]. On every level, there is an 'ultimate customer': the consumer on the infill level, the housing corporation or developer on the support level, and the municipality on the tissue level (Fig. 1).

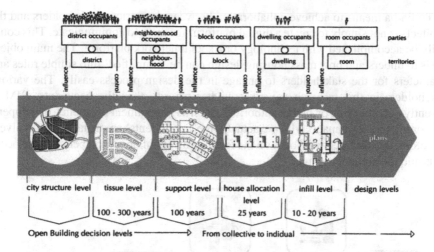

Fig. 1. Open building (John Habraken, 1961)

"Open design" is made possible from the two previous definitions; open source provides information, and open building provides the methodology. The main characteristics in open design are that professionals and laypersons are on equal footing; only then can communication and collaboration occur smoothly. Any stakeholder who shares an interest in the design will be able to influence it.

Open design examines the two main aspects, social optimization and technical optimization, which cannot be separated. "A professional design also incorporates the social views of the professionals and therefore implicitly includes their social group optimum. And a social design incorporates the technical views of the non-professionals, thus implicitly including their technical group optimum." [41].

Mass housing is one of the building typologies that requires open design. The outcomes from the design process should not be dictated, but rather communicated. Much housing that is built by architects or governments is based on past experience, and proven concepts and methods. For example, new urban areas in Amsterdam appear to have come from this process due to the authorities following rules and proven designs, creating dissatisfaction among the residents [41]. Although it is in an urban context, mass housing is the same. In fact, housing demands much more individuality, as it aims to house a single family compared to urban areas, which serve the general public.

3 Collaboration of Open Mass Housing Design

Collaboration poses an enormous challenge, especially in the mass housing context. As spatial preference is very personal, conflicts are sure to arise and are mostly difficult to resolve. This is usually because the decision-making models in current practice are all 'black box', in which the control unit is closed and often fixed [41]. In order for collaboration to work, the decision model should be a 'glass box' instead, in which the decision variables and parameters are open and transparent.

To find a means to achieve collaboration between the various stakeholders and the architects is not simply to create a digital platform for them to communicate. This could easily be accomplished with technology or a social network platform. The main objective is to understand how mass housing design can be 'simplified' into simple rules and parameters for the stakeholders to engage in the design process easily. The various stakeholders in this research are given higher priority than the occupants. BIM is currently only focusing on higher authorities, such as government personnel, developers, and contractors. Occupants who are actually the 'real clients' are usually not involved. Therefore, this research will focus on the facilitation of collaboration between the occupants and the architects (Fig. 2).

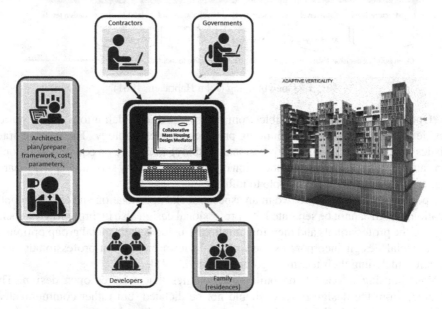

Fig. 2. Collaboration between occupants and architects

Considering this objective, there are sub-questions that need to be addressed. Since the focus is on the occupants, there are some social aspects that need to be examined. Especially in the mass housing context, many sensitive issues could hinder this research. Instead of resolving these issues, this research aims to increase those possibilities. One such possibility is the introduction of a computational platform to engage the occupants at the early stage of the design process to build up the community bond. By setting the parameters optimally, the platform could achieve a balance such that there is fair play among everyone. The controls have to be optimized so that the collaboration of the occupants will not dictate the design too much, which might cause the design to lose control, yet will not be too constrained to the extent that participation is meaningless. In addition, these parameters have to be simplified, such that anyone can easily understand them to ensure the possibility of collaboration. Another sub-question is how to enable the stakeholders to change their decisions during any point of the design process. For an open system to work, the goals and criteria of the occupants have to be incorporated. This must also be done in such a way that they can reach a consensus at some point. Thus, the modeling process in this case has to be 'free', so that it can be discussed, negotiated, and changed during use. This is where the digital platform comes into play. As the modeling process has become part of the design process, with changes becoming constant throughout, the speed and efficiency of computers is necessary to organize the unstructured collection of possibilities.

To quite a great extent, these also revolve around the parameters used. The organization of the design options have to be controlled in an optimized manner such that it is easy to manipulate, yet manageable at the same time. In addition, the parameters must also be controlled such that the design provided will not go out of control yet maintain the freedom available to achieve individuality among the occupants. Essentially, this research actually focuses on the design parameters and the workflow process that could encourage collaboration and enhance data management.

4   Studio 1: Preliminary Work (Manual)

To further understand the possible problems that would occur in collaborative design, a preliminary design studio is set up to explore the progress without any digital tools as an aid. The only use of computer software is to generate the final design outcome. The studio is conducted with 16 students with various levels of design background. They play the role of designers, designing for a group of occupants which is set by them. The duration is only one semester, which is usually not enough to conduct a fully detailed collaboration process. However, it is somewhat enough to obtain data to analyze and understand the needs of the process.

4.1   Description

The studio observed the struggle between flexibility and control, i.e., the conflict of the top-down versus bottom-up approach. It investigated the potential problems faced while designing parts of a building. With each designer having his or her own ideas and goals, the research focus was to monitor their collaboration. Two groups of eight MArch students were given a brief summary to examine the parameters of housing designs that designers would tend to choose. The studio was organized into four phases:

Phase One. This phase was with reference to the open building concept, in which the housing design was divided into support and infill. In a top-down manner, a main architect (the authors) developed a building form in terms of layout and structure, in this case, typical mix-use building with commercial at the bottom and residential at the top (Fig. 3). The latter, the focus of this research, was fragmented into a certain grid for flexible selection and customization.

Phase Two. This phase relied on a bottom-up approach, in which each designer acted as a potential occupant with specific demands-and-needs, and a design to accommodate them. In order to examine how the level of constraints would impact the designers' choice, two groups of eight designers were given different sets of parameters to follow

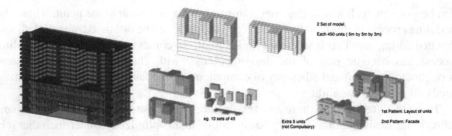

Fig. 3. Setup of the design

during the design process (Fig. 4). In a grid system, the designers arranged the massing units into habitable spaces. Functioning as a potential occupant, each of them had the chance to choose their neighbors.

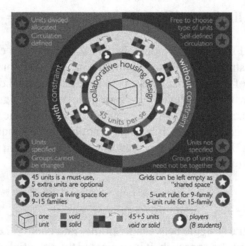

Fig. 4. Parameters for the two groups (Serdar, 2014)

Phase Three. In this step, collaborative decision-making for the unit distribution, circulation and common area organization, and green/planted area allocation were observed. The designers assessed their options.

Phase Four. At this stage, the design addresses the façade part of the building. Each designer had to decide on opening types and material. Privacy issues were taken into account, which necessitated reassessing the decisions made in the previous stages. The main architect would step in to maintain a semi-controlled process.

4.2   Studio Progress and Outcome

The designers could change the constraints as they saw fit, as long as both the whole group and the main architect (the authors) agreed. Especially in the first group with more constraints, some constraints had to be removed in order to open up more space for

Fig. 5. Manual collaboration process from using colored cubes to allocate desired space to spatial plans

Fig. 6. Design proposal of a mass housing building assembled using colored cubes after one week of discussion

more optimized design outcomes. Regarding the group without much constraint, new rules were developed to ensure a certain 'style'. The constraints in each group were then compared to determine the type of parameters, so that the main designer could define the overall building level. This allowed an optimal control versus freedom by which the individual designer's creativity was enhanced.

Under the condition of a plan layout fixed by the main architect, the designers were given a number of unit cubes to fill up the plan. The designers then worked together to generate a circulation such that each space was accessible. Safety and fire escape issues were considered minimally. The basic requirement was that the circulation should reach the core. The main architect then assessed the designers for moving to the next stage (Fig. 5). The more the discussions continued, the more the cubes shifted around.

Problems occurred constantly, as well. For example, crashes of model components, inconsistent plan organization, and issues of privacy due to windows placements occurred. At the same time, the main architect would request each group to provide additional public spaces or to increase the porosity of the building for more ventilation. Physical models were built for better and faster simultaneous assessment. This encouraged another level of discussion, which might necessitate returning all of the way back to the planning stage (Fig. 6).

After every conflict was settled, the façades were designed individually. One of the groups established that each façade had to have strong vertical elements. They also tried more parametric relationships through computational tools, such as Grasshopper, while the other group focused on virtual visualization and physical modelling (Fig. 7).

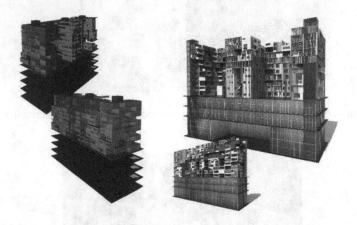

Fig. 7. Final design results of the two groups

At the end of the studio, a survey was given to every designer to obtain feedback with respect to this design methodology. Although they encountered many difficulties, 95 % of them expressed the desire to use this design method, if available, to design a place of their own in the future.

5   Studio 2: System Development (Computer-Generated)

The information collected from the first studio was used to design a digital platform. The objectives of this platform were that the design parameters could be controlled better, communication could be recorded, and data collection could be managed more efficiently.

5.1   ModRule: Mass-Housing Design Platform

By integrating the concept of open architecture, we developed a collaborative design platform, named "ModRule". By setting the best rules and parameters, the modular system is able to work diversely to generate a wide variety of design options for every individual occupant. It is a system that allows the architect to work more closely with potential inhabitants. The setup, therefore, is quite different from a normal design process. In ModRule, the housing design process is divided into four parts: (i) the overall form; (ii) the spatial layout of units; (iii) structure; and (iv) architectural components. The architect uses ModRule to plan a framework within which prospective users of the system are engaged (Fig. 8).

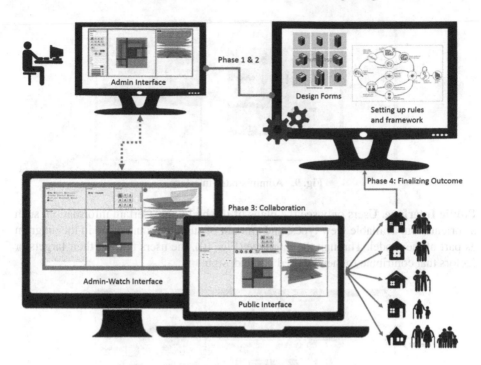

Fig. 8. Workflow of ModRule

The ModRule platform (version 0.1), although it is divided into two main groups, i.e., the administrator for the architects and the public for the users, has three kinds of interfaces: (i) admin interface – in which the architect sets the initial design rules and parameters; (ii) public interface – in which the public interacts with the model to 'design' its desired living space; and (iii) admin-watch interface – in which the architect communicates with the public and oversees the whole collaboration process with data gathered from each individuals' movement.

Admin Interface. The administrator interface (Fig. 9) is where the architect prepares his or her framework of the design. With reference to most games, "gridding" the plans helps to simplify the collaboration process. The architect can grid the plans with respect to his or her plan geometry, i.e., it does not need to be a square grid if the architect is designing a unique housing plan.

Next, the architect sets the parameters of each grid, giving each grid a value for any factors that are desired by the inhabitants. For example, the most apparent parameter will be the cost of each grid. The architect can also set the daylight factor, sky-view factor, privacy, and views. In addition, some grids can be set as "fixed", in which users will not be able to select them. These are mainly spaces, such as the core of the building, the circulatory systems, utilities, and even public spaces where sole control would belong to the architect.

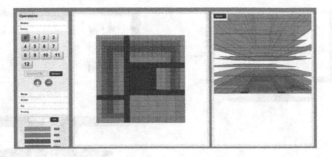

Fig. 9. Administrator interface

Public Interface. Users only see the plans of the buildings. Certain information, such as orientation, available view types, and amount of sunlight is indicated in the diagram as part of the model. Through the interface (Fig. 10), the users first set their targets or factors that contribute to their desired home design.

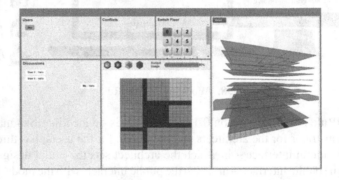

Fig. 10. Public interface

In any collaboration process, it can be assumed that conflicts will exist. To address this, an interface in ModRule 0.1 appears for any conflict that a participant has with other users. Negotiations are then necessary. A resolution of the conflict can be negotiated by referring to the pre-established target values of the participants. The architect acts as "judge" in this case and facilitates a successful solution of the conflict.

Admin-watch Interface. In the administrator interface, there is an additional feature, in which the architect can oversee the entire "playing" process (Fig. 11). The interface is quite similar to the public interface. Every conflict is visible, and the architect would have to consider the targets of each user to provide the best win-win situation for everyone involved. For example, the user with "view" as the first target will have a higher priority to choose units with a high view value compared to another user with "view" as the second target. However, if the former user has already achieved 80 % or more of his or her target, the latter would then be given priority to achieve his or her target.

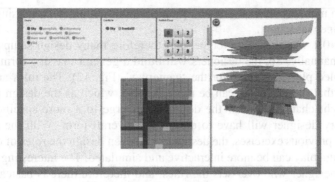

Fig. 11. Admin-watch interface

After all of the prospective inhabitants fulfil their targets, the architect moves on to the next phase, in which every individual user plans his or her interior spatial layout. The process is simplified such that users with no knowledge of design will still be able to utilize it fully. The users will only need to drag the room types, make the connections, and the plan will appear immediately.

5.2   Studio Progress and Outcome 2

The second design studio was conducted in ModRule 0.1. There was no group of individual designers. Each designer was responsible to setup his or her own parameters and
rules. Moreover, no constraint was defined beforehand, so that they were freer to setup
their design than was the case in the previous studio. Since the setting up requires a
certain level of understanding of rule-setting and parametric design thinking, the
designers, MArch students, were exposed to a series of programs.

Firstly was 'Prison Architects', a game designed for people to design their own
prison. Although it is a game, the rules set, the parameters, the design components, and
even the spatial relations are setup very comprehensively for the players to design their
own prison. This game relates to BIM to a great extent. For example, by telling the
system what space it is, the players can only include certain furniture and require certain
amounts of utilities, such as water and electricity. Although it is as complex as architectural design, the way that they provide guidance and requirements for each spatial
type enables the players to design the prison without much difficulty. However, as simple
as it may be, players still have to play a few times in order to truly grasp the whole
gameplay. This is very similar to housing design, in that the players should 'play around'
and configure their living space as much as possible to determine which one best suits
their needs and works out practically. Yet, this is in the end still a game, and the result
is just a two-dimensional plan with agents moving around.

Secondly, the designers were introduced to 'Starlogo TNG', a system developed by
a research group at MIT to teach programming to children. The interface is designed to
be very intuitive, yet the interaction with the system is very rich. The objective in this
exercise is to allow the designers to have some hands-on experience with setting up

rules. To gain more established skills for programming, coding in Processing Programming Language was taught.

ModRule 0.1 was then a prototype, and therefore many design setups had to be established manually. So, the designers will build a general massing form, and write down a detailed plan to prepare for the 'gameplay' (Fig. 12). The rules are set quite generally so that the gameplay can be more flexible, which as the design progresses, the rules might change to allow the design to diverge to a more specific outcome. Initially, every designer will have to design one overall form. With the experience gained in the previous exercises, the designers can even design the roles of each player so that the gameplay can be more interactive and simulated. The interesting part is that there is one designer who over-sets the rules, and therefore there is basically little or no freedom for the players to choose their desired spot in the building design. Not only did the designers set the parameters, the unit types are also specified for every role such that the players are just finding suitable spots to place their units (Fig. 13). The outcome is very limited, and the players experienced difficulty most of the time. The result was very similar to what the designer planned.

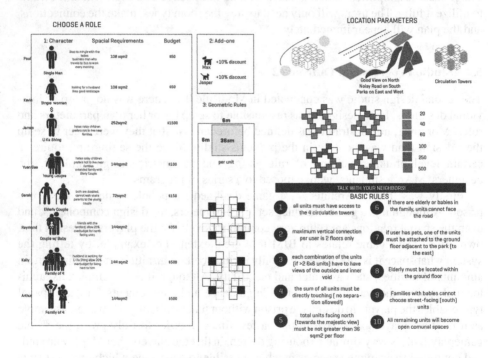

Fig. 12. Rules and parameters set by one of the designers

After every designer has set his or her design framework and parameters, discussion and even trial play is done with each design to rate its advantages and disadvantages in terms of flexibility and constraints of the set parameters. One design is then chosen (Fig. 14) for further development into a full design building. Everyone played the specific role assigned by the designer of the chosen design to achieve the requirement. For

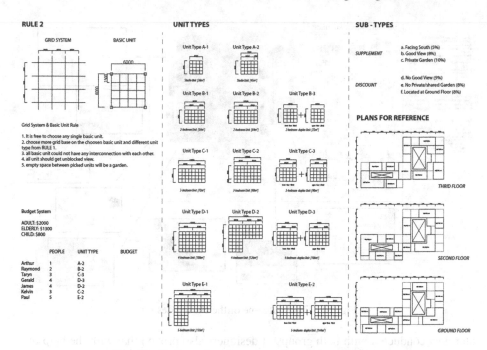

Fig. 13. Rules and parameters set by another designer

example, a family of four should not be located beside a single family who hates children, an elderly family is preferably located at the lower level and closer to the loft core to have better access to the ground level, etc. In order for every role to fulfil their desired living environment, another round of discussions and negotiations has to be performed. The digital platform enables the design to change and adjust easily. The parameters enhanced the negotiation with a clearer understanding of each other's needs and criteria. Lastly, the designers will return to do what they do best – design the units for the role that they played. The detailed plans are then generated from the abstract units to define the function of the houses. The outcome (Fig. 14) was successful to a great extent, as the demands of every role are almost fulfilled.

As compared to the previous preliminary study, the designers showed better under-standing in rule-based collaborative design. The exposure of various games and programs before introducing ModRule 0.1 gave the designers a better understanding of the purpose and flow of ModRule. During the planning of their rule sets and parameters, the designers know what to look for to ensure collaboration and a design language to be communicated. As compared to the previous study, the previous group took a longer time to reach the stage of generating rules. In addition, the rules generated by the previous group caused quite a lot of conflict among each other and a substantial amount of time was spent to have the design adjusted and refined. For the current group, however, although the users only played a role that did not reflect what they would really demand, fewer conflicts appeared, as the players attained their targets and aims. The only setback was that the architects need to have a different design thinking (computationally) to be able to set up the model parametrically to allow this collaboration to work. A post-design

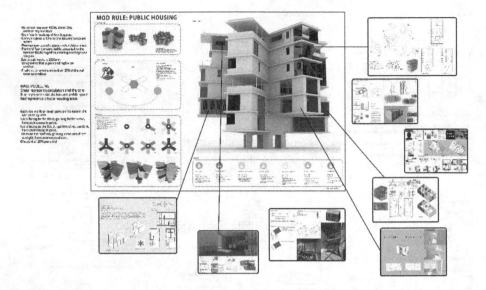

Fig. 14. Final outcome of the chosen design

interview conducted with both groups of designers also proved that with the help of a digital platform, the designers have an easier and more effective way to engage with the users.

6 Further Development

Remote Discussion. ModRule is designed to host discussions between experts and laypersons. To encourage participation, gamification techniques are exhausted in the first version. Further improvement requires these methods to be more prevalent in both their interface types and structure. Gamification provides intrinsic motivation for the players to interact with the system and collaborate with other players. The next version is planned to focus on designing Points, Badges, and Leaderboards (PBLs). In the previous studio work, the designers often needed to meet physically, i.e., remote discussion occurred only at a minimal level. To test the impacts of collaboration from different destinations, ModRule 0.2 will use PBLs to encourage virtual discussion during the process.

Virtualization-and-Visualization. ModRule 0.1 is substantially lacking in visual capability and setting up the context of the design. The current studies are done by designers imagining the site condition. The availability of views, the amount of daylight, and orientation are all drawn on paper and referred to during the collaboration process. Even designers participating in the research studio have difficulties imagining it. One development is to fuse the system with a visually advanced software which relates very closely to BIM – *Fuzor,* which is an interactive and real-time virtual reality visualization and evaluation plugin for *Revit*™ developed by Kalloc (2014). To be able to answer the research question more directly, visual enhancement is necessary. The aim is to provide a much more visually clear model so that the public can understand the design and objective intuitively instead of requiring an explanation of the details of the models, since the public is not architecturally trained and the current abstract building form is quite difficult for the public to understand. The availability of a visualization of site environment and conditions will aid the public to set their desired living condition more clearly (Fig. 15), and hence enable the research to be conducted with much more fruitful results.

Fig. 15. Screenshot of user interacting with model in *Fuzor* – a *Revit*-Plugin by *Kalloc*

Developing Spatial/Parametric Relationships. Last, but not least, our research focus is mainly on turning the rule-based design system of ModRule 0.1 into more parametric relationships. In other words, Space Syntax methods exploited in the previous two design studio works will be enhanced with parametric spatial relationships through shape grammar. ModRule 0.2 will be primarily focused on remote discussion and visualization. However, with the third version, our target is to integrate shape grammar into the system.

7 Conclusion

ModRule is a user-centric mass-housing design platform. Mass-housing includes different levels of understanding. It is designed and developed to promote and facilitate collaboration between architects and future occupants during the design stage of mass housing buildings. But it is much more than just an architectural design instrument; it is also social, political, and economic. Its aim is to bifurcate the decision-making process toward the end-user. The system utilizes gamification methodologies as a reference to promote incentives and user-friendliness for the layperson who has little or no architectural background. Therefore, ModRule focuses on different aspects to translate a design environment into a digital platform and to improve on remote control discussions, visualizations, and profound parametric design techniques. The collaboration tool instills a greater sense of belonging to the people, as well as giving the providing architects with a better understanding and control of how to give people more control over their living spaces. The adopted open-source strategy and open-collaborative design approach of this research developed a platform for a bottom-up design methodology that allows for mass-customization, and maintains efficiency and cost-effectiveness in the housing industry. Future developments of ModRule will allow a better connection to BIM software and a refinement of the algorithm allowing more parameters to be set. The here presented studies have shown that ModRule not only enables stakeholders to engage seamless in a collaborative process, but also that the resulting design successfully expresses the design desires of users and architects leading to a novel architecture.

References

1. Bauer, C.: Social questions in housing and community planning. J. Soc. Issues 7(1–2), 1–34 (1951)
2. Bech-Danielsen, C.: De-signed ecology. In: Oksala, T., Lasker, G.E. (eds.) Acta polytechnica Scandinavica. Design. Evolution, Cognition. Selected and edited papers from DEcon 1994 Symposium: Civil engineering and building construction series no. 105, Helsinki, pp. 3–11 (1996)
3. Benrós, D., Duarte, J., Branco, F.: A system for providing customized housing. In: Proceedings of the 12th International Conference on Computer Aided Architectural Design Futures, Sydney, Australia, pp. 153–166 (2007)
4. Blessing, M.: Types of Family Structures. LoveToKnow: http://family.lovetoknow.com/about-family-values/types-family-structures (n.d.)
5. Britannica, T. E.: Prefabrication. Retrieved from Encyclopædia Britannica, 20 August 2013. http://global.britannica.com/EBchecked/topic/474611/prefabrication
6. Case, K., Shiller, R.: Forecasting prices and excess returns in the housing market. Real Estate Econ. 18(3), 253–273 (1990)
7. Chien, S., Shih, S.: Design through information filtering. In: de Vries, B., van Leeuwen, J., Achten, H. (eds.) Computer Aided Architectural Design Futures, pp. 103–110. Springer, Netherlands (2001)
8. Chuen, H., Huang, J., Krawczyk, R.: i_Prefab Home - customizing prefabricated houses by Internet-Aided design. In: Communicating Space(s), pp. 690–698 (2006)
9. Cuperus, Y.: An introduction to open building. In: Proceedings of the 9th Annual Conference of the International Group for Lean Construction, Singapore (2001)
10. Deterding, S., Dixon, D., Khaled, R., Nacke, L.: From game design elements to Gamefulness: defining "Gamification". In: Proceedings of the 15th International Academic MindTrek Conference, (MindTrek 2011), Tampere, pp. 9–15 (2011)
11. Fabian, E., Janssen, P., Lo, T.: Group forming: negotiating design via web-based interaction and collaboration. In: Open Systems: Proceedings of the 18th International Conference on Computer-Aided Architectural Design Research in Asia (CAADRIA 2013), Singapore, pp. 271–280 (2013)
12. Frazer, J.: An Evolutionary Architecture. Architectural Association, London (1995)
13. Gao, Y., Su, Y.: Computational design research for high density social housing in China. Glob. Sci. Technol. forum J. Eng. Technol. (2012)

14. Gao, Y., Lo, T., Chang, Q.: Integrated open source architectural design for high density. In: Proceedings of 4th Annual International Conference on Architecture. Athens, Greece (2014)
15. Gerber, A., Molefo, O., Van der Merwe, A.: Documenting open source migration processes for re-use. In: Kotze, P., Gerber, A., van der Merwe, A., Bidwell, N. (eds.) Proceedings of the SAICSIT 2010 Conference - Fountains of Computing Research, pp. 75 – 85. ACM Press (2010)
16. Grimes, O.: Housing for Low-income Urban Families: Economics and Policy in the Developing World. World Bank (1976)
17. Guneet, K.: Participatory approach/community involvement in planning. In: 43rd ISOCARP Congress (2007)
18. Wright, G.: Building the Dream: A Social History of Housing in America. MIT press, Cambridge (1983)
19. Herr, C., Fischer, T., Wang, H., Ren, W.: Demand-driven generative design of sustainable mass housing for China. In: The Fifth China Urban Housing Conference, China (2005)
20. Huizinga, J.: Homo Ludens: A Study of the Play element in Culture. Routledge & Kegan Paul, London (1955)
21. Hunicke, R., Leblanc, M., Zubek, R.: MDA: a formal approach to game design and game research. In: 19th National Conference of Artificial Intelligence, p. 5 (2004)
22. Israel, N.: Okohaus, los límites de la participación. La civdad viva: http://www.laciudadviva.org/blogs/?p=14164. Accessed 15 June 2012
23. Kalloc: Fuzor, 30 January 2014. www.kalloctech.com
24. Kapp, K.: The Gamification of Learning and Instruction—Game-Based Methods and Strategies for Training and Education. Wiley, San Francisco (2012)
25. Kelly, A.: Decision Making Using Game Theory: An Introduction for Managers. Cambridge University Press, Cambridge (2003)
26. Kendall, S.: Managing Change: the application of Open Building in the INO Bern Hospital. In Design & Health Congress. www.designandhealth.com/Media-Publishing/Papers.aspx. Accessed 29 September 2009
27. Kernohan, D.: User Participation in Building Design and Management: A Generic Approach to Building Evaluation. Butterworth-Heinemann, Oxford (1992)
28. Kim, J., Brouwer, R., Kearney, J.: NEXT 21: A Prototype Multi-Family Housing Complex. University of Michigan, College of Architecture and Urban Planning, Michigan, Ann Arbor (1993)
29. Lefaivre, L.: Top Down Meets Bottom-up, Spontaneous Interventions: design actions for the common good. Architect Magazine, August 2012
30. Lo, T.T., Schnabel, M.A., Gao, Y.: Collaborative mass housing design practice with smart models. In: International Conference on Digital Architecture (DADA), Beijing, China (2013)
31. Madigan, R., Munro, M., Smith, S.J.: Gender and the meaning of the home. Int. J. Urban Regional Res. **14**(4), 625–647 (1990)
32. Madrazo, L., Sicilia, A., González, M., Cojo, A.: Barcode housing system: integrating floor plan layout generation processes within an open and collaborative system to design and build customized housing. In: Tidafi, T., Dorta, T. (eds.) Annual Joining Languages, Cultures and Visions: CAAD Futures, PUM, pp. 656– 670 (2009)
33. Mayer, C., Somerville, C.: Residential construction: using the urban growth model to estimate housing supply. J. Urban Econ. **48**(1), 85–109 (2000)
34. Nikos, A.: Design methods, emergence, and collective intelligence, new science, new urbanism, new architecture? In: Towards a New 21st Century Architecture, Katarxis no. 3 (2004)

35. Op-ed.: Open Source Architecture (OSArc). domus. http://www.domusweb.it/en/op-ed/2011/06/15/open-source-architecture-osarc-.html. Accessed 15 June 2011
36. Record.: Largest LAN Party. Guinness World Record. http://www.guinnessworldrecords.com/world-records/3000/largest-lan-party. Accessed 1 December 2007
37. Sass, L., Botha, M.: The instant house: a model of design production with digital fabrication. Int. J. Archit. Comput. 4(4), 109–123 (2006)
38. Schnabel, M.: Interplay of Domains. Learning from the Past a Foundation for the Future, Special Publication of Papers Presented at the CAAD Futures 2005 Conference, pp. 11–20. Vienna University of Technology, Vienna (2005)
39. Schnabel, M., Kvan, T.: Spatial understanding in immersive virtual environments. Int. J. Archit. Comput. 1(4), 435–448 (2003)
40. Schnabel, M., Kvan, T., Kruijff, E., Donath, D.: The first virtual environment design studio. In: Proceedings of Architectural Information Management, 19th eCAADe Conference, Helsinki, Finland, pp. 394–400 (2001)
41. Van Gunsteren, L., Binnekamp, R., Van Loon, P.: Open Design, a Stakeholder-oriented Approach in Architecture, Urban Planning, and Project Management. Research in Design Series, vol. 1. IOS Press, Delft (2006)
42. Zichermann, G., Linder, J.: The Gamification Revolution: How Leaders Leverage Game Mechanics to Crush The Competition. McGraw-Hill, Boston (2013)

Structural Design Based on Performance Applied to Development of a Lattice Wind Tower

Marina Borges[✉] and Ricardo H. Fakury

Federal University of Minas Gerais, Belo Horizonte, Brazil
marinafborges@gmail.com, fakury@dees.ufmg.br

Abstract. This paper studies the process of parametric and algorithmic design, integrating structural analysis and design for the generation of complex geometric structures. This methodology is based on the Performative Model, where the shape is generated using performance criteria. In the approach, the development of complex structures is only possible by reversing the process of thinking to generate the form with established parameters for geometry, material and loading aspects. Thus, the structural engineer no longer only participates in the evaluation phase but also appears in the early stages, creating a process of exploration and production of common knowledge among architects and engineers. To research performance-based design, the development of a conceptual lattice for a wind tower is proposed. Thus, a system is made to generate geometries using Rhinoceros software, the Grasshopper plugin, and the VB programming language, integrated with stress analysis through the Scan & Solve plugin.

Keywords: Structural design · Parametric and algorithm architecture · Structural analysis · Performative model · Lattice wind tower

1 Introduction

The development of digital technologies has enabled significant changes in architectural design processes, engineering and the construction industry. CAD (Computer Aided Design) allowed the development of 2D and 3D representation techniques in the digital environment, and BIM (Building Information Modeling) added information to models through parametric relationships. Until recently, the CAD and BIM technologies continued to be associated with a traditional design process, with a sequence of decisions involving synthesis of architectural form and subsequent evaluation, which in the case of structural design, happens through structural analysis.

In the early 2000s, the architecture methodology changed with the evolution of the form shown digitally to the form digitally generated, where the computer is used to explore possibilities. In this new way of designing, the architect stop to model shapes to articulate an internal logic to generate shapes [1]. In this context of changing paradigms that opened the simulation possibilities of form through a process of optimization or generation, architects have begun to develop performance-based projects. The parametric and algorithmic architecture allows architects to design based on parametric

© Springer-Verlag Berlin Heidelberg 2015
G. Celani et al. (Eds.): CAAD Futures 2015, CCIS 527, pp. 255–271, 2015.
DOI: 10.1007/978-3-662-47386-3_14

relations and through scripts, which use mathematical data as the basis for form generation. According to Terzidis [2], for the first time perhaps, a paradigm shift is being formulated that outweighs previous ones, where algorithmic design employs methods and devices that have no precedent.

Thus, this work puts forward the following questions: Can the work of architects and structural engineers converge from emerging digital practices? Are the digital tools available sufficient for the development of a performance-based model or is this type of methodology still inaccessible outside the elite of world architecture? How would this model be developed with the resources available in Brazil for a small project?

To apply the methodology for structural design, New Structuralism of Oxman and Oxman [3] was used as a conceptual foundation for the reverse process of the development of the structure. The hypothesis is that the methodological reversal applied to the structural design provides innovative results because the project is not the reproduction of an existing pattern but a solution generated through forces and specific parameters for the problem in question.

As the methodology application object was proposed a lattice wind tower 140 m high composed of circular section bars manufactured by Vallourec of Brazil (the only national manufacturer of this product). The project is part of a need to generate sustainable energy in Brazil, mainly in the countryside. For the use of wind power in the mountain regions, the tower must be high enough to capture the wind. Therefore, the towers require an optimized solution from a structural point of view, but they also need an aesthetic solution that does not create visual pollution, as they are often placed in areas with a great influx of people, and even at tourist sites. The tower design is of paramount importance to the work and is the main factor that demands the participation of the architect in the design process of the structural shape. Because structural issues are intrinsically related to the shape, the proposal is to use a collaborative design process with digital tools to reach a shape that has a transparency and aesthetic lightness through the combination of generative techniques and structural analysis.

The Canton Tower, built in 2009 in the city of the same name in China, was an aesthetic and design methodology reference. The design of the structure was the result of a collaborative process between the Dutch architects Mark Hemeland and Barbara Kuitwith and the British engineering company Arup, who was responsible for the structural optimization. The shape was developed with the aid of digital tools for parametric design using genetic algorithms [4].

For the lattice wind tower, the methodology proposed to design the structure was divided into two stages. In the first step, a shell was developed using parametric modeling, resulting in a shape with a minimal surface through the established geometric parameters. This shell was submitted to the ultimate combination of actions (the actions are increased by safety factors) and subdivided into 14 modules of 10 m each along the vertical axis to determine the maximum Von Mises stresses in each module. These stresses are compared to the maximum permissible stress.

The maximum stresses were compared to a maximum allowable stress determined with the global factor for steel resistance in an approximate way, using the possibility of instability occurrences under axial compression. To ensure that the Von Mises stress does not exceed the allowable stress, the thickness of each shell module was suitably adjusted. These thicknesses were the connection between the structural design of the shell and the bar structure generated in the second step. This transition was made by converting the shell thickness to the sum of the equivalent thickness of circular tubes in each module. Using the commercial tables of the tubular circular profiles from Vallourec [5], the programming converted the numeric data into geometric models based on the shape of the shell designed in the first step.

Based on the proposed questions, the available digital tools were first identified, and then whether these tools were able to develop an experimental application was determined. The parametric modeling plug-in Grasshopper was used combined with algorithmic programming in Visual Basic. The plugin Scan & Solve, which is based on the finite element method, was chosen for the structural analysis, though it does not have the same principle of mesh generation. Grasshopper and Scan & Solve operate in the same database of the Rhinoceros software. These plugins were chosen considering the criterion of interoperability, allowing virtually iterative operation.

This paper experimentally develops a performance-based model of structural design through reversing the form design process. Shea [6] said that "the next phase in digital design lies in considering the computer as a collaborative partner in the design process that is capable of generating new design ideas and stimulating solutions over difficult tasks". Emerging digital tools, which can combine the development of geometry with structural analysis, were explored along with the benefits of better relations between the architect and structural engineer by redefining the attitudes of both professionals.

2 Architectural Design Based on Performance and the *New Structuralism*

The performance-based design in digital processes is an instrument that contributes to the development of innovative projects, with the integration of simulation and generation mechanisms, requiring collaboration between architects and engineers during the design process. Kolarevic [7] states that qualitative and quantitative performance issues should be the technological principles that guide new design approaches.

The implementation possibilities of generative processes have grown significantly. In the early 2000s, only elite offices with teams of programmers, such as Foster + Partners, had resources for the development of these processes. Currently, parametric software such as Grasshopper has made this an increasingly accessible methodology. Performance-based design reflects the changes in the very profession of architects and changes in philosophy, where partner professionals, especially the structural engineers, are of fundamental importance in the design of the form.

In a contemporary approach to the development of structural design, the sequence of design decisions begins with the structure and material, and the shape is defined later. This approach was called by Oxman and Oxman [3] the *New Structuralism*. Traditionally, the form is designed by the architect and later analyzed and optimized by the structural engineer. To Oxman and Oxman [3], the structural engineer designs optimization and generation with the architectural concepts, reversing the way of thinking of form, strength, structure and performance.

The *New Structuralism* is the integration of design, architecture, structural engineering and digital technologies. The study of complex geometries and architectural design possibilities through algorithms are redefining the possibilities of structural design. Parametric software was extremely important in the development of these concepts. This software is a means of producing generative, structural and iterative design through collaborative processes between architects and engineers.

The design paradigm based on performance focuses less on formal and aesthetic issues and more on material and design intelligence. The layout is not as relevant, but instead the logic that defines it is the most important. According to Grobman [8], a new type of architecture based on data and performance is gradually being developed, in contrast to architecture focused on typology.

3 Digital Process of Architectural and Structural Design Based on Performance

3.1 Model Application Object

Digital tools and performance-based structural design can create non-standard solutions to structural problems, where the shape is not just pre-designed and optimized later, but the design emerges from the complexity required for the problem solution [9]. For study and experimentation of the performative model methodology, the design of a lattice wind tower was proposed. The geometry of the tower is the result of a combination of settings as the geometric parameters, aesthetic references and forces applied due to the equipment, wind and the weight of the tower itself (Fig. 1).

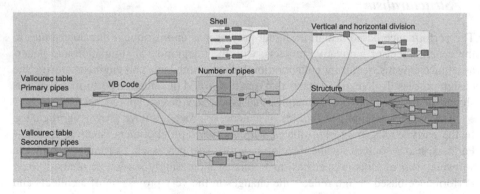

Fig. 1. Symbolic diagram of design relationships

To Dimcic [10], the integration of the three areas of knowledge (architecture, structural analysis and programming) allowed for the generation and the static analysis of any structure. For this study object, geometric modeling software, programming language and a structural analysis plugin were used. The specific tools used were the geometric modeling software Rhinoceros, the plugin Grasshopper and the Visual Basic programming language, which provides the creation of parameters for the generation of form. In this process, the structural analysis is incorporated at an early development stage of the project through the plugin Scan&Solve (Fig. 2).

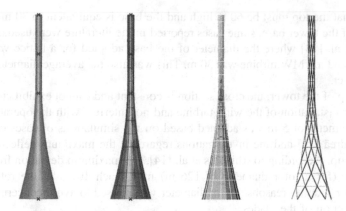

Fig. 2. Workflow incorporated for the structural analysis

3.2 Geometric Parameters for the Development of the Lattice Wind Tower Design

The wind tower requires a solution that reconciles aesthetic and structural optimization. For this generation, the proposal is to combine the required parameters of geometry with the forces applied to the structure. This project aims to considerably increase the use of wind energy due to its characteristics of sustainability and innovation. Currently, only 1 % of Brazil's total energy demand is met by wind power, and the installed wind power capacity accounts for 2 % of the energy matrix of the country [11]. Developing wind farms in the mountain region has great interest, but the conventional tubular towers of 60–80 m high, used in coastal areas, do not met the required criteria (Fig. 3).

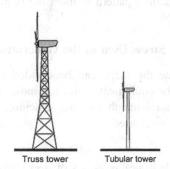

Truss tower   Tubular tower

Fig. 3. Difference in height between truss and tubular towers

The lattice wind tower to be developed in this project is proposed to best capture the highest wind currents, where the higher power turbines of can be more efficient. For this to happen, a height of 140 m was set. For the definition of the geometric parameters and loading of the project, the choice of turbine was key. For these definitions, a 3 MW turbine with a rotor diameter of approximately 120 m with three blades was chosen, taking as a reference the GWT-3.0 MW [12]. Consequently, the rotor diameter was defined as that the top must be 60 m high and the base is equivalent to 80 m high. For the design of the tower base, some cases reported in the literature were used, such as in Engström et al. [13] where the diameter of the base adopted for a lattice wind tower 150 m high and a 3 MW turbine was 30 m. This was also the average diameter adopted for the project.

At the top of the tower, the cross section is constant and cannot exhibit curvature to allow proper installation of the wind turbine and not interfere with the operation of the blades. A diameter of 5 m was adopted based on the simulations of cases of extreme loads in Andreä [12] and the investigations regarding the maximum deflection of the tower blade tip. According to Rhizoids et al. [14], the maximum deviation from the tip to the tower (for a rotor diameter of 126 m) may reach 10 % of the rotor radius. Therefore, for security reasons, a 5 m diameter was chosen to avoid concerns with the limited deflection of the blades.

With the above definitions, Table 1 shows the sizing for the generation of the tower geometry.

Table 1. Tower design parameters

Overall height	140 m
Base height	80 m
Height of the top	60 m
Base diameter	30 m
Top diameter	5 m

Such geometry definitions served as the initial parameters for geometric modeling. Starting from this data, the best way to make the project was studied, defining the best material, bar section and structural pattern to meet the requirements.

3.3 Forces and Resistant Stress Used in the Generation of the Form

The forces acting to generate the shape can be divided into the self-weight of the structure, the forces due to the equipment (wind turbine), including the effect of wind on the blades, and the wind strength on the structure. Table 2 summarizes the mechanical properties of the steel used.

Table 2. Mechanical properties of steel VMB-350 Cor

Yield strength	350 MPa
Ultimate strength	485 MPa
Modulus of elasticity	200,000 MPa
Poisson's ratio	0.3

For the resistant strain calculation, the following value was assumed for the maximum allowable stress:

$$\sigma_{Rd} = \frac{\chi f_y}{\gamma_{a1}} \tag{1}$$

where f_y is the yield strength of the steel, in this case equal to 350 MPa, γ_{a1} is the global factor for steel resistance, equal to 1.10, and χ is the reduction factor associated with the compressive strength (takes into account the global instability of the compression bars). This expression was used considering that all the bars, depending on the direction of the acting horizontal loading, will be subjected to axial compression or axial tensile, where compression is the most unfavorable situation. To simplify, χ was assumed to be 0.80, corresponding to a non-dimensional slenderness of approximately 0.90 (see Brazilian Standard ABNT NBR 16239:2013 [15]) because in the lattice space to be projected, the bars will have reduced length and the non-dimensional slenderness should not exceed this value. Local buckling was not considered because Vallourec's rolled circular hollow sections have a small proportion between the diameter and the thickness, precluding the occurrence of this failure mode.

Applying f_y, χ and γ_{a1} to Eq. (1), one obtains σ_{Rd} equal to 254.54 MPa, which in structural analysis is the maximum tension. Above this value, the analyzed form was considered inappropriate. For the analysis, the values of F_{Hres}, F_z and M_{res} design actions (Fig. 4) were selected among the highest values between all the action combinations, representing conservative final design values in the structure. The force F_z represents the self-weight of the structure and the weight of the equipment. To calculate the weight of the equipment, a load applied in the amount of 2.78×10^6 N was considered. The horizontal force F_{Hres} is caused by the wind on the structure and on the equipment, and it was applied in a simplified manner on top of the tower with a value of 0.955×10^6 N. The resulting total moment M_{res} applied on top of the structure refers to the sum of the moment caused by the self-weight of the machine and the moment caused by the wind on the equipment.

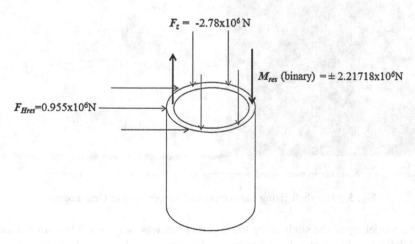

Fig. 4. Application of F_{Hres}, F_z and M_{res} at the top of the tower

3.4   Step One: Geometric Modeling and Structural Analysis of the Shell

For structural analysis, the plugin Scan&Solve [16] was chosen because it does not require sophisticated user knowledge in structural analysis or finite element mesh. The generated model is a simplification of a finite element mesh, a mesh free technology patented by the company. According to the supplier, the model is advantageous because it creates a separation between the geometric and physical representation of the object, combining them when necessary without spend much time with conversion and error correction and preserving most of the advantages of the classic method of analysis by FEM. Thus, the Scan & Solve is viable structural analysis software for architects to use for a preliminary design.

To test the reliability of the analysis made by Scan & Solve, two experiments were conducted to compare the analytical solution and the solution given by the program for tension and displacement. The purpose of the experiment was to validate the computational solution compared to the analytical solution. A tube with a loading applied at the top was first tested, followed by a beam fixed at both ends with a distributed load. In both cases, the structures were tested at various mesh settings; for smaller meshes the result was always the same, but the stress results were closer to the analytical solution in the medium meshes.

For the development of the tower project, the first step was generating an initial geometry shape as a shell through Grasshopper (Fig. 5). The traditional solution from an engineering point of view would be a cylinder on the top with a frustocone at the base. To find a solution that meets the aesthetic factors, the Gestalt principles were used, especially those that suggest the continuity and the roundness of the shape [17].

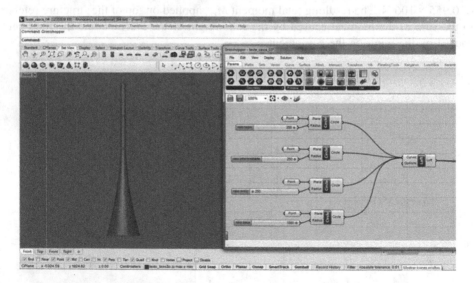

Fig. 5. The shell sizing parameters in Rhinoceros and Grasshopper

The modeling of the shell using these principles was only possible with the use of the NURBS tool by approaching a more fluid stroke as in the hand drawings, allowing the development of increasingly more complex shapes and lightweight aesthetics. Because the rotor revolves around the tower to capture the wind in any direction, the shape of the top must be symmetrical, excluding any possibility of asymmetry. To ensure the same eccentricity at the top and at the bottom, the base should have the same axis of the top, thus creating symmetry on all sides of the structure.

The purpose of first generating a shell was to define an initial aesthetic form and through the structural analysis via Scan & Solve to determine the required thickness of the shell in each module so that the design stress does not exceed the maximum allowable stress of 254.54 MPa. The shell was divided into 14 modules with varying thicknesses. These thicknesses were used as a reference in the choice of the lattice structure profiles.

Finding the equivalent maximum thickness in each shell module was necessary for a reference thickness for the analysis, taken as equal to 10 cm. Requesting the maximum stress of each module (σ_{Sd}) obtained an equivalent thickness for the development of the truss, given by:

$$t = \frac{\sigma}{f_{yd}} \times 10 \qquad (2)$$

Thus, it was possible to find the ring area in each module and convert the area into an equivalent number of tubes. For stress analysis, Scan & Solve allows a mesh

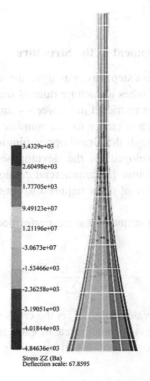

3.4329e+03
2.60498e+03
1.77705e+03
9.49123e+07
1.21196e+07
-3.0673e+07
-1.53466e+03
-2.36258e+03
-3.19051e+03
-4.01844e+03
-4.84636e+03
Stress ZZ (Ba)
Deflection scale: 67.8595

Fig. 6. Maximum stress for mesh with 201100 elements

refinement of 9999-500000 elements. As described above, the best results were found in the meshes with intermediate values (Fig. 6).

After obtaining the maximum stresses in MPa, Eq. (2) was applied, and the equivalent thickness in each module was found, as shown in Table 3.

Table 3. Relationship between the thickness and the maximum design stress in each module

Module	Maximum design stress (MPa)	Thickness (cm)
1	-8.39	0.3
2	-18.50	0.7
3	-24.10	0.9
4	-34.00	1.3
5	-42.70	1.7
6	-48.40	1.9
7	-48.40	1.9
8	-36.00	1.4
9	-25.90	1.0
10	-18.40	0.7
11	-13.80	0.5
12	-11.30	0.4
13	-7.84	0.3
14	-7.42	0.3

3.5   Step Two: The Development of the Structure

The second project development step was to analyze the shell thickness data and relate it to the equivalent number of tubes in each module of the tower. The number of tubes to be used in each module was restricted to between 4 and 12. The bottom area of the ring of each module served as a reference for the number of tubes needed according to the stress analysis. Thus, through the Grasshopper plugin and VB programming language, an algorithm was developed for the development of a lattice composed of tubular profiles using the Vallourec [3] commercial catalog of circular tubular sections to relate the shell to the number of pipes required to produce the final form tower, as shown in Table 4.

The calculations of the tube quantity were performed according to the following expression:

$$N = \frac{A_c}{\sum A_t} \tag{3}$$

where N is the number of equivalent tubes, A_c is the cross-sectional area in each module of the shell, and A_t is the cross-sectional area in each tube. With these settings, the development of the generator lattice algorithm using Grasshopper was possible (Diagram 1).

Table 4. Calculations of the number of tubes needed for each module

Module	Ø for bottom section of shell (cm)	Bottom section area of shell (cm²)	Number of tubes necessary for Ø = 355.6 mm and t = 25 mm
1	500	517.13	2
2	500	1139.37	4
3	500	1483.61	6
4	500	2091.43	8
5	500	2624.79	10
6	500	2973.84	11
7	630	3749.99	14
8	760	3368.71	13
9	990	3159.69	12
10	1270	2880.92	11
11	1580	2688.71	10
12	2000	2787.20	11
13	2500	2417.46	9
14	3000	3234.00	12

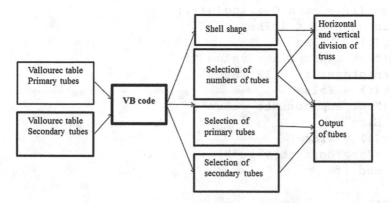

Diagram 1. Arrangement of the algorithm for the structure

Programming in Visual Basic was necessary to control the output of the smallest number of tubes determined by the thickness found in Table 3 in an automated manner. The minimum number was 4 tubes per module, and the maximum number was 12, such that the bars would not have inclinations smaller than 30°. Tables of the selected tubes were connected directly to VB code as input parameters for the conditional settings. In addition of the tables, the input parameters were also the thickness of the shell and the outer radius of the section. As an output parameter, the values were classified as appropriate and not appropriate (Diagram 2).

The output of the tubes is directly connected to the division of the modulation parameters and the diameters of the defined commercial tubes through the conditional in the VB code:

```
Private Sub RunScript(ByValShellThickness As Double,
ByValOuterRadius As Integer, ByValTubeDiameter As List(Of
Double), ByRef A As Object, ByRef B As Object)
    Dim CrossSectionAreaAs Double
    Dim InnerRadiusAs Double
    Dim TubeArea(0 To 2) As Double
    Dim iAs Integer
    Dim result(0 To 2) As Boolean
Dim n(0To 2) As Double
Dimninteger (0To 2) As Integer
InnerRadius = OuterRadius-ShellThickness
CrossSectionArea = 3.14*((OuterRadius^2) -
(InnerRadius^2))
    For i = 0 To 2
TubeArea(i) = 3.14 * ((TubeDiameter(i) / 2) ^ 2)
n(i) = CrossSectionArea / TubeArea(i)
ninteger(i) = math.Ceiling(n(i))
If  ninteger(i) < 4 Then
result(i) = False
print("not appropriate value ")
ElseIfninteger(i) > 12 Then
result(i) = False
print("not appropriate value")
    Else
result(i) = True
print ("appropriate value")
    End If

Next

A = ninteger
B = result

End Sub
```

With the possible combinations of tube numbers between 4 and 12, obtaining various configuration options for the truss was possible. Figure 7 shows the workflow developed to obtain the best solutions through a combination of geometric modeling and structural analysis.

After obtaining some solutions with between 4 and 12 tubes, some criteria were established to find the best solution considering quantitative and qualitative factors. First, double modules for creating trapeze forms were discarded, which do not

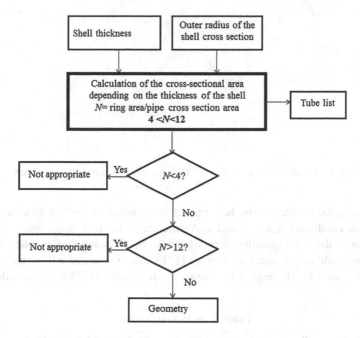

Diagram 2. Conditionals for geometrical generation of the structure with pipes

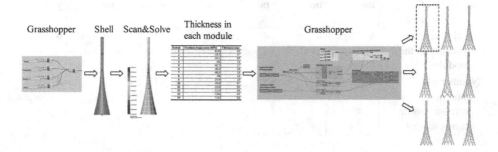

Fig. 7. Workflow developed to obtain the best results

contribute to structural efficiency and aesthetically are not significantly better than the simple modules.

For the profile definition, the catalog of a domestic manufacturer was used, and the biggest profile available was Ø355.6 mm. Using this profile, some modules had a quantity greater than 12 tubes, which does not meet the established conditions. Therefore, the possibility of combining 3 profiles of the commercial catalog (Fig. 8) to allow larger sections was allowed. However, this combination would not be the ideal situation and so was avoided.

To compare the tube combinations, Table 5 lists other criteria that were instrumental in choosing the best structure. The most efficient structure was one that did not need to combine three tubes, had minor profile variations along the tower and had the smallest number of modules without profile combinations.

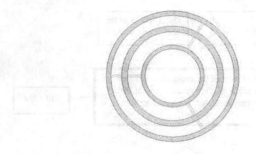

Fig. 8. Combination of 3 tubes: Ø355.6 mm, 273 mm and 168.3 mm

Examining these criteria, the best results were obtained for the structure with 8 tubes and the combination with 8 and 4. Aesthetically, the preference would be for the continuation of the same quantity of profiles with the least number of tubes, based on the continuity rule as proposed by Gestalt [17]. Thus, the tower with 8 tubes has the best results (Table 5), although it has many modules with Ø355.6 mm profile.

Table 5. Selection criteria

Combination of tubes	8	8_4	10	10_5	12	12_6	6
Necessity of using 3 tubes	no	no	no	yes	no	no	yes
Profile variations throughout the modules	6	6	8	11	3	6	6
Number of modules without profile combinations	4	4	5	2	12	12	3

Thus, the best geometry found through this methodology would be 8 tubes along all 14 modules (Fig. 9), with a primary tube diameter of 355.6 mm and a secondary diameter of 168.3 mm. This geometry maintains the same aesthetic aspect for all modules, which provides a visual unit structure. Moreover, all the tubes are connected at the same point, preventing pattern variations for the connections.

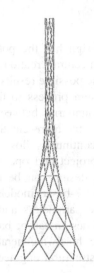

Fig. 9. Selected geometry with 8 pipes

According to Celani [18], a generative system can be used to optimize (convergence) or vary (divergence) by generating multiple alternatives. This process tends towards optimization by convergence, combining geometric and structural criteria. Thus, the selected structure fulfills the prerequisites for geometry by applying the

Fig. 10. Photomontage of wind tower lattices

performative model and its structural efficiency has been further demonstrated in the preliminary study phase (Fig. 10).

4 Conclusion

The parametric and algorithmic design has the potential to enable an architectural process in which the process of architectural creation is connected to data management. The end result comes from one of the possible results within a multitude of alternatives generated, which can open the design process to the collaboration of other professionals. This opening lowers the boundaries between design and construction, while separation is greatly strengthened by the representative project process.

The digital process creates a continuous flow of design and production. With greater possibilities linked to the project and opening participation to other professionals in the design of the form, design can be based on more rational and less intuitive rules. Therefore, performance-based models are being developed where the building's priority is to meet some parameters and the shape is a consequence of these responses. Performance-based design can be based on only optimizing the shape designed by the architect or can cover his own generation. In both cases, a collaborative process is essential, involving the structural engineer from the preliminary stages of the project.

The methodology presented here shows a great potential for the development of complex structures. Future work could increase the possibilities of structural analysis, study connections, and evaluate second-order analysis as part of the process. Other members of the project could be incorporated through a more complex object and the correlation of more than one component to generate forms and to assess the performance. Design integration with digital fabrication and with the manufacturing and assembly process could also be further discussed. Furthermore, cost and time parameters could also be incorporated into the generation of the shape and manufacturing processes.

Although we cannot say that the performance-based model improves the quality of the project, it substantially increases the design solutions and improves the structural efficiency even in the preliminary study. The collaborative process dilutes the questions of authorship, which generally causes conflicts between the authors (architects) and the evaluators and builders (engineers), in favor of better project performance through investigative and experimental procedures.

References

1. Kolarevic, B.: Architecture in the Digital Age: Design and Manufacturing. Spon Press, New York (2003)
2. Terzidis, K.: Algorithmic form. In: Ahlquist, S., Menges, A. (eds.) Computational Design Thinking, pp. 94–101. Wiley, London (2011)

3. Oxman, R., Oxman, R.: The new structuralism: design, engineering and architectural technologies. AD **80**, 15–23 (2010)
4. Canton Tower. http://www.cantontower.com
5. Vallourec Tubos do Brasil: Tubos Estruturais, Seção Circular, Quadrada e Retangular, catalogue, São Paulo (2014)
6. Shea, K., Aish, R., Gourtovaia, M.: Towards integrated performance-driven generative design tools. Autom. Constr. **14**(2), 253–264 (2005)
7. Kolarevic, B.: Performative Architecture Beyond Instrumentality. Spon Press, New York (2005)
8. Grobman, Y.J.: The various dimensions of the concept of "performance" in architecture. In: Grobman, Y., Neuman, E. (eds.) Performalism: Form and Performance in Digital Architecture, pp. 9–13. Routledge, Oxon (2012)
9. Schwitter, C.: Engineering complexity: performance-based design in use. In: Kolarevic, B. (ed.) Performative Architecture beyond instrumentality, pp. 113–122. Spon Press, New York (2005)
10. Dimcic, M.: Structural optimization of grid shells based on genetic algorithms. Ph.D. thesis, Institute of Building Structures and Structural Design, Stuttgart University (2011)
11. Abeeólica. http://www.portalabeeolica.org.br
12. Andrea, A.: Condensed version of Technical Report TR-04R0-2014-An: Estimation of Tower Design Loads for a Generic 3 MW Wind Turbine, Salvador (2014)
13. Engström, et al.: Tall towers for large wind turbines. Elforsk, Estocolmo (2010)
14. Riziotis, V., Voutsinas, S., Manolas, D., Politis, E., Chaviaropoulos, P.: Aeroelastic Analysis of Pre-Curved Rotor Blades. http://proceedings.ewea.org/
15. ABNT NBR 16239: Design of steel and steel and concrete composite structures for buildings with tubular profiles, Brazilian Association of Technical Standards (2013)
16. Scan&Solve: *Scan&Solve* ™ 2014 Plug-in for Rhino, version 2014.6.16.0, Intact Solutions, Madison (2014)
17. Filho, J.: Gestalt do Objeto: Sistema de Leitura Visual da Forma. Editora Escrituras, São Paulo (2000)
18. Celani, G.: Algorithmic Sustainable Design, uma visão crítica do projeto generativo, Vitruvius, 10, 116.03, São Paulo (2011)

Parametric Modeling of Bamboo Pole Joints

Olivia Espinosa Trujillo[(⊠)] and Tsung-Hsien Wang

University of Sheffield, Sheffield, England, UK
arq.oet@gmail.com, tsung-hsien.wang@sheffield.ac.uk

Abstract. This paper describes the development of a parametric modeling system that enables the design of customized bamboo pole joints, where the geometry of each bamboo piece becomes the main design constraint. Rules of design are identified in traditional bamboo-jointing practice through the analysis of a bamboo catalogue. This knowledge informs the constructive principles of the system. Output data of the system successfully formulates the design of a customized bamboo jointing system. The effort of this paper suggests that further development of an application or software to facilitate the design of parametric bamboo joints is a feasible project that could help bamboo to have a solid presence in modern building industry. Lastly, the paper hints that transference of parametric technology is a promising domain that could potentially be applied to streamline the use of other natural materials.

Keywords: Bamboo · Pole joints · Design rules · Parametric modeling

1 Introduction

Bamboo is a natural resource with renewable properties that is expected to play a bigger role in the building industry. With a lightweight profile and fast growing rate, bamboo rises as a fair candidate to replace timber in the future [6, 10]. Despite the vast list of benefits that bamboo has to offer, its domestication by the building industry is still at an early stage. Dealing with geometrical complexity and irregularities of bamboo poles remains a problem yet to be solved, especially when it comes to designing efficient jointing elements.

Joints play a key role in the construction of any structural system, providing continuity among different parts of a structure. Janssen [5] argues that mastering jointing techniques is an essential step needed to guarantee the use of any material at a large-scale scenario and optimize its structural performance. Bamboo, therefore, needs to efficiently master the art of jointing before it can have a solid presence in modern building industry.

In traditional bamboo-jointing practice, joints have a modular design approach, this means that the joint is not properly acknowledging the individual geometry of each element and, frequently, bamboo pieces end up being adapted to the jointing system itself. In most cases, the result of this situation is the construction of a faulty structural

© Springer-Verlag Berlin Heidelberg 2015
G. Celani et al. (Eds.): CAAD Futures 2015, CCIS 527, pp. 272–290, 2015.
DOI: 10.1007/978-3-662-47386-3_15

system, where the strength of the canes is usually lost. This paper proposes a different jointing design approach, in which, the jointing system adapts to the physical characteristics of the bamboo elements to be jointed. In this manner, each joint will be customized to respond exclusively to a particular configuration.

Parametric modeling is a design approach that has made mass customization a feasible reality at present. In a parametric model, a set of unchangeable parameters is formulated to respond to different scenarios, thus, design outcomes are constantly altered. This design approach has gained strength and popularity over the last years due to proliferation of parametric software [2]. Materials like concrete, steel and timber have successfully incorporated this promising technology to improve its performance. It is argued here that bamboo could also benefit from this technology to overcome its limitations. The main objective of this paper is, therefore, to explore how parametric modeling could be used to facilitate the design of customized bamboo joints.

2   Research Background

2.1   Material and Geometric Considerations for the Design of Bamboo Joints

Bamboo is a giant grass that can be described as a hollow tube-like structure divided by a series of nodes. The microstructure of bamboo reveals a system of parallel cellulose fibers acting as reinforcement bars along the axial direction of the cane [5]. The distribution of cellulose fibers increases towards the outer layer of the cane. This arrangement explains why bamboo behaves as a strong material with high tensile properties when loads are applied in the direction of its fibers. However, when loads are applied on the opposite direction, bamboo becomes a brittle material due to the lack of sufficient radial fibers and the hollowness of the cane. Scholars therefore, describe bamboo as a longitudinal reinforced material with little transversal capacity [1, 3, 5]. Given the arrangement of the fibers, common failures in bamboo specimens are crushing and splitting. Efficient joints should aim to work in favor of mechanical properties of bamboo by transmitting forces along the longitudinal direction of the cane to facilitate continuous flow of efforts, or else, reinforcing the cane, when forces are applied on the transversal direction [1].

Bamboo is a natural material that shows a wide diversity and, although the geometric structure of most bamboo species is similar (Fig. 1), dimensions are not. Every bamboo is different. The culm of some species reaches up to 30 meters height and a diameter that ranges from 10 to 30 cm [9]. Additionally, most specimens are tapered, curved, hollow and nearly round. Wall thickness usually varies along the culm and the location of nodes is rather random. The fact that every bamboo is different means that structural behavior varies from one specimen to another and, acknowledgement of these variations could help to optimize the performance of the jointing system. Shape and size adaptability, consequently, are one of the key issues to consider when designing joints.

Finally, it is important to consider that bamboo, as a natural resource, is vulnerable to insects and fungi and has high levels of humidity. The use of dry canes with protection against the attack of living organisms is fundamental to preserve the structural behavior of bamboo [4]. Joints should consider protection of the cane against the attack of living

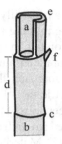

Fig. 1. Bamboo Structure: Interior wall (a), exterior wall (b), node (c), internode (d), wall thickness (e) and branch (f)

organisms, especially at open ends. Also, dry bamboos should be used in order to prevent loose joints. In summary, effective jointing design should focus on maximizing the use of bamboo canes by taking full advantage of its good properties, while avoiding or minimizing the impact of the bad ones.

2.2   Traditional Bamboo Jointing Practice

The complexity embedded in the design of bamboo pole joints has not prevented the use of bamboo on a local-scale. Bamboo jointing techniques have been instinctively developed through trial and error from generation to generation. Due to the lack of sufficient information on the topic, it appears to some as if bamboo-jointing practice is an arbitrary process that cannot be efficiently rationalized [5]. Although there are several examples of traditional joints, a survey of the literature review and different bamboo projects, identifies six types of joints commonly used in construction Fig. 2:

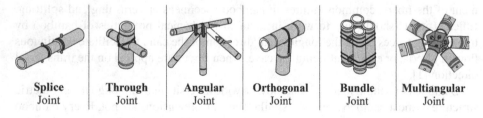

| Splice Joint | Through Joint | Angular Joint | Orthogonal Joint | Bundle Joint | Multiangular Joint |

Fig. 2.   Types of bamboo joints commonly used in construction

Traditional bamboo jointing development has invested most of its efforts on finding modular solutions that best adapt to the geometric complexity of bamboo; this has not always being the best approach. At present, the environmental benefits of using bamboo as a building material have inspired designers, architects and constructors to understand more about traditional jointing practice and streamline this knowledge into the development of more effective jointing techniques [7].

2.3 Parametric Modeling Considerations

Parametric modeling is a design approach in which the designer has to trace the logic behind a problem and understand clearly how all the elements embedded in a process affect each other [11]. The designer has to identify input variables, constants and expected outputs in a problem. The success of a parametric model lies in the establishment of constants or rules of design [12]. Different variables are applied to a sequential set of rules; hence, results change accordingly. The rules remain as constants in the whole process and, due to a previous analysis of the problem, these rules become applicable to different scenarios. The result of this iterative process is the design of customized objects.

3 Steps Towards the Development of a Parametric System

The main aim of this research is to build a system that enables the parametric modeling of customized bamboo joints, where the geometry of each bamboo piece becomes the main design constraint. A parametric model, as stated before, requires input data, constraint data or rules of design and output data. For the purpose of this research, the geometry of each bamboo piece became input data. Rules of design were found in the implicit knowledge of traditional bamboo-jointing practice. Finally, the system formulates customized joints as output data. The first part of the methodology focused on finding implicit rules of design through the analysis of a bamboo joint catalogue, whereas; the second part focused on the development of a preliminary parametric system.

3.1 Searching for Implicit Rules of Design

In order to map out rules of design to inform the parametric system, a catalogue of ninety joints was compiled. As mentioned earlier, there are six common types of bamboo joints used in construction. These types of joints determined the scope of the catalogue. Hence, fifteen joint examples were collected per each type of joint commonly used in construction. The analysis of each type of joint allowed the identification of the following data:

- Purpose of the Joint
- Uses in construction
- Design Configurations
- Main Rules of Design

3.2 Development of the Parametric System

The development of a parametric modeling system that integrates all the information gathered in the catalogue is a process that needs to be gradually done. Ideally, the system should facilitate the design of the six types of joints previously mentioned. At this early stage of the research, however, only one type of joint was chosen to explore the incorporation of bamboo geometry data and implicit rules of design in a parametric system. The joint was selected according to its present relevance in the field of construction.

The preliminary parametric system was developed with the use of Grasshopper, a parametric and algorithmic plugin for Rhinoceros 3D Software. The steps undertaken for the construction of the parametric modeling system are summarized in the following diagram Fig. 3:

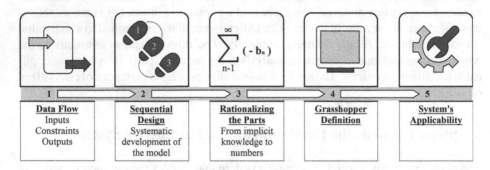

Fig. 3. Steps to develop a parametric modeling system

4   Implicit Rules of Design

From the analysis of the catalogue is possible to conclude that there are general design rules that applied to all types on joints, and, there are also particular design rules per type of joint. General design rules seek to protect and maximize the performance of bamboo canes, whilst particular rules seek to solve the main purpose of each type of joint.

4.1   Splice Joint

The main purpose of the splice joint (Fig. 4) is to increase the length of a bamboo piece by attaching an additional piece to it. This type of joint is frequently used to connect plumbing pipes. On a smaller scale, it is also used to repair or elongate structural elements with low bearing capacity. It is not advisable to use it in large structures, since the joint itself can create a weak point in a load transference system.

Fig. 4. Common design configurations of splice joints

The main rules of design for this type of joint are:

- This system only solves the attachment of two bamboo members.
- Bamboo canes are aligned one after another to create a longitudinal element.
- An additional attachment mechanism is needed to fix bamboo members.
- Reinforcement of the attachment area is needed.

4.2 Through Joint

The main purpose of the through joint (Fig. 5) is to resolve the intersection of two bamboo members with different diameters. The piece with smaller diameter is fully or partially embedded in the piece with bigger diameter. Through joints are predominantly used for the construction of railings and fences. They are also used, with less frequency, as grid-wall reinforcement systems and structural frames with low bearing capacity.

Fig. 5. Common design configurations of through joints

The main rules of design for this type of joint are:

- Bamboo pieces with smaller diameter are partially or completely embedded in the pieces with bigger diameter.
- An additional mechanism is used to secure the attachment of the canes at the cross point.
- Reinforcement of the cross point area is needed.

4.3 Angular Joint

The purpose of this joint (Fig. 6) is to fix, at a cross point, a number of pieces that meet at angles other than 90°. Angular joints are important elements in a structural system. These joints are largely used for the assembly of roof trusses and bracing elements. They are used to give rigidity to frames and to efficiently transfer loads to supporting elements.

Fig. 6. Common design configurations of angular joints

The main rules of design for this type of joint are:

- When a single bamboo piece is used as bracing element, it needs to be reinforced with a perpendicular element.
- When two or more pieces are jointed, an external element is used to secure the attachment of the canes.
- Reinforcement is needed at the cross point area when two or more elements are jointed.
- Supported ends of the canes are cut to form a saddle.

4.4 Orthogonal Joint

The purpose of the orthogonal joint (Fig. 7) is to fix, at a cross point, two elements that meet at 90° angles. This type of joint is usually used for the construction of window frames, doorframes and as a connector of horizontal and vertical elements. It is also used for the construction of grid structures, railings and furniture.

Fig. 7.   Common design configurations of orthogonal joints

The main design rules for this type of joint are:

- The system only solves the intersection of two bamboo elements.
- An external fixing element is used to secure the attachment of the canes at its cross point.
- Reinforcement is needed at the cross point area.

4.5 Bundle Joint

A bundle joint (Fig. 8) is used when more than two bamboo pieces are joined to behave as a single structural bearing element. The main purpose of the joint is to maintain all the pieces together and aligned. Bundle joints are used for the construction of structural elements submitted to heavy loads such as columns. Most bundle systems provide seating for horizontal elements.

Fig. 8. Common design configurations of bundle joints

The main design rules for this type of joint are:

- The joint solves the rigidity and alignment of more than two elements.
- Additional elements are used to provide rigidity and alignment of the canes.
- Several reinforcement elements are needed along the element to guarantee attachment of the canes.

4.6 Multiangular Joint

The purpose of the multiangular joint (Fig. 9) is to hold together a number of bamboo pieces that rotate around a central point in multiple angles. Given its flexible configuration, this joint can be used in a variety of projects. It is frequently used in the construction of curvilinear structures, supporting elements, space frames, geodesic domes and planar grids.

Fig. 9. Common design configurations of multiangular joints

The main design rules of this type of joint are:

- A central joint holds all pieces together.
- Bamboo pieces rotate around the centroid of the joint.
- Reduction of bamboo ends is advisable for a better load transference.
- An external anchor system is used to fix bamboo pieces inside the central joint.
- Reinforcement of every bamboo member is needed at its ends.

4.7 General Rules of Design

- Nodes are more resistant to splitting than internodes. Joints therefore, are formed at or near nodes
- Holes reduce the strength of the cane. If making a hole in the cane is unavoidable, then it should be placed near a node.

- If a hole is made near a node, it is important to reinforce the cane near the node.
- A joint should reinforce the cane against splitting and crushing.
- The joint should solve the problem of size adaptability.
- The jointing system should transfer forces in the axial direction of the fibers.
- Collection of forces in a joint should be from the inside, the outside or from the cross section of the cane.

5   Development of a Parametric System for Multiangular Joints

The multiangular joint was chosen for the development of a preliminary parametric model due to its promising application in a wide range of projects. The flexibility of this joint is of particular interest for the building industry, since it enables the use of bamboo in curvilinear and rectilinear structures.

In order to inform the development of a multiangular parametric system, the mechanical behavior of the multiangular jointing system as a whole was outlined (Fig. 10). First, the central joint receives the impact of a load and distributes it along its surface (a). Secondly, the anchor systems distribute the load towards the cross section of all bamboo members (b). Finally, after the surface created by the cross section of the bamboos receives the impact of the distributed load, the efforts are directed in the longitudinal direction of the canes, along the direction of its fibers (c). Since the connections between the central joint and the bamboo members is crucial to achieve a liner flow of forces, these usually happen near nodes and, reinforcement of the cross section is needed to prevent future failures.

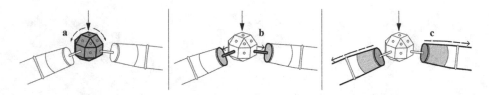

Fig. 10. Mechanical behavior of the multiangular jointing system

Exterior diameter, interior diameter and node distance are key elements to consider for the achievement of efficient load transference. The angle of each member is also important, since it indicates the direction of the load after it impacts the central joint. Finally, the total length of bamboo members represents the distance that the distributed load will travel until reaching another joint or structural element.

5.1   Data Flow Inside the Multiangular Parametric System

Geometry and configuration of every bamboo piece, deducted from the mechanical analysis of the jointing system, represents input data of the parametric system. Identified rules of design for multiangular joints serve as constructive principles of the system. Finally, output data formulates the design of a customized multiangular jointing system. Data flow inside the system is summarized in the next diagram Fig. 11:

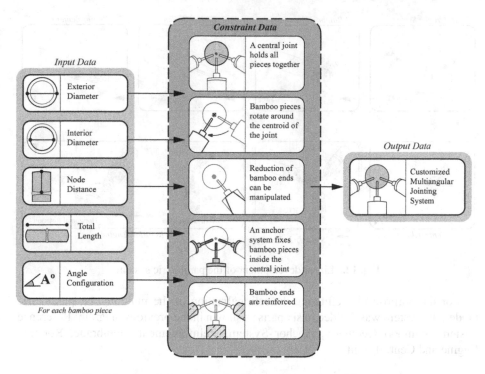

Fig. 11. Diagram of data flowing inside the parametric multiangular system

5.2 Sequential Development of the Parametric System

The parametric system is designed to evolve in a logical linear workflow. A set number of consecutive steps (Fig. 12) are systematically executed every time a new multiangular jointing system is designed.

The first step determines the starting point of the system (**1**). At this stage, the system establishes the location of a central point and an anchor point to fix the geometry of each bamboo piece. In the second step, information about the geometry of the first bamboo piece (**2**) is provided in order to build a 3-dimensional representation. Following this, a customized anchor system (**3**) is derived parametrically from the bamboo geometry. A customized reinforcement membrane (**4**) is then generated in consideration with the anchor system and bamboo piece. In the next step, the horizontal and vertical rotations (**5**) of the bamboo piece, the anchor system and the reinforcement membrane are calculated around the central point that was established in step one.

After positioning the first bamboo piece in the multiangular system, steps 1, 2, 3, 4 and 5 are executed for each piece in the jointing system (**6**). Once all pieces have been positioned, the final step is the design of a central joint (**7**). The centroid of the joint is equal to the central point defined in step one and, the groove depth of the anchor system determines the size of the joint.

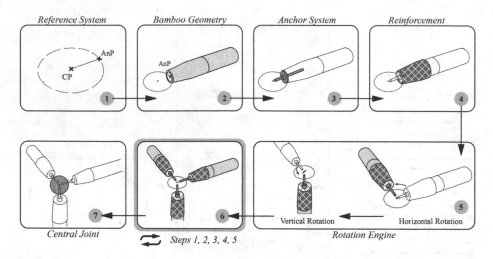

Fig. 12. Linear development of the parametric system

For the purpose of facilitating the rationalization of the multiangular parametric model, the system was divided in six parts as shown in the previous diagram: Reference System, Bamboo Geometry, Anchor System, Reinforcement Membrane, Rotation Engine and Central Joint.

5.3 Rationalizing the Parts

Reference System (Fig. 13)

1. Central point (CP) = 0,0
2. Distance from Central Point to Anchor Point (AnP) = Radius of the circle that circumscribes the polygonal figure formed by all bamboo pieces.
3. Anchor Point is placed along the circumference.
4. The designer can change the position of the Anchor Point (mAnP).

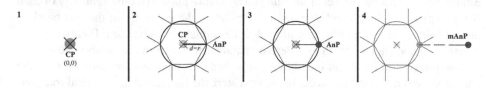

Fig. 13. Rationalization of reference system

Bamboo Geometry (Fig. 14)

For this part, the designer needs to input the following data of each bamboo piece: exterior diameter, interior diameter, node distance and total length.

1. C1 = Representation of bamboo end, anchored at modified anchor point (mAnP).

2. C2 = Representation of the start of the cone reduction. The designer provides distance from anchor point, but it has to be smaller than the node distance.
3. C3 = Representation of the node. Distance from anchor point is equal to node Distance (Nd).
4. C4 = Representation of the opposite bamboo end. Distance from anchor point is equal to the total length (Tl) of the bamboo.
5. The first bamboo end (C1) can be reduced.
6. Final representation of the geometry, using the circle line profiles as generative forms.

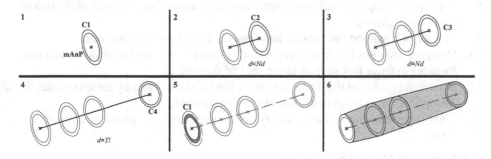

Fig. 14. Rationalization of bamboo geometry

Anchor System (Fig. 15)

1. Central Point of the plate is fix at the modified anchor point (mAnP).

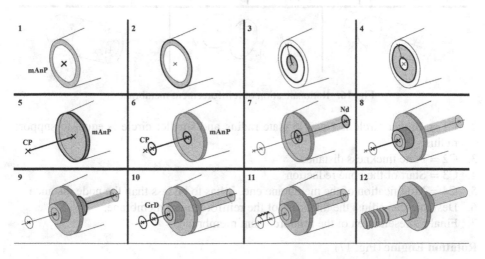

Fig. 15. Rationalization of anchor system

2.   Plate radius is equal to the exterior diameter of the first bamboo end.
3.   Bolt Radius is greater than 0 and less than half of the distance from anchor point to the inner diameter of the first bamboo end.
4.   Bolt Support Radius is greater than bolt radius and less than the distance from anchor point to the inner diameter of the first bamboo end.
5.   Plate thickness is greater than 0 and less than a quarter of the distance from central point (CP) to modified anchor point (mAnP).
6.   The start of the bolt is greater than plate thickness and less than the distance from central point (CP) to modified anchor point (mAnP).
7.   The end of the bolt is less than the node distance (Nd).
8.   Exterior bolt support thickness is less than the distance from the start of the bolt to the plate thickness.
9.   Interior bolt support thickness is less than the end of the bolt distance
10. Designer provides the groove depth (GrD), but it has to be less than the distance from the exterior bolt support to the start of the bolt.
11. The thread profile of the thread system of the bolt is restraint by the groove depth. The number of profiles in the thread can be modified.
12. Final representation of the geometry, using the circle line profiles as generative forms.

Reinforcement Membrane (Fig. 16)

1.   Reinforcement system will start at the central point of the anchor system plate (Plp).

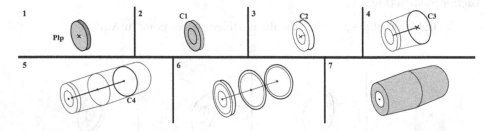

Fig. 16.   Rationalization of reinforcement membrane

2.   C1 = Bigger circle is equal to plate radius and smaller circle is equal to support radius.
3.   C2 = Plate thickness distance
4.   C3 = Start of the cone reduction
5.   C4 = Modification of the membrane end. It has to be less than the node distance.
6.   Designer can adjust the thickness of the reinforcement membrane.
7.   Final representation of the reinforcement membrane.

Rotation Engine (Fig. 17)

1.   Geometry is fixed to the anchor point (AnP).

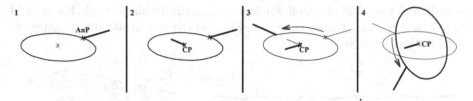

Fig. 17. Rationalization of the rotation engine

2. A line perpendicular to the longitudinal direction of the geometry is drawn at the central point (CP)
3. The geometry and the line rotate around the central point.
4. Geometry rotates around the perpendicular line in a vertical direction.

Central Joint (Fig. 18)

1. Centroid of the Central Joint is equal to Central Point.

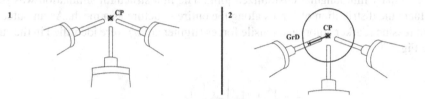

Fig. 18. Rationalization of the central joint

2. Joint Radius is equal to the distance from Central Point (CP) to Groove Depth (GrD).

5.4 Grasshopper Definition

The rationalized parts of the parametric system were built in Grasshopper as customized components. An additional customized component was also designed to help the designer specify and organize the geometric input data of each bamboo piece as well as its angular configuration. The Grasshopper Definition was designed to develop multi-angular joints for three to ten bamboo pieces.

5.5 Applicability of the Multiangular Parametric System

To exemplify how the customization of multiangular joints can improve structural performance by acknowledging geometric configurations, a multiangular joint was designed with the parametric system, taking as reference the structure of the German-Chinese House[1] (Fig. 19). The applicability of the multiangular parametric system was

---

[1] The German-Chinese House was a bamboo pavilion designed for the Shanghai Expo 2010. Markus Heinsdorff and MUDI architects developed the project. Information about the project can be found at: www.heinsdorff.de/en/work/installations/expo-shangai.

tested through a series of structural simulations, performed with the plugin Karamba 3d [8], to articulate how a parametric customized joint can help to take full advantage of the properties of bamboo.

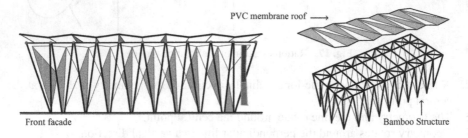

Fig. 19. German-Chinese house, used as design reference

The corner joint of the Chinese-Chinese House was chosen to inform the design of a preliminary multiangular customized joint. The first structural simulation was set to evaluate the distribution of forces along the entire structure as a mesh. As an outcome, compression (darker color) and tensile forces (lighter color) were identified in the structure Fig. 20.

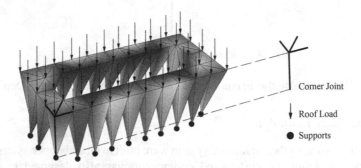

Fig. 20. Structural analysis of the German-Chinese house

Once the distribution of forces was identified for the entire structure, a structural analysis was carried out on the edges of the mesh to identify the stresses of every bamboo member as structural beams. The analysis was then narrowed down to the corner joint. As can be seen in the image below (Fig. 21), the corner joint is formed by four bamboo members and a central joint (a), a load from the roof is applied on the central joint, whilst P1, P2, P3 and P4 are anchored to other structural elements on its opposite ends (b). The analysis of the structure shows that members P1 and P3 are submitted to compression, while P2 and P4 are submitted to tension (c).

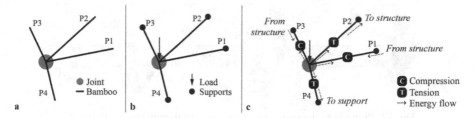

Fig. 21. Structural analysis of the corner joint of the German-Chinese house

After defining the stresses to which the corner joint would be submitted to, the next step was to input the geometric configurations of each bamboo member in the parametric system. The original Chinese-House was built with giant bamboo pieces with an average diameter of 230 mm. With the purpose of acknowledging individual geometric constraints, the pieces were considered to have diameters that ranged from 210 mm to 270 mm. The following table summarizes the information that was used as input data for the design of a customized parametric corner joint Table 1:

Table 1. Input data for the design of a multiangular jointing system

	Piece 1	Piece 2	Piece 3	Piece 4
Exterior diameter (in mm)	230	210	240	270
Interior diameter (in mm)	195	180	200	230
Node distance (in mm)	550	500	500	600
Total length (in mm)	2500	2500	2500	7000
Horizontal angle (0°–360°)	0°	45°	90°	45°
Vertical angle (0°–360°)	0°	0°	0°	60°

Once the system receives the input information, a customized joint is constructed with the option to further adjust the components of the multiangular joint. The resulting output is set as a mesh. In order to avoid random alteration of components, the resulting mesh was analyzed as a structural element, using as input data the structural information of the corner joint. In this manner, every time a variable was changed, the multiangular joint was structurally re-analyzed with the appropriate changes. This process allows the designer to optimized the multiangular jointing system according to the geometry of each bamboo and the structural demands of each member. The following image (Fig. 22) illustrates how the alteration of the joint size and reduction of bamboo ends contribute to achieve a better load performance. The smaller the surface of the joint, the quicker the efforts are transmitted to bamboo members. Distance between the joint and bamboo pieces is also important to control the velocity of load transmission. Finally, the area of the cross section of bamboo can also be reduced to create a quicker load transmission to the longitudinal section of the cane.

Fig. 22. Sample of the structural analysis of the parametric corner joint

After exploring different configurations for the multiangular parametric corner joint and analyzing its structural performance, a structurally optimized corner joint was proposed (Fig. 23). Reduction of bamboo ends is desirable, especially for members P1 and P2, which are submitted to tension (a). Although the configuration of each anchor system is particular for each bamboo piece, the recommended diameter of the anchor bolt should range between 12 mm to 18 mm, depending on the diameter of the bamboo end (b). Ideal size of the central joint should be smaller than the average diameter of bamboo pieces attached to it (c). Reinforcement membranes for P1 and P3 should be longer to provide reinforcement for bamboo fibers acting under tension; while reinforcement for P2 and P3 should be thicker, in order to reinforce the cane against common failures of elements submitted to compression (d).

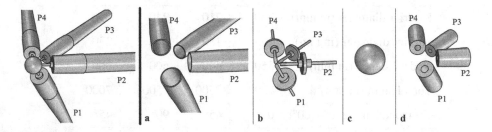

Fig. 23. Customized corner joint

The design of the customized corner joint suggests that acknowledgement of the geometric and mechanical properties of bamboo, as well as information about the expected structural behavior of the jointing system could help to enhance the structural performance of bamboo as a building material and also rationalize its design process. Under this approach, using bamboo as a building material becomes a hybrid process, where tradition is transferred to a digital realm to facilitate its construction methods. Outputs of the parametric system are thrown as digital meshes that can later become inputs for Computer Aided Manufacturing tools; hence the production of the customized jointing system can also be achieved through digital means in a short period of time.

This design approach enables the designer to have more freedom when using bamboo in a project. For instance, a particular design could require bamboo supports to be thicker than bamboo beams and, bracing elements could have their ends reduced to ensure optimal load transference. With a parametric system, attaining such detailed structural demands is possible; the designer just needs to input this data and the system will automatically perform the operations needed to generate a joint that adapts exclusively to that configuration.

6 Further Work and Relevance

The development of a parametric modeling system that compiles traditional knowledge of the other five joints commonly used in construction is still at an early stage. Rules of design have been outlined for all types of bamboo joints and, the development of the multiangular jointing system serves as reference to guide the development of the other jointing systems. Further analysis of each type of joint can help to improve the performance of the system. Additionally, characteristics like curvature of the culm, taper shape, nearly round ends and wall thickness variations can be added to the parametric system as design inputs. Although there is a considerable amount of work ahead, the effort of this research seems to suggest that the development of an application or software to facilitate the design of customized pole joints is a feasible project for the near future.

Materials are usually adapted to the needs of a project, adapting a material with random size, like bamboo, is a task hard to achieve with traditional means. Parametric modeling embraces the irregularities of bamboo, begging the system to adapt to these irregularities and not the other way around. Under this approach, bamboo's geometry has a saying in the design and, as a result, a better structural performance. Optimization of bamboo's shape, through the design of customized joints, can help to bridge the gap that separates bamboo from being used as a large-scale building material in permanent structures. Moreover, the rationalization of low-tech materials, like bamboo, urges the building industry to acknowledge that construction with low environmental impact is a reality that can be achieved.

In conclusion, parametric modeling is an exciting domain that can help to embrace the use of low-tech materials in the building industry and, most importantly is good to remind the reader that the scope of this research can be streamlined to other natural materials with implicit knowledge waiting to be discovered by the parametric designer.

References

1. Arce -Villalobos, O.A.: Fundamentals of the design of bamboo structures, Published Ph.D. Dissertation, Eindhoven University of Technology, Netherlands (1993)
2. Dunn, N.: Digital Fabrication in Architecture. Laurence King Publishing Ltd., London (2012)
3. Ghavami, K.: Bamboo: low cost and energy saving construction materials. In: Xiao, Y., et al. (eds.) Modern Bamboo Structures, pp. 5–21. CRC Press/Balkema, London (2008)
4. Hidalgo- López, O.: Manual de Construcción con Bambú, Colombia. Estudios Técnicos Colombianos Ltda., Colombia (1981)
5. Janssen, J.J.A.: Designing and building with bamboo. © International Network for Bamboo and Rattan, Netherlands (2000)
6. Jayanetti, L., Follet, R.: Bamboo in construction. In: Xiao, Y., et al. (eds.) Modern Bamboo Structures, pp. 23–32. CRC Press/Balkema, London (2008)

7. Kries, M., et al.: Grow Your Own House: Simón Vélez and Bamboo Architecture. Vitra Design Museum, Weil am Rhein (2000)
8. Preisinger, C.: Linking Structure and Parametric Geometry. Archit. Des. **83**, 110–113 (2013). doi:10.1002/ad.1564
9. Quintans, K.N.: Ancient Grass, Future Natural Resource: The National Bamboo Project of Costa Rica: A Case Study of the Role of Bamboo in International Development. INBAR, New Delhi (1998)
10. Vellinga, M., et al.: Atlas of Vernacular Architecture of the World. Routledge, Abingdon – Oxon (2007)
11. Whitehead, H.: Foreword. In: Woodbury, R.: Elements of Parametric Design. Routledge, London and New York, p. 1 (2010)
12. Woodbury, R.: Elements of Parametric Design. Routledge, London and New York (2010)

Assisted Construction of Non-standard Wooden Walls and Envelope Structures by Parametric Modeling

Oscar Gámez$^{(\boxtimes)}$, Jean-Claude Bignon, and Gilles Duchanois

School of Architecture of Nancy, Nancy, France
gamezbohl@univ-lorraine.fr,
{bignon, duchanois}@crai.archi.fr

Abstract. We introduce a parametric modeling method in the field of computer-aided architectural conception, which aims to produce non-standard wooden walls and envelopes with CNC machinery. This method explores the application of polygonal cellular structures (as patterns) on facade and envelope interventions for new and old projects. We innovate by bringing the 3D production environment complexity into the conception model to improve the production of manifold woodworking items by CNC (Computer Numerical Control) 3D fabrication. A recent experimentation, tests the entire workflow from parametric modeling to production of two full-scale prototypes. The results prove the range of inputs offered by the method to be functional, though it needs various improvements in order to optimize parametric modeling and digital fabrication procedures. Future research will focus on treating a wider range of joints via parametric modeling and deal with joint creation regardless wall deformation to expand the morphological approach of non-standard wooden walls design.

Keywords: Non-standard walls · Computer-aided architectural design · Wood construction · Parametric modeling · CNC fabrication · Mass customization

1 Introduction

The present paper shows the results obtained through a parametric modeling method that aims to create non-standard wooden walls composed by cell structures as part of the development of a new computer-aided architectural design tool. It deals with the subdivision of Nurbs surfaces by cell patterns as a method to create façade walls and envelopes with non-standard features associated to the shape and/or the characteristics of its parts. Cell patterns offer a variety of complex morphological problems associated with the feasibility of architectural objects dealing with such concept.

In a cell-patterned wall every cell has to respond to structural efforts, nevertheless the wall remains being light and easy to build, a fact that is true if we compare it to a standard wood frame wall. Taking into account that a wood frame standard wall weights up to 21.5 kg per sqm[1] [1, 2], Table 1 shows a reduction of 3.25 kg per sqm as

---

[1] Calculated using 2 × 4 studs and 9 mm OSB sheathings. No top or bottom plates are considered.

© Springer-Verlag Berlin Heidelberg 2015
G. Celani et al. (Eds.): CAAD Futures 2015, CCIS 527, pp. 291–308, 2015.
DOI: 10.1007/978-3-662-47386-3_16

the prototypes described herein have an average weight of 18.255 kg per sqm.[2] A future goal for us is to incorporate insulation material into every wall-cell, in order to take prefabrication of non-standard cellular wooden walls to a more industrial level, and then we will compare the weight facts including insulation components.

Table 1. Weight facts of a cellular wooden non-standard wall.

CELLULAR GRID WALL. WEIGHT FACTS		CELLULAR VORONOI WALL. WEIGHT FACTS	
Area per wood sheet (m2)	3.050	Area per wood sheet (m2)	3.050
Weight per sheet (kg)	17.970	Weight per sheet (kg)	17.970
Volume per sheet (m3)	0.037	Volume per sheet (m3)	0.037
Grid wall area (m2)	14.429	Voronoi wall area (m2)	11.050
Grid wall, wood volume (m3)	0.546	Voronoi wall, wood volume (m3)	0.420
Grid Wall total weight (kg)	262.821	Voronoi Wall total weight (kg)	202.170
Wall weight per sqm (kg)	18.215	Wall weight per sqm (kg)	18.296
Average weight per sqm	18.255 kg		
** insulation, top plates and bottom plates are not considered for this calculation.			

Another criterion is the use of materials. In a cellular wall every cell can be proportionally big compared to the whole wall, a fact that represents a saving in material consumption and mounting times because of the "puzzle" nature of cellular patterns.

Using the non-standard approach can lead to understand that those procedures are only suitable for new projects, which is the point that allows us to widen the application field of our method. As several old buildings are structurally stable but their aesthetics are poor, the presented method could contribute to rehabilitate old facade walls and turn them into aesthetically and energetically well-functioning components, a feature that would be particularly useful in constructions with poor energetic performance (like some flat buildings from the 60's and 70's). These are the main reasons why we chose to deal with cellular structures (represented as walls) as a subject of exploration in the non-standard environment.

Precedent works focus on creating structures using a modeling system that treats structural elements as bi-dimensional units that, once assembled, generate tridimensional complex architectural shapes. Such is the case of the Instant House [3] and the SUTD Library Pavilion [4] in which the use of a modeling procedure leads to a 2D cutting system that allowed the construction of complex standard and non-standard plywood structures; in both cases, regardless of the morphological approach of the structures, the model used for their conception dealt with the high degree of complexity derived from automated CNC fabrication.

In this context, we propose to create non-standard façade walls and envelopes conceived and produced by parametric modeling and 3D CNC means, with the aim to

---

[2] Data obtained from the prototyping experiment described herein.

develop a conception-to-production design tool based on the concept of mass customization that considers *"new processes to build using automated production, but with the ability to differentiate each artifact from those that are fabricated before and after"* [5].

As a test of the capabilities of our method at its initial development stage, we present the conception and production of two full-scale prototypes presented on a student contest organized in May 2014 by The School of Architecture of Nancy (ENSAN) and the Superior National School of Technologies and Wood Industries (ENSTIB) in the town of Epinal, France. It involved the modeling and production of two walls with different cell-morphologies that meant a different approach for assemblies, joints and item fabrication using a five axis industrial robot. The CAD to CAM interface proved to be complex as it strongly depends on software capabilities to produce fabrication commands, which finally turned out to be critical and had a heavy influence over the parametric model settings before starting its digital production.

2 Background: Non-standard Wooden-Cellular Structures

The non-standard approach, largely discussed in academic and professional environments, emerges as an alternative to the Euclidean paradigm and the Fordian serial model. It is underpinned on the principles of shape freedom and automated production, encouraged by the informatics avant-garde and the existence of more efficient robotic tools. Those aspects turned into novel design and production technics directly linked through the contemporary computational environments in which they work.

Hereby, the non-standard concept not only defines the formal properties of an architectural object like curvature, deformation, volume variation or the absence of stasis [6] but the techniques and tools that allow to produce those architectural geometries.

It is worth to tell that the equipment that allows the production of non-standard architectural shapes is the same used to accomplish the typical tasks of mass production, however, the way to master it defines its non-standard way of use. That is the case of the Times Eureka Pavillion by Nex Architecture [7] (Fig. 2A) in which a collection of Voronoi cells of different shapes and sizes is produced with industrial robots, however, the task of programming and defining special cut paths requires special capabilities from the designer [8] to customize the cut tasks that lead to produce such unique pieces without sacrificing time and/or material. So the non-standard concept is also applied to the method used to produce these special architectural objects.

This approach evidences the complex link between digital technology and architectural culture [9] in which the conception of form and its materialization merge as one problem. Hardly, with the contemporary techniques, a gridshell, a blob line-network structure or a cellular structure are conceived without implicitly calculating the way it will be achieved by automated means. In works like the Parasite Project [10] the modeling algorithm has to go deep into assembling details in order to make the cells which conform the structure not only feasible but stable.

Those works dealt with the creation of cell joinery in different ways. Whilst the Parasite project (Fig. 1A) worked on a 2D interface to fold the items, assemble the cells and rigidify a structure; the Eureka pavilion (Fig. 2A) worked on a 3D fabrication approach to customize the joinery cutting paths of every item cell according to the angle of incidence between them.

A project of the same kind executed by Fabian Scheurer had the same approach. In the Swissbau pavilion [11], the miter joints between the cell frame items were solved by 3D cutting. Figure 1B shows how the miter has two cuts. The first one creates the miter and a second profiled-cut gives room to a wood-fastener that binds the pieces together.

The examples cited so far (and others like them), apply the non-standard conception and fabrication approach to ephemeral structures, most of them represented by pavilions. However, to find these concepts applied to cellular structures in permanent walls (or other kind of permanent structures) is rare but not absent. The Andrée Chedid library [12] in Paris, introduces a honeycomb patterned wall as part of an extension project for a library (Fig. 2B). The side walls of the auditorium are produced following the same principle of modeling and CNC 3D fabrication discussed by Fabian Scheurer in his lectures [8], but this time, the cellular approach deals with a permanent construction that must respond to strict requirements in matters of insulation and stability. As the walls are not curved, the non-standard concept lies in the application of the pattern to a wall that is made of wood and whose production is founded on the principles of mass customization, which is one of the aspects that characterize non-standard production.

Another example is the pavilion for the EDF solar energy central at Toul-Rosières in France (Fig. 2C) conceived by the studio Cartignies + Canonica. It is a wooden-sphere composed by rectangular cell-boxes arranged in a running bond pattern in which cells are prefabricated by using CNC milling machines, despite the fact of the design not being entirely achieved by parametric means, the approach to the non-standard concept for wooden-walls is valid.

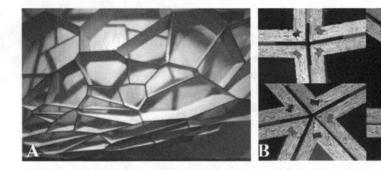
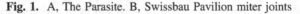

Fig. 1. A, The Parasite. B, Swissbau Pavilion miter joints

The building is composed by a self-holding monolithic spherical wall in which the boxes (cells) are mounted prior to injecting a fiber glass insulation compound. A vapor control layer covers the structure before giving way to the final layer of steel panels which give finish to the pavilion.

Given this background, for us, the non-standard architectural concept refers to the diverse morphological and constructive approaches not bounded to stylistic paradigms but to the potential of digital modeling and fabrication. It is related to the morph-geometric aspects of architectural objects conceived through parametric modeling and the technical features of their components (details, joints, assemblies). As for the non-standard wooden-walls, the concept characterizes the non-Euclidean architectural object whose physical elements have different shapes, dimensions or materials.

Based on that context the use of patterns have a great potential to create cellular structures applied to our field of study as an alternative to explore new morphological-structural possibilities different from the traditional standard ones.

Since patterns can take various morphologic approaches, they are a good mecha-nism to explore cells as structural components created by parametric modeling, in which case we call them "boxes". Those "boxes" are the product of paneling a Nurbs surface by dividing it with a cell pattern (Fig. 6A).

To test the capabilities of the method (further described), an experiment involving the modeling and production of two non-standard wall prototypes was executed in May 2014 as part of an academic event known as the wood challenges - Défis du Bois in French - (UMR MAP/CRAI 3495, 2014). The contest took place at Cours park in the town of Epinal, France, from the 13th to the 20th of May; its conception began 73 days earlier at the facilities of the Center for Research in Architecture and Engineering (C.R. A.I, by its French acronym) at the School of Architecture of Nancy, France. Fabrication and assembling took place at the ENSTIB and a total of 80 days were necessary to conceive and build the prototypes using ½" × 4' × 8' plywood sheets for structural components (boxes), ½" × 3½" bolts for box attachment and #6 × 1" screws for box assembling.

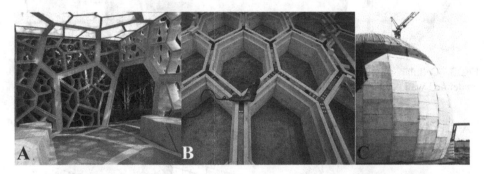

Fig. 2. A, Eureka Pavilion Voronoi Structure. B, Andree Chedid Library honeycomb wall structure. C, Solar Energy Pavilion running bond cell structure -image courtesy of Cartignies-Canonica Architects.

3 Method

Herein we present a method intended to create and produce non-standard facade walls with cellular "wood-box" structures through parametric modeling and 3D digital fab-rication. To achieve those goals, the method has two approaches:

(a) Parametric Modeling of Non-standard Walls. The process begins by acquiring information from the wall context. It can be a free shape (as is the case) or a fragment of an old or new dwelling that defines the intervention limits and its geometric characteristics which are merged into a Nurbs surface (Fig. 3B).

To create the base surface it is possible to use any modeling software capable of dealing with Nurbs geometry which is later imported into Rhinoceros and Grasshopper (henceforth named RGH). To explain the process more accurately, let us imagine a given wall whose properties such as height, curvature, thickness and openings are already defined (Fig. 3A). The abstract form of that wall is represented by a Nurbs surface (Fig. 3B) which inherits the wall's morphological and geometric features; given the tools offered by the RGH environment we panelize [13] that surface and divide it into small sub-surfaces by using a grid (Figs. 3C and 4A). The density and variations of the grid will help to define the features of a pattern that will serve as a modifier of the Nurbs surface. RGH allows exploring the way points on a grid are linked to each other by lines; the rhythm and frequency of those connections generate the patterns we intend to use in order to produce what we have already defined as non-standard wooden walls. The acquired pattern (Fig. 4B) is now associated to a predefined geometric morphology and becomes the base element to redefine the wall's inner structure and turn it into a cellular one (Fig. 4C).

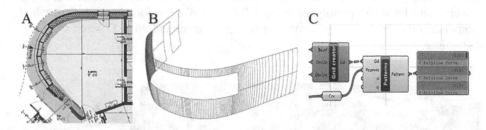

Fig. 3. Cellular structure derived from an actual wall. A, Wall. B, Base surface extracted from predefined wall. C, Grid and pattern algorithms. Refer to next figure.

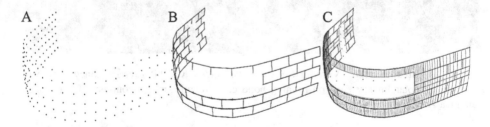

Fig. 4. Patterned surface. A, point grid. B, pattern obtained by linking points on a grid. C, pattern associated to a wall's base surface.

Regarding the prototyping experiment described herein, we did not use a predefined wall but free surfaces instead in order to accomplish one of the contest's constraints: limited time for conception and production.

The parametric algorithm defines the walls constraints and adds curvature to one of them in order to test how complex the assemblies could be as curvature and shearing of a given structure increase.

The various obtainable patterns, give the designer the ability to choose between different valid models. Prior to a pattern choice for exploration an analysis to evaluate the complexity of patterns was performed considering the following aspects:

Pattern Density: Being a pattern derived from a collection of points placed in a container (grid) and the size of each pattern module (cell) defined by the proximity between these points; the closer the points are, the smaller the cell gets, resulting in an increasing number of structural components and therefore of junction points. This means that the number of elements to deal with, in function of their quantity, is harder to manage (more complex) from the computational and production point of view.

Pattern Typology: once again, the complexity concept is bounded to the logical and computational processes needed to render the pattern into a wall structure. Honeycomb patterns and quad patterns, for instance, are more like regular patterns in which the variables are easier to be controlled from the modeling point of view as the produced cells will always have the same number of vertices so that resulting data trees are not very complex. But for others like the Voronoi pattern, is different. A Voronoi pattern is more complex since the number of variables to treat cell vertices increases in function of the number of sides of every cell, resulting in cutting paths that are less regular and more demanding to program. Nesting is also different. With a regular pattern there is more chance to get an optimal use of plywood sheets to avoid waste, but with irregular ones, the amount of waste increases resulting in a harder material optimization task.

Other aspects of this analysis remain out of the scope of the present paper, however it demonstrates that due to its computational backgrounds, the parametric modeling of cell structures refers its complexity to the concept of disorganized complexity [14] in which the number of variables of a problem do not follow parallel but random paths.

We tested the morphological possibilities of various patterns (Fig. 5) so that a surface can be divided by projecting a pattern onto it therefore obtaining a series of panels later treated as cells and as parts of a structure (Fig. 6C and D).

As the goal is to get a feedback from pattern complexity, we used which seemed to be the less and the most complex patterns: a regular quad pattern and a Voronoi pattern (Fig. 5A and B).

The parametric model uses a series of inputs to create a structure out of a pattern. At the scale of the wall they determine (or adapt to) curvature, pattern morphology,

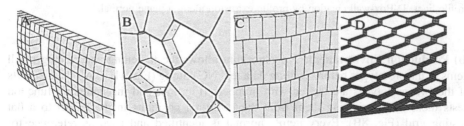

Fig. 5. Exploration patterns. A, Quad. B, Voronoi. C, Running bond. D, Hexagonal.

cell density, surface paneling (cell creation), cell size and redefine wall thickness (constant or variable).

At the scale of the "box", inputs define their properties by taking information from the production environment such as file exchange, CNC programming, CNC execution, assembling and mounting. Those inputs are thickness of cell-walls and cell-covers (inherited from the wood sheet in use), joint management (miters and rabbets), cell connector placement (fasteners) and drillings (Fig. 7). Since a box is derived from the paneling of a surface by means of a pattern (Fig. 6A), the acquired panel outline defines the edges of a box (Fig. 6B) and thus its contour walls and covers which inherit thickness from the chosen material (½" plywood) – (Fig. 6). The intersections between these items (box-covers and box-walls) are treated as wood joints (Fig. 6C, Figs. 7 and 12A).

Joints are obtained by means of heuristic filtering from data trees. To do so, the box edges are extracted in order to perform a series of intersections from which a collection of junction points are obtained (Figs. 7 and 12A) and systematically ordered to create the defining profiles of wood joints (miters and/or rabbets).

The acquired profiles (Figs. 6C and 7) allow the geometry of structural boxes to be split, so the process becomes a sequence of splitting, cutting and capping operations that lead to create box items (Fig. 6D) and consequently the prototype structures.

Though, some difficulties appeared. First, the point extraction method is unforgiving in matters of curvature. Excessive curvature of the base surface proved to be less tolerated by the parametric model as some points were lost or their order was changed resulting in wrong joint profiles and an erroneous output. Diminishing curvature gave a positive result towards fabrication, although the general idea is to achieve curved structures, as shown on Fig. 3A, without having this problem.

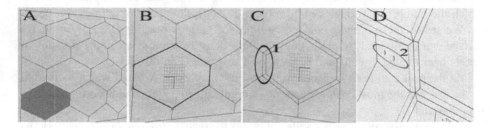

Fig. 6. Box generation. A-Surface subdivision by a pattern. B-Loop (box) creation by a closed polyline and work plane extraction. C- Box-wall thickness defined by patch subdivision with profile lines. D-Box-wall creation by profile extrusion along a plane normal.

(b) Production Environment. The algorithm allows the flattening and nesting of all items in the prototypes before sending data to CNC cutting (Fig. 11C). All the elements of the two prototypes are tagged with numbers (Fig. 8A) and the flattening function nests them by re-orienting them from their original positions in the model to a flat nesting grid (Fig. 8B). Every item's normal is identified and used as reference for tagging and positioning items into the flat grid. Considering that items are grouped into a data tree, the initial plane and final plane must have the same data structure to preserve the order of elements and tags.

The nesting's final optimization was made manually to save material and time when cutting; however, it will be necessary to adopt a different nesting technique in order to optimize the 3D cutting procedure. Before passing to execution, two production constraints were considered and integrated into the parametric model:

CNC Machine: Güdel industrial 5-axis robot with an ABB controller
Machine tools: A 25 mm coarse tooth mill and 15" saw

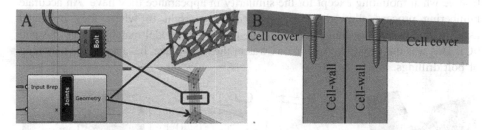

Fig. 7. Joints. A, Voronoi-wall. Generation of Miter joints by point-to-line profiles and cell-fixing bolts. B, Grid-wall rabbet joints treatment.

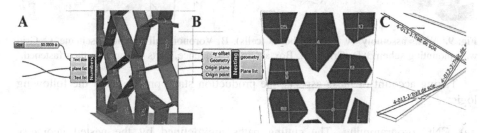

Fig. 8. A-On-model tagging. B-Nesting. C-Cadwork BTL instructions.

Some parameters were adjusted to match these conditions. For instance, angle cuts in rabbet operations were not possible because of the diameter of the mill-end (25 mm) which led to eliminate curvature and shearing of the structures on axis Z, resulting in all rabbet joints being forced to a 90° angle (Figs. 7B and 14D).

Other operations like transportation, assembling and mounting had their influence on the parametric model as well. As all boxes had to be prefabricated, their size should be easy to manage by one person and adequate to fit in a small truck.

An execution time projection per plywood sheet established that producing the structures would take more time than it was available, this forced a reduction in cell density of both structures to improve the production schedule in 48 working hours by reducing the grid structure from 60 to 24 boxes and the Voronoi structure from 38 to 18 boxes.

Once the model is complete it implicitly sets the assembling procedure of components. A Voronoi cell, for instance, is assembled based on its cover (Figs. 9A and 12C). Since the cover is the item containing the final shape of the box, the box-walls are assembled using its borders as reference. Miter joints are then put together, glued and fastened with screws to keep the joint stable, which is the same for rabbet joints (Figs. 7b and 9D).

The general layout of every wall gives an idea of the process that will be used for mounting as every box acts like a module that, in some cases, fits in one way only. This is quite obvious for the Voronoi prototype (Fig. 9B) but not for the grid one, this is where numbering the boxes counts.

For the grid structure, all items fit in almost the same way so there is not much trouble when mounting except for the similarity in appearance they have. An accurate numbering process allowed positioning the boxes right to where they belonged assuring that the bolt drillings defined in the parametric model matched (Figs. 7A and 9C). This was the way to know if a box was in the right place, because of the matching of bolt drillings.

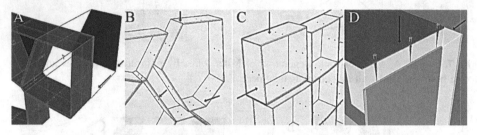

Fig. 9. Walls assembly. A, Voronoi boxes (cells). B, Voronoi wall mounting scheme. C, Grid wall mounting scheme. D, Grid-wall. Box assembly sequence, parts fit together then fastened.

Taking account of these aspects, the production stage process uses the following logic:

(a) CNC programming. The cutting paths are defined by the nested geometry exported from RGH into Cadwork, a program that identifies the milling operations and converts them into CAM commands (Fig. 11A) which are exported into LignoCAM to turn the cutting commands readable by the robot controlling software (ISO code).

(b) CNC cutting. The cutting paths are verified with the simulation tools of the Güdel robot software (Fig. 11B), later, the plywood sheets are cut using these cutting paths (Fig. 11C).

(c) Item classification: Items are manually tagged, grouped and placed.

(d) Verification: unsuccessful items are refabricated. If the robot is not available, they are repeated using standard machinery: electric saws for straight cuts, shapers for miters and rabbets and drills for bolt perforations.

(e) Box assembling: Classified items are manually assembled. Rabbets and miters serve as assembling joints fastened with screws and stabilized with glue (Figs. 7B and 12B).

(f) On-workshop mounting: Boxes must be pre-installed in order to find defective boxes and fix them before sending them to the work site (Fig. 13A and C).
(g) Transportation and mounting: The structural components have to be classified by prototype and sent in that order to the work site (Figs. 13B, D and E). Mounting takes up to two people per prototype using standard tools: Screwdrivers, jigsaws, hammers and sanders.

Figure 10 resumes the necessary workflow with which our method works to achieve conception and production of a non-standard cellular wall.

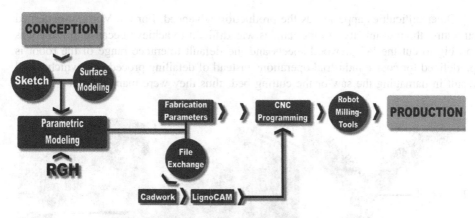

Fig. 10. Conception to production workflow

4   Conception to Production

This stage uses the nested elements modelled with Grasshopper and exports them in a Step format (**.stp) to Cadwork. We use Cadwork to create the BTL files [15] needed by the CAM interface (LignoCAM) to communicate with the robot controller (Fig. 8C). Despite its large database of milling operations, some complications emerged when Cadwork did not get to read some modeling operations from the imported geometry, which led to manual programming of several BTL instructions (Fig. 11) to create the necessary ISO code that feeds the robot controller and thus to create the machine trajectories, resulting in significant delays. Such situation was particularly usual with some rabbets (for the grid structure) and miters (Voronoi structure).

Once the set of instructions for CNC cutting are created, the machining process started proving to be fast. Processing a plywood sheet takes 18 min in average, including fastening, cutting, numbering, clearing and sorting of items.

The cutting interface of the robot allows the user to simulate the fabrication routine before launching it (Fig. 11B), providing information about invalid cutting trajectories to correct them directly in the CAM interface, avoiding unnecessary delays by repeating file exchange procedures.

Concerning the situation found with Cadwork not reading some machining operations to turn them into BTL language, several of the affected items were cut by CNC but some woodworking operations (especially miters) were made manually.

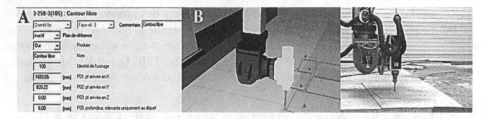

Fig. 11. A, Cutting path commands. B, Cutting path simulation. C, CNC cutting.

Other difficulties appeared as the production advanced. For the Voronoi-patterned structure, the multiplicity of miter angles was difficult to achieve because the saw was too big to cut the ½" plywood sheets and the default tolerance range of the robot is predefined for coarse industrial operations instead of detailing procedures, which could result in damaging the saw or the cutting bed, thus they were manually cut.

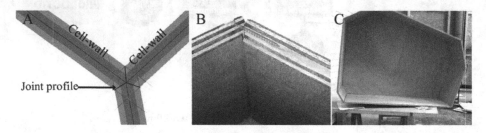

Fig. 12. Voronoi box assembly. A, Miter profiles on cell-walls. B, Miter +fastening. Angles not matching well after cutting. C, Assembled box. Some miters do not fit well.

An important issue was found when trying to create the CAM commands for the voronoi cell-walls. The milling command database of Cadwork did not get to create a numerical definition for miter cuts so that manual programming was necessary. Being the number of items to be cut as big as about 150 elements, the manual programming of each milling operation could take about 10 min, which means 3.5 working days for programming.

Account taken of that fact, it was decided to cut a part of the miter joints manually and the other with the robot. In both cases there were cutting mistakes either because of the lack of precision of standard machines (i.e. manually cut items) or because of errors when programming the cutting paths. A constant issue was the mirroring of cutting trajectories and/or angles, which resulted in inversed miter angles and consequently in useless items.

Aside of these complications, once items were cut and classified, the boxes were assembled and a mounting test was performed before sending the wall components to the construction site to be installed (Figs. 13A and C). All boxes left the facility numbered and referenced along with their fastening accessories and bottom plates for support; it took two days to mount the prototypes.

Though the achieved results are acceptable, optimization is needed to avoid the creation of an ISO code for the cutting paths to be readable. Aware of the potential of robotic simulation tools given by the HAL plugin within grasshopper, one of the next steps is to achieve the creation of cutting paths by using a tool like this instead of making a file exchange between several programs, however, the prototyping sessions heavily rely on the capabilities of the available equipment.

Fig. 13. Mounting of prototype structures. A, grid-wall on-workshop mounting. B, grid-wall on-site mounting; boxes positioned by bolt drillings. C, Voronoi wall on-workshop mounting test. D.E, Voronoi wall on-site mounting.

5   After Production Evaluation

The prototype structures were exposed from the 20th May 2014 until the end of the summer under open-air conditions, without showing extreme changes caused by moisture or sudden temperature changes (Fig. 16).

However, an important production problem related to the CNC cutting process was identified and its causes evaluated to check for possible solutions in future prototyping tests. The problem, first identified as a calibration issue, led to wrong rabbet and miter profiles. Using visual inspection and a lasegrammetry equipment to evaluate a group of defective items, we could establish the deviation amount of the milling tool on axis Z of the cutting path.

As plywood thickness is only ½", the deviation proved to be too high in relation with the given thickness of the affected items. The visual analysis was carried out on 3 box components randomly chosen from the installed prototypes (Fig. 14C) and the lasergrammetry test was executed on an item that could not be used due to the fabrication defects on two of its rabbets (Fig. 14A).

The acquired data from produced items, showed rabbet depth differences in a range from −8 % to 50 % compared to the theoretical depths of the parametric model. This means that a rabbet that should be 6 mm deep after milling, in fact was 9 mm deep (50 %) or 5 mm deep (−8 %) (Fig. 15). An example is the box # 4 of the grid-pattern wall, in which the height on rabbet "A" was 50 % higher than it should be (9 mm instead of 6 mm) and height on rabbet "D" was 33 % deeper (8 mm instead of 6 mm) (Figs. 14C and 15).

Not all of the defective items were rejected; an error tolerance was determined in order to accomplish the execution of the structure in time. As all the boxes participate of the structural efforts of the structure and joints do not assume them all, we decided to assemble the boxes with items having less than a 50 % deviation on the cutting path error (refer to Fig. 12B).

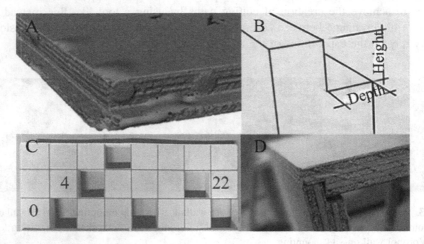

Fig. 14. Prototype evaluation. A-Defective joint lasergrammetry test. B- Rabbet measurement parameters. C-Evaluated boxes. D-Successful rabbet joint

In an effort to study the causes that led to these problems two questions arose in order to make this situation clear:

a. Was the path deviation problem caused by a lack of calibration of the machine?
b. Was there a human mistake when attaching the plywood sheets to the cutting bed?

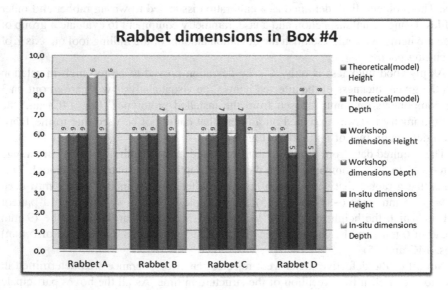

Fig. 15. Rabbet cutting deviation analysis.

With these questions in mind, the ENSTIB made an inspection to the axis calibration setup of its Güdel robot finding that a new setup is mandatory to avoid such lack of precision in the future.

Regarding the "b" point, there was a mistake during the production stage when fixing the wood sheets to the cutting table resulting in excessive sheet vibration when milling, though a more accurate procedure will be implemented in future full-scale prototyping experiments to avoid it.

6 Discussion

The method described herein, deals with the conception by parametric modeling and the digital fabrication of non-standard wooden walls suitable for new and old projects whereby they can get to perform as energetically passive architectural elements. To do so, once the structural and construction challenges will be solved, an analysis on thermal conductivity including insulating components will be performed in order to prove that this system can act as a passive solution for energetic performance improvement according to the scope described in chapter one.

The execution of two non-standard wall prototypes allowed us to test the capabilities of our method in its initial stage of development by participating of an academic event in which the prototypes were mounted and exhibited (Fig. 16).

The tested actions focused on the development of a 3D fabrication routine to produce two typical woodworking joints applied to pattern-generated non-standard wooden structures. We test two joint types: rabbets and miters. The parametric model with which we conceive the prototypes manages to create the necessary data to fabricate those joints and repeat them over different shaped structural items, regardless of the chosen pattern or the variations over the architectural element of which they make part.

As CNC machining facilitates the fabrication process, there are aspects to keep in mind when working with CNC machinery that lead to an ideal work environment. For instance, machinery and tools must be adequate to the scale of the intended structure.

The parametric algorithm can always receive feedback from its production environment and adapt the structure as necessary to achieve its digital fabrication, although having the right tools adds freedom to execution and improves the workflow efficacy.

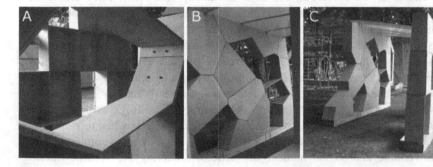

Fig. 16. Final result. Mounted non-standard-wall prototypes. A, Grid Wall. B Voronoi wall. C, Walls mounted.

It is important to emphasize that not all of the process is optimized by automation; there are tasks that remain analog and need human intervention to be done, nevertheless, parametric modeling and digital fabrication both reduce the amount of specialized workmanship needed since all structural items are numbered and referenced. Tasks like modeling, programming, fastening and clearing plywood sheets, numbering, sorting, assembling and mounting require human abilities; however, the most accurate part, which is cutting, is achieved through automation giving an important boost to the process along with the simulation advantages of parametric modeling.

7 Conclusions

This paper exposes the achieved results of testing a method whose purpose is to produce non-standard wooden walls with cell-pattern morphologies, as part of the initial development of a design tool in the field of computer-aided architectural conception. It is intended to be applied on old and new projects as a an exploration design tool which is based on the principle of cellular subdivision of surfaces by patterns, turning them into structures suitable for façade and envelope walls, using wood as primary material.

Two wall prototypes were conceived and built by using the mentioned method, in which digital fabrication is the first step in the production chain of structural components. As each one of the prototypes has a particular morphological approach (Voronoi and grid patterns) some differences and similarities were found when conceiving and materializing them. The common point is the base procedure of modeling which uses a Nurbs surface and a pattern to panelize that surface and convert it into a collection of panels later transformed into cells which, once grouped, create a wall. However, the differences arise when focusing on the specific qualities of each wall according to the complexity of the pattern from a computational point of view.

The wall with the quad pattern is easier to achieve in terms of modeling and production because of the pattern regularity (Fig. 16A). As all the cells have the same number of sides, identifying the vertices of every cell is quite a serial process that requires no complex calculations regardless of the variations of curvature and shearing that the structure might suffer in the modeling process. Programming is also simple. Since the angles of incidence between cells are always the same, there are neither special cutting paths to define nor special angles to cut either, meaning that the reference point for the machine to cut the plywood sheets remains invariable.

The assembling and mounting process adopt the same simplicity as the precedent operations (refer to Fig. 9; however, special care has to be taken in order to not confuse items when they are being classified because of their aspect similarity, which can lead to an erroneous classification and thus in delays when assembling.

The wall with the Voronoi pattern, on the contrary (Fig. 16B), evidences some difficulties in modeling and execution. The most remarkable issue when modeling lies on joint creation. Given the fact that no cell is similar to any other, the number of sides per cell is variable and so the number of vertices, rendering the vertices filtering operation for joint creation into a complex data tree that needs an accurate criterion for sorting random series of points.

Concerning the production process, the nesting operation for saving material is complex as well since arranging irregular items is more demanding and the automated process cannot make it on its own, so human intervention is necessary to accommodate the items into a plywood sheet, reducing at the same time, the waste of material. Assembling the Voronoi prototype is also demanding. Because of all the cells being different in shape and size, the items composing every cell are different too. The tagging and assembling operations take about 40 % more time to be executed than with a regular patterned structure however, once assembled, the process is more intuitive.

As joinery is the most complex modeling and fabrication operation to perform, our aim is to generate a database with several joint types usable with different pattern morphologies, creating a generic set of functional assemblies regardless of the shape variations of structural items composing a non-standard wooden wall. So far, two joint types are being tested. The success in mastering these joints with different cell morphologies will open the way to test other joint techniques and render the method into a more generic tool.

Future research will seek for other joint types to be included and managed via parametric modeling in order to expand the morphological options of this approach. In addition, the integration of insulating components will be studied as a means to test the energetic performance of non-standard pattern-generated wooden walls.

Acknowledgements. The described work was possible with the funding of the Lorraine region as well as the technologic and human support of the ENSTIB and the Laboratory for Studies and Research in Wood (LERMAB) at Epinal, France; the Map C.R.A.I and the School of Architecture of Nancy and the team of the wood challenges (*défis du bois*). Special thanks to Anis Bouali (CNC programming), Julien Lallemand (robot operation), Marie Claude Plourde and Esmael Moussavi (assembling and mounting).

References

1. Structural Board Association: Oriented Strand Board in Wood Frame Construction. Structural Board Association, Ontario, Canada L3R 5L9 (2005)
2. Ziff, M.: WEIGHT OF WALL AND PARTITIONS IN - Weights of Materials.pdf. http://www.interiorarchitecture.ohiou.edu/ziff/hcia350/Weights%20of%20Materials.pdf
3. Botha, M., Sass, L.: The instant house: design and digital fabrication of housing for developing environments. Caadria 2006, Kumamoto (Japan) (2006)
4. Sevtsuk, A., Kalvo, R.: A freeform surface fabrication method with 2D cutting. In: Gerber, D., Goldstein, R., Tampa, F. (eds.) 2014 Proceedings of the Symposium on Simulation for Architecture and Urban Design, pp. 109–116 (2014)
5. Anzalone, P., Vidich, J., Draper, J.: Non-uniform assemblage: mass customization in digital fabrication. In: Without a Hitch: New Directions in Prefabrication Architecture |. UmassAmherst (2008)
6. Lynn, G.: Animate Form. Princeton Architectural Press, New York (1999)
7. Dempsey, A., Piasecki, M., Chung, J.: Times Eureka Pavilion (2011). http://www.nex-architecture.com/projects/times-eureka-pavilion/
8. Scheurer, F.: Materialising complexity. Archit. Des. **80**, 86–93 (2010)
9. Migayrou, F., Mennan, Z.: Architectures non standard, Paris (2003)

10. Kolarevic, B.: Architecture in the Digital Age: Design and Manufacturing. Taylor & Francis, New York (2005)
11. Design to Production: designtoproduction - Swissbau Pavilion, Basel (2005). http://www.designtoproduction.ch/content/view/11/43/
12. D'HOUNDT+BAJART: MEDIATHEQUE ANDREE CHEDID, TOURCOING - D'HOUNDT+BAJART architectes&associés. http://www.dhoundtplusbajart.fr/MEDIATHEQUE-ANDREE-CHEDID-TOURCOING
13. Issa, R.: Paneling tools (2011). http://wiki.mcneel.com/_media/labs/panelingtoolsmanual.pdf
14. Weaver, W.: Science and complexity. Am. Sci. **36**, 536–544 (1948)
15. Sema, C.: design2machine - the data transfer interface for wood constructions - btl v10. http://www.design2machine.com/btl/index.html

Building Information Modelling (BIM)

A BIM-Compatible Schema for Architectural Programming Information

Ehsan Barekati[✉], Mark J. Clayton, and Wei Yan

Texas A&M University, College Station, USA
{ehsan.barekati,mark-clayton,wyan}@tamu.edu

Abstract. Architectural programming, although a key part of AECFM processes, has not been well integrated into Building Information Modeling (BIM). Having access to architectural programming information throughout the lifecycle of a building can add value to design evaluation, facility management, renovation and extension. There is not currently a comprehensive and standard data model to store architectural programming information. Our research is producing a universal format for an architectural program of requirements (UFPOR) that can connect the architectural programming information to the IFC BIM schema. The result is a data model for architectural programming that is inherently interoperable with BIM standard schema. A graphical user interface facilitates data creation and manipulation. The schema and effectiveness of the bridging fields has been tested by entering the content of three two different architectural programming documents into the UFPOR database.

Keywords: BIM · Architectural programming · Data modelling · Interoperability · IFC

1   Introduction

BIM as an information ecosystem is now an established way of communication between the stakeholders in AECFM projects. As BIM becomes more prominent, the data interoperability amongst different BIM applications becomes more essential as well [1, 2]. In an environment of mobile devices and constant wireless networking, communication becomes more and more important [3]. Although BIM has provided a platform to connect different disciplines in the AECFM industry, architectural programming is still disconnected from BIM models [4]. Having access to architectural programming information throughout the lifecycle of a building can be invaluable in different disciplines such as design evaluation, facility management, renovation and extension. The lack of a comprehensive and standard data model to store architectural programming information is a major current challenge to further smoothing AECO processes. The authors are addressing that challenge by developing a universal format for an architectural program of requirements (UFPOR) [5]. In this paper, enhancements to the UFPOR are presented and we further examine the potential of the UFPOR in connecting architectural programming to a BIM schema.

Achieving interoperability between the UFPOR and BIM requires coordinating the data schema. The International Foundation Classes (IFC) are a widely accepted open

© Springer-Verlag Berlin Heidelberg 2015
G. Celani et al. (Eds.): CAAD Futures 2015, CCIS 527, pp. 311–328, 2015.
DOI: 10.1007/978-3-662-47386-3_17

standard for storing a BIM. While all the data fields defined in the UFPOR are not directly covered by the standard BIM schema such as IFC, many of the data fields and object models can be shared between the two data schema. These shared data fields allow creation of an overlay between the UFPOR and BIM schema. By using the same schema and naming convention to model the overlapping area in a BIM and the respective UFPOR, a pipeline is formed through which the two schema can communicate. The result is a data model for architectural programming which is inherently interoperable with BIM standard schema. The pipeline will increase the accessibility of architectural programing information in a BIM data model by eliminating the cost and inaccuracy involved in any type of data conversion.

To test this model, we have created a digital database for the UFPOR schema capable of storing architectural programming information. A graphical user interface was added to the database to facilitate data creation and manipulation. We have tested the proposed schema and the effectiveness of the bridging fields by entering the content of three different architectural programming documents into the UFPOR database. The comprehensiveness of the proposed schema (UFPOR) is measured by the success rate in entering information from manual documents into the digital database. Failure in covering all the pieces of information included in manual architectural programs reveals areas in UFPOR where additional data fields should be added. The success in connecting architectural programming discipline to a BIM schema is measured by the success in populating the bridging fields.

2   Formats of Architectural Programming and UFPOR

Formats of architectural programming are a long debated topic in architecture industry [6]. Several authors have published their thoughts on architectural programming and proposed formats to structure the architectural programs [7–9]. The authors have reviewed several of those formats and have proposed a universal format for a program of requirements based on their finding [5]. The process and the results have been discussed in detail in a separate paper. UFPOR is based on five base classes: environment, people, activity, need, and assessment. Below we describe each class briefly:

- Environment. We define an Environment as any entity that is capable of containing human beings or other environments. Based on this definition a kitchen is an environment since it can contain people. A house is also an environment since it contains human beings as well as other environments (e.g. a kitchen). Our definition, because it is recursive, is scale independent, meaning that a city is also an environment.
- People. Architectural environments are intended for the use of people. People can have different roles regarding a specific environment. Occupants, clients, authorities and even the society are all subclasses of people.
- Activity. Activities are the connection between people and the environments. Activities are what people do in environments. A good environment is equipped to host at least one activity properly.
- Need. Accommodations of needs (also referred to as goals, requirements, etc.) are the main reason for creating an environment. Throughout the architectural

programming process by studying people needs we discover what activities should be included in the program and by analyzing those activities, we can determine which spaces should be considered for the project.

- Assessment. The fulfillment of each need is a process of assessment, which we have encapsulated into a class. This class contains all the criteria, methods, and potentially the people involved in the evaluation process as well as the results.

Figure 1 shows a UML diagram that depicts all the five main classes, their key variables and their connections.

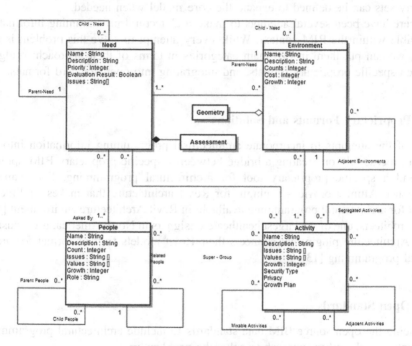

Fig. 1. UFPOR UML diagram

3 Architectural Programming and BIM

Having access to architectural programming information is critical to the operation of several parties within the AECFM community. During the design process, architects and planners constantly evaluate their design against the programming criteria. After the construction, facility managers need access to the architectural programming information for a full understanding of the facility [10]. Integrating programming information more smoothly into BIM intensifies requirements for interoperability amongst the parties within the AECFM industry. While there is a consensus within the industry on what BIM is and what it should do, there are several implementations of BIM. Some vendors have branded implementations of BIM which rely on the vendor's data models, file formats, and graphical user interfaces. Autodesk Revit and Graphisoft ArchiCAD are two examples of BIM implementations. Open standards are a contrasting strategy for BIM. Over the past few years IFC has become the standard way to share data among BIM applications. IFC definitions are created through a public, non-profit committee process, the definitions are openly published and freely distributed, and it has been adopted by the International Standards Organization (ISO).

Because the AECFM industry is diverse and the intended uses of BIM are pervasive, any BIM implementation is continually evolving. Proprietary commercial products are being updated regularly with new releases. IFC includes a flexible way to define and utilize data standards to enable incremental growth [11]. The most common classes and their attributes are part of the core IFC, but data models and custom property sets can be defined to expand the core model when needed.

There have been several attempts to make architectural programming information accessible within the BIM context. While every attempt to solve this problem is different, we can put them in two main categories in terms of their approach: bridging between specific proprietary formats, and integrating into open standard formats.

3.1   Proprietary Formats and Solutions

Some of the attempts to incorporate architectural programming information into the design process rely on creating a bridge between a specific proprietary BIM application and a specific proprietary tool for architectural programming. For example, Trelligence Affinity provides a plugin for Revit architecture that makes Trelligence format for architectural programming available in Revit Architecture environment [12]. HKS Architects, one of the largest healthcare designers in North America, use a custom Revit Architecture plugin that connects their Revit models to their format for architectural programming [13].

3.2   Open Standards

Enhancing the open source BIM data standards to include architectural programming information is the other approach to solve the problem.

IFC promotes creation of sub-standards within IFC by adding custom property sets that are geared toward the needs of a specific subset in AECFM industry [14]. For example, IfcWall is an entity dedicated to define a wall in IFC that supports all the common attributes that are of interest to the majority of the stakeholders. Meanwhile, the structural engineers may need to further define the structural behavior of the wall and thus need additional attributes. A custom property sets may be defined and attached to IfcWall class resulting in creating a sub-standard. These sub-standards are known as MVDs (Model View Definitions) and will be supported only by the applications that the structural engineers may use. Currently there are several MVDs that are recognized by IFC and can be accessed through the buildingSMART portal including Coordination View Version 2.0, Coordination View Version 1.0, Structural Analysis View.

In this study, we are focused on defining a BIM compatible format for UFPOR by taking the second approach. We have created a MVD for UFPOR.

4   IFC and Architectural Programming Information

There have been several initiatives to define an IFC model view definition that is capable of capturing such information. Here we discuss three of the models that are closer to our definition of an architectural programs than the others.

4.1   IFC AR-5

IFC AR-5 is one of the first attempts to expand IFC capabilities to host architectural programing data. The project was active between 2002 and 2004 with the results incorporated into IFC 2*2 [15]. The goal was to extend the capabilities of the IFC schema to allow inclusion of early design decisions and requirements. The motive was to make the data available throughout the design process. The solution is based on adding "What is required" to an IFC model to support tools later in the process to assess whether the requirements were met or not. Four primary stages in the AECFM process were considered: Analysis of Alternatives, Blocking and Stacking, Bubble Diagram, Review and Revision.

AR-5 defines two type of spaces, building and functional. Building spaces are the ones that define the anatomy of the building such as rooms, circulation spaces, cores, and structural depth. Functional spaces accommodate identifiable actions on the part of the users such as the reading area in a library.

4.2   Spatial Compliance Information Exchange (SCie)

SCie addresses the need of access to architectural programming information throughout the lifecycle of a facility in public projects [16]. The process of initiating a new facility starts with an architectural program. Based on the program, the request for a new facility is approved or denied. The architectural program is also used to aid initial estimates of the cost of design and construction. By maintaining the architectural programming information in BIM models throughout the lifecycle of a facility, organizations can estimate their functional capacities at any time by referring to the architectural program. SCie focuses on the delivery of the architectural programming related information on a facility as part of the handoff from construction to maintenance phase.

SCie is defined as a subset of COBie standard. COBie stands for Construction-Operation Building Information Exchange. COBie is a simplified version of IFC where all the geometric information is eliminated. Figure 2 shows the first ten rows of the space table from SCie.

SCie creates an abbreviated version of the architectural program that is tailored toward facility maintenance and management. It is missing information about needs, goals, activities, and spatial composition and adjacencies, but provides detailed measurements on spaces such as rentable and plannable areas.

The SCie information can then be delivered in a COBie file or as a standalone file.

WORKSHEET NAME	Space		
CONTENT	Spaces identified within a given floor		
REQUIRED	Yes		
PRIMARY AUTHOR	Designer		
ALTERNATE AUTHOR	Construction Contractor (updates with as-built data)		
Column	**Column Title**	**Data Type**	**Reqd**
A	SpaceID	Integer (LUID)	Yes
B	FloorID	Integer (Foreign Key)	Yes
C	SpaceFunction	Classification(OmniClass13)	Yes
D	SpaceReferenceID	Integer (Local Key)	If Needed
E	ExternalSystemName	Text (50)	If Needed
F	ExternalNameID	Text (50)	If Needed
G	SpaceNumber	Text (50)	Yes
H	SpaceName	Text (50)	Opt
I	SpaceDescription	Text (255)	Opt
J	SpaceUsableHeight	Positive Decimal Number	Opt

Fig. 2. SCie space table (first 10 rows)

4.3   Building Programming Information Exchange (BPie)

Comparing to SCie, BPie is a more recent effort to capture Architectural Programming information through a BIM compatible format [17]. While SCie is more focused on providing architectural programming information for the FM industry, BPie offers the following definition: "Building programming is the process of collecting all requirements the building must fulfill". BPie also regards an architectural program as a dynamic document that changes through the lifecycle of the project; therefore it should be included in BIM models and be available for modification. BPie gathers the requirements posed by an architectural program to support evaluation of the design against them. The difference between the use cases of the two standards reflects on their content. SCie addresses the as-built information regardless of whether they fulfill the requirements or not. SCie relies on architectural programming information since it is a reflection on the functional capacity of the facility, while BPie regards architectural programming as a collection of requirements. While BPie might include information regarding the required ventilation air flow of a specific space, such information is not of use in SCie.

The other major difference between the two standards relies on the data model upon which that they are based. SCie is defined as a subset of COBie as it is meant to support the FM industry COBie is a stripped down version of IFC which essentially provides a less elaborated data model. BPie is defined as a direct MVD within the IFC data model and provides a more flexible data model that can capture a wider array of information.

BPie relies on five different entities from IFC data model to capture architectural programming information. The five entities are: Project, Building, Story, Space, and Zone. The requirements are captured by attaching additional properties to these five entities. These properties are grouped together under several property sets Fig. 3.

Property Group	Property Name	Definition	Further Explanations
Dimensional requirements	Net Floor area		
	Minimum net height		
Common relations	Functional membership	Relationship to the function or sub function that this space belongs to. A space is only member of one function	
	Space decomposition	Complex (multiple spaces), elemental (room), or partial (part of a room) and link to an elemental space (decomposition tree)	I
	Occupancy schedule per day	The point of time during the day when the space will normally	Example would be 9:00 - 18:00 expressed as 09:00/18:00

Fig. 3. A partial view of BPie space attributes

BPie focuses on the "Need" class in the UFPOR, naming it the "requirements". The BPie provides several classes (Space, Story, and Building) that were abstracted into the UFPOR Environment class. "Zone" defines a concept that is more close to "Activity" in UFPOR model. UFPOR offers different types of relationships between different entities through parameters that point to other entities. For example, by having reference parameters in UFPOR we could define child/parent relationships. All the custom parameters that are added to the IFC entities by BPie are primary parameters such as text, number, and Boolean (yes/no) parameters.

While BPie provides "requirements" that have helped to elaborate the "Need" class in UFPOR, UFPOR covers more ground than requirements.

5 Implementing the UFPOR with IFC

We have implemented the UFPOR using IFC standards to support a first stage of testing.

5.1 Introduction to IFC File Format

To better understand the examples below, a short introduction to reading a text-based IFC file will suffice. IFC provides file formats where each object is represented by a line of text [14, 18]. Common concepts in object-oriented programming such as inheritance and relationships can be captured by IFC file format. The following lines describe a vector and a three dimensional direction as well as their relationship. Ifc-Vector has two parameters, the first parameter refers to an instance of IfcDirection and represent the orientation (#21) while the second parameter (2000.0) represents the magnitude.

```
#20=IFCVECTOR(#21,2000.0);
#21=IFCDIRECTION((0.0,-1.0,0.0));
```

Each object starts with an identification number (#20) followed by a type (IFC-VECTOR). The rest is the attribute values provided for each object. The values are mapped to the attributes based on their location in comparison with the entity definition provided by IFC. Figure 4 shows the definition of IfcVector from IFC 4 schema.

EXPRESS specification:

```
ENTITY IfcVector
  SUBTYPE OF (IfcGeometricRepresentationItem);
    Orientation        : IfcDirection;
    Magnitude          : IfcLengthMeasure;
  DERIVE
    Dim                : IfcDimensionCount := Orientation.Dim;
  WHERE
    WR1     : Magnitude >= 0.0;
END_ENTITY;
```

Fig. 4. IfcVector definition in IFC 4 schema

Each object can establish a direct relationship with other objects through their ID; in result, the referred object will form an inverse relationship with the referee object. Inverse relationship are not shown in the physical file format; however they are part of the schema.

The IFC schema is divided into four main layers: the domain schemas, the shared schema, the core schema, and the resources schema.

5.2 Defining an MVD for UFPOR

IFC is a large collection of classes that can be used to represent a very large array of information in the AECFM industry. Usually the applications in the AECFM industry support a predefined subset of IFC. On top of that, the vanilla flavor of IFC entities can be further enriched with custom property sets. To use IFC as a data transfer standard specific subset of IFC need to be defines. These subsets are called Model View Definitions [14].

A standard IFC format for UFPOR depends upon a subset of IFC that is specialized for architectural programming information. buildingSMART has a standard way of creating MVDs that is documented in the Information Delivery Manual format, IDM (also ISO29481). MVDs are documented in a format called MVDXML. building-SMART has published an application called "ifcDoc" that can be used to create MVDs in MVDXML format. Alternatively a text (or xml) editing application can be used to create or edit an MVD as long as all the rules defined by MVDXML are followed.

To propose an MVD that can represent UFPOR, we need to find one or more entities in IFC for each UFPOR class and attach. custom property sets if enhancement is needed. A collection of property sets geared toward architectural programming information is available through the previous efforts to use IFC to capture such information. IFC entities will be evaluated in three capacities. First, their definition and the category that they belong to should match the respective UFPOR class. Second, they should be capable of representing the same attributes either directly or through custom property sets. Third, the selected classes should be able to represent UFPOR relationships. IFC provides a wide array of choices to connect entities together and choosing the right method requires attention to the details.

5.3   UFPOR Environment Class

IFC already has a good structure to support the Environment class in UFPOR. In IFC, any physical object (such as environments) can be defined through a combination of subclasses of IfcObject and IfcTypeObject. The subclasses of IfcTypeObject represent the generic properties that are shared by all the instances of a class. On the other hand, subclasses of IfcObject are used to represent the specific characteristics that are unique to each instance (such as location). Using type properties reduces data duplication in IFC data files.

To represent an Environment in IFC, we used two base classes IfcSpatialElement and IfcSpatialElementType. According to the definition "IfcSpatialElementType defines a list of commonly shared property set definitions of a spatial structure element and an optional set of product representations. It is used to define a spatial element specification (the specific element information that is common to all occurrences of that element type)." IfcSpatialElementType entity is well suited for an architectural program since it is common in architectural programs to define abstract and generic requirements that should be met by all the instances that share the type. IfcSpatialElementType has two main subclasses: IfcSpatialZoneType and IfcSpaceType.

According to the definition of IfcSpatialElement "A spatial element is the generalization of all spatial elements that might be used to define a spatial structure or to define spatial zones." IfcSpatialElement has more subclasses that IfcSpatialElementType. The subclasses of IfcSpatialElement should be used to form a spatial hierarchical representation of the project by using different classes such as IfcSite, IfcBuilding, IfcBuildingStory, IfcSpace. There is a logical order that should be followed in creating the hierarchical structure of the spaces. An IfcSite can hold instances of IfcBuilding, IfcBuilding can hold instances of IfcBuildingStory and IfcBuildingStory can hold instances of IfcSpace. IfcRelAggregates will be used to create the relationships.

To create space groupings such as departments and sections, IfcSpatialZone should be used. Through IfcRelAggregates, different instances of IfcSpace, IfcSpatialZone, or other subclasses of IfcSpatialStructureElement can be grouped together to form a spatial zone. Instances of IfcSpatialZone can have an independent location and geometry representation.

Note that "ContainsElement" property is to create connections between a space and subclasses of IfcProduct by using instances of IfcRelContainedInSpatialStructure. This relationship cannot be used to create a relationship between spaces and is reserved for the relationship between spaces and other products such as furniture and equipment.

5.4   UFPOR Need Class

IfcConstraint is designed to assign requirements to properties and objects. According to the definition "IfcConstraint is used to define a constraint or limiting value or boundary condition that may be applied to an object or to the value of a property." Through the ConstraintGrade property, a constraint strength level can be associated to a constraint. Constraints can hold a strength level of hard, soft, advisory, user defined, or not defined. If "Userdefined" is selected then the UserDefinedGrade property on IfcConstraint should be filled. The CreatingActor attribute holds an optional reference to a person or an organization as the creating authority.

IfcConstraint has two subclasses: IfcObjective and IfcMetric. As the names explain, IfcObjective is used to assign qualitative requirements while IfcMetric is used for quantitative requirements.

5.4.1   Defining Adjacency Requirements

To create an adjacency requirement between two or more spaces, we have used a combination of an instance of IfcObjective and an instance of IfcRelAssociatesConstraint. Through IfcObjective we defined a constraint grade and also the creating actor. The name and description will indicate that the constraint defines adjacency requirements between spaces and should follow the internal standards of a specific MVD. An instance of IfcRelAssociatesConstraint will be used to assign the constraint to the respective instances of IfcSpatialElement. The spaces will be declared through the RelatedObjects property in IfcConstraint entity. Note that the same instance of IfcConstraint can be used multiple times to define adjacency requirements between different spatial elements.

5.5   UFPOR People Class

IfcActor is the only IFC entity that is appropriate for People in the UFPOR. According to the definition, "The IfcActor defines all actors or human agents involved in a project during its full life cycle. It facilitates the use of person and organization definitions in the resource part of the IFC object model. This includes name, address, telecommunication addresses, and roles."

As you can see, this definition is for specific individuals who are involved in the project. While that would cover a large number of groups that UFPOR would represent, it seems difficult to make the definition work for the generic users that are defined in UFPOR. For example, in creating a UFPOR for a school we may have an instance of People called students that represents the 5th grade students. This is a generic group of people; we only care about common attributes such as age and gender and not their name and addresses as IfcActor would suggest.

IfcActorRole might be a better fit for what UFPOR People tries to accomplish, but IfcActorRole can only exist attached to the instances of IfcActor.

IfcActor extends another concrete superclass called IfcOccupant. In cases where we try to represent the space users through UFPOR People, IfcOccupant might be a more appropriate class to use. A custom property set can be defined to capture all the information such as Description, Count, Issues and values. We can use a custom property set similar to the one proposed for IfcZone.

IfcGroup and IfcRelAssignsToGroup can be used to create the parent child relationships between different instances of IfcOccupant and IfcActor.

5.6   UFPOR Activity Class

Amongst all the classes in UFPOR, activity is more exclusive to an architectural program and thus it is more difficult to find the right structure in IFC schema for activities. We identifed three different potential objects to accommodate activities in the IFC schema: IfcProcess, IfcSpatialZone, and IfcZone. Amongst all three choices, IfcZone proved to be the better fir for UFPOR Activity.

In contrast with IfcSpatialZone, IfcZone provides a more loose association between different zones and does not provide geometrical representation attributes. According to the definition "A zone is a group of spaces, partial spaces or other zones". Zone structures may not be hierarchical (in contrary to the spatial structure of a project). That means one individual IfcSpace may be associated with zero, one, or several instances of IfcZone. IfcSpace instances are grouped into an IfcZone by using the objectified relationship IfcRelAssignsToGroup as specified at the super type IfcGroup."

While the name of IfcZone still implies a different concept than UFPOR activity, the data structure seems like a good fit to represent the required data.

5.7   Results

Figure 5 provides a hierarchical illustration of all the IFC entities that are used in replicating UFPOR. The image does not include the attributes for each entity nor the relationships between the entities. Custom property sets defined by BPie and SCie will be added to enrich the MVD and make it compatible with other methods for representing a POR.

6   Software Prototype

While the proposed model can be evaluated without software implementation, a prototype increases the credibility by enabling other researchers to interact with the data model. Such implementation also increases the robustness of the system by revealing the areas that are not covered in sufficient details. Software implementation requires translation of all the descriptions to machine-readable and executable code. Machine-readable code is a very intense form of logical argumentation as it leaves no room for ambiguity.

In our prototype, the user can provide the system with architectural programming information and receive an IFC file in return. The system will also provide a data persistence mechanism that allows the user to save the data for future uses. It also gives the users the capability of reusing the requirements in several projects. Figure 6 shows all the main parts of the system and how they are connected to each other.

6.1   User Input

The user input consists of a graphical user interface enabling the user to enter pieces of architectural programming information by filling out forms and answering questions.

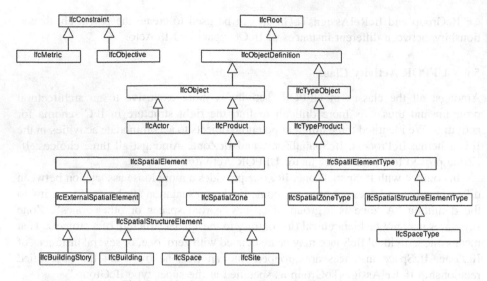

Fig. 5. IFC classes that are part of UFPOR MVD

The human computer interaction can be facilitated through a touch screen interface or the more traditional mouse/keyboard combination. The system incorporates feedback and guidance to assure the user has provided the most accurate information possible.

6.2 Data Models

The IFC entities structure represented in Fig. 5 has been replicated by classes in an object-oriented system. It also includes the property sets proposed by SCie and BPie. The classes are instantiated and populated based on the user input.

6.3 Data Persistence

The data models must be persistent by writing to a database for future use. The persistence layer can create a bridge between a relational database and the data models or it can take advantage of an object-oriented database. There are advantages and disadvantages in both approaches; however, that discussion is out of the scope of this paper.

6.4 IFC Output

The IFC file consists of a header reflecting general information about the file and the main content section representing all the objects. The content of each class is converted to a line in an IFC physical file format to create the IFC file.

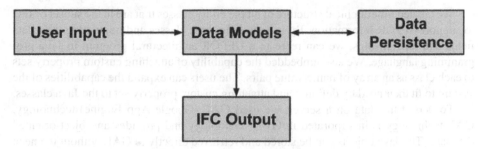

Fig. 6. UFPOR prototype architecture

7 Selecting the Implementation Platform

Given the nature of the application and all the entities recognized in the architecture diagram, we identified two main alternatives to implement the system.

First, the system can be implemented as a standalone desktop application similar to many applications used by the AEC industry, such as MS Word, and Autodesk AutoCAD. Through the application, the user can store architectural programming documents in IFC format. The system could feature a binary file format as the persistence layer. The User Input layer can be in accordance to the operating system for which the application is implemented. The system will support one or several operating systems depending on the implementation technology.

Second, the system can be implemented as a web application. In that case, the User Interface layer will run in a browser. The user input will be sent to a server where an application on the server populate the data models. The data models then are stored in a central database [19].

There are advantages and disadvantages for both systems. The first approach is less complicated to implement; however the users need to download and install the application. The application may or may not run on their computer depending on the operating system. It also has limitations in sharing the models with other users.

The second approach provides greater accessibility since it will run in a browser without any software installation required; however such implementation is more complicated because it involves both client and server computers. A central database is required to access, modify and add new data. With a central database, security becomes another issue as the users need to be authenticated and authorized to access the data.

After reviewing the pros and cons of both options, we decided to select the second option to provide higher visibility. This choice will enable us to test the prototype and gather feedback from as many users as possible.

We selected GWT (Google Web Toolkit) as the framework to develop the prototype. GWT is a development toolkit that facilitates development of complicated applications in a browser [20]. By using GWT, developers can write every layer of a web application in Java programming language. GWT compiles the Java code to Javascript which is the language that browsers understand. Java is inherently an object-oriented programming language and can accommodate complicated logic and data models more efficiently [21].

We created a hierarchical structure of all the entity classes that are in the subset of IFC to support UFPOR information. By instantiating these classes and populating their data fields and relationships, we can recreate a UFPOR architectural program in Java programming language. We also embedded the capability of attaching custom property sets to each class as an array of name/value pairs. The users can expand the capabilities of the system to fit their need by defining and attaching custom property set to the Java classes.

To persist the data on a server, we used GAE (Google App Engine) technology. GAE technology is incorporated in GWT technology and provides an object-oriented database. The Java objects can be stored and retrieved directly to GAE without the need for designing a relational database. Figure 7 is a screenshot of the application running in a browser. Below is the IFC file created by the application after receiving the basic information including project name, measuring units, and minimum and maximum accepted total area for the project. You can see how several entities from the IFC 4 schema were used by the program to store that information in IFC format. The following section is the IFC file produced by the application based on the information entered by the user.

```
SO-10303-21;
HEADER;
FILE_DESCRIPTION (
('Test 35538Long'),
'2;1');
FILE_NAME (
'Test 35538.ifc',
'2015/01/26T08:34:15',
('test@example.com'),
('test@example.com'),
'UFPOR APP 0.0.1',
'UFPOR DEMO beta',
'gmail.com');
FILE_SCHEMA (('IFC4RC4'));
ENDSEC;
DATA;
#1= IFCPROJECT ('0eknmBJtf6sfk8GqHIIdwb', $, Test 35538, $, $, Test 35538Long, $, $, #2);
#2= IFCUNITASSIGNMENT(#3,#4,#5);
#3= IFCSIUNIT(*, .LENGTHUNIT, $, .METRE);
#4= IFCSIUNIT(*, .VOLUMEUNIT, $, .CUBIC_METRE);
#5= IFCSIUNIT(*, .AREAUNIT, $, .SQUARE_METRE);
#6= IFCQUANTITYAREA(NetFloorArea, *, *, 0.0, *);
#7= IFCMETRIC ('MAX_VALUE', null, HARD, null, *, *, *, LESSTHANOREQUALTO, null, 1200.0, *);
#8= IFCMETRIC ('MIN_VALUE', null, HARD, null, *, *, *, GREATERTHANOREQUALTO, null, 1000.0, *);
#9= IFCOBJECTIVE ('null', *, HARD, *, *, *, *, (7,8), LOGICALAND, REQUIREMENT, *);
#10= IFCRESOURCECONSTRAINTRELATIONSHIP(*, *, 9, 6);
#11= IFCELEMENTQUANTITY(1tnh4kFOD05Pc9BntWuJvm, *, *, *, *, (6));
#12= IFCRELDEFINESBYPROPERTIES(2N2yC1D6P9UBxhMfYL3MjA, *, *, *, (1), 11);
ENDSEC;
END-ISO-10303-21;
```

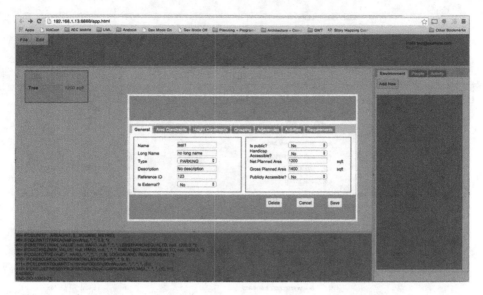

Fig. 7. A screenshot of UFPOR prototype user interface

8 Testing the Prototype

We tested the prototype by entering the data from two different POR documents to our prototype. The PORs are related to a hospital and an office building designed by two different design firms in North America. Both of the design companies are among the ten largest firms in the USA. The name of the companies and some of the programming information are obfuscated to respect the privacy of the companies and their client.

8.1 Test Case 1. The Office Building

Within this firm, the POR is organized into a collection of MS Excel worksheets. The first worksheet summarizes the project by listing all the departments and sections within each department. The other worksheets break down each section into sub-sections and spaces. For each space, sub-section, section, and department the work-sheets include information on count and existing area (in case of a renovation project), headcount, seat count and area (planning phase 1), and seat count and area (planning phase 2). Figure 8 is a screenshot of the summary worksheet.

The circulation area was included in each space area. The program includes an estimated add-on factor of 1.14 to account for the building elements such as walls and columns.

Entering the content of the program into our data model via the user interface showed some weaknesses and some strength on our system. The four level space structure was fully supported by our system as we did not put any limitations on the depth of space structure. Adding the attribute for each space type was also fully supported. The net and gross areas were defined as an internal circulation factor that

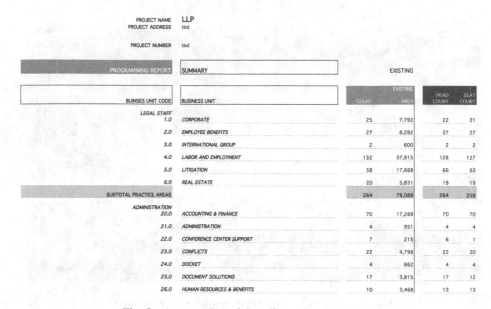

PROJECT NAME	LLP
PROJECT ADDRESS	tbd
PROJECT NUMBER	tbd

PROGRAMMING REPORT	SUMMARY			EXISTING	
BUINSES UNIT CODE	BUSINESS UNIT	EXISTING COUNT	EXISTING AREA	HEAD COUNT	SEAT COUNT
LEGAL STAFF 1.0	CORPORATE	25	7,792	22	21
2.0	EMPLOYEE BENEFITS	27	8,282	27	27
3.0	INTERNATIONAL GROUP	2	600	2	2
4.0	LABOR AND EMPLOYMENT	132	37,915	128	127
5.0	LITIGATION	58	17,668	66	63
6.0	REAL ESTATE	20	5,831	19	19
SUBTOTAL PRACTICE AREAS		264	78,088	264	259
ADMINISTRATION 20.0	ACCOUNTING & FINANCE	70	17,269	70	70
21.0	ADMINISTRATION	4	951	4	4
22.0	CONFERENCE CENTER SUPPORT	7	215	6	1
23.0	CONFLICTS	22	4,798	22	20
24.0	DOCKET	4	862	4	4
25.0	DOCUMENT SOLUTIONS	17	3,815	17	12
26.0	HUMAN RESOURCES & BENEFITS	10	3,468	13	13

Fig. 8. A screenshot of the office building program

Mount Carmel St. Ann's **Hospital**   **Departmental Space Program**

SUMMARY

Department	7/12/10 Program DGSF	7/12/10 Calculated NEW BGSF	7/12/10 Calculated RENOV.	Master Plan SF	Difference SF[1]	Comments
1 New Patient Tower and Connected Spaces						
2 LOWER LEVEL						
3 BED STORAGE and REPAIR	913	1,214	0		1,214	
4 DISCHARGE LOBBY	462	614	0		614	
5 STERILE PROCESSING & DISTRIBUTION	53,946				0	Added Surgery Staff Lockers/Lounge to space allocations
6 MECHANICAL / ELECTRICAL ROOM						
7 CENTRAL ENERGY PLANT ADDITION				1,800		
8 SUMMARY - LOWER LEVEL	55,321		0		1,828	
9 GROUND FLOOR LEVEL						
10 INTERVENTIONAL CARDIOLOGY SUITE	25,515	25,515		26,000	-485	
11 SUMMARY - GROUND FLOOR LEVEL	25,515			26,000	-485	
12 FIRST FLOOR LEVEL						
13 SURGERY DEPARTMENT (Expansion)	6,390		6,390		6,390	
14 CARDIOVASCULAR UNIT (30 Beds)	21,812	26,174			26,174	
15 SUMMARY - FIRST FLOOR LEVEL	28,202		0		32,564	
16 SECOND FLOOR LEVEL						
17 ORTHO / NEURO / SPINE UNIT (30 Beds)	21,835	26,202		26,202	30 Beds	
18 SUMMARY - SECOND FLOOR LEVEL	21,835		0		26,202	
19 Subtotal	239,911	79,719	6,390	53,800	94,017	
20						

Fig. 9. A screenshot of the healthcare facility

was added to each department (35 %). There was an estimated ad-on factor of 14 % added to the project to account for building elements such as walls and columns. The system fell short in providing a project attribute for the add-on factor, although the net and gross areas were supported. The system also fell short in reflecting how requirements may change through time. We consider that a minor modification, as it can be included to the data models by adding a time span for each requirement.

8.2 Test Case 2. The Healthcare Facility

The second test case study was a small health care facility. The POR was kept as a MS Excel file with a very similar structure to the first example. Figure 9 is a screenshot of the summary page.

While the general structures of the two programs were the same, the second program contained more requirements information. The departments were assigned to floors. The second program contained a few more categories in the space structure to include Department, Section, Sub-section, and furniture. The net and gross areas were calculated in ways similar to the first program with the exception of calculating the building add-on factor for each department. The attributes for each space types were unit area, quantity and comments.

Similar to the first case study, the system fully supported the space structure while the building add-on attribute was missing from the data structures.

9 Conclusion

The previous efforts to exercise IFC capabilities in capturing architectural programming information have been very fruitful. The newer versions of IFC have made it easier to capture architectural programming information thus a new MVD for architectural programming can take advantage of this new capacity.

The current state of IFC is capable of capturing architectural programming information; however some of the entities are not well suited to fit all the needs of an architectural POR. For example we had to use IfcZone to represent UFPOR activities, Based on IFC documentation IfcZone is an aggregation of spaces or other zones, however in UFPOR an activity is an independent concept. Custom property sets can enhance IFC schema in capturing all the extra data that is demanded by architectural programming documents.

Web applications are an ideal platform to implement a data management system for architectural programming information. They maximize accessibility and security for the user data. UFPOR is capable of supporting the typical architectural programming formats used by major architectural firms in North America. IFC can be used as a native format for a universal format for architectural programming documents without compromising data entities and accuracy.

References

1. Eastman, C.M.: BIM Handbook: A Guide To Building Information Modeling for Owners, Managers, Designers, Engineers, and Contractors, pp. xiv, 490 p., 4 p. of plates. Wiley, Hoboken (2008)

2. Bilal, S.: Building information modelling framework: a research and delivery foundation for industry stakeholders. Autom. Constr. **18**, 357–375 (2009)
3. Björk, B., Laakso, M.: CAD standardisation in the construction industry — a process view. Autom. Constr. **19**, 398–406 (2010)
4. Kiviniemi, A.: Requirements Management Interface, vol. 161 (2005)
5. Barekati, E., Clayton, M.J.: A universal format for architectural program of requirement - a prerequisite for adding architectural programming information to BIM data models. In: The 32nd eCAADe Conference, pp. 385 (2014)
6. Cherry, E.: Programming for Design: From Theory to Practice, pp. xxiii, 327. Wiley, New York (1999)
7. Duerk, D.P.: Architectural Programming: Information management for Design, pp. xiv, 258. Van Nostrand Reinhold, New York (1993)
8. Peña, W., Parshall, S.: Problem Seeking: An Architectural Programming Primer, p. 224. Wiley, New York (2001)
9. Sanoff, H.: Methods of Architectural Programming, pp. xi, 184. Dowden, Hutchinson & Ross, Stroudsburg (1977)
10. Hershberger, R.G.: Architectural Programming and Predesign Manager, pp. xix, 506. McGraw-Hill, New York (1999)
11. Liebich, T., Wix, J.: Highlights of the development process of industry foundation classes. In: Proceedings of the 1999 CIB W78 Conference, pp. 18 (1999)
12. Anonymous: Affinity, vol. 2012
13. Barekati, E.: HKS BIM+Programming. In: Fiatech 2012 Technology Conference and Showcase (2012)
14. Liebich, T.: IFC2x Edition 3 < br /> Model implementation guide. In: buildingSMART International (2009)
15. Anonymous: information requirements specification – [AR-5] early design. In: International Alliance for Interoperability- UK Chapter (2004)
16. East, W., Nisbet, N.: Spatial Compliance information exchange (SCie). buildingSMART alliance (2009)
17. East, W.: Building Programming information exchange (BPie) (2012)
18. Liebich, T., Adachi, Y., Forester, J., Hyvarinen, J., Richter, S., Chipman, T., Weise, M., Wix, J.: IFC4 OFFICIAL RELEASE. buildingSMART International Ltd (2013)
19. Shklar, L., Rosen, R.: Web application architecture, Principles, Protocols and Practices. Wiley, Chichester (2009)
20. Dewsbury, R.: Google web toolkit applications, Pearson Education, 2007. Horstmann, C.S., Cornell, G.: Core Java 2: vol. I, Fundamentals, Pearson Education (2002)

A Framework for Speech-Oriented CAD and BIM Systems

José Luis Menegotto(✉)

Federal University of Rio de Janeiro, Rio de Janeiro, Brazil
jlmenegotto@poli.ufrj.br

Abstract. This article discusses the development of a Speech Oriented Graphics Interface embedded in CAD and BIM software. The aim is to provide the means to work with complex 3D BIM models with minimal touch operations. We can cite the growing need for tools and user interfaces to assist designers in handling complex models, minimizing the risk of producing changes accidentally. In this area, the integration of a graphical database in BIM applications can be seen as an advantage over traditional CAD applications. However, we can note a difficulty in this integration, due to the need to maintain the constant levels of mental concentration required in order to effectively manage a larger inter-connected graphical database. Specifically in this area, voice interfaces can help by avoiding the need of "touch" to work with the 3D models, looking for improving its robustness and consistency. In addition, SR is used in order to reduce cognitive stress among the users, trying eliminating the need to memorize and remember commands, names and locations in GUI interfaces.

Keywords: Accessibility · Text to speech · Speech recognition · CAD-BIM

1 Introduction

Since the 1950s, two techniques linking the field of Linguistics with Information Technology have attracted attention to research in these areas. They are *Automatic Speech Recognition* (ASR) and *Text to Speech* (TTS) [1]. Programs of automatic recognition of speech, or simply speech recognition (SR), seek to define and optimize mechanisms that confer on the computer the capacity to recognize phrases spoken by a human agent. Inversely, TTS programs seek to define mechanisms with the capacity to transform alphanumeric data into synthesized sounds that simulate human voices.[1]

Nowadays, it is increasingly more frequent to find these technologies integrated in telephone systems or present in widespread computer environments, controlling computational devices, which do not use the traditional means of inputting data such as keyboard, mouse or touch sensitive screens. Although there are libraries and Application

---

[1] In the 1920 s, a toy called Radio Rex was sold in the United States. It functioned using a sound recognition mechanism, which reacted to a frequency of 500 Hz, close to the sound of the letter "e" of the word "Rex". More robust recognition mechanisms were created from the 1950 s at Bell Labs. [8].

© Springer-Verlag Berlin Heidelberg 2015
G. Celani et al. (Eds.): CAAD Futures 2015, CCIS 527, pp. 329–347, 2015.
DOI: 10.1007/978-3-662-47386-3_18

Program Interfaces (APIs) which make SR and TTS capabilities available, it can be said that the technology has not yet been disseminated significantly within the graphic environments traditionally used in architectural and engineering projects. It could be assumed that this is because drawing is a highly gestural activity. The CAD systems have adopted the mouse and the keyboard as input devices and, recently, have begun to incorporate interactive devices such as touchscreen, screens and multi-touch tables [6], which have recuperated and even expanded the gestural aspect of graphic activities. In terms of incorporating voice into graphic interfaces, it can be seen that there have been few advances.

From the traditional perspective of the Computer Aided Design and Drafting discipline, another phenomenon can be observed: the need for designers to count on the assistance of complementary tools and interfaces, which permit them to manipulate models of increasing complexity. In spite of the sophistication reached by the new interfaces, the task of aggregating and managing construction elements in complex 3D models continues to be a task that requires care and attention. The complexity of the 3D models of buildings brings with it the risk of producing erroneous alterations in the geometry due to an accidental touch of the cursor on the objects modelled. Although the evolution of graphic interfaces GUI (*Graphic User Interface*) has shown constant advances and development of locking and filter tools, the risk of an inadvertent touch continues.

In terms of the specific BIM applications, the integration of the graphic database, which permits the manipulation of the geometrical and logical information of a project, can be highlighted as an advantage in relation to traditional CAD applications. However, a problem can be seen in this possibility of integration, arising from the difficulty of maintaining the constant levels of mental concentration needed to manage the increasingly complex graphic databases efficiently. For the same 3D construction model, the geometric complexity in CAD and BIM should theoretically be equal. This is not the case when one compares the amount of construction data and relationships incorporated in the BIM models. Creating a BIM model with a wealth of links and dependences between construction components, defining and manipulating design phases or design alternatives, and controlling and coordinating all the disciplines of a project efficiently are activities that bring with them additional cognitive pressures for the designer.

In relation to workflow, BIM environments are regarded as facilitators of work in collaborative teams. However, thanks to the integration potential of the technology, it has become possible for a single professional, highly qualified in the diverse areas, to project and take on many, if not all, of the disciplines necessary to conclude a conventional building project. Once again, it could be pointed out that this way of approaching the project is cognitively very demanding, as in addition to dealing with the requirements of the project, one must deal with diverse interfaces, memorizing, operating and associating specific commands and procedures of the project. Voice user interfaces would appear to be an additional alternative to help in reducing the weight of mental fatigue. Perhaps it would be desirable for the interfaces of graphic applications to evolve, gradually eliminating many of the elements currently present, such as keys, windows, browsers, menus, etc. In this way, VUIs (*Voice User Interfaces*) can provide their contribution in the CAD-BIM field.

A VUI applied to a graphic system allows one to carry out operations of creation, editing and control without the need of contact with the model. The lack of "touch" implies a profound change in the graphic activity, as currently drawing is a highly gestural task and suddenly we are faced with the possibility of eliminating this gestural aspect. Thinking beyond this it is not difficult to imagine, in a not too distant future, that it will be possible to control devices without the need for voice input, given the initial results achieved in research into sub-vocal recognition. Through the technique of capturing electromyogram (EMG) signals carried out by the Chuck Jorgensen group at the *Ames Research Center at NASA* [4]. Connecting external sensors to a person's neck, Jorgensen captured the nerve signals close to the vocal chords, permitting the transformation of the stimulation of the nerves provoked by the silent reading of the words before they are voiced. According to him, various techniques tested managed to obtain a success rate of between 73 % and 92 % in the identification of the 10 numerical digits and five words (*stop, go, left, right, alpha*) [4]. A graphic application with a sub-vocal recognition interface would eliminate the problem of the ambient noise interference and would permit the act of creating a project to become a totally intellectual operation, eliminating all that remains of the tactile or gestural sense from the task of drawing.

Another situation where voice interfaces show their potential is in the support they give to professionals who suffer from some type of disability and who cannot execute motor actions. They can benefit from interfaces that avoid the use of control devices such as the mouse and the keyboard. Experiments focusing on assisting people with special needs have reported successes, such as those conducted and related by Burnett in 1985 [2] or by Corine Bickley, Hong Tan and David Horowitz, at the beginning of the 1990s [3]. The Bickley group conceived and tested a voice recognition interface for AutoCAD. According to the researchers, the graphic environment prepared with a VUI interface allowed a quadriplegic architect, to return to design work. He controlled the software through voice commands. Software companies such as Infoquest Technologies and Enact Technology have also developed applications to execute voice commands in graphic modelling systems. We see great value in the possibility of continuing to integrate voice technologies (SR and TTS) in CAD systems and at the same time in computational environments directed towards BIM.

2 The Experimental VUI Application

The focus of the experimental TTS/ASR application presented in this work is related to the configuration of a voice interface VUI which permits designers to interact with the model, avoiding mediation through cursors or traditional inputting devices, present in interfaces of the GUI type. Its aim is to seek to enter and manipulate information orally, permitting the user to use forms of expression close to natural language and within the specific lexicon of each discipline of the project.

This interface mode aims to avoid or diminish the need to know the names of the commands and their location within the GUI graphic environment. The working hypothesis is that by eliminating the mental load, which involves memorizing commands and processes, the application learning curve could be reduced. Another objective is to permit, at least in theory, a freer, more fluid and comfortable interaction for the project designer, liberating him/her to think on the concrete issues of the project. It is important to clarify that this article presents the first results of the experiment integrating the VUI and GUI interfaces. In the tests, they were treated in a complementary fashion and without one interfering in the other.

There are two modes of using SR technology: in the dictated mode or controlled by previously defined grammar. In the dictated mode, the recognition mechanism is dependent on the speaker. As each user has an individual timbre, modulation and inflection, a sample of the sounds of the voices which will be recognized needs to be collected. This means that each speaker must previously train with the recognition mechanism through the reading of texts. In this mode, the timbre and the inflection of the voices are entered and stored in a databank of sound profiles, which the interpreter will use during the recognition. The second mode is independent of the speaker. In these cases, the recognition mechanism requires the creation of a data structure, called grammar. This structure must contain three basic elements:

- The lexicon permitted which will be recognized as input by the SR mechanism;
- The rules of the lexical combinations;
- The output returned, which will be passed on to the graphic application.

In this experiment, the use of SR was restricted to the second mode. Therefore, a set of grammatical rules was developed and registered in specially formatted XML files. Two programs that are widely in use in project offices were used: AutoCAD and Revit. The users can cumulatively customize the grammar rules developed, as when stored in independent XML files, they can have new locutions, words and verb forms added to them in accordance with the cultural preferences and/or technical terms of the users. As well as permitting the model to be controlled by remote commands, the SR/TTS technology permits the creation of recorded message services, which can contain spoken reports on the data of the model. These reports can be exchanged between the designers in collaborative teams through the available communication networks.

2.1   TTS/SR Components and Environment

In order to create the application, was used the components library .Net API System. Speech, that contains a speech recognition device for the Windows operational system. It can be embedded in clients or in desktops and accepts training for the recognition of various users, including a dictation grammar. The application was tested running on Windows 8.0, AutoCAD 2014 and Revit 2014.

2.2   Referencing NameSpaces in the Project

The *System.Speech* library was referenced inside the application project. This permits the recognition functions to be loaded, declaring the following *Namespaces* that contain methods, properties and events divided into three specific categories.

- *System.Speech.Recognition*: specifies the methods, properties and events to carry out the speech recognition process (SR).

- *System.Speech.Synthesis*: specifies the methods, properties and events to carry out the transformation of texts into speech (TTS).
- *System.Speech.AudioFormat*: specifies the methods, properties and events to create and manipulate the audio files generated.

Once the necessary references and the *Namespace* have been declared, the configuration of the classes of the application begins. A class containing a synthesizing object (*SpeechSynthesizer*), to return the spoken messages, and an object for the recognition mechanism (*SpeechRecognitionEngine*) were created.

3   The Grammar Structures

The formalization of the grammatical structure, containing the valid sets of recognizable phrases and the rules to combine them, is one of the key factors in the process to create a VUI system. No less important is the set of procedures that will be activated by the solicitations and the mode in which the man-machine communication will be established. In this way, the recognition system can be limited to perform a spoken command, which will be executed immediately. Thus, the SR mechanism is used in only stage. However, it is more interesting to use the mechanism within a flow of man-machine dialogical communication, in which moments of recognition SR are interspersed with moments of data requisition by the TTS mechanism as well as being integrated into the specifically programmed algorithmic procedures (Fig. 1).

Fig. 1.   One and multiple communication stage mechanism

The human factor is present in this mode of operation, a fact that makes it more complex. The individual way in which each person interacts with the machine to perform a certain task means that the grammar project must be carried out in conjunction with the application structure project. The output collected during the recognition process can supply the class properties or the parameters of the methods programmed in the application.

The grammar presented in this article concentrates on the automation of tasks involving only one or, at most, two stages of communication. The definition of the grammar tested follows the recommendations published by the W3C organization. This consortium publishes guidelines for the organization of the syntactic structure, which should be respected when creating voice controls. These guidelines are consolidated in the document called SRGS (*Speech Recognition Grammar Specification*) [5]. The grammar can be written either in the *Augmented BNF* (ABNF) language or in XML. In this work was adopted the XML format.

Below a small extract of the grammar is presented in which the various possible locutions are defined. The recognition mechanism will understand as valid voice input to determine a single stream of characters (out = "A_Z1") as output which will be sent to the application to perform a specific instruction.

```
<item>
        <one-of>
            <item>setar vista              </item>
            <item>seta vista               </item>
            <item>sete vista               </item>
            <item>por favor sete a vista   </item>
            <item>prepare vista            </item>
            <item>preparar vista           </item>
            <item>mostrar vista            </item>
            <item>quero ver                </item>
            <item>gostaria ver             </item>
            <item>mostre me                </item>
        </one-of> <tag> out = "A_Z1";      </tag>
</item>
```

In this example, each pre-defined locution is enclosed in a simple structure:

```
<item>Locution</item>
```

The locutions are grouped within a larger structure < *one-of* > </*one-of* > permitting the recognition mechanism to select one from among many pre-defined locutions inside the structure. Some of the items were defined by more direct expressions, while others were prepared in a colloquial way. The aim of the work is to make it possible for the VUI interface to acquire characteristics which approximate to interfaces of the NVUI (*Natural Voice User Interface*) type, but limiting the concept of "natural" just to less stilted communication.[2]

As the items can be nested, the grammatical structures can be treated separately giving them the statute of a rule. The project seeks to construct a non-redundant lexicon. When certain locutions are repeated inside a rule, it is re-examined to reduce the expression to the minimum and, if possible, permit that in the future it can be inserted inside locutions that are more extensive or ones that have other purposes. Verbs are treated as independent rules.

```
<rule id="Rule1">
        <one-of>
                <item> Locution1 </item>
                <item> Locution2 </item>
        </one-of>
</rule>
```

---

[2] In this work, it is understood that speaking with a machine is not natural behaviour, while not completely artificial.

Dividing into smaller rules, it is possible to form a complete lexicon of expressions that would serve to direct the outputs sent to the modelling application. However, it is clear that registering all the locutions (creation, modification, selection, search, configuration, comparison, etc.) that a user could use during an architectural or engineering project would be unfeasible because of the quantity.

To try to cover an increasingly wide aspect of situations in geometric modelling using oral communication, the GUI interface was used as a guide, as it already has a structure embedded in it. Therefore, the grammar was divided in XML files containing requests for creation, modification, visualization or filter controls, initially imitating a division of tasks proposed by GUI. However, this decision does not mean that there was an attempt to reproduce a GUI interface. We agree with Harris [7] when he points out the substantial differences, which exist between a VUI interface and a GUI interface. It was decided to separate and distribute the grammar into specialized XML files, dividing them by types of action or procedures. During a recognition process, the active grammar can be loaded and unloaded at any moment. Below is an example of a function for uploading a specific grammar in the recognition mechanism.

```
Grammar Gra = Carga_Gramatica("Estudo_solar.xml", "Gra");
RecEn.LoadGrammarAsync(gramar_name);
```

The tests carried out showed that separating the grammar in independent files makes the recognition process more efficient, as the verbal requests are less subject to suffer semantic ambiguities. By segmenting the work contexts, words or fragments of locutions can be repeated in different action contexts. In order to develop the specific technical lexicon of this experiment, the study of speech in context constantly had to be taken into consideration. In this experiment, the human factor was limited because the user and grammar programmer were the same person.

3.1 Activation of Recognition in Revit and AutoCAD

To activate the recognition process inside the AutoCAD and Revit programs, event handlers associated with the recognition class were prepared. The function of the handler is to trigger the process that interprets the sound of the locution emitted by the user. In AutoCAD the event handler has the following content:

```
RecEn.SpeechRecognized += new
EventHandler<SpeechRecognizedEventArgs>(Listen);
acadApp.Idle += new EventHandler<IdlingEventArgs>(Act);
RecEn.RecognizeAsync(RecognizeMode.Multiple);
```

In Revit the process was similar, only varying the references of the names of methods and the handler acadApp.Idle for an event App.Idling. This event handler triggers the process of interpreting the speech of the user.

```
RecEn.SpeechRecognized += new
EventHandler<SpeechRecognizedEventArgs>(Listen);
App.Idling += new EventHandler<IdlingEventArgs>(Act);
RecEn.RecognizeAsync(RecognizeMode.Multiple);
```

During a session of drafting or modelling, the locution recognition process remains active and in the background, without interfering with the functioning of the traditional GUI interfaces. The recognition object, activated through the event handler, will return the result heard (*recres = e.Result*). This result must be processed for a semantic value to be assigned within a specific and previously stipulated technical domain.

To this purpose, an interpretation function was prepared. This function has two well-defined tasks. The first filters the value of the locution heard by some type of criterion; the second concatenates the filtered locutions in a more extensive stream of meanings. The objective of a function of this type, such as the one presented (Semantics), is to assemble an output which contains the sum of the partial meanings contained in the spoken phrase, concatenating the outputs of the smaller segments formatted in the grammar. Once the phrase has been concatenated, the result heard is derived to execute the corresponding actions in the application. In general, the outputs returned are passed on as the properties of classes or parameters of the specific methods of each class of the application. Some outputs are used to commute between contexts or to finalize the recognition mechanism. The following presents an extract of the function as an example:

```
public void Semantica(RecognitionResult res)
{
string itens = "-";
if (recres.Semantics != null)
{
foreach(KeyValuePair<String, SemanticValue> child in
res.Semantics)
{
string key = child.Key;
string val = child.Value.Value.ToString();
switch (key)
{
case "acc" : Accion=valor; itens=itens+"-"+Accion; break;
case "obj" : Objeto=valor; itens=itens+"-"+Objeto; break;
case "qua" : Quanti=valor; itens=itens+"-"+Quanti; break;
case "uni" : Unidad=valor; itens=itens+"-"+Unidad; break;
case "let" : Letras=valor; itens=itens+"-"+Letras; break;
case "num" : Numero=valor; itens=itens+"-"+Numero; break;
....}
```

The key (parameter key), which itself contains a filtering criterion, is interpreted as one of the semantic categories defined in the rules listed in the XML file. In other words, the locution can signify an object, a number, a letter, an action (verb) or any type of category that has previously been stipulated as a rule and registered within a lexical structure of interpretation of the semantic domain. Next are presented the definitions of the semantic categories in an XML file related to the previous example.

```
<rule id="Comandos" scope="public">
<item><ruleref uri="#acc"/><tag>out.acc=rules.acc;</tag></item>
<item><ruleref uri="#obj"/><tag>out.obj=rules.obj;</tag></item>
<item><ruleref uri="#qua"/><tag>out.qua=rules.qua;</tag></item>
<item><ruleref uri="#uni"/><tag>out.uni=rules.uni;</tag></item>
<item><ruleref uri="#let"/><tag>out.let=rules.let;</tag></item>
<item><ruleref uri="#num"/><tag>out.num=rules.num;</tag></item>
        .
        .
        .
</rule>
```

Concatenated in this way, the locutions can acquire different meanings. The concatenation of rules permits more extensive phrases to be assembled which link, for example, an action to various elements of the predicate, such as a number, an object, a relation or a free locution. The free locutions are important to manage the uncertainty and to introduce a degree of naturalness in the man-machine communication. They use two resources offered in *SRGS:* the pre-defined rules NULL and GARBAGE.

```
<rule id="Free_Exp">
  <one-of>
            <item><ruleref special="GARBAGE"/></item>
            <item><ruleref special="NULL"/>    </item>
  </one-of>
</rule>
```

When introduced inside other rules, they make it possible for a determined expression to be found in spite of some word not having been said or, on the contrary, the user saying words which are not defined in the rule (Table 1).

Table 1. Concatenation of results.

Input (Speech)	Semantic structure	Output
Move	Action	A_E1
Draw a wall	Action + Object	A_D1 + O_01
Window	Object	O_02
Copy 10 Doors	Action + Number + Object	A_D02 + 10 + O_03
Delete last Door	Action + Relation + Object	A_E01 + R01 + O_03

A locution can start an action, which is executed immediately or needs some data to proceed. In this case, the application can load a grammar that belongs to another context and ask for spoken data in order to continue or finalize the action. The request "Copy 10 doors", for example, will need more definitions such as "Which doors?" or "Copy them where?" In this case, there must be co-ordination between the context of the grammar and the objectives of the application. The general structure of a locution rule to set a scale #seta_escal contains four elements:

- Rule for an action (for example: "accion_setar")
- Rule for an Object (for example: "escala")
- Rule for the interpretation of articles and/or adverbs (for example: the, in, it, by)
- Free locutions (for example: Please)

The result of the locution rule #seta_escal is formed by the concatenation of these elements (rules and free locutions) leading to the catalogued action, such as this example, A_Z033, to which is added as a parameter the numerical value of the scale which is the value of the numerical value spoken (Fig. 2).

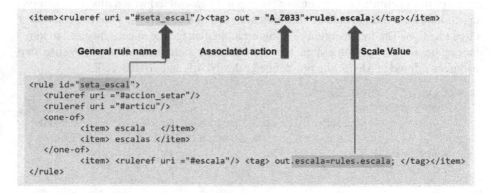

Fig. 2. Scheme of the rule for the action "set a scale"

As the grammar rule with the value of the scales was isolated as an independent rule with a name, it can be inserted in various other action rules that need a numerical definition of value of scale. The free locutions can make the mode of communication more natural from the point of view of the user. Below are some of the phrases related to the configuration of the scale (Fig. 3).

Setar a escala 1/100
Escala 100
Sete escalas 1/50
Por favor setar as escalas 1/50

From the point of view of the machine, some functionalities of the TTS synthesizer permit adjustments to diverse characteristics of the modulation of the synthesized voice. The speed of speech (Rate), the emphasis of speech (*PromptEmphasis*) and the language used can be adjusted. In the tests carried out, no meaningful differences were observed in terms of the control of emphasis of the voices spoken. However, in terms of the speed of speech emitted by the TTS mechanism, the difference between rapidly executed locutions and slow ones was clearly perceived. The adjustment chosen for the rate of speech was medium speed but when using the interface for dictation assistance to confirm model data (the machine lists objects for the designer) care should be taken with

```
<rule id="escala"> <one-of>
<item>natural                <tag> out =   "1"; </tag></item>
<item>un                     <tag> out =   "1"; </tag></item>
<item>uno                    <tag> out =   "1"; </tag></item>
<item>dos                    <tag> out =   "2"; </tag></item>
<item>dois                   <tag> out =   "2"; </tag></item>
<item>cinco                  <tag> out =   "5"; </tag></item>
<item>dez                    <tag> out =  "10"; </tag></item>
<item>diez                   <tag> out =  "10"; </tag></item>
<item>veinte;                <tag> out =  "20"; </tag></item>
<item>vinte;                 <tag> out =  "20"; </tag></item>
<item>vinticinco;            <tag> out =  "25"; </tag></item>
<item>veinticinco;           <tag> out =  "25"; </tag></item>
<item>cincuenta              <tag> out =  "50"; </tag></item>
<item>cien                   <tag> out = "100"; </tag></item>
<item>ciento cincuenta       <tag> out = "150"; </tag></item>
<item>doscientos             <tag> out = "200"; </tag></item>
<item>doscientos cinquenta <tag> out = "250"; </tag></item>
<item>duzentos cinquenta     <tag> out = "250"; </tag></item>
<item>quinientos;            <tag> out = "500"; </tag></item>
<item>mil                    <tag> out = "1000"; </tag></item>
<item>mil quinientos         <tag> out = "1500"; </tag></item>
<item>dos mil                <tag> out = "2000"; </tag></item> </one-of> </rule>
```

Fig. 3. Rule for the value of a scale

this parameter, as medium speed speech can be tiring during long responses. The function which executes the machine speech is Speak().

4 The Language Issue

The mechanisms to perform the speech recognition depend on language packs for the recognition of each specific language. At the time of programming this experiment, there were language packs to recognize locutions in the following languages: English, French, Spanish, German, Japanese, simplified Chinese and traditional Chinese. A recognition mechanism in the Portuguese language for the environment tested (Windows 8.0, AutoCAD and Revit) was not yet available. However, despite this limitation, the recognition mechanism was tested with Spanish, as Spanish and Portuguese share many words and phonemes. The option was taken to configure the grammars using locutions that were the same in both languages (*vista, planta, ampliar*, etc.) or to state the locution in Portuguese if its phoneme exists in Spanish. A phoneme is an acoustic phenomenon, the smallest sound element capable of establishing a distinction between words. Therefore, although a word may not exist, what the recognition mechanism interprets is the sound profile of the word. The two following locutions are comprehensible to the Spanish interpreter although the words "*quero*" and "*gostaria*" do not exist in this language.

```
<item>quero ver      </item>
<item>gostaria de ver</item>
```

Meanwhile, for the inverse process, in other words, the transformation of Text to Speech (TTS) there are voices available in Portuguese with the Brazilian variant. In this experiment, some specific grammar was tested mixing locutions in Spanish and Portuguese. The following operations were created and tested with the VUI interface.

- Create structural grids and building levels.
- Search structural elements by its name in a grid.
- Create columns, beams and slabs.
- Load families.
- Count and inform about construction objects.
- Set view templates.
- Apply zooms.
- Adjust the point of view in 3D views.
- Adjust the section box of a 3D view.
- Automatically slicing the project in different 3D views.
- Perform solar studies.
- Carry out general units operations and view modes configuration.

The number of levels of meanings of the operations depends on the complexity of the operation to be carried out. For this experiment, it can be said that the type of communication established between the individual and the machine is determined by a well-defined closed grammar within a specific technical domain. The system does not have special mechanisms of inference, which can anticipate or infer the solicitations that the user makes. This type of mechanism could be embedded in the application, considering the grammar project inserted in an artificial intelligence work context.

Three strategies were used in order to facilitate the modelling operations and broaden the communication possibilities between man and machine. The first relates to the possibility of customizing the locutions registered in the XML file. This possibility is a natural structural consequence of an application formed by grammar. For example, a rule for the solicitation of the configuration of a sun chart can be:

```
<rule id="solar">
        <item> <one-of>
                <item>solar        </item>
                <item>carta solar</item>
        </one-of> </item> </rule>
```

However, a user could add new locutions to this rule. According to his/her technical culture, the user can add new forms of solicitation to the previous solicitations to execute the same operation orally. In this example, solicitations with more technical vocabulary can be added such as *"analemma"* or *"heliodon"*, as well as other locutions, which approximate to lay communication (Fig. 4).

```
<rule id="solar">
    <item> <one-of>
              <item>sol              </item>
              <item>solar            </item>
              <item>carta solar   </item>
              <item>rayos de sol </item>
              <item>raios solares</item>
              <item>rayos solares</item>
              <item>analemma       </item>
              <item>heliodon       </item>
         </one-of> </item> </rule>
```

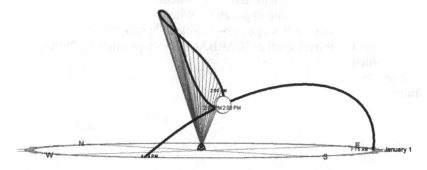

Fig. 4. Solar analemma rays during a year at weekly intervals at 2.00 PM

The second strategy relates to the possibility of establishing a dialogical communication of question-response (Solicitation by the user – response from the system – response from the user…), similar to the modes of operation with traditional GUI interfaces. The difference is that the solicitations made by the system to the user are spoken which makes them more evident, if compared with text messages which mix with other elements in the peripheries of the interfaces of the screen.

The messages are spoken taking advantage of the possibility of TTS translation. Their textual content can be registered in the application, as well as combining alphanumerical data collected during the execution of the commands. In this way, in order to proceed with carrying out a task, a command can orally solicit some missing data. In this example, after activating the grammar for the solar studies, it was necessary to establish which type of solar study will be calculated: over a year, a month, a week or a day, as well as requiring the specific time. The options required for this information were registered in independent rules, which deal with time (Fig. 5).

The third communication strategy was to create independent grammar for the verbs used with greater frequency, registering their verbal moods in the infinitive, the present and the imperative. In the rules related to adverbs, articles, modes of courtesy and comparatives (greater than, less than, parallel to, etc.) there was a rule of free locution in their body to allow them to be vocalized or not.

```
<rule id="tempo_solar">
  <one-of><item>
              <one-of>
                  <item>diario      </item>
                  <item>un día      </item>
                  <item>día         </item>
                  <item>por día     </item>
              </one-of><tag> out = "ESolar01"; </tag> </item>
          <item> <one-of>
                  <item>anual       </item>
                  <item>un año      </item>
                  <item>año         </item>
                  <item>por año     </item>
              </one-of> <tag> out = "ESolar02"; </tag> </item>
          <item> <ruleref special="GARBAGE"/> <tag> out = "....";</tag>
          </item>
  </one-of>
</rule>
```

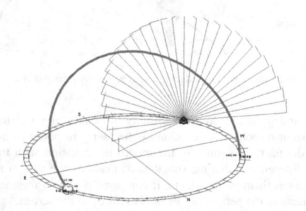

Fig. 5. Solar rays and their normal during a day with intervals of 30 min

In this stage of the programming of the CAD-BIM system oriented by voice, the tests were individually performed by the author and in parallel with the programming of the functions. The project intends to begin a second stage in which it will seek to test the VUI interface in a real production environment with various users. The preliminary observations indicate that although certain types of operations can be activated and executed more quickly with the VUI interface than with the resources of a traditional GUI interface, even so, the habit of operating with a mouse and keyboard is a factor that interferes in the evaluation. Of the tasks tested, some were shown to be more suitable to be activated by voice. In general, they are those that do not require the manipulation of relations between various objects, such the zoom control; configurations of units and scales; the controls of modes of visualization and the selection of views. The creation of objects, which involve relations with other objects, makes the voice interface more of a challenge, as in addition to finding suitable grammar, it is necessary to overcome the habit of the gesture. In this sense, the hand does not relax. We can point to this human factor as a complicating issue. In the case of the BIM model, which depends on a well-structured and specialized database, the voice interface takes advantage of the model structure. It is possible to carry out some operations of quick selections without the intervention of the GUI interface. For example, "*Select columns in axis 4*" or "*Select column B2*". The launching of a set of structural axes and reference levels, and the counting and checking of the existence of objects and loading of families were operations that were tested and evaluated with a positive outcome (Fig. 6).

```
<rule id ="Carga">
   <one-of>
            <item>cargar </item> <item>carregar </item>
            <item>cargue </item> <item>carregue </item>
            <item>carga  </item> <item>carrega  </item>
   </one-of>
</rule>

<rule id ="Familias">
<one-of>
  <item>coluna de concreto<tag> out = "/Structural Columns/Concrete"; </tag></item>
  <item>pilar de concreto <tag> out = "/Structural Columns/Concrete"; </tag></item>
  <item>coluna metálica   <tag> out = "/Structural Columns/Steel";    </tag></item>
  <item>pilar metálico    <tag> out = "/Structural Columns/Steel";    </tag></item>
  <item>portas            <tag> out = "/Doors";                       </tag></item>
  <item>ventanas          <tag> out = "/Windows";                     </tag></item>
 </one-of>
</rule>

<item> <ruleref uri ="#Carga"/>
       <ruleref uri ="#Familias"/>
       <tag> out = "A_M001" + "*" + rules.Familias;</tag>
</item>
```

Fig. 6. Grammar for the loading of families

There is no way to predict what will happen during the phases of conception of the project. Which elements will be incorporated and which eliminated? Which manufacturer or component will be used? Which name will be given to the rooms? Therefore, some grammars had to be constructed automatically on the fly during a modelling session. They are created from the reading of the updated state of the graphic database at a certain moment. If a *ViewTemplate* or a new level is created, they must be incorporated as content of a grammar, so that the user can call them. The code below shows a on the fly construction mechanism.

```
newoption = "<item> <one-of> <item> " + option + "</item>
</one-of> <tag> out = "+ "\"" + option + "\"" + "; </tag>
</item>";
sw.WriteLine(newoption);
```

A complicating factor for operations by voice to have a greater presence relates to the naming of the elements and the mix of languages in the production environments. There are moments when it is necessary to manipulate or load objects in a different language from that used in the work environment. In these cases, inserting a word in the grammar - without obeying the original spelling in order to simulate the phonetics - is a partial solution. Another problem experienced relates to the verbal solicitation of elements with technical names which include silent characters ("_", "-", "#") or unpronounceable codes. In order to resolve these cases, the option was taken to construct a graphic interface (dialogue box) which, by showing a numbered list with the names of the elements, solicits the option desired. The integer number is used as a hot-word for the oral solicitation. In these cases, the difficulty occurs when the lists are extensive. The solution then is to spell the code, which makes the operation laborious for long codes.

5 Conclusions

The research related here was guided by certain aims. The first aim was to develop an alternative interface to the traditional GUI. The second aim was that the interface should avoid traditional entry devices, and the third was to conceive a system that as far as possible avoided the need for touch between the cursor and the elements of the BIM model. In parallel, during the course of the work, our attention was drawn to the fact that the SR and TTS technology, in spite of having made the first steps in the field during the 1980s and 1990s [2, 3], has still not been widely diffused three decades later. In this article, we have speculated that among the factors which might account for this situation can be numbered the fact that graphic activities in the great part require the intervention of the gesture. We based this speculation on direct observation, which arose during the programming of the grammar and the tests with spoken commands that were carried out and have been related in this work. The automatic movement of the hand, seeking to execute a command on the GUI interface, often anticipated the vocalization of the VUI orders that were being programmed, tested and adjusted. As the GUI and VUI interfaces were active at the same time during the tests, the interference of the mechanical habit was inevitable. In this sense, we could not fail to notice the tension, which exists between the intellectual aspect, that conceives the action, and the sensorial and motor aspect that executes it.

We also speculated that the VUI interfaces would be useful to help reduce the level of attention required to manipulate 3D models, which are becoming increasingly complex and rich in data. Working on this question, we focused on the programming of four types of grammar: grammar to create new objects; grammar to configure the working environment; grammar to search for and quantify objects; and, finally, grammar for selection in order to diminish the need to touch the objects of the model with the cursor. These tasks were facilitated by the well-defined data structures available in the BIM models. Selecting elements inside a 3D model which are outside the direct reach of the cursor is an activity that requires the mediation of filters, locking tools to protect other objects and changes in the positioning of the views. Tasks that selection by voice have facilitated. In our experience, the VUI interface was positively evaluated in these four types of operations, although we should highlight the need to increase the offer of grammar, as well as the need to test the system outside the laboratory, in real working situations. One of the points that requires special attention is voice control in work environments in which coexist various different languages. Finally, we would like to make some speculative considerations about the future use of SR/TTS technology in CAD-BIM environments.

In the recent past, the passage from traditional drawing to drawing with CADD tools has permitted architects, engineers and designers to stop using squares, rulers, pencils and compasses. This change has also meant a substantial reduction in the gestural aspect of graphic work. In other words, the movements of the draughtsman have been reduced to small movements involving the use of one hand and the fingertips. The form, as a geometric materialization, has moved away from the gesture. It has found refuge and new impulses in the Algorithm Aided Architectural Design techniques, in which the form is understood as the abstract support of the project. Currently, some research groups have been developing tactile interfaces and devices, such as interactive multi-touch tables combined with 3D digitalized models [6]. These developments point in the direction of the recuperation of the gestural aspect as a necessary condition for spatial knowledge. VUI interfaces place the gestural question on another plane. The remaining gestures that traditional GUI interfaces still permit or the gestural potential that the new multi-touch interfaces point to as the future of interactive design could disappear completely if the control of the interface comes to be vocalized. The VUI interfaces transform the graphic activity, which traditionally combines an intellectual aspect with a sensorial, gestural and mechanical aspect, to a solely intellectual one, where only the visual sense remains as the evaluator of the formal results. If the research into sub-vocal recognition [4,9] develops favorably, it is reasonable to imagine the emergence of a project process in its purest intellectual state. Perhaps, the development of voice recognition interfaces in the near future will mean that the mouse and keyboard suffer the same fate as the pencil and squares, being left to one side at the workstations. The leap to a totally intellectual design activity which does not depend on contact or interactivity with drawing devices, in which the participation of the sensorial is reduced to the

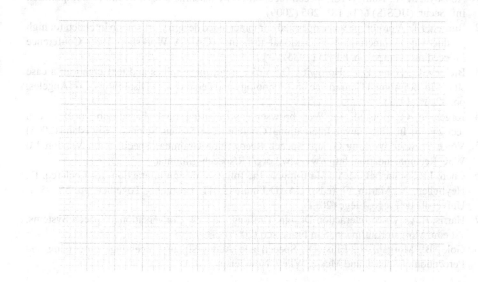

Fig. 7. A speculative white sheet VUI interface

minimum, appears to be a scenario which is technically possible. In other words, a return to the blank page, thanks to new interfaces and graphic programs which make it possible to completely eliminate all the current elements of inputs from GUI interfaces, does not seem out of reach (Fig. 7).

We know that locutions of the type *"Draw a volume of 3 floors"*, *"Tell me if any tubing interferes in the structure"* or *"What is the best angle for this window?"* can, today, be interpreted and translated as sequences of commands. The various strategies and design methods with Algorithm Aided Architectural Design techniques can also take advantage of the integration of SR-TTS verbal communication. However, if we wish to communicate in a more natural way, a lot of work remains to be done to integrate the SR technology within intelligent CAD-BIM project environments.

In the face of this "intellectual-sensorial" tension, it is worthwhile turning to an observation present in a manuscript of the Austrian philosopher Ludwig Wittgenstein who said *"How small a thought it takes to fill a whole life!"* [10]. In a certain way, this statement makes us remember the difficulty of adjusting our thoughts to the reality. In the field of design, thoughts can be expressed in words, words translated into shapes, and shapes materialized into buildings. Or, would it be better to say, gestures induce thoughts, thoughts crystalize into shapes, and shapes materialize into designs? If there are no great barriers to overcome before 100 % VUI graphic interfaces are developed, it remains to be seen if drawing and the project, activities that require the intervention of gestures, will lose this characteristic letting the intellectual aspect take the place of the remaining sensorial aspect. For the moment, we are inclined to think that solutions, which combine both aspects, will be more efficient.

References

1. Anusuya, M.A., Katti, S.K.: Speech recognition by machine a review. Int. J. Comput. Sci. Inf. Secur. (IJCSIS) 6(3), 181–205 (2009)
2. Burnett, J.J.: A prototype voice operated computer aided design workstation intended for high productivity commercial & educational use. In: ACADIA Workshop 1985 Conference Proceedings Tempe, pp. 83–95 (1985)
3. Bickley, C., Hong, Z.T., Horowitz, D.: Voice input for graphics and text creation: a case study. In: 8th Annual Conference on Technology and Persons with Disabilities, Los Angeles, pp. 32–36 (1993)
4. Jorgensen, C., Binsted, K.: Web browser control using EMG based sub vocal speech recognition. In: 38th Hawaii International Conference on System Sciences, Big Island (2005)
5. Voice Browser Working Group: Speech Recognition Grammar Specification Version 1.0 W3C Recommendation. http://www.w3.org/TR/speech-grammar
6. Chen, I.R., Schnabel, M.A.: Multi-touch: the future of design interaction. In: Leclercq, P., Heylighen, A., Martin, G. (eds.) CAAD Futures 2011: Designing Together, pp. 557–571. Université de Liège, Liège (2011)
7. Harris, R.A.: Voice Interaction Design: Crafting the New Conversational Speech Systems, 1st edn. Morgan Kaufmann, San Francisco (2005)
8. Gold, B., Morgan, N., Ellis, D.: Speech and Audio Signal Processing: Processing and Perception of Speech and Music. Wiley, New Jersey (2011)

9. Meltzner, G.S., Sroka, J., Heaton, J.T., Gilmore, L.D., Colby, G., Roy, S., Chen, N., De Luca, C.J.: Speech recognition for vocalized and subvocal modes of production using surface EMG signals from the Neck and Face. In: 9th Annual Conference of the International Speech Communication Association, pp. 2267–2270. ISCA, Brisbane (2009)
10. Wittgenstein, Philosopher of Cultures. Conference in Akademia Ignatianum Krakowie. http://www.wf.ignatianum.eu/konferencja-Wittgenstein

Development of BIM Performance Measurement System for Architectural Design Firms

Jihye Shin, Jungsik Choi$^{(\boxtimes)}$, and Inhan Kim

Kyung Hee University, Seoul, South Korea
{shj9025,junsikchoi,inkim}@khu.ac.kr

Abstract. Despite the effort of Korean government to vitalize BIM adoption in AEC industry, the domestic adoption of BIM is still in its initial step. Particular in design field where medium and small firms being the majority, shows lower level of BIM adoption. The primary reason for this can be considered as lacking of necessities caused by uncertain benefits of BIM. Therefore, it is time to develop the objectives, quantifiable and qualitative measurement system of BIM performances. The purpose of this study is to suggest the BIM Performance Measurement System for architectural design firms. In achieving this, the authors have developed Balanced Scorecard (BSC) and validated its appropriateness by questionnaire survey with experts and performing statistical analysis. This development can be contributed to the voluntary BIM adoption by visualizing the detailed benefit of BIM and to the improvement of enterprise competitiveness by facilitating management of design process and estimating future outcome.

Keywords: Building information modeling (BIM) · BIM adoption · BIM benefit · Performance measurement system (PMS) · Balanced scorecard (BSC) · Critical success factors (CSF) · Key performance indicators (KPI)

1 Introduction

1.1 Overview

BIM is a technology for improving the productivity and efficiency of the construction industry, by taking advantage of the information generated throughout the life period of the facility to a consistent system to maximize production efficiency and utilization of their information [1]. In order to vitalize the adoption of BIM in the construction industry, Korean government applied mandates to implement BIM in more than 50 billion won turnkey project and design competition from 2012. Moreover, government-led efforts, such as mandating BIM design apply to all procurements of Public Procurement Service from 2016 and distribution of BIM application guideline for architectural field, have been continued.

Nonetheless, BIM is still tend to be perceived as a visualization tool and is only applied to fulfill at a level that meets the requirements of owners in Korea. In addition, active use of BIM in private sectors have shown limitations with a high technical

© Springer-Verlag Berlin Heidelberg 2015
G. Celani et al. (Eds.): CAAD Futures 2015, CCIS 527, pp. 348–365, 2015.
DOI: 10.1007/978-3-662-47386-3_19

barriers and key technologies absent. Despite the government's aggressive movements to the introduction of BIM, the adoption of BIM is still staying on the initial level due to failure in realizing the effects of BIM, which makes investment profitability unclear.

Design phase, in where the key decision and information is made, can create the greatest value through BIM adoption. In the case of domestic architectural and design firms, there is a wide spectrum from companies utilizing BIM actively to the ones that do not take into account of BIM at all. The recent survey shows that 75 % of the architects has been identified as non BIM project experience.[1] Therefore, the environment where adoptable visualization of financial and non-financial values of BIM in design phase as the successful case of BIM adoption and the preliminary data for the improvement of competitiveness, should be established in order to enable the voluntary application of BIM at the corporate level. Currently BIM performance evaluation tool tailored for the characteristics of each country are being developed and operated, such as the BIM I-CMM and bimScore of United States and BIM3 of Australia.

The development of BIM performance evaluation tools suitable for architectural practice is still inadequate. Furthermore, it is harder to evaluate the IT investment than other industry due to the lack of case for benchmarking assessment. To evaluate properly the effect of BIM adoption as IT technologies, the multilateral evaluation including tangible effect which can be objectively measured and quantified and intangible effects(for example, improved product quality, better decision-making capabilities, increased availability of data) is required [2].

1.2 Research Objective

To activate the BIM application, this paper derives the BIM performance Measurement framework and Key Performance Indicators (KPI) in the design phase at the corporate level as the basic research on development of BIM Performance Measurement System (PMS). Therefore, the concrete measures about each KPI has not been taken account of in this study. It is the goal of this paper to provide the environment to which the design firms could be able to measure and compare the performances themselves from a realistic and systematic perspective to promote the voluntary adoption of BIM.

1.3 Methodology

In the effort to revitalization of using BIM, the authors developed indicators for BIM performance measurement based on the results from the analysis of the design firm's purpose in the adoption of BIM. This study focuses on the design firms above medium scale (20 people or more), where the roles of organization within the business are clearly separated to consider the organizational characteristics of the design firm. The research of this paper consist of four parts:

---

[1] The result of the survey of 442 architecture design firms, "BIM performance and readiness survey" conducted by Korean Architects Association, 2014.5.

- Part 1: an analysis of literature regarding BIM performances and performance management system
- Part 2: an analysis of BIM guidelines to deduce the general purpose of adopting BIM in design firms
- Part 3: development of the indicators for BIM performance measurement; and conduct advice requisition to the BIM experts to reflect the domestic architecture practice on the indicators
- Part 4: conduct the survey among the BIM experts who have BIM project operating experiences; and regression analysis with SPSS 21[2] to identify the cause-and-effect relationship

2 Literature Review

2.1 BIM Benefits

In this paper, Building Information Modeling (BIM) is considered as an investment in Information Technology (IT) to achieve a specific purpose in corporates. IT investment performance means the value of the overall behaviors and relationships based on IT, from ensuring competitiveness through IT investment to the level of connection between business operation/strategy and each corporate activities [3]. This includes the reducing cost through IT investment, improvement of quality, flexibility and operational efficiency and increase customer satisfaction [20]. Specifically the problem is that it is hard to quantify in monetary terms and to evaluate objectively.

IT benefit could be categorized in three areas: (1) tangible benefits: quantifiable in monetary terms; (2) semi-tangible benefits: quantifiable, but not in monetary terms; and (3) intangible benefits: non-quantifiable, described qualitatively [2]. BIM as the one type of the IT, also makes tangible, semi-tangible or intangible benefits [4]. Therefore, the BIM performances should include the economic values occurred by BIM adoption as well as positive effects and the achieved goals of corporate by BIM system and operating process based on BIM. The performances of BIM is defined as financial, non-financial, quantitative and qualitative effects made by adopting BIM which substantially contributes to the goal of corporate.

2.2 Literature Review

The literature review was conducted to analyze the current research regarding to the benefits derived from BIM and methodology for its measurement. Researches related to BIM performances are classified into evaluation of design firm's BIM capacity, measurement of satisfaction degree for BIM-based project, Return on Investment (ROI), analysis for adopting BIM and development direction of a BIM performance assessment tool in Table 1. These reviewed papers are published within past five years.

---

[2] SPSS (Statistical Package for the Social Sciences) developed by IBM is typical in software for data analysis in the social sciences.

Table 1. Literature review about measurement of BIM performances

Reference	Level of measurement	Subject to measurement	Developed measurement system
Lee and Lee [5]	Corporate level	BIM capacity	BIM capacity evaluation model based on CMM
Song and et al. [4]	Project level	Satisfaction degree for BIM construction Project	BSC based Measurement system of Satisfaction Degree for BIM
Seo and Choo [6]	Corporate level	The Cost-effectiveness of BIM-based Design process	Cost-benefit factors for visualizing the economic effects of BIM
Kang and et al. [8]	Project level	BIM performances	Direction and Considerations for development BIM performance assessment tool
Barlish and Sullivan [7]	Project level	BIM performances	Return and investment metrics for quantifiable BIM performance

These are the researches on which the measurement systems was developed, from the perspective of design organization to activate adopting BIM. Lee and Lee developed CMM-based BIM capability evaluation model, divided into the technical part and the management part, with reflecting the characteristic of the design organization [5]. Song and et al. [4] suggested that BSC based satisfaction degree management system for design firms adopting BIM.

On impact of business perspective, Seo and Choo [6] deduced the cost-benefit factors to quantify the economic impact of BIM in design phase. In a similar point of view, Kristen Barlish and et al. [7] developed the return and investment metrics for quantifiable and monetary BIM performances (e.g. schedule, design changes, expense and RFIs) for providing the competitive performance evaluation environment. Kang and et al. [8] analyzed various BIM performance evaluation tool and interviewed BIM experts to derive to the basic direction for development of BIM performance assessment tool.

The related researches to date have shown limits to establishing the system which can review and analyze the level of achievement on established strategies. Furthermore, absence of clear criteria for measurement of performances prompts as a difficulty for application in real practice. The multilateral and macroscopic assessment about BIM performance in the corporate level is considered as necessary to the situation in lacking of research on intangible value from BIM.

2.3 BIM Performance Management System Review

The BIM Performance Management System (PMS) has been developed by around the United State, Australia and Netherlands. The most representative systems are

BIM I-CMM[3] and bimScore[4] which are developed in U.S and BIM3[5] developed in Australia. These tools measure the performances at the project level, thus there are the limitations to the representation of such for the BIM performances at corporate level. In order to evaluate the BIM performances in enterprise unit, PMS supporting corporate governance are needed. IT investment performance measurement systems is a tool for managing the values of IT investment in corporate or organization, the degree of contribution to economic performance and the level of achieving enterprise objective. This section reviewed the IT investment PMS to select the suitable system for applying to BIM PMS. IT investment PMS is largely categorized in four areas:

- Financial approach: The financial evaluation methods are the way to financial assessment based on the risk assessment in conjunction with the use of IT-related indicators. When pure financial technique is used, there is the disadvantage of which only the flow of money could be identified. However, many methodologies are based on this approach, thus there is the advantage to be understood easily within the field.
- Qualitative approach: The methods belonging to this approach mainly evaluate qualitative value, with focus on the organization, process and technology. These methods are mainly used for evaluating IT strategy or portfolio analysis.
- Multi-Criteria Approach: This approach considers both financial and non-financial indicators. In general, a number of indicators are considered to evaluate any systems. This approach has the advantage of being able to take into account a number of indicators at the same time.
- Probabilistic Approach: This approach assesses the value of IT through a scientific method using statistical and mathematical models. It is mathematically sophisticated. Therefore, there is a difficulty to illustrate the performance in business language in some cases.

BIM performance measurement should evaluate extensively the financial, non-financial, tangible and semi-tangible/intangible values occurred by adopting BIM. Therefore, this study determined that *Multi-Criteria Approach* on IT investment performance management system is appropriate to apply to BIM PMS.

2.4 IT BSC Model of Grembergen

Balanced Scorecard (BSC), the one of the methodology of Multi-Criteria Approach, is developed by Kaplan and Noton in 1992. The proposed system evaluated the value from the results of execution in the balanced four *Perspectives* and each *Perspective*

---

[3] BIM I-CMM is the BIM maturity measurement software based on CMM model of software engineering. It is developed by FIC (Faculty Information Council) in NIBS (National Institute of Building Science) in 2007.

[4] bimScore is the BIM maturity measurement service model based on BSC which is developed by bimScore Inc, from 2013. (https://www.bimscore.com/).

[5] BIM3 (BIM Maturity Model) is a performance evaluation tools related to BIM practice, developed by the University of Newcastle, Australia.

has cause-and effect relationship to each other [9]. The four *Perspectives* are as follows: Financial perspective, Customer perspective, Internal Business, Learning & Growth perspective. IT BSC is the performance management framework of redesigned BSC considering the characteristics of IT. In other word, it is the management model to evaluate the activities performed by IT organization [10]. The IT BSC model of Grembergen depicted in Fig. 1 are used most commonly.

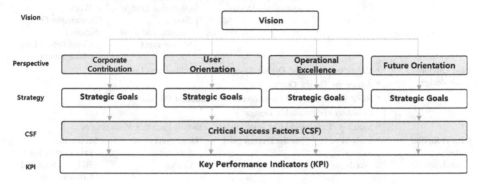

Fig. 1. The structure of Grembergen's IT BSC model

In view towards the adoption of BIM as an IT investment, IT organization means an organization that performs BIM-related work in the design firms. The BIM PMS developed in this study is based on Grembergen's IT BSC model to offer the environment of a balanced evaluation in BIM performances with financial, non-financial, quantitative, qualitative, result and process measurement indicators.

3 Development of IT BSC- Based Key Performance Indicators of BIM Performance

3.1 The Purpose of BIM Adoption in the Design Firms

IT investment performance measurement is defined as the act of analyzing the substantial degree of contribution to the corporate strategy and suggesting a plan for the identified problem to maximize the effects [11]. In order to develop the BIM PMS, the *Vision*, which be ultimately accomplished, and *Strategies* for the four *Perspectives* should be firstly defined. Subsequently, Critical Success Factors (CSF) for each *Strategies* and Key Performance Indicators (KPI) for each CSFs are to be developed to measure the degree of achievement for *Vision* and *Strategies*.

In this chapter, analyses were performed to deduce general *Vision* and *Strategies* about BIM adoption in design firms from domestic and international BIM guidelines. The analyzed guidelines are as follows: Basic BIM Guidelines for Facilities Project (Public Procurement Service), BIM Guideline for Design(Korea Land and Housing Corporation), BIM Adoption Design Guidelines(Virtual Construction Research Team), Common Criteria for Building Information Modeling/Delivery(Korea Institute of Construction Technology) and BIM Guide(GSA). Please see Table 2.

Table 2. Purpose of BIM adoption in BIM guidelines

BIM Guideline	Design phase			
	Pre-design	Schematic design	Design development	Construction document
Basic BIM guidelines for facilities Project		*Assure the Design Quality *Output Accurate Drawings *Sustainable Design	*Assure the Design Quality *Output Accurate Drawings *Sustainable Design *Efficient Construction Cost Management	*Increase Maturity of Design *Secure Information for Construction Work *Sustainable Design *Efficient Construction Cost Management
BIM Guideline for design	* Utilize the Advanced Digital Systems and Architectural Information * Assure the Design Quality * Build the Effective and Reasonable Construction Process * Induction of Sustainable Design * Induce to Economical Construction and Efficient Facilities Management			
BIM Adoption design guidelines	*Analysis of Owner's Needs	*Set the Design goal	*Development of Schematic Design	*Secure the Information for Bid, Contract and Construction Work
	*Planning the Execution of Design Work	*Evaluation of Design Alternatives and Determination of Best Solution	*Clarify all sorts of Material, Equipment	
Common criteria for building information modeling/ delivery	* The Goal of Quality standards: Design Review, Space Requirements Review, Workability Review * 22 Utilizations of BIM Listed in the Guide: Design Modeling, Design Review, Design History Records, Workability Review, Design Review, Energy Analysis, Cost Estimate etc.			
BIM Guide	* Define the Document needed in The early Stages of Design * Clarification of Design Information * Increase the Understanding about Design Intent and Assessment on Program * Build the Sustained and Efficient Design Information * Reduce the Rework			
Common issues	* Secure the quality of design * Clarification of design information * Establish efficient design processes * Build the sustained and efficient design information			

The result of the comparison analysis on BIM guidelines is represented in Table 2. Although the Guidelines have some differences objective of BIM adoption, they share the ultimate context. The five BIM guidelines imply the common purpose of BIM: (1) Assure the Design Quality; (2) Clarification of Design Information; develop the efficient Design Process; (4) Build the Sustained and Efficient Design Information. In addition, they suggest similar application of BIM, such as 3D Modeling, Design Review, Output Accurate and Energy Analysis. Therefore, the author has defined the general purpose of BIM adoption as Secure high quality and value of design & Establish the efficient design process.

3.2 BIM Balanced Scorecard Framework

The authors developed the BIM PMS framework based on IT BSC, reflecting the purpose of the adoption of BIM in design firm derived from the previous section. This study titled it as BIM Balanced Scorecard (BIM BSC). The definition of each *Perspective* and Strategy is presented in Table 3.

- Vision: The *Vision* of the BIM BSC represents the ultimate goal of BIM realization in design firms. Reflecting to the result of the previous section, improvement of design quality and efficiency of design works has defined as the general *Vision* of BIM BSC.
- Four Perspectives: The *Perspective*, the subdivision of the *Vision,* forms the bases for performance measurement to express clearly the pursuing value of organization [12]. To establish the *Perspectives* and *Strategies* of BIM BSC, the basic *Perspectives* of IT BSC were revised and reconstituted according to the BIM characteristics.

Table 3. The developed BIM BSC Framework

Business contribution	User orientation
*Definition: Assess the degree to business contribution against BIM investment and adoption in design firm ***The strategic objectives**: Achieving high performance through the adoption of BIM	***Definition**: Assess the satisfaction of owner and user about BIM and BIM-based projects ***The strategic objectives**: Improvement the satisfaction of client and BIM organization
Operational Excellence	Future Orientation
*Definition: Evaluate how BIM-based design process is operated efficiently and effectively	***Definition**: Evaluate the technical innovation ability and BIM project capability responding to the future BIM technological changes
*The strategic objectives: Construct the effective BIM-based design process	***The strategic objectives**: Acquiring the technical skills to improve the design competitiveness

The Business Contribution perspective and Future Orientation perspective of BIM BSC is composed similar to the concept of IT BSC Model. The characteristics of design firm on the subject of BIM technology development and utilization are also reflected into the User Orientation perspective. Therefore, this *Perspective* is defined by means of evaluating the satisfaction of owner and user about BIM-based projects though the variance of existing *Perspective* of IT BSC, which is divided into technology providers and users. Since the BIM technology is not developed by organization of design firms, the Operational Excellence perspective has reconstructed with a focus on operations of BIM-based design process.

3.3 Development of Critical Success Factors and Key Performance Indicators

BSC is a methodology to convert the metaphysical *Vision* of enterprise into Key Performance Indicators (KPI) to realize to be specific and visible [13]. Critical Success Factors (CSF) are specific factors required to be achieved in order to accomplish the *Vision* and *Strategy* of each *Perspective*; while KPI measure the degree of CSF achievement. To utilize effectively BSC, CSFs and KPIs must be monitored and managed by the company. The running targets of corporate should be also integrated clearly into the KPIs [14].

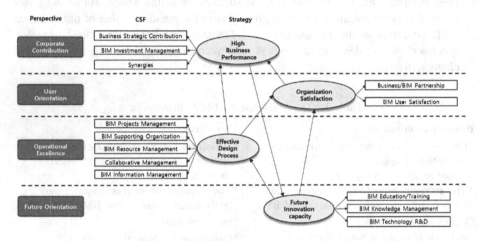

Fig. 2. Preliminary BIM BSC models

The preliminary indicators were collected from related researches on IT BSC and BIM [9, 17–19] to develop the measurable CSFs and KPIs of BIM BSC in design firms. Because the objective of this study is to establish measurement framework and select KPIs for development of BIM PMS, the detailed measurement methods of each KPI are not taken into account of.

The preliminary BIM BSC comprised of 13 CSFs and 32 KPIs has been revised and developed with based on the classification of CSFs and KPIs [9] and development process for PMS of IT-organization [15]. Figure 2 shows the suggest Preliminary BIM BSC Model, of which each CSFs have the cause-and-effect relationship.

3.4 Supplementation of BIM BSC

Individual interview with experts who has the experience in BIM projects and works for medium-scale design firms were conducted in order to reflect on the practice to CSFs and KPIs of BIM BSC and review the compatibility of BSC BIM. The four experts of three different type of design firms, (1) design firm A which is part of conglomerates, (2) large-scaled design firm B, (3) medium-scaled design firm C.

The respondents showed similar opinions on BIM BSC framework and most of the indicators, with small differences in suitability of KPIs.

All of them especially agreed on the fact that there is difficulty in evaluating BIM performances under the current domestic working environment where work and business is not managed by Man-Hour system. In addition, they suggested that clarification of the indicators is needed for users to understand easily the meaning of KPIs and how much *Strategies* have been achieved. They also said that the consideration toward satisfaction of owner which determine the success or failure of projects and role of BIM manager who decide adoption of BIM on project should be reflected on KPIs. Nonetheless, the KPIs of Operational Excellence perspective and Future Orientation perspective were rated to be appropriate for utilization in practice. Based on the advisory opinions, BIM BSC has been complemented with 4 *Perspectives,* 16 *CSFs* and 33 *KPIs* like Table 4. In order to clearly define, KPIs have classed by two types as quantitative indicator or qualitative indicator.

4 Verification of BIM BSC

4.1 Data Collection and Analysis Method

BSC must provide a complete view of the business and performance. This could be achieved by well-constructed balance between performance indicators of 4 *Perspectives* [21] and clear cause-and-effect relationships to represent the complicated performance [16]. If their relation is more complicated, it is more enable to build sophisticated inspection system and to maximize the utility value of the performance assessment tool. Therefore, the level of balance and importance should be identified by analyzing casual relationships between each *Perspectives* and indicators. In order to evaluate the value and effects occurred by BIM adoption, the indicators of BIM BSC must have the proper balance and clear cause-and-effect relationships between each other. Regression analysis has been conducted with this study to test validity of BIM BSC by explicating the correlation among the CSFs.

To collect the data for regression analysis, the authors has conducted the survey on importance to the each *Perspectives*, CSFs and KPIs. The importance of each sector of BIM BSC has been measured by a Likert 5-point scale. The survey was conducted by sending e-mail and visiting site during one month. The questionnaire survey target s are the BIM experts and executives from the 50 small and medium-sized design offices which has BIM-based project experience. The reason for setting survey target limit is that minimum over 10 years practice experience is needed to evaluate the importance of BIM performance. Please see the Table 5.

The survey was distributed to the recipient from October 13, 2014 to November 14, 2014. A total of 32 respondents completed the survey. The collected data through the survey and analysis by SPSS 21, the statistical analysis tool.

Table 4. CSFs and KPIs of BIM BSC

Perspective	CSF	KPI	KPI Type
Corporate contribution	Business Strategic Contribution	Ratio of BIM Project Order against Total amount of Order	Quantitative
		Ratio of Profit margins per Capita of BIM Project against Total project's	Quantitative
		Achieved Rate on BIM Project Budget Execution Plan	Quantitative
	Productivity Improvement	Improvement Ratio of BIM Project's Schedule Compliance against Normal Project's	Quantitative
	Synergy Effect	Marketing Effectiveness through BIM Adoption	Qualitative
		Ratio of Estimate cost of outsourcing against Total cost of BIM Project	Quantitative
Operational excellence	BIM/Business Partnership	The Ratio of BIM Related Strategies of Management Strategies	Quantitative
		Level of Construction of BIM Execution Plans	Qualitative
	BIM-based Design Process Management	Level of BIM Application	Qualitative
		Level of Construction of Design Process based on BIM	Qualitative
Operational excellence	BIM Supporting Organization	Retention Level of BIM supporting Organization/Department	Qualitative
		Management of BIM Technology Supporting System	Qualitative
		BIM Experts Percentage of the Total Design Organization	Quantitative
	BIM Resource Management	BIM S/W Retention Level	Quantitative
		BIM H/W Build Level	Quantitative
	BIM Collaboration System Management	Management of BIM Collaboration System	Qualitative
		Level of Data Compatibility with cooperator (structural, MEP part)	Qualitative
		Development Level of Integrated Management Sever for BIM Collaboration	Qualitative
	BIM Design Information Management	Development Level of BIM Standard Framework	Qualitative
		BIM Library Management	Qualitative
		Level of Data Compatibility between S/W	Qualitative
		Management of BIM Design Quality Assurance System	Qualitative
User orientation	Improving Design Quality	Quality review Rate on BIM Project against non-BIM Project	Quantitative
	Owner Satisfaction	Satisfaction of Owner on BIM Project	Qualitative
	BIM User Satisfaction	Satisfaction of BIM Supporting Organization on BIM project	Qualitative
Future orientation	BIM Education/ Training	Construction Level of BIM Education/ Training Program	Qualitative
		Management of Implementation for BIM Education Program	Qualitative
	BIM User's Capability	BIM Manager's capability on Operating Project	Qualitative

(Continued)

Table 4. (*Continued*)

Perspective	CSF	KPI	KPI Type
		Proficiency of BIM User	Quantitative
	BIM Knowledge Management	Construction Level of BIM Information Management System	Qualitative
		Knowledge Management for the Migration of Closed Project	Qualitative
	BIM Technology R&D	The Ratio of BIM Budget against Investment for Technology	Quantitative

Table 5. Overview of survey

Research period	2014.10.13. ~ 2014. 11. 14
Research object	The practitioners over the leader level of 50 small and medium-sized design offices which ranked Top 50 on design offices of BIM Application performance by buildingSMART Korea in 2014
Research method	Sending E-Mail and visiting site to distribute and collect the questionnaires (1 questionnaire distributed per company)
Survey contents	Work Experience of respondent and BIM adoption level of enterprise
	Priority investigation by *Perspectives*, CSFs, KPIs of BIM BSC
Analysis method	Regression analysis with SPSS 21
Return rate	64 % (32 companies response on survey)

4.2 Establishment of Hypothesis

In this study, the hypothetical model like Fig. 3 is established to analyze the level of balance between *Perspectives* and cause-and-effect relationships between CSFs. Each hypothesis is constructed with reflecting the result of expert interview.

To identify the correlation and balance between CSFs, the authors established the hypotheses as follows:

- H_1: The variables related to Future Innovation Capacity affects the variables of Effective Design Process
- H_2: The variables related to Future Innovation Capacity affects the variables of Organization Satisfaction
- H_3: The variables related to Future Innovation Capacity affects the variables of High Business Performance
- H_4: The variables related to Effective Design Process affects the variables of Organization Satisfaction
- H_5: The variables related to Effective Design Process affects the variables of High Business Performance
- H_6: The variables related to Organization Satisfaction affects the variables of High Business Performance

- H_7: The variables related to High Business Performance affects the variables of Future Innovation Capacity

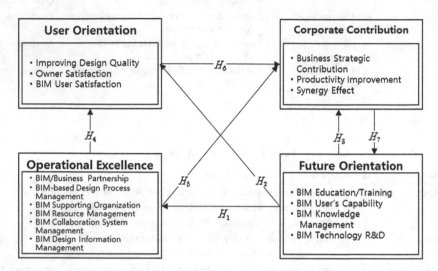

Fig. 3. Hypothetical models

4.3   Statistical Verification of BIM BSC

Method of Statistical Verification. In this study, Simple linear regression model has been utilized to analyze significant relationship between CSFs. Simple linear regression model describe the cause-and-effect relationship between Dependent Variable(Y, result variable) and Independent Variable(X, reason variable). The higher the Standardized Coefficient (β), the bigger the effect of independent variable for dependent variable is [22]. α means constant and ϵ means possible error.

$$Y = a + \beta X + \epsilon \tag{1}$$

The regression analysis has performed on the established hypothesis with 95 percent accuracy level. The verification result of the regression analysis has been analyzed at the significance level of $p \leq 0.05$ and reviewed the goodness of fit based on the significance probability, p, and the coefficient of determination, R^2.

When the p value is smaller than 0.05, this study reads the analysis result into the meaning which the hypothesis is adopted and shows the high correlation. In addition, the case of that R^2 is close to $1 (R^2 \leq 0.5)$, the authors interpret regression model as a suitable model.

The Result of Statistical Verification. Regression analysis was performed to develop performance indicators for achieving a balance in various aspects. Causal analysis and criticality assessment between 16 CSFs of BIM BSC conducted. A total of 105 single regression model were analyzed by assuming dependent and independent variables differently according to each hypothesis. Only 47 regression models among 105 models have been identified as statistically significant models ($p \leq 0.05$). All of these model has R^2 values higher than 0.5. Therefore the 47 regression models has been assessed as suitable models. The statistically significant model from each hypothesis is expressed in Table 6.

- H_1: The 10 models of 24 regression models (41.7 %) showed a statistically significant result. The most of *Dependent Variables* are compositively influenced by more than 2 *Independent Variables*. Therefore, authors evaluated that hypothesis is adopted because it clearly describes the relationship between CSFs.
- H_2: The 9 models of 12 regression models (75 %) showed a statistically significant result. The most of *Dependent Variables* are compositively influenced by more than 3 *Independent Variables*. Therefore, authors evaluated that hypothesis is adopted

Table 6. The result of regression analysis

Hypothesis	Dependent variable(Y)		Independent variable(X)		β	p	R^2
H_1	Operational Excellence	BIM/Business Partnership	Future Orientation	BIM Technology R&D	0.848	0.015	0.719
		BIM-based Design Process Management		BIM User's Capability	0.901	0.006	0.812
				BIM Knowledge Management	0.825	0.016	0.681
		BIM Supporting Organization		BIM Education/ Training	0.709	0.05	0.503
				BIM Technology R&D	0.813	0.017	0.661
		BIM Resource Management		BIM Technology R&D	0.763	0.033	0.582
		BIM Collaboration System Management		BIM User's Capability	0.796	0.022	0.634
				BIM Knowledge Management	0.869	0.012	0.755
		BIM Design Information Management		BIM Knowledge Management	0.714	0.049	0.510
				BIM Technology R&D	0.741	0.041	0.549
H_2	User Orientation	Improving Design Quality	Future Orientation	BIM User's Capability	0.714	0.049	0.510
				BIM Knowledge Management	0.897	0.007	0.805
				BIM Technology R&D	0.749	0.038	0.561
		Owner's Satisfaction		BIM User's Capability	0.892	0.008	0.796
				BIM Knowledge Management	0.776	0.028	0.602
				BIM Technology R&D	0.763	0.033	0.582
		BIM User's Satisfaction		BIM Education/ Training	0.719	0.048	0.517
				BIM Knowledge Management	0.768	0.032	0.590
				BIM Technology R&D	0.714	0.049	0.510
H_3	Corporate Contribution	Improving Design Quality	Future Orientation	BIM Knowledge Management	0.714	0.049	0.510

(Continued)

Table 6. (*Continued*)

Hypo thesis	Dependent variable(Y)		Independent variable(X)		β	p	R^2
H_4	User Orientation	Improving Design Quality	Operational Excellence	BIM/Business Partnership	0.796	0.021	0.634
				BIM Supporting Organization	0.759	0.036	0.576
				BIM Collaboration System Management	0.848	0.015	0.719
		Owner's Satisfaction		BIM-based Design Process Management	0.768	0.032	0.590
				BIM Design Information Management	0.804	0.019	0.646
		BIM User's Satisfaction		BIM Supporting Organization	0.726	0.046	0.527
				BIM Resource Management	0.796	0.021	0.634
H_5	Corporate Contribution	Productivity Improvement	Operational Excellence	BIM-based Design Process Management	0.759	0.036	0.576
		Synergy Effect		BIM Supporting Organization	0.726	0.047	0.527
H_6	Corporate Contribution	Business Strategic Contribution	User Orientation	Owner's Satisfaction	0.879	0.011	0.773
		Productivity Improvement		Improving Design Quality	0.911	0.003	0.830
		Synergy Effect		Improving Design Quality	0.892	0.008	0.796
				BIM User's Satisfaction	0.879	0.011	0.773
H_7	Future Orientation	BIM Education/ Training	Corporate Contribution	Synergy Effect	0.857	0.014	0.734
		BIM User's Capability		Business Strategic Contribution	0.714	0.049	0.510
				Productivity Improvement	0.719	0.048	0.517
		BIM Knowledge Management		Productivity Improvement	0.789	0.025	0.623
		BIM Technology R&D		Productivity Improvement	0.753	0.037	0.567

because it clearly describes the relationship between CSFs and shows the well-established balance.

- H_3: The 1 models of 12 regression models (8.3 %) showed a statistically significant result. Although there is one model which is statistically significant, the rest of regression models are not suitable to describe cause-and-effect relationship between CSFs. Therefore, authors denied this hypothesis.
- H_4: The 7 models of 18 regression models (39 %) showed a statistically significant result. Each *Dependent Variables* are compositively influenced by more than 2 *Independent Variables*. Therefore, authors evaluated that hypothesis is adopted because it clearly describes the relationship between CSFs.
- H_5: The 2 models of 18 regression models (11 %) showed a statistically significant result. Although there is two models which are statistically significant, the rest of regression models (89 %) are not suitable to describe cause-and-effect relationship between CSFs. Therefore, authors denied this hypothesis.

- H_6: The 9 models of 4 regression models (44 %) showed a statistically significant result. Each *Dependent Variables* are influenced by more than 1 *Independent Variables*. Therefore, authors evaluated that hypothesis is adopted because it clearly describes the relationship between CSFs.
- H_7: The 5 models of 12 regression models (41.7 %) showed a statistically significant result. Each *Dependent Variables* are influenced by more than 1 *Independent Variables*. Therefore, authors evaluated that hypothesis is adopted because it clearly describes the relationship between CSFs.

The regression analysis shows that CFIs of four *Perspectives* have the complex and organic relationships to each other. In this analysis, CSFs from the developed BIM BSC have clear connected relationships with CSFs of other *Perspectives*. Furthermore, R^2- value shows that the BIM BSC Model follows the established hypotheses at significant level. This means that significant relationship is not focused on a particular success factor or *Perspective*. Therefore, it could be assumed that each CSFs are closely connected and the values which are intended to be achieved are well-represented through the CSFs.

Through the process of the regression analysis, it is identified that the developed BIM BSC could be utilized sufficiently to provide the measurement environment for achieving degree of targeted *Vision*. In addition, this BIM BSC which possesses the various balanced cause-and-effect relationships across the *Perspective,* would make multidisciplinary evaluation possible.

5 Conclusion

As the solution to the reduced productivity problem in construction industry, the application of BIM has gradually increased and movements by government to the introduction of BIM are also becoming more active. Adopting BIM is the urgent issue especially in the design field because of its inefficient work process and continuous loss of the information. However, lacking of recognized necessity caused by uncertain benefit from BIM and high barriers of technology introduction still limit the various utilization of BIM in design phase.

This study suggested the BIM Performance Measurement System (PMS) to visualize benefits and effects of BIM as the method for vitalizing adoption of BIM. The benefits of BIM include tangible, intangible and semi-tangible values alike IT investment performance. IT BSC, one of the IT PMS in Multi-Criteria approach, was applied to develop the BIM PMS offering the multifaceted evaluation. BIM BSC, the result of this study, is composed of 4 *Perspectives*, 16 CSFs and 33 KPIs. Compliance Review of BIM BSC has conducted through the interview with BIM experts. In addition cause-and-effect relationship and balanced state was validated by analyzing regression models. It is identified that BIM BSC has sophisticated management system based on closed connected relationship between *Perspectives* and complicated correlation between CSFs. However, BIM BSC has the limitation of identifying degree of influence of specific factors and has the insufficiency to reflect the weight on achieving vision to each factors. In order to compensate for these limitations, the analysis of the weight to CSFs is necessary with reflecting empirical feasibility and usefulness.

The developed BIM BSC is target for the contribution to design firm's voluntary of BIM adoption and to the improvement of corporate competitive power by facilitating management of design process and estimating future outcome. The development made in this paper is the fundamental study for BIM PMS. The research for actual measurement methodology have yet been conducted. The result of this study could be used as the guidelines and extensible basic data for development of BIM PMS in the various type of design firms. This study has a significance for establishing foundational environment in which measure and compare BIM performance in realistic and systematic perspectives. Further research with be conducted to develop the applicable BIM performance evaluation system to various type of design firms.

Acknowledgements. This work was supported by the National Research Foundation of Korea (NRF) grant funded by the Korea government (MEST) (No. 2010-0029196). This research was supported by Basic Science Research Program through the National Research Foundation of Korea (NRF) funded by the Ministry of Education (No. 2013R1A1A2065654).

References

1. Kim, W., et al.: Survey and Implications of Utilizing BIM in Construction Company. Construction & Economy Research Institute of Korea, Korea (2012)
2. Becerik-Gerber, B., Rice, S.: The percieved value of building information modeling in the U.S. building industry. ITcon **25**, 185–201 (2010)
3. Radhkrishnan, A., et al.: A process-oriented perspective on differential business value creation by information technology: a empirical investment. Omega **36**, 1105–1125 (2008)
4. Song, M., et al.: BSC based measurement of satisfaction degree for based BIM construction project. Korean J. Constr. Eng. Manag. **12**, 117–129 (2011)
5. Lee, J., Lee, J.: A study on BIM capability evaluation for design organizations. J. Archit. Inst. Korea Planning Design **27**(6), 257–266 (2011)
6. Seo, J., Choo, S.: A study on cost-benefit analysis of BIM-based integrated design process in Korean architectural offices. Int. J. CAD/CAM **15**, 261–270 (2010)
7. Barlish, K., Sullivan, K.: How to measure the benefits of BIM – a case study approach. Autom. Constr. **24**, 149–159 (2012)
8. Kang, T., et al.: A Study on the Development Direction of a BIM Performance Assessment Tool. Korean J. Space Inf. **21**, 53–62 (2013)
9. Im, J.: Study on using BSC framework to develop CSF & KPI for IT performance measure on IT organization and examining the relation of cause and effect in indicators, Master dissertation, Yonsei University (2006)
10. Grembergen, W.: Information Technology Governance Through the Balanced Scorecard, pp. 199–211. IDEA Group Publishing, Hershey (2001)
11. Lee, Y.: IT performance of small and medium firms : a comparison between manufacturers and non-manufacturers, Master dissertation, Hankuk University of Foreign Studies (2014)
12. Olve, N., et al.: Performance Drivers : A Practical Guide to Using the Balanced Scorecard. Haneon Books, Seoul (2000)
13. Choi, D.: (Easy to Know) BSC. KOMIT Publishing, Seoul (2004)
14. Min, J.: Performance evaluation of knowledge workers in knowledge-based organization. Korean J. Manag. Sci. **25**, 137–154 (2000)

15. Kim, H.: A case study on the establishing public IT organization's performance measurement model through the IT BSC, Master dissertation, Soongsil University (2008)
16. Kaplan, S. and Noton, P.: Using the Balanced Scorecard as a Strategic Management System, Harvard Business Review, January-February, 75–85 (1996)
17. Seo, J., et al.: The development of an evaluation model for the work environment of the BIM-based architectural design firms. J. Archit. Inst. Korea Planning Design **28**(5), 95–105 (2012)
18. Cha, S., Kim, T.: Developing measurement system for key performance indicators on building construction projects. Korean J. Constr. Eng. Manag. **9**, 120–130 (2008)
19. Kim, E., et al.: A Study on Building the Work Environment to Utilize BIM for Domestic Architectural Firms. J. Archit. Inst. Korea Planning Design **30**(3), 121–128 (2014)
20. Kim, J., Lee, Y., Kim, S.: Perceived IT performance and contextual factor of small firms in Korea: an explorative study. J. Inf. Prof., pp. 23–41 (2004)
21. Caleb&Company: Performance drivers, pp. 36–129. Hanun, Seoul (2000)
22. Won, T., Jung, S.: Statistical Research SPSS PASW STATISTICS 18.0, pp. 343–357. Hanara Academi, Seoul (2010)

Facilitating Fire and Smoke Simulation Using Building Information Modeling

Chengde Wu[✉], Saied Zarrinmehr, Mohammad Rahmani Asl,
and Mark J. Clayton

Texas A&M University, College Station, USA
{chdwu22,szarinmehr,mrahmaniasl,dr.mjclayton}@gmail.com

Abstract. CFAST is a two-zone model which simulates fire growth and smoke transport. Manually modeling a building using CFAST user interface is a time consuming and error-prone process. In addition, the limitations in CFAST structure impede data transfer between CFAST and BIM (Building Information Modeling). In this research, we identified major limitations of CFAST, proposed solutions to the limitations, and developed a system for data interchange between BIM and CFAST. This greatly facilitated fire and smoke simulation. We further developed a visualization module to visualize the simulation results to overcome the problems when using SmokeView, an application developed by NIST (National Institute of Standards and Technology). A pilot test is conducted using this system. The simulation process was done in just a few minutes. This is expected to help architects to design buildings safer from building fires, and help students in learning building safety and fire related building codes.

Keywords: Fire simulation · Building information modeling (BIM) · CFAST · Building fire evacuation

1 Introduction

Building fires cause many fatalities each year, but architectural design process typically does not incorporate smoke simulation or evacuation simulation [1]. There were more than 10,000 building fire deaths each year in 27 industrialized countries from 2007 to 2009 [2]. Expanding populations are increasingly moving to cities and living in high density development, where fire risks are greater. Protecting occupants from building fires is one of the major tasks when architects design buildings. To predict whether all occupants can be safely evacuated from the building in case of a building fire, researchers have developed various building simulation models. These simulation models can be classified into two categories: fire/smoke simulation and occupant evacuation simulation. Fire/smoke simulation models simulate the air status of the spaces in the building in temporal sequence. Indicators of the air status include temperature, soot, oxygen, toxins (such as CO, HNC, and heavy metal vaporized from burning paints and synthetic polymers). Occupant evacuation simulation models simulate how occupants react to the

© Springer-Verlag Berlin Heidelberg 2015
G. Celani et al. (Eds.): CAAD Futures 2015, CCIS 527, pp. 366–382, 2015.
DOI: 10.1007/978-3-662-47386-3_20

fire conditions, and how many of them can be safely evacuated in the adverse conditions. Current fire simulation software tools are stand-alone programs with poor or no interoperability to design tools. Our research is motivated by the speculation that designers could better understand the consequences of design decisions on fire safety if the simulation tools were integrated with design tools. We wish to discover how to integrate fire simulation tools with Building Information Modeling (BIM) software that is becoming the standard in practice.

1.1 Problem Statement

At present, smoke simulation software is not well integrated into design processes. Collecting information and inputting it to the simulation is often a cumbersome and time-consuming activity. To simulate fire and smoke of a building, we need to manually model the building in simulation applications according to special-purpose definitions. This is a tedious process. In CFAST smoke simulation model, as an example, a room is defined as the coordinate of the base point (X, Y, and Z values), and the three dimensional measurements, width, depth, and height respectively. The spaces connected by an opening have to be manually assigned to denote the linkage of the spaces. Because of this extensive manual work using text-based and non-graphical interfaces, modeling a building in a fire/smoke simulation application is time consuming and error-prone. In addition, manual work must be repeated every time the design of the building changes. A building design usually changes many times before it is ready for construction. Because of its cumbersome input process, fire simulation is rarely used during building design process. Because of the richness of BIM representations, using BIM for fire/smoke simulation could greatly reduce manual work. A software tool that enables a BIM to provide input to CFAST could reveal the issues in integrating smoke simulation with BIM and demonstrate the benefits that could accrue to designers and students.

1.2 Research Objectives

We developed a software system that extracts the necessary information from BIM, and rearranges it to accommodate the requirements in CFAST, a fire/smoke simulation application. The simulation results are brought back into BIM for further use such as to support crowd evacuation simulation and visualization. This will automate the modeling process for fire/smoke simulation. Furthermore, this software is expected to help architects and engineers to easily simulate building fire safety. This software also could be of great use as an educational tool to enable students and architects to understand better fire safety issues.

1.3 Research Scope

Fire/smoke simulation depends upon given parameters of architectural aspects, mechanical systems, and fire source. The scope of this research is limited to the architectural aspects. Mechanical systems and fire source will not be covered.

2 Previous Studies

Fire simulation has been a subject of research for many years. Physical characteristics of fire are the basis of fire simulation. These characteristics include ignition point, heat release ratio, yield of the combustion products, spread of smoke, etc. As these characteristics are unveiled with countless experiments, mathematic models and computer models have been developed to enable prediction of fire and smoke behavior.

2.1 Fire Experiments

Understanding the physical characteristics of fire and smoke is the essential key to model fire and smoke. Since 1970s, researchers have extensively experimented with fire to unveil various characteristics of fire and smoke. Many researchers tested ignition behavior of various flammable building materials. Moghtaderi et al. [3] tested piloted-ignition on various types of wood. An ignition equation with three key parameters, ignition temperature, heat flux, and moisture, was defined which can be used for fire simulations. The time to ignite, heat release rate (HRR), weight loss, yield of the combustion products including CO and CO_2, heat of combustion and oxygen depletion rate were also measured during the experiments. The ignition behavior of the following materials are also tested: polystyrene, epoxy [4], wood (pine and oak), cardboard, newspaper, canvas, cotton cloth, rubber strip, polyurethane foam [5]. Kishore and Mohan Das [6] determined flammability index of 24 polymeric materials.

Heat Release Rate (HRR) is another important factor in fire simulation. HRR is the energy released per unit of time, and this is considered as the most important factor in building fire. Not surprisingly, extensive experiments have been done to determine HRR of variety of building materials and furniture including upholstered furniture [7], chairs, sofas, closets [8], fiber reinforced polymer (FRP) composites [9], dry partition walls [10], silicones (foams, elastomers, and resins; [11]), different species of wood [12, 13], Polystyrene–Clay Nano-composites [14], and many others. Huggett [15] calculated HRR, based on Thornton's [16] findings, by measuring oxygen consumption which was proved in his experiment to be quite accurate. Janssens [17] provided a set of equations to determine HRR by oxygen consumption.

Researchers also have done extensive research on how building fire spreads, horizontally and vertically, one object to another. Quintiere [18] reviewed full-scale and scaled model experiments to study fire growth and spread in building compartments. Quintiere and Harkleroad [19] tested ignition temperature, thermal inertia, and flame spread speed of 36 building materials caused by radiation. Hasemi [20] conducted experiments on flame spread of vertical walls with combustible surface. Cheney et al. [21, 22] developed fire spread/time curve to show the fire growth and acceleration. Heskestad and Delichatsios [23] studied heat transfer by convection in a fire. Larson and Viskanta [24] studied flame radiation, wall heat conduction, and laminar convection. For the spread of smoke, many researchers agree on a two-zone model that warmer smoke floats on the top layer because of convection, while cooler air stays at the bottom layer [25–27]. He and Beck [28], based on their experiment of burning a multi-story building, confirmed the existence of the two-zone on the same floor, but two-zone model does not apply to vertical spaces such as stair cases. While the smoke rises in vertical shafts, the temperature of the smoke cools down quickly and the air become murky instead of forming two distinctive layers.

During pyrolysis process, smoke is released along with heat. Smoke contributes to deaths in two ways: incapacitating victims or causing deaths directly by toxic gases, or indirectly inhibiting people from escaping because of reduced visibility. Fire smoke can contain more than a dozen types of gas, but CO is proved to be the major toxicant directly causing deaths. There is not enough evidence that any other toxic gases such as HCN or HCl directly cause deaths, although they might have contributed to the early incapacitation [29, 30]. Low density of CO is not lethal. People can stay in 0.3 % of CO for 15 min without risking their lives [30]. However, people become incapacitated at COHb (carboxyhemoglobin) level of 30 %, and 50 %–60 % of COHb is lethal [31]. Scarcity of oxygen is another threat. When oxygen drops under 7 % people can become incapacitated or even die. However, low oxygen levels only occur when the air (smoke) is very hot, approximately 600 °F [31]. Terrill et al. [30] also concluded that the threat order is CO is greater than heat, which is greater than oxygen deficiency. Bernard and Duker [32] listed the distance people can travel in different concentration of CO. In an experiment on mice, toxic gases other than CO shortened time to deaths [31, 33].

2.2 Smoke Models

As physical characteristics of fire have been revealed with countless experiments, researchers have tried to model building fire and smoke in mathematical equations and further in computer simulation [34–39].

Zone models are very commonly used in computer simulation. One-zone models assume each room as one homogeneous space. In two-zone models, a room is stratified into upper zone which is filled with hot and toxic smoke, and lower zone which is filled with fresh air. Multi-zone models divide a room into many (e.g. hundreds of) zones to simulate micro environment. CFAST [40] is a two-zone model developed at NIST. Based on a set of conservation equations, CFAST can simulate upper layer and lower layer temperature, layer interface position, gas species concentration, fire pyrolysis and heat release rate, and other parameters [39]. CESARE-SMOKE is another two-zone model similar to CFAST. He and Beck [28] experimented with multi-story building fire and confirmed Hokugo's [41] finding that smoke temperature dropped rapidly in the stair case, which is call the chimney effect. He and Beck also found that stratification is not dominant at the rooms that are remote from the origin of fire. They suggested that for these rooms one zone model would be more appropriate.

Some computer models are based on Computational Fluid Dynamics (CFD) to simulate fire and smoke spread. FDS, a CFD based model developed by NIST, simulates thermally-driven smoke flow of building fires. Compared to zone models, CFD models provide more details on distribution of smoke temperature, toxic gas concentration, etc. The trade-off for this is that it takes longer to process. Zone models usually run in a few minutes, but CFD models run for hours to days.

On the whole, mechanism of fire spread has been known to the researchers for decades, and the computer models simulating fire and smoke spread are well developed with sound validation. In this research, we chose CFAST as a relatively easy to use, accurate, and speedy simulation tool. Its interfaces are well documented in publicly available documents to aid our software development effort.

2.3   Validity of CFAST Model

Many researchers have validated the CFAST model besides NIST. Naval Research Lab [42] conducted experiments of real scale fire in vessel compartments induced by the enormous heat of launching rockets on the deck. The data was collected and compared to CFAST simulation results. They found that although there are some mismatches, CFAST simulation '*predictions compared reasonably well with experimental results*'. Peacock et al. [25] compared results of experimental data with CFAST simulated data using five test cases. The comparison results shows that CFAST is reasonably close to actual experiment data. Peacock et al. [43] conducted validation tests on eight out of 15 fire phenomena for nuclear power plants. They concluded that the simulation results of hot gas layer temperature and height, oxygen and carbon dioxide concentration are consistent with experiments, but smoke concentration tended to be over-predicted. Travel delay of the smoke in corridors [44] and chimney effect in vertical shafts [27] are also validated with experimental data.

2.4   BIM

In conventional CAAD systems, buildings are represented as drawings. BIM, on the other hand, represents buildings as models made of collections of building components such as walls and windows. BIM also contains the information about the relationship of the building components, such as that a roof is connected to a wall or a window is hosted by a wall, and non-spatial information, such as materials and physical attributes. A great number of processes can be automated using BIM because of its data structure. Myriad of studies have been done on extracting BIM data and connecting it to cost estimating, structural engineering, construction simulation, energy simulation, acoustic simulation, facility management, urban design, etc. In addition, BIM software is constructed to allow the user to extend the data structure to represent additional values. Our study explored whether sufficiently rich models can be built easily with BIM software to enable smoke and evacuation simulations. We used Autodesk Revit as our BIM software system, and its Application Programming Interface (API) in C# programming language for software development.

3   Interoperation Between BIM and CFAST

BIM and CFAST were developed independently to serve totally different purposes. They have intrinsically different data structures for representing building elements. When CFAST was first developed in 1990s, 2D CAD was dominant in the field, and BIM was still in its theoretical phase. CFAST assumed that 2D CAD was the state of the art for representing buildings. Today, BIM has many more capabilities than CFAST to support rich and accurate representation of a building. In this section, the major limitations of CFAST are listed, the solutions to compensate these limitations are proposed, and a system is developed for data interchange between BIM and CFAST based on the solutions.

3.1 Workflow in CFAST Simulation

A room or a space is defined as a compartment in CFAST. To simulate fire and smoke in CFAST, four major categories of data are needed as input: compartments, openings connecting the compartments, fire source, and mechanical devices including fire detection and suppression system. These information units can be documented either using CFAST interface, or writing a text file as input (Fig. 1).

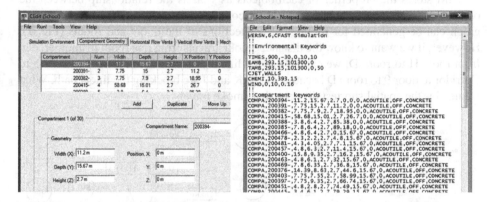

Fig. 1. Modeling building using CFAST interface (left), or by writing text input file (right).

The conventional workflow is to study a CAD drawing, either in paper format or electronic format, to detect the values to define the input, and then use the CFAST interface to enter the necessary values. After initiating and completing a run with CFAST, the output must be analyzed and interpreted by inspection. Using CFAST interface is a time-consuming and error-prone process. By using the API of Revit, we are able to produce txt input file from a BIM model that has the Level Of Development [45] of 200 or higher. The software initiates the run of CFAST and then collects output for visualization within the original BIM. The workflow in our system is encapsulated entirely in the Revit interface.

3.2 Major Limitations in CFAST

There are three major technical limitations in CFAST as described in the user manual [46]. (1) The maximum number of compartments CFAST can simulate is limited to 30 in the latest version of the software. (2) A compartment has three parameters determining its shape, i.e. width, depth, and height. Therefore all compartments only can take box shapes. Location and the orientation of the compartments do not affect simulation results. (3) The maximum size of the building CFAST can simulate is 100 m × 100 m on each floor. These limitations require that the software user must interpret and transform a real building design to conform to the abstraction that can be computed by CFAST.

3.3   Solutions to the Limitations

The major part of this research has been defining algorithms for converting the relatively less abstract representations in BIM into the more abstract representation in CFAST. Our first step was to overcome the limitation in CFAST to the maximum number of 30 compartments so the software could be used on larger buildings. Our algorithm identifies the first 30 compartments that smoke strikes. We used the 30 rooms that have the shortest distance from the room caught fire. This is true under the assumption that all the doors have similar height.

BIM stores the properties of each objects as well as the relationship between the objects. A door knows which two rooms are connected through it. Therefore a network graph can be generated for the logical connections of the doors and rooms (Fig. 2). However, if we want to know the distance smoke travels from one room to another, e.g. from room H to room D, we cannot use the lineal distance from room H to door 5 to Corridor to door 9 to room D because rooms K and J are blocking the lineal path. What we need is the spatial shortest distance that smoke travels.

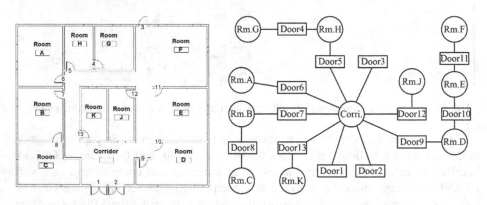

Fig. 2. Network graph for logical connections of doors and rooms

To calculate the spatial shortest distance, another network graph is generated using the openings and the vertices of each room as nodes, and the spatial distance as the weight of the link between the nodes. Figure 3 shows the links between the nodes of the corridor, and Table 1 shows the adjacency matrix of the corridor. If the lineal path between two nodes do not intersect with the boundary of the room, the distance of the two nodes is set as the weight of the two nodes. If they intersect, on the other hand, the weight is set to infinity. Once the adjacency matrices are set based on the network graphs, we used shortest path algorithms, a combination of Floyd algorithm and Dijkstra algorithm, to calculate the shortest spatial distances. By connecting all the network graphs, we can get the first 30 compartments that have the shortest spatial distance from the room that caught fire.

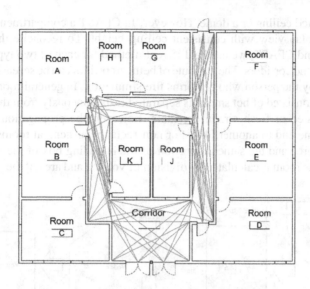

Fig. 3. Network graph for spatial connection in a room

Table 1. Adjacency matrix of corridor. D stands for door, V stands for vertex. The corridor contains 9 doors and 14 vertices.

	D1	D2	D3	D5	D6	D7	D9	D12	D13	V1	V2	...
D1	0	1.9	∞	∞	∞	∞	∞	∞	∞	5.5	∞	
D2	1.9	0	∞	∞	∞	∞	∞	∞	∞	6.5	∞	
D3	∞	∞	0	∞	∞	∞	15.2	7.9	∞	∞	7.0	
D5	∞	∞	∞	0	1.2	2.9	∞	∞	7.3	8.3	7.7	
D6	∞	∞	∞	1.2	0	1.8	∞	∞	6.5	7.4	8.3	
D7	∞	∞	∞	2.9	1.8	0	∞	∞	4.9	5.8	∞	
D9	∞	∞	15.2	∞	∞	∞	0	7.4	∞	7.5	8.3	
D12	∞	∞	7.9	∞	∞	∞	7.4	0	∞	∞	0.9	
D13	∞	∞	∞	7.3	6.5	4.9	∞	∞	0	0.9	∞	
V1	5.5	6.5	∞	8.3	7.4	5.8	7.5	∞	0.9	0	∞	
V2	∞	∞	7.0	7.7	8.3	∞	8.3	0.9	∞	∞	0	
...												

Shape of the Compartments. Real rooms can take various shapes other than a rectangular shape. BIM authoring tools can likewise accommodate non-rectangular rooms. The plan view of a room can be a circle, a trapezoid, or any other shape. A room also can have a slanted ceiling or a dome. However, In CFAST a compartment only can be rectangular in plan view with consistent ceiling height. To reconcile this difference between BIM and CFAST, we used a different method for each of two types of rooms: general rooms, and corridors. The attribute of being a corridor can be set easily in CFAST dropdown list by the person who performs fire simulation. In general rooms, the upper layer which is consisted of hot smoke is separated instantaneously from the lower layer which is consisted of fresh air. In corridors, however, the propagation of smoke is delayed from one end to another [44]. For non-rectangular general rooms, a rectangle with the same area and the same proportion of the bounding box of the room is used. The height of the room is calculated by division of volume and area of the room (Fig. 4).

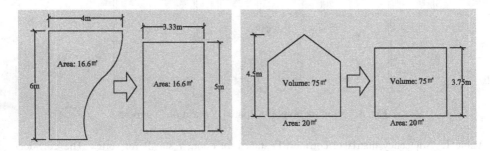

Fig. 4. Transformation of a non-rectangular room to a compartment. Plan view (left) and section (right)

The method used for general rooms are inappropriate for corridors. This is because of delayed smoke propagation and the shape of the corridors. In Fig. 5, if we transform T shaped corridor or a donut shaped corridor with a courtyard using the same method, the simulation result will not accurately represent real situation. Smoke behaves totally differently in the two spaces. Therefore we used another method for corridors.

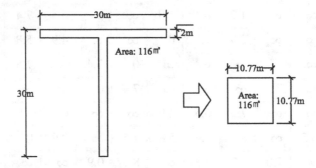

Fig. 5. Transform corridors using the same method. Smoke in the two space will behave in totally different ways.

In Fig. 6 (left), when room A has caught fire, point p1 is where smoke first enters the corridor. Point p2, furthest point from p1, is the last point smoke reaches. The distance of p1 to p2 (d1 + d2) is used as the length of the corridor; area divided by length is used as the width of the corridor; and volume divided by area is used as the height of the corridor (Fig. 6 right). This ensures that the longest smoke travel time is equal in both spaces.

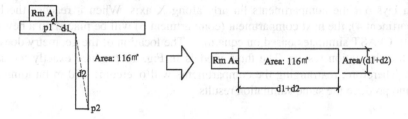

Fig. 6. Transforming a corridor

An alternative to the methods explained above could be dividing a non-rectangular space to multiple rectangular compartments, and defining the overlapping boundary as an opening (Fig. 7). However, this method has two major problems. First, it uses up 30 compartment limit quickly. Second, the simulation result is not as accurate because CFAST counts temperature drop effect at openings. In Fig. 8, two square compartments are aligned perfectly, and the overlapping wall is defined as full opening. A fire source is put at the middle but belongs to compartment1. Although the two compartments should have the same temperature and air composition, the simulation results shows that there are differences between the two compartments at certain point of time.

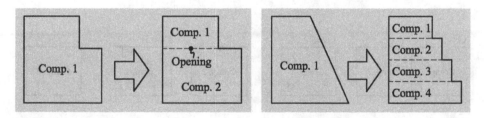

Fig. 7. Dividing a non-rectangular space, and define the overlapping wall as an opening

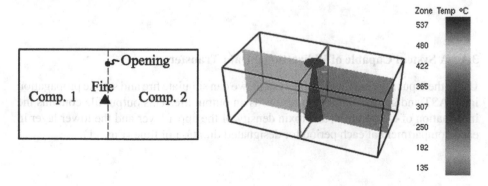

Fig. 8. Difference in the simulation results in two compartments

Maximum Size of the Floors. The maximum size of one floor in CFAST is set to 100 m × 100 m. This will cover most buildings. However, there are some buildings longer than 100 m, such as many train stations, airports and other transportation buildings. For these buildings, the compartments are rearranged to meet 100 m limit. The system lays out the compartments linearly along X axis. When it reaches the limit (compartment 4), the next compartment (compartment 5) will be placed on a new row (Fig. 9). CFAST simulates based on equations. The location of the geometry does not affect the simulation results. The three models in Fig. 10 produce exactly the same results. Therefore, rearranging the compartments will overcome 100 m building size limit and produce the same simulation results.

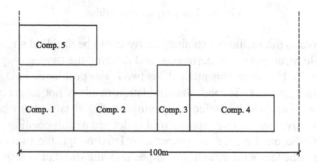

Fig. 9. Rearranging the layout of the compartments

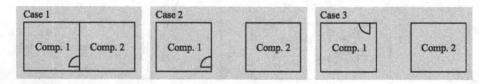

Fig. 10. Compartment2 and the door are placed at different locations. The door is set to connect compartment 1&2 in all three cases. The simulation results remain the same.

3.4 A System Capable of Bidirectional Data Transfer

Using the input file generated by the system, we can simulate fire and smoke propagation in CFAST and get the simulation results as an output file. This output file contains the information of temperature, and toxin density of the upper layer and the lower layer in each compartment at each period for designated duration of time (Fig. 11).

```
Time =      30.0 seconds.

Compartment   Upper    Lower    Inter.   Upper          Upper     Lower      Pressure   Ambient    Floor
              Temp.    Temp.    Height   Vol.           Absorb    Absorb                Target     Target
              (C)      (C)      (m)      (m^3)          (m^-1)    (m^-1)     (Pa)       (w/m^2)    (w/m^2)
--------------------------------------------------------------------------------------------------------
200394-       30.90    20.11    2.022    1.19E+02( 25%) 0.159     5.868E-02  -1.112E-03 11.8       10.9
200391-       20.38    20.00    2.697    0.30   ( 0%)   0.500     1.000E-02  2.145E-03  3.120E-02  2.893E-02


Upper Layer Species
Compartment   N2       O2       CO2        CO       HCN      HCL      TUHC     H2O      OD        CT          T
              (%)      (%)      (%)        (ppm)    (ppm)    (ppm)    (%)      (%)      (1/m)     (g-min/m3)  k
--------------------------------------------------------------------------------------------------------------
200394-       78.3     20.3     9.183E-02  26.9     0.00     0.00     0.00     1.26     0.793     0.282       0.
200391-       78.3     20.5     7.253E-03  2.13     0.00     0.00     0.00     1.18     6.473E-02 2.479E-03   0.


Lower Layer Species
Compartment   N2       O2       CO2        CO       HCN      HCL      TUHC     H2O      OD        CT          T
              (%)      (%)      (%)        (ppm)    (ppm)    (ppm)    (%)      (%)      (1/m)     (g-min/m3)  k
--------------------------------------------------------------------------------------------------------------
200394-       78.4     20.5     0.00       0.00     0.00     0.00     0.00     1.16     0.00      0.00        0.
200391-       78.4     20.5     0.00       0.00     0.00     0.00     0.00     1.17     0.00      0.00        0.
200382-       78.4     20.5     0.00       0.00     0.00     0.00     0.00     1.17     0.00      0.00        0.
200415-       78.4     20.5     0.00       0.00     0.00     0.00     0.00     1.17     0.00      0.00        0.
```

Fig. 11. Information in the output file

Data flow in many simulation models based on BIM is unidirectional. This means that data can be transferred from BIM to simulation model, but not the other way around. For this system, we stored the object IDs of the components in the BIM model throughout the simulation process. By doing so, the simulation result can be brought back to BIM model using the object IDs. The simulation result data can be stored in the BIM on the appropriate rooms and elements, retrieved through visual query, or visualized, this allows other BIM-based simulation models such as building optimization models or crowd evacuation simulation models to use the fire/smoke propagation data, and simulate how people react to these adverse conditions.

3.5 Fire Source

Fire is not included in this system because BIM typically does not contain fire information. Furthermore, feeding fire information in BIM or in CFAST will take the same amount of effort. CFAST does not contain fire growth model which sets adjacent furniture on fire when it reaches ignition temperature. It is left to the users to specify the time-dependent fire source explicitly which is an open issue [47].

4 Demonstration

As a pilot test case, we used a building floor plan with more than 30 rooms. The floor plan is modeled in Revit Architecture, a BIM authoring tool. A room (in blue) is set as the room that first caught fire by click of a button (Fig. 12). An input file for fire simulation is produced using the system, and fed to CFAST to conduct the simulation (Fig. 13). This fire simulation process can be done easily by a building designer just in a few minutes.

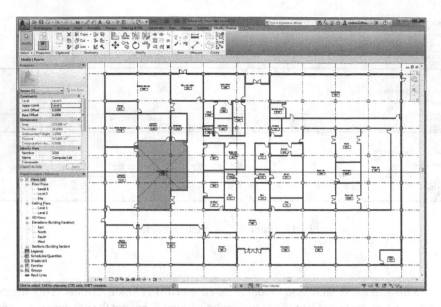

Fig. 12. Revit model

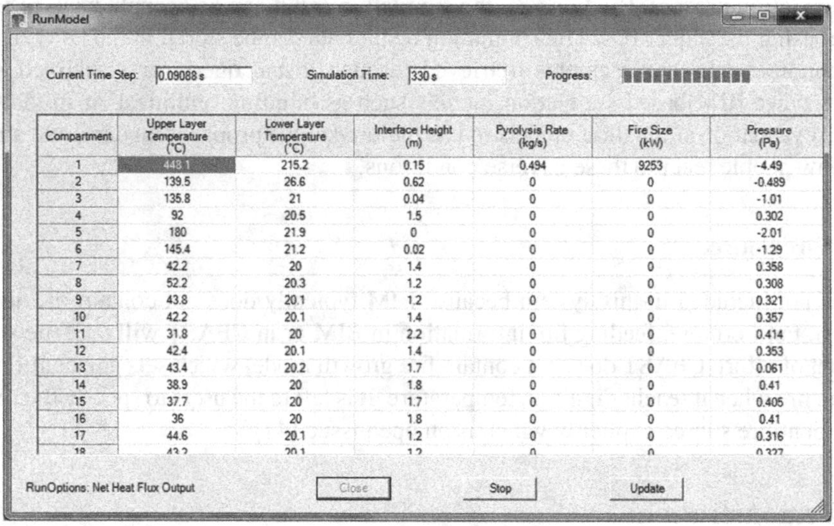

Fig. 13. Simulation of the input file in CFAST

Simulation result file can be visualized in SmokeView, an application developed by NIST. However, it is hard to match the floor plan with the result displayed in SmokeView (Fig. 14). This is because not all rooms are rectangular; not all rooms are simulated; and the compartments are rearranged.

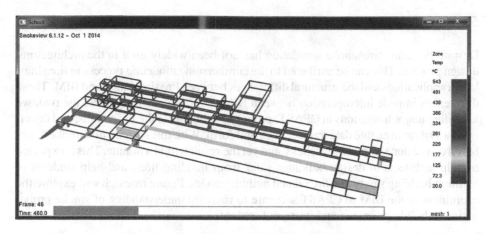

Fig. 14. Simulation result visualization in SmokeView

We brought the simulation result back into BIM and visualized it using the module we developed (Fig. 15). As the time slider changes, the color and the values for each room change based on the simulation output file. Among the huge amount of data in the output file, we displayed seven of the most important factors including smoke height (m), upper layer temperature (OC), lower layer temperature, upper layer oxygen (%), lower layer oxygen, upper layer carbon monoxide (ppm), and lower layer carbon monoxide. The color of each room denote smoke height. When smoke gets lower, the color gets darker with black meaning full of smoke. The rooms that are not in the first 30 compartment list remains white regardless of time slider.

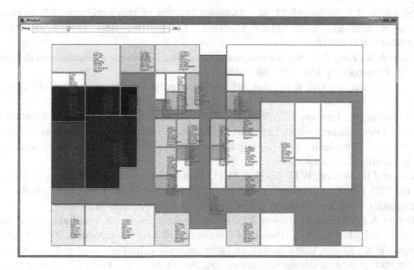

Fig. 15. Simulation result visualization

5 Conclusion

Despite its value, fire/smoke simulation has not been widely used in the architectural design process. This can be attributed to the cumbersome modeling process in fire simulation applications and the structural differences between fire simulation and BIM. These differences impede interoperation between BIM and CFAST. To connect the two, we identified major limitations in CFAST; proposed solutions to the limitations; and developed a system to enable data transfer back and forth. With this system, fire/smoke simulation can be done by just a few clicks, and get the result within a minute. This is expected to help architects to design buildings safer from building fires, and help students in learning building safety and fire related building codes. Future research will explore the usefulness of the BIM to CFAST software to increase understanding of smoke propagation in buildings among architects and students.

Acknowledgements. Funding of his research is provided by Natural Science Fund of China (grant No. 51308377).

References

1. Tunstall, G.: Managing the Building Design Process. Routledge, London (2006)
2. WFSC: World Fire Statistics Centre Bulletin, vol. 28 (2012). https://www.genevaassociation.org/media/186703/ga2012-fire28.pdf. Accessed
3. Moghtaderi, B., Novozhilov, V., Fletcher, D.F., Kent, J.H.: A new correlation for bench-scale piloted ignition data of wood. Fire Saf. J. **29**(1), 41–59 (1997). doi:10.1016/S0379-7112(97)00004-0
4. Ohlemiller, T.J., Summerfield, M.: Radiative ignition of polymeric materials in oxygen/nitrogen mixtures. Symp. (Int.) Combust. **13**(1), 1087–1094 (1971). doi:10.1016/S0082-0784(71)80106-6
5. Smith, W.K., King, J.B.: Surface temperatures of materials during radiant heating to ignition. J. Fire Flammability **1**(4), 272–288 (1970)
6. Kishore, K.: Mohan Das, K.: Flammability index of polymeric materials. Colloid Polym. Sci. **258**(1), 95–98 (1980)
7. Babrauskas, V., Lawson, J.R., Walton, W.D., Twilley, W.H.: Upholstered furniture heat release rates measured with a furniture calorimeter. US Department of Commerce, National Bureau of Standards (1982). http://www.nist.gov/manuscript-publication-search.cfm?pub_id=106922. Accessed
8. Lawson, J.R., Walton, W.D., Twilley, W.H.: Fire Performance of Furnishings as Measured in the NBS Furniture Calorimeter: Part I. US Department of Commerce, National Bureau of Standards (1984). http://fire.nist.gov/bfrlpubs/fire84/art002.html. Accessed
9. Mouritz, A.P., Mathys, Z., Gibson, A.G.: Heat release of polymer composites in fire. Compos. A Appl. Sci. Manuf. **37**(7), 1040–1054 (2006). doi:10.1016/j.compositesa.2005.01.030
10. Chow, W.K., Leung, C.W.: Survey on partition walls commonly used in Hong Kong and estimation of the heat release rates during fire. Archit. Sci. Rev. **44**(4), 379–390 (2001). doi:10.1080/00038628.2001.9696918
11. Buch, R.R.: Rates of heat release and related fire parameters for silicones. Fire Saf. J. **17**(1), 1–12 (1991). doi:10.1016/0379-7112(91)90009-N

12. Harada, T.: Time to ignition, heat release rate and fire endurance time of wood in cone calorimeter test. Fire Mater. **25**(4), 161–167 (2001). doi:10.1002/fam.766
13. Tran, H.C., White, R.H.: Burning rate of solid wood measured in a heat release rate calorimeter. Fire Mater. **16**(4), 197–206 (1992). doi:10.1002/fam.810160406
14. Zhu, J., Morgan, A.B., Lamelas, F.J., Wilkie, C.A.: Fire properties of Polystyrene–Clay nanocomposites. Chem. Mater. **13**(10), 3774–3780 (2001). doi:10.1021/cm000984r
15. Huggett, C.: Estimation of rate of heat release by means of oxygen consumption measurements. Fire Mater. **4**(2), 61–65 (1980). doi:10.1002/fam.810040202
16. Thornton, W.: The relation of oxygen to the heat of combustion of organic compounds. Phil. Mag. J. Sci. **33**, 196–203 (1917)
17. Janssens, M.L.: Measuring rate of heat release by oxygen consumption. Fire Technol. **27**(3), 234–249 (1991). doi:10.1007/BF01038449
18. Quintiere, J.G.: Growth of Fire in Building Compartments. Fire Standards and Safety. In: ASTM STP 614, pp. 131 – 167 (1977)
19. Quintiere, J.G., Harkleroad, M.T.: New concepts for measuring flame spread properties. fire safety: science and engineering. In: ASTM STP 882, American Society for Testing and Materials, pp. 239–267 (1985)
20. Hasemi, Y.: Thermal modeling of upward wall flame spread. fire safety science. In: Proceedings of the First International Symposium (1986)
21. Cheney, N.P., Bary, G.A.V.: The propagationof mass conflagration in a standing eucalyptus forest by the spotting process. In: Mass Fire Symposium, vol. 1 (1969)
22. Cheney, N., Gould, J.: Fire growth and acceleration. Int. J. Wildland Fire **7**(1), 1–5 (1997)
23. Heskestad, G., Delichatsios, M.A.: The initial convective flow in fire. Symp. (Int.) Combust. **17**(1), 1113–1123 (1979). doi:10.1016/S0082-0784(79)80106-X
24. Larson, D.W., Viskanta, R.: Transient combined laminar free convection and radiation in a rectangular enclosure. J. Fluid Mech. **78**(01), 65–85 (1976). doi:10.1017/S0022112076002334
25. Peacock, R.D., Jones, W.W., Bukowski, R.W.: Verification of a model of fire and smoke transport. Fire Saf. J. **21**(2), 89–129 (1993). doi:10.1016/0379-7112(93)90038-R
26. Zukoski, E.E., Kubota, T.: Two-layer modeling of smoke movement in building fires. Fire Mater. **4**(1), 17–27 (1980). doi:10.1002/fam.810040103
27. Jones, W.W., Forney, G.P.: Improvement in predicting smoke movement in compartmented structures. Fire Saf. J. **21**(4), 269–297 (1993). doi:10.1016/0379-7112(93)90017-K
28. He, Y., Beck, V.: Smoke spread experiment in a multi-storey building and computer modelling. Fire Saf. J. **28**(2), 139–164 (1997). doi:10.1016/S0379-7112(96)00081-1
29. Birky, M.M., Halpin, B.M., Caplan, Y.H., Fisher, R.S., McAllister, J.M., Dixon, A.M.: Fire fatality study. Fire Mater. **3**(4), 211–217 (1979). doi:10.1002/fam.810030406
30. Terrill, J.B., Montgomery, R.R., Reinhardt, C.F.: Toxic gases from fires. Science **200**(4348), 1343–1347 (1978). doi:10.1126/science.208143
31. Alarie, Y.: Toxicity of Fire Smoke. Crit. Rev. Toxicol. **32**(4), 259–289 (2002). doi:10.1080/20024091064246
32. Bernard, T.E., Duker, J.: Modeling carbon monoxide uptake during work. Am. Ind. Hyg. Assoc. J. **42**(5), 361–364 (1981). doi:10.1080/15298668191419884
33. Esposito, F.M., Alarie, Y.: Inhalation toxicity of carbon monoxide and hydrogen cyanide gases released during the thermal decomposition of polymers. J. Fire Sci. **6**(3), 195–242 (1988). doi:10.1177/073490418800600303
34. Yan, Z., Holmstedt, G.: CFD and experimental studies of room fire growth on wall lining materials. Fire Saf. J. **27**(3), 201–238 (1996). doi:10.1016/S0379-7112(96)00044-6

35. Xue, H., Ho, J.C., Cheng, Y.M.: Comparison of different combustion models in enclosure fire simulation. Fire Saf. J. **36**(1), 37–54 (2001). doi:10.1016/S0379-7112(00)00043-6
36. Karlsson, B.: Modeling fire growth on combustible lining materials in enclosures (dissertation). Lund University (1992). http://lup.lub.lu.se/record/1669903. Accessed
37. Hadjisophocleous, G.V., Mccartney, C.J.: Guidelines for the use of CFD simulations for fire and smoke modeling. ASHRAE Transactions. American Society of Heating, Refrigerating and Air-conditioning Engineers 111(2), pp. 583–594 (2005). http://cat.inist.fr/?aModele=afficheN&cpsidt=18780300. Accessed
38. Mouilleau, Y., Champassith, A.: CFD simulations of atmospheric gas dispersion using the fire dynamics simulator (FDS). J. Loss Prev. Process Ind. **22**(3), 316–323 (2009). doi:10.1016/j.jlp.2008.11.009
39. Peacock, R.D., Forney, G.P., Reneke, P.A., Portier, R.W., Jones, W.W.: CFAST, the consolidated model of fire growth and smoke transport. National Institute of Standards and Technology Gaithersburg, MD (1993). http://fire.nist.gov/bfrlpubs/fire93/art001.html. Accessed
40. NIST: Fire Growth and Smoke Transport Modeling with CFAST (2010). http://www.nist.gov/el/fire_research/cfast.cfm. Accessed
41. Hokugo, A., Yung, D., Hadjisophocleous, G.: Experiments to validate the nrcc smoke movement model for fire risk-cost assessment. Fire Saf. Sci. **4**, 805–816 (1994). doi:10.3801/IAFSS.FSS.4-805
42. Bailey, J.L., Tatem, P.A.: Validation of Fire/Smoke Spread Model (CFAST) Using Ex-USS SHADWELL Internal Ship Conflagration Control (ISCC) Fire Tests. No. NRL/MR/6180–95-7781. Naval Research Lab, Washington DC (1995)
43. Peacock, R.D., Reneke, P.A.: Verification and validation of selected fire models for nuclear power plant applications, Volume 5: Consolidated Fire Growth and Smoke Transport Model (CFAST). NUREG-1824. US Nuclear Regulatory Commission, Washington, DC (2007)
44. Bailey, J.L., et al.: Development and validation of corridor flow submodel for CFAST. J. Fire. Prot. Eng. **12**(3), 139–161 (2002)
45. BIM forum: Level Of Development Specification (2013). http://bimforum.org/wp-content/uploads/2013/08/2013-LOD-Specification.pdf. Accessed
46. Peacock, R.D., Reneke, P.A. Forney, G.P.: CFAST – Consolidated Model of Fire Growth and Smoke Transport (Version 6) User's Guide. NIST SP 1041r1. National Institute of Standards and Technology (2013). http://nvlpubs.nist.gov/nistpubs/SpecialPublications/NIST.SP.1041r1.pdf. Accessed
47. Floyd, J.: Comparison of CFAST and FDS for Fire Simulation with the HDR T51 and T52 Tests. US Department of Commerce, Technology Administration, National Institute of Standards and Technology (2002)

A Semantic Web Approach for Built Heritage Representation

Stefano Cursi[1], Davide Simeone[1(✉)], and Ilaria Toldo[2]

[1] Sapienza University of Rome, Rome, Italy
{Stefano.cursi,davide.simeone}@uniroma1.it
[2] University of Southern California, Los Angeles, CA, USA
toldo@usc.edu

Abstract. In a built heritage process, meant as a structured system of activities aimed at the investigation, preservation, and management of architectural heritage, any task accomplished by the several actors involved in it is deeply influenced by the way the knowledge is represented and shared. In the current heritage practice, knowledge representation and management have shown several limitations due to the difficulty of dealing with large amount of extremely heterogeneous data. On this basis, this research aims at extending semantic web approaches and technologies to architectural heritage knowledge management in order to provide an integrated and multidisciplinary representation of the artifact and of the knowledge necessary to support any decision or any intervention and management activity. To this purpose, an ontology-based system, representing the knowledge related to the artifact and its contexts, has been developed through the formalization of domain-specific entities and relationships between them.

Keywords: Built heritage · Knowledge-based model · Ontology-based systems · Building information modeling · Semantic web technologies

1 Introduction

Architectural heritage is a substantial, dynamic repository of knowledge whose significance and authenticity must be preserved. Each heritage object, considered as a unique and irreplaceable source of aesthetic, historical, and cultural values, needs to be recorded and documented in order to prevent any loss or damage and ensure well-informed activities of maintenance, repair, and change of use.

The process of research and investigation of an heritage asset is a complex set of activities that produces a large amount of measured surveys, describing in detail the physical, dimensional, mechanical, and chemical configuration of an artifact at a given point of time (tangible knowledge), and other baseline data not collected through direct survey activities such as any historical, social, political, economic, and cultural issue related to its context (intangible knowledge), in a systematic way. Recording such a large stock of information is a prime responsibility of everybody involved in the conservation process and requires the participation of professionals from different fields of expertise and interests [1]. Moreover, records' accuracy and completeness are crucial

© Springer-Verlag Berlin Heidelberg 2015
G. Celani et al. (Eds.): CAAD Futures 2015, CCIS 527, pp. 383–401, 2015.
DOI: 10.1007/978-3-662-47386-3_21

for all the activities of investigation, intervention, and maintenance of historical buildings and any inconsistency or lack of knowledge can bring to irreparable damage to the artifact or, in the worst case, even to its loss.

The recent interest in the development of more suitable tools able to manage the knowledge related to architectural heritage is due to the actual difficulty that the actors involved in the conservation process find in accessing information related to the artifacts. In fact, information management in heritage processes is still mainly document-based and the representation of the artifacts is just the sum of documentation provided by different professionals and collected into different databases and, as a result, its comprehensive understanding is difficult to be gained. Therefore, built heritage representation usually suffers of:

- Difficulty in checking the information stored and finding errors and inconsistencies in the different data sets;
- Lack of integration, coherence, and coordination among different documentation sets generated by different activities during the heritage process;
- Poor information management with consequent lack or duplication of data;
- Actors' difficulty to share knowledge and to collaborate in the investigation and restoration phases.

Over the past few years, some research focuses on the use of Building Information Modeling (BIM) in order to achieve a more complete integration of tangible and intangible knowledge in built heritage representation. The chance to couple abstract properties, such as structural, thermal, chemical, historical. And temporal, with the geometrical representation of an object, typical of BIM systems, intended as object-based systems that employs an integrated data repository in order to generate, manage, and store building information and domain knowledge from conceptual design to demolition [2, 3], is the main feature of a potential instrument able to allow for different kinds of reasoning. In this kind of 3D knowledge-rich parametric models, the representation of building components is not only a coherent geometrical representation of the reality, but also solves the redundancy problems typical of 2D representations while parametric rules and constraints can facilitate the creation of a rich model. Furthermore, BIM, as a process data stream system able to provide a "complete, live, interactive, and accurate" description of the entire building and of the relationships between its elements in a dynamic virtual environment where any information can be constantly shared and transformed [4], is particularly suitable to represent and manage the changes that occur during time in architectural heritage. It can potentially allow for an effective exchange of information between different domains and platforms and for the creation of enriched models in which the level of detail of the objects from approximation moves to a more precise description.

Nevertheless, this representation system has its own limits. The parametric description of heritage objects in a BIM environment, at the current stage of its development, results problematic since BIM systems were originally conceived as an answer to the standardization of new construction elements. The uniqueness of heritage artifacts demands, instead, for the possibility to create in the model non-standardized objects with a customizable set of functional, semantic, and topological rules.

In this context, the hereby presented research investigates the possible use of semantic web technologies in the perspective of providing a new modeling approach, able to comprehensively represent all the knowledge collected, used and shared during the activities of investigation, survey, intervention and conservation of an architectural heritage artifact.

2 Previous Works on Built Heritage Representation

2.1 Virtual Reality GIS

At present, Virtual Reality Geographic Information Systems (GIS) are the main tools used for storing and visualizing as geometrical information the geographical features, referring those data by means of map projections and 3D spatial coordinates.

One of the most widespread application of Virtual Reality GIS is the CityGML international standard, which is able to represent objects in relation to their geometrical, topological, semantic and appearance properties. This approach extends the capabilities of Virtual Reality modeling: if in the past 3D models have been used primarily for visualization purposes, with the addition of topology and semantic information, more complex analysis and 3D spatial queries can be carried out.

Although CityGML was designed for city modeling (e.g. for planning or disaster management), because of its capabilities and interoperable design, some studies have tested its effectiveness in built heritage modeling. For instance, D'Andrea [5] focused on future perspectives for archaeological documentation where CityGML was assessed for the management of spatial and geographic documents, while Delgado [6] adopted CityGML as an approach to semantic modeling of existing buildings in order to support intervention and monitoring of architectural heritage. Both research works show that an effective extension of Virtual Reality GIS framework to built heritage field cannot be achieved without the implementation in these models of additional, domain-specific semantics. In the typological classification of GIS, these application attempts on existing buildings matches a thematic and methodological distinction but not a technological innovation, at least for now.

In fact, despite the presence of some new VR GIS applications in this field, even with special interfaces and new algorithms, a specific modeling framework for built heritage representation has not yet been designed, except perhaps some specific intra-site applications. As a result, the standardization of VR GIS application to existing buildings is still far from having consistent results, hindered also by issues in terms of integration of VR GIS technologies with existing documentation and coding databases, both at regional and national level.

2.2 Advantages and Limits of Building Information Modeling to Built Heritage

Despite the growing interest of the AEC Industry in the use of Building Information Modeling to support life cycle, maintenance, and deconstruction management of new buildings, the research in BIM implementation for existing buildings is rather neglected. In literature, articles published in academic journals and applied publications that contribute to BIM implementation for existing buildings can be found starting from 2007, while the research on the use of BIM specifically for architectural heritage is a quite recent phenomenon and only a few publications in this field have been taken during the last few years. Nevertheless, the trend of BIM publication on this topic is significantly increasing.

Among all the papers related to the use of BIM as a support in the heritage conservation process, a consistent number of publications concentrates on the acquisition of the geometrical asset for existing structures through high-tech systems for field data acquisition, such as laser scanner and other photogrammetry techniques. One of the first applications of 3D geospatial information translation into an efficient 3D as-built BIM creation can be found in the concrete cracking analysis of the Solomon R. Guggenheim Museum in New York conducted by Robert Silman Associates in 2007 [7]. In order to keep track of concrete cracks and define their cause, the engineers worked with a digital survey company to create a full model of the building in a finite element modeling software. Measurements of the movements of the building have been collected for one year in order to calibrate the model and determine guidelines to settle the problem. This first experience pointed out the advantages of a rich 3D model integrated with specific information in the management of an existing building.

Starting from 2008, further studies have concentrated more on the development of enriched models adding intangible information to a component-based 3D BIM for heritage. Pauwels [8] proposed an approach similar to BIM, called Architectural Information Modeling (AIM), in which he theoretically describes a system obtained blending historical building information with a 3D model in a structure that can be implemented as soon as information is collected. At the Dublin Institute of Technology, Dore et al. [9] showed the advantages in using parametric and procedural modeling techniques typical of BIM systems for digitally recording architectural heritage. In their proposed model, named Heritage Building Information Modeling (HBIM) [10], a library of heritage objects has been designed following parametric rules and constraints deduced from historic manuscripts and architectural patterns book, which is able to automatically generate 3D models from the original survey data, allowing at the same time for manual refinements. Despite the interesting use of the Geometric Descriptive Language (GDL), the enrichment of the model with semantics, topology and appearance properties has not been made within BIM but through the transposition of the model in a 3D GIS environment where data related to built heritage artifacts have been used for further analysis.

These advances point out that the main advantage in the use of BIM for representing historical artifacts can be seen in the construction of a realistic 3D model able to store information related to each object such as morphology, type, construction data, etc.

Indeed, as for the AEC industry, BIM systems can ensure some benefits also in the built heritage field such as:

- Geometrical description of the object;
- A comprehensive and endowed description of each element by means of properties that can wide object's meanings;
- Semantic richness, able to provide different kinds of relationships which can be assessed for analysis and simulations;

- Integration of data in a single repository ensuring their consistency, accuracy, and accessibility.

On the other hand, their application still have some limits:

- Many BIM's default families regard only modern and contemporary buildings. Therefore, they are not useful to describe existing architectures, which require the creation of ad hoc families;
- BIM software automatically applies to constructive elements some characteristics (e.g. the horizontality of the pavements or the regularity of the vertical surfaces) that do not regard heritage contexts;
- The asymmetric and geometrically irregular constructive elements of many historic buildings (as well as archaeological remains or fragments) are not compliant with the BIM features;
- Archaeological objects' modeling requires new libraries that contain specific families: they should be able to describe this domain and its peculiar characteristics.

Although these approaches are particularly suitable for achieving a realistic and substantial representation of the artifact, BIM and GIS systems, as data repositories, do not allow for any further kind of reasoning. Even if it is extremely useful to include all information in a single model all the information needed for a complete understanding of heritage assets, knowledge, meant as an awareness understanding of the artifact achieved through experience or education, cannot be exclusively associated to a BIM component.

At present, knowledge acquisition involves complex cognitive processes of perception, communication, and reasoning and is usually embed in designers' mind. Even if it is difficult to represent knowledge trough parameters, there are some application that can associate a higher level of semantics to each object, enhancing its understanding and helping professionals in the decision-making processes.

Over the past few years, in order to overcome these shortcomings and enhance the collaboration between different profiles operating in the heritage conservation fields, some research has been made on the development of integrated systems in which Building Information Modeling is combined with semantic web technologies, a technology already in use in the AEC industry for new constructions. As partially suggested by Pauwels [11], this kind of integrated model, in which information is digitalized, documented, archived, and enriched with a higher level of semantics, could also provide a valuable support in the process of investigation, interpretation, and conservation of architectural heritage increasing the level of knowledge of the artifact and its management.

2.3   Current Knowledge Representation for Built Heritage Documentation

The field of built heritage is certainly a context in which the use of Communication and Information Technologies, has found a strong distribution and use, as well as one of the disciplines in which there is more debate concerning which of them should be used and in which way. One of the main issues in their current applications is the representation of the many changes of the architectural artifact during both its life and the following process of conservation: the current method of building documentation in the Historic Structure Report (HSR) provides a significant amount of information but it is only a snapshot in time. It cannot respond to changes, renovations, and repairs. It does not serve as an up-to-date reference for understanding the current state of a building. It is static and quite difficult to use since information related to different states of the artifact is spread in different archives and databases, usually not accessible, nor well-organized or structured.

In fact, current IT applications to heritage documentation process merely consist in the creation of large databases that have the task of gathering a wide range of information asynchronously provided by the different actors involved. This approach led to the proliferation of a wide variety of digital databases related to cultural heritage, mainly characterized by a great heterogeneity concerning the transmission formats used, the level of accessibility and the consistency of the information represented.

One of the first models for collecting information used in this context, perhaps the cause of most of the previously mentioned problems and limitations, is the record-oriented model based on "virtual catalog sheet" of objects, an approach directly derived from the traditional bibliographic one.

In this database, the information were represented mainly by textual descriptions of every single aspect of the object considered, thus preventing complex operations on data and resulting inappropriate for fully covering the complexity of historical objects and of their relationships.

This led to the creation of data models in which the information is fragmented in several basic entities, described by a list of properties associated with them, resulting in different computer applications based mostly on large relational databases. In this case, the main limitation continues to be the central role attributed to objects: the description of their features through a list of properties has led to a representation of the information often redundant and too simplified, highlighting the inability, through this data model, to represent semantic associations between objects and other parts of knowledge pertinent to other disciplines. It is therefore essential to use a technological infrastructure that allows to represent concepts relying on a knowledge representation and to perform high formal reasoning and inferences.

Ontologies are the primary tool used to overcome these problems, as they allow to represent objects and concepts not only through the description of their features but also by the description of the relationships that exist between them, paying attention to the meaning of the terms and the structure and nature of the different knowledge domain involved.

Several national and international organizations and commissions, including the ICCD (Central Institute for Cataloguing and Documentation) and the CIDOC (International Committee for Documentation of the Council of Museums) [12, 13] have focused their efforts towards the establishment of standards that indicated more precise and detailed criteria for structuring heritage-related knowledge. The CIDOC Conceptual Reference Model represents one of the main examples of this sort, as it provides a specific language for representing information on cultural heritage to mediate between different sources of information, such as the ones stored by museums, libraries and archives, also related to the concepts of space and time. While this model has been developed to manage cultural heritage documentation mainly for its cataloguing, other domain-specific ontologies have been progressively introduced to represent specific aspects of heritage conservation. The more emblematic is the Information System for Monument Damage Description (MONDIS) [14] that focuses on an ontological framework able to coordinate an automated reasoning behind the documentation of built heritage damages, their diagnosis and possible interventions.

Those examples show the potentialities of applying ontology-based models to heritage representation, documentation and analysis. Nevertheless, at present, these experiments are still too domain-specific and a more general knowledge-based model, able in particular to formalize in a homogenous way all the information related to an architectural heritage artifact, is still missing.

3   A Knowledge-Based Model for Built Heritage Representation

3.1   Conceptual Framework and Research Methodology

Investigating and operating on a built heritage artifact is a complex process where a large amount of heterogeneous data is collected, provided, used and shared by different specialists in many different ways.

The objective of this research was to develop a computational informative model for providing a homogeneous representation and integration of all the information collected and used during of the activities of investigation, intervention, use and management of heritage buildings. In the hereby presented model, a knowledge-based representation of different domains related to the heritage artifact and its multiple contexts, oriented to include and integrate any information necessary for its full comprehension, is proposed by means of ontologies. In the AEC field, several researchers have shown how ontologies can be effectively used to overcome the traditional difficulties of knowledge integration and sharing among the different specialists involved in an architectural design process [15–17].

The built heritage scope is not so different from the AEC ones. Several specialists – with their own expertise, models, tools and jargon - are usually involved in the process of investigation and restoration of a Built heritage artifact, and each of them is both user and provider of a large amount of knowledge to share with the others actors involved. In addition, heritage artifacts usually require a wider knowledge base for their full comprehension, including crucial information such as those related to their historical context and their evolution along time. An ontology-based representation system, with its hierarchical and relational modeling features, is potentially able to represent in a consistent way all the knowledge derived from the different domains, and to integrate it in a single, coherent and up-to-date model. The main advantage of using ontologies is the ability of homogenously representing concepts, relationships, functions, rules and constraints in a unified semantic network. In fact, usually, concepts are indicated as specific nodes, while relationships are displayed as oriented interconnections/vectors between two concepts. Properties are variables' values stored in slots of each concept, while functions, rules and constraints are algorithms that can be executed to 'walk' through the semantic network in order to search, access, compute and verify the information stored.

Indeed, ontologies have already been introduced in heritage conservation field as a way to represent and manage information and knowledge related to specific domains and disciplines (i.e. the previously mentioned CIDOC and MONDIS). Nevertheless, these models are very limited in terms of domain of application (historical documentation in the case of the CIDOC system, damage representation in the case of MONDIS) and can only partially being applied to Architectural Heritage representation. As a consequence, their being so domain-specific reduces one of the main potentialities of semantic web technologies, the possibility of enhance knowledge sharing and collaborations among different specialists. In this context, we illustrate a research aimed at using ontologies in order to develop a more general knowledge-based model able to integrate these domain-specific representations in a single, comprehensive relational database.

The presented research is mainly based on a constructive methodology: the general ontology-based modeling approach for architectural objects representation (and in particular on the one previously developed by the authors [18]) have been adapted to built heritage scope and then integrated with other domain-specific models. Where previous ontology-based models were not available, the conceptualizations implemented in the model have been developed by involving some specialists in the related field. This integration has been provided for peculiar fields such as the ones related to biological, chemical and microclimate analysis. After the construction of different semantic networks for the different knowledge domains considered, a process of mapping has been performed in order to depict the entities and the properties shared among different specialists and these entities behave as intersections among the different knowledge areas.

During the conceptual development of the modeling framework and the implementation of the platform by means of ontologies, the system has been progressively applied to the investigation process of the Castor and Pollux roman temple (located in Cori, a small town 50 km South of Rome). While the various survey and analysis were performed on the artifact, the platform was used to formalize and integrate the resulting information. As usual, the investigation process of the heritage artifact is asynchronous and spread along time; in this case, the proposed platform was able to represent also information provided by previous investigation activities and accessible through archival resources.

Despite the limitation of Building Information Modeling application for Built Heritage shown in the second chapter, a BIM platform has been used to provide a tridimensional representation of the physicality of the artifact and of its components, including also a representation of their properties. This connection between the database of the ontology-based system and the BIM database is possible because of their similar approach to the modeling of the architectural object. In fact, both of them rely on a component-based approach oriented to depiction of the single entities that compose the building (or, as in our case, the built heritage artifact) assigning to them a set of properties in accordance to the specifications of their class (defined as "families" in the BIM environment). Conceptually, this connection was provided by assigning the same label to both the representations of the entity in the two modeling environments (the BIM and the OWL database) and controlling the passage of information from one database to the other. As matter of fact, in this model the BIM platform was mainly used to display data and values stored in the ontology-based system.

From the computational implementation perspective, the platform was developed by using the ontology-editor Protégé (4.3 version + WebProtégé for the final users' interface and VOWL for graphical visualization) while Autodesk Revit Architecture (2014 version) as BIM platform with the additional plugin DB-Link for the database exporting. For the connection between the two databases, an application prototype previously developed by the research group has been reused [13].

3.2 The Knowledge-Based Model and Its Formalization

Representation of existing and historical buildings information involves many and complex domains of interest in which is present both what UNECAP [19] defines as tangible and intangible knowledge. The previously presented analysis showed how the major limitations of most of the technologies used for this purpose are due to the difficulty of organizing a very large amount of data, usually extremely heterogeneous, without a structure that could underline the semantic links between the information. As mentioned above, because of the multitude of data with a very high semantic value and their particular aptitude to be interconnected, the Built Heritage field results to be an ideal candidate for the Semantic Web technologies application.

Ontologies allow users to exchange information in new ways and to create connections and understanding relationships that were previously hidden, revealing an added value otherwise invisible. Differently from their philosophical meaning, the ontologies used by the Semantic Web technologies only describe relationships between concepts that interest specific applications.

Defined by a set of primitives consisting of classes, properties and relationships (or rules), the ontologies, also due to their independence from lower level data models, are used for integrating heterogeneous databases, enabling interoperability among disparate systems and specifying interfaces to independent, knowledge-based services [20]. Moreover, the definitions of the representational primitives include information about their meaning and constraints and their logically consistent application.

As mentioned above, any ontological entity involved is fully described through three main features representing a synthesis of the concepts necessary for its formal characterization. By defining a class and thus assigning to it different meanings we can give a description of the entity in relation to the different knowledge domains considered; properties, instead, are necessary to represent all the descriptive aspects related to the concerned element such as geometrical, physical and behavioral features; rules, finally, can be divided into relationship rules and reasoning rules.

The relationship rules can link lower level entities and higher complexity ones as results of multiple entities' assembly, ('Part-Of', 'Whole-Of') or define hierarchical relationships ruling entity generality stratifications in terms of Father/Son, Prototype/Instance ('Is-A', 'Instance-Of').

This kind of knowledge formalization is capable of characterizing the entities linked through the relations that occur among them, and which belong to the family of logical descriptions. In this way, we are able to manipulate also the type of an entity's structure, allowing not only to change the inheritance of an entity but also to mix entity assemblies.

Reasoning rules can be made of: algorithms and formal codes for analyzing, checking and evaluating concepts associated to specific entities with inferential procedures of 'If-Then' type; cardinality constraints defined for each class; consistency rules formalized to check values, parameters, attributes, instances, relationships and properties referring to the specific meanings associated to each entity in the specific context in which it is used; empirical rules, best practice codes and concepts that represent part of the reasoning process of any actor on his/her own specific disciplinary domain during the investigation, interpretation an intervention process.

By means of this reasoning layer, able to match rules among the considered entities belonging to the same ontology, the system allows operators to use in a coherent manner different levels of abstraction and to exploit a real interoperability of concepts.

3.3   The Knowledge Domains

In order to provide a comprehensive and accurate description of a Built Heritage artifact and of its multiple contexts, we decided to depict and formalize all the conceptual entities considered necessary for its representation, and to classify them within four knowledge macro-domains: the Artifact, the Historical Context, the Heritage Process and the Actors, mutually interconnected by strongly structured relationships.

The model is based on the assumption that the representation of the involved knowledge domains is the result of a complex, dynamic and interactive system of many modeling entities - some related to physical objects, others to abstract concepts - each characterized by a class definition, a set of properties and a set of relationships with other entities.

The Artifact Domain. With reference to the architectural object, the heritage artifact has been investigated and modeled by relying on the definition of two macro-systems: the 'Spatial Class' and the 'Technological Class'. The first includes the spaces delimited by physical elements and their aggregations, while the second embeds all the physical elements (components) and their aggregations, which make up the constructive aspect of the artifact [21].

All the Classes belonging to the artifact knowledge structures have been defined by means of two iterative processes:

* an inductive approach in which entities have been first defined in terms of meaning, performances and requirements, and then instantiated by assigning all the required values and establishing connections, relationships and rules between them;
* a deductive approach in which every actor associated meanings, properties and rules to each entity starting from their geometrical definition.

All the identified entities has been agreed with a group of specialists in the restoration area in order to use definitions, methods and representative classification methodologies already consolidated in this field as those provided by the ICCD cataloging scheme. This correspondence aims at ensuring the consistency of data with the standards defined at a national level, thus guaranteeing the uniformity of the information, considered indispensable for correct usage and sharing among the specialist involved in the conservation process.

Furthermore, the freedom ensured by this structure enables to compose an entity of a class also with entities of other classes belonging from heterogeneous domains (for example an entity belonging to the class of the spaces with one belonging to the one of the components). In our case, we have implemented the structure of spaces which, together with the system of components, contributes to completely define the building; so that the two structures (usually separated) can be interfaced directly through an inversion of the inheritance relationship (Is-A), allowing an assembly of mixed entities by means of the composition relationships (Whole-Of/Part-Of) (Fig. 1).

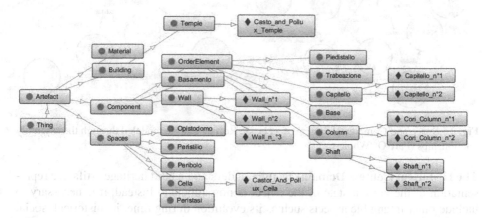

Fig. 1. Artifact knowledge domain modeled by means of ontologies – *Spaces* and *Components* classes (yellow bullets) are represented through the 'Is-A' relationship, while Individuals (purple diamonds) are linked to the class they belong through the 'Instance-Of' relationship (Color figure online).

In the presented case study, the definition of the artifact knowledge structure started with the formalization of the classic elements that are present in a Roman Temple, both in terms of spaces (e.g. Cella, Pronaos, Peribolos, etc.) and in terms of components (e.g. Column, Capital, Architrave, etc.) with the related construction materials. Subsequently, starting from the defined classes, the temple specific spatial and constructive entities - deduced from the geometric survey - have been instantiated in the ontology editor and related each other through the assembly properties.

Since is not always possible to univocally identify the different components of ancient buildings, as often happens at the beginning of an investigation process, it has been necessary to develop some classes in order to represent unknown objects in terms of their geometric and material features, waiting for a later interpretation that will associate them to the proper class.

By assigning an entity to a class, it inherits all the properties of its representation template helping the specialist to understand the already available information and which data are still missing; thus, operators can see which entities are still unidentified and, on the bases of their knowledge and experience, provide suggestions for their interpretation (Fig. 2).

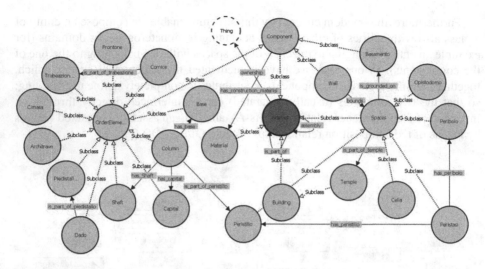

Fig. 2. Space and Component system of a classic Roman temple modeled through the assembly relationships (Part-Of/Whole-Of).

The Historical Context Domain. To fully understand a built heritage artifact, a representation of the current state of the object is not sufficient. Instead, it is necessary to include other intangible aspects such as its evolution during time, its historical, social and technological contexts, its intended functions and uses along time, the origin of the construction materials and other information usually collected by studying the archival sources.

The representation of physical evolution and functional architectural artifact, or rather the modifications that this has undergone over time, have been represented within the model through a set of classes defined Historical Context Entities.

The structure of this macro-domain has been designed by adapting the CIDOC-CRM international standard, nowadays largely accepted as a reference system for structuring the documentation of cultural heritage and by establishing interconnections and interoperability between different data structures.

The driving principle is the explicit modeling of *Event* entities (e.g. Beginning/Ending of Existence, Transformation, Modification, etc.) to be linked with the concepts of Space-Time, Material/Immaterial Object in order to allow the formalization of metadata and the connection of facts into a coherent representations of the history.

The normal human way to analyze the past is to split up the evolution of matters into discrete events in space and time. Thus the documented past can be formulated as series of events involving *Persistent Items* like *Physical Things* and *Persons*, while *Conceptual Objects* are items that can be created but can reside on more than one physical carrier at the same time (e.g. a book, a computer disk, a painting, etc.), including human thought.

Only *Temporal Entities* - such as Events - can be linked to time while other objects (Conceptual and Physical Actors/People and Places) cannot be directly linked to time.

Physical Things are destroyed when they cease to be functional and therefore destruction is not necessarily linked to physically disappearing. A thing could be physically destroyed and transformed into something else preserving parts of it. That new thing then becomes part of our domain of interest (Fig. 3).

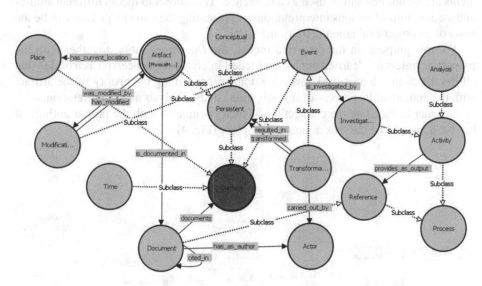

Fig. 3. Model of the historical building life-cycle in its physical and functional evolution together with the representation of the related archival sources.

Starting from the event of its construction (formalized by means of the *Beginning of Existence*) the case study temple has been modeled as a *Physical Man-Made Thing* (subclass of *Persistent Item* and equivalent to the *Artifact Macro Domain*). Then, through the *Transformation* and *Modification* classes (sub-class of *Event*) all its different configurations over the centuries have been represented, including for instance its transformation into a house during the middle ages. The changes of physical configuration have also been represented in the BIM environment, so that the different components of the different configurations can be filtered in accordance to the selected time span.

In fact, it was necessary to represent complex aspects such as morphology mutations, use changes and even destructions or relocation of building elements; for instance some columns of the case study were moved from their original position during time and reused in the medieval age as part of new walls. For this purpose, a specific set of data-properties has been implemented in order to represent if the element is in place or not, the age, the period of realization, and the different phases of the heritage object life it was in.

Another relevant part of the Historical Context Domain is the representation of archival sources. Although in the CIDOC template there is a class defined as *Document* (subclass of Information Object) and a specific property 'documents/is documented in' that allow to connect an entity with a document, this representative structure does not allow to model the authors of the document, nor other elements such as citations and scholars of the source.

In fact, in order to model the study of the artifact it is necessary to represent not only the sources that document the object, but also subsequent studies in which these documents are mentioned and/or used as a reference. This allows to model different studies and assumptions of various interpretations, representing the knowledge that will be the basis of an object evaluation/definition.

For this purpose, in the proposed model, the *Document* entity, together with the properties 'refers to', 'carried out by' and 'cited in', has been conceived as a bridge that allows the connection of the knowledge domain concerning the history of the artifact with the domain of its process of investigation, study, analysis and interpretation.

In order to facilitate the connection of such documents with the proper authors, it has been introduced the 'has as author' property (Fig. 4).

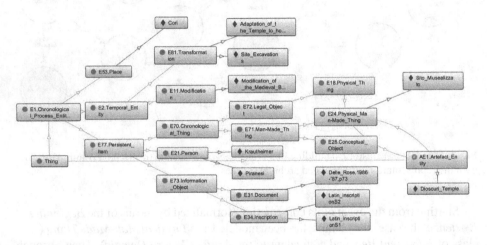

Fig. 4. Historical Context domain modeled by means of ontologies – *Events* and *Persistent Item* classes (yellow bullets) are represented through the 'Is-A' relationship, while Individuals (purple diamonds) are linked to the class they belong through the 'Instance-Of' relationship (Color figure online).

The Heritage Process Domain. In this model, the formalization of the knowledge concerning the macro-domain of heritage conservation and restoration processes comprises all the activities of investigation, analysis, and interpretation related to the artifact.

While, on one hand, the application of CIDOC system has allowed for testing its potential in modeling the knowledge associated to the artifact's life cycle, on the other hand, it has shown its limits in the representation of study, analysis, investigation, survey, and intervention activities, not just for the ongoing ones, but also in recording the previous ones. Concerning the historical documentation, the entities are points of conjunction with the classes related to the heritage process.

In analogy to the Historical Context, four main components have been identified and subsequently formalized in order to represent the Heritage Process domain: *Heritage Process Activities*, *Resources*, *Actors*, and *Reference Information Objects*.

With the aim of following the logical steps carried out by the operators during an historical building investigation, we have chosen to formalize the activities related to the investigation, analysis, and interpretation as subclasses of the process activity domain.

Resources entities were introduced to represent tools, methodologies and samples used by operators during the activities described, while the reference information objects represented information and concepts used as input and provided as output during the various activities.

Through specific Interpretation Activity classes such as the *Attribute Assignment* and *Appellation Assignment*, it is possible to connect the activities of investigation and analysis to the possible interpretations and deductions, which edit and/or increase the knowledge concerning an entity of the artifact (Fig. 5).

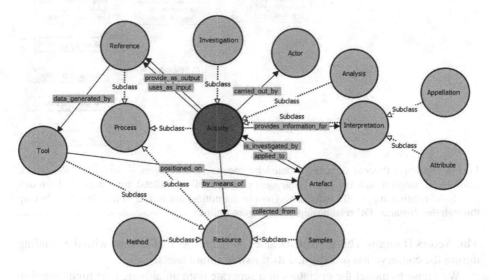

Fig. 5. Modeling framework of the investigation, analysis and interpretation activities related to the Heritage Process knowledge domain.

Particular relevance has been given to the Attribute and Appellation classes, whose purpose is to assign a definition/interpretation (respectively in terms of meanings and data) to an artifact entity. In this way, it is possible through an appropriate rule of reasoning to highlight the presence of multiple definitions assigned to an object, thus signaling problems or inconsistencies in its interpretation. Those entities must be associated with a suitable data property that could represent a range in the reliability of the attribution/definition.

Furthermore, in order to connect the different components of the artifact and the related knowledge, it has been necessary to model a set of properties related to the Heritage Process domain with a sufficiently generic range of application (Fig. 6).

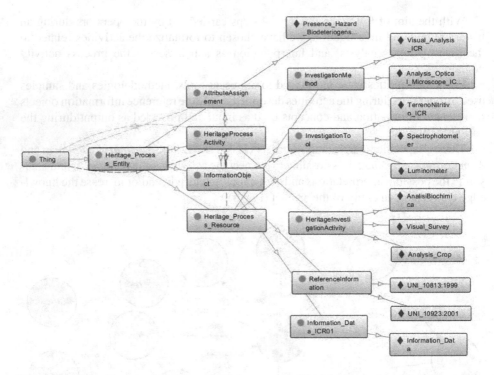

Fig. 6. Heritage Process domain modeled by means of ontologies – *Activities, Resources, Information Objects* and *Attribute Assignment* classes (yellow bullets) are represented through the 'Is-A' relationship, while Individuals (purple diamonds) are linked to the class they belong through the 'Instance-Of' relationship (Color figure online).

The Actors Domain. This domain includes all the actors that interact with the building during the conservation process and its possible future users.

We chose to model the operators in a separate domain although, as highlighted in the previous paragraphs, they are among the entities involved in the representation of both the Heritage Process activities and the Events of the Historical Context knowledge domain.

Formalizing the actors in a dedicated domain is mainly due to the necessity of knowledge management. In fact, in order to improve collaboration among the specialists involved in the process activities, the actors are required to interact with the entities of the other domains and control their specific features in relation to their needs.

To do so, the proposed template for knowledge modeling represents each entity primitive by different actors' perspective: by using this model, architects as well as conservationists can represent entities in terms of their discipline-specific definition (since the same entity can have different meanings according to different actors), properties and rules, pointing out special requirements and intents. At the specialist level, the right formalization of each actor's knowledge helps him/her in checking the coherency, congruence, and consistency of the ongoing investigation, interpretation, and intervention activities.

By means of this formalized knowledge structure, collaboration, intended as "problem sharing", is enhanced as common concepts and entities are shared and agreed by all the actors involved, helping avoid misunderstandings, misinterpretations and lacks of data.

4 Conclusions and Future Developments

In this paper, we presented the results of a research conducted through a constructive methodology and aimed at conceiving an ontology-based model for Built Heritage knowledge representation. The presented model was developed by adapting to the Built Heritage scope the conceptual framework of an ontology-based modeling approach already well-known in AEC field. In fact, while ontologies have shown their great potentials in supporting knowledge representation and sharing in new building design processes, no attempts were made for their application to the built heritage field. By integrating this knowledge structure with the semantic networks related to some of the different disciplines involved in a heritage investigation process and by mapping the entities (physical or abstract) shared among them, we were able to generate a semantically rich representation of the artifact and of the knowledge necessary for its full comprehension.

This is a first, innovative step in built heritage information management field; it means moving from a documentation-based informative system, where information about the artifact is stored in incremental, not structured archives (or databases) to a model-based system, where every piece of information is a part of a coherent, interconnected and up-to-date representation.

The proposed model provides a solution to several problems of current informative systems, such as inconsistency and duplication of data, or incoherence between different representations of the same aspects of the built heritage artifact, are solved.

On the other side, the introduction of this modeling approach opens for the necessity of addressing new issues in terms of knowledge managing protocols and filters. Among the others, we can cite the relevant topic of "property" of the knowledge shared through this system, or the one related to representation of reliability of information, that in built heritage processes are often results of interpretation or interpretative analysis. Among the others, our current work is focusing on improving semantic filtering between different domains and disciplines in the heritage practice, and on investigating how Building Information Modeling approach and the Knowledge-based one can be integrated more effectively.

Acknowledgements. This research was partially supported through a Research Project of National Interest ("Built Heritage Information Modelling/Management - BHIMM", 2012) funded by the Italian Ministry of Education University and Research.

The authors are grateful to Gianfranco Carrara from Sapienza University of Rome and Karen Kensek from University of Southern California for supporting this research with useful comments, suggestions and feedbacks.

References

1. Letellier, R., Schmid, W., Le Blanc, F.: Recording, Documentation, and Information Management for The conservation of Heritage Places Guiding Principles. The Getty Conservation Institute, Los Angeles (2007)
2. Lee, G., Sacks, R., Eastman, C.M.: Specifying parametric building object behavior (BOB) for a building information modeling system. Autom. Constr. **15**, 758–776 (2006)
3. Eastman, C.M., Teicholz, P., Sacks, R., Liston, K.: BIM Handbook: A Guide to Building Information Modeling for Owners, Managers, Designers, Engineers and Contractors. Wiley, New Jersey (2011)
4. Kensek, K.M.: Building information modeling. In: Smith, E.R. (ed.) Pocket Architecture: Technical Design Series. Routledge, Taylor & Francis Group, London (2014)
5. D'Andrea, A.: Sharing 3D Archaeological Data: Tools and Semantic Approaches. In: 14th International Conference on Virtual Systems and Multimedia, Limassol, Cyprus, pp. 149–156 (2008)
6. Delgado, F., Martínez, R., Hurtado, A., Finat, J.: Extending functionalities of Management Systems to CityGML. In: eWork and eBusiness in architecture, engineering and construction, pp. 409–415, CRC Press (2010)
7. Ayón, A.: Historic fabric vs. design intent: authenticity and preservation of modern architecture at Frank Lloyd Wright's Guggenheim Museum. J Archit. Conserv. **15**, 41–58 (2009)
8. Pauwels, P., Verstaeten, R., De Meyer, R., Van Campenhout, J.: Architectural information modelling for virtual heritage application. In: Digital Heritage, 14th International Conference on Virtual Systems and Multimedia, Lymassol, Cyprus, pp. 18–23 (2008)
9. Dore, C., Murphy, M.: Integration of historic building information modeling (HBIM) and 3D GIS for recording and managing cultural heritage sites. In: Virtual Systems in the Information Society, VSMM 2012, 18th International Conference on Virtual Systems and Multimedia, Milan, Italy, pp. 369–376 (2012)
10. Murphy, M., McGovern, E., Pavia, S.: Historic building information modelling (HBIM). Struct. Surv. **27**, 311–327 (2009)
11. Pauwels, P., Bod, R., Di Mascio, D., De Meyer, R.: Integrating building information modelling and semantic web technologies for the management of built heritage information. In: 1st International Congress on Digital Heritage, Marseille, France, pp. 481–488 (2013)
12. The CIDOC conceptual reference model, references http://www.cidoc-crm.org/references.html
13. Doerr, M.: The CIDOC conceptual reference module: an ontological approach to semantic interoperability of metadata. AI Mag. **24**(3), 75–92 (2003)
14. Cacciotti, R., Blasko, M., Valach, J.: A diagnostic ontological model for damages to historical constructions. J. Cult. Heritage **16**(1), 40–48 (2015)
15. Beetz, J., van Leeuwen, J.P., de Vries, B.: An ontology web language notation of the industry foundation classes. In: the 22nd CIB W78 Conference on Information Technology in Construction, CIB-W78, Dresden, Germany, pp. 193–198 (2005)
16. Carrara, G., Fioravanti, A., Loffreda, G., Trento, A.: Conoscere Collaborare Progettare, Teoria tecniche e applicazioni per la collaborazione in architettura. Gangemi Editore, Roma (2014)
17. Yongwook, J.: Mediating semantics for multidisciplinary collaborative design. PhD dissertation, Berkeley University of California (2008)

18. Simeone, D., Cursi, S., Toldo, I., Carrara, G.: BIM and Knowledge Management for Archaeological Heritage. In: ACADIA 14: Design Agency - Proceedings of the 34th Annual Conference of the Association for Computer Aided Design in Architecture, Los Angeles, pp. 681–390 (2014)
19. UNECAP: Cultural Tourism Sites Management - A Training Manual for Trainers in the Greater Mekong Subregion. United Nations, Economic and Social Commission for Asia and the Pacific (2008)
20. Gruber, T.: Ontology, Encyclopedia of Database Systems. In: Liu, L., Tamer, M.O. (eds.) pp. 1963–1965 (2008)
21. Carrara, G., Fioravanti, A., Novembri, G.: Knowledge-based System to Support Architectural Design. In: Penttila, H. (ed.) Architectural Information Management, Proceedings of eCAADe 01 Conference, Helsinki, pp. 80–85 (2001)

Fabrication and Materiality

Migratory Movements of Homo Faber: Mapping Fab Labs in Latin America

David M. Sperling[1(✉)], Pablo C. Herrera[2], and Rodrigo Scheeren[1]

[1] University of Sao Paulo, Sao Paulo, Brazil
sperling@sc.usp.br, rodrigoscheeren@gmail.com
[2] Peruvian University of Applied Sciences, Lima, Peru
pablo@espaciosdigitales.org

Abstract. The present paper is a mapping study of digital fabrication laboratories in Latin America. It presents and discusses results from a survey with 31 universities' fab labs, studios and independent initiatives in Latin America. The objective of this study is fourfold: firstly, to draw the cultural, social and economic context of implementation of digital fabrication laboratories in the region; secondly, to synthesize relevant data from correlations between organizational structures, facilities and technologies, activities, types of prototypes, uses and areas of application; thirdly, to draw a network of people and institutions, recovering connections and the genealogy of these fab labs; and fourthly, to present some fab labs that are intertwined with local questions. The results obtained indicate a complex "homo faber" network of initiatives that embraces academic investigations, architectural developments, industry applications, artistic propositions and actions in social processes.

Keywords: Digital fabrication · Fab labs · Latin america · Mapping

1 Introduction and Precedents

What makes us humans is our capacity to make things. From this perspective, for the philosopher Vilém Flusser [1], looking critically to present manufacturing methods is an effective way to think over our time. In the same way, to discover about the past of our species we should dig ruins of factories. If one asks about future scenarios s/he needs to begin by the stage of factories in the future. Flusser projects the factory into the future as a more adaptable place where "the creative potential of homo faber will come into its own" [1], and where he will recognize the action of manufacturing as the same of learning, acquiring information, producing it and disseminating it. It is possible to see these concerns of Flusser about the factories in the future as a previous conception of what we are experiencing nowadays as, despite their differences, maker spaces, hackerspaces and fab labs [2].

Recovering these ideas, this article aims to exhibit the current state of the art of digital fabrication in the field of architecture in Latin America,[1] looking to its recent

---

[1] For the sake of this paper, Latin America is been represented by countries of the fab labs that answered the survey presented here, with emphasis in South America.

© Springer-Verlag Berlin Heidelberg 2015
G. Celani et al. (Eds.): CAAD Futures 2015, CCIS 527, pp. 405–421, 2015.
DOI: 10.1007/978-3-662-47386-3_22

past and to its present, allowing the delineation of future trends. Digital fabrication, one of the last unfoldings of the CAAD field, coexists in Latin America with a context of late and recent industrialization - dated from XX century. It brings new perspectives of innovation to the uneven and combined development in the region, that still has big challenges for economic investment and infrastructure oriented to research.

The present paper is a mapping study of digital fabrication initiatives in Latin America. It presents and discusses some results from a survey performed in 2014 with 31 universities' fab labs,[2] studios and independent initiatives in Latin America. For Abrams and Hall, mapping "has emerged in the information age as a means to make the complex accessible, the hidden visible, the unmappable mappable (…) mapping refers to a process – ongoing, incomplete and of indeterminate, mutable form." [3].

A previous study about digital fabrication in Latin America has been conducted by Herrera and Juaréz [4], categorizing 18 laboratories under three types of initiatives: experiences of master and doctoral students; external academic/commercial circuit, and self-learning. Mapping was also used before by Rocha [5] for the purpose of delineate a computational emergence in architecture between 1960–80, exposing the role of theory within computational practice, connections and influences of people and universities between UK and USA. The thesis focuses on five research centers both in the UK and in the USA, constructing a broader context to be able to understand a historical scenario that influenced the formation of our contemporary architectonic computational culture [5].

The objective of our study is fourfold: firstly, to draw the cultural, social and economic context of implementation of digital fabrication laboratories in the region; secondly, to synthesize relevant data from correlations between organizational structures, facilities and technologies, activities, types of prototypes, uses and areas of application; thirdly, to draw a network of people and institutions, recovering connections and the genealogy of these fab labs; and fourthly, to present some fab labs that are intertwined with local questions.

2 Context of the Region

The development of Latin American fab labs is taking place in a progressive way. In a first stage due to the high costs of equipment of Rapid prototyping the major initiatives were linked with the large industry and to universities and research organizations. With the reduction of costs for acquisition of equipment and the expiration of some patents [4], began to emerge fab labs consolidated at smaller scales and more appropriated for "home users", focused on product design and interdisciplinary practices, of which only recently began to receive greater attention from architects. And, finally, with the growth of the "maker movement" (or DIY), independent initiatives emerged and started to

---

[2] In this paper we use "fab labs" without capitals to differentiate independent laboratories from the Fab Lab network of MIT.

expand [6]. Recently the creation of fab labs became part of the public policy of Latin American cities such as Bogota and Sao Paulo, in the context of "creative cities".[3]

Even though the creative inspiration of digital fabrication lab's in our region is effervescent, the scenario is very different from other places in North Hemisphere. The MIT Fab Lab's network installed in South America is an indicative of present challenges in local context. According to Benito Juárez – coordinator of Fab Lab Lima and of the South America MIT Fab Lab's network – actually the network has more than 250 laboratories around the world with an exponential growth in recent years. Despite they present itself as an inclusive project, 75 % of Fab Labs are located in developed countries (40 % in Europe e 35 % in USA) and 25 % in developing countries, with only 5 % in Latin America. Juarez points out that some cultural factors cause that the concept of "technological democratization" - conceived in developed nations - differs from the reality in our region [7].

The first challenge is the extension of the "innovative thinking", inverting the consumer's framework to another about technological development. The second challenge is the substitution of "competitive thinking" for "cooperative thinking", overcoming the win /lose logic present in low degree innovation environments. The third challenge is the optimization of "economic and administrative factors", with cutting rates and bureaucracies to purchase equipment [7, 8], besides encouraging local production of machinery and technology.

The local situation in front of the expansion about what is being considered as a new cultural, economic, educational and industrial revolution [9–13] has received a growing interest from the region and from outside of it, in recent articles [4, 8, 14], exhibitions,[4] a round table,[5] a thematic symposium[6] and a lecture.[7]

---

[3] Prefeitura de SP anuncia 12 Fab Labs em São Paulo [SP City Hall announces 12 Fab Labs in Sao Paulo], Estado de Sao Paulo, February 03, 2015, URL: http://blogs.estadao.com.br/link/prefeitura-de-sp-anuncia-12-fab-labs-em-sao-paulo/.

[4] Exhibitions: New Territories: Laboratories for Design, Craft and Art in Latin America, MAD Museum, New York, November 4, 2014 to April 5, 2015, URL: http://madmuseum.org/exhibition/new-territories; Homo Faber. Digital Fabrication in Latin America, Vila Penteado, Faculty of Architecture and Urbanism of the University of Sao Paulo, upcoming next July as part of CAAD Futures 2015, URL: http://caadfutures2015.fec.unicamp.br/index.php/exhibition1/.

[5] Round table "New Mediums: Digital Fabrication in Latin America", MAD Museum, December 11, 2014, with the designers Guto Requena (Brazil) and Sebastian Errazuriz (Chile), URL: http://www.madmuseum.org/events/new-mediums-digital-fabrication-latin-america.

[6] Thematic Symposium: "Laboratórios de produção digital em arquitetura – experimentações em ensino, pesquisa e extensão no Brasil" [Digital Production Labs in Architecture – teaching, research and extension experiments], coordinated by prof. David M. Sperling (USP, Brazil), in the III Encontro da Associação Nacional de Pesquisa em Arquitetura e Urbanismo [III Encounter of the National Association of Research in Architecture and Urbanism], Sao Paulo, October 20–24, 2014. URL: http://www.anparq.org.br/dvd-enanparq-3/htm/XFramesSumarioST.htm.

[7] Herrera, P.: Towards an Identity: Digital Fabrication in Latin America. Lecture at Symposium AA Visiting School: Politics of Fabrication Laboratory, Valparaíso, Chile, May, 13th (2011). Available at URL: http://issuu.com/pabloherrera/docs/towards_an_identity_digital_fabrication_in_latin_a/1.

3 Mapping Latin American Fab Labs

It is broadly known that the MIT Fab Labs are mapped and their profile is public,[8] with 39 operating in region: Argentina (7), Brazil (14), Chile (4) Colombia (5), Ecuador (2) and Peru (7). Knowing the existence of several other fab labs that do not participate in this network, the research is directed to them, even it includes three MIT Fab Labs by the representativeness of their work (Brazil: 2; Peru: 1).

In order to capture the institutional profile, infrastructure, operation and activities of these laboratories, we performed a mapping based on a survey using an online form. This survey was submitted in July 2014 to 48 fab labs, of which 31 laboratories from 06 countries answered (Argentina: 2; Brazil: 22; Colombia: 1; Chile: 4; Peru: 1; Uruguay: 1).[9]

The survey was oriented to capture institutional information (name, affiliation, city/country, current coordinator, current staff, date of foundation, brief history, association with nets, email/website) and infrastructure (machines), operating and work data (summary of current activities/workshops/courses, fabrication technologies, number/types/brands of equipment, uses of digital fabrication and applications of the fabrication processes/fabricated objects). The possibilities of the multi-choice answer for "uses of digital fabrication" were: "fabrication of architectural components", "fabrication of architectural models", "fabrication of construction molds", "fabrication of machines", "prototyping of small objects", or "others". And for "applications of the fabrication processes/fabricated objects" the multi-choice possibilities were: "design prototypes (visualization and/or simulation and/or analysis)", "pedagogical models", "components for the construction industry", "models for art and museology", "models of historical buildings", "objects for impaired people", "objects /processes for development of communities", "pedagogical objects", or "others".

---

[8] URL: https://www.fablabs.io/map (March 26, 2015).

[9] Argentina: CID - Centro de Informática y Diseño - FADU/Universidad Nacional del Litoral; Instituto de la Espacialidad Humana - Laboratorio de Morfología – FADU/UBA; Brazil: Aleph Zero; CADEP - Centro Avançado de Desenvolvimento de Produtos – FAAC/UNESP; Centro de prototipagem experimental – FCT/UNESP; DT3D - Divisão de Tecnologias Tridimensionais Centro de Tecnologia da Informação Renato Archer; Estudio Guto Requena; Fab Lab Universidade de São Paulo – FAU/USP; Fab Social; Garagem Fab Lab; GEGRADI, Grupo de Estudos para o Ensino/aprendizagem de Gráfica Digital – FAU – UFPel; LAGEAR - Laboratório Gráfico para Experimentação Arquitetônica – FAU/UFMG; Lamo3D – Laboratório de modelos 3D e Fabricação Digital – FAU/UFRJ; LAPAC / Laboratório de Automação e Prototipagem para a Arquitetura e Construção – FEC/UNICAMP; Laboratório de Prototipagem Rápida Mackenzie – FAU/Mackenzie; LEAUD - Laboratório de Estudo das Linguagens e Expressões da Arquitetura, Urbanismo e Design – DAUR/UFJF; LED | Laboratório de Experiência Digital – FAU/UFC; LM + P - Laboratório de Modelos e Prototipagem – DA-CT/UFPA; Nomads – IAU/USP; PRONTO 3D - Laboratório de Prototipagem e Novas Tecnologias Orientadas ao 3D – Design/UFSC; Rede Brasileira de Fabricaçao Digital; SimmLab – Laboratório de Simulações e Modelamento em Arquitetura e Urbanismo – FAU/UFRGS; SUBdV Architecture; ViD_Virtual Design – Design/UFRGS; Chile: Area Computacional - Universidad Tecnica Federico Santa Maria; gt2P - Great things to people; Lab CNC FAU/Uchile; Producción Digital UC / Fabhaus UC – PUC-Chile; Colômbia: Frontis3D R + D; Peru: Fab Lab Lima; Uruguay: LabFabMVD - FArq/Universidad de la República.

3.1 Institutional and Infrastructure Profile

Initially, it is important to note that most of the answers came from Brazilian fab labs (22 of 31) linked to research institutions /universities (15 of 31). Although one participant started his work in the year 2000 (DT3D-CTI Renato Archer – Fig. 1), most of the survey respondents (24) began their work after from 2010. Furthermore, the answers to the survey showed that most fab labs in Latin America were created in the last 3 years (19).

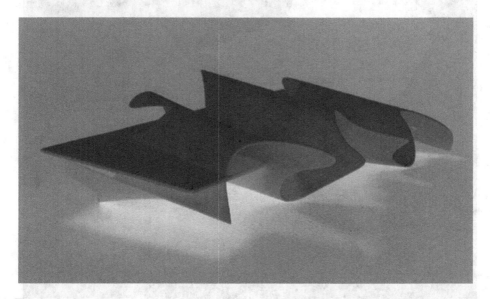

Fig. 1. Surface Homeomorphism. Design by David Sperling, SLS model – DT3D-CTI Renato Archer (2001)

The initiatives were classified according to their legal constitution (academic research institute or private studio), and were evaluated by the capacity of their machinery - variability and quantity - that is, their level of autonomy in manufacturing. So there are two axes and correspondent subdivisions to the installed capacity (Fig. 2).

The first axis, "academic research institutions", marks 22 laboratories that have emerged and operate at universities, technical institutes and research centers.[10] The first subdivision of the axis, "research and development centers", considers only one facility in Brazil, which has an extensive and diverse rapid prototyping machinery frame (DT3D-CTI Renato Archer, the first fab lab installed in the region[11]). The second subdivision refers to "university laboratories with high-capacity installed", which characterizes the initiatives that have at least one of each types of machinery - 3D

---

[10] Into this axis, one institution is bond to MIT Fab Lab and is installed in an university (Fab Lab SP – Faculty of Architecture and Urbanism, University of Sao Paulo).

[11] http://www.cti.gov.br/tecnologias-tridimensionais.

Printer, Laser Cutter, CNC router and /or any other - giving them autonomy in the manufacture of objects. There are 12 fab labs that meet this configuration: 9 in Brazil, 2 in Chile and 1 in Uruguay.

Fig. 2. Map of fab labs mapped and their institutional profile in comparison with the number of MIT Fab Labs in the region.

The third subdivision, "laboratories in universities with an average installed capacity", considers the fab labs that work with only two of the main types of machines - 3D Printer, Laser Cutter, CNC Router. There are 6 fab labs in this configuration: 5 in Brazil and 1 in Chile. In the last subdivision, "laboratories in universities with low installed capacity", that characterizes fab labs which have only one type of machine, we mapped 3 initiatives: 2 from Argentina and 1 from Brazil.

The second axis, "private studios", includes 9 labs that were created by the private sector. The first subdivision of the axis, "laboratories bond to networks (FabLab or RhinoFab)" - which requires a minimum of machine framework to receive the label - has 3 initiatives: 2 in Brazil and 1 in Peru. Under the second subdivision, "independent laboratories" - that do not have one of the listed equipment or don't have some external link -, 6 initiatives were mapped: 4 in Brazil, 1 in Chile and 1 in Colombia.

Overall, from 31 of the fab labs, 29 have at least one 3D printer; 23 have a laser cutter; 21 have a CNC Router; and 14 have other digital fabrication machines (scanner, vinyl cutter, experimental machine, etc.) and 11 fab labs outsource machinery services.

3.2 Workshops and Courses

All laboratories answered that they provide workshops and courses. While most fab labs are in academic institutions (24) and the emphases of their work are on teaching and research, private studios (7) direct their activities to courses /workshops and to design objects.

Among the synthesized categories, 16 laboratories provide software training and modeling – Rhinoceros 3D, Grasshopper, BIM and CAD software -, 12 provide preparation courses about files for digital manufacturing - F2F -, 7 provide workshops about objects, prototypes and furniture design, 6 about architecture and urban design projects, 2 about programming language and only one provide courses about robotics.

3.3 Uses of Digital Fabrication

Within the categories presented in the survey, the uses made of the machinery is firstly oriented to prototyping of small objects (31 fab labs), then used to the fabrication of architectural models (27 Labs) and fabrication of architectural components (27 Labs), fabrication of construction molds (15), fabrication of machines (10) and Others (7).

3.4 Applications of the Fabrication Processes/Fabricated Objects

From the categories presented in the survey, the following applications have been identified by fab labs, in descending order: design prototypes - visualization and /or simulation and /or analysis (28), pedagogical objects (26), components for the construction industry (16), models for art and museology (16), objects /processes for development of communities (15), models of historical buildings (14), objects for impaired people (10) and others (02).

3.5 Correlations

The mapping highlights a recent context of starting and development of fab labs in Latin America. While the first activities started 15 years ago, 2/3 of fab labs were created in the last 3 years. In this scenario, the majority of the fab labs surveyed are bond to academic research institutions and half of them have a high capacity installed. These are followed by fab labs linked to universities or private studios with medium or low capacity.

While the results of "Applications" show, for example, the predominance of the production of small objects in relation to the manufacture of molds for construction or manufacturing machines, the "Uses" results indicate a more equal division in several areas. After the predominance of design prototypes and models for teaching, uses targeted to industry, art and heritage and actions in social process (communities and impaired people) have similar results.

Fab labs mapped in this survey are geared to a variety of activities involving the training of human resources, design processes and research of different uses and applications of digital manufacturing - with few cases showing a narrow specialization.

4 Migratory Movements

The emergence of digital fabrication labs in Latin America countries has happened in very diverse scenarios, initiatives and institutions in recent years. As a migratory movement, its ideas and programs were transmitted from more advanced research centers, with a history of consolidated research - such as North America and Europe - to be implemented in Latin America. Therefore, this movement was driven by multiple actors and sources of information, as well as work strategies and funding agencies (Fig. 3).

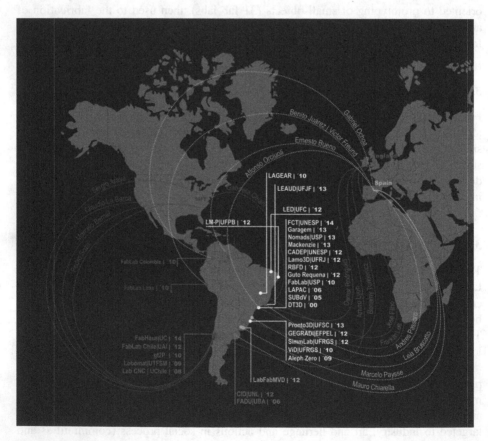

Fig. 3. Map of migratory movements: master and doctoral experiences in USA and Europe and the organization of fab labs.

4.1 Global Connections, Local Work and Network

Two differences mark the implementation of emerging digital technologies, between the northern and southern Hemisphere [15, 16]. While in the former, the use in the profession and self-learning are two recurring patterns, in Latin America, from the beginning these experiences have been part of academic implementations organized in short workshops, gradually forcing the profession to adapt them to their ventures, experimentally.

In a global context, at ABB 2010: Machinic Processes [15], from the 55 professionals and 27 architecture leading architecture schools, Latin America still showed the embryonic state of its process, with no applications that would go beyond the academic context, and no local connection. Neither are there representatives of the region in "Fabricating the Future" [17], which sought to demonstrate the impact of digital manufacturing in professional practice.

Some of the labs mapped in this research appear as early as the 90 s, driven by local academic requirements: in the case of Brazil, a Government act from 1994 determined that all architecture programs were required to teach 'Informatics Applied to Architecture'. Since then, computer labs were created in virtually all architecture schools [18]. However, as shown in the present research, in some cases there 20 years were needed to some of these computer labs go from visualization and simulation to fabrication with 3D printers, CNC equipment and laser cutters.

Thus, it can be said that during the first years of the 21st century, the migratory movement of academics and students in Master and Doctorate programs, brought digital technologies to different Latin American universities that were being experimented at the same time in the USA and Europe. Never before Latin America had an approach so disruptive [16] and generalized as in those almost ten first years. Programming and scripting were at the beginning of a phase in which design and fabrication dialogued in the same work platform.

In 2007, Margaret Dewhurst, then a student at AA Intermediate Unit 2 [19], won with "Bad Hair" the Architectural Association Summer Pavilion, adapting a definition created by Guillermo Parada, founder of gt2P [20], that originally produced a Grid Shell or Waffle, to another that allowed to section double-curved surfaces in non-parallel structures.

The immediacy in which information produced in workshops could be shared, allowed local experiences to connect globally with no additional cost, under free platforms such as blogs, websites and repositories. Between 2006 and 2010 the number of new blogs about digital fabrication raised from 7 to 26 in the USA, from 6 to 46 in Europe, and from 1 to 12 in Latin America [21]. This shows the exponential growth in the resources that eliminated previous limitations, such as the need for the people to wait for courses in order to learn about these technologies, as demonstrated by Senske, who wrote that the "technology moves much faster than pedagogy can possibly adapt. Students must often teach themselves in order to keep up with new programs and techniques" [22].

Under these two contexts, after the first decade, the influence of the first academics grew stronger thanks to two simultaneous situations: cheaper 3D equipment [4] and the experiences in a local reality that was looking into its own traditions to generate a major impact.

After a first phase of creating labs from experiences of researchers abroad, the current dynamics is an internal nucleation, with expertise sharing between researchers and professionals in the region. This happened, for example, in Brazil as emblematic case. After her PhD at MIT, Gabriela Celani created the Laboratory for Automation and Prototyping for Architecture and Construction (LAPAC) at the University of Campinas (UNICAMP)[12] in 2006. One of her fomer students, Regiane Pupo, has started to seed a network of labs in the South of the country, creating Rede Pronto 3D,[13] in 2013. More recently, other former students of Celani have started the creation of a new fab lab in a Northern Federal University (UFRPE).

5 From Local to Global to Local

A majority tendency of introduction of fab labs in Latin America - mainly in laboratories linked to universities - can be described by experimentation with design and manufacturing of scale models, objects and pavilions, associating parametric software and laser cutters/CNC. On one hand, the trend has appeared (and is still presented) as a way of learning to use new design tools and production routines. On the other, it can be characterized as a connection with initiatives undertaken before or synchronously in the US and Europe.

After a period of introduction and critical review, this work marked by a strong global accent based on devices (parametric modeling + digital fabrication) is sharing space with initiatives with a local accent based on the technological, cultural and social reality of the region (local reality + parametric modeling + digital fabrication).

These initiatives point to other possible interpretations of modernization and technological development, in front of dual narratives that reinforce relations between developed and developing countries, between center and periphery. And in this sense, they can be approached from studies on the theory of uneven and combined development and their correlation with Latin America, such as the Brazilian sociologist José Domingues, who states that:

> '[facing] a homogeneous space-time configuration of global social life and social evolution (...) there are regionalized space-time constructions, with their own rhythms, configurations, densities (...) in a multi-linear evolutionary process in which collective subjectivities exercise their creativity. Those space-time settings can remain in tension with each other, finding themselves now, however, irremediably intertwined and generally subordinated to the dynamic centers that drive modernity. Latin America is one of those space-time constructions - crossed by heterogeneity since its inception' [23].

Such initiatives can also be approached from certain aspects of the concept of 'appropriate modernity' developed by Chilean architect Cristian Fernandez Cox as a counterpoint to the vision of a European and American normative modernity

---

[12] http://lapac.fec.unicamp.br/.

[13] http://www.redepronto3d.com/.

continually being received out of step by Latin America. This notion, conceived during the heat of the debates of the 1980s about a Latin American architectural identity could be recovered to think about the heterogeneous situation of Latin America in the technological context.[14] Cox defines what it means by 'appropriate modernity':

> 'Here we find the opportune linguistic coincidence of the triple meaning of the term. Appropriate as adequate. To the reality in question, useful to it, to its service, from it, consistent with it, harmonic with it. Appropriate as made own. (...) In the precisely condition that we make a previous distinction from the critical digestor of our identity, and what suits to our reality, let us know to adapt and harmonically incorporate to it, that is, appropriating it in the sense of make it your own. Appropriate as own. There are peculiarities fairly abundant that are objectively own, and it is only possible to respond with own solutions' [24].

The possibility of other viewpoints for the technological processes in the Latin American hybridization context, such as responses to overcome social challenges and the creation of cultural artifacts, is the result of tactical actions in the face of technologies such as processes of appropriation that may be termed as 'technophagy'.[15] One could think about these tactical actions according to what has proposed the Czech-Brazilian philosopher Flusser, the action of play by the operator of the apparatus could be a possibility to open the programs that constitute themselves, expanding the playing field:

> '(...) freedom is a strategy by which chance and necessity are submitted to human intention. In other words, that freedom 'equals playing against the apparatus'. (...) They know that they are playing against the apparatus. However, even they are not aware of the extent of what they are doing. They are not fully aware that they are trying, through their activities, to answer the question of 'freedom' in a context of apparatus' [25].

Of the 31 fab labs mapped in the region, we selected three cases among other possible that work amid the challenges mentioned, from a close bond with the local reality and a tactical view on technology. These fab labs are investigating uses possibilities of digital fabrication to act within social and urban problems in slums (Lagear-Brasil); to act within social and environmental questions in Amazonia (FabLab-Lima); and to act with cultural and technological hybridization (gt2P).

5.1 Lagear – Belo Horizonte, Brazil[16]

In the same way as all installed laboratories in Brazilian public universities, the activities of Lagear (Graphics Laboratory for Architectural Experience - School of

---

[14] Herrera and Juárez [8] reported to the Argentinian critic of architecture Marina Waisman (La Arquitectura Descentrada, Bogota, Editorial Escala, 1995) which deals with technological modernization processes in the region. The author argues that while for European and American technological modernization happened in response to the circumstances, in Latin America it appears as a symbol of progress and apparent modernity. This is associated to what Cox [16] says about the modernization process in the region carried out from outside and by regulatory pressure, i.e. disconnected from local realities.

[15] We refer here to the concept of 'antropofagia' coined by Oswald de Andrade in the 1920 s, in the context of Brazilian modernist movement, according to which the creation of a genuine national culture would only be possible through the consummation and critical reworking of both culture national and foreign influences.

[16] http://www.mom.arq.ufmg.br/lagear/.

Architecture - Federal University of Minas Gerais) are oriented to teaching, research and extension. Founded in 1993, it is a significant case of the Brazilian context laboratories linked to schools of architecture dedicated to visualization and simulation, which started to work with digital fabrication in recent years, with funding of FINEP, CNPq and other Brazilian public agencies.

In the 2000s, the research developed in the laboratory about CAD and multimedia practices converged on the possibilities of its application in social contexts, encompassing design and physical computing interfaces such as interfaces to support participatory design processes with residents of social housing complex (Mutirão São Gabriel) and interfaces for community involvement and visualization of urban problems in the scale of the city, the neighborhood and the individual (Ituita).

Under the coordination of the professors José dos Santos Cabral Filho and Ana Paula Baltazar (which had a significant part of their training held in foreign Schools as the University of Sheffield, McGill University, The Royal College and Bartlett School of Architecture) low-cost interactive projects and remote environments connections associated with physical computing systems and simple electronics mechanisms are investigated. In this context, since 2012 the laboratory began to explore parametric design process and digital fabrication.

In reference to cybernetics - as to the ethical imperative of cyberneticist Heinz von Foerster "act always so to increase the number of choices" [26] - the research group works with the focus on social contexts of low income and aims to explore digital fabrication as a way to expand the possibilities to respond to informal architectural issues and complex characteristics of the Brazilian context [27].

One of the works in this line, developed as part of MArch of Marcus V. Bernardo is the use of digital fabrication in housing construction processes in slums - a high precariousness context and reusing materials. Among the adopted initiatives such as the development, availability, sharing and the construction of open source equipment and software, stand out a Grasshopper programming that allows unify the stages of build and cut from the specificity of the collected materials by the locals that have different sizes and the enhancement of a CNC equipment (Fig. 4). It happens with the installation of ultrasonic distance sensors, data projector and camera, to enable feedback in real time between model and equipment, software and machine, preserving the context of high variety [28].

5.2   Fab Lab Lima – Lima, Peru[17]

In 2009, Fab Lab Barcelona and the Spanish government, through AECID, chose Lima as headquarters for MIT's first Fab Lab project in Latin America, which included scholarships to Fab Academy (2009–2010). The commitment of each fellow was to return home and lead the implementation. In Lima, Benito Juaréz (architect) and Victor Freund (industrial designer) were selected, and the National University of Engineering, located on the outskirts of Lima, was the venue for infrastructure. Although scholars,

---

[17] http://fablabuni.edu.pe/.

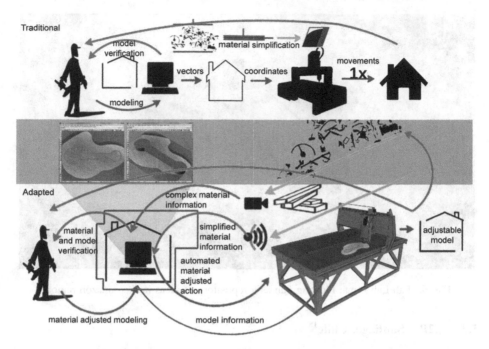

Fig. 4. LAGEAR: feedback improvements and investigation of introduction of a digital fabrication process in auto-construction in slums.

turned into administrators, came back to Lima in 2010, it was not until late 2011, when the Fab7 was performed, that the equipment arrived and it was finally possible to commence operations.

The context of a state university and its geographic location quickly connected it to real situations and, at the same time, limited economic resources. So, from brief workshops, they were able to propose solutions to the common people, recycling or using inexpensive materials. Being an initiative from foreign sources, the academic relationship with professors and students was not direct, the Lab served as a service space for the students, rather than being used for experimentation.

Management was changed in 2012, and the original fellows moved the initiative, still supported by MIT, and founded Fab Lab Met, with funds from the Municipality of Lima. This brought them even closer to projects with a strong cultural, social and environmental link.

Amongst its multiple initiatives, in 2014 the "Fab Lab Floating" project started (Fig. 5), under the Creative Commons License. It seeks to be a repository of ideas for building its infrastructure, and that this in turn promotes the importance of conservation the Amazon region. This region, with a wide variety of resources, many of them still unexplored, is the starting point to explore new materials, reusing waste and propose alternatives aimed at raising the responsibility for our environment.

Fig. 5. Fab Lab Lima: Floating Fab as a repository of ideas in the Amazon region.

5.3   gt2P – Santiago, Chile[18]

The Higher Education Quality Program (MECESUP) which is in its third phase (2012–2016) foresees an investment of more than US$ 80 million in Chilean Universities. Since 1999, this fund has allowed the implementation of digital fabrication equipment in schools of architecture. The case of the Catholic University of Chile (MECESUP 2003), the University of Chile (MECESUP 2008) and UTFSM (MECESUP 2009) have enabled many students to integrate these technologies into their projects, thus providing for its application in the practice of architecture; in other cases, it's just a service for cutting or prototyping.

The self-managed initiatives are also involved in different funding sources, with Santiago de Chile being the first seat of a Mini Maker Faire in Latin America (2012).[19]

Great things to people (gt2P) was founded in 2010 and its current partners are Guillermo Parada, Tamara Pérez, Sebastián Rozas and Eduardo Arancibia. Since before its foundation, their partners' familiarity with programming techniques in Rhinoscripting and later in Grasshopper allowed them to approach to design and fabrication processes. They not only create unique objects, but also focus on solutions that would later become the DNA of a family of products.

---

[18] http://www.gt2p.com/.

[19] Maker Faire is one of the four brands promoted by Maker Media, a global platform born with the scope of leading the Maker movement. It focuses on do it yourself (DIY) and/or Do it with others (DIWO). According to Maker Media, "Maker Faire features innovation and experimentation across the spectrum of science, engineering, art, performance and craft." The first Maker Faire took place in San Mateo, CA, in 2006. In 2012 and 2013, Santiago de Chile was the only Latin American proposal and became and important platform for showing the different Fab Labs generated during the last few years.

Their early works are focused on exploring the variability of shape and fabrication, taking as a starting point G. Parada's experience in the Grid Shell technique, applied to the project "Sectionimal" (coffee table). Afterwards they worked on "Furrow Fields" (centerpiece), "Voro Twins" (shelves) and "Heart Days" (vase). In 2010, gt2P was awarded twice with money by the Technological Innovation Fund of Chile for parametric design and digital fabrication of furniture. In his essays with metal, ceramic and wood, it is evident their aim to interpret the utility of those materials, producing then families like "Supple Series" (aluminium fixation system and bronze 2011) and "Gudpaka" (plywood and alpaca wool 2011).

The group moved its studio in 2011 to a larger space and then experimented with low-tech knowledge, reaching out to the reality of local production. Representative cases are the "Royal Mahuida" (ceramic in bronze 2012), "Vilu Ligth" and "Shhh the hope keeper" (2013), and "Less CPP No. 2: Porcelain vs Lava Lights" (2014). These experiences lead them to implement "Digital Crafting" as a working methodology. The result of these processes lead to the project "Losing My America", currently on display at the Museum of Art and Design in New York. In the latter, they highlight the interpretation of craft and indigenous traditions and the use of 3D scan, FDM printing, Progressive Polygonal Reduction Piece and CNC carving of molds, using different materials like copper, porcelain, ceramic, glass or plaster.

In contrast to the Brazilian and Peruvian examples, gt2P rescues artistic practices powered by technology, experimenting not only with materials and equipment from third parties, but producing their own machines, as in the project "Less No.1 Catenary Pottery Printer" (2014) or distorting the result of an object made by a FDM technology 3D printer, which is incorporated in the process of reading, interpreting, hacking and writing, to produce alterations they called "Dysgraphia" (Fig. 6).

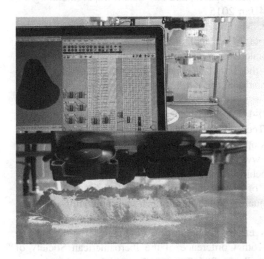

Fig. 6. gt2P: Dysgraphia: "programmed errors" in the language of 3D printers

6 Final Remarks

The set of information synthesized in this research (economic, cultural and social local context, data of existing laboratories, a network of people and institutions, and local cases) indicate the varied "homo faber" network of initiatives of digital fabrication that embraces academic investigations, architectural developments, industry applications, design of objects, artistic propositions and actions in social processes.

Until now, the frame installed in Latin America indicates a double scenario. On the one hand, there is a transition of an initial situation of seeding laboratories from the outside, to a current process of internal nucleation within a context that still has lag in relation to existing infrastructure and human resources in dynamic centers in the area. On the other hand, there is a coexistence of expertise with strong global accent and initiatives in close dialogue with the region's specificities.

In this dialogue with local necessities and potentialities, as shown by the cases presented, we recognize that still reside major challenges and open possibilities to be explored in the future of Latin American fab labs. For this, we imagine that a greater diffusion and acting face to installed practices and the extension of local collaborative networks can be fruitful paths to explore.

Acknowledgements. We thank Gabi Celani (LAPAC-UNICAMP) for the suggestions and comments made during the development of this work.

References

1. Flusser, V.: The Factory in The Shape of Things. Reaktion Books, London (1999)
2. Van Holm, E.J.: What are Makerspaces, Hackerspaces, and Fab Labs?. http://dx.doi.org/10.2139/ssrn.2548211. (2015). Accessed 24 Jan 2015
3. Abrams, J., Hall, P. (eds.): Else/where: Mapping. New Cartographies of Networks and Territories, p. 12. University of Minnesota, Minneapolis (2006)
4. Herrera, P.C., Juaréz, B.: Fabrication Laboratories: Problems and possibilities of implementation in Latin America. In: Proceedings of the Fab 9 Research Stream. Yokohama, Keiko University SFC. http://www.fablabinternational.org/fab-lab-research/proceedings-from-the-fab-9-research-stream (2013)
5. Rocha, A.J.M.: Architecture theory 1960–1980: emergence of a computational perspective. PhD Thesis. Massachusetts Institute of Technology (2004)
6. Gaona, N.: Changing the way industries operate is driving force behind maker movement, Future Source Summit, México http://www.futuresourcesummit.com/news/changing-the-way-industries-operate-is-driving-force-behind-maker-movement/ (2014)
7. Smith, E.: Benom Juarez on the future of digital fabrication in Peru, make:, April, 24th http://makezine.com/2014/04/24/benom-juarez-on-the-future-of-digital-fabrication-in-peru/ (2014)
8. Herrera, P.C., Juaréz, B.: Perspectivas en los Laboratorios de Fabricación Digital en Latinoamérica. In: Proceedings of the 16th Conference of the Iberoamerican Society of Digital Graphics, SiGraDi, Fortaleza, Brazil, pp. 285–289 (2012)
9. Hatch, M.: The Maker Movement Manifesto: Rules for Innovation in the New World of Crafters, Hackers, and Tinkerers. McGraw-Hill Professional Publishing, New York (2013)

10. Blikstein, P.: Digital Fabrication and 'Making' in Education: The Democratization of Invention. In: Walter-Herrmann, J., Büching, C. (eds.) FabLab: Of Machines Makers and Inventors, pp. 203–222. Transcript Publishers, Bielefeld (2013)

11. Rifkin, J.: The Third Industrial Revolution How Lateral Power is Transforming Energy, the Economy, and the World. Palgrave Macmillan, New York (2011)

12. Anderson, C.: Makers: The New Industrial Revolution. Crown Publishing Group, New York (2012)

13. Troxler, P.: Making the Third Industrial Revolution – The Struggle for Polycentric Structures and a New Peer-Production Commons in the FabLab Community. In: Walter-Herrmann, J., Büching, C. (eds.) FabLab: Of Machines, Makers and Inventors, pp. 181–198. Transcript Publishers, Bielefeld (2013)

14. Celani, G.: Digital Fabrication Laboratories: Pedagogy and Impacts on Architectural Education. Nexus Netw. J. **14**, 469–482 (2012)

15. Leach, N., Weiguo, X.: Machinic Processes: Architecture Biennial Beijing 2010. Tsinhua University, Shangai (2010)

16. Herrera, P.C.: Tecnologías Disruptivas: Programación y Fabricación en Latinoamérica. In: Proceedings of the 14th Conference of the Iberoamerican Society of Digital Graphics, SiGraDi, Bogotá, Colombia, pp. 213–216 (2010)

17. Yuan, P.F., Leach, N.: Fabricating the Future. Tongji University Press, Shangai (2012)

18. Soares, L.: EduCAAD: An X-ray of CAAD education in Brazil. In: Proceedings of the 16th Conference of the Iberoamerican Society of Digital Graphics, SiGraDi, Fortaleza, Brasil, pp. 255–258 (2012)

19. Self, M., Walker, Ch.: Making Pavilions: AA Intermediate Unit 2 2004–09. Architectural Association, London (2011)

20. Herrera, P.C.: VBScritp en la educación del arquitecto: Estrategias y métodos durante y después de la implementación In: Proceedings of the 12th Conference of the Iberoamerican Society of Digital Graphics, SiGraDi, La Habana, Cuba, 368–371 (2008)

21. Herrera, P.C.: Rhinoscripting y Grasshopper a través de sus instructores: Un estudio de Patrones y usos. In: Proceedings of the 15th Conference of the Iberoamerican Society of Digital Graphics, SiGraDi, Santa Fé, Argentina, 179–182 (2011)

22. Senske, N.: Fear of Code: An Approach to integrating Computation with Architectural Design. MSc Thesis. Massachusetts Institute of Technology (2005)

23. Domingues, J.M.: A América Latina e a modernidade contemporânea: uma interpretação sociológica, Belo Horizonte, Editora UFMG (2009)

24. Cox, C.F.: Modernidad y Postmodernidad en América Latina, Bogotá, Escala (1991)

25. Flusser, V.: Towards a Philosophy of Photography. Reaktion Books, London (2000)

26. Poerksen, B.: Ethics of enabling ethics. Cybernetics Human Knowing (Exeter: Imprint Academic) **18**(3–4), 143–149 (2011)

27. Cabral, F.J.S., Baltazar, A.P.: Por uma produção arquitetônica interativa para além do paradigma da representação: a experiência do LAGEAR. In: Anais do III ENANPARQ - 2014, São Paulo (2014)

28. Bernardo, M.V., Cabral F., J.S.: Fabricação digital e variedade fora do contexto industrial. In: Proceedings of the 18th Conference of the Iberoamerican Society of Digital Graphics: Design in Freedom, pp. 320–323 [=Blucher Design Proceedings, v.1, n.8]. Blucher, São Paulo (2014)

A New Machinecraft

A Critical Evaluation of Architectural Robots

Cristina Nan[(✉)]

HafenCity University, Hafencity, Germany
cristina_nan87@yahoo.com

Abstract. This paper intends to develop an understanding of the new role robotics occupy in the architectural process, from the early stage of conceptualization to the final stage of its materialization. This issue will be addressed on two levels of discourse. While the first level discusses the theoretical-philosophical framework behind the architectural integration of robots, the second investigates the resulting methodological implications on an applied research project. A critical evaluation of the use and the self-development of robots or robotic devices by architects is being aspired to. The attempt to redefine the status of the machine in general, and specifically of the robot, seeks to illustrate the robot as an active design agent.

Keywords: Robotic printing · Robotic fabrication · Construction strategy · Machinecraft

1 Introduction

This paper intends to develop an understanding of the new role robotic machines or systems occupy in the architectural process from the early stage of conceptualization to the final stage of its materialization. This issue will be addressed on two levels of discourse. While the first level discusses the theoretical-philosophical framework behind the architectural integration of robots, the second investigates the resulting methodological implications on an applied research project.

The main aim is to provide a framework for redefining the status of the robotic machine in architecture. The attempt to redefine the status of the machine in general, and specifically of the robot, seeks to illustrate the robot as an active design agent, which influences the whole architectural process.

2 Theoretical Framework

The last 25 years of architectural development have been significantly influenced by the profound digitalization of the discipline. At the beginning of the digital turn the main fascination with the new digital tools was primarily focusing on digitally influencing and controlling form generation. Digital fabrication tools were not completely excluded

© Springer-Verlag Berlin Heidelberg 2015
G. Celani et al. (Eds): CAAD Futures 2015, CCIS 527, pp. 422–438, 2015.
DOI: 10.1007/978-3-662-47386-3_23

from the agenda of interest, but only after the first wave of form generation exuberance faded away, architects turned their focused attention also towards the means of digital fabrication and production. During this time span, the interest moved from multi-axial milling machines to laser cutters then to 3D-printers and reaching finally the robotic arms. A look at academic research pavilions suffices to read this development. The academic student pavilions mirror best the implementation order of the digital fabrication tools and act as an indicator for the shift of the technological attention allocated by professionals.

The implementation of the digital tools in the two areas of form generation and the making of form led to vast polemical discussions over the impact and the relevance the new processes will have over time. During these debates a multitude of paradigm shifts have been evoked, the shift from mass production to mass customization, the shift from the analog to the digital just to mention a few. But leaving aesthetic and form-orientated debates aside and concentrating on the constructive substance of architecture, the most relevant shift was probably *'the paradigm shift in the production conditions of architecture'* (Gramazio et al. 2014a) caused by the new generation of digital fabrication tools. Founding the first worldwide architectural fabrication laboratory to include robots, Gramazio and Kohler argue that the division between the design process, understood as an intellectual act, and the fabrication process will be easily overcome through the use of robots by architects, as robots directly involve the architect to all processes (Gramazio et al. 2014b). It is important to not only concentrate on the use of these technologies and their implementation in the fabrication of architectural elements, but also to observe the changes which deviate, on an operational and structural level, from the use of robotic machines as direct tools of the architect. Gramazio and Kohler have coined the term of digital materiality, which in their opinion *'is generated through the integration of construction and programming in the design process'* (Gramazio et al. 2014a). Digital materiality is a relevant concept of which architects and designer involved in digital fabrication techniques need to be aware of, as is brings the aspect of material and the new type of materiality which results from digital manufacturing, into the architectural discourse. It underlines the connection between material and tool and the fact that a any type of discourse on one of this topics must implicitly involve the other. Through the means of digital fabrication tools, mostly the robot, the relationship of the architect to the used material alters significantly, as *'digital materiality leads us from the design of static forms to the design of material processes. [...] We design the relationships and sequences that inhabit architecture and that merge as its physical manifestation.'* (Gramazio and Kohler 2008).

One of the biggest advantages of the insertion of the robot in the architectural practice is the omission of an intermediary agent between architect and the fabrication tool. The architect himself is in control of the robot, by defining a set of instructions. By observing the way of evolution of today's robots and their integration in the design, material and constructive processes, the concept of architecture machines (Negroponte 1969) seems to be reactivated. In his article dedicated to the theorization of such machines, Nicholas Negroponte demonstrates a foresight in terms of defining the role such robots can take. Bearing mind that the written article dates from 1969, architecture machines are not seen as mere tools, but as a almost equal protagonists:

'the partnership of an architect with such a device is a dialogue between two intelligent systems - man and the machine - which are capable of producing an evolutionary system.' (1969, pp. 9).

The variability and variation of the design and thus of the design series is a topic which has been often evoked in architecture (Lynn 1998). Digital fabrication tools and mass customization guarantee the unproblematic buildability of various design series. The variability of the machine according to a specific project would represent the next step. A move towards this direction was already taken by using robotic arms. A second approach consists in leaving the idea of the non-specific robotic arm aside and instead developing for every project customizable robots or machines, as project specific tools, which are able to react specifically to the multifarious constraints of the project. This is where the self-developed term *machinecraft* ties in. Machinecraft describes the ability of the architect to be involved in machine development, adapting and customizing machines according to design and material requirements.

Thus, besides controlling the design, material and informational processes, the architect would be also in charge of designing machine devices and the corresponding robotic strategies. Apart from being the operator of the machine, he would also be to a certain extent its inventor. By involving the architect in the development of machine systems, he sets a bidirectional process in motion: the adaptation of the design to the machine, and of the machine to the design.

The architectural theorist Mario Carpo suggests in his book *The Alphabet and the Algorithm* the existence of two main paradigm which describe the profile and work method of the architect: the paradigm of Brunelleschi and the paradigm of Alberti. The paradigm of Brunelleschi, an Italian architect mostly active in Florence, depicts the architect as a master-builder, closely working with craftsmen and who handles equally all aspects of building. Design, material, craft, fabrication processes, all of these are supervised and coordinated by him. Opposed to this, the paradigm of Alberti, a coeval Italian humanist from Rome, understands the role of the architect as a purely intellectual one, separated from the processes of construction and the craftsmanship. Following this concept, the architect's occupation finishes with the delivery of a complete set of plans, which describe in detail the appearance of a building. These plans shall be delivered to the construction group, whose whole purpose lies in achieving the depicted image of the building, as shown on the architect's plans. The way of achieving this, for instance construction details and the underlying way of fabrication, are irrelevant to the architect. While the first paradigm is based on the idea of unification, the second paradigm is based on the notion of intellectual separation. Carpo arguments that through the digitalization of architecture, so the apparition of CAD and CAM technologies, which are digitally based upon each other, the architect moves towards the paradigm of the master-builder (2011, pp. 63).

So the multidisciplinarity of the discipline would be once again extended in the spirit of the master-builder's paradigm after Brunelleschi (Carpo 2011). The architect would be the organizer of a conceptual strategy which covers the areas of design, material, structure and machine development. The forgotten relationship between the architect and the machine as an invented tool of fabrication would be revitalized. Like this the link between the design, the image of what is to be constructed, and the making of the materialization of this image is being reinforced.

3 Machinecraft

In order to redefine the importance and relevance of the machine, including robots, for the whole of the design and fabrication processes in the discipline of architecture, the author presents the theoretical concept of **machinecraft**.

The idea of understanding machine engineering as an integral part of the architectural profession is not a new concept, though it might have fallen into oblivion for a long time. Already Vitruvius, considered to be the spiritual father of architecture, stated that the discipline of architecture is formed by three main parts: the art of building, gnomonics, meaning the art of constructing sundials and machine building. In his "De Architecture Libri Decem" Vitruvius completely dedicates the last book of this series to the theme of building and developing needed construction machines, in order to facilitate the building process (1987, pp. 30). The Roman practitioner and theorist recognizes the crucial importance for the architect of controlling the tools and means of fabrication and the best way of achieving this, is by being actively implicated in their making. Based on this historical ground, the relationship between architecture and the machine as a fabrication tool has been reinvestigated, a process which led to the development of the concept of machinecraft.

The new term machinecraft, coined by the author of this paper, is a juxtaposition of the words 'machine' and 'craft', two words which are antagonistic. Machine refers to an automated process, while craft rather relates to manual ones.

Machine describes a mechanically working device, designed by man to carry out a task in order to simplify or completely delete an assignment from his or her task list. Machines operate by conducting a series of predefined operations and following exact instructions, thus being in general considered as high precision tools. Craft on the other hand describes a way of working, a profession of its own. The word craft designates the human as the main driver, which will revert to the use of tools or machine to support his undertaking. The activities of craftsmanship are based on acquired skills, experience and intuition, the last resulting from the ability to anticipate. Craftsmanship relies on the detailed control of the deployed tools and the explicit understanding of the interaction between tool and material. Adequately using tools and material, understanding material logics and applying them to the design logics are working methods which define the work of craftsmen.

The concept of machinecraft intends to combine the two operational ways which are being represented by its word composition. Machinecraft describes the process of developing a fabrication strategy which satisfies the requirements of design, material and machine parameters. It is based on a closed informational circuit in which design, material and machine information constantly complement and influence each other. Machinecraft addresses the ability to extend the area of control over the machine, just like a craftsman controls his tools, this meaning to be able to manipulate the technical, mechanical configuration of a machine, in order to attune it to material and design requirements. This manipulation can be done in two ways. If in possession of advanced engineering skills, the change of the machine configuration can be done actively by the user, in this case the architect. In the second case of highly complex systems, the adaptation of machine configuration will be achieved by collaborating with mechanical engineers or the machine developers and giving indications to how and why the mechanistic operating mode should be changed. This last step can be only done, if a preliminary examination and understanding of the operational system has been done, so that the implications which result from conducted changes consort with the desired outcome.

The concept of machinecraft is rooted in the assumption, that just as architects gradually engage in the customization of design software through scripting, in the development of customized materials or material systems (Menges 2008) in order to increase the optimization and effectiveness of both design and making, the same should be valid for their engagement with customizing themselves machines. Using material properties, simulation data as valid parameters of design is the state of the art, the same approach should be followed in terms of the fabrication tools: interpreting the robot, more broadly the machine, as a design agent. In order to avoid misunderstandings on the level of semantics, it is important to state that, in the context of this paper, the word machine is used as a collective term, succeeding the following dictionary definition: '*a mechanically, electrically, or electronically operated device for performing a task*'. (Merriam-Webster 2014) No other technology or machine type lends itself better to fulfilling this purpose than robots. Representing non-specific fabrication devices, industrial robotic arms constitute ideal customizable machines, as they can be equipped with any end piece, which seems fit to the user. Additionally supported by the fast spreading of the maker movement, desktop fabrication tools and open source communities, the self-development of robots becomes extensively accessible to non-professionals (Anderson 2013).

Tools of fabrication are subject to a set of technical limitations, which the architect has to consider and respect in his design processes in order to assure the practicability of his proposal. The concept of machinecraft represents a break with former paradigms because it entitles the architect to overcome the limitations of the machine by being able to constantly and flexibly move these boundaries according to the specific needs of a project. By disposing of knowledge in the field of machine engineering, this represents the main and most valuable opportunity which arises from the use of robots.

Concluding, the introduction of the concept of machinecraft intends to point out at the potential which arises from the integration of robots in the architectural process. The importance of holistic fabrication strategies, not just singular processes, developed by architects, holds the potential to achieve a profound reconnection on multiple layers between design and fabrication, which are still often handled as consecutive, self-enclosed phases. A beneficial secondary effect would lie in the increase of control level for the architect.

The Role of the Machine Placed in a Historical Context. Following this argumentation, from a historical point of view a number of important moments can be enumerated which illustrate the importance and the role played by the ability of the architect to be directly involved in the development of machines. Using tools or machines as part of the fabrication process represents the most common practice. The inherent nature of this activity implies that the architect is bound to the technical limitations of the employed tools or machines. Whatever the technical boundaries of these are.

To better demonstrate the intention behind the concept of machinecraft, two historical examples will be offered as to exhibit the sometimes conditional relationship
between architecture and machine engineering. Looking at the historical development
of the architectural discipline two time periods stand out pertaining to the role and impact
the architect's comprehension and inclusion in the developing and construction of
machines might have. At the break between what is considered in more general terms
the middle ages and the Renaissance, a generation of master builders started to increasingly devote time and attention to the matter of machine invention. These diverse efforts
culminated in terms of the invention of construction site machines in the endeavors of
particularly one Italian representative known as Fillippo Brunelleschi. The master-
builder Brunelleschi was assigned with the construction of the Florentine dome, a
construction requiring a span of approximately 40 m (Jesberg 1996, pp. 51). To better
understand the amplitude of the Florentine ambitions, Fanelli states that since the
building of the Roman Pantheon such a span was unequaled and since then an attempt
to build cupola with a similar diameter had not been undertaken (1988, pp. 11). Considering these circumstances Brunelleschis design for the cupola and the realization of it
depended on the ability to develop the needed construction strategy which covered a
suitable design, building machines and material knowledge. This idea and the role
machine development played in the endeavor is best expressed by Paolo Galluzzi when
he makes the following remark:

> "Perhaps the most striking feature of Brunelleschi's construction machines is the close inter-
> relationship between their structure and the worksite's operating requirements and physical
> characteristics. One cannot help thinking that, in Brunelleschi's mind, the definition of the
> structural arrangement of the project and the design of the main construction machines
> proceeded on parallel, strictly symmetrical tracks. From the formulation of the project concept,
> he must have moved directly to defining the techniques and instruments needed to achieve it
> economically, quickly, and safely." (1997, pp. 21).

The second example to be given refers to the age of the Industrial Revolution and the
building of the Crystal Palace. While it is common knowledge that the Crystal Palace
can be considered as the architectural expression of new means of production, meaning
machines, which appeared during and through the Industrial Revolution, the wide audience is not familiar the fact that Joseph Paxton had to develop himself as well as offer
guidance and assistance in the development of a series of machines which facilitated the
construction of his pavilion. Chup Friemert describes in great detail the complexity of
processes connected to the construction of the Crystal Palace as well as the influence
and role which was played by the construction machines and necessary implication of
Paxton in these processes (Friemert 1984).

The point to be made by these two examples is that often the buildability of architectural design depends on the ability of the architect to manipulate and develop the
means of construction, so the employed machines, according to the needs of the proposed
design and by this to enlarge the possibilities these offer in terms of the construction
technique and strategy.

4   Case Study Minibuilders

The previously described theoretical approaches and constructs will be exemplified and demonstrated on an applied case study. The case study at issue, bearing the name Minibuilders, was developed as a robotic research conducted as a group project at the Institute for Advanced Architecture of Catalonia in Barcelona.[1] Minibuilders is a project which deals with architectural robotics and the development of a robotic fabrication strategy based on the use of a multiple robotic system which uses a material distribution system similar to the current 3D-printing.

4.1   State of Research

The following presented technologies and approaches represent variations of additive manufacturing techniques developed in the field of architecture. The three project are representative examples of the ongoing attempt to implement the concept of rapid prototyping and robotics as viable fabrication methods in architecture. During the research phase of the Minibuilders, these projects were viewed with a detailed attention regarding their underlying processes and methodological approaches.

4.2   Variable Property Rapid Prototyping

The work and research of Neri Oxman at the MediaLab of the Massachusetts Institute of Technology had a strong impact on the layout and development of the project. Oxman engages in a holistic approach, developing a strategy which covers and intrinsically unites the processes of design and fabrication: variable property modeling (VPM) and variable property rapid prototyping (VPRP). Starting from biological examples, such as wood, shells or antlers, she sets the observation focus on material properties, material formation on micro and macro-levels, material distribution, and their interdependence on functional factors. Following the example of highly optimized natural material distribution, Oxman explains as follows her methodology and approach:

> *'Variable property modelling is investigated as a theoretical and technical framework by which to model, analyze and fabricate objects with graduated properties designed to correspond to multiple and continuously varied functional constraints. In order to implement this approach as a fabrication process, a novel fabrication technology, termed - variable property rapid prototyping has been developed, designed and patented.'* (2011, pp. 16).

Through this technology, Oxman proposes to move away from the comparable simplistic approach of structural reinforcement, which is being executed only on a macro-level and to start the process of structural and functional optimization on the material micro-level: *'VPRP [...] offers gradation control of materials within one 3D print with the aim of increasing mechanical efficiency and reducing energy inputed.'* (2010, pp. 4) At the current state, VPRP is a technology which is mainly appropriate

---

[1] Further detailed information on the framework of the project can be found at the end of the paper, at the section Acknowledgements.

for the scale of industrial design objects and not yet applicable for the construction site. One reason lies in the use of resins as construction material, while the second is connected to the size of the used machine. The chaise longue named 'Beast', designed and fabricated by using VPM and VPRP, consists of 32 separate pieces which required a post-production assembly. In this way the size of the machine depicts a considerable limitation to itself.

Opposite to the approach of Oxman, two further showcases must be named in the context of robotics and 3D-printing technologies in architecture: D-Shape and Contour Crafting. Both technologies solely engage with the fabrication stage.

4.3 D-Shape

Developed by the inventor Enrico Dini, D-Shape represents a fabrication process which is very similar to general 3D-printing technologies which are based on a horizontal layer-by-layer material depositing system. For this technology a custom-made material was developed, consisting of sand and a mineral binder. The result is similar to artificial sandstone. Other than the resin and plastic composites used at other 3D-printing technologies, the custom-made material of D-Shape seems to implicate considerable benefits in terms of its sustainability and material resistance. The developer describes the material as having:

> '[…] a resistance and traction much superior to Portland Cement, so much so that there is no need to use iron to reinforce the structure. This artificial marble is indistinguishable from real marble and chemically it is one hundred percent environmentally friendly.' (Dini 2014).

Thus the most beneficial aspect of this technology lies in the development of a sustainable and ecological construction material. While other the developers of other similar additive technologies concentrate their efforts on solely the technology itself and rely on the use of existing materials, which mostly aren't neither suitable for big scale construction nor sustainable, Dini simultaneously addresses the material problem and offers a viable solution for it. Contrary to VPRP, D-Shape proposes an undifferentiated material depositing system and can be considered a scaled-up version of an industrial 3D-printer. The printing frame represents a ground surface of 6 × 6 m with a height of 1 m. The printing volume of D-Shape is a multiple of the one of a Connex500 multi-material printer, deployed for VPRP purposes. Regardless of its increased printing area and the deployed material, which is suitable for structural purposes, no large scale architectural structure has yet been constructed with this technology. The developer indicates that future steps will follow in employing D-Shape for the development of a construction system (Jakupovic 2013, pp. 87).

4.4 Contour Crafting

Prof. Behrokh Khoshnevis, head of the Center for Rapid Automated Fabrication Technologies (CRAFT) at the University of Southern California developed the technology of contour crafting (CC), defined as:

'a method of layered manufacturing (LM) process that uses polymer, ceramic slurry, cement, and a variety of other materials and mixes to build large scale objects with smooth surface finish.' (Khoshnevis et al. 2006, pp. 302).

Other than the two previously showcased projects, CC represents a fabrication method which implements the 3D-printing technology at the scale of architecture. The technology is designed to print structures of large dimensions and distinguishes itself by taking various aspects of the construction site into account, which are neglected by most comparable projects. Besides offering a wide material range, from smart concrete to ceramics, it offers automated solutions for the integration of reinforcement elements, plumbing, electrical wiring and even tiling (Khoshnevis 2004) Compared to D-Shape, CC does not only represent a scaled 3D printer which keeps its technical attributes, but it further enlarges the technological complexity in accordance to the intricate demands of architecture.

The three presented technologies showcase the different approaches, architects, and builders can represent, in the attempt to integrate the 3D printing technology in the architectural construction practice. While VPRP focuses on the parallel development of both a design and fabrication strategy, which transforms the fabrication tool into an active design parameter, D-Shape concentrates on simultaneous machine-material development and CC illustrates the ambition of developing a robotic fabrication strategy which satisfies the procedural demands of the construction site. These ongoing endeavors exemplify research models which carry out an in depth examination of a technology which was non-specific to architecture and the attempt to implement it in a beneficial way into the construction discipline.

4.5 Project Agenda

The main aim of the project consists in the development of a robotic fabrication strategy which is suitable for the on-site construction use and offers additional substantial benefits to existing technologies.

Prior to starting to develop a precisely detailed project agenda, the first step of the research consisted in collecting data about the current utilization of robotics and the appendant employed materials. A multitude of diverse robotic technologies, most of which originating from car design, ship building and aircraft industry, were investigated. Close attention was given to the academic field, as it offers a higher variety of experimental robotic applications. Another centre of interest concentrated on 3D printing technology and its architectural applications. As a second step, the collected data of multiple case studies was analyzed and evaluated, in due consideration of predefined comparative criteria.

Subsequently the four following limitations of robotic arms were identified as main impediments in achieving a more complete implementation of robotics into the applied field of architecture:

- Limited reaching area.
- Limited mobility. In order to extend the reaching distance, robotic arms need to be moved on tracks or placed on moving platforms, which implies the input of additional effort and the creation of an infrastructure.

- Weight and size. The average weight of an industrial robot arm amounts to approx. 600 kg. This weight can represent an impediment in terms of fast and flexible motion. On the construction site it represents an additional load which needs to be taken into account. The size of industrial robots corresponds to their weight, so that they can be considered as large-scale fabrication tool. A restricted accessibility can derive out of this.
- Restrained range of application. Excepting very few examples, such as the ICD/ITKE fibre-woven pavilion 2013/14, where the robot engages in a continuous construction workflow which results in a finished pavilion, robot arms are normally used to perform only parts of the fabrication, construction or assembly processes. Therefore, if we look at the entirety of building processes, they rather represent auxiliary, supporting tools assigned with secondary activities.

The identified disadvantages, enumerated in this list, represent features which can be interpreted as such from the builder's standpoint, having in mind the construction site. In the context of their area of use, such as performing at an assembly line, these features represent high-value assets.

Resulting from the afore detailed analysis and the elaborated determining factors, the research group concluded on the following three objectives, as detailed below, to be covered by the developed project:

- The main set goal is defined as developing a robotic strategy which covers the construction process as a whole and is designed for on-site use.
- The second requirement aims at technical specifications regarding the aspect of scale. Other than industrial robot arms or building site equipment, the developed machines should exhibit the following features: lightweight, small size and autonomous mobility. Satisfying these demands leads to flexible, easy maneuverable machines. Yet, the reduced size and weight should impose no limitation to still being able to construct normal scaled structures.
- Sustainability in relation to material usage represents the third set goal. Taking into account the general bias towards the non-standard curvilinear designs, the decision was taken to focus on offering a solution for fabrication challenges which derive from such geometries. Building curvilinear shapes often implies the use of an on-site scaffolding, an elaborate production of casting moulds or high figures of material offcuts. Thus material usage, energy footprints and labour time can be reduced, just by developing a technology which is not reliant on the use of scaffolding or moulds.

4.6   Robotic Construction Strategy

Preliminary it is important to state that all focus and effort have been invested in the developing of an operational construction methodology. Therefore, this paper is concentrating on the attempt to highlight the relevance of self-developed robots and the importance of the interrelation between design-material-machine. Due to this approach, profound technical details concerning aspects of mechanical engineering or programming will not be described extensively. Following the same reasoning, the design depicted in the following pictures is irrelevant in terms of its formal aesthetics and was deliberately kept minimal.

Fig. 1. Minibuilders. From left to right: Grip robot, foundation robot, vacuum robot.

To meet the previously mentioned requirements a robotic strategy for on-site fabrication was developed. The strategy is predicated on the development of a series of mobile robots, which can act independently from one another and thus fulfill separate functional demands. The three developed machines (Fig. 1) with their built-in technology represent a hybrid betweens robotics and 3D printing: while the mechanic specifications corresponds to the ones of robots, the integrated material deposition system correlates in its procedural features to the functioning of 3D printers. The drafted strategy relies on dividing the on-site construction processes into three phases, according to functional necessities. The three phases are consecutive and each correlates with the use of a different robot.

The first robot, the foundation robot, to come into operation is responsible for raising up the first ten to fifteen layers which form the foundation of the future structure (Fig. 2). Subsequently, after the foundation is finished, the second robot continues depositing the following layers and finalizes the design. Whereas the foundation robot is capable of moving on the ground, the second robot, named grip robot, needs to be manually positioned on top of the finished foundation layers. According to the task it needs to fulfill, the grip robot is designed as a type of climber robot. After being placed in its position, the grip robot, equipped with a suitable climbing mechanism, continues with the successive deposition of the layers. As the deployed material is a fast hardening two-component resin system and the grip robot features two heating devices, which if activated, reduce the curing time, the extruded layers can accurately set on time and thus ensure structural stability and support for the grip robot to continue its movement. The grip robot is the robot which completes the form and which is responsible for the main construction task.

Fig. 2. Minibuilders connected to industrial extruder on the construction site. From left to right: Foundation robot, close up of grip robot, grip robot finishing structure.

As both the foundation and the grip robot deposit horizontal layers, any resulting structure, independent of its shape, will exhibit a restricted structural stability. Naturally, the cause of this lies in the absence of vertical reinforcement. In order to counteract this effect and to offer an increased structural stability, vertical layers along the horizontal ones must be added. Concluding, the third phase seeks to address this problem and deals with the construction of the earlier mentioned reinforcement layers. This stage is based on the utilization of the vacuum robot. Whereas the foundation and grip robots follow a horizontal line of movement, the vacuum robot is designed for ensuring a vertical motion. As indicated by its name, the robot creates a vacuum between himself and the surface of the structure in order to be able to advance vertically. Similar to its predecessor, also this robot needs to be manually placed on the structure. It then moves along the structure, by following predefined paths. These pathways originate from a previous, detailed structural analysis of the design. They derive from force flow lines and represent abstractions of these lines, which were simplified for printing purposes. After the completion of this last layer, design and construction process can be considered as finalized.

4.7 Material Supply and Depositing Strategy

All three robots are connected to an external, industrial extruder which contains two buckets filled with a custom-made, two-component resin system. The custom material was developed simultaneously and in accordance with the robots. In this case, robots and material are intrinsically connected to one another. Information on the material behavior, which was gained from conducting a series of material experiments, operated as determining factor concerning the mechanical development of the robots. Material viscosity, mixing ratio and curing times would influence the extrusion rates, movement speed up to the physical elaboration of the robots.

During the extrusion, the two-component system is being mixed together and then deposited as consecutive layers by the robots. Being a resin based system, after its mixing, the chemical reactions induce the curing of the material. Depending on the layer thickness, the outside weather conditions (temperature and humidity) and the adding of an external heat source, the curing time can vary or be deliberately influenced. Curved surfaces can be easily achieved without the use of a supporting structure. This was solved by exploiting the material behavior of the developed resin system. The adhesion between the consecutive layers is so high, that even curved elements with an overhang can be printed (Fig. 3).

Fig. 3. From left to right: Grip robot finishing structure, vacuum robot moving vertically and depositing reinforcement layers, printed curved wall element.

The applied robotic printing strategy and the operating mode of conventional 3D printing devices are similar in nature, but differ in so far as the way of the material depositing is concerned. A diverse range of different 3D printing processes exists, starting from fused deposition modeling to selective laser sintering. All these processes are based on printing consecutive parallel cross-sections of the model. The grip robot discussed here follows a slightly different material depositing strategy. It deposits the layers as a continuous spiral and not as a sequence of parallel cross-section layers. This means that the finished design model is processed by a custom-made script which redefines the shape that is to be constructed as a continuous spiral.

4.8   Benefits and Limitations

Taking into account that the project Minibuilders was developed as case study holding the ambition of representing a proof of concept of the adequacy of an independent and lightweight multiple robotic system for the on-site use. The most valuable achievement lies in the coherent development of a fabrication strategy, which unifies in a reasonable way robotics and 3D-printing for architectural purposes. The project is not predicated on the up-scaling of technologies from other disciplines and then in retrospect searching for adequate applications. Instead it is based on a problem-solving approach, mainly orientating itself after specific observations and architectural requirements. But besides achieving these objectives, by being an experimental project it exhibits a series of limitations.

The used material is a resin-based composite and as such not appropriate for a large scale use in the building industry. Epoxy resins are associated with a number health risks if the user is exposed to large amounts, from causing irritations to possible intoxications, in case of extreme exposure. Simultaneously the used material is not biodegradable and because of its composition not sustainable. In consequence, for further investigations also on a larger scale, a different material variety should be exploited.

Regarding the technological aspects a number of constraints respectively further development areas can be enumerated. In conducted experiments with the robots, curved wall elements with an overhang were achieved. However, a completion of a full ceiling, though in theory possible, was never undertaken. During the construction of the experimental structure, the climber and vacuum robot were placed manually on the structure, due to the lack of a local positioning system. As the shape of the printed structure is from a geometrical point of view simplistic and symmetric, manual positioning did not represent an issue. This might change in the case of more complex geometries. Also another aspect lies in adapting the steering of the minibuilders in order to master even very narrow and steep types of curvature.

4.9 Future Fields

A first step in the broader development of the showcased project would lie in the refinement of functional subdivisions according to the necessitated architectural elements. For now the foundation, walls and ceiling as one unit and structural reinforcement were addressed. Extending the list, for instance by adding windows, differentiating between exterior and interior elements, would lead to an increased number of specialized robots.

One further advancement of the technology could lie in not only extending the types of robots but also the material range. Besides the simple extension, a refinement of the depositing strategy is worth pursuing in order to reach a high level of optimization according to structural and functional requirements. For accomplishing this goal Variable-Property Rapid Prototyping (Oxman 2010) could serve as an indicative paradigm. This technology relies on the use of multiple materials, which can be variantly deposited, ideally influencing even individual material properties, such as density, according to the specific structural or functional needs of the printed area.

Another desirable and beneficial enhancement of the technology could lie in extending this additive manufacturing procedure by equipping the robots with the capability of simultaneously adding and subtracting material, so that small construction or material deposition errors can be rectified in real time.

Autonomous architectural robotics is still in the early stages of development. In terms of architecture, judging by the number of academic on going research projects, this field depicts one of today's main areas of research and focus. Efforts are being made to further implement these technologies in architecture and by this to catch up with other related industrial fields, such as transportation or industrial design, where robots represent an essential component and activity without them is unconceivable.

5   Conclusions

The described project with its underlying construction strategy depicts schematically both a work approach and a procedural method which are in an early beginning stage. Nevertheless, it illustrates the benefits of the involvement of the architect in the assembly of a comprehensive strategy which covers aspects of design, fabrication and machine construction.

In terms of the educational benefits, this project shows that instead of educating students to only make use of new technologies and to try to integrate them in their endeavors by artificially making space for questionable applications, a reversed approach can be followed. Future architects can be encouraged and empowered to actively participate at the development of technology according to specific project needs or in order to offer solutions for problems which are from the architect's perspective commonly encountered while making use of certain devices, machines or technologies. This process of educating architecture students in the field of mechanical engineering and programming may be at its start, but as demonstrated before, a tradition of dealing with machine engineering can be traced in architecture. If the historic precedents will be admitted as indicators for the future potential, then a fruitful expansion of the technological boundaries of architecture can be expected.

Engaging the architect into robotic development, he can implement and adjust fabrication or construction strategies which are fully adapted to architectural specific needs. Being involved in the mechanical development of the construction tools asks for a complete understanding and participation of the architect in the material research. By a detailed understanding of the material and through the collaboration with material scientists, it should be possible to generate modified materials according to the specific needs and demands of both the design and the machine, so that they best fulfill the requirements of the developed construction strategy. The machine turns into a design agent of equal importance with other parameters which influence the design and its materialized quality. Through the integration of self-developed machines or robotic devices as an autonomous design agent in the architectural process a complete liberalization and democratization of the discipline could be achieved (Anderson 2013).

As mentioned before, industrial robots are non-specific fabrication tools. This means that the architect can decide over the type of effector which will be deployed and he can also decide over the operating way of the robot, meaning that the sequence of executed movements and fabrication steps can be exactly defined by the architect. Thus through the use of robots and the ability of manipulating them, the architect can overcome the limitations of fabrication tools and not be restricted by their limitations. The effort of exerting a complete control over the tools of fabrication facilitates the development of an intelligent and sustainable fabrication strategy, which can fully meet the specific need of a project without obliging the builder to engage with unnecessary compromises on the level of both design and construction. This leads to the acquired competence of the designer to not only create shape and space but to also develop a fabrication strategy which respects design requirements, material logics and machine logics.

The high level of skepticism regarding the dematerialization of architecture through the extensive use of digital fabrication tools proves itself to be superfluous. Gramazio and Kohler argue in benefit of the deep impact robotic arms had, claiming *"that the robot engenders a fundamental alteration in the discipline's constructive understanding of itself"* (2014a, pp. 182). Following the line of argumentation initiated by Gramazio and Kohler, the robot is seen as a catalyst between architecture and construction, which strengthens further this relationship. If the potential of the digital is understood correctly and applied in a suitable way, the digital can lead to the reinforcement of the material and constructive nature of architecture. Through the use of robots or robotic machines a convergence of architecture and a new type of handcraft is being facilitated.

A common approach lies in using technology from other industrial fields such as the automotive industry, aircraft or shipbuilding and undertaking big efforts to implement the chosen technology into architecture. Such undertakings can only result in limited success. The intrinsic way the technology or the machine work, its underlying operating logics, needs to be understood by the designer or architect, whose projects are going to be built with it. By doing so, the designer allows himself to overlap the operational logic of the machine, with the operational logic of the developed design and the selected material range. Thus the architect can actively influence and even coordinate the meaningful and reasonable adaptation of the technology to best support his design.

Yet there has to be considered that as projects evolve in their size a boundary is set to the architects involved in handling alone all of the aspects of programming and machine development. But by possessing the basic knowledge over these aspects, just as in the presented cases of Brunelleschi and Joseph Paxton, the aim consists in enabling the architects to play a decisive, productive and competent part in the unrolling of these processes, to guide them and to be able to formulate the correct and appropriate demands towards a team of specialist. The interdisciplinary work would be reinforced and the architect could take the lead. The main competence of the architect remains in developing spatial programs according to a wide series of aspects and developing construction strategies and organizational structures which imply a complete control and manipulation of the fabrication information and corresponding tools.

This paper pleads for a more technology orientated occupational profile of the architect. By acquiring profound knowledge on the technical functioning of used machines, including here robots, 3D-printers and others, a beneficial extension of the area of expertise, influence and control can be achieved. The architect's role should not just be limited at operating machines and accepting their performance as a given, but in the case of adequacy, necessity and usefulness demanding it, to be able to be constructively involved in the mechanical development.

The following quote by Kieran and Timberlake summarizes most adequately the potential which can derive from the simultaneous reengagement of the architect with different fields of specialization:

'While we cannot return to the idea of the masterbuilder embodied in a single person, the architect can force the integration of several spun-off disciplines or architecture - construction, product engineering and material science - all with the aim of reuniting substance with intent.'
(2003, pp.)

Acknowledgements. This paper and the presented theoretical part relies on the author's PhD thesis, completed under the guidance of Professor Dott. Arch. Paolo Fusi, conducted at the HafenCity University Hamburg and funded by the DFG, the German Research Foundation.

Minibuilders, the here described research project, was developed during the Open Thesis Fabrication program 2013/2014 at the Institute for Advanced Architecture of Catalunya. The OTF program is constructed on the idea of offering a suitable academic framework and guidance for its participants to conduct individual or group research according to a self-imposed research agenda. Minibuilders was conducted by a group consisting of six international researchers, under the guidance of Prof. Areti Markopoulou and with the help of multiple staff members of the mentoring institute. Further information on the individual members of the research team, the extended academic support, sponsorship and collaborators can be viewed on the official webpage dedicated to this project: http://iaac.net/printingrobots/.

References

Anderson, C.: Makers: The New Industrial Revolution. Random House Business, London (2013)

Carpo, M.: The Alphabet and the Algorithm (Writing Architecture). MIT Press, Cambridge (2011)

Dini, E.: http://www.d-shape.com/tecnologia.htm (2014). Accessed 10 Dec 2014

Fanelli, G.: Brunelleschi. Scala, Florence (1988)

Friemert, C.: Die Gläserne Arche. Kristallpalast London 1851 und 1854. Prestel Verlag, München (1984)

Galluzzi, P.: Renaissance engineers from Brunelleschi to Leonardo da Vinci: [Florence, Palazzo Strozzi, June 22, 1996–January 6, 1997]. GIUNTI, Florence (1997)

Gramazio, F., Kohler, M., Willmann, J.: The Robotic Touch: How Robots Change Architecture. Park Books, Zürich (2014a)

Gramazio, F., Kohler, M., Willmann, J.: Authoring robotic processes. In: Gramazio, F., Kohler, M. (eds.) Made by Robots: Challenging Architecture at a Large Scale, Architectural Design. Wiley, London (2014b)

Gramazio, F., Kohler, M.: Digital Materiality in architecture. Lars Müller Publishers, Zürich (2008)

Jakupovic, A.: Large Scale Adddtive Manufacturing. Department of Engineering and Architecture, University of Triest, Trieste (2013)

Jesberg, P.: Die Geschichte der Ingenierbaukunst aus dem Geist des Humanismus. Deutsche Verlags-Anstalt, Stuttgart (1996)

Khoshnevis, B., Hwang, D., Yao, K., Yeh, Z.: Mega-scale fabrication by contour crafting. Int. J. Ind. Syst. Eng. 1(3), 301–320 (2006)

Khoshnevis, B.: Automated construction by contour crafting - related robotics and information technologies. J. Autom. Constr. Spec. Issue (The best of ISARC 2002) 13(1), 5–19 (2004)

Kieran, S., Timberlake, J.: Refabricating Architecture: How Manufacturing Methodologies are Poised to Transform Building Construction. McGraw-Hill Professional, United States (2003)

Lynn, G.: Fold, Bodies and Blobs: Collected Essays. Lettre Volee, New York (1998)

"machine" Merriam-Webster.com 2014: http://www.merriam-webster.com/dictionary/machine (2014). Accessed 02 Dec 2014

Menges, A.: Integral Formation and Materialisation: Computational Form and Material Gestalt. In: Kolarevic, B., Klinger, K. (eds.) Manufacturing Material Effects: Rethinking Design and Making in Architecture, pp. 195–210. Routledge, New York (2008)

Negroponte, N.: Toward a theory of architecture machines. J. Archit. Educ. 23(2), 9–12 (1969)

Oxman, N.: Material-based Design Computation. http://hdl.handle.net/1721.1/59192 (2010). Accessed 10 Dec 2014

Oxman, N.: Variable property rapid prototyping. Virtual Phys. Prototyp. 6(1), 3–31 (2011)

Vitruv, M.: Baukunst. Artemis Verlag für Architektur, Zürich and München (1987)

Formal Descriptions of Material Manipulations

An Exploration with Cuts and Shadows

Benay Gürsoy[1(✉)], Iestyn Jowers[2], and Mine Özkar[3]

[1] Istanbul Bilgi University, Istanbul, Turkey
`benaygursoy@gmail.com`
[2] The Open University, Milton Keynes, UK
`i.r.jowers@open.ac.uk`
[3] Istanbul Technical University, Istanbul, Turkey
`ozkar@itu.edu.tr`

Abstract. Shape computation in design is never purely limited to visual aspects and ideally includes material aspects as well. The physicality of designing introduces a wide range of variables for designers to tackle within the design process. We present a simple design exercise realised in four stages where we physically manipulate perforated cardboard sheets as a case to make material variables explicit in the computation. The emphasis is on representing sensory aspects rather than easily quantifiable properties more suitable for simulations. Our explorations demonstrate the use of visual rules to represent actions, variables and form as well as how to control the variables to create new results, both desired and surprising, in materially informed ways.

Keywords: Material computing · Shape rules · Making

1 Introduction

Seeing is very personal and perceptual with a ubiquitous role in design. Most prominent studies on design feature its visual aspects and highlight the ambiguities in seeing as the key factor for design creativity and productivity. These studies approach design as a way of visual thinking and reasoning, often indicating an immaterial and cognitive process either separate from or prior to materialization. The "see-move-see" model of design advocated by Schön and Wiggins [1] upholds the "reflective conversation with the situation" through visual reasoning [2]. Similarly Goldschmidt [3] refers to a dialogue between "seeing that" and "seeing as" in the course of design sketching, where "seeing that is reflective criticism" and "seeing as is the analogical reasoning and reinterpretation of shapes that provokes creativity".

Pioneering studies within the new material computing research area challenge the long existing understanding of design as an immaterial and cognitive process with visual thinking in the spotlight. This research area has emerged through the extensive use of digital fabrication tools and technologies in design. Material practices commonly

© Springer-Verlag Berlin Heidelberg 2015
G. Celani et al. (Eds.): CAAD Futures 2015, CCIS 527, pp. 439–457, 2015.
DOI: 10.1007/978-3-662-47386-3_24

reappear at the centre of design activity, seeking potential effects of material information on design while aiming to define a framework where "material has the capacity to compute" [4]. The link between physical materialization and computing finds strength mostly in "advanced machine capabilities" [5]. Material-based design now is "a computational informing process that enhances the integration between structure, material, and form within the logic of fabrication technologies" [6]. This integration of "computational design, advanced simulation and robotic fabrication" considerably opens up our design spaces [7]. Moreover, form comes together with forces and material in a "new generative logic of form-finding" [8] and scholars now report on experimental design research with cutting-edge fabrication tools to show "how material information could become a generative driver rather than an afterthought in design computation" [9].

In parallel, there is a growing interest in revisiting the relation between the analogue and the digital how-tos. Thomsen & Tamke [10] discuss the "narratives of making" through the ways in which "new digital design practice introduces computational thinking into making" and "the means by which architectural practice changes as new digital tools become ubiquitous in architectural making." The knowledge embodied in crafts regarding material and process as a means of design results in new means of making with computer controlled toolsets [11]. Nevertheless, the existing literature summarized above is limited firstly in its approach to computation as the use of computational tools and technologies whereas computation encompasses reasoning in general. Secondly, although rigorous and imposed formalisms exist due to the technical interfaces with digital tools, there is a lack of computational formalism to represent the sensory aspects of working with materials. In one of the few studies that focus on filling this void, Knight & Stiny [12] propose making grammars to extend the shape grammar formalism from computations with shapes to computations with material things. They consider designing as a kind of making itself where the designer perceptually and bodily engages with materials. Suitably, shape grammar computations are a "highly sensory, action-oriented" kind of computational making where "shapes are the materials that one works with by hand and by eye" [12].

In this paper, we consider making as a personal and perceptual act of material manipulation in design with visual and haptic means rather than with numbers. We make use of shape grammars to represent the visual thinking in design and to establish sharable grounds to talk about it as a visual calculation process [13]. The distinctiveness of shape grammars over other approaches to recording and reporting visual thinking lies in its ability to handle uncertainties of seeing. In return, its rule-based approach enables the creative exploration of design spaces and generation of novel alternatives. Visual rules in shape grammars are not determinate. They support embedding. In the course of a shape computation, it is possible to see new shapes that emerge from the application of shape rules. The user can decide what shapes to see and which rules to apply. This is what makes visual calculating both "perceptual and improvisational" [12].

Along similar lines, we report in this paper ongoing research on exploring how shape grammars can extend beyond the abstract shapes that compose sketches, drawings and digital design models in CAD systems, to incorporate material shapes that have a physical and tangible existence. Theory suggests that material manipulation in design can relate and translate to shape computing, but the physicality of material introduces a range of properties beyond visual form. A key challenge lies in deciphering the causal links between interventions on the material and our shape making, so that both can be integrally represented in shape rules that support formal computation. Our main objective has been to clarify and handle the creative outcomes of the translation of material manipulations to shape computing. We postulate that we can apply shape rules creatively, as is possible when shapes are viewed as abstract visual objects, without the physical character of material forcing us to conform to highly determinate rules.

We present our arguments with reference to a particular experimentation in which sheet materials with systematically varied cuts are manipulated in specific ways. The process is short and simplistic but embodies controlled action that can be traced easily and, most importantly, embodies emerging shapes that are characteristic of design processes. In the end, we are interested in formalising the emerging shapes and the material manipulations that bring them about. We aim at formally modelling the material properties of the sheets by relying on visual rules and weight definitions according to the theory of shape grammars.

2   Formalising Material Aspects of Design

Being able to express a process in a formal way, e.g. as an algorithm, shows a deep understanding of the process [14] and the resulting formal description is useful in communicating this understanding to others. For design processes where visual thinking dominates, shape computations have been shown to provide appropriate formal descriptions that give insight on processes of shape transformations. For example, Prats et al. [15] describe how explorative sketching in a design process can be formalised according to shape rules, and Paterson [16] presents a series of studies where shape rules formalise explorative prototyping, including physical model-making. In both these works shape computations give formal descriptions of creative design processes, with a focus on the transformation of representations, and this description is then used to analyse the processes, giving insight based on objective external evidence, rather than designers' recollections of their internal thought processes. Both works exemplify practical applications of Stiny's schemas of shape computation [13], which generalise shape transformations according to a small set of possibilities. While basic, schemas are powerful, giving a high-level visual language to describe transformations of design representations.

Visual rules and schemas are well suited to design explorations involving sketches or digital models. However, they are not yet explored as modes of representations that have a physical and tangible existence. Designers' interactions with physical models, either through craft-like process of making, or via interaction with digital fabrication tools, cannot be fully described as visual interactions. The materiality of such representations introduces physical considerations imposed by the material world: the fact that orientation is not homogenous, because of gravity; the need for support material, to resist gravity; the occlusion of internal shapes by external surfaces; etc. Even though the materiality results in decisions of form, visual representations do not capture the full range of interactions that designers employ as they explore and discover the properties of material form. Instead designers use other senses to augment their visual interaction, most importantly the tactile exploration that arises from touching, lifting, and manipulating objects in space. In our exploration, we create rules with labels and weights to capture some of these aspects.

3   Case Study

We conducted a three day workshop in Istanbul Technical University with the participation of graduate level computational design students. The aim was to guide the participants to explore material manipulation in design with a computational perspective. The participants worked on two simple design related tasks. The first group of students worked with a knitting machine and systematically explored the machine knitting process. The second group of students were asked to cut slivers into sheet materials (cardboards of different thicknesses) to play with surface flexibility. Both groups were introduced to shape computing after a half day hands-on exploration working on the tasks. They were guided towards defining visual rules and weight definitions, using shape grammars to represent their shape making process of generating the cutting and knitting patterns. Afterwards, they were asked to physically explore their material samples and define a formal way to relate their shape making and interactions with the material.

All generated sets of material samples from the cutting experiments are shown in Fig. 1. In the examples shown in Fig. 1a and b the participants explored the variable

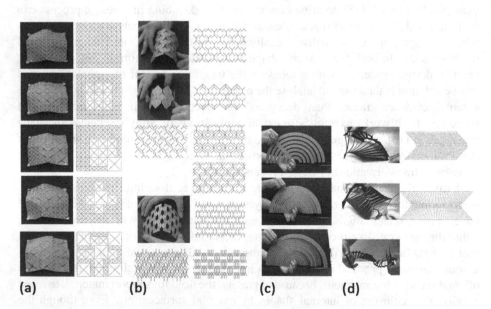

(a)   **(b)**   **(c)**   **(d)**

Fig. 1. Student work from workshop. Details of the material experiments from the knitting and cutting groups' works can be examined at http://materialcomputing.wix.com/knittingcutting.

bending capacity of cardboard by cutting repetitive patterns on planar sheets. Figure 1c shows an exploration where the flexibility of the planar surfaces under twisting motion is controlled by cutting concentric radial slits of varying density. In Fig. 1d, discrete lines cut the planar surfaces and the sequential change in the angle of the lines alters the final forms of the samples when pulled from both ends.

We have since extended the exploration in Fig. 1a to develop our approach to material computing. First, we generated our own set of cut samples for a more systematic inquiry into the variables affecting the material outcome. Our aim has been to put forth the relations between our shape computations which alternate the cut patterns and our material manipulations, and to find a formal way to correlate the two. Following the starting set of schemas for the cuts and the manipulative action (bending), we did not start with a clear design goal but engaged with the material in an exploratory manner. In the process, we observed that while the cuts have an effect on the overall flexibility of the surface, as previously explored by the participants of the workshop, they are also differentiated in light transmittance as well. Considering light as a design variable, we concentrated mainly on manipulating it with our cut sheets. We saw that variations on the cut patterns generated different shadow-light configurations. When the cut sheets are held towards a light source, different patterns emerge as light and shadow on projected surfaces. While the emergent light patterns simultaneously change with their relative position to the cut sheets, they also change with reference to the form of the surface of the cut sheets. Bending a cut sheet correspondingly changes the light-pattern. Since bending capacity depends also on the changes in material specifications (i.e. thickness of the material), same patterns cut from cardboards of different thicknesses do not bend to the same form, causing different light patterns to emerge. We systematically explored and documented these various material outcomes and take out "formally" represented our explorations with shape rules.

3.1 Shape Manipulation: Generating the Cut Patterns

In exploring the links between our shape making and our material manipulations, we have designed a systematic process with a simple set of material samples. The simplicity of the set mostly lies in the symmetry of the square shaped cut sheets with 4 fold rotation axes and 4 mirror planes. The sheets are cut with repeating symmetrical patterns which contain symmetrical shapes. The meticulous use of symmetry is to create homogeneous surfaces of which the material properties are shaped by the cut slivers. We change the variables of the cut patterns consistently. The samples obtained at the end can be explored in relation with each other, in a systematic way, according to the changes in the variables. Below, we present the shape rules and computations which generate our samples. This first set of rules also serves as a reference point for all other rules in our explorations.

Rule 1 and Rule 2 describe the division of a square shaped whole into identical parts (Fig. 2a). We can thus obtain square grids of varying sizes from an initial square. We choose to derive three specific grids for our study (Fig. 2b).

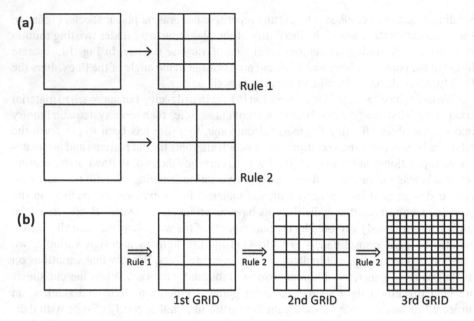

Fig. 2. (a) Rules and (b) the computation that transform the square to grids

Another rule, describes how squares transform into crossing lines (Fig. 3a). We can thus generate repetitive patterns of crossing lines based on the square grids (Fig. 3b). Rule 3 is altered with a label that changes the length of the crossing lines, and with a weight that affects the width of the crossing lines. (Fig. 3c and d) These variations of Rule 3 describe our initial systematic manipulations on the material and serve as devices of control.

By using the above four Rule 3 variations, we obtain 12 different cut patterns. We cut these samples from cardboards of three different thicknesses (0.2 mm, 0.8 mm, and 1.2 mm). We refer to the cardboard thickness as *material weight* in the rules. All of the cut patterns we obtained are shown in Fig. 4 as a systematic exploration of the effects of the variables on the material outcome.

3.2   Material Manipulations

The exploration that corresponds to a simplified design process has been realised in four stages. We physically manipulate the cut sheets in four ways in each stage. In the first, where bending is applied to observe the altering degrees of perforations and smoothness in the material, the exploration led to observing the altering degrees of light intensity on the surface. We considered this as design emergence and established a setup to observe light systematically as it goes through the perforated surfaces (Fig. 5). The simple setup is inspired by traditional shadow plays where light transmitting through the perforations of the cut sheets generates light and shadow configurations on the screen. In the following three stages, we manipulated the distance between the screen in the set up and

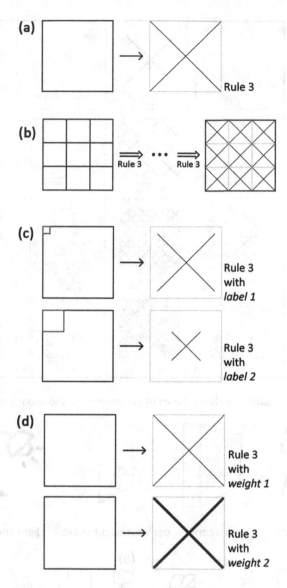

Fig. 3. (a) Rule 3 that transforms the square to a cross, (b) the computation that shows the transformation of the grid to the alternate grid of diagonal lines, and variations of Rule 3 (c) with labels and (d) with weights

the cut sheets, rotated, and layered them. These manipulations result in patterns of light on the screen. We photograph these patterns and by recognising the emergent shapes, we trace new patterns in a different medium. In these experiments, we consider light almost as a material with which we generate new patterns.

Below we identify the actions and the variables for each exploration then represent these with visual rules.

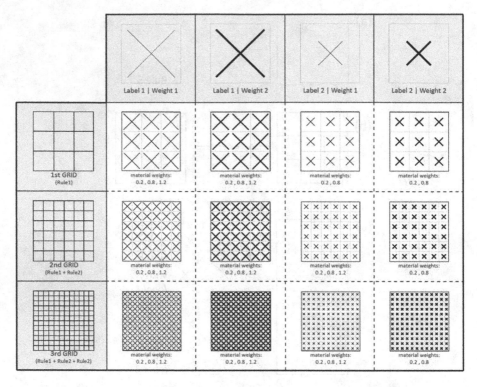

Fig. 4. The matrix that shows the set of cut patterns we use in our exploration

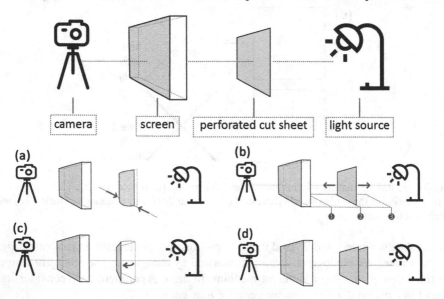

Fig. 5. The setup to observe light and the four variations of the setup in each of the four stages of the exploration: (a) by bending the cut sheets, (b) by changing the distance between the screen and the cut sheet, (c) by rotating the cut sheet, and (d) by layering.

Exploration #1

Actions: Bending.
Variables: 1. Cut patterns, 2. Material weights

For this exploration we have three rule sets: for materializing the cut patterns, for bending, and for light patterns. In the rules that materialize the cut patterns, a weight (mw) is introduced as an indicator of the thickness of the material samples (Fig. 6a). In the rules that bend the cut samples, labels are used to denote the points where the samples are held to enable bending. A weight (w1) defines the intensity of the force applied for bending. We represent this weight with a point on a gradient scale bar. The lightest colour in the middle indicates flat position, darker left parts indicate bending forwards, and darker right parts indicate bending backwards. Different weights can be introduced for left hand thumbs and right hand thumbs. Here, to symmetrically bend the cut samples, we make use of a single weight, which controls both thumbs in the same way (Fig. 6b). Lastly, we evaluate light transmittance and the last set of rules generates the visual patterns on the screen (Fig. 6c). We present in Fig. 7 various computations in which the initial abstract shape is the same. We apply to this initial shape the rules that materialize this shape, the rules that bend the materialized shape and the rules that generate light patterns, in a sequential order. Applying the same bending rule with different labels and weights generates a considerable amount of variations in the materialized shapes, resulting in variations in the light patterns as well.

Exploration #2

Actions: Moving the cut sheets on an axis perpendicular to the screen
Variables: 1. Cut patterns, 2. Distance between the screen and the cut sheet

The first exploration with bending the cut sheets shifted our design intent to manipulating the light effects. In the second exploration, without any physical intervention to the cut sheets, we explore the changes in the patterns emerging on the screen by gradually moving the cut sheets between three spots on an axis perpendicular to the screen. For this exploration we have three rule sets: for materializing the cut patterns, for generating the light patterns, and for translating the emerging light patterns to drawings. Rules for materializing the cut patterns do not require a weight to control the thickness of the material samples since the cut sheets are not physically manipulated (Fig. 8a). Labels in the set of rules that generate the light patterns denote the three spots where we place our material samples: the far left label indicating the closest distance to the screen and the far right, the farthest among the three (Fig. 8b). This transition from abstract shapes to material shapes back to abstract shapes can be observed as a generative process in the various computations we present, with a new rule that translates the light patterns to a new medium as drawings (Fig. 9).

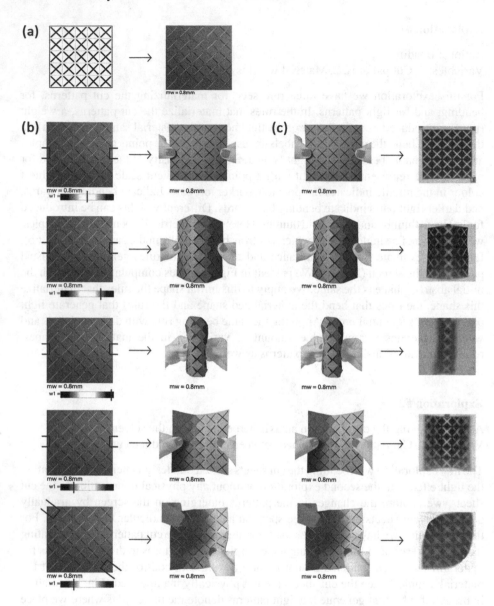

Fig. 6. Shape rules of the first exploration: (a) Rules to materialize the cut patterns. (mw) is a weight indicating the thickness of the material sample. (b) Variations of the rule that bend the material samples with labels and weights. Labels indicate the handling points for bending. (mw) and (w1) are weights. (mw) indicates the thickness of the material sample. (w1) controls the intensity of the force applied for bending. (c) Rules to generate the light patterns. Bent cut sheets generate distorted light patterns.

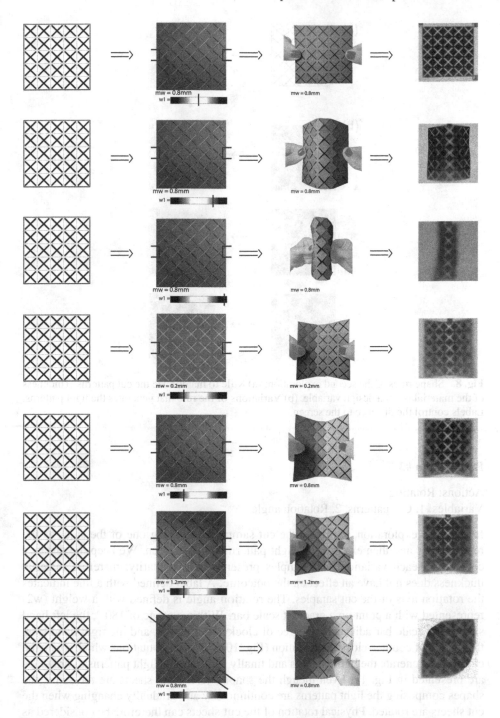

Fig. 7. The initial abstract shape common in the computations generates a considerable amount of variations of the materialized shapes (as both bent sheets and light patterns), when the labels and weights defined in the rules are changed.

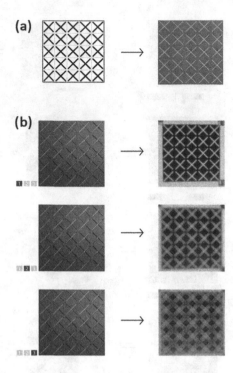

Fig. 8. Shape rules of the second exploration: (a) Rule to materialize the cut patterns. Thickness of the material is not a design variable. (b) Variations of the rule that generates the light patterns. Labels control the distance to the screen.

Exploration #3

Actions: Rotating.
Variables: 1. Cut patterns, 2. Rotation angle

In the third exploration, we rotate the cut samples by setting one of the sides as the rotation axis and then examine the light patterns on the screen. We keep the distance constant in each variation. Cut samples preserve their planarity, therefore material thickness does not have an effect on the outcome. A label defined with a line indicates the rotation axis of the cut samples. The rotation angle is defined with a weight (w2) represented with a point on a gradient scale bar. Within a range of 180 °, the left hand side of the scale bar adjusts the degree of clockwise rotation, and the right hand side, the degree of counter-clockwise rotation (Fig. 10b). The computations which rotate the cut sheets, generate the light patterns and finally translate the light patterns to drawings are presented in Fig. 11. Even though the shapes on the cut sheets are the same, the shapes composing the light patterns are continuously and gradually changing when the cut sheets are rotated. Physical rotation of the cut sheets can therefore be considered as a generative tool within the setup we present.

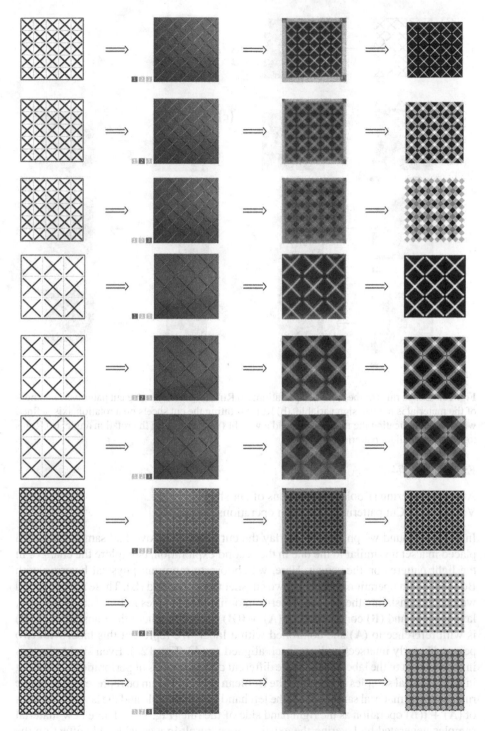

Fig. 9. The computations which show a transition from abstract shapes to material shapes, back to abstract shapes with a last rule translating the light patterns to drawings.

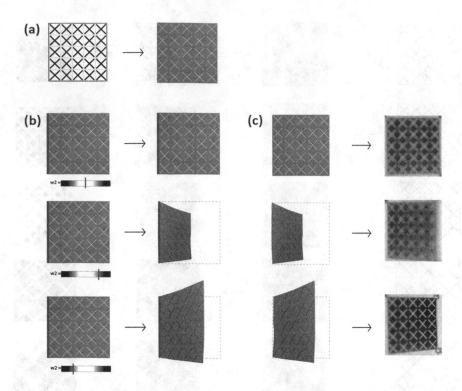

Fig. 10. Shape rules of the second exploration: (a) Rule to materialize the cut patterns. Thickness of the material is not a design variable. (b) Rules rotating the cut sheets on a rotation axis defined with a label indicating the rotation axis and a weight (w2) indicating the rotation angle. (c) Rules to generate the light patterns.

Exploration #4

Actions: Layering (Boolean Operations of cut shapes).
Variables: 1. Cut patterns, 2. Boolean operations

In the final round we physically overlay the cut sheets. The overlaid samples are then placed in a set up similar to the one in the second exploration, to explore the changes in the light patterns on the screen. Here, we choose to represent physical layering with Boolean union operations of at least two cut sheets, say (**A**) and (**B**). These are generated with rules translating the two cut patterns into material samples in Fig. 12a. Materially, layering (**A**) and (**B**) corresponds to (**A**) + **t**(**B**) operation where the translation of (**B**) is with reference to (**A**) and controlled with a label. We represent this label with two perpendicularly intersecting lines, each aligned to (**A**) (Fig. 12b). Even slight changes in the position of the label of (**B**) create different configurations of perforations, resulting in new material samples (Fig. 12c). The Boolean operations can be represented as shape rules with the material sample (**B**) as the left hand side of the rule and the layered samples of (**A**) + **t**(**B**) operation as the right hand side of the rule (Fig. 13a). These new material samples generated by layering the existing ones, result in a considerable effect on the

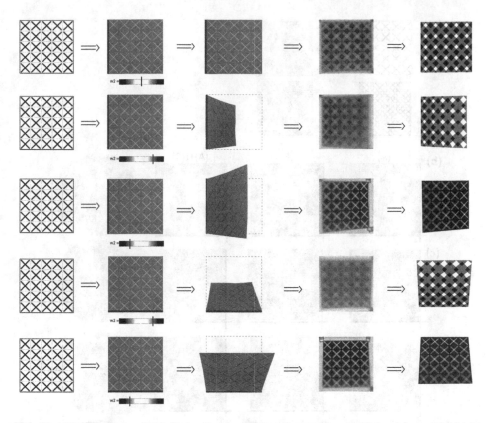

Fig. 11. Shape rules sequentially applied in computations with an additional last rule which translates the light patterns to drawings.

light patterns on the screen (Fig. 13b). The 4 fold rotational symmetry with 4 mirror planes of the cut patterns changes to a symmetry with a single mirror plane when layered. Also, while physically layering the cut sheets denotes a union operation, the resulting patterns on the screen correspond to a product operation where the shapes are the perforations on the cut sheets. If the same exploration was realised with translucent sheets instead of opaque cardboards, physically overlaying the sheets would correspond to a product operation. Simultaneously the light patterns on the screen would be the result of a union operation. This shows how schematized representations can be misleading in describing the material manipulations in design.

The computations with the rules in Fig. 13a, b and an additional rule to translate the light patterns to drawings are presented in Fig. 13c.

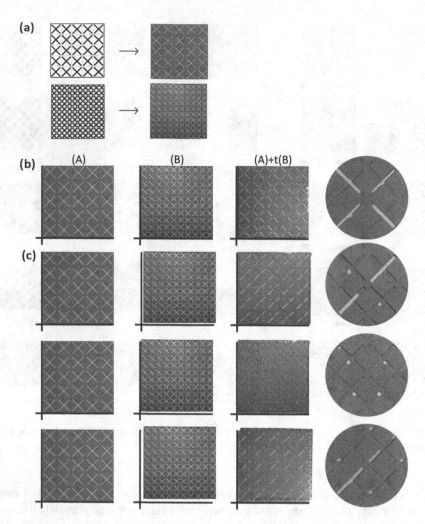

Fig. 12. Final exploration: (a) Rules that generate the material samples. (b) Labels control the translation of (B) with reference to (A) in a Boolean union operation. (c) Slight changes in the position of the label of (B) create different configurations in perforations.

4 Discussion

With open source sharing being a growing ethical practice, it is imperative more than ever that design process is traceable. Traceability is especially relevant in design studio environments where students are asked to communicate their acts and decisions with instructors and peers for the sake of learning how to reason in design. More than just for accountability to fellow humans, formalising reasoning as design computations, allows the individual designer to have control over the design process, to be able to

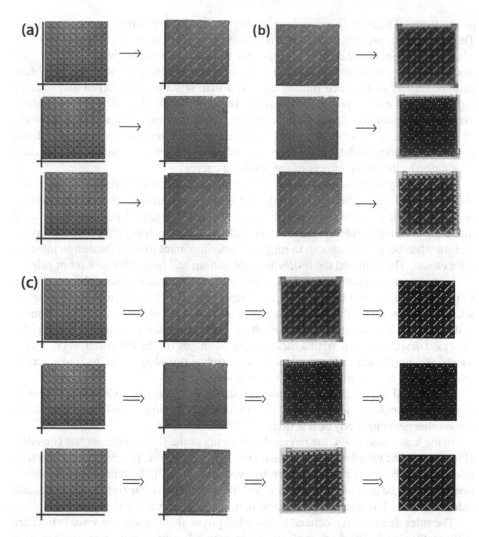

Fig. 13. Rules of the last exploration: (a) Boolean operations represented as shape rules (b) Rules generating the light patterns and (c) the computations which layer the material samples, generate the light patterns and translate the light patterns to drawings

determine how and why unexpected outcomes emerge and how to turn them into design ideas. Yet, design computation is not widely inclusive of multisensory design processes. Due to their complex interfaces, digital fabrication tools already impose particular formalisms and require computation in design implementation. Nevertheless, there is still a need in the field to computationally represent the sensory aspects of working with materials in design.

The utilization of shape rules as analytical and creative tools have been demonstrated in the shape grammar literature. In addressing the need above, we attempt to extend this utilization by integrally representing the causal links between interventions on the material and our shape making in shape rules that support formal computation. The research we present is ongoing. We have reported on a select set of explorations where we manipulate the three dimensional form of cut samples and light as a case study to show shape computation that is informed by material interventions. Our exploration has so far been limited only to a narrow scope of material and sensory aspects. These can be recapitulated as the texture composed of slits cut on a sheet material, the manually applied physical force to bend the material, and the light effects of perforations, as observed by the subjective eye. All three are very much in direct connection to form with the exception of bending which involves tactile manipulation in addition to the visual effects of the resulting curve.

The four explorations demonstrate the use of visual rules to represent actions, variables and form. In the first, it is visible that bending axes impact the visual outcome. According to the axis, the slits allow the sheet material to behave differently. The causal link is partially represented in the tools. In addition to the changing effects of the surface texture when bent, from smooth to rugged, it was important to shift the design intent to light effects. This initiated the following explorations and hence the new set of rules.

In the second exploration, we describe a process of transition from abstract shapes to material shapes, and back to abstract shapes. The slits transform to light patterns, which inspire new visual patterns that can be translated to yet another medium. Similar to the emergence in the first exploration, this supports our quest to formalise a materially informed design process. With a focus on the 2d shapes (of the cut patterns, on the cut sheets and on the screen) our attempts to correlate our shape making and material manipulations are communicated in a simple way.

In the third exploration, uniformly cut sheets are physically rotated resulting in different light patterns with gradual and continuous variations. We denote rotation as yet another generative physical action.

In the final exploration, the physical overlaying of the sheet materials has considerable effect on the visual patterns on the screen. Here, we choose to represent the Boolean operations with the cut patterns rather than visual rules. Still, the representations of the operations can be considered as rules where the column to the far right is the right hand side of the rule. The result is unexpected new shadow patterns on the screen.

The rules that we have defined to show the physical cause and the visual effect are still mostly visual. The final exploration elevates rule representation to another level where material layering leads to the visual product and making switches into seeing.

In each exploration, explicitly representing the cause and the effect allows for controlling the variables and for alternating them to create new results. Whereas the desired results assure the designer of the causal link, the surprising results indicate a materially informed emergence. The simplicity of this exercise is suitable for the studio context but, further research can extend the demonstration to more sophisticated processes of material manipulation and their causal links to form creation. Rather than quantifiable properties useful for exact simulations, our emphasis has been on representing sensory aspects in order to sustain a designer-centered formalism where the level of abstraction matches the sensory involvement. In the future, the formalism may be inclusive of inhabitants' experiences in designs at the urban scale.

Acknowledgements. We would like to thank George Stiny for early feedback at the Knitting, Cutting, and Material Computing workshop and the student participants of the workshop (Aslı Aydın, Begüm Hamzaoğlu, Benan Şahin, Ebru Ulu, Ege Özgirin, Ezgi Baştuğ, Hande Karakaş, Kaan Karabağlı, Oğuz Kurtuluş, Oytun Gür Günel, Özde Özdal, Yusuf Reşat Güner, Zeynep Kırım). All of the images are created by Benay Gürsoy.

References

1. Schön, D., Wiggins, G.: Kinds of seeing and their functions in designing. Des. Stud. **13**(2), 135–156 (1992)
2. Schön, D.: The Reflective Practitioner. Basic Books, New York (1983)
3. Goldschmidt, G.: The dialectics of sketching. Creat Res. J. **4**(2), 123–143 (1991)
4. Menges, A.: Material computation: higher integration in morphogenetic design. Archit. Des. **82**(2), 14–21 (2012)
5. Menges, A., Schwinn, T.: Material reciprocities. Archit. Des. **82**(2), 118–125 (2012)
6. Oxman, R.: Informed tectonics in material based design. Des. Stud. **33**(5), 427–455 (2012)
7. Fleischmann, M., Knippers, J., Lienhard, J., Menges, A., Schleicher, S.: Material behaviour: embedding physical properties in computational design processes. Archit. Des. **82**(2), 44–51 (2012)
8. Kotnik, T., Weinstock, M.: Material Form and Force. Archit. Des. **82**(2), 104–112 (2012)
9. Menges, A.: Material resourcefulness: activating material information in computational design. Archit. Des. **82**(2), 34–43 (2012)
10. Thomsen, M., Tamke, M.: The narratives of making: thinking practice led research in architecture. In: Proceedings of the Conference Communicating Communicating (by) Design. Brussels (2009)
11. Tamke, M., and Thomsen, M.: Digital wood craft. In: Tidafi, T., Dorta, T. (eds.) Joining Languages, Cultures and Visions: CAADFutures, PUM, pp. 673–686 (2009)
12. Knight, T., Stiny, G.: Making Grammars: from Computing with Shapes to Computing with Things, Retrieved June 2014, from Computational Making, Workshop at the 6th International Conference on Design Computing and Cognition (DCC'14) http://descomp.scripts.mit.edu/computationalmaking (2014)
13. Stiny, G.: Shape: Talking About Seeing and Doing. The MIT Press, Cambridge (2006)
14. Knuth, D.E.: Computer science and its relation to mathematics. Am. Math. Mon. **81**(4), 323–343 (1974)
15. Prats, M., Lim, S., Jowers, I., Garner, S., Chase, S.: Transforming shape in design: observations from studies of sketching. Des. Stud. **30**(5), 503–520 (2009)
16. Paterson, G.: Form Generation in Design. PhD Thesis, The Open University (2009)

Super-Details: Integrated Patterns from 3D Printing Processes to Performance-Based Design

François Leblanc[(⌧)]

McGill University, Montréal, Canada
francois.leblanc4@mail.mcgill.ca

Abstract. Performance-based architecture has predominately been influenced by computational advances in simulating complex organizations. The advent of 3D printing, however, has introduced a new approach to generate complex forms, which is redirecting focus from shape-centric design to material design, namely, innovative structures and properties generated by the process itself. This article investigated the multiscale approach potential to design using extrusion-based 3D printing techniques that offer novel geometric organizations that conform to desired performance. It was found that 3D printed toolpaths adapted to extrusion-based systems render an anisotropic behavior to the architectural object that is best optimized by designing tessellated surfaces as the primary structural shape from which small-scale periodic surfaces can be embedded within a larger geometric system.

Keywords: 3D printing · Multiscale design · Extrusion-based systems · Porous material · Topology · CAD integration

1 Introduction

Over the past several years, experimental architecture using 3D printing technology has gained considerable attention as a potential alternative technique for construction [1, 2]. Although most projects have been developed in research facilities and remain proto-typical in nature, some have been fully implemented on construction sites. This was the case for the *3D Print Canal House* project by Dus Architects (Hans Vermeulen, Martine de Wit, and Hedwig Heinsman), which is currently under construction in Amsterdam. This three-story building constructed of extruded polymer aims to attain the title of the first 3D printed building [3]. Aside from plastics, much of the current research into 3D printing is focused on exploring the utility of concrete and cements, materials widely used in construction that are relatively inexpensive and accessible. The recent partnership between the construction firm Skanska and the architectural firm Foster + Partners aims to develop further prototypes under the *Freeform Construction* project developed by the Loughborough University School of Civil and Building Engineering research team, which demonstrates the growing enthusiasm in the application of 3D printing in architecture.

Throughout the 25-year development of 3D printing technologies, the layer-based process has been mostly confined to relatively small objects, initially to fabricate rapid

© Springer-Verlag Berlin Heidelberg 2015
G. Celani et al. (Eds.): CAAD Futures 2015, CCIS 527, pp. 458–473, 2015.
DOI: 10.1007/978-3-662-47386-3_25

prototypes and more recently to produce functional components (also referred to as direct part production). A multitude of commercial and desktop 3D printers are now capable of producing high quality objects due to the ongoing optimization of 3D technology [1, 4]. Owing to the recent interest in architecture of this technology, however, these processes have yet to be optimized for large structures in terms of time to production, waste generation, and post processing of parts, which limit 3D printing applicability and competitiveness within the construction industry. Moreover, the technology is only partly scalable. This means that additional constraints need to be addressed for the optimization of larger scale fabrications. These architectural structures are described in this paper as larger than one meter that are infeasible with current commercial 3D printers.

This article argues that the answer to such issues partly resides in forcing change related to design thinking, namely, the implementation of new geometric models designed specifically for 3D printing that can integrate different levels of detail. With the increasing availability of tools developed for parametric design, a wealth of information and architectural detail can be programmed with efficiency. Coupled with superior control over form and geometry, 3D printing now makes it possible to envision multiple scales of detail for the design of a single component. This approach is termed multiscale design or architectural synthesis as suggested by Dillenberger and Hansmeyer, and is defined as the integration of a number of distinct dimensional geometric qualities in a 3D model that pertain to shape, texture, porosity, and local functionality [5, 6]. Given that this approach was largely influenced by mechanical engineering, however, no guidelines currently exist for architectural structure design standards utilizing 3D printing with regards to providing a clear integration of geometric models optimized for fabrication processes and material performance [7]. How can multiple scale designs be integrated from toolpath modeling to the optimization of form and functionality to assembly while providing feedback to designers at each stage of the process? This article will demonstrate the usefulness of the multiscale approach in generating optimized large-scale 3D printed structures through the examination of patterns stemming from (1) layer-by-layer material deposition, (2) topological interaction of small subelements, and (3) performance-based façade grids.

1.1 Multiscale Design – Olson's Three-Links Chain Model

'If material is considered through a hierarchy of structure, the act of designing synthetic materials is one of enforcing control over these structures at various dimensional scales to exhibit properties of our choosing.' [6]

A multiscale design approach mimics the optimization of natural formations, especially those pertaining to life itself. For such material systems, multiple levels of organization exhibit specific properties that are expressed from the material level to the overall structure. As Srinivasan suggested, there is no distinction between material and structure in natural systems [8]. The optimization of form occurs at the same time as its material configuration and is therefore multiscale in nature. While it is improbable that designers will design a specific material for each product, a multiscale approach implies the introduction of small details that describe pores throughout the internal structure, namely, a topological array of small subelements in the order of few millimeters. Such specific geometric organizations found largely in nature are capable of determining a specific localized behavior within the structure, transforming the property of the overall structure concomitantly [9] (Fig. 1).

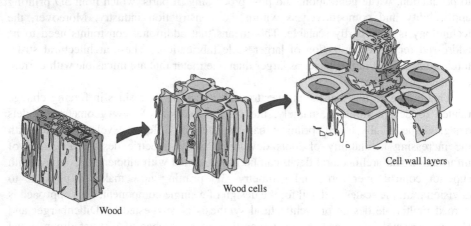

Fig. 1. The different scales integrated in the structure of wood, wood cells, and cell wall layers show a similarity of form that procures an optimized material behavior.

This hierarchy of scale was defined in the three-links chain model first demonstrated by Olson as a means to integrate material science and mechanical engineering by overlapping the two design processes [10]. For this model, three groups of interaction are defined as process-structure, structure-properties, and properties-performance. On one hand, the process determines the structure, namely, the type of fabrication and machining that creates a specific pattern. In the case of 3D printing, the structure is influenced by the material deposition technique utilized that, for extrusion-based systems, will exhibit anisotropic behavior due to the layer-by-layer configuration inherent to the process. On the other hand, material properties are chosen to better match the desired performance of the designed object. This larger scale response to Ashby's material selection charts was designed to obtain the appropriate material optimized for two properties, such as compliance-stiffness for lightweight structures or price-stiffness for more competitive and affordable structures [11]. Olson's argument is that the material process itself has a direct influence on the performance of a given object, and a third link should therefore integrate the structure of the material to the property favored to further control desired behavior. By using the faculty of 3D printing to produce minute detail, material structure can act as a geometric organization (pore distribution, density variation, toolpath deposition orientation, etc.) designed specifically for optimal performance (Fig. 2).

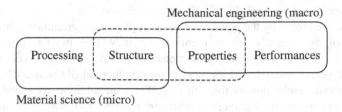

Fig. 2. Olson's three links chain model.

2 Machine Patterns

Different 3D printing technologies are distinguished from one another by the manner in which the material is laid or fused from layer to layer, producing different material structures. Two main material processes dominate 3D printing technologies. The first and more widely available process is an *extrusion-based system* that pushes a paste-like material through a nozzle while heating the media (polymers) or by employing a curing agent into the mix that will force it to quickly solidify after deposition (cement and concrete being examples). Control and placement of material is governed by a toolpath whose function is translated in G-code that is defined by linear vector (point-to-point directions) and speed. It generally prohibits freeform fabrication but can easily be implemented on larger scales by modifying the thickness of each layer. The second process uses a leveled bed of powder on which the printing head(s) fuses (*powder-bed fusion*) or bonds (*binder jetting*) to the surface of the bed. For this process, a dotted matrix characterizes material structure where each drop of liquid or laser impulse is projected on the surface of a layer. Although it can effectively enable a freeform fabrication, removal of powder once the object has been fabricated can quickly become an issue in larger scale productions. Each of these two processes has drawbacks in term of scalability. In seeking to obtain specific material behavior through a multiscale approach, the full potential of these two 3D printing processes is realized when they (1) deliver a good level of accuracy, namely, a resolution small enough to allow for finer details without compromising build time; (2) prevent the need for post-processing that results from requisite support material or high variation in the accuracy of the print; and (3) are compatible and scalable with robotic technology employed in digital fabrication.

How can a pattern that results from the fabrication process influence the performance of an object?

Under a multiscale design approach, it is critical to choose the appropriate resolution for which the part will be printed. For example, low accuracy would otherwise generate bulky elements with no possible internal variation in structural organization. This was the case for early experiments in and around 2004, applying industrial processes to cement and concrete-based prototypes. The *contour crafting* technique patented by Behrokh Khoshevis is well-suited to large prototypes, but each layer only has a 13 mm resolution, resulting in straight extrusions [2]. This 3D printing invention essentially transfers masonry techniques through an automatized construction process that provides modest changes in designing new morphologies. A similar drawback applies to the *binder jetting D-Shape* technology developed by Enrico Dini whose giant gantry is capable of no less than a 10 mm resolution. The lack of control in the absorption of the binder by the powder results in high surface granularity, hindering the application of finer details not to mention the inevitable manual post-processing involved (namely, removing three cubic meters of powder with a shovel).

In recent years, research and innovation on commercial 3D printers have considerably improved resolutions to finer than 100 μm in addition to speeding up the fabrication process itself. Although production remains too costly for architectural application as yet, some projects have taken advantage of the opportunity. In 2013, for example, Benjamin Dillenberger and Michael Hansmeyer exhibited *Digital Grotesque*, a 3 m tall installation whose 3D model was composed of nearly 260 million facets. Using an industrial 3D printer employed for large sand-mold making, the 3D model was discretized in 8 billion voxels, used as a tridimensional Cartesian grid intended for fabrication. Owing to its precision, the process is appropriate for multiscale design, however, the binder was only developed to be short-lived, requiring the object to be infused with an epoxy [5].

Unveiled at the same time was the successful implementation of large-scale 3D printing initiatives for which the construction of the *3D printed Canal House* project in Amsterdam is an example. This project demonstrates the scalability of extrusion-based systems. The project's robotically-driven fabricator, the Kamermaker, was indeed a very large and unique version of Ultimaker, a desktop 3D printer that extrudes polymer (PLA) pellets. Although it did not achieve the same resolution as the previous project, the 2 mm thickness of each layer allows enough detail to construct a multiscale design, especially for large modules. This method has several advantages:

– Material variety available for extrusion (polymers, clay, cement, concrete, and porcelain) is currently used in the construction industry and is economical and durable.
– Extruders necessary to control material flow can be easily adapted and mounted on robotic arms as end-effectors.
– Process scalability allows for the production of models as well as end products while using the same 3D model.
– Resolution can be adjusted by changing the nozzle in accordance to different types of production or even variable resolutions can be conducted with a flexible nozzle.
– Post-processing output is not required thereby saving time and avoiding damaging finer elements during manipulation.

Nevertheless, choosing an unsupported structure during fabrication limits the geometry that can be employed. For the *Freeform Construction* project, De Kestelier demonstrated that, for extrusion-based techniques, direct control of the toolpath during the modeling phase can overcome manufacturing constraints, pointing to the need to support complex geometries and the time to fabrication of complex material organizations [12]. This article looked at developing strategies that could enable self-supporting geometries with the aim of avoiding the use of supports by linking toolpath logic of extrusion-based systems to optimized topological configurations.

2.1 Toolpath and Shell-like Structures

Whereas 3D mesh representation for models were adequate enough to transmit fabrication information in terms of geometry, large-scale 3D printing processes, as it relates to fabrication and scale, require different modeling strategies. The STL file format developed by 3D Systems, which is the most common format for rapid prototyping, describes only an approximation of the object surface. It is convenient for small models that would otherwise be inundated by material. On larger scales, however, surface accumulation generated in the model can lead to extremely large files, especially for curvilinear surfaces. As described by Buswell et al., data conversions using STL format causes certain issues, such as (1) large files (duplicate edges and vertices), (2) inaccurate geometries derived from highly curved objects, (3) reparation (holes/gaps/ missing facets, non-manifolds, degenerated facets/collinear edges, overlapping facets), and the necessity for the application of third party software during post-processing [7]. Moreover, small details can be compromised due to the approximation of a 3D mesh. For information-rich models suitable for multiscale design, a model is best suited using spline and NURBS descriptions.

Boundary representation modeling, whether meshes or BRep, is typically coupled with a slicing algorithm that transforms the model into layers, providing a boundary defining solid/void binary information. It functions in a similar manner to a concrete formwork. For large-scale applications, filings are unnecessary and are often to be avoided. Therefore, models require careful planning of internal voids by designing toolpaths. To better improve workflow between the design stage of functional design and production, Doubrovsky stated that geometric design, CAD modeling, and toolpath generation should be integrated within a single process [13]. In other words, the toolpath itself should be part of the design strategy to derive synchronized material behavior.

Numerous examples of extrusion-based systems using multi-axis robotic apparatuses have demonstrated the potential utility offered by modeling toolpaths for 3D printing [3], [14–16]. Designing continuous toolpaths have several advantages, such as the optimization of material deposition (laying the footprint to take advantage of empty spaces that will reduce the weight of the module) and the reduction of time required for fabrication, two key factors related to the implementation of large-scale fabrication. Moreover, for robotically-driven 3D printers, avoiding sharp angles improves deposition quality while maintaining a regular speed rate. However, two different strategies are necessary in the creation of continuous paths.

Spiral Path. The first strategy is a *offset* or *spiral path* that generates the full plane of a layer by connecting different parts of the path through juxtaposition. The *Building bytes and the 3D printed Solar Bytes pavilion* by Brian Peters is representative of this technique, applying continuous section by section deposition using a robotic arm. For each layer built, the toolpath is carefully positioned to draw the silhouette of an object, including some intricate features, such as peripheral attachments and internal connections. This option is preferred for its higher level of accuracy. Moreover, the toolpath is continuous and homogenous and avoids crossing itself, which would cause excessive material to buildup at junctions. The important factor with regard to complex geometries is to assure that tangent curves merge adequately during material extrusion, especially when using polymers, to consolidate a structural shape to such tangent curves.

Weaved Path. The second strategy is the *loop* or *weaved path*. This process involves crossing itself to generate internal junctions, assuring surface stability during the creation of subsequent layers by giving support to walls. The *FabClay* project developed by Nasim Fashami, Sasa Jocik, and Starski Nay Lara, using clay as the primary medium, successfully implemented this strategy which works well with the more malleable properties of this medium. Adapted to the design of a column, this particular project applied geometry borrowed from roulette curves (namely, hypotrochoids and epitrochoids) to create spiral elliptical paths in the shape of a flower [17].

Superposed Interconnected Paths. To create 3D objects, the aforementioned paths are stacked together to form an extruded surface. To avoid use of temporary supports, the maximum overhang allowance of the material limits the position of the subsequent layer. Large-scale prototypes limit further overhanging due to the weight of the material itself, thereby limiting the potential freedom of geometries unless interconnections between multiple walls are generated. A good example is *Building Bytes* designed by Brian Peters, showcasing possible undulations of 3D printed clay [14].

Stacking layers of continuous paths derive from a careful manipulation of variable surfaces described as NURBS, which have a direct impact during 3D printing module modeling. By keeping each toolpath independently controlled as part of a surface subset, they can be the smallest definition of a geometric object and be parametrically manipulated to vary according to specific parameters. Therefore, such variations together with 3D printing module resolution respect the manufacturing constraints mentioned earlier without affecting the fabrication process itself. They instead play along its specificities (Fig. 3).

3 Topological Patterns

As stated earlier, a more efficient method in which to design large-scale 3D printed objects is to avoid compacting geometries into solid forms. Voids allow for the potential of manipulating finer structures on smaller scales. Topological patterns are the link between the structure revealed by the process and the overall performance projected for the final product, and are the core of multiscale design. They form a geometric organization that responds to the desired property (structural, thermal, visual, etc.) [18]. To be truly topological, such patterns must define a set of interconnected subelements, each acting locally to optimize the specific behavior defined for the entire structure. To be effective, though, the size of each subelement should be sufficiently small, sufficiently numerous, and disposed in a tridimensional array.

Topological patterns act as open-cell structures (or porous structures) that are defined by an extremely low solid fraction of the total elements involved. Such lightweight structures are widely found in nature where energy is cheap and material costly. It provides a considerable microgeometric library that ranges from crystal shapes to foam bubbles. One advantage of foam structures is their associativity potential with simulation-based algorithms used to optimize configurations with environmental or structural parameters [19]. Cubic lattices are the most popular form of discretization for such structures on account of the Cartesian disposition of repeated unit cells on x-, y-, and z-axis. These open-cell structures exhibit variable porosities

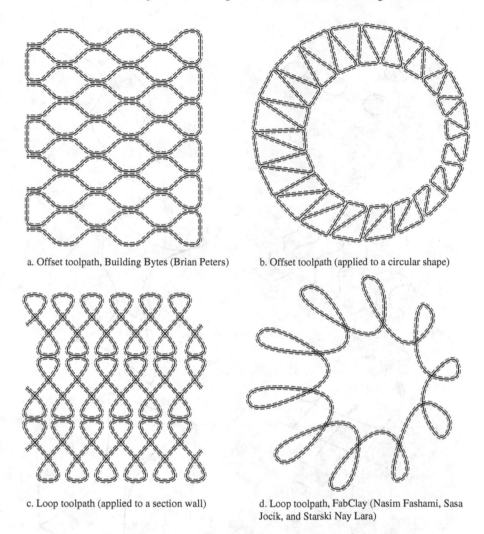

a. Offset toolpath, Building Bytes (Brian Peters)   b. Offset toolpath (applied to a circular shape)

c. Loop toolpath (applied to a section wall)   d. Loop toolpath, FabClay (Nasim Fashami, Sasa Jocik, and Starski Nay Lara)

Fig. 3. The different uses of toolpath for 'spiral' and 'weave' strategies.

defined by the fraction of solid material contained in each unit and take the shape of interconnected strut configurations, namely, a thickened wireframe.

3.1 Volumetric Surface Tessellations

Under a multiscale approach, such patterns are dependent of the process, which limits the choice of geometry under constraints, such as the direct support for material deposition and the maximum deviation angle allowed for layers to remain in place. Most cell units are unsuitable for this process. Powder bed fusion technology has been used as an alternative to explore their full potential and to considerably reduce their

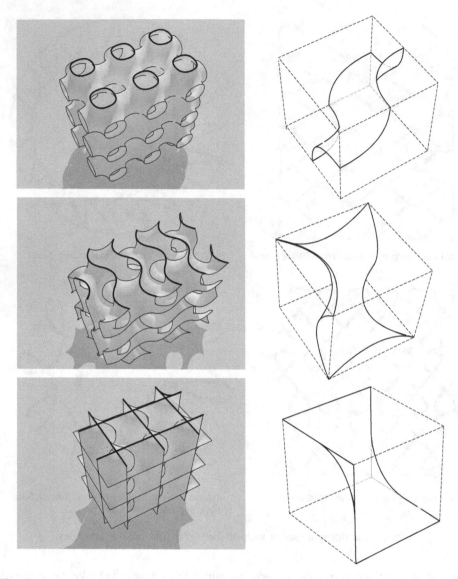

Fig. 4. (From top to bottom) 1. Triply periodic minimal surface Schwarz 'Primitive'. It is characterized by a toolpath discretization following an offset of the centroid more or less circular. 2. Triply periodic minimal surface Schwarz 'Gyroid' Its repeated sinuous toolpath changes direction when reaching half of the cell unit. 3. Triply periodic minimal surface Schwarz 'Diamond'. It connects in the pattern a grid between each units but otherwise draws a parallel toolpath.

scale, creating a material of its own. For large-scale applications, this article proposes to apply surface tessellation to build each cell, using, for example, minimal surfaces and origami folds, in three dimensions instead of struts.

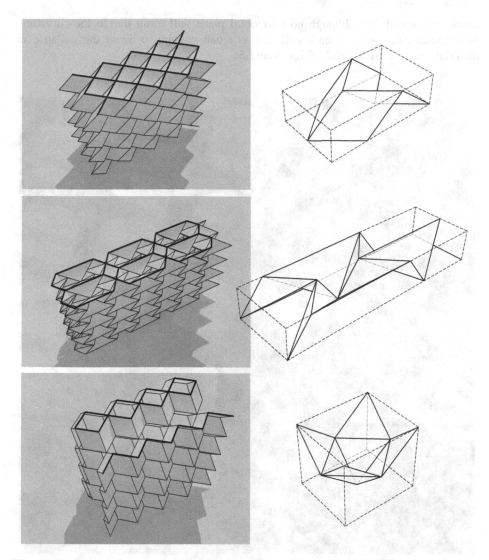

Fig. 5. (From top to bottom) 1. Miura Ori Tessellation. The packing of multiple folded Miura Ori surfaces procures several internal channels describing a vertical zigzag. 2. Diagonal Tessellation. 3. Egg Shell Tessellation.

Triply Periodic Minimal Surfaces. Minimal surfaces are light structures that uniformly distribute structural stress by reducing their mean curvature to zero. The resultant surface describes a minimal area connecting the wireframe, similar to soap film. This category of surface has a great potential for implementation as a topological pattern, especially for Schwartz minimal surfaces. Possessing three planes of symmetry (genus 3) they fit within a cubic cell and can be repeated to form a lattice structure in addition to being able to morph easily into other space-filling polyhedron. The main issue concerning such geometries is the control of the layer-to-layer angle that in some cases can exceed 45°, although no horizontal plane will result due to the curvature. Nevertheless, the scale of each cell unit is small enough to avoid the collapse of material due to it own weight (Figs. 4 and 5).

Fig. 6. 3D-printed lattice structure using the triply periodic minimal surface Schwarz 'Primitive'. Each tessellation varies in shape and density according to local stress obtained through topology optimization simulation.

Origami Tessellations. Origami tessellations are folded shell structures that have the ability to generate tridimensional lattices when juxtaposed together. As demonstrated by Schenk et al., the foldable nature of such geometry can enable the metamaterial to function kinetically, providing frictionless hinges [20]. The advantage for large-scale 3D printing is the control over layer-to-layer angles, which provides a better overall surface quality. The different patterns possible are diverse and exhibit a wide range of behavior due to their compressibility, such as auxetic properties of materials that

Fig. 7. 3D-printed lattice structure using the triply periodic minimal surface Schwarz 'Primitive'.

produce a negative Poisson ratio. Common types of origami tessellations are Miura Ori, Diagonal, and Egg Shell patterns.

Both of the above strategies have the ability to be paired with simulation-based algorithms by either varying the localized thickness of the surface (by duplicating toolpaths) or by amplifying the fold of each discretized unit to generate variable properties.

4 Performance-Based Patterns

On architecture scale, it is necessary to apply a discrete element approach, providing better performance for the whole process. Performance-based patterns connect local variations to global organization, provided with topological patterns, via simulation

Fig. 8. 3D-printed lattice structure using the triply periodic minimal surface Schwarz 'Primitive'.

software [21]. From the pattern is resulting the optimization the properties and the global organization described in Olson's Three-links chain model. Indeed, recent developments in parametric tools now available to architects and designers have led the way from monolithic and uniform design to fractioning of architectural elements, mostly façades, with the individuation of subelements, each responding to local variations. The myriad of paneling tools available to architects and designers highlights a shift toward a more responsive architecture that embeds environmental variation into tridimensional grids.

Traditional construction techniques are comprised of multiple components, which are layered and assembled together for the following three reasons: manipulation, production space, and material behavior as a result of changing environmental conditions (soil deformation, wind pressure, and thermal stress). Although some large-scale 3D printing experiments have explored monolithic building structures using concrete [2], such initiatives are likely to miss the opportunity to implement smaller details owing to topological patterns resulting from the limited capacity of such technologies in providing finer detail. To create an effective multiscale design, this article explored variable modular units as a way to bridge topological patterns with architectural components that provide a common geometric organization.

4.1 Topology Optimization

Under parametric design, surfaces are useful to define the boundary condition for simulating a macro material organization. Topology optimization is a generative design method that seeks at distributing voids in a given domain linking the material properties (micro) to the boundary conditions of a given domain (macro). The simulation provides a lightweight global structure by minimizing local stresses. It typically treats the domain of optimization as mesh geometries on account of the topological organization of nodes that define grid intersections and generate an ordered cell structure. The two types of two-dimensional cell shapes are triangle and quadrilateral, the hexagonal grid being a collection of triangles.

Under a multiscale approach, paneling (the association of shapes on a grid or lattice) is the interface of geometry that is in direct contact with sub-levels of material organization. It must therefore interact with the same logic. Patterns used for panels necessitate conformity to the associative tridimensional topological pattern used, which can be cubic or tetrahedral. The hierarchy that arises from the toolpath, internal structure, and performance-based patterns is similar to wood structures. Indeed, tree shape is optimized by environmental factors, resulting in a specific form and orientation that is the *wood*. On smaller scales, wood cells internally orientate to wood structure but distribute stress by varying thickness and density. The construction of each unit is made of cell wall layers that generate a microstructural pattern that in effect makes the wood a material. Paneling is therefore the final scale that connects material behavior to architectural design.

5   Conclusion

This article demonstrated the potential of a multiscale approach for large-scale 3D printing to generate small details tailored to the improvement of structural properties. Scalability of extrusion-based systems enables the integration of topological patterns by using surfaces that describe a collection of toolpaths. Geometric organization linking deposition patterns to paneling of façades provides a better control of both material and form under formal logic. Furthermore, this method helps integrate multiple objectives on different scales, from internal structures to overall performance. 3D printing has the potential to couple complexity and geometry to facilitate the optimization and integration of functionality in architecture from material to form. Super-detail has therefore arrived (Figs. 6, 7, and 8).

Acknowledgements. The author would like to thank professor Aaron Sprecher, director of LIPHE laboratory, for the development of large-scale 3D printing and the valuable experience gained from the Evo DeVO project, together with Clothilde Caillé-Lévesque and Zhongyuan Dai for the development of prototypes. The research have been funded by the SSHRC grant.

References

1. Buswell, R.A., Soar, R.C., Gibb, A.G.F., Thorpe, A.: Freeform construction: mega-scale rapid manufacturing for construction. Autom. Constr. **16**(2), 224–231 (2007)
2. Khoshnevis, B., Hwang, D., Yao, K.T., Yeh, Z.: Mega-scale fabrication by contour crafting. Int. J. Ind. Syst. Eng. **1**(3), 301–320 (2006)
3. 3D Print Canal House: http://3dprintcanalhouse.com/ (2015). Accessed 29 Jan 2015
4. Wohlers, T.T.: Wohlers report 2012: additive manufacturing and 3D printing state of the industry. Wohlers Associates, Fort Collins (2012)
5. Dillenburger, B., Hansmeyer, M.: The Resolution of Architecture in the Digital Age. In: Zhang, J., Sun, C. (eds.) Proceedings of 15th International Conference CAAD Futures: Global design and local materialization. Springer, New York, pp. 347–357 (2013)
6. Beckett, R., Babu, S.: To the micron: a new architecture through high-resolution multi-scalar design and manufacturing. Archit. Des. **84**(1), 112–115 (2014)
7. Buswell, R.A., Thorpe, A., Soar, R.C., Gibb, A.G.F.: Design, data and process issues for mega-scale rapid manufacturing machines used for construction. Autom. Constr. **17**(8), 923–929 (2008)
8. Srinivasan, A.V., Haritos, G.K., Hedberg, F.L.: Biomimetics: advancing man-made materials through guidance from nature. Appl. Mech. Rev. **44**(11), 463–482 (1991)
9. Smith, C.S.: A Search for Structure: Selected Essays on Science, Art, and History. MIT Press, Cambridge (1981)
10. Olson, G.B.: Computational design of hierarchically structured materials. Science **277**(5330), 1237 (1997)
11. Ashby, M.F.: Materials Selection in Mechanical Design. Butterworth-Heinemann, Burlington (2005)
12. De Kestelier, X., Buswell, R.A.: A digital design environment for large- scale rapid manufacturing. In: D'Estrée Sterk, T., Loveridge, R., Pancoast, D. (eds.) Proceedings of the 29th annual conference of the Association for Computer Aided Design in Architecture, pp. 201–208 (2009)
13. Doubrovski, E.L., Verlinden, J.C., Geraedts, J.M.P.: Exploring the links between CAD model and build strategy for inexpensive FDM. In: International Conference on Digital Printing Technologies, pp. 500–506 (2011)
14. Peters, B.: Building Bytes: 3D-Printed Bricks. In: Proceedings of the 33rd Annual Conference of the Association for Computer Aided Design in Architecture, Cambridge, pp. 433–434 (2013)
15. Malé-Alemany, M., Portell, J.: Soft tolerance: an approach for additive construction on site. Archit. Des. **84**(1), 122–127 (2014)
16. Vander Kooij, D.: http://www.dirkvanderkooij.com/ (2015). Accessed 29 Jan 2015
17. FabClay: https://fabbots.wordpress.com/2012/12/09/fabclay-2/ (2015). Accessed 29 Jan 2015
18. Doubrovski, Z., Verlinden, J.C., Geraedts, J.M.P.: Optimal design for additive manufacturing: Opportunities and challenges. In: Proceedings of the ASME Design Engineering Technical Conference 9, pp. 635–646 (2011)

19. Chu, C., Graf, G., Rosen, D.W.: Design for additive manufacturing of cellular structures. Comput. Aided Des. Appl. **5**(5), 686–696 (2008)
20. Schenk, M., Guest, S.D.: Geometry of Miura-folded metamaterials. Proc. Natl. Acad. Sci. U.S.A. **110**(9), 3276–3281 (2013)
21. Bendsøe, M.P., Sigmund, O.: Topology Optimization: Theory, Methods, and Applications. Springer, Berlink (2003)

Architecture Meets Gaming and Robotics: Creating Interactive Prototypes and Digital Simulations for Architects

Taro Narahara[✉]

New Jersey Institute of Technology, Newark, NJ, USA
narahara@njit.edu

Abstract. This paper presents an approach to producing an interactive physical kinetic prototype and its digital simulation for architects using a series of proposed methods. Conventional architectural CAD applications alone are not always sufficient for illustrating ideas for adaptable and responsive architecture that can conditionally change its states over time. The use of technologies from game design and robotics has a potential to extend the role of architects beyond merely providing static formal design solutions to various spatial problems. The paper introduces methods for rapid prototyping and real-time interaction between physical kinetic prototypes and a digital application environment for simulation using readily available commodity hardware, such as Arduino microcontrollers, 9 g servo motors, Kinect sensors, and Unity 3D game engine software with its computational physics. The paper also presents case studies using the approach and discusses possible applications and assessment of this approach.

Keywords: Interactive prototypes · Simulation · Game engine · Robotics

1 Introduction

Today, smart products, adaptive designs, and intelligent spaces are in the forefront of current artistic discourse. They are critical components in sustainable designs where products monitor their own performance and respond to consumers' real-time needs and environmental factors. Nowadays many architects are starting to incorporate sensors, actuators, and microcontrollers into their architectural prototypes to represent their interaction ideas. However, the realization of these prototypes requires architects to use skills that are foreign to most of them, and the production of such prototypes occasionally becomes costly and requires many hours of work. This paper introduces an effective, rapid, and inexpensive solution to interface digital and physical environments for their interactive prototypes using a systematic approach that can be adopted by architects. The paper explores potential new application areas with this new ability for architects to implement interactivity.

© Springer-Verlag Berlin Heidelberg 2015
G. Celani et al. (Eds.): CAAD Futures 2015, CCIS 527, pp. 474–490, 2015.
DOI: 10.1007/978-3-662-47386-3_26

The proposed approach allows real-time interaction between physical kinetic proto-types and a digital application environment for simulation using readily available commodity hardware, such as Arduino microcontrollers, 9 g servo motors, and Kinect sensors, and software such as the Unity 3D game engine [23]. Firstly, through basic examples from robotics such as a delta robot and a quadruped robot, the author demon-strates how complex kinematic conditions in such examples can be rapidly fabricated and how they can be interfaced with a digital application environment for controls and simulations using mouse, keyboard-based, and 3-D gestural interfaces. The game engine platform comes with libraries equivalent to those used for professional programming languages such as C++, while it still maintains ease of use for relatively inexperienced users in architecture. The use of the game engine platform allows for implementations of computational physics and any user-defined logic through its embedded scripting language. The method takes advantage of these features and can be used as a tool for architects to create kinetic physical prototypes and digital simulations.

The paper further explores computational methods to acquire kinetic behaviors for prototypes based on user-defined conditions using algorithms and focuses on explaining its applications in architecture by showing several conceptual case studies. The use of technologies from game design and robotics has a potential to extend the role of archi-tects beyond merely providing static formal design solutions to various spatial problems. This will give architects an opportunity to actively propose inclusion of interaction-based features in their designs.

2   Methods

This paper introduces an approach that consists of a series of methods to produce phys-ical prototypes and digital simulations. One of the proposed techniques is a digital fabri-cation technique that allows architects to rapidly produce kinetic physical models.

2.1   Rapid Fabrication Approach

A number of prototyping approaches using toolkits have been previously introduced. For example, [14, 16] demonstrated the use of toolkits to make prototyping more feasible, and design patterns have been widely utilized in architecture, design, and computer science, as Alexander [1] advocated in A Pattern Language. The author's proposed method focuses on a rapid fabrication technique to produce an interactive kinetic model that can be used for a speedy verification of architects' concepts with the use of inexpensive and readily available components. In this section, to improve ease and speed of physical prototyping, the author introduces a toolkit with fabrication design template patterns. The author explains a proposed method through production of a delta robot that can be controlled by user interfaces. The author has conducted several short-term tutorials using the example in this section as a module to demonstrate the method to beginning architects who were interested in producing interactive prototypes at the author's institution.

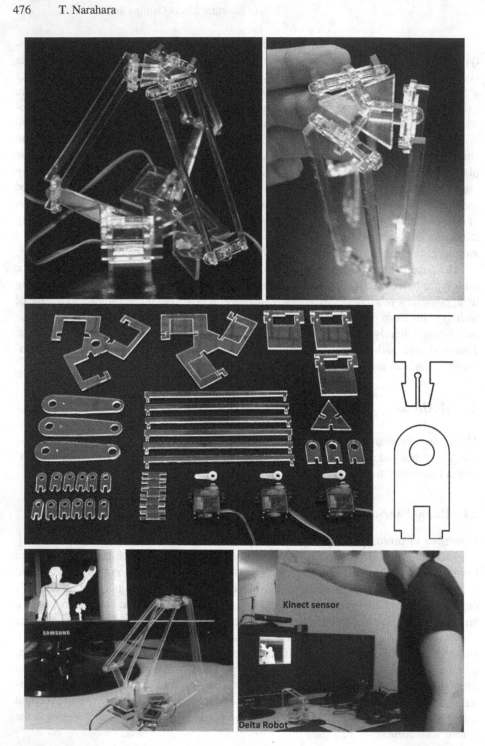

Fig. 1. A delta robot was used to explain inverse kinematics (top). Laser-cut Plexiglas parts (middle-left). Snap-in friction-fit joints for FAB (middle-right). Demonstrations using the Kinect sensor (bottom).

A delta robot consists of three arms connected to universal joints at the base, allowing a parallel motion of a head in 3-D space. The toolkit demonstrates how such a complex mechanism can be rapidly fabricated by cutting planar materials (Plexiglas) with snap-in friction-fit joints using a laser cutter, without using expensive metal fittings or adhesives excessively (Fig. 1). The laser cutter is a fast and economical option for professionals and students in architecture. All parts work with a size and specification of a 9 g servo motor that has a reasonable size and torque for a conceptual scaled study model for an architectural kinetic prototype. This servo motor is readily available anywhere in the world at an inexpensive price. Thus the entire assembly can be done in a day, and CAD drawings for parts can be modified and reused when architects decide to make kinetic models with different configurations. Additionally, while the toolkit provides required basic shapes for mechanical movements, it can be customized in aesthetically pleasing ways in CAD software.

After the fabrication, the author introduces template codes that can control the delta robot with mouse-based user interfaces and 3-D gestural interfaces using a Kinect sensor from Microsoft. The author prepared template codes first using Processing language [22] to introduce these features, but the same features were implemented on the Unity 3D game engine, which will be introduced in the next section in detail. A reduction to simple programming elements was used for instructions for architects. The author highlighted the primary lines of code that are important for architects to understand when they need to implement their own custom instructions. In this case, the important part is where user-input coordinates from a mouse or a sensor are converted to movements of effectors using servo motors. For example, to utilize a Kinect sensor, architects at least need to know where in the code the coordinates for tracked joints are converted and sent as outputs for servo motors – effectors. This requires architects to have exposure to concepts of inverse kinematics through learning how a function finds three motors' rotation angles to move an end-effector to a specific target location in a 3-D space. The inverse kinematics of a delta robot can be solved geometrically using trigonometry and ordinary algebraic equations without recourse to advanced calculus [7], and awareness of this logic allows architects to determine the joint parameters, such as rotation angles, that achieve a desired configuration. These ideas can be applied by architects to possible original projects that require mechanical movements. By going through this process, architects can learn how to produce efficient kinetic motions by fabricating mechanical systems composed of appropriate gears and joints from the author's toolkit. Through a minimum number of actuators and modest power requirements (achieved by reducing redundancy in mechanical systems), there is an opportunity to derive various complex motions using the toolkit.

2.2 Connecting Digital with Physical

The author's approach utilizes technologies from computer gaming, virtual reality, and robotics for development of a method for architects to create interaction between virtual (digital) simulation and physical architectural prototypes. The proposed method uses the physics engine in the Unity 3D game development system to calculate the user's physical interactions with virtual game objects and control the movement of physical prototypes with microcontrollers, sensors, and actuators to simulate interactivity. While CAD software applications such as AutoCAD and Rhinoceros are reliable for static representations of architecture, they alone are not always sufficient for producing and communicating ideas for adaptable and responsive architecture that can conditionally change its states over time. Game engines allow users to implement custom interaction logics for any component (for example, behaviors of enemy characters) and can demonstrate them in real time. As game engines have the capability to import 3-D models from CAD file formats, they are a promising platform for architects to visualize systems that can change their states and improve their performance based on evaluations of given conditions on a real-time basis.

Software offering similar visual interaction capabilities to physical prototypes has been available for architects. For example, Firefly [5] in the Grasshopper plug-in [10] for the Rhinoceros 3D CAD application allows near real-time data flow between the Grasshopper plug-in and other input/output devices such as an Arduino microcontroller [2], and there are a number of other plug-ins available for Grasshopper to experiment with many aspects of design, including the Kangaroo plug-in [15] for physics simulation. The Processing language also offers various libraries to create visual interactive applets and can be connected with hardware such as an Arduino microcontroller and Kinect using serial communication [22].

The Unity 3D game engine, which has been widely used among digital designers, is equipped with powerful capabilities to develop challenging computer games that can sustain a user's interest. Unity 3D allows for implementation of GPU-accelerated computational physics – powerful 3D physics engine NVIDIA PhysX Physics [20], which is sufficiently fast to simulate user interaction with game objects and controls the physical prototype/robot to provide a sense of virtual touch. While Unity animation operates at the computer screen refresh rate (~100 frames/s), its physics can operate at a higher frequency required for proper haptic perception. In addition, game-defined logic is implemented through its embedded scripting platform using C# that integrates seamlessly with its state-of-the-art real-time rendering capabilities. Due to these particular characteristics and advantages of the game engine, including its speed and accuracy for computational physics and compatibilities with various CAD model formats common among architects, the author selected Unity 3D and its C# scripting language as a main platform to develop proposed methods in this paper.

The author has done physical computing projects interfacing a commodity microcontroller, an Arduino microcontroller, with Unity 3D. An Arduino microcontroller is the current primary means for many architectural researchers to control their physical prototypes [2]. The versatility, usability, and adaptability of Unity have been proven as the author has already developed interfaces between Unity and Arduino using the Transmission Control Protocol (TCP) through a C# script.

The author introduces a simple robotic device to explain the method in this section. The device has a one degree of freedom arm with a servo motor to rotate the arm, a potentiometer to encode its rotation angle, and a force sensor to sense a push by a user's hand (Fig. 2.) This device is connected to a virtual environment in Unity 3D using the aforementioned TCP. Every 0.001 s. a force sensor detects the user's intended movement/rotation through a push of the device's arm, and drives an admittance controller to move the arm to a new position based upon Newton's Second Law. Thus, the device carefully follows the user's wishes, while amplifying the strength of the arm by adjusting the allowable rotation range from the servo motor. Meanwhile, the virtual environment in Unity 3D displays a user's hand as a 3-D model of a hand in real time, and the physics engine of Unity 3D will be incorporated into this admittance loop so that when a user's arm contacts a virtual object, the device's movement is modified so that the user is given the virtual sense of touching the object. The physics engine will determine whether or not the touched object deforms or moves based on the user's applied force. The user will feel resistance in the device when the virtual hand makes contact with the objects. Figure 3 shows a block diagram of the development of a stereo vision loop and addition of Unity 3D to a simple robotic device that assimilates the admittance control loop.

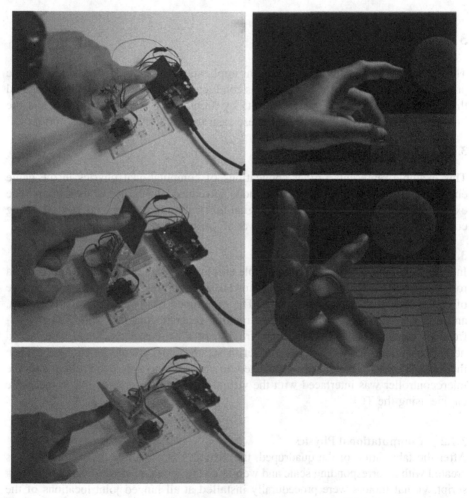

Fig. 2. A simple robotic device with a haptic feedback system and its simulation in a 3-D virtual world.

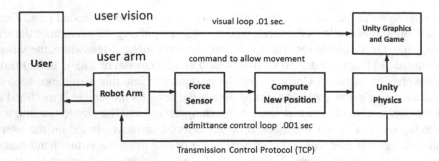

Fig. 3. A block diagram of the addition of Unity 3D as the graphics and physics engine for the haptic feedback device

3   Case Studies

Three case studies in this section present applications of methods introduced in the previous sections. The first case study was conducted by the author, and the second and third case studies were short-term results by architecture students who had had the instruction about the methods prior to these case studies at the author's institution.

3.1   A Quadruped Robot

This example represents further applications of computational physics in the game engine environment in addition to methods introduced in the previous section. The example highlights three main issues: digital fabrication techniques, interactions using computational physics, and an active use of algorithms for more generative purposes.

3.1.1   Digital Fabrication
In terms of digital fabrication, this example employs the same technique from the delta robot example using the CAD template for laser-cutting that works for a specific size of components such as a servo motor. The quadruped has twelve 9 g servo motors, and this approach allows the author to rapidly generate four legs with 3-degree-of-freedom mechanical joints using only friction-fit Plexiglas parts. Small screws and holes were additionally provided in order to secure joints around kinetic parts. Then the twelve servo motors were connected to an Arduino microcontroller, and the microcontroller was interfaced with the virtual environment created inside the game engine using the TCP.

3.1.2   Computational Physics
After the fabrication of the quadruped, the virtual 3-D model of the quadruped was created with a corresponding scale and weight of the actual quadruped, and using a C# script, virtual motors were procedurally installed at all hinged joint locations of the quadruped's legs with a proper torque and speed that simulate the physical servo motor's specifications in the virtual world. The script using the TCP allows bi-directional

communication between the quadruped robot and the digital environment by exchanging data through a serial port. Similar to the delta robot, the inverse kinematic function that can derive rotation angles of three motors at joints from a 3-D coordinate of a toe location for each leg was written using a C# script. Firstly, the author hard-coded the gait motion by providing a trajectory of a toe movement during one gait cycle, and this trajectory can be parametrically adjusted according to the change in the location of a quadruped's center of mass, posture, and heading direction. The physics engine also has parameters to adjust material properties including dynamic and static friction and a damping factor (bounciness) to replicate actual physical conditions of surface and materials for the robot. A graphic user interface was implemented in order to control a connection to the physical robot, rotations of motors using sliders, and the speed and direction of the robot. The setting for the interface was designed to accommodate user-defined conditions to some extent, and (for example) users can add more joints with new configurations.

There are a number of virtual representations in gaming and architectural visualization that rely on conditionally applied pre-recorded animations to simulate kinetic elements to demonstrate smooth and realistic movements. However, the above settings enable the quadruped to use its legs to literally push the ground and move its body weight forward using computational physics inside the game engine, and to allow for a fairly precise simulation of the physical robot motion in real time. This approach can simulate movements based on computational physics while a user sees the performance of the tangible prototypes. A user can easily modify the virtual environment by placing 3-D obstacles to match any physical constraints existing in a real-life environment. The physics in the virtual world can be adjusted in accord with the actual performance of physical prototypes at the outset and can be used as a test bed tool to foresee potential behaviors of the prototype using user-defined conditions.

3.1.3   Generative Approaches: A Gait cycle Generation and Simulation

There is another advantage of connecting digital and physical environments. The digital simulation platform can also be used to derive possible behaviors of prototypes based on certain user-defined objectives under certain conditions by providing appropriate algorithmic descriptions. For instance, instead of providing a hardcoded trajectory of a quadruped's toe movement as in the previous section, users can use a computer to search for a better gait cycle pattern based on a distance that virtual quadrupeds can travel within a certain period inside the computational physics environment. This way of thinking is common among engineers and computer scientists, and there are many successful virtual robotics experiments that have evolved optimal behavioral patterns for physical robots to accomplish certain objectives given by researchers [3, 12, 13, 17]. These experiments by scientists use programming languages such as C++ with physics engine libraries which require extensive technical knowledge and skills, and they are often overwhelmingly complex for architects. The author found that the same approach can be explored by architects without having them write an extensive code through the use of the environment template produced by the author inside the game engine. Although this approach requires architects to do some level of scripting to implement custom conditions, using the author's template is far more approachable than writing one's own application and scripts from scratch (Fig. 4).

Fig. 4. A physical quadruped robot (top right) and a screenshot of a digital environment with a user interface (top left) and a robot character constructed with virtual motors at its joints using computational physics (second row left). A slope created from a rigid board and a cylinder: A user can modify the virtual environment to match physical constraints existing in a real-life environment (third row). Interactions of multiple quadrupeds can be simulated inside a game engine environment (bottom row).

For the particular case of the quadruped example, one of the common approaches to acquire a gait motion is use of an artificial neural network (ANN) inside an optimization loop that evolves the NN generation by generation. The author implemented this common approach among computer scientists [13, 17] inside the game engine environment and verified the usability of the physics engine and the environment as customized by the author. This NN can output signals to the virtual quadruped's twelve motors based on inputs from four virtual sensors installed at its toes that detect whether they are in contact with the ground plane. The NN can have different output patterns for movements of quadrupeds based on how the NN's links are weighted with a different combination of weight values. The author started with a population of one hundred NNs initialized with randomly generated weights. Then, the physics engine simulated a quadruped with each NN scheme, and recorded the distance that the quadruped traveled. The algorithm selects above a certain percentage of NNs that can cause quadrupeds to travel further, and these elite NNs are copied and modified to reproduce a new set of NNs which will be tested again in the next simulation as a new population. To produce a new population, crossover and mutation processes commonly used in a genetic algorithm [11] are used for the elite NNs' weight values. After repeating this process over 50,000 generations for multiple times, several reasonable gait motions were generated from this implementation of the method in the game engine environment. Due to the nature of stochastic selection, results vary with each trial and might not have derived the best optimal gait solution. It requires further improvements on optimization methods with a higher number of trials. One unique byproduct of this approach is that it can derive non-trivial strategies such as hopping and rolling movements by quadrupeds that are not typically conceived by human designers as a conventional solution, and this fact sheds light on this approach's unique characteristics and additional potentials. The author will discuss further how these approaches could be made more applicable in architectural design in Sect. 5, "Discussion."

3.2 Interactive Façade System

This project was produced directly from revising the method and the toolkit for the delta robot in Sect. 2 and demonstrates an architectural application of the method tested by users. The entire production was done in two weeks by two architecture students after they studied the method introduced in Sect. 2. They proposed an interactive façade system that can locally change its opacity based on a user's gesture in order to shade certain areas to prevent direct sunlight. It can also open certain areas to reveal a desired partial exterior view to users while it maintains opacity in other areas to provide privacy for users on the inside. They were interested in using a series of operable louvers with twisted vertical strips to locally vary opacities in the façade. In order to make the rotation angles of louvers variable, they attached servo motors at the top and bottom of each vertical strip. Strips were made of flexible fabric, and the differential in the rotation angles of servo motors at the top and bottom could control the vertical location of a crease to add a dynamic vertical motion. The relationship between the crease location in height and the differential in rotation angles was thoroughly studied (Fig. 5.) By

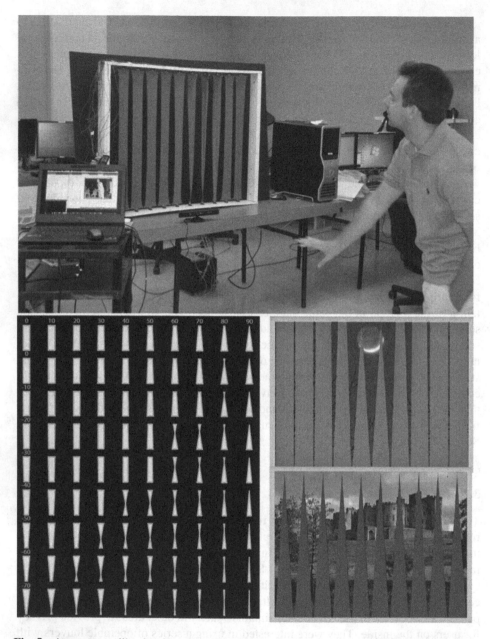

Fig. 5. A user controlling local opacity of the façade using a Kinect sensor (top). Differentials in rotation angles can control the vertical location of a crease (bottom left). Concept sketches show possible uses of the interactive façade (bottom right). Source: A project by students Krystian Krepa and David Solano at NJIT.

arraying the vertical strips in a horizontal direction, the louver system can move the position of an open area by varying the locations of creases both vertically and horizontally. By sending the right set of rotation angles to servo motors, based on a corresponding user's hand location in front of the louver system, an open area created by creases can be controlled by the user in real time.

Using the depth information acquired from the Microsoft Kinect sensor, a user's skeleton using simple vector graphics can be constructed in real time. A simple template code, which was previously demonstrated through the method using the delta robot, was used to track a hand's location. First, a user's body motion is tracked by the Kinect located at the bottom of the façade system. Then the algorithm from the Open Natural Interaction (OpenNI) framework [21] inside the template code proceeds to create a skeleton from a silhouette of the user and starts tracking a user's right hand location. The x and y coordinates of the right hand location are sent to the Arduino microcontroller using serial communication through a USB cable. Subsequently, the program stored inside Arduino receives the x and y coordinates as inputs and returns rotation angles to servo motors to move creases to the corresponding user's right hand location. The above procedures are executed simultaneously in real time as the user moves his or her hand.

3.3   A Haptic Glove

This is another short-term case study, carried out by one student, who applied the author's method using the game engine introduced. The project's goal was to create a haptic glove to rehabilitate people with weak muscle strength in their arms. The haptic glove allows users to feel virtual space and also allows them to have haptic interactions when using a Kinect without any controllers such as a mouse or joystick. The glove has five flexion sensors that change resistances depending on the amount of bend of each finger and five small vibration motors (typically used inside smart phones) at each fingertip. These components are connected to an Arduino microcontroller that is already interfaced with the game engine environment using the author's script with the TCP introduced in Sect. 2.2. The number of sensors and actuators that are interfaced with the author's environment can be easily adjusted and changed based on a user's preference. Inside the virtual space, various objects are floating in the space, and a user can interact by touching or grasping these virtual objects which neither exist nor possess any weight in the real world. The Kinect sensor tracks the physical hand location of the user relative to the virtual world, flexion sensors read bends of each finger, and the 3-D model of a hand inside the virtual space replicates the motion in real time. When the user interacts with virtual objects, a haptic sensation occurs through vibrations of motors connected at the user's fingertips along with visual effects such as an explosion or movements of objects inside the virtual world. In the next section, "Discussion," the author would like to speculate as to how these methods can be integrated into our current and future discourse in architecture (Fig. 6).

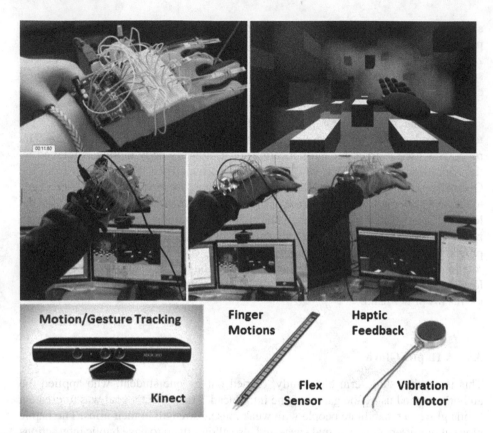

Fig. 6. A haptic glove with flexion sensors and vibration motors (top left). Objects in a virtual space (top right). A user interacts with virtual objects using a haptic glove tracked by a Kinect sensor (bottom). Source: A project by a student, Amanda Cronce, at NJIT.

4   Discussion

In this paper, in order to highlight essential concepts of each method, examples with relatively simple and clear mechanisms were selected. They are generic enough for further applications in various contexts, and some approaches can be applied in combination. The quadruped robot and haptic glove described in this paper are not directly related to applications in architecture. However, they may suggest potential applications of computational physics and haptic technology in architecture. Many adaptable concepts for architecture can benefit from kinetic components for buildings, and methods for the delta robot and the quadruped can be used for production of mechanically movable architectural prototypes and digital simulations using computational physics. The same approach used for their joints can be easily applied (for example) to joints for kinetic variable trusses that can sense local loading conditions or operable systems for enclosures.

The generative approaches introduced in Sect. 3.1.3 show a way to find proper behaviors for a system that possesses spatiotemporal dynamics, and we anticipate having more examples of architecture that possesses some level of active performative characteristics in the near future, judging by recent growing interest in (demand for) adaptable and responsive architecture. These approaches are effective when problems are extremely complex, and no trivial solution is available. The algorithmic method used in the section is often categorized as "evolutionary computation" by computer scientists [4], and applications of these processes in architectural design have been introduced by architectural researchers such as Flazer [6] and Gero [8]. Also, more recent papers, for example [9], have presented architectural design and planning options produced on the basis of criteria such as energy performance factors, using current state-of-the-art software. The author intended to show the potentials of these approaches not only for seeking static design solutions in planning stages but also for finding dynamic spatiotemporal behaviors for certain systems with active adaptable features for building operations.

The approaches in this paper are particularly effective for finding appropriate behaviors for architectural details with control mechanisms that utilize multiple input/output variables in a spatiotemporal context. Figure 7 shows a conceptual, yet more architectural, example that may take advantage of these approaches. The project was previously developed by the author [18, 19]. The architectural modular panels equipped with locally embedded light sensors and microcontrollers were linked with two-degree-of-freedom joints, which allows them to reconfigure their orientations with respect to dynamically changing local lighting conditions. At the time, the author used Nelder-Mead method – a commonly used multi-dimensional heuristic search method – to seek better configurations that can maximize the average light value from panels using a directly sampled resulting utility value from the physical prototypes for each trial. However, the approach required many trials for the prototype to reconfigure and to sample the value from physical space, and made it impractical for implementation in any real-life application with the additional complexity resulting from physical dynamics of panels' movements and their balances. Digital simulations with precise computational physics introduced in this paper allow faster parallel processing of multiple instances simultaneously and are advantageous for development of architectural prototypes that require population-based optimization algorithms such as genetic algorithms. The example in Fig. 7 was still highly abstract and conceptual, yet the twisting louvers from 3.2 may also add another slightly more architectural application of these approaches. The interactive louvers can also be applied as an envelope scheme for all sides of any building structure with the use of similar algorithmic techniques to seek better operational movements for each louver for different times of the day under varying conditions, such as weather or events that are occurring inside or outside of the structure. Unlike the example in 3.2, which only employed a single user's movement for the interaction, the case requires finding appropriate behaviors of multiple louvers under possibly conflicting multiple objectives (e.g., more light versus more privacy), and this is the case where methods of evolutionary computation may become effective.

Methods introduced in the haptic glove and the interactive façade may also allow architects to conceive more interactive ways to interface with buildings. The author is well aware that examples such as the haptic glove are not readily applicable to our

Fig. 7. A previously developed conceptual architectural robotics project by the author [18].

current conception of architecture. However, the author speculates that future roles of architects may include not only to provide physical envelopes for human activities and living, but also to design infrastructure for active interactions among all components of buildings with humans, and this will involve interdisciplinary collaborative efforts among specialists from diverse technical backgrounds. The kinds of knowledge that architects traditionally possess through their practice, such as spatial design based on behavioral science, human factors, and ergonomics, are all essential for the implementation of such integration for design and interactivity among buildings and users. There are emerging application areas of architectural robotics – interactive façade design, integration of assistive technologies with spatial design, therapeutic interactive spatial elements inside medical facilities, and so on. Readers may think these are not the first priority for the applications, though demands for such innovations might be expected in order to cope with the current trend in population ageing or a possibly more egalitarian social structure in the near future. By way of example, the author has currently started collaborating with biomedical engineers at his institution to develop therapeutic games and robotics for disabled people while seeking new application areas around architecture and communication. Further exploration of more architectural applications using these methods is under consideration by the author.

5 Conclusions

This paper has introduced a series of technical methods for architects to speedily fabricate physical prototypes and to connect them to virtual digital simulations, and three case study projects using the proposed approach were presented. The production of interactive prototypes and digital simulations requires us to take a holistic approach to design in both physical and virtual environments. Thus the result of the paper was not limited to introducing a technique from one area. The author intended to propose a concise yet comprehensive approach that consists of techniques in fabrication, digital and physical interfaces, computational physics, and generative approaches as a whole.

Unlike design using software applications inside a digital environment, design of architectural physical kinetic prototypes requires students and even experienced professionals to go through a number of trials and errors to make things work properly. There are numerous things preventing us from the completion of such systems – for example, unexpected friction between gears, endless reassignments of threshold values in codes for actuation of certain components, lengths and sizes of segments relative to torque of actuators, and so on. It is almost impossible to come up with a perfect physical model with active interaction features from the outset, and it is impractical to use the most expensive inflexible materials that do not allow any revisions for design development by architects. Thus, the approaches to use lower-cost commodity hardware, readily available and adjustable materials and methods, and flexible and familiar software platforms for architects, are useful in architectural kinetic prototyping.

The selection of the game engine platform to develop the tool was one unique feature in this paper compared to several platform precedents listed in Sect. 2.2. The Unity 3D game engine and its flexible C# scripting language allowed the author to incorporate its powerful and precise computational physics engine and extensibility for implementations of interaction logic. The game engine also has excellent compatibility with CAD model formats for architects to import their assets. In Sect. 3.1.3, the author presented the method of using the simulation environment to acquire possible movements of quadrupeds algorithmically under certain objectives in a generative manner. This approach, using computational physics, can be applied to a search for possible behaviors of architectural prototypes, for example, aforementioned adaptable trusses under a certain loading condition. The physics engine can also simulate structures under other forces, such as wind pressure. The current state of the author's tool is only compatible with physics-based criteria, though it is technically possible to consider incorporating other environmental or social criteria, such as solar radiation, lighting, pedestrian flows, zoning regulations, location-based social factors, and so on, to search for new possible behaviors for architectural prototypes using the flexible scripting platform in the game engine to implement custom logic by architects.

The author has included parametrized features in the graphic user interface so users can customize their conditions. For example, to some extent, topological linkages of kinetic joint configurations can be reconfigured without coding. However, implementation of more complex custom conditions requires users to have some ability to write their own scripts in the proposed methods. For example, incorporating user-defined criteria for acquiring prototype behaviors through simulation is one such case. Further active development of more adaptable interfaces can be anticipated in order to enhance this approach. The author had an opportunity to introduce the methods to architects at a relatively early phase of their training with a short amount of time; this work developed into the case studies introduced in this paper. An obvious next step is to test the methods with advanced users, allowing for more professional goals, real-life project constraints, and a longer project duration.

Acknowledgements. First, I would like to thank my students: Amanda Cronce, Krystian Krepa, and David Solano. Without their dedicated contributions this paper would not have been possible. I would also like to thank my current employers, Dean Urs Gauchat and Professor Glenn Goldman, and my current collaborator, Professor Richard Foulds at the Department of Biomedical Engineering at New Jersey Institute of Technology, for their generous academic support. Finally, I would like to thank my former academic advisers, Professor Martin Bechthold and Professor Kostas Terzidis at Harvard University, and Professor Takehiko Nagakura at the Massachusetts Institute of Technology, for their insightful guidance and constant support.

References

1. Alexander, C.: A Pattern Language: Towns, Buildings Construction. Oxford University Press, Oxford (1977)
2. Arduino: http://arduino.cc/en/ (2015). Accessed 27 Jan 2015
3. Bongard, J., Zykov, V., Lipson, H.: Resilient machines through continuous self-modeling. Science **314**(5802), 1118–1121 (2006)
4. Eiben, A.E., Smith, J.E.: Introduction to Evolutionary Computing. Springer, Berlin (2003)
5. Firefly: http://www.fireflyexperiments.com/ (2015). Accessed 27 Jan 2015
6. Frazer, J.: An Evolutionary Architecture. Architectural Association, London (1995)
7. García, J.M.: www.jonmartinez.neositios.com/ 2013. (Inverse - Forward Kinematics of a Delta Robot: 2010) Accessed 15 Dec 2013
8. Gero, J.S., D'Cruz, N., Radford, A.D.: Energy in context: a multicriteria model for building design. Build. Environ. **18**(3), 99–107 (1983)
9. Gerber, D.J., Lin, S-H.: Geometric Complexity and Energy Simulation: Evolving Performance Driven Architectural. In: Stouffs, R., Janssen, P., Roudavski, S., Tunçer, B. (eds.), Proceedings of the 18th International Conference on Computer-Aided Architectural Design Research in Asia (CAADRIA 2013), pp. 87–96 (2013)
10. Grasshopper: http://www.grasshopper3d.com/ (2015). Accessed 27 Jan 2015
11. Holland, J.: Genetic algorithms. Sci. Am. **267**(1), 66–72 (1992)
12. Hornsby, G.S.P., Jordan, B.: The Advantages of generative Grammatical Encodings for Physical Design, Congress on Evolutionary Computation (2001)
13. Hornby, G.S.: Generative representations for evolutionary design automation. Ph.D. Dissertation, Brandeis University Department of Computer Science, Waltham (2003)
14. Hudson, S.E., Mankoff, J.: Rapid construction of functioning physical interfaces from cardboard, thumbtacks, tin foil and masking tape. In: Proceedings of the 19th annual ACM symposium on User interface software and technology, ACM Press, Montreux, Switzerland, pp. 289–298 (2006)
15. Kangaroo: http://www.food4rhino.com/project/kangaroo?ufh (2015) Accessed 27 Jan 2015)
16. Lee, J.C., Avrahami, D., Hudson, S.E., Forlizzi, J., Dietz, P.H., Leigh, D.: The calder toolkit: wired and wireless components for rapidly prototyping interactive devices. In: Designing interactive systems: processes, practices, methods, and techniques, ACM, pp. 167–175 (2004)
17. Lipson, H., Pollack, J.B.: Automatic design and manufacture of artificial lifeforms. Nature **406**, 974–978 (2000)
18. Narahara, T.: Self-Organizing Computation: A Framework for Generative Approaches to Architectural Design, Doctor of Design Dissertation. Harvard University Graduate School of Design, Cambridge (2010)
19. Narahara, T.: Design for constant change: adaptable growth model for architecture. Int. J. Archit. Comput. (IJAC) IJAC **8**(1), 29–40 (2010)
20. NVIDIA PhysX Physics: http://www.geforce.com/hardware/technology/physx (2015). Accessed 27 Jan 2015
21. OpenNI: http://www.openni.org/ (2015). Accessed 27 Jan 2015
22. Processing: http://processing.org/ (2015). Accessed 27 Jan 2015
23. Unity 3D: http://unity3d.com/ (2015). Accessed 27 Jan 2015

Shape Studies

Design Patterns from Empirical Studies
in Computer-Aided Design

Rongrong Yu[1(✉)] and John Gero[2,3]

[1] The University of Newcastle, New South Wales, NSW, Australia
rongrong.yu@uon.edu.au
[2] George Mason University, Fairfax, VA, USA
john@johngero.com
[3] University of North Carolina at Charlotte, Charlotte, NC, USA

Abstract. This paper presents the results from studying the effect of the use of computational tools on designers' behavior in terms of using design patterns in the conceptual development stage of designing. The results are based on a protocol study in which architectural designers were asked to complete two architectural design tasks with similar complexity, one in a parametric design environment and one in a geometric modeling environment. To explore the development of design patterns during the design process, the technique of 2nd order Markov model was used. The results suggest that there were more design patterns adopted in the parametric design environment than in the geometric modeling environment. Also, there are more design patterns related to structure in the parametric design environment than in the geometric modeling environment.

Keywords: Design pattern · Markov model · Protocol studies

1 Introduction

In computational design environments, designers often adopt existing design patterns based on their experience of using their design knowledge and their experience in using computational tools. Design patterns have been studied in architectural design: The reuse of existing problem-solution pairs extracted from a designer's own or others' professional experience makes the design process more efficient [1]. This idea has been widely applied in the software design domain. However, this phenomenon has not been adequately studied and evaluated in computer-aided architectural design environments (CAAD).

To improve our understanding of the possible use of design patterns while designing in CAAD, the results of a cognitive study in which designers were asked to complete two architectural design tasks with similar complexity in a parametric design environment (PDE) and a geometric modeling environment (GME) are presented. Protocol analysis was employed to study the designers' behavior. The technique of Markov model analysis is used to analyze the protocol data collected. From the Markov model analysis results describing the occurrence design patterns in computational design environments are derived and discussed.

G. Celani et al. (Eds.): CAAD Futures 2015, CCIS 527, pp. 493–506, 2015.
DOI: 10.1007/978-3-662-47386-3_27

2   Background

2.1   Selected Computational Design Environments – PDE and GME

Design media have significant effects on designers' thinking processes [2, 3]. Past research has suggested that sketching can assist design thinking as an effective design medium [4, 5]. In a similar way, with the increasing application of digital design tools, researchers have started to study the influence of computational design tools on design processes [6–9]. Oxman [10] argues that design media are knowledge-intensive computational environments. Designers share the design knowledge that can be represented and employed in computational environments.

Geometry modeling tools have largely replaced 2D drafting tools in many design practices. GMEs as 3D digital design tools are more effective in assisting in the design process than 2D drafting tools in various ways [6], for example, better visual representations including the ability to produce perspective and walk-through animations, and better coordination of documentation. 3D geometry modeling tools applied in architecture include ArchiCAD, AutoCAD, Microstation, Sketchup, 3ds Max, Maya, Rhino, and many others. In this study, for comparison, we chose Rhino as an example of a GME, Fig. 1(a). In the late 1990s, with the growth in importance of 3D digital tools in the design industry, architects began to identify a range of ways where these were superior to previous 2D computer-aided design systems [6, 11]. More recently another shift has begun to occur, with BIM and parametric software tools beginning to challenge the role played by 3D geometry modeling software in the AEC industry.

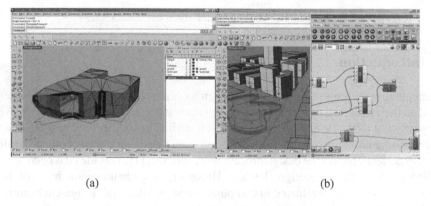

(a)   (b)

Fig. 1. (a) Design environment – GME, (b) design environment – PDE

Parametric design is a dynamic, rule-based process controlled by variations and parameters, in which multiple design solutions can be developed in parallel. According to Woodbury [12], it supports the creation, management and organization of complex digital design models. By changing the parameters of an object, particular instances can be altered or created from a potentially infinite range of possibilities [13]. The term "parameters" means factors which determine a series of variations. In architecture, parameters are usually defined as building parameters or environmental factors. In the architectural design industry, parametric design tools are utilized mainly on complex building form generation, multiple design solution optimization, as well as structural and sustainability control. Parametric design, in a computational form, is a new way of thinking about architectural design. Its impact on designers' processes has not been adequately explored. Currently, typical parametric design software includes Generative Components from Bentley Corporation, Digital Project from Gehry Technology, Grasshopper from McNeel. Scripting tools include Processing based on the Java language, Rhino script and Python script, based on the VB language from McNeel. In this study, Grasshopper was chosen as the parametric design environment, Fig. 1(b). Grasshopper is both an advanced environment for facilitating conceptual design and is in relatively wide-spread use in the architectural profession. Each software classified as a GME or a PDE has its unique features for designing. The selection of Rhino and Grasshopper as the GME and PDE in this study is due to their features, which are representative of the main characteristics of GMEs and PDEs.

2.2   Basis for Protocol Coding Scheme – FBS Ontology

As one of the main design ontologies, Gero's FBS ontology [14] has been applied in numerous cognitive studies [9, 15, 16]. Researchers argue that it is potentially capable of capturing most of the meaningful design issues and design processes [14] with the transitions between design issues clearly classified into eight design processes. The FBS ontology, Fig. 2 shows the three classes of ontological variables: Function (F), Behavior (B) and Structure (S). Function (F) represents the design intentions or purposes; behavior (B) represents the object's derived behavior (Bs) or expected behavior from the structure (Be); and structure (S) represents the components that make up an artifact and their relationships. The ontology as the basis of a coding scheme includes two additional design issues that can be expressed in terms of FBS and therefore do not require an extension of the ontology. These are requirements (R) and descriptions (D). The first of these represents requirements from outside design and the second, descriptions, mean the documentation of the design. Figure 2 shows the FBS ontology indicating the eight design processes—formulation, analysis, evaluation, synthesis, and reformulation I, II and III. Formulation defines the process that generates functions and then expected behaviors, i.e. sets up expected goals from the requirement, while synthesis generates a structure as a candidate solution. Analysis produces a behavior from the existing structure and evaluation compares Bs and Be to determine the success or failure of the candidate solution. Reformulation is the process from the structure back to itself, to the behavior or to the function, which is a reconstruction or reframing process. Among the eight design processes, the three types of reformulation processes are considered to be the dominant processes that potentially capture creative aspects of designing by introducing new variables or new directions [17]. The FBS ontology is claimed to be a universal coding scheme for various design environments [15]. By calculating the transitions between design issues from empirical data, various analyses can be conducted. In this study, the FBS ontology is utilized as the basis of the coding scheme in the protocol analysis.

In the present study, which explores designers' behavior in both a PDE and a GME, an instantiation of the coding scheme is required. Gero's FBS ontology has been applied

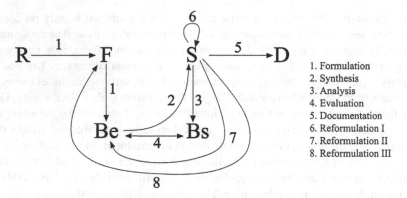

Fig. 2.   The FBS ontology (after [14]).

in many cognitive studies where it has been demonstrated as potentially capturing most of the meaningful design processes [15] and recording clear transitions between design issues. The FBS ontology is founded on the requirements of coverage and uniqueness: the categorical concepts that make up the ontology need to cover all the attributes of a design and there can be no overlap of categorical concepts. A major outcome of the FBS ontology is that design processes are a consequence of the transitions between ontological elements and do not require a separately produced ontology of processes. The FBS ontology has been used widely in the domains of mechanical engineering, architecture, software engineering, civil engineering, cognitive psychology, manufacturing, management and creativity research. The behavior of designers, using the FBS ontology as the basis, can be measured from empirically derived data from protocol analysis. With this ontology it becomes possible to compare designing independent of researcher, independent of domain, independent of education, independent of whether an individual or a team is designing, independent of location or co-location, independent of the use of tools, independent of design experience and independent of design task. Prior to this such empirically derived data from different researchers was generally not comparable and it was difficult to build directly on the research of others. Kan and Gero [18] applied the FBS ontology to a study of software designers' behavior, suggesting that the method is effective for encoding programming or rule-based activities across different design disciplines. Given that PDEs enable scripting and programming activities, similarly the FBS scheme will be able to encode both geometric modeling and rule-based algorithmic activities effectively. Therefore, in this study it is introduced as a conceptual foundation for developing the coding scheme for the protocol analysis.

3   Research Method

3.1   Protocol Analysis

Protocol analysis is a method for turning qualitative verbal and gestural utterances into data [19, 20]. It has been used extensively in design research to develop an understanding of design cognition [17, 21, 22]. According to Akin [23], a protocol is the record of behaviors of designers using sketches, notes, videos or audio. After collecting the protocol data, a coding scheme is applied to categorize the collected data, enabling detailed study of the design process in the chosen design environments. As Gero and Tang [24] state, protocol analysis has become the prevailing experimental technique for exploring the understanding of design.

Usually in protocol analysis, concurrent and retrospective protocol collection methods can be applied in design experiments [19, 25]. A concurrent protocol involves participants in an experiment verbalizing their thoughts when working on a specific task – also called the "think aloud" method – whereas a retrospective protocol explores what designers were thinking while designing, a process which is applied as soon as they have finished the design task. Some studies have compared these two protocol collection methods. For instance, Kuusela and Pallab [26] argue that concurrent protocols are more suitable for examining the design process and can generate larger numbers of segments, while retrospective protocols are more suitable for examining design outcomes. Another example of this comparison is Gero and Tang's [24] study exploring design processes. Their results show that concurrent and retrospective protocols lead to very similar outcomes in terms of exploring designers' intentions during design processes. But they also conclude that concurrent protocols are an efficient and applicable method by which to understand design processes. Retrospective protocols are commonly believed to be less intrusive to the design processes.

Importantly, protocol analysis of this type deals with a relatively small number of samples, but it enables an in-depth exploration of the samples. Thus, a study of the cognitive behavior of eight designers is both acceptable and in keeping with past research in this field because of the quality and depth of information that is recorded and analyzed. However, for this reason we also cannot generalize the results of this research to describe the actions or behaviors of a much larger population of designers. Nevertheless, from such studies important patterns, which are repeated by designers can be used to provide an increased level of understanding of the design process.

3.2 Markov Model Analysis

A Markov model describes the probabilities of moving from one state to another [27, 28], it demonstrates the tendency of future design moves. Kan and Gero adopt the Markov chain model using the FBS ontology to describe cognitive design processes [15, 29]. Within the context of the FBS ontology, the Markov matrix can be applied as a quantitative tool to study design activities based on the transition probabilities between design issues or between design processes. Within the FBS context, two types of Markov models have been found to be useful: the 1st order Markov model and the 2nd order Markov model. The 1st order Markov model presents the probability of moving to a future state depending only on a knowledge of the current state, without considering the past states, Fig. 3.

The 2nd order Markov model includes the memory of the past state. That means a future movement is dependent on both the current state and its preceding state. For example, if the current design activity is Be, and the previous one was F, which is a formulation design process, then we use the 2nd order Markov model to calculate the probability of next state being S if the previous design process was formulation, Fig. 4.

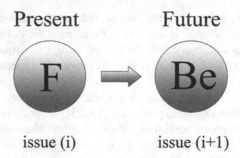

issue (i)   issue (i+1)

Fig. 3. An example of the foundation for a 1st order Markov model using the FBS ontology

Jiang [30] applies both the 1st order and 2nd order Markov model to study multidisciplinary designers' behavior. The result of his study shows that the main transition models match the original FBS ontological processes. Compared to the 1st order Markov model, the 2nd order Markov model presents a longer probability passage of transitions, which contains three sequential steps. This research utilizes the 2nd order Markov model to explore the utilization of design patterns in the CAAD environments.

An example of a 2nd order Markov model is shown in Fig. 4.

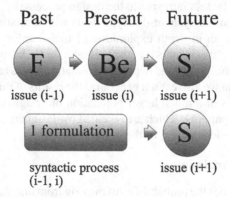

Fig. 4. An example of a 2nd order Markov model using the FBS ontology [30]: a 2nd order Markov chain, this is the interpreted as a transition from a design process to a design issue.

4   Experiment Setting

4.1   Selection of Subjects

In the any experiment, the selection of participants is important as it can influence the objectivity and reliability of the final results. The principle behind the selection is to reduce as much as possible individual differences and other subjective influences. The criteria of selection for the eight architects was that they should each have more than five years' architectural design experience and no less than two years' experience using parametric design tools, to ensure that the participants are experienced both in architectural design and in operating parametric design software. The requirements of two years' experience using parametric design tools is based on the fact that Grasshopper, as a parametric design software, was developed in 2007 and gained wider adoption only during the 2010s. By the time this research was conducted, most parametric designers have only gained two to three years' experience with the tool. Previous protocol studies often selected subjects with experience levels ranging from five to ten years as expert designers [11, 31]. However most parametric designers tend to come from a younger generation. Therefore, architects with five years' architectural design experience are considered as sufficiently experienced designers amongst the younger generation and are suitable for the current study. Additionally, participants' abilities regarding creative design and manipulating software should be at a similar level so that individual differences would not greatly affect the final results. In the end, eight designers were found who could satisfy the selection criteria. Architects were recruited from architectural design companies, tutors of parametric design workshops, and lecturers (four practitioners and four academics). Among the participants were two female designers and six male designers, five of the participants are from Australia and three from outside Australia. The standard deviations of the measurements are the bases for determining whether these demographic variations are significant. If the standard deviation for a particular measurement is low then the effect of the demographic variation in the subjects is not statistically significant.

4.2 Design Brief

For applications of protocol analysis, it is suggested that the experiment normally be limited to around one hour in length, meaning that the design task should not be too complex. In real cases, an architectural design task usually takes weeks or months. A previous studies has shown that the design behavior of designers across long-term, multiple design sessions shows only minor variations [32]. In the current research due to the restriction of research method, the selection of a one hour design task with an appropriate complexity level in a simulated experiment environment is reasonable to explore designers' cognitive behavior during the conceptual design stage. Many previous studies used simple product design tasks, such as a computer mouse, packaging or even a symbol design. In the architectural field, design tasks are also simplified, such as rearranging furniture or producing a home office layout [33]. However, parametric design tools are appropriate for generating complex geometries. If the design task is too simple, the advantages of parametric design tools are difficult to express.

In the present experiment, each designer was required to complete two different design tasks with similar levels of complexity, one using Rhino (GME) and one using Grasshopper (PDE). Designers were given 40 min for each design session, but were allowed to continue for an extra 20 min, if required, in order to complete the task. Considering the time necessary for a conceptual design task, as well as the time involved for later data analysis of the results, 40 min is a reasonable time constraint. Task 1 is a conceptual design for a community center and Task 2 is a similar study of a shopping center, with both containing some specific functional requirements. These functional requirements are the main differences between the two tasks. In all other ways the two design tasks are similar, including the site provided, the required building size, and the extent of the concept development. A pre-modeled site, shown in Fig. 5, was provided to the designers for each task. Because the present study is focused on exploring designers' behavior at the conceptual design stage, the designers were required to only consider concept generation, simple site planning and general functional zoning. No detailed plan layout was required. Both tasks focus on conceptual design in general to enable the design process to be completed in a relatively short time period, and therefore to be captured and analyzed using the protocol analysis method. The tasks were both open and general enough to provide designers with the freedom to enable various possible design strategies to be applied during parametric design. As a result, the designers were allowed to exhibit different ways of approaching parametric design, which are similar to the actual practices of parametric design and therefore useful in order to examine the findings about parametric design. The design sessions and tasks were randomly matched among different designers. During the experiment designers were not allowed to sketch, ensuring that almost all of their actions happened within the computer. This ensured that the design environment was purely within either the PDE or the GME.

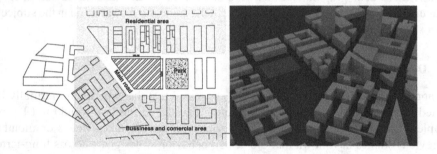

Fig. 5. Site model provided

4.3 Experiment Procedures

Before the data collection part of the experiment commenced a "warm-up" process was used to familiarize participants with the equipment. According to some current studies, the "think aloud" method for protocol data collection may influence participants' perception during design processes [19, 22]. As a consequence, designers may not be used to talking while they are designing, which could lead to incomplete data from such experiments. The purpose of the warm-up training is to explain to the participants the significance of the research and to provide training to practice the "think aloud" skills required [34] so that they can better verbalize their thoughts during the experiment.

The experiment is divided into two parts. In the first part, participants are required to speak aloud what they are thinking while designing. A screen capture program records both their words and actions. If there is not sufficient verbal data produced, in the second part the retrospective protocol method is used to produce complementary verbal data.

That means that, after finishing the design task, the videos are played back and participants are asked to make additional comments about what they were thinking while designing. The data collected, therefore include verbal information about participants' design intentions as well as visual information about their activities.

5   Analysis

5.1   General Analysis

This study employs an integrated segmentation and coding method. The segmentation and coding process are based on the "one segment one code" principle [35]. It means there is no overlapped code or multiple codes for one segment. If there are multiple codes for one segment, the segment will be further divided. Table 1 provides the general information of the coding coverage. The values shown in the table are the average of the eight protocols. The average overall numbers of segments are respectively 244 in the PDE and 224 in the GME. Designers, on average, spent more time in the PDE session (48 min) than in the GME (44 min). On average over 92.2 % of segments can be coded as FBS codes. Non-coded segments include communication and software management. The design speed is very similar between the two design environments, with means of 5.11 and 4.78 segments/min and low standard deviations. The individual speed of design varies between 3.06 and 6.86 segments/min, especially in the GME session. That indicates that designers have their own design habits or strategies or that some designers may think and act faster than others.

Table 1. General coding information of design sessions. Low standard deviations in these results indicate that the demographic variation in the subjects is not significant.

	Design environment	Time (min)	Number of segments	Coded percentage (%)	Speed (segments/min)
Mean	GME	44.0	224	92.2	5.11
	PDE	48.0	244	92.2	4.78
SD	GME	11.2	45.3	4.3	1.20
	PDE	7.4	29.7	3.5	0.53

After transcription, two rounds of segmentation (the division of protocols into individual segments based on their content) and coding were conducted. The coding was conducted by one researcher with a time interval of two weeks between the two rounds of coding. Following this an arbitration session (to make decisions on any disagreements between codes) was carried out to produce the final protocol. The agreement between the two rounds of coding is 84.8 % (GME) and 83.5 % (PDE). The final arbitrated results were 92.1 % (GME) and 91.5 % (PDE). The high level of agreement suggests the reliability of the coding results.

5.2   2nd Order Markov Analysis Results

The 2nd order Markov model analysis is presented in Table 2. It shows that all the transitions with higher probability are related to S. The 2nd order Markov model produces a larger pattern that includes two transitions. As shown in Table 2, the highest transition probability is from reformulation 3 to S, reformulation 3 refers to transition S to F, which means that the transition S-F-S is the most likely to occur pattern. The obvious difference between GME and PDE is the transition after reformulation 3 to S and the transition after reformulation 3 to Be. Reformulation 3 to S means that, after the designer has carried out the process reformulation 3, which is from S to F, the designers' consideration goes back to S. This transition, which is F to S is part of a larger pattern, which is S-F-S.

Table 2.   The 2nd order Markov model analysis

	R		F		Be		Bs		S	
	GME	PDE	GME	PDE	GME	PDE	GME	PDE	GME	PDE
Formulation	0.04	0.02	0.22	0.20	0.24	0.19	0.24	0.22	0.26	0.37
Synthesis	0.00	0.00	0.04	0.05	0.14	0.24	0.36	0.28	0.45	0.43
Analysis	0.01	0.00	0.06	0.06	0.21	0.15	0.25	0.25	0.47	0.54
Evaluation	0.02	0.01	0.06	0.06	0.17	0.23	0.23	0.28	0.52	0.43
Reformulation 1	0.01	0.00	0.03	0.06	0.15	0.18	0.39	0.31	0.43	0.45
Reformulation 2	0.01	0.00	0.09	0.06	0.22	0.16	0.24	0.34	0.45	0.44
Reformulation 3	0.06	0.00	0.13	0.06	0.30	0.07	0.17	0.18	0.34	0.69

6   Design Patterns in Computational Design Environments

6.1   The Design Pattern S-F-S

A descriptive diagram of the 2nd order Markov model analysis in the GME and the PDE is presented in Fig. 6. The circles labeled with the FBS codes represent the design issues, and the size of circle represents the frequency of occurrence of the design issue. Each arrow shows the transition from one state to the other, and the thickness of the line represents the transition probability between design issues. To demonstrate the main activities of the designers, we select those transitions with the probability value larger than 0.4 and highlight them in Fig. 6. The value 0.4 is selected as threshold to abstract the model based on a transition probability that is 2 times that of the random transition probability. In the FBS model, each variable has 5 other states to go to, which means that the random probability is 0.2, therefore 0.4 is set as the threshold.

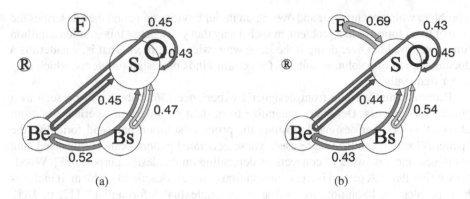

Fig. 6. (a) Primary transitions of the 2nd order Markov model in the GME, (b) primary transitions of the 2nd order Markov model in the PDE.

Applying 2nd order Markov model analysis, the results in Fig. 6 suggest that there are significantly more S-F-S transitions in PDE than in GME. During the F–S process, designers select an existing structure/solution for the particular design problem based on their experience or knowledge, which is a process of using an existing design pattern to the problem. The S-F-S transitions refer to a consideration to a structure issue (S) followed by the adoption of the design pattern (F-S). That is to say, design patterns usually based on the consideration of geometrical structure. From this result we can infer that when architects apply programming and scripting in their design, such as in a PDE, they exhibit the characteristic of using design patterns when building the structure of the geometry.

Within the context of the FBS ontology, this process of transitioning directly from function (F) to structure (S) is excluded from routine ways of design (excluded from the eight design processes expressed in FBS model). Previous research suggests from the study of software designers' behavior, that F to S is a typical design process that occurs frequently [18]. During the F–S process, designers select an existing structure/solution for the particular design problem based on their experience or knowledge, which is a process of selecting and applying an existing design pattern to the problem. This matches the concepts behind Alexander's "pattern language" [1]. Since software designers use design patterns when programming and scripting [36, 37], we can infer that when architects apply programming and scripting in their design, such as in a PDE, they exhibit the similar characteristic of using design patterns.

Design patterns are an important concept in both architectural design and software design. In software design, it assists software designers in working more efficiently and makes the programming and scripting process traceable. In the PDE, if we can generalize some useful design patterns, it would assist architects in their scripting process.

6.2 Design Patterns in Computational Design Environments

From the Markov model analysis results, we found design patterns are adopted in both GME and PDE, with more patterns in the parametric design environment. The idea of design patterns was first introduced by Christopher Alexander: "each pattern describes a problem which occurs over and over again in our environment, and then describes the core of the solution to that problem, in such a way that you can use this solution a million times over, without ever doing it the same way twice." [1, p. x]. That is, a pattern is a documentation of a solution suitable for certain kinds of design problems, which may occur frequently.

Patterns usually come from designer's experience [36], which can be seen as a "induction" process. Designers generalize from their own design experience or from observation of other designers, abstract the problem-solution pair, and formalize the "patterns" which can then be re-used. These generated patterns can be improved, and combined into a network of connections depending on the design purpose [38]. Woodbury writes that: "A pattern is a generic solution to a well-described problem. It includes both problem and solution, as well as other contextual information." [12, p. 185]. A design expert has accumulated a large number of examples of problems and solutions in a specific domain [39]. The pattern itself is an abstraction of that experience, when designers apply the patterns, they could revise them based on their own preference, or on the specific context of the current design task.

In the software design domain, educators found that Alexander's work on design patterns is suitable in software design pedagogy. For example, Gamma et al. [37] define patterns as a tool to describe compositional ideas in computer programming. This matches our analysis results that in parametric design, design patterns are developed and used.

7   Conclusion and Future Work

This paper has presented the results of a protocol study that explores the phenomenon of using design patterns in computational design environments. It compared the design patterns found in a parametric design environment (PDE) with those found in a geometry modeling environment (GME). The main finding is that: firstly, the adoption of design patterns is found in both computational design environments – PDE and GME. Secondly, significantly more design patterns are used in the PDE than in the GME. Since the main differences between the two design environments is that there is rule algorithm feature in the PDE, we can assume that the more rule algorithm features in the computational design environment, the more design patterns tend to be used during design process; Thirdly, the occurrence of design patterns is mainly based on the consideration of geometry. This claim is based on the higher number of S-F-S transitions in the PDE than in the GME. During this process designers' attention first focus on building the geometric pattern, followed with a design pattern. This is to say, when designers consider the structure of geometry, they tend to adopt design patterns based on their professional experience or knowledge.

The existence of design patterns implies that some aspects of the design processes in computational design are potentially generalizable and transferable, and can be learned by architectural designers and students. The design patterns identified from the current study can be potentially customized for different design scenarios and embedded as generic components in the system to allow designers to apply computer-aided design tools more effectively. These protocol analysis results suggest that some designers currently define design patterns by themselves and repeatedly use them in a computational design process.

The future work based on this study will focus on exploring the development of design patterns in the PDE over time. This has pedagogical implications in terms of both teaching and learning.

Acknowledgements. This research has been supported in part by the National Science Foundation grant CMMI-1161715. Any opinions, findings, and conclusions or recommendations expressed in this material are those of the authors and do not necessarily reflect the views of National Science Foundation.

References

1. Alexander, C., Ishikawa, S., Silverstein, M.: A Pattern Language: Towns, Buildings, Construction. Oxford University Press, New York (1977)
2. Chen, S.-C.: The role of design creativity in computer media. In: Architectural information management, 30th eCAADe conference, Helsinki, Finland (2001)
3. Mitchell, W.J.: Beyond Productivity: Information Technology. Innovation and Creativity, Washington, DC (2003)
4. Black, A.: Visible planning on paper and on screen. Behav. Info. Technol. **9**(4), 283–296 (1990)
5. Schön, D.A.: The Reflective Practitioner: How Professionals Think in Action. Basic Books, New York (1983)
6. Bilda, Z., Demirkan, H.: An insight on designers' sketching activities in traditional versus digital media. Des. Stud. **24**(1), 27–50 (2003)
7. Fallman, D.: Design-oriented human-computer interaction. In: 21th ACM CHI Conference on Human Factors in Computing Systems, Florida, USA (2003)
8. Kim, M.J., Maher, M.L.: The impact of tangible user interfaces on spatial cognition during collaborative design. Des. Stud. **29**(3), 222–253 (2008)
9. Gero, J., Tang, H.-H.: concurrent and retrospective protocols and computer-aided architectural design. In: 4th CAADRIA conference, Shanghai (1999)
10. Oxman, R.: Design media for the cognitive designer. Autom. Constr. **9**(4), 337–346 (2000)
11. Kan, J.W.T., Gero, J.S.: The effect of computer mediation on collaborative designing, in between man and MACHINE? Integration, Intuition, Intelligence. In: Proceedings of 14th CAADRIA conference, Yunlin, Taiwan (2009)
12. Woodbury, R.: Elements of Parametric Design. Routledge, New York (2010)
13. Kolarevic, B.: Architecture in the Digital Age: Design And Manufacturing. Spon Press, New York (2003)
14. Gero, J.S.: Design prototypes: a knowledge representation schema for design. AI Mag. **11**(4), 26–36 (1990)
15. Kan, J.W.T., Gero, J.S.: Using the FBS ontology to capture semantic design information in design protocol studies. In: McDonnell, J., Lloyd, P. (eds.) About: Designing. Analysing Design Meetings, pp. 213–229. Taylor & Francis, New York (2009)
16. Kan, J.W.T., Gero, J.S.: Can entropy indicate the richness of idea generation in team designing? In: Digital Opportunities, 10th CAADRIA conference, New Delhi, India (2005)
17. Kan, J.W.T., Gero, J.S.: Acquiring information from linkography in protocol studies of designing. Des. Stud. **29**(4), 315–337 (2008)

18. Kan, J.W.T., Gero, J.S.: Studing software design cognition, In: Petre, M., Hoek, AVd (eds.) Software Designers in Action: A Human-Centric Look at Design Work. Chapman Hall, London (2009)
19. Ericsson, K.A., Simon, H.A.: Protocol Analysis: Verbal Reports as Data. MIT Press, Mass (1993)
20. Gero, J.S., Mc Neill, T.: An approach to the analysis of design protocols. Des. Stud. 19(1), 21–61 (1998)
21. Atman, C.J., et al.: A comparison of freshman and senior engineering design processes. Des. Stud. 20(2), 131–152 (1999)
22. Suwa, M., Tversky, B.: What do architects and students perceive in their design sketches? A protocol analysis. Des. Stud. 18(4), 385–403 (1997)
23. Akin, O.: Psychology of Architectural Design. Pion, London (1986)
24. Gero, J., Tang, H.-H.: The differences between retrospective and concurrent protocols in revealing the process-oriented aspects of the design process. Des. Stud. 22(3), 283–295 (2001)
25. Dorst, K., Dijkhuis, J.: Comparing paradigms for describing design activity. Des. Stud. 16(2), 261–274 (1995)
26. Kuusela, H., Pallab, P.: A comparison of concurrent and retrospective verbal protocol analysis. Am. J. Psychol. 113(3), 387–404 (2000)
27. Ching, W.K., Ng, M.K.: Markov Chains: Models, Algorithms and Applications. Springer, New York (2006)
28. Meyn, S.P., Tweedie, R.L.: Markov Chains and Stochastic Stability. Cambridge University Press, Cambridge (2009)
29. Kan, J.W.T., Gero, J.S.: Exploring quantitative methods to study design behavior in collaborative virtual workspaces. In: New Frontiers, Proceedings of the 15th International Conference on CAADRIA (2010)
30. Jiang, H.: Understanding senior design students' product conceptual design activities— a comparison between industrial and engineering design students. National University of Singapore, Singapore (2012)
31. Gero, J.S., Kannengiesser, U.: Commonalities across designing: empirical results. In: Proceedings of 5th International Conference on Design Computing and Cognition, College Station (2014)
32. Gero, J.S., Jiang, H., Vieira, S.: Exploring a multi-meeting engineering design project. In: Chakrabarti, A., Prakash, R.V. (eds.) ICoRD'13 conference, Springer, India (2013)
33. Kim, M.J.: The effects of tangible user interfaces on designers' spatial cognition key centre of design computing and cognition. Faculty of Architecture, Doctor of Philosophy (2006)
34. Nguyen, L., Shanks, G.: Using protocol analysis to explore the creative requirements engineering process. Information Systems Foundations Workshop, pp. 133–151. ANUE Press, Canberra (2006)
35. Pourmohamadi, M., Gero, J.S.: LINKOgrapher: An analysis tool to study design protocols based on FBS coding scheme. In: Culley, S., et al. (eds.) Design Theory and Methodology, pp. 294–303. Design Society, Glasgow (2011)
36. Fowler, M.: Patterns of Enterprise Application Architecture. Addison-Wesley, Reading (2003)
37. Gamma, E., et al.: Design patterns: abstraction and reuse of object-oriented design. In: Manfred, B., Ernst, D. (eds.) Software Pioneers, pp. 701–717. Springer, New York (2002)
38. Alexander, C.: The Timeless Way of Building. Oxford University Press, Oxford (1979)
39. Razzouk, R., Shute, V.: What Is Design Thinking and Why Is It Important? Rev. Educ. Res. 82(3), 330–348 (2012)

Shape Grammars for Architectural Design:
The Need for Reframing

Pieter Pauwels[1(✉)], Tiemen Strobbe[1], Sara Eloy[2], and Ronald De Meyer[1]

[1] Ghent University, Ghent, Belgium
{pipauwel.pauwels,tiemen.strobbe,ronald.demeyer}@ugent.be
[2] Lisbon University Institute, Lisbon, Portugal
sara.eloy@iscte.pt

Abstract. Although many shape grammars and corresponding implementations have been proposed, shape grammars are not widely adopted by architectural designers. In this paper, we therefore look for the barriers of implementing and using shape grammars for architectural design. We do this by outlining several implementation strategies of shape grammars, we briefly point to our own graph-based design grammar system, and we analyse the resulting overview using theories on how designers think and act upon incoming information. Based on this analysis, we develop and suggest how design grammars might best be implemented and used for architectural design relying on the information technologies available at this particular moment of time.

Keywords: Architectural design · Design space exploration · Design thinking · Shape grammar

1 Introduction

Shape grammars have often been proposed as possible support mechanisms for architectural designers [1]. An implemented shape grammar allows the rapid production of alternative shapes following one grammar. As architectural designers often seem to use a grammar when designing, one might theoretically opt to try capturing the grammar used by a specific architect and make it available to computer algorithms in the form of a computer-implemented grammar. We propose to distinguish here between *shape grammars* and *design grammars*, the former focusing only on geometric shape and the latter taking also into account semantically more meaningful concepts, such as walls, windows, or other object types. This is obviously a theoretical distinction, as most grammars include both geometry and more complex semantical concepts. Theoretically, if one would be able to implement a design grammar, the system that has access to this implemented design grammar would be able to generate design alternatives for specific new design situations.

The theory and idea behind shape grammars were introduced by George Stiny and James Gips in the seventies, with their early work on the composition of form [2, 3]. Based on this work, Stiny developed the ice ray lattice grammar [4] and the Palladian grammar, together with William Mitchell [5], both before the eighties. Also the

© Springer-Verlag Berlin Heidelberg 2015
G. Celani et al. (Eds.): CAAD Futures 2015, CCIS 527, pp. 507–526, 2015.
DOI: 10.1007/978-3-662-47386-3_28

grammars produced by Terry Knight can be counted among the first shape grammars [6–8]. Experiments have been made to produce similar shape grammars for other designs and design languages. A lot of the earlier shape grammar examples hereby focus on geometry. Another example of this focus can be found in Heisserman's 3D Koch snowflake grammar of 1990 [9]. Many of the later shape grammars, on the contrary, appear to focus on capturing design grammar (meaning - semantics) rather than shape grammar (geometry - syntax). Two examples are the Malagueira Houses grammar for Alvaro Siza [10] and the Prairie House grammar for Frank Lloyd Wright (FLW) [11]. In both cases, realised houses appear to follow rather clear design rules, so they appear to be amenable for being captured in a shape grammar. In contrast to the Koch snowflake grammar, which is quite simple and purely geometric, the Malagueira grammar and the FLW grammar include a greater number of semantically more complex concepts (including notions like *'left'*, *'right'*, *'street side'*, *'courtyard'*, and so forth). Consequently, they tend to consist of hundreds of rules, resulting in a considerable complexity that keeps them from being used effortlessly.

From these two different examples (geometry and syntax vs. meaning and semantics), one can already see that it is not so straightforward to just take the original idea of a shape grammar, which acts primarily upon geometric concepts and generates rather diverse and almost random shapes (purely syntactic), and use it to also construct grammars that have a considerably larger and more complex semantics, which is the case for Alvaro Siza's houses and Frank Lloyd Wright's houses. So, although many efforts have already been made to implement a shape grammar so that it can generate as complete design alternatives as possible for a realistic design situation, there appears to be an inconsistency or impossibility in the notion of using a shape grammar for semantically more complex situations.

We consider two types of practical implementations of shape grammars for explicit usage in an architectural design context. First, computer implemented design grammars might be used to capture a more or less fixed and proven grammar, comparable to an architectural style that is constructed over years of experience by an architectural designer. Alvaro Siza's Malagueira house grammar and the FLW grammar can be considered examples of such a grammar. A practical application of this grammar then allows to reproduce new designs in the same style. This practical usage scenario is closer to what is referred to as an *analytical grammar*. Most of the effort goes in building a complete and consistent grammar. As a result, the more buildings are designed according to the implemented grammar, the more effective the grammar implementation is. As a second option, computer implemented design grammars might be built from scratch by designers who did not yet decide which style or grammar they would like to use. In this case, a system would be needed that allows a designer to efficiently set up a new or modified design grammar that is complete and consistent in a short amount of time. This usage scenario is closer to what is referred to as an *original grammar*. The system should then be able to provide useful insights to the designer, thereby relying on the design grammar input earlier by the designer. In this case, the system that allows building and modifying the grammar is of key importance. The more intuitive and flexible this system is, the more benefit is experienced by an architectural designer.

In this paper, we will look more closely into the second, 'original' scenario, because implementations of such grammars are rarely found. In support of this investigation, we developed and implemented a system in which a designer is able to define custom grammars with custom rules, in which a designer is able to specify an initial design situation from which the system can start executing the custom rules in the custom grammar, and in which a designer is able to interactively intervene by selecting or deselecting rules and by manually modifying any of the suggested design alternatives at a particular moment in time so that it can be used as a new seed in the implemented system. We do not present the actual system or its implementation here, as this is not the topic of this paper. Please refer to [12] for details on the implemented system. We do present the more theoretical conclusions that we could make based on our own experiences in building, implementing and using the system. These theoretical conclusions focus on what might be needed to provide designers with the desired functionality, namely a system that autonomously provides new insights that are of value to the designer and his 'active design grammar' (see original grammar scenario above).

Our conclusions indicate a 'need for reframing'. Currently available systems, including our implementation, appear unable to autonomously 'make a shift' (reframing) in the design grammar that they rely upon. In other words, they are able to shift from one design state into another, while remaining in one and the same grammar. As human designers are typically able to shift from one design state into another *by* (modestly) *changing* the underlying design grammar (thinking out of the box), it would be desirable if a system would allow to do such reframing as well. This functionality would allow the system to provide precisely those insights that could bring real added value to the designer. Hence, we make a suggestion on how design grammars might best be implemented and used for architectural design, namely as part of a system that does not accommodate (or do) reframing on its own, but that allows a form of 'supervised reframing' by the designer.

2 The Theory Behind the Usage of Shape Grammars

2.1 The Early Proposal by George Stiny

Shape grammars were originally introduced as a way of analysing and synthesising paintings by George Stiny [2]. They were later extended [13] and their application in various application domains was considered, one of these application domains being architectural design. George Stiny defines a shape grammar as *'a set of transformation rules applied recursively to an initial form, generating new forms'* [13]. The originally proposed shape grammars are rule production systems that generate geometric shapes or solids in Euclidean space (E^2 or E^3). At the core thus lies a *simple rewrite rule system*. A shape grammar G is a 4-tuple $< V_T, V_M, R, I >$, with:

- a finite set of terminal shapes V_T,
- a finite set of marker shapes V_M,
- a finite set of shape rules R, and
- an initial shape I, which is a subset of V_T and V_M.

The shapes defined in the set V_T and V_M form the basic elements for the definition of shape rules in the set R and in the initial shape I. New shapes are generated by iteratively applying shape rules to the initial shape. A shape rule is described as an *IF-THEN* statement $A \rightarrow B$, with a left-hand side (LHS) A and a right-hand side (RHS) B. A shape (rewrite) rule can be applied when the pattern shape A (*IF*-part or LHS) can be detected in a given shape C. This matching process can occur under certain Euclidean transformations t to find more possible matches: translation, rotation, scaling and other linear transformations. Rule application results in subtracting the transformed shape A from C, and adding the transformed replacement shape B (*THEN*-part or RHS). This results in a new shape $C' = C\text{-}t(A) + t(B)$.

This basis was originally mainly used for geometric shape grammars, including the ice ray lattice grammar, the Palladian grammar and the 3D Koch snowflakes grammar. Yet, architectural design was present as a targeted domain of application. In this context, shape grammars were primarily intended for analysis of real-world designs and generation of new design alternatives in the same language. This includes Frank Lloyd Wright's Prairie Houses [11], Palladian columns and villas [5], suburban Queen Anne Houses [14], Alvaro Siza's Malagueira houses [10], and so forth (see also [9] for early intended usage examples). The shape grammars were supposed to capture the formalism and rationale behind designing according to each of these specific styles, so that they could generate solutions for alternative design situations using the same grammars.

2.2   Towards an Optimal Application Path for Executing Rewrite Rules

An important next step after the early proposals by Stiny and Gips was suggested by Cagan and Mitchell [15, 16] in their proposal to implement a *shape annealing* algorithm in combination with the original shape grammars. The argument was made that the traditional mechanisms did not really provide any indication of how the system would choose which rule to apply next. So, it appeared that the original idea was to generate as much as possible alternatives and make them viable. Cagan and Mitchell suggest to use the principle of simulated annealing in the context of forming shapes, so that the derivation of alternatives by the system is controlled. By making this modification, the complete process of applying rules can conceptually be placed more closely to the area of problem solving, because an explicit optimisation criterion is taken into account. '*We formulate the design problem as an optimisation problem with a quantifiable objective function and a set of design constraints. [...] The result is an optimally directed design solution.*' [15].

The approach suggested by Cagan and Mitchell [15, 16] is one of the first steps towards what is now known as *directed search*. By using explicit optimisation criteria, the system can deploy a shape grammar in a particular direction that is considered most optimal. From the start, it is clearly stated that it cannot be the objective to attain a globally optimal solution for a particular design situation, but rather that the purpose is to direct the search in at least some suboptimal regions in the space of design solutions [15, 16]. Important in this setup is the use of design constraints within the design rules. From the beginning, a number of constraints is defined as part of the design rules, together with a quantifiable objective function and an initial state. Rules can only be executed if the constraints within the rules are satisfied.

2.3   Lexicon: Design States in the Design Space

From this early research on the application of shape grammars, a certain lexicon developed, consisting of terms like 'design space', 'design states', 'design rules' or 'shape rules', 'paths', and so forth. These terms are typically associated with a formal or structured representation. For example, the *design space* is commonly formalised as a network structure, with the nodes representing *design states* and the arcs representing the *paths* between two of the design states (Fig. 1). The set of shape rules *R* and the initial shape *I* are the key elements in any shape grammar *G*. The initial shape *I* corresponds to the 'root design state' in Fig. 1. As the system applies rules selected from the set of shape rules *R*, the initial design state transforms into new design states (1a, 1b, 1c, etc. in Fig. 1). Also these *design states* are typically interpreted as well-structured formalisations of more complex real-world design states.

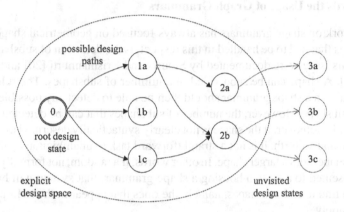

Fig. 1. A sample design space consisting of nine design states and nine paths connecting the root design state with explicitly derived (1a, 1b, 1c, 2a, 2b) or derivable design states (3a, 3b, 3c)

The language of the grammar $\mathcal{L}(G)$, which is the set of shapes that can be generated using the grammar *G*, designates a *design space*. Using a carefully developed grammar, this language $\mathcal{L}(G)$ defines a potentially vast and coherent design space that can be explored systematically. The exploration process is terminated when either no applicable rules are found or when a given goal state is satisfied. Presumably, the closer the formalisation of the design space is to the design space as it is in the designer's mind, the more useful it can be for that designer.

In this early interpretation on the usage of shape grammars for architectural design support, the design process is put right in the middle of a problem-solving context. Although it is rightfully made clear that it is not the purpose to get *the* global solution to a particular design situation, the system using a shape grammar is nevertheless aimed at finding suboptimal solutions [15, 16]. Using this interpretation, the resulting tools are considered to support a creative design process by amplifying a designer's capabilities to represent and search a design space [17]. This task is commonly referred to as *design space exploration*, which involves (1) the representation of many design alternatives in a structured network called the design space, (2) searching and navigating this space by traversing paths in the network and (3) evaluating design alternatives towards design goals [18].

If information systems were capable of design space exploration, they would theoretically be able to traverse the design space autonomously and in a useful/reasonable fashion. As such, these systems might become specialised 'agents' that act like assistants in a creative design process. Moreover, such agents can learn from interaction with the designer and actively anticipate to suit a designer's needs. Existing agent applications provide specific functionality in a wide variety of application domains, including text editing, web browsing, information visualisation, etc. To some extent, information systems for design space exploration might thus also be implemented and used as intelligent agents, leading the way forward towards a more agent-like role for computers in architectural design, rather than their more limited role as oracles or draughtsmen [19].

2.4   Towards the Usage of Graph Grammars

The early work on shape grammars has always focused on geometrical shapes. One of the key issues that had to be handled in this respect, is the detection of subshapes. Some details on this issue were documented by Stouffs and Krishnamurti [20] and by Krishnamurti [21]. A shape can be subdivided in a number of subshapes. The rules that are made available in a shape grammar should then be able to detect any possible subshape in this overall shape. However, the number of subshapes that can be detected in a shape is infinite, and, moreover, if the shape is not clearly syntactically described in rectangles, lines, points, and so forth, it is not a straightforward task to unambiguously identify the desired subshape from a larger shape. In other words, if a random, not formally presented shape is presented to a system housing a shape grammar, that system will have a very hard time to find useful subshapes, namely the ones that appear in the LHS parts of the rules it can apply.

Hence, proposals were made to represent the shape in a less ambiguous manner. This opened the way to a number of alternative formal grammars, among which graph grammars. A graph grammar, in short, does not act on shape per se, but it acts upon graph representations (which often represent geometrical shape). A good description of the workings of a graph grammar and a number of sample references is given by Chakrabarty [22]. In short, the rules deployed by a graph grammar system include graphs in their LHS and RHS parts, and the initial design state is not a geometrical outset, it is also a graph. As the rules can be interpreted now as graph rewrite rules, a number of rule applications transforms the meaning of the initial design state, which is semantically represented in the directed labelled graph captured in the initial graph, into new design states, which are also semantically represented as directed labelled graphs. Considering their higher level of semantical complexity, the Malagueira house and the FLW grammar should be good candidates for graph grammar implementations.

2.5   The More Recent Shape Grammar Implementations

From this evolution onwards, the more recent shape grammar implementations notably increased in semantic complexity and size. A review of these recent research and implementation efforts is given in the work of Gips [23], and a review of more recent shape grammar implementations is given by McKay et al. [1]. In addition to the shape grammar implementations that we already briefly mentioned above, a number of the more recent shape grammar implementations rely on an underlying graph representation [24–26]. Recent work of Grasl [27] demonstrates several advantages of a graph-based representation, including the ability to recognise subshapes and support parametric shape rules. These previous implementation approaches are thus directed towards parametric rule support and subshape detection, while navigation and design comparison are less supported. Other example shape grammar implementations of relevance here are suggested in [24, 28–31]. Also the prototype implementation that we briefly outline in the following section is based on a graph grammar.

3 A Graph-Based Prototype Implementation for Investigating Key Implementation Barriers

3.1 The Prototype Implementation

Details about our graph-based shape grammar implementation can be found in an earlier article [12], hence we will not go in detail on this implementation. An indication of the graphical user interface (GUI) is given in Fig. 2. The GUI provides a navigation toolbar (top), a list of rules (upper left), and a visualisation of the initial design state (lower left). The current design path is indicated in grey. The implementation relies entirely on graph representations, both of design states and of rules in the design grammar. These graphs unambiguously define geometry and semantics of design states and rules. Figure 2 mainly shows that the designer is presented with the geometric representation of the graphs, annotated with the semantics that is captured in the graphs.

The main idea of this implementation is to provide custom design space exploration to an architectural designer. This is closer to the second, original grammar scenario that we outlined in the introduction of this paper. The implementation is thus not meant to use only one specific shape grammar, such as the FLW prairie houses grammar or the Malagueira houses grammar, and repetitively apply this shape grammar. Rather, it is meant to allow designers to specify their own grammars, so that the system can interpret these and produce design alternatives according to these custom grammars. Additionally, designers are allowed to closely interact with the design alternatives produced by the shape grammar system. For example, they are able to edit the graph underlying the resulting geometry, thereby manually changing the design. They are able to traverse back and forth through the visualised design space (see left to right in Fig. 2), so that they can manually indicate to the system in which direction it should preferably direct its search. In order to keep track of visited design states, all design states are stored in a tree-like data structure (left in Fig. 2 represents the root, right in Fig. 2 represents the leaves). This allows a designer to navigate the design space and consider multiple design alternatives at the same time. By providing this kind of functionality, a designer is allowed to interact with the system and the design space used by that system, at his own use and benefit. Furthermore, instead of using purely geometrical node types, as is the case in the work of [24–26], for example, we also allow other node types for various other concepts and elements, such as walls, windows, and so forth.

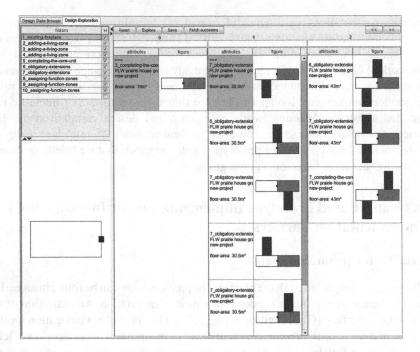

Fig. 2. Screenshot of the graphical user interface of the developed software system. The user interface provides a navigation toolbar (top), a list of rules (upper left), and a visualization of the initial design state (lower left). The current design path is indicated in grey.

3.2   Representation of Design States and Design Rules

Graphs provide a powerful data structure to represent a shape and by extension, a complete design. We use graphs to represent both the design states and the design rules that are used by the system (see also [32]). As an example, Fig. 3 shows a design state that represents a simple rectangular space enclosed by four walls. The resulting attributed topology graph is hybrid, consisting of both geometrical node types (*vertex* and *edge*) and semantically more complex architectural node types (*wall* and *space*). All geometrical shapes shown in the GUI (see Fig. 2) have such an underlying graph representation. The design rules used by the system (upper left in Fig. 2) are graph rewrite rules (*LHS → RHS*), which can be represented using the same representation language as the one used for the representation of the graphs.

3.3   Design Space Exploration

The representation of design states and design rules provides a flexible and stable basis for building a system that allows designers to define their own rules and initial design states from scratch. These are two essential first steps in bringing the power of shape grammars back to the designer. Yet, there remains a key question present. Namely, how should the actual design space exploration now be implemented on top of this basis, so

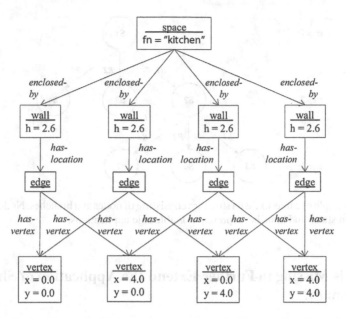

Fig. 3. A simple rectangular kitchen space represented with an attributed topology graph

that it provides appropriate support to the designers? At this point, rule application can be done in several ways. They can either be applied manually (total supervision), for example through priorities assigned to rules or through a user-defined sequence. Alternative, one may choose to allow fully automatic rule selection (totally unsupervised), which typically causes the generation of random-like design states.

At this moment, we allow designers to let the system apply rules in any of these ways, thus leaving maximum flexibility with the designer. To further streamline this flexibility, we provide, at the moment, an equally flexible navigation panel (Fig. 2), thus also targeting maximum flexibility in the exploration of the design space. More precisely, the navigation panel always offers a tree-like view on the design states that are generated and available at each step in the exploration by the system. The designer is then allowed to focus on exploration and selection of alternatives. Additionally, the designer can keep track of visited design states using the tree-like navigation structure. The tree root represents an initial design state, the branches represent possible rule applications and the nodes correspond to specific states in the design space. The a priori unknown design space is further explored by applying rules to a chosen design state, thereby generating a new set of design states. The set of all leaf nodes that are available for expansion is called the frontier. The process of expanding nodes on the frontier continues until either a design state meets a certain goal state or there are no more states to expand. Figure 4 shows an example of such a tree. Node *S1* represents an initial design state, upon which several rules (*R1*, *R2* and *R3*) can be applied. At each step in the exploration process, the designer can select a design state that will be further expanded (from left to right in Fig. 2).

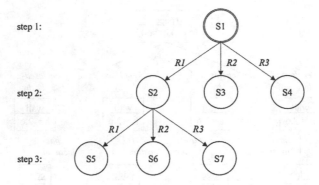

Fig. 4. An example of a tree-like data structure consisting of nodes and branches. Nodes represent specific design states and branches represent possible rule applications.

4   What is Missing to Further Extend the Application of Shape Grammars?

The documented system differs from earlier implementations in the sense that designers should be able to more easily develop their own grammars and browse through the suggestions made by the system using any one of these custom grammars. It thus focuses on the concept of design space *definition* and *exploration*, rather than on exploration (search) only. In this section, we will indicate how we think that this can be a valuable improvement for an architectural designer and what we think can still be improved to further extend the application of shape grammars to active designers.

4.1   The Ill-Structured Nature of Design Activity

The concept of shape grammars has been suggested multiple times before with the aim of improving or supporting the architectural design process. Yet, in many cases, focus is almost immediately put on the implementation of the shape grammar, so that it can be used for the repetitive generation of design solutions following that one particular static grammar (see analytical grammar scenario in the introduction). Little investigation is made of what actually happens in the mind of the architectural designer when making design decisions, either with or without using the implemented grammar, resulting in little or no support for designers in an original grammar scenario (designing without a particular grammar in mind). The best that is thus offered by shape grammar implementations to architectural designers, is an environment that allows to generate a number of design alternatives for a particular design problem, after which the designers can select the best design alternative(s) to proceed from.

This functionality matches rather well with a well-structured type of problem solving, in which the (design) problem and the rules to solve problems are unambiguously given [33]. Architectural design, however, is often, if not always, characterised as a specific kind of problem-solving in which the design problems and the design solutions are not only *ill-defined* [34], but also *co-evolving throughout the design process* [35, 36]. In other words, not only is it impossible to capture design problems and solutions in *unambiguous, closed and complete* representations; even if some feasible representation is found, it is continuously changing due to an impacting design context. In particular, the design problem is highly constrained by quantifiable and non-quantifiable requirements, and their formulation is often part of the design problem itself. According to this characterisation, design problems belong to the category of ill-defined, ill-structured or even wicked problems [33, 37]. Typical examples of such design problems can be found in the domain of architectural design, urban planning, product design, and so forth. The same applies to the rules used by the architectural designers. These can only seldom or to a very limited extent be disambiguated into a complete and consistent rule set.

As an example, we can consider Alvaro Siza's Malagueira houses and the associated Malagueira house shape grammar. These function very well in an analytical grammar usage scenario, but considerably less in an original grammar usage scenario. Obviously, it is highly unlikely that Alvaro Siza, when he started designing his first Malagueira house design, elaborated a full shape grammar in his mind, and then decided to rationally implement and build a whole range of design alternatives following that same Malagueira grammar. This would be the well-structured way to solve this particular problem. If we look at this from a more 'ill-structured' perspective, in which a designer is continuously in a reflective conversation with his design situation [38], a different process appears to be more viable instead. In this perspective, Siza likely aimed at designing a first Malagueira house as good as possible, while continuously reframing the design context in the design process for this first Malagueira house (gradually building an original shape grammar). In a number of following design situations, he likely found elements in the design situation similar to his first design, which made him opt to make similar choices. But, for any of these following design situations, the design grammar used was likely different from the previous ones, even if it were only in some minor details. Presumably, after a good number of such iterations, clear parallels can be found across the diverse design alternatives. It might indeed be possible to put these returning features in a fixed analytical grammar and try to apply them to any future design situation, yet, this is likely not the same as Alvaro Siza designing a new Malagueira house, which requires an original grammar. Yet, *design space exploration* remains to be a compelling and good model. In a sense, Alvaro Siza is indeed considering the diverse alternatives for any future design situation through a continuous exploration of the active design space. The key difference between the design space in Alvaro Siza's mind and the one in an implemented Malagueira shape grammar system, also if it were implemented in our system (Sect. 3), is that the former changes every second according to new interpretations or information (original grammar), whereas the latter is far more static (analytical grammar).

A cognition-oriented discussion of design space exploration is given by Goldschmidt [39]. The author argues that exploration is an important part of inquiries or experiments taken by designers. These inquiries or experiments are to be understood against the backdrop of Schön's theory [38] on the designer as a 'reflective practitioner'. Schön [38] describes design as a combination of different kinds of experiments: exploratory experiments, move-testing experiments and hypothesis testing. The inquiry starts by formulating the design situation, after which the designer can perform exploratory experiments to either find new design solutions (move testing) or alter the design space (hypothesis testing). Under the effects of these inquiries or experiments, the design space evolves and both the design problem and corresponding solutions, which are implicitly contained within that design space, co-evolve as well. This does not occur in an implemented system housing a design space: the implicit design space remains the same, as it is disambiguated during the implementation phase of the system, or, in our system, when the designer defines a new custom grammar (initial state I and a set of rules R). This is fine when aiming at the usage of an analytical shape grammar, but not when aiming to build, use and interact with multiple original shape grammars.

4.2   Design Space Exploration in the Human Mind

Although we do not have direct access nor evidence of what happens in a designer's mind, we can safely make certain assumptions on how the designer's mind works, thereby relying on earlier theoretical studies [34–39]. We will assume here that at least some sort of representation of a real-world design situation is maintained in the designer's mind. One such representation at any particular moment in time can be understood as a design solution or a *design state* (cfr. × symbols in Fig. 5). At any moment in time, the designer takes decisions that lead him from one design state to the next, following a particular *design path* (bold arrows in Fig. 5). The collection of design states that is traversed over time by the designer, is then called the *explicit design space* (ellipse in Fig. 5). The collection of design states that could have been traversed if the designer had followed different paths, is called the *implicit design space* (the collection of *all* design states in Fig. 5).

In every design state in the designer's mind, available information is reduced to a more manageable level that is suited for a design process and for decision-making within this design process. This reduction is often referred to as a 'bounded rationality', a term coined by Simon [41] to indicate that designers always take into account only a part of the design information available in the real world. Defining the design space thus heavily relies on removing detail from a complex design situation and reducing it to a set of necessary design features (or variables). This process is often called abstraction or disambiguation [34]. Once the design space is defined, a designer can reflect upon the design paths that are available starting from the current disambiguated design state. Because of the bounded nature of the information taken into account in any disambiguated design space, a fully optimal goal design state cannot be reached by the designer, not in an information system, not in the human mind. As a result, we can talk about the design process as a process of 'satisficing' (see [41]). Satisficing, a combination of 'satisfy' and 'suffice', directs exploration for design alternatives towards criteria for adequacy within a bounded rationality, rather than towards a fully rational solution. When aiming for original shape grammars, it is thus similarly useful to aim for bounded shape grammars as well, allowing satisficing.

In reflecting and choosing for particular design paths, the designer receives feedback and he can subsequently revise, further develop or even entirely reject and rebuild the design space. By choosing for particular design paths, a design act is performed against

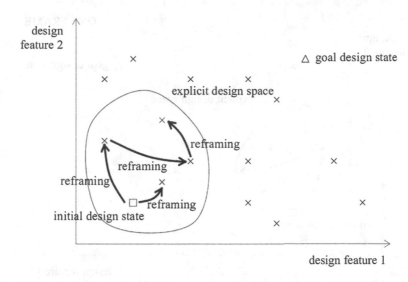

Fig. 5. The design space consists of design states and design paths. The initial design state (□), goal design state (Δ) and other design states (×) are related by design paths (bold arrows). The implicit design space consists of the complete field of design states and design paths shown here. The explicit design space is indicated by the ellipse and contains all visited design states.

the current design state, thereby changing it into a new design state (see arcs in Fig. 5). So, in other words, a designer engages in a dialogue or 'conversation' with the external world during the design process. In continuously changing design state, the designer continuously *reframes* the design problem and associated design solution [38, 42], resulting in the effect of co-evolution of design problem and solution as we identified it in the introduction [35, 36]. When reframing the design problem and design solution, which occurs every time a design move is made and an arc can be drawn as in Fig. 5, important concepts in the design change, resulting in a different semantic structure of the entire design problem and design solution, and thus also of the entire design space. *Every design move* (cfr. 'reframing' arrows in Fig. 5) *essentially alters the structure of the design space, even if it is only slightly.*

4.3 Design Space Exploration in an Information System

In the context of an information system, the above situation of design space exploration looks a bit different. First and foremost, most of the terms in Fig. 5 (design space, design state, path) are typically associated with a formal or structured representation, as we already saw in Sect. 2.3. Presumably, the closer this formalisation of the design space is to the design space as it is in the designer's mind, the more useful it can be for that designer. When considering the shape grammar implementations documented in the previous sections, the design spaces acted upon by graph grammar implementations (e.g. Malagueira house grammar) are presumably more similar to what is in the designer's mind then those acted upon by the purely geometric shape grammars (e.g. Palladio grammar).

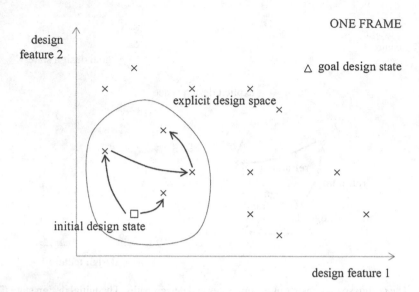

Fig. 6. In a straight-forward implementation of a design space in an information system, the design space is a formal representation of a design problem and the available set of design solutions as it is framed once by the person who prepared the formal representation (preferably the designer).

When considering only such graph grammar implementations, the design space typically includes an initial design state, represented as a root design state, and a goal formulation or a set of goal design states (Fig. 6), similar to what we had in Fig. 5. The set of goal design states that meet the goal formulation constitutes only a small part of the design space. Based on a set of formalised design moves or design acts, the system is able to generate a design space consisting of the various design states that can be reached through any number of design paths using one or more of the available formalised design acts. The designer is then given the opportunity to explore the design space as it is generated and represented in the information system.

It is important to distinguish in this matter between the implicit and the explicit design space [17]. The implicit design space is understood, in the context of an information system, as the collection of all design states and design paths that can be generated by the information system by applying any number of design moves within the expressiveness of the implemented formalisation of the design space (root design state, goal design states, available design moves). The explicit design space is the record of design states that are in fact visited by the designer in exploring the available implicit design space.

One might say that there hardly is any difference between the procedure in an information system (Fig. 6) and in the human mind (Fig. 5). There is, however, one key difference. Namely, design space exploration in the human mind is not limited by the expressiveness of the implemented formalisation of the design space. During design space exploration in the human mind, the implicit design space changes at every design move that is made, every arc in Fig. 5. During design space exploration by an information system, the implicit design space is just as static as the formalisation of the design space.

They basically do not change over the course of the design process, resulting in limited usability within the actual design process. This is caused by one important difference between the human mind and an information system, namely, that an information system is, unlike the human mind, *unable to disambiguate or make abstractions*. Hence, the *reframing* steps, which are so characteristic of design thinking (Fig. 5), do not occur in current (mostly analytical) shape grammar implementations. As a result, a system that implements a shape grammar will only be capable of showing the design space associated with *one frame* of the problem (Fig. 6). It is of course an option to let a system make decisions without providing it a capacity for reframing, but in that case, the decisions that are made will be very different from the creative decisions that are typically made by a designer *in the sense that these decisions will remain stuck in one formal representation of a design state*. If designers are not aware that they should somehow still manually include these reframing steps themselves, then their expectancies will be far too high compared to what shape grammar implementations currently can offer.

4.4   Design Space Exploration in the Proposed Implementation

In the design space exploration system that is documented in [12] (see Sect. 3), no reframing step is included either. In a sense, much of the functionality offered is similar to what is offered in other shape grammar implementations. With our focus on flexibility, however, we do try to offer designers an interface in which they are at least capable of manually modifying the formalisation of the shape grammar, and thus also of the implicit design space. In theory, this corresponds to a procedure as depicted in Fig. 7: designers can interact with a design space as it is traditionally available (no reframing, design exploration in one direction – see design feature 1 and 2 on the axes of the diagram in Fig. 7), but they are also capable at any moment in time to make alterations to the design grammar, resulting in a reframed design space (bold arrow between Frames A and B in Fig. 7). This arrow then represents an explicit reframing step, allowing for renewed design exploration in an alternative direction (see design feature 3 and 4 on the axes of the lower diagram in Fig. 7).

This strategy responds to the statement by Chakrabarty et al. [22]: '*However, a main roadblock to achieving wider impact, especially in conceptual design, has been to support designers in the iterative development of a grammar, without having to program it directly, and its application to rapidly generate alternative designs.*'. Designers should be able to develop their shape grammars themselves. Where Chakrabarty et al. [22] mention the option to either build sophisticated grammar interpreters or either build self-learning shape grammar implementations, the system that we suggest fits entirely within the former (sophisticated grammar interpreter). The key features of an information system aimed at design space exploration should thus be (1) providing the designer the possibility to change the formal representation of the design space so that it becomes more dynamic and (2) allowing the designer to do this in an interactive and intuitive manner. If these features are provided, a designer should be capable of relatively easily changing the formal representation used by the system and thus manually reframing that system (cfr. Figure 7). A profitable and useful interaction can then be realised between the designer and the tool that he uses for enhancing his exploration capabilities.

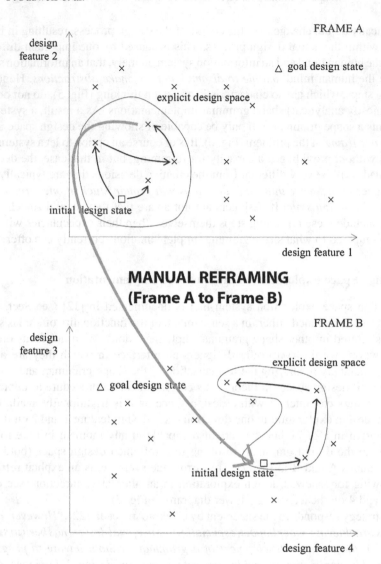

Fig. 7. A flexible and user-friendly system is needed, in which a designer is able to manually reframe one (bounded) design space (Frame A in top of Figure) into an alternative, yet related (bounded) design space (Frame B in bottom of Figure).

4.5   Implications to Take into Account in Future Implementations

There is one very important implication that needs to be considered here. It is rather easy to state that *'a user should be able to change the entire grammar used by a program so that that program is capable of generating entirely new solutions to a particular problem'*. This is not so easily realised in practice, especially not if the designer has to be kept out of environments that involve a programming language [22]. Namely, as soon as one of the elements in a shape grammar is changed, a whole lot of other elements typically have to be modified as well in order to keep the whole grammar consistent and closed under logical consequence. A good insight in this change propagation task requires from the designer a high level of familiarity with the existing grammar. This rapidly becomes a problem for any architectural designer if this existing grammar becomes large and complex.

For a complex grammar, such as the Malagueira house grammar, this is likely to be impossible. One change to the original grammar likely results in an entirely inconsistent and thus unusable grammar. For a simpler grammar, such as the Koch geometric grammar, this issue becomes notably less of an issue. Note that also the (rather straightforward) boundary solid grammars that were proposed by Heisserman [9] suffered from inconsistency, even without making any change to it. As the solid models were transformed by both local (acting upon specific objects only) and global rules (acting upon complete compositions of objects), some of the rules could result in geometrically inconsistent models, such as self-intersecting geometric elements. These inconsistencies needed to be handled by a specific 'police-like' kind of rule: the *unary operation* [9]. The sole job of the unary operation was to fix the geometry so that it would be consistent again. So, even when handling with 'simple' geometric shapes, keeping the resulting design alternatives consistent is a challenge. Of course, it will be an even harder challenge in a grammar that takes into account elements and concepts with a semantics beyond mere geometry.

In our proposal, we do not solve this issue. We do address it, however, (1) by encouraging and allowing designers to build their own grammars (which increases the odds for the designers of being able to change their grammars while keeping consistency), and, more importantly, (2) by encouraging designers to only build small-scale and approximate (bounded rationality [40]) grammars for shape generation rather than fully detailed, complex, all-including grammars. Through these features, a designer will be more inclined to follow a procedure as depicted in Fig. 7, in which there is a place for manual reframing of the design grammar used.

5   Conclusion

Many shape grammar systems have been proposed in the past, aiming at an application in an architectural design context. A distinction should be made between analytical and original shape grammars, the former focusing on the one-time formalisation of a particular architectural style, and the latter focusing rather on the types of design rules that are generated and used on the spot, during the design phase, by the designer. Whereas analytical shape grammars have their applications, original shape grammars are not commonly used in architectural design contexts. It appears to be interestingly challenging to implement a shape grammar system that is commonly usable in very diverse design situations. This message also comes across from the brief literature review made in this paper. Multiple shape grammars have been implemented, ranging from the simpler geometric shape grammars to the semantically far more complex graph grammar implementation. None of them seems to be aptly used by an architectural designer at the moment.

In this paper, we investigate the reasons behind this situation. Why is it so hard to prepare a single shape grammar implementation able to support architectural designers? We do this investigation by outlining several existing implementation strategies of shape grammars, including also our own graph-based design grammar system, and we analyse the resulting overview with theories on how designers think and act upon incoming information. From this comparison, it appears that one crucial element is typically unavailable in the implemented systems (including our own), namely, the ability of the system to *reframe* its grammar, and the associated design space, into a slightly changed version of that grammar, and the associated design space. In other words, any implemented shape grammar is currently only able to generate the design alternatives that are inherently present in its implicit design space, whereas an actual architectural designer is also capable of generating design alternatives that are beyond that particular design space.

What is needed, is a system that is capable of reframing its grammar. In our belief that it is, at the moment, highly unlikely that a system can be developed that is capable of doing this through any unsupervised learning mechanism, we propose the development of a system that allows an architectural designer to aptly modify the grammar used by a shape grammar implementation. In our implementation, we therefore focus on providing to the designer (1) all possibilities and tools to construct full representations of design states and graph rewrite rules and (2) a highly flexible navigation panel that allows highly flexible navigation through a design space (including any previous design states or even design states in entirely different branches). These features allow a designer to adapt, store and restore design states and design spaces. The main difficulty in using this kind of shape grammar system and its capacity of changing the grammar used by the system, is that the grammar can very quickly become inconsistent and thus unusable. We do not have any hard resolution to this challenge, besides recommending designers to keep the grammars that they use manageable and sizeable.

Acknowledgements. The authors of this article greatly acknowledge the support received by the IWT Flanders and by the Special Research Fund (BOF) of Ghent University.

References

1. McKay, A., Chase, S., Shea, K., Chau, H.H.: Spatial grammar implementation: From theory to useable software. Artif. Intell. Eng. Des. Anal. Manuf. **26**, 143–159 (2012)
2. Stiny, G., Gips, J.: Shape grammars and the generative specification of painting and sculpture. Inf. Proc. **71**, 1460–1465 (1972)
3. Stiny, G.: Two exercises in formal composition. Envir. Plan. B **3**, 187–210 (1976)
4. Stiny, G.: Ice-ray: a note on the generation of Chinese lattice designs. Environ. Plan. B **4**, 89–98 (1977)
5. Stiny, G., Mitchell, W.J.: The Palladian grammar. Environ. Plan. B **5**, 5–18 (1978)
6. Knight, T.W.: Languages of designs: from known to new. Environ. Plan. B **8**, 213–238 (1981)
7. Knight, T.W.: The forty-one steps. Environ. Plan. B **8**, 97–114 (1981)
8. Knight, T.W.: Transformations of languages of designs. Environ. Plan. B, 10, Part 1: 125–128, Part 2: 129–154, Part 3: 155–177 (1983)

9. Heisserman, J.: Generative geometric design and boundary solid grammars. Ph.D. thesis, Carnegie Mellon University (1990)
10. Duarte, J.P.: A discursive grammar for customizing mass housing: the case of Siza's houses at Malagueira. Autom. Constr. **14**, 265–275 (2005)
11. Koning, H., Eizenberg, J.: The language of the prairie: Frank Lloyd Wright's prairie houses. Environ. Plan. B **8**, 295–323 (1981)
12. Strobbe, T., Pauwels, P., Verstraeten, R., De Meyer, R., Van Campenhout, J.: Towards a visual approach in the exploration of shape grammars, Artificial Intelligence for Engineering Design, Analysis and Manufacturing (2015, in press)
13. Stiny, G.: Introduction to shape and shape grammars. Environ. Plan. B **7**, 343–351 (1980)
14. Flemming, U.: More than the sum of parts: the grammar of Queen Anne houses. Environ. Plan. B **14**, 323–350 (1987)
15. Cagan, J. and Mitchell, W.J.: Shape Annealing: A New Approach for Controlling Shape Generation, Tech. Rep., Carnegie Mellon University - Engineering Design Research Center (1991)
16. Cagan, J., Mitchell, W.J.: Optimally directed shape generation by shape annealing. Environ. Plan. B **20**, 5–12 (1993)
17. Woodbury, R., Burrow, A.: Whither design space? Artif. Intell. Eng. Des. Anal. Manuf. **20**, 63–82 (2006)
18. Gero, J.S.: Towards a model of exploration in computer-aided design. In: Gero, J., Tyugu, E. (eds.), Formal Design Methods for CAD, North-Holland, pp. 315–336 (1994)
19. Lawson, B.: Oracles, draughtsmen, and agents: the nature of knowledge and creativity in design and the role of IT. Autom. Constr. **14**, 383–391 (2005)
20. Stouffs, R., Krishnamurti, R.: The complexity of the maximal representation of shapes. In: Preprints of the IFIP Workshop on Formal Methods for Computer-Aided Design, pp. 53–66 (1993)
21. Krishnamurti, R.: The maximal representation of a shape. Envir. Plan. B **19**, 267–288 (1993)
22. Chakrabarti, A., Shea, K., Stone, R., Cagan, J., Campbell, M.J., Vargas-Hernandez, N., Wood, K.L.: Computer-Based Design Synthesis Research: An Overview. Journal of Computing and Information Science in Engineering **11**, 9–10 (2011)
23. Gips, J.: Computer implementation of shape grammars (1999)
24. Grasl, T., Economou, A.: From topologies to shapes: parametric shape grammars implemented by graphs. Environ. Plan. B **40**, 905–922 (2013)
25. Heisserman, J.: Generative geometric design. IEEE Comput. Graphics Appl. **14**, 37–45 (1994)
26. Correia, R., Duarte, J.P., Leitao, A.: GRAMATICA: A general 3D shape grammar interpreter targeting the mass customization of housing. In: Achten, H., Pavlicek, J. Hulin, J., Matejdan D. (eds.), Digital Physicality - Proceedings of the 30th eCAADe Conference, pp. 489–496 (2012)
27. Grasl, T.: On shapes and topologies: graph theoretic representations of shapes and shape computations. Ph.D. thesis, TU Vienna (2013)
28. Tapia, M.A.: A visual implementation of a shape grammar system. Environ. Plan. B **26**, 59–73 (1999)
29. Hoisl, F., Shea, K.: An interactive, visual approach to developing and applying parametric three-dimensional spatial grammars. Artif. Intell. Eng. Des. Anal. Manuf. **25**, 333–356 (2011)
30. Trescak, T., Esteva, M., Rodriguez, I.: A shape grammar interpreter for rectilinear forms. Comput. Aided Des. **44**, 657–670 (2012)
31. Keles, H.Y., Özkar, M., Tari, S.: Embedding shapes without predefined parts. Environ. Plan. B: Plan. Des. **37**, 664–681 (2010)

32. Strobbe, T., De Meyer, R., Van Campenhout, J.: A generative approach towards performance-based design: using a shape grammar implementation. In: Stouffs, R., Sariyildiz, S. (eds.), Computation and Performance - Proceedings of the 31st eCAADe Conference, pp. 627–633 (2013)
33. Simon, H.A.: The structure of ill-structured problems. Artif. Intell. **4**, 181–201 (1973)
34. Cross, N.: Designerly ways of knowing. Des. Stud. **3**, 221–227 (1982)
35. Maher, M.L., Poon, J.: Modelling design exploration as co-evolution. In: Microcomputers in Civil Engineering. Chapman and Hall, London, pp. 195–210 (1996)
36. Dorst, K., Cross, N.: Creativity in the design process: coevolution of problem and solution. Des. Stud. **22**, 425–437 (2001)
37. Rittel, H., Webber, M.: Dilemmas in a general theory of planning. Policy Sci. **4**(2), 155–169 (1973)
38. Schön, D.: The Reflective Practitioner: How Professionals Think in Action. Temple Smith, London (1983)
39. Goldschmidt, G.: Quo vadis, design space explorer? Artif. Intell. Eng. Des. Anal. Manuf. **20**, 105–111 (2006)
40. Simon, H.A.: Models of Man: Social and Rational. John Wiley and Sons, New York (1957)
41. Simon, H.A.: Rational choice and the structure of the environment. Psychol. Rev. **63**, 129–138 (1956)
42. Cross, N.: Designerly Ways of Knowing. Birkhauser, Basel (2007)

From Idea to Shape, from Algorithm to Design: A Framework for the Generation of Contemporary Facades

Inês Caetano[1(✉)], Luís Santos[2], and António Leitão[1]

[1] University of Lisbon, Lisbon, Portugal
{ines.caetano,antonio.menezes.leitao}@ist.utl.pt
[2] University of California, Berkeley, Berkeley, CA, USA
luis_sds82@berkeley.edu

Abstract. Nowadays, there is a growing interest in buildings' envelops presenting complex geometries and patterns. This interest is related with the use of new design tools, such as Generative Design, which promotes a greater design exploration. In this paper we discuss and illustrate a structured and systematic computational framework for the generation of facade designs. This framework includes (1) a classification of facades into different categories that we consider computationally relevant, and (2) an identification and implementation of a set of algorithms and strategies that address the needs of the different designs.

Keywords: Generative design · Facades · Algorithms

1 Contemporary Facades

The history of Architecture provides many examples of styles that were adopted, rejected, and then re-adopted in a similar or changed form. Before Modernism, buildings' facades were the canvas where architectural style was celebrated. On this canvas architects imprinted their personal interpretation of the current cultural stylistic models, with their metrics and canons. However, with the birth of Modernism, and its hygienic and austere aesthetic, composing a facade was an architectural task that lost some of its prestige. After Modernism (or since Post-modernism), we witness an increasing interest in facade composition and, nowadays, designing a facade is reassuming an important role in architecture practice due, in part, to the support of digital technologies [1].

This trend of highly textured building envelopes celebrates again the ornament in architecture and the composition of architectural facades. There are historical and cultural reasons for this renewed interest, such as the reinterpretation of Modernist aesthetics, the reintroduction of symbolism and historical precedent by Post-Modernism [2], and the diligent look and revisit of vernacular precedent proposed by Critical Regionalism [3]. However, there is also a technological reason: algorithmic approaches made it easier to conceive, deploy and adapt the design of architectural surfaces with complex and intricate textures, and differentiated levels of porosity. As an example, consider the highly sophisticated Erwin Hauer "Continua series" sunscreens patterns

© Springer-Verlag Berlin Heidelberg 2015
G. Celani et al. (Eds.): CAAD Futures 2015, CCIS 527, pp. 527–546, 2015.
DOI: 10.1007/978-3-662-47386-3_29

(Fig. 1), which nowadays can be treated as a programming exercise in some parametric design courses.

Fig. 1. Continua screen, design 1 - pattern developed by Erwin Hauer in the 1950's [4].

Unfortunately, new facade designs still require a lot of effort to invent, experiment, and produce. It is important, then, that this effort be as small as possible. The work presented here proposes a systematic methodology for the development and composition of algorithmically-based facade patterns. As we will show, our methodology promotes the design exploration of facades and simplifies its adaptation to the ever-changing design process conditions.

2   Algorithmic-Based Processes in Architecture

Creativity is characterized by unconsciousness and inaccuracy [5] and, thus, is better served by a design process that embraces change. Traditional tools do not easily support change because they require too much time and effort to modify models. On the other hand, the computer became a very important tool for the design process, which changed, and is still changing, the way architects design [6]. Recent technologies allow design exploration to go far beyond the traditional possibilities, thus promoting the development and proliferation of complex shapes, new patterns and advanced production techniques. Computers "*do not eradicate human imagination but rather extend its potential limitations…it provides the means for exploration, experimentation, and investigation in an alternative realm*" [7].

Generative design (GD) is an approach to design which creates shapes through algorithms [7]. This approach enables the generation of various solutions in a short period of time, avoiding the tedious and repetitive tasks needed when the modeling work is done manually, even with state-of-the-art CAD/BIM (Computer Aided Design/ Building Information Modeling) software. In addition, GD enables and facilitates the manufacturing of complex solutions, by extracting information directly from the model to CAM (Computer Aided Manufacturing) or Digital Fabrication. Through GD, instead of going directly from the idea to the design, architects produce an intermediate algorithmic-based description of a design [8]. Parametric Design is a GD approach in which the parameters of a particular design are declared, rather than its shape [6]. This approach has the ability to generate different instances of a design where each instance represents a unique set of transformations based on the actual parameters [9], allowing the designer to freely explore a larger solution space of the design briefing/program. Ultimately, this leads to the assessment of solutions that would be difficult to generate with traditional design methods. An algorithmic-based design method can easily accommodate changes in the proposed solutions, as the dynamics of the design process alter the state of the design brief and its programmatic nature.

3   A Framework for the Generation of Contemporary Facades

In this paper, we discuss the development of a computational framework for the design of facades. Our work started with an analysis of a large corpus of contemporary facades. The wide variety of contemporary facades has already promoted several different classifications, which were based on different concepts, such as Depth and Affect [10] and facade's Articulation [1]. However, as our framework aims to help the designers with the *generation* of facades, we propose a different classification which is more helpful to the designer that intends to use a computational approach.

In our work, facades are classified into different categorical dimensions that we consider computationally relevant. This multidimensional classification guides the designer towards a library of functional operators, each addressing the generation of different designs of facades. By using this library, designers match their ideas with the categorical dimensions, which guide them in the selection of the most appropriate computational approaches for the generation of the idealized facades.

Given that facades are, in many cases, a composition of different designs, it is not reasonable to expect that this matching process yields a complete computational solution. Instead, the designer is responsible for the division of the whole design into parts, for establishing the dependencies between them, for instantiating and combining the different computational functions that handle each part, and for the additional scripting that might be needed to handle specific circumstances of the design brief.

4   Design Stages

There are several stages in the design of facades and the presented framework takes them into account. These stages are in accordance with the computational logic of the facade design and each one corresponds to one or more dimensions of our classification. The stages are:

1. The definition of the facade's geometry.
2. The generation of the facade's elements, which includes the definition of their geometry, type of deformation and size variation.
3. The distribution of the elements, which is responsible for mapping and rotating the elements on the facade.
4. The generation of the facade's final appearance, which produces the type of facade's finish and selects the material or color to apply.

In the next sections we discuss each categorical dimension and its role in the different steps of the facade generation.

5   Categorical Dimensions

The framework is organized in eight categorical dimensions: (1) Facade's Geometry, (2) Element's Geometry, (3) Element's Distortion, (4) Element's Size, (5) Element's Distribution, (6) Element's Rotation, (7) Material & Color, and (8) Facade Articulation, where each dimension corresponds to a set of related computational functions. This classification generates a multi-dimensional space where parts of a facade can be located. The important result of our work comes, then, from the identification and implementation of a set of algorithms and strategies that address the needs of the different dimensions of this space. Some of the locations in this multi-dimensional space can use a specific computational approach that is adequate for the creation of the designs that match the intended facade. Other locations, representing less common kinds of facades, might not have a specific computational solution, but our experience shows that is possible, using the range of tools that we developed, to quickly implement the particular solution required by that facade.

Table 1 shows, synthetically, all the categorical dimensions. Each box describes one dimension and the corresponding algorithms. In the next sections we discuss each of these dimensions.

Table 1. Classification synthesis: the dimensions are at the top of each box and below there are the corresponding algorithms.

FACADE'S GEOMETRY	ELEMENT'S GEOMETRY	ELEMENT'S DISTORTION	ELEMENT'S DISTRIBUTION		
STRAIGHT CYLINDRICAL SPHERICAL UNDULATE S-ELLIPSE TORUS FREE-FORM	CIRCULAR CYLINDRICAL SPHERICAL OVAL TRIANGULAR PYRAMIDAL SQUARED RECTANGULAR	TWISTED UNDULATED INTERLACED BENDED	1D IN COLUMNS IN ROWS ALTERNATED: COLUMNS OR ROWS	2D REGULAR GRID CHESS GRID ALTERNATED GRID RECURSIVE GRID PICTORIAL GRID	3D
ELEMENT'S ROTATION	CUBOID HEXAGONAL PENTAGONAL STRIPES PICTORIAL	**ELEMENT'S SIZE**	**MATERIAL & COLOR**	**FACADE ARTICULATION**	
HORIZONTAL VERTIVAL PICTORIAL RANDOM		FIXED INCREASING ATTRACTED PICTORIAL RANDOM	WOOD METAL CONCRETE ONE COLOR MULTI-COLOR PICTORIAL RANDOM COLOR	PERFORATED APPLIED STACKED JUXTAPOSED LAYERED	

5.1   Facade's Geometry

Given that designers want their models to be flexible, when they define the underlying principle of a geometry, they want to control and change it easily, so that many design instances can be generated within the same geometrical principle. This idea guides our first dimension, named Facade's Geometry. For each different geometry, our framework provides a $\mathbb{R}^2 \rightarrow \mathbb{R}^3$ parametric function that describes the shape of the facade. For example, $f(u,v) = XYZ(u \times 5, 0, v \times 10)$, where XYZ is the Cartesian coordinate function, represents a five-by-ten rectangle on the XZ plane. Naturally, other coordinate systems can be used, such as the Cylindrical, represented by function CYL, and the Spherical, represented by the function SPH, to which can be applied transformations, such as translation, rotation, etc. The coordinate system transformations are related to a spatial location of reference, capable of codifying the transformed referential, which, for brevity, we will omit. To simplify the presentation, each parametric function $S(u,v)$ will range over the domain $0 \leq u \leq 1, 0 \leq v \leq 1$.

To make the framework more flexible, we also rely on the use of anonymous functions, i.e., functions which do not have a name, and higher-order functions (HOFs), i.e., functions that receive other functions as arguments and/or compute other functions as results [11].

As an example, consider the facade of the Formstelle Office Building (Fig. 2), which is completely planar. This is classified in the Facade's Geometry dimension as Straight, which, depending on a width w and height h of the facade, is defined by (1):

$$Straight(w, h) = \lambda(u, v).XYZ(u \times w, 0, v \times h) \tag{1}$$

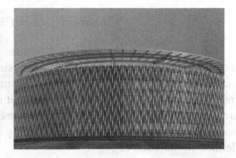

Fig. 2. Facade geometry: straight facade - formestelle office building, in töging am inn, Germany.

Fig. 3. Facade geometry: cylindrical facade - suzhou snd district urban planning exhibition hall, in jiangsu, China.

Note that Straight is a HOF that returns an anonymous parametric function that represents a delimited region on the XZ plane. The λ symbol is the λ-calculus notation for an anonymous function [11].

Although it is perfectly possible to explicitly define functions such as Straight, our framework goes deeper than that by providing a set of more fundamental functional operators that can be arbitrarily combined. One such operator represents a one-dimensional linear variation: $linear(a,b) = \lambda(t) \cdot a + (b - a)t$. Another, represents a (paradoxical) constant "variation": $constant(c) = \lambda(t) \cdot c$.

Given that the facade geometry domain is two-dimensional, it is also useful to extend the domain of the above one-dimensional variations into $\mathbb{R}^2$. To this end, we define the HOFs $dim_u(f) = \lambda(u,v).f(u)$ and $dim_v(f) = \lambda(u,v).f(v)$. A final but important operator is the generalized composition of functions

$$\circ(f, g_1, \cdots, g_n) = \lambda(x_1, \cdots, x_m).f(g_1(x_1, \cdots, x_m), \cdots, g_n(x_1, \cdots, x_m)) \qquad (2)$$

In order to allow a simplified notation, we define $a \otimes b = dim_a(linear(0, b))$, we treat all numbers n that occur in a function context as $constant(n)$, and we treat any ordinary first-order function f that is used with functional arguments $g_1, \cdots, g_n$ as $\circ(f, g_1, \cdots, g_n)$. This means, e.g., that $sin \times cos$ is the same as $\circ(\times, sin, cos)$.

The use of HOFs allow us to move from the numeric space, where numbers are combined using numeric operators, into the function space, where functions are combined using functional operators. In this space, the Straight function presented above can be equivalently defined as

$$Straight(w, h) = XYZ(u \otimes w, 0, v \otimes h) \qquad (3)$$

For a different example, consider the Suzhou SND District Urban Planning Exhibition Hall (Fig. 3), which, for radius r and height h, is described by the following function (4):

$$Cylindrical(r, h) = CYL(r, u \otimes 2\pi, v \otimes h) \qquad (4)$$

Finally, consider the sinusoidal facades which are very common in recent architecture (see Figs. 4 and 5). The sinusoidal HOF is: $sinusoid(a, \omega, \phi) = \lambda(x).a \times \sin(2\pi\omega x + \phi)$, where a is the amplitude of the sinusoid, ω is the angular frequency, i.e. the number of cycles per unit length, and ϕ is the phase. However, there are more than one type of sinusoidal surfaces. Some, such as the one in Fig. 4, have the undulation in the XY plane, thus producing a horizontal wave. This type of surface is defined by function (5):

$$Sb(w, h, a, \omega, \phi) = XYZ(u \otimes w, u \otimes sinusoid(a, \omega, \phi), v \otimes h) \qquad (5)$$

Others, such as the Boiler house at the Guy's Hospital, in London (Fig. 5) have the undulation along two axes and are defined by (6):

$$Se(w, h, a, \omega, \phi) = XYZ(u \otimes w, u \otimes sinusoid(a, \omega, \phi) \times v \otimes sinusoid(a, \omega, \phi + \pi/2), v \otimes h) \qquad (6)$$

On the other hand, there are facades with completely irregular shapes, like the Selfridges Building in Birmingham (Fig. 6), which are classified in the Facade's Geometry dimension as Free-Form. In this last case, the designer creates the shape manually, and imports it into our framework where it is represented as another parametric function that results from an interpolation process.

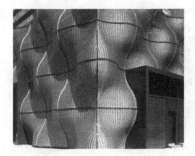

Fig. 4. Facade geometry: facade with horizontal waving - apartment house in Tokyo.

Fig. 5. Facade geometry: sinusoidal and co-sinusoidal facade - boiler house at guy's hospital, in London, UK.

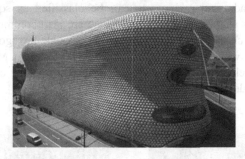

Fig. 6. Facade geometry: free form facade - selfridges building in Birmingham, UK.

We will now look into the Elements' Geometry, the next relevant dimension of our classification.

5.2 Elements' Geometry

There are several examples of facades where a particular kind of element is repeated, as is visible in Fig. 7. As we saw in the previous section, the facade's geometry defines the surface on which the elements will be placed, but before considering the placement of the elements, we need to describe the algorithms that shape them. This dimension is called Element's Geometry and, as it happens with the Facade's Geometry, it provides several pre-defined functions representing geometric shapes. In many cases, these elements can be described by the same functions that describe the facade geometry but, here, the geometry is more standardized, allowing us to provide pre-defined functions such as circle, triangle, square, hexagon, etc.

Contemporary facades with round elements are also very common and can be classified as cylindrical, spherical, circular, etc. The New Center for Manufacturing Innovation (Fig. 7), is an example of a facade with circular elements. Another example is the facade of the Hanjie Wanda Square (see Fig. 8), which is covered by several metallic spheres.

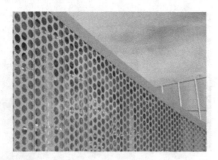

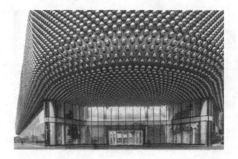

Fig. 7. Element's geometry: circular elements - new center for manufacturing innovation, in Monterrey, Mexico.

Fig. 8. Element's geometry: spherical elements - *Hanjie Wanda Square*, in China.

Facades with quadrangular elements can be classified as squared, rectangular, cuboid, etc. Elements shaped as regular-polygons are also common in contemporary facades and can be classified as hexagonal, pentagonal, hexagonal-prism, etc. An example of a facade with hexagonal elements is The Cube in Milano (see Fig. 9). Facades with striped elements are classified as stripes, producing continuous elements along the whole facade (Fig. 10).

Fig. 9. Element's geometry: hexagonal elements - the cube, in Milan, Italy.

Fig. 10. Element's geometry: stripes elements - aspen art museum, in Aspen, USA.

Besides the regular geometries, this dimension provides algorithms for more specific geometries, which are classified as Pictorial. These algorithms generate elements whose shape is determined by an image. An example of a facade with pictorial elements is Mayfair House, in London (Fig. 11).

After selecting the facade's geometry and the element's geometry, it is time to combine them to define the complete facade. One of the advantages of the functional representation is that it makes this combination a trivial composition of functions. As an example, a facade such as the one in Fig. 7 (circular elements on a straight facade), is defined by $\circ(circle, Straight(w, h), constant(r))$ or, in simplified notation, $circle(Straight(w, h), r)$.

Fig. 11. Element's geometry: pictorial elements - mayfair house, in London, UK.

It is important to note that the previous function is a continuous function that generates an infinity of circles in a delimited rectangle on the XZ plane. This means that we are not yet representing the actual distribution of circles, a topic that will be described in a later section.

5.3 Elements' Distortion

Distortion is a type of transformation where the natural form of the element is changed, for example, by twisting it along some dimension. To this end, it is possible to use pre-defined operations, such as Sweeping, which displaces the element's section along a curve, possibly rotating it and/or scaling it.

Twisted elements, such as those visible in the Huaxin Business Center (Fig. 12), result from a helical movement around their own axis. These particular elements are described by the following function, where c is a curve in the facade's surface, w and e are the dimensions of the cross-section of the element and, finally, ϕ is the twisting angle:

$$\lambda(c).sweep(c, rectangle(w, e), \phi) \tag{7}$$

Another type of distortion is named Undulated, which is a particular case of sweeping, where the guiding curve is sinusoidal (Fig. 13).

Interlaced elements use the same method described above but the elements are strategically placed so that they are weaved (Fig. 14). This is achieved by alternating the value of the sinusoid's phase, in both vertical and horizontal elements.

Finally, Bended is a deformation similar to a Zig-Zag, which flexes the elements according to the angles defined by the user (Fig. 15).

5.4 Elements' Size

As is visible in Fig. 16, it is common to find modern facades where the element has a size that varies along the facade. For this dimension-Element's Size-we have pre-defined a set of functions capable of producing the most common types of variations. For example, if we assume that we have a straight facade where the element is a circle whose radius changes linearly from r_0 to r_1 along the v dimension, the corresponding function is given by

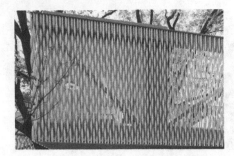

Fig. 12. Element's distortion: twisted elements: huaxin business center, in Xuhui, China.

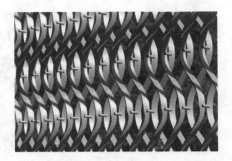

Fig. 13. Element's distortion: undulated elements - visitor pavilion national museum palace in Het Loo, Apeldoorn, Netherlands.

Fig. 14. Element's distortion: interlaced elements - argul weave building, in Bursa, Turkey.

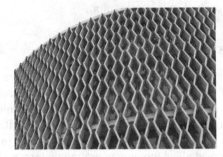

Fig. 15. Element's distortion: bended elements - pan American health organization building, Washington DC, USA.

$$circle(Straight(w, h), dim_v(linear(r_0, r_1))) \tag{8}$$

In another frequent example the size varies according to the distance to a point or a curve (Fig. 17). These cases are classified as Attracted and we provide a set of corresponding functions for their computation.

Elements with a size variation that reproduces an image are classified as Pictorial (Fig. 18). For these cases, an image is provided as input, where each pixel color value controls the size of the element.

Finally, elements with a random size variation (Fig. 19), are classified as Random because the element function has a size parameter controlled by a random function. As an example, we can modify the linear size variation illustrated above to use randomness instead:

Fig. 16. Element's size: increasing - the tourist office and landscaping of Quinta do Aido, Portugal.

Fig. 17. Element's size: attracted - quality hotel friends, in Sweden.

Fig. 18. Element's size: pictorial - hästsportens hus, in Sweden.

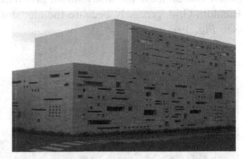

Fig. 19. Element's size: random - cascais house, in Portugal.

$$circle(Straight(w, h), \lambda(u, v).random(r_0, r_1))\qquad(9)$$

5.5 Elements' Distribution

So far, we have described functions and functional operators that allow the construction of a functional description of the facade that includes its geometry, the element's shape, its transformation and its size variation. As previously mentioned, this description is a continuous function. However, most facades are discretized, in the sense that the function is not evaluated in its entire domain but, instead, in a sampling of its domain. It is this sampling that characterizes the Element's distribution, that is, the placement of the elements along the facade. In other words, the functional description of the facade is mapped, not on a continuous domain, but on a discrete domain. This is accomplished by a discretization function that, given a continuous domain and the intended number of samples, computes a set containing the discretization of the domain. Depending on the dimensionality of the domain, we might also need to compute the Cartesian product of the discretization of the independent domains.

The use of discretization functions allows different patterns of mapping. For example, in the Huaxin Business Center (Fig. 12) the elements are distributed in alternated columns with opposite rotations. Another example is the Quality Hotel Friends (Fig. 17) where elements are disposed in a regular grid, i.e. aligned horizontally and vertically. A third example occurs when there is an overlapping of two grids, as it happens with the Hanjie Wanda Square (Fig. 8). We classify this type of distribution as Alternated Grid.

A Recursive Grid is an interesting example of a composed distribution: it occurs when a surface is divided into a regular grid which is further randomly subdivided into sub-grids (Fig. 20). Another composed distribution, classified as Pictorial Grid, maps the elements according to the design or image provided by the designer, i.e. the elements' distribution outlines the geometry in the picture (Fig. 21). The last composed two-dimensional distribution, pre-defined within this sub-group, is classified as Random-Grid, precisely because the element's distributions are based on randomness (see Fig. 19).

Fig. 20. Element's distribution: recursive grid- the cube, in Birmingham, UK.

Fig. 21. Element's distribution: pictorial grid - podcetrtek sports hall, in Podcetrtek, Slovenia.

In the last sub-group, 3D distribution, the mapping of the elements is done along three dimensions. Two of them belong to the surface geometry and the third one represents an additional spatial or temporal dimension. In this last case, the placement of the elements varies with the course of time (Fig. 23).

The functionality here described is summarized in Fig. 22 for the one-dimensional and two dimensional discretization cases.

5.6   Element's Rotation

In some facades, such as the one in Fig. 12, elements can be distinguished according to its rotation. This categorical dimension, Element's Rotation, is responsible for defining the rotation angle to be applied to each element. The most common types of rotation are pre-defined in our framework and include elements horizontally rotated and elements

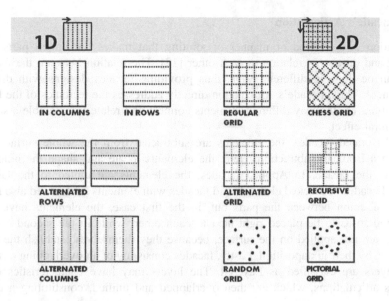

Fig. 22. Explanatory scheme of the available types of distributions. The set on the left represents one-dimensional distributions (1D), and the set on the right the two-dimensional distributions (2D).

vertically rotated. Facades whose element's rotation produces a general image or pattern are classified as Pictorial-Rotation. The mechanism is similar to the dimension Pictorial-Size, but uses rotation angles instead. The last type of rotation is classified as Random-Rotation, and it applies a random rotation angle to each element (Fig. 24).

Fig. 23. Element's distribution: 3d distribution - megafaces pavilion sochi 2014 winter olympics, in Russia.

Fig. 24. Element's rotation: pictorial rotation - winery gantenbein, in Switzerland.

5.7   Facade's Articulation

Articulation is a method or manner of jointing that makes the united parts clear, distinct, and precise in relation to each other [12]. The relation between the facade's parts can be done in different ways, thus providing facades designs with different appearances. Thus, Facade's Articulation directly addresses the tectonics of the facade composition, i.e. the way different elements connect and relate to assemble a specific architectural effect.

In Perforated facades, the elements are subtracted from the whole surface, thus requiring a Boolean subtraction. Here, the elements locate and shape the holes that constitute the facade. In Applied facades, the elements are united to the façade's surface. Facades of Stacked elements and facades with elements Juxtaposed also have a relation of union between the parts but, in the first case, the elements have to be distributed so as to be placed right next to each other, while in the second case the elements are not applied on the surface, because they themselves establish the building's skin, by their juxtaposition. Lastly, facades consisting of an overlapping of two or more layers are classified as Layered. The layers may have characteristics of the previous articulations, which are then overlapped and unified, constituting a unique facade.

5.8   Material and Color

The last categorical dimension is in charge of giving the materiality to the facade's model. If the facade has the material in sight, the layer of the facade will have the name of the chosen material and will also present the chosen materiality. If the facade has colors in its final appearance, the process is the same but with the color name. For more specific uses of colors, if there is an apparent use of random colors, the layer name will have a certain randomness that, consequentially, produce random colors - Random Color. If there is an apparent use of color to produce an overall image or pattern, the name of the layer will be submitted to the same process as the coordinates already explained, Pictorial-Size and Pictorial-Rotation, but this time receiving tones - Pictorial Color.

6   Practical Application

In practical terms, the end result of our research is a library of functional primitives and functional operators usable in different programming languages and a set of guidelines that helps a designer select and combine the most useful operators to implement a design for a particular facade.

As an example, consider a facade with Straight geometry and with Juxtaposed elements. The elements have a Pictorial geometry and a linearly increasing Size variation. The distribution of the elements is in a Regular Grid, and the color of the facade is classified as White. For each of these classifications, we can select the appropriate function, which we will combine using the functional operators. The end result is visible in Fig. 25. The chosen classification is highlighted in the following table:

FACADE'S GEOMETRY	ELEMENT'S GEOMETRY	ELEMENT'S SIZE	ELEMENT'S DISTRIBUTION 2D	FACADE ARTICULATION	MATERIAL COLOR
STRAIGHT	CIRCULAR	FIXED	**REGULAR GRID**	PERFORATED	METAL
CYLINDRIC.	SQUARED	**INCREASING**	CHESS GRID	APPLIED	CONCRETE
SPHERICAL	HEXAGONAL	ATTRACTED	ALTERNATE GRID	PRINTED	...
UNDULATED	TRIANGULAR	PICTORIC	RECURSIVE GRID	**JUXTAPOSED**	**WHITE**
FREE-FORM	**PICTORIAL**	RANDOM	PICTORIC GRID	LAYERED	BLACK

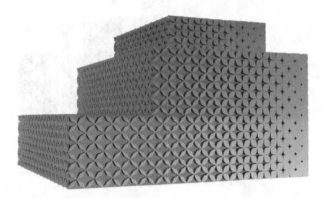

Fig. 25. An example of a facade generated through the framework operations: Straight facade; pictorial elements with increasing sizes; regular-grid distribution; Color white and juxtaposed surface.

Now, imagine that we replace the size variation, from linearly increasing to randomized. This change produces the facade visible in Fig. 26.

Now, if we change the type of element's distribution to become a Recursive Grid, and keep the type of size variation classified as linearly increasing, we generate the facade in Fig. 27.

Lastly, imagine that this facade has now the distribution of the elements in a Chess Grid, but keeps the geometry and the size variation of the elements as in the previous example. The facade articulation is Juxtaposed but also Layered, where the first layer is classified by the color White and the second layer by the color Black. After exploring this pattern, it is applied on a surface with undulated geometry. The generated facade is represented by Fig. 28.

7 Evaluation

In order to evaluate our framework we used it to reproduce some existing facades. Table 2 presents (on the left) a selection of projects which we classified (in the middle) according to our categorical dimensions and which we modeled (on the right) using the functional representation suggested by the classification.

FACADE'S GEOMETRY	ELEMENT'S GEOMETRY	ELEMENT'S SIZE	ELEMENT'S DISTRIBUTION 2D	FACADE ARTICULATION	MATERIAL COLOR
STRAIGHT	CIRCULAR	FIXED	**REGULAR GRID**	PERFORATED	METAL
CYLINDRIC.	SQUARED	INCREASING	CHESS GRID	APPLIED	CONCRETE
SPHERICAL	HEXAGONAL	ATTRACTED	ALTERNATE GRID	PRINTED	...
UNDULATED	TRIANGULAR	PICTORIC	RECURSIVE GRID	**JUXTAPOSED**	**WHITE**
FREE-FORM	**PICTORIAL**	**RANDOM**	PICTORIC GRID	LAYERED	BLACK

Fig. 26. An example of a facade generated through the framework operations: Straight facade; pictorial elements with random sizes; regular-grid distribution; Color white and juxtaposed surface.

We can conclude, from the comparison between each project and the corresponding model generated using our framework, that we can achieve a high degree of fidelity. Equally important is the effort required to use our framework. Our empirical evaluation shows that the classification step requires between five and ten minutes, while the selection, composition, and testing of the functions suggested by the classification takes between fifteen minutes and one hour, depending on the complexity of the facade.

8 Related Work

There are already some tools that attempt to solve the problems here described, such as the Paneling Tools plug-in for Rhino and Grasshopper, the Lunch Box add-on to Grasshopper, and ParaCloud Gem, a stand-alone toolkit that adds generative capabilities to any CAD system that supports *.obj, *.stl, *.collada, and *.dxf file formats. All of them are capable of creating grids of points on a surface, mapping elements in different ways, applying attractors to control elements size, etc.

The nature of their limitations is three-folded: (1) its use is entirely manual, thus mainly promoting iterative user-driven processes, which can be tiresome and error-prone; (2) when using such toolkits in the context of an Application Programming Interface (API) or as plug-ins to a domain-specific programming language, such as

FACADE'S GEOMETRY	ELEMENT'S GEOMETRY	ELEMENT'S SIZE	ELEMENT'S DISTRIBUTION 2D	FACADE ARTICULATION	MATERIAL COLOR
STRAIGHT	CIRCULAR	FIXED	REGULAR GRID	PERFORATED	METAL
CYLINDRIC.	SQUARED	**INCREASING**	CHESS GRID	APPLIED	CONCRETE
SPHERICAL	HEXAGONAL	ATTRACTED	ALTERNATE GRID	PRINTED	...
UNDULATED	TRIANGULAR	PICTORIC	**RECURSIVE GRID**	**JUXTAPOSED**	**WHITE**
FREE-FORM	**PICTORIAL**	RANDOM	PICTORIC GRID	LAYERED	BLACK

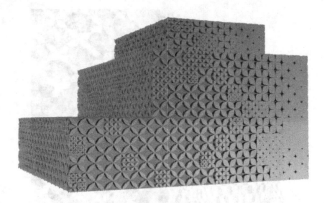

Fig. 27. An example of a facade generated through the framework operations: Straight facade; pictorial elements with increasing sizes; recursive-grid distribution; Color white and juxtaposed surface.

Grasshopper, a certain level of automation is obtained, however, the designer is always bound to the specific functionalities provided by the tool, thus limiting its agency in exploring different combinations of operations and extending the capabilities of the tool's pre-defined operations; (3) these tools are more used for generic panelization, subdivision, and population of surfaces thus, although they have been used to generate complex facade patterns, they are not fully architectural oriented which means that they do not directly address relevant concepts in facade design such as materiality or the tectonic relation between the facade elements.

We should also mention recent domain-specific programming languages, such as Dynamo for Revit and Grasshopper for Rhino, which allow users to implement the functionalities proposed in this paper. In addition, some of the pre-defined components have similar purpose to some of the HOFs which we presented. However, the freedom of connection allowed by these tools becomes difficult to manage in complex facades [13]. In these cases, a more structured and systematic approach like the one we propose is more manageable.

In summary, with the current framework the architect is limited by the non-domain specificity of existing tools. In order to extend their capabilities he needs to build from scratch the necessary functionalities or use a mix of different tools that most of the time

FACADE'S GEOMETRY	ELEMENT'S GEOMETRY	ELEMENT'S SIZE	ELEMENT'S DISTRIBUTION 2D	FACADE ARTICULATION	MATERIAL COLOR
STRAIGHT	CIRCULAR	FIXED	REGULAR GRID	PERFORATED	METAL
CYLINDRIC.	SQUARED	**INCREASING**	**CHESS GRID**	APPLIED	CONCRETE
SPHERICAL	HEXAGONAL	ATTRACTED	ALTERNATE GRID	PRINTED	...
UNDULATED	TRIANGULAR	PICTORIC	RECURSIVE GRID	**JUXTAPOSED**	**WHITE**
FREE-FORM	**PICTORIAL**	RANDOM	PICTORIC GRID	**LAYERED**	**BLACK**

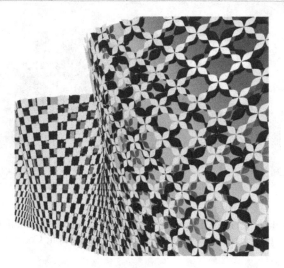

Fig. 28. An example of a facade generated through the framework operations: Layered facade with undulated geometry on top of a reflective surface. Each layer is composed by juxtaposed pictorial elements with increasing sizes and chess-grid distribution. The outer layer uses color white and the inner layer, simulating a shadow of the outer layer, uses color black.

Table 2. Table synthesis with some of the framework's applications

PROJECT	CLASSIFICATION	MODEL	PROJECT	CLASSIFICATION	MODEL
	STRAIGHT FACADE **PICTORIAL** ELEM. **FIXED** SIZE **REGULAR-GRID** **LAYERED** ARTICU.			**FREE-FORM** FACADE **SPHERICAL** ELEMENT **FIXED** SIZE **ALTERNATED-GRID** **APPLIED** ARTICULA.	
	STRAIGHT FACADE **CYLINDRICAL** ELE. **FIXED** SIZE **REGULAR-GRID** **JUXTAPOSED** ART.			**STRAIGHT** FACADE **PICTORIAL** ELEM. **FIXED** SIZE **ALTERNATED-GRID** **APPLIED** ARTICULA.	
	STRAIGHT FACADE **HEXAGONAL** ELE. **ATTRACTED** SIZE **ALTERNATED-GRID** **PERFORATED** ART.			**STRAIGHT** FACADE **STRIPE** ELEMENT **FIXED** SIZE **UNDULATED** ELEM. **ALTERNATED ROWS** **JUXTAPOSED** ART.	

are not compatible. This work extends the state-of-the-art by: (1) systematizing and structuring, in an architectural-oriented framework, the parametric generation of a wide range of facade typologies, and by (2) operationalizing it resorting to a simple algorithmic approach that uses and combines different functional operators that directly implement facade design concepts.

9 Conclusions

The exploration of architectural facades is not new. However, by resorting to recent digital technologies, architects can once again focus on facade design, promoting a growing interest in the exploration of complex patterns and geometries.

In this paper we presented a methodological framework that helps designers generate different facade designs, through the use of a set of functional operators. The current implementation of the framework was done using the Rosetta IDE [14], allowing its exploration in different programming languages.

In order to systematize the use of the framework, we proposed a classification of facades based on several categorical dimensions which we considered to be computationally relevant. These categorical dimensions guide the selection of the functional algorithms that handle each part of the facade. These might then be used directly, or might be combined using functional operators, promoting a systematic exploration of designs which ultimately aims to a higher productivity by: (1) improving the time of scripting tasks, and (2) adding flexibility to the designers' workflow. Due to the simplicity of the functional composition, this framework accommodates the ever-changing nature of a design process by facilitating the test of several design concepts, or instantiations of the same idea, in any design stage.

In the near future, we plan to expand the set of functional algorithms and operators, covering a wider range of facades. In order to make this framework more usable, we are particularly interested in conducting a wider field study of its application, to identify weaknesses of the proposed processes and opportunities for extensions.

Acknowledgments. This work was partially supported by national funds through Fundação para a Ciência e a Tecnologia (FCT) with reference UID/CEC/50021/2013, and by the Rosetta project under contract PTDC/ATP-AQI/5224/2012 and by the PhD grant under contract SFRH/BD/98658/2013.

References

1. Pell, B.: The articulate surface - ornament and technology in contemporary architecture. Birkhauser (2010)
2. Venturi, R.: Complexity and Contradiction in Architecture. Museum of Modern Art, New York (1966)
3. Frampton, K.: Towards a critical regionalism: six points for an architecture of resistence. The Anti-Aesthetic: Essays on Postmodern Culture (1983)

4. Hauer, E.: Continua, Architectural Screens and Walls. Princeton Architectural Press, New York (2004)
5. Bukhari, F.A.: A hierarchical evolutionary algorithmic design (head) system for generating and evolving buildings design models. Ph.D. thesis, Queensland University of Technology (2011)
6. Kolarevic, B.: Architecture in the Digital Age - Designing and Manufacturing. Taylor & Francis, London (2003)
7. Terzidis, K.: Introduction em Expressive Form - A Conceptual Approach to Computational Design, pp. 1–8. Spon Press, New York (2003)
8. Leitão, A.: Teaching computer science for architecture. In: Proceedings of 1st eCAADe Regional International Workshop, University of Porto, Faculty of Architecture (Portugal), pp. 95–104, 4–5 April 2013
9. Barrios, C.: Transformations on parametric design models. In: CAAD Design Futures 2005, Vienna, Austria (2005)
10. Moussavi e, F., Kubo, M.: The Function of Ornament. Actar, Cambridge (2006)
11. Leitão, A.: Improving generative design by combining abstract geometry and higher-order programming. In: em CAADRIA - Conference on Computer-Aided Architectural Design Research in Asia, Kyoto (2014)
12. Borson, B.: Life of an architect. http://www.lifeofanarchitect.com/words-that-architects-use/ (2010). Accessed 08 Nov 2010
13. Leitão, A., Luis Santos, J.L.: Programming languages for generative design: a comparative study. Int. J. Archit. Comput. 10(1), 139–162 (2012)
14. Lopes e, J., Leitão, A.: Portable generative design for cad applications. In: em ACADIA, Calgary, Canada (2011)

Pattern, Cognition and Spatial Information Processing

Representations of the Spatial Layout of Architectural Design with Spatial-Semantic Analytics

Kai Liao[1], Bauke de Vries[1(✉)], Jun Kong[2], and Kang Zhang[3]

[1] Eindhoven University of Technology, Eindhoven, The Netherlands
{kliao,b.d.vries}@tue.nl
[2] North Dakota State University, Fargo, USA
jun.kong@ndsu.edu
[3] University of Texas at Dallas, Dallas, USA
kzhang@utdallas.edu

Abstract. In this paper, we review and extend the idea of Alexander's "pattern language", especially from the viewpoints of complexity theories, information systems, and human-computer interaction, to explore spatial cognition-based design representations for "intelligent and adaptive/interactive environment" in architecture and urban planning. We propose a theoretic framework of design patterns "with spatial information processing", and attempt to incorporate state-of-the-art computational methods of information visualization/visual analytics into the conventional CAAD approaches. Focused on the spatial-semantic analytics, together with abstract syntactic pattern representation, by using "spatial-semantic aware" graph grammar formalization, i.e., Spatial Graph Grammars (SGG), the relevant models, algorithms and tool are proposed. We testify our theoretic framework and computational tool *VEGGIE* (*a Visual Environment of Graph Grammar Induction Engineering*) by using actual architectural design works (spatial layout exemplars of a small office building and the three house projects by Frank Lloyd Wright) as study cases, so as to demonstrate our proposed approach for practical applications. The results are discussed and further research is suggested.

Keywords: Pattern language · Complex adaptive systems · Spatial cognition · Design representations · Spatial information processing · Artificial intelligence · Visual language · Spatial graph grammars (SGG) · Spatial-semantic analytics

1 Introduction

In the past decades, the CAAD approaches with emphasis on complexity theories, information systems, and human-computer interaction, were widely accepted. Among those pioneer explorations, Alexander's work on patterns might be a notable one. Although Alexander developed the methodologies for his "pattern language" with "aggregation in an associative network" [2, 3], in-depth investigations into a formalized

© Springer-Verlag Berlin Heidelberg 2015
G. Celani et al. (Eds.): CAAD Futures 2015, CCIS 527, pp. 547–562, 2015.
DOI: 10.1007/978-3-662-47386-3_30

framework, the process and mechanics of pattern formation, and pattern-based design methodologies are still absent [13, 43, 45] (especially comparing with the paradigms, such as, "Pattern Grammars and Syntax-Directed Analysis" [19] developed by K.S. Fu in 1960 s and "Design Patterns" [20] in software engineering, pattern recognition, and other relevant academic fields).

We argue that the main bottlenecks are spatial-structural complexity and the spatial cognitive limitations of human beings (either for designers and users) (Fig. 1), considering (1) complex dynamics in human-environment coupled systems; and (2) the spatial-locational characteristics of planning and design work [4–6, 9, 10, 26–28, 32–34, 36, 37].

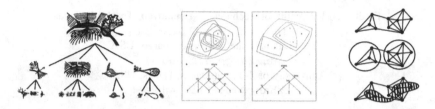

Fig. 1. Tree vs. semi-lattice (Alexander's representations of "structural complexity" [2, 3])

To address the issue, our research is focused on the exploring of the relation of design cognition and spatial organization, i.e. the representations of the spatial layout of architectural design, and the relevant computational design methodologies and tools for design thinking and spatial-semantic analytics in design process.

The subsequent sections of this paper are organized as follows: Sect. 2 briefly reviews existing design representations, and detail analysis on these methods is discussed; Sect. 3 presents a novel representation for spatial-structural complexity (focused on dynamic hierarchies and adaptive layouts with spatial-semantic awareness) based on Spatial Graph Grammars (SGG) [31, 46]. A formalized framework of the process and mechanics of pattern formation is proposed; Sect. 4 applies this presented method in design representation of spatial layouts in actual architectural works, and detailed examples are illustrated. Finally, the paper is summarized in Sect. 5.

2 Design Representations

Architectural design activities and design thinking depend upon multiple representations, which afford distinctive opportunities for communicating and transforming ideas during the process of design analysis, synthesis and evaluation [1, 14, 15, 21]. From the viewpoint of cognitive-developmental linguistics [49, 50] and the complex adaptive systems [4, 9, 10, 35], representations are rooted to spatial information processing, i.e., the interaction between human beings (designers and users) and environment. Thus, we should consider representations as "design media" [41], either acting as the intermedium between designers with others, or designers themselves (Fig. 2).

The academic discussions on design representations date back to the Vitruvius' treatise, on the role of plan, elevation and perspective in architectural practice. The Renaissance architects indulged in geometry, and also adopted the physical model. Nowadays,

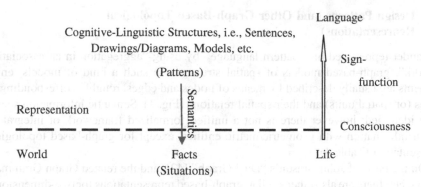

Fig. 2. Representations of patterns within various cognitive levels – a viewpoint of complex adaptive systems and cognitive linguistics [4, 8, 50]

architects employ different representational modes and strategies, from various drawings, diagrams, physical or digital models, to various forms of analysis, written or text/linguistic specifications, and so on [16]. From the perspectives of human cognition and spatial information processing, we conduct a brief review on the representation models of spatial layout design, mainly in the computational medium as follows.

2.1   2D Drawing

The representation model is applied to modeling physical space by using orthographic projections – plans, sections, and elevations. Within the drawings, each Cartesian point has its own correspondence within real or proposed physical space. Disjoint spatial domains within a two-dimensional projective plan are delineated by lines on papers. As attributes are also ascribed, all spatial information – about its dimensions, shape, and attributes – is available [17].

This representation model emphasizes both of topological and metric consider-ations of spatial layouts. From the cognitive perspective, it is a static, low-level, and the fundamental model of design representations (Table 1).

2.2   Bubble Diagram (and Other Diagrams)

The "Bubble Diagram" or "Relationship Diagram" is a simplified graphic description that consists of roughly drawn round/elliptical bubbles (to represent individual con-figurational/spatial entities) connected by various lines (to specify the relation between them), drawn to explore ideas and solutions in the early, conceptual phases of design.

Including many other kinds of diagram, they are usually freehand drawings, emphasizing topological relations and/or architectural images without adequate metric/ shape specifications [14]. Thus, a diagram might be recognized as *'a set of simple symbols (glyphs) and a set of spatial relations between them'* [23]. From the viewpoint of design cognition, they are abstract, cognitively high-level and intuitively closed to human mind and memory (Table 1).

2.3   Design Patterns (and Other Graph-Based Topological Representations)

Alexander represented his "pattern language" by using "aggregation in an associative network", graph-based models of spatial structure. In such a kind of models, environments are usually described by means of nodes and edges, roughly corresponding to places (or spatial units) and their spatial relations (Fig. 1). Semantic information seems to be identified; however there is not a unified formalized framework of integrating design information with geometric/metric entities, except for graph-based topological representation (Table 1).

On the basis of John Grason's "Dual Graph" [42], and the related Graph Grammars approaches, there are also other similar, graph-based representations for two-dimensional spatial layouts existed in CAAD [11, 22].

2.4   Shape Grammars

As "a specific class of production systems" of generating geometric shapes, a shape grammar consists of (1) shape rules (a start rule, at least one transformation rule, and a termination rule) that define how an existing shape (or a part of shape) can be transformed; and (2) a generation engine that selects and processes rules. [43].

Owe to the generative mechanics within its recursive structure, the shape patterns could be emergent with using transformational rules [28]. Thus, we may consider it as a certain kind of dynamic model of design representations. However, due to lack of adequate architecture-specific spatial-feature modeling, the widespread use has not being found in architectural design applications (Table 1).

2.5   Ontologies and Semantics

Distinct with visual-image category of design representations, spatial ontologies approach is related to the technologies of natural language processing and information systems. With the model, the transformation could be implemented between building schema and semantic expression. It has been successfully applied as '*a semantic enabler of communication between both users and applications of building information modeling in AEC domain*' [12, 39].

However, as far as we known, there is no investigation of the formal ontological/semantic modeling on spatial information processing during design process. Therefore, our proposed representation model is designed for spatial cognition-based layout design to integrate both spatial and spatial-related semantic information modeling, i.e., spatial-structural, pattern-based "design semantics" [44] (Table 1).

2.6   Spatial Cognition- and Knowledge-Based Model

One of the key problems of CAAD is to connect computational design methodologies and tools with the representation of design knowledge and integrate both of them into design systems. The relevant research on representation, description and the cognitive processes in design could be found in the early explorations since 1960s [18, 24, 25], and the lasting works in recent years [1, 40, 41].

However, for the relevant theoretic models, there is a cognitive gap between low-level spatial data/information and high-level design knowledge. This deficiency prevents a direct cross-linking between spatial-coordinate information and generic knowledge representation during the design process (Table 1).

2.7 Summary

These existing representation models could be roughly distinguished into the main categories: topology, geometry/metrics, semantics, and so on. However, all of them are hybrids combining with various levels-of-abstraction from the perspective of spatial cognition (Table 1).

Table 1. A comparative analysis of the multiple representations < $\sqrt{}$ = Yes; ($\sqrt{}$) = Maybe >

Design representation models	Complex systems dynamics	Topology	Metrics	Semantics	Spatial-semantic analytics
2D Drawing		$\sqrt{}$	$\sqrt{}$	($\sqrt{}$)	
Diagram		$\sqrt{}$		($\sqrt{}$)	
Design Patterns		$\sqrt{}$		$\sqrt{}$	
Shape Grammar	$\sqrt{}$	($\sqrt{}$)	$\sqrt{}$		
Ontologies				$\sqrt{}$	$\sqrt{}$
Knowledge-Based		$\sqrt{}$	$\sqrt{}$	$\sqrt{}$	($\sqrt{}$)
Proposed Model	$\sqrt{}$	$\sqrt{}$	$\sqrt{}$	$\sqrt{}$	$\sqrt{}$

Aims to a unified and formalized framework, our proposed model attempts to cover all capabilities of these models, being focused on the pattern formation with complex dynamics (a recursive production mechanics) [4–6, 32–34] and spatial-semantics [44].

3 A Generic Representation and Spatial-Semantic Analytic Model

On the basis of the above theoretic explorations, we propose a representation model for the "structural complexity" of two-dimensional spatial layouts, with dynamic, multi-level hierarchies, inspired by the information theory of complex systems [4, 35–37], and the spatial semantics of cognitive linguistics [49, 50]. In our model, patterns are no longer pre-dominated beings, but becoming (which is out of dynamic hierarchies and structural information emergence). The pattern formation results from dynamic hierarchies and adaptive layouts (driven by complex dynamics, and controlled by the relevant "spatial-semantic aware" specifications) within various cognitive levels (Figs. 4, 7 and 13). The proposed model consists of abstract syntax, together with the consistent rules of spatial-semantic compositionality.

3.1   Overview of Solution

At the technical level, we present a computational analytic method and design representation by using the spatial graph grammar formalism (SGG) [31, 46]. Pattern-based design is formalized as a process of specifying multi-level, dynamic hierarchies using the SGG, with (1) graph-based descriptive and generative model of the spatial topology; and (2) spatial-semantic analytic model for layout geometric/metric specifications, on the basis of spatial information processing for patter formation.

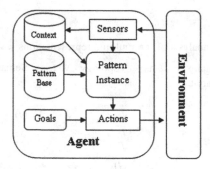

Fig. 3. Pattern formation with agent's spatial-semantic intelligence [8]

With the proposed generic analytic representation, a formalized pattern formation language would be developed, with the essential features: normativity/conventionality (communicable to context information), representation, and intentionality (accessible to human mind) [49, 50]. Within a design system [24, 25], each pattern or "design unit" [18] (driven by its innate pattern formation mechanics) acts as an agent (with its spatial-semantic awareness/intelligence) interacting with other patterns or units, and their environment (Fig. 3).

3.2   Spatial Graph Grammar (SGG)

SGG has been successfully applied to a number of areas, including adaptive webpage design and webpage interpretation [29, 30], which are in principle similar to environmental plans and designs. Graph grammars with their well-established theoretical background can be used as natural and powerful syntax-definition formalism for visual languages, which model structures and concepts in a two-dimensional fashion.

Various grammar formalisms have been proposed for different purposes. Most of those formalisms use nodes to represent objects and edges to model relations between objects in the abstract syntax. Distinctive with other conventional graph grammar formalisms, SGG is enhanced context-sensitive graph grammar formalism, with its unique extension of "spatial-semantic awareness" by introducing a set of spatial-semantic notations as a complement to the abstract syntax. The "direct representation of spatial-semantic information" into the abstract syntax makes grammatical rules (i.e., productions) easy to understand since grammar designers often design rules with similar appearances as the represented graphs (Figs. 4 and 5). In other words, it is consistent with the concrete representation by using spatial-semantic information to directly model relationships in the abstract syntax.

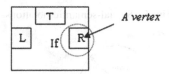

Fig. 4. A node with a hierarchical structure (consists of its low-level multiple vertexes) within various levels of granularity (also see Fig. 7)

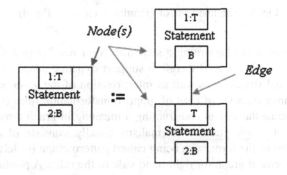

Fig. 5. A graph grammar production

In a word, allowing designers to specify design knowledge in both spatial-structural and spatial-semantic properties simultaneously, the SGG approach is ideal for specifying dynamic hierarchical structures and their adaptive layouts, and well-adopted into our model.

3.2.1 Spatial-Semantic Notations
SGG is context-sensitive graph grammar formalism, with a set of notations for spatial-semantic specifications: direction, topology, distance and alignment (Fig. 6).

3.2.2 Spatial Granularity and Spatial Hierarchy
There is a hierarchical structure inside a node, consisting of multiple vertexes within various levels of granularity (Figs. 4 and 7).

3.2.3 Layout Production and Spatial Hierarchy
SGG also supports the syntax-directed computation through action code. An action code is associated with a production, and is executed when the production is applied.

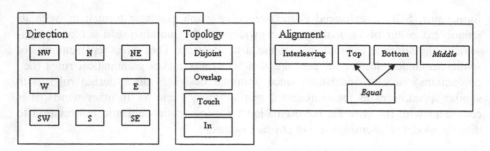

Fig. 6. Spatial-semantic notations

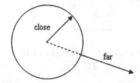

Fig. 7. The first level of granularity (also see Fig. 4)

Writing an action code is like writing a standard event handler in Java programming language. This mechanism would therefore support dynamic adaptation of any specified two-dimensional structure, as well as interpretation of the given structure.

A graph grammar consists of a set of graph transformation rules (i.e. productions) (Fig. 5), which dictate the way of constructing a meaningful graph through a variety of nodes. Formally, a graph grammar formalism usually consists of a set of graph transformation rules of the form, with being called pattern graph (or left-hand side) and being called replacement graph (or right-hand side of the rule). A production is applied to the host graph by searching for an occurrence of the pattern graph (pattern matching) and by replacing the found occurrence by an instance of the replacement graph.

Since all possible inter-connections among the nodes have been stated in the grammar, any connection between a pair of objects in a graph with a valid meaning can be eventually derived from a sequence of production applications, which incrementally rewrite one graph to another. Conversely, an un-expected connection signals a violation on structural requirements. Given a graph grammar, beginning from the initial graph, a generating process, i.e. a graph grammar is applied in a forward direction, can generate all well-formed graphs defined by the graph grammar; a parsing process, i.e. a graph grammar is applied in a reverse direction, can evaluate the structural validity of a graph, which is usually called a host graph (Fig. 12).

3.2.4 Layout Transformation

To reduce the representation space while maintaining the original spatial structure, the adaptive layout transformation method applied, which includes: distance transformations, zooming transformations, and location transformations (Figs. 8 and 9).

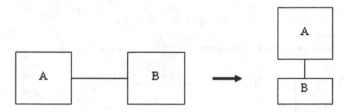

Fig. 8. Spatial-semantic zooming for a layout adaptation

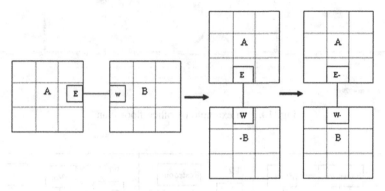

Fig. 9. Applications of spatial-semantic zooming, and distance rules, to achieve the effect in Fig. 8 (The first step: location/direction adapting and downsizing with the notation of "-B"; and the second step: distance reducing with the notations of "E-" and "W-")

4 Examples and Applications

Figure 10[1] presents an office floor plan. Assuming the floor plan follows a general guideline, i.e. a set of layout rules that can be formally defined as a graph grammar; we can then automatically verify any other floor plans conforming to the guideline. In the grammar formalization, nodes represent different entities in the floor plan, such as rooms or office workstations/workspace (WS), and links indicate an adjacent relation between two entities (or entity groups). Spatial relations among different entities are implicitly specified through the layout of the right graph in a production.

More specifically, Fig. 11 illustrates a spatial graph grammar, which summarizes the essential properties (i.e. the given guideline) of the above floor plan. The entire floor plan includes three major areas (i.e., left, center and right) from left to right, as defined in Production 9 (Fig. 11, P9). The left area is denoted as a non-terminal node left in P1, includes three rooms, i.e., reception, store and meeting, and the right area (P2) includes two rooms, restroom and kitchen. The center area indicates the office space, which has a set of office workstations/workspace (WS). Workstations can be organized in different ways. Four workstations, two workstations or one workstation can form one block, as defined in Productions 3, 4 and 5, respectively. Finally,

---

[1] Source from: http://www.officelayouts.org/office-renovation/detail-31.html.

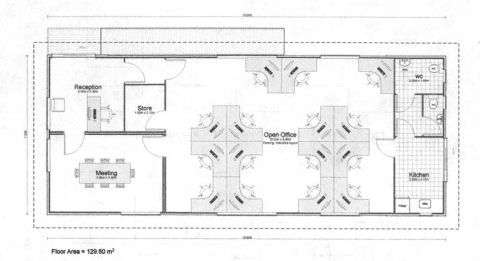

Floor Area = 129.60 m²

Fig. 10. An example of office floor plan

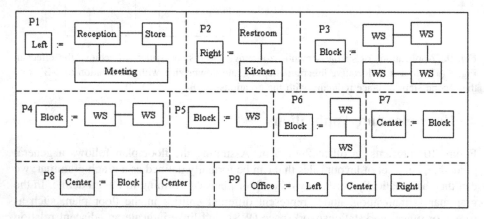

Fig. 11. A graph grammar < WS, An acronym of office workstations/workspace >

Productions 6, 7 and 8 integrate blocks together as the whole office space. Figure 12 illustrates a host graph, which is an abstraction of the floor plan in Fig. 10, which is one instance of the floor plan conforming to the defined graph grammar. Based on the graph grammar, the generation process can produce all possible instances of the floor plan that conform to the graph grammar definition.

A graph grammar specification, parsing and induction tool, called *VEGGIE* (*a Visual Environment of Graph Grammar Induction Engineering*) (Figs. 15 and 16) developed by Zhang and Kong [7, 31, 46]. A designer could use VEGGIE to specify his/her design in the spatial graph grammar and VEGGIE would be able to automatically validate any correct instances of the design meeting the requirements specified in the graph grammar.

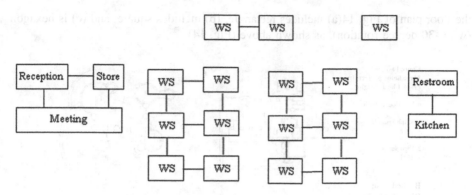

Fig. 12. A host graph representing the floor plan in Fig. 10

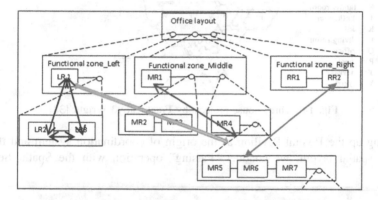

Fig. 13. The diagram of layout hierarchical structure, with possible spatial-semantic information interactions between their nodes (and vertexes), for the pattern-based design evolution using grammar induction and graph transformation [30, 47, 48]

The same specification principle also applies to any architectural layouts that follow a given set of design regulations. We select the three house projects by Frank Lloyd Wright as our second study case for experimental design.

According to the analysis of March and Steadman [38, p. 27–28], the spatial organization in the three house design is sharing in the same/similar design pattern (in terms of spatial topology) (Fig. 15).

However, through parsing with SGG, we would be able to represent, retrieve and pertain to those multiple, complemented and combined features of relevant design knowledge and spatial information (either in spatial-topological and spatial-semantic recognition and representations) for both precedent design analysis and novel design synthesis, for instance, automatic searching for design solutions with case-based reasoning via "Spatial-Semantic Analytics" (Fig. 17).

For the three house design by F.L. Wright, we suggest that a "Pivotal Pavilion" (locates at "F", the family room area for each) acts as the circulation nexus, social communication hub and visual/compositional crux of the layout design. Respectively, the floor plan of Fig. 14(a) includes rectangle, (b) includes square, and (c) is hexagon (with -30 degree rotation), as shown above (Fig. 14).

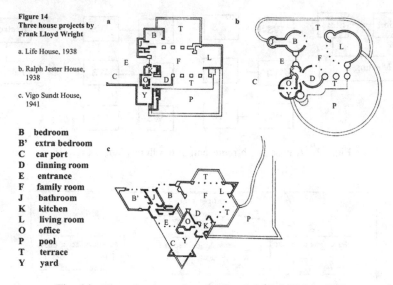

Figure 14
Three house projects by
Frank Lloyd Wright

a. Life House, 1938

b. Ralph Jester House,
   1938

c. Vigo Sundt House,
   1941

B   bedroom
B'   extra bedroom
C   car port
D   dinning room
E   entrance
F   family room
J   bathroom
K   kitchen
L   living room
O   office
P   pool
T   terrace
Y   yard

Fig. 14. Three house projects by Frank Lloyd Wright [38]

Setting up the Pivotal Pavilion as the origin of coordination system and the start point of spatial layout, we conduct "Parsing" operation with the Spatial-Semantic

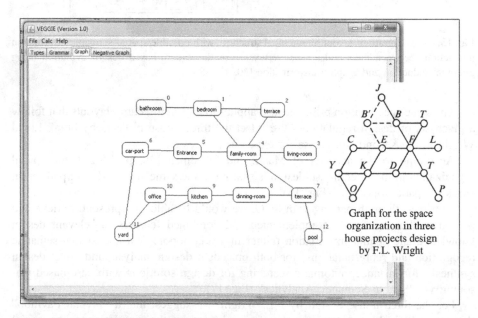

Graph for the space
organization in three
house projects design
by F.L. Wright

Fig. 15. The screenshot of a VEGGIE-generated, task-specific spatial-semantic analytic map (spatial-semantic attributed graph, etc.) for the spatial organization in the three house design

Analytics on the layout design using the VEGGIE system, so as to generate the graph grammar and the Spatial-Semantic Analytic Maps (Fig. 15).

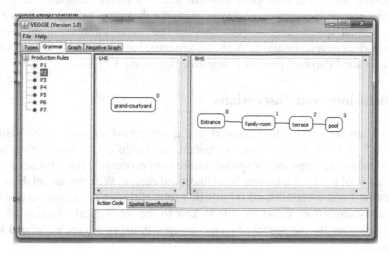

Fig. 16. A screenshot image of the graph grammar, the Production (**grand courtyard**) := (**Entrance - family room – terrace – pool**) for the large block of E- F-T-P (with a "grand courtyard") (Figs. 14 and 15)

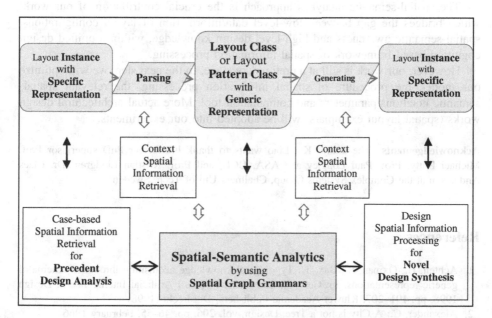

Fig. 17. A conceptual model of "spatial information processing" with *multiple* design representations towards "spatial-semantic analytic intelligence" for design-pattern mining, retrieving, (re-)configuring, transforming and adapting to a variety of context conditions

By the "Parsing" with the VEGGIE Spatial Semantic Analytics, we might be able to obtain the "systematic spatial information" of layout design patterns formally, consisting both of the spatial topology of design configuration and/or composition/compositional units, and their correspondent spatial-semantic attributes, in terms of spatial organization in architectural design. With the three house design case, we try to present a formal spatial-semantic paradigm for the spatial information processing in design knowledge representations. A spatial-semantic representation and layout design analytics for the "Parsing" process is implemented using VEGGIE.

5   Conclusions and Discussions

Our work presents a theoretic framework and a conceptual solution of the "structural complexity" problem in Alexander's "pattern language", i.e., introducing spatial-semantic analytic intelligence for spatial information processing into abstract syntactic representation of the spatial layouts in architectural design. With the model, both of the configurational and compositional information (out of design cognition) as additional/complement connections could be able to knit to the topological structure of spatial layouts (validated by the spatial-semantic compositionality which is defined by the design goal).

A formalized and operable method of design representation for various complex structures/patterns is developed, and implemented by using SGG. With the above the preliminary case study, we testify our theoretic framework and computational tool to demonstrate our proposed approach for practical applications.

The spatial-semantic analytics approach is the crucial contribution of our work, which bridges the gap between low-level data/information of layout configurations, spatial-semantic awareness and high-level design knowledge, within a unified design cognition-based framework of spatial information processing.

However, our work is still at a preliminary stage. In the next step, we will optimize our model, the procedure of spatial information processing, the relevant spatial-semantic notations/parameters and computation tool. More actual architectural design works (spatial layout exemplars) will be adopted into our experiments.

Acknowledgements. The author Kai Liao wants to thank his former PhD supervisor Prof. Michael Batty, Prof. Paul Longley at CASA, UCL, and Prof. Kristian Lindgren, Dr. Claes Andersson at the Complex Systems Group, Chalmers Uni of Tech, Sweden.

References

1. Achten, H., Oxman, R., Bax, T.: Typological knowledge acquisition through a schema of generic representations. In: Gero, J., Sudweeks, F. (eds.) Artificial Intelligence in Design 1998, pp. 191–207. Kluwer Academic Publishers, Dordrecht (1998)
2. Alexander, C.: A City is not a Tree, Design, vol. 206, pp. 46–55, February 1966
3. Alexander, C.: A Pattern Language. Oxford University Press, New York (1977)

4. Andersson, C.: Ontogeny and ontology in complex systems modeling. In: Albeverio, S., et al. (eds.) The Dynamics of Complex Urban Systems, pp. 43–58. Springer, Heidelberg (2008)
5. Andersson, C., Frenken, K., Hellervik, A.: A complex network approach to urban growth. Environ. Plan. A **38**(10), 1941–1964 (2006)
6. Andersson, C., Hellervik, A., Lindgren, A.: A spatial network explanation for a hierarchy of urban power laws. Phys. A **345**(1–2), 227–244 (2005)
7. Ates, K.L., Zhang, K.: Constructing VEGGIE: machine learning for context-sensitive graph grammars. In: Proceedings of 19th IEEE International Conference on Tools with Artificial Intelligence, pp. 456–463 (2007)
8. Barouni, F., Moulin, B.: A framework for qualitative representation and reasoning about spatiotemporal patterns. In: Hernandez, N., Jäschke, R., Croitoru, M. (eds.) ICCS 2014. LNCS, vol. 8577, pp. 79–92. Springer, Heidelberg (2014)
9. Batty, M., Longley, P.: Fractal Cities: A Geometry of Form and Function. Academic Press, London (1994)
10. Batty, M.: Cities and Complexity. The MIT Press, Cambridge (2005)
11. Baybars, I., Eastman, C.M.: Enumerating architectural arrangements by generating their underlying graphs. Environ. Plan. B **7**(3), 289–310 (1980)
12. Beetz, J., van Leeuwen, J., de Vries, B.: IfcOWL: A case of transforming EXPRESS schemas into ontologies. Artif. Intell. Eng. Des. Anal. Manuf. **23**(01), 89–101 (2009)
13. Coyne, R.D., Gero, J.S.: Design knowledge and sequential plans. Environ. Plan. **12**(4), 401–418 (1985)
14. Do, E.Y.L., Gross, M.D.: Thinking with diagrams in architectural design. Artif. Intell. Rev. **15**(1–2), 135–149 (2001)
15. Do, E.Y.L., Gross, M.D., Neiman, B., Zimring, C.: Intentions in and relations among design drawings. Des. Stud. **21**(5), 483–503 (2000)
16. Eastman, C.M.: The evolution of CAD: integrating multiple representations. Build. Environ. **26**(1), 17–23 (1991)
17. Eastman, C.M.: Representations for space planning. Commun. ACM **13**(4), 242–250 (1970)
18. Eastman, C.M.: Explorations of the cognitive processes in design, Technical Report, Carnegie Mellon University (1968)
19. Fu, K.S., Swain, P.H.: On syntactic pattern recognition. In: Tou, J.T. (ed.) Computer and Information Sciences-1969, Software Engineering, vol. 2, pp. 155–182. Academic Press, New York (1971)
20. Gamma, E., Johnson, R., Johnson, J., Helm, R.: Design Patterns: Elements of Reusable Object-oriented Software. Addison-Wesley, Reading (1994)
21. Goldschmidt, G., Porter, W.L. (eds.): Design Representation. Springer, London (2004). (with the reviews by N.J. Habraken and C.M. Eastman)
22. Grasl, T., Economou, A.: Palladian graphs: using a graph grammar to automate the palladian grammar. In: Future cities: 28th eCAADe Conference Proceedings, pp. 275–283 (2010)
23. Gross, M.D.: Indexing visual databases of designs with diagrams. In: Koutamanis, A., Timmermans, H., Vermeulen, I. (eds.) Visual Databases in Architecture. Avebury, Aldershot (1995)
24. Habraken, N.J.: The Structure of the Ordinary: Form and Control in the Built Environment. The MIT Press, Cambridge (1998)
25. Habraken, N.J.: The Appearance of the Form. Awater, Cambridge (1985)
26. Haken, H., Portugali, J.: Information Adaptation: The Interplay Between Shannon Information and Semantic Information in Cognition. SpringerBriefs in Complexity, p. XIV. Springer, Heidelberg (2015)
27. Harary, F.: The city is a tree; the real world is not a tree! Geogr. Anal. **43**(4), 347–357 (2011)

562   K. Liao et al.

28. Terry, K., Stiny, G.: Classical and non-classical computation. Inf. Technol. 5(4), 355–372 (2001)
29. Kong, J., Barkol, O., Bergman, R., Pnueli, A., Schein, S., Zhang, K., Zhao, C.: Web interface interpretation using graph grammars. IEEE Trans. SMC-Part C 42(4), 590–602 (2012)
30. Kong, J., Ates, L., Zhang, K.: Adaptive mobile interfaces through grammar induction. In: Proceedings of 20th IEEE International Conference on Tools with Artificial Intelligence, pp. 133–140 (2008)
31. Kong, J., Zhang, K., Zeng, X.: Spatial graph grammars for graphical user interfaces. ACM Trans. Comput.-Hum. Interact. 13(2), 268–307 (2006)
32. Liao, K., Han, C.Y.: Collective pavilions: a generative architectural modeling for traditional Chinese pagoda. In: Martens, B., Brown, A. (eds.) The CAAD Futures 2005: Learning from the Past, pp. 129–138. Oesterreichischer Kunst- und Kulturverlag, Vienna (2005)
33. Liao, K., Li, D.: An analysis of traditional Chinese architecture and garden design from the viewpoint of chaos theory and fractal geometry. J. Wuhan Tech. Univ. Surv. Mapp. (WTUSM) 23–3, 189–203 (1997)
34. Liao, K.: From Feng-shui to Chaotic/Fractal architecture: transformation of urban space design concept of Chinese Shan-shui (mountain and water, landscape) city. In: Huang, G., et al. (eds.) Proceedings of International Symposium on Sustainable Development of Human Settlements in Mountainous Regions, pp. 77–91. Science Press, Beijing (1997)
35. Lindgren, K: Information theory for complex systems. Lecture Notes (Jan 2003), Department of Physical Resource Theory, Chalmers and Göteborg University (2003)
36. Lindgren, K., Moore, C., Nordahl, M.: Complexity of two-dimensional patterns. J. Stat. Phys. 91(5–6), 909–951 (1998)
37. Lindgren, K., Nordahl, M.G.: Evolutionary dynamics of spatial games. Physica D: Nonlinear Phenom. 75(1), 292–309 (1994)
38. March, L., Steadman, P.: The Geometry of Environment: An introduction to Spatial Organization in Design. MIT Press, Cambridge (1974)
39. Niemeijer, R., de Vries, B., Beetz, J.: Freedom through constraints: user-oriented architectural design. Adv. Eng. Inform. 28(2014), 28–36 (2014)
40. Oxman, R.: The thinking eye: visual re-cognition in design emergence. Des. Stud. 23, 143–158 (2002)
41. Oxman, R.: Design media for the cognitive designer. Autom. Constr. 9, 337–346 (2000)
42. Simon, H.: The Sciences of the Artificial. The MIT Press, Cambridge (1969)
43. Stiny, G.: Shape: Talking About Seeing and Doing. The MIT Press, Cambridge (2006)
44. de Vries, B., Jessurun, A., Segers, N., Achten, H.: Word graphs in architectural design. AI Eng. Des. Anal. Manuf. 19(4), 277–288 (2005)
45. Yessios, C.: Formal language for site planning. In: Eastman, C.M. (ed.) Spatial Synthesis in Computer-Aided Building Design, pp. 147–183. Applied Science Publishers, London (1975)
46. Zhang, K.: Visual Languages and Applications. Springer, Heidelberg (2007)
47. Zhao, C., Kong, J., Dong, J., Zhang, K.: Design pattern evolution and verification using graph transformation. In: Proceedings of 40th Annual Hawaii International Conference on System Sciences, pp. 290–296 (2007)
48. Zhao, C., Kong, J., Dong, J., Zhang, K.: Pattern-based design evolution using graph transformation. J. Vis. Lang. Comput. 18(4), 378–398 (2007)
49. Zlatev, J.: Spatial Semantics. Oxford University Press, Oxford (2010)
50. Zlatev, J.: The Semiotic Hierarchy: Life, Consciousness, Sign and Language. J. Cogn. Semiot. 2009(4), 169–200 (2009)

The Geometry of Chuck Hoberman
As the Basis for the Development of Dynamic Experimental Structures

Márcia Anaf[✉] and Harris Nogueira de Camargo Ana Lúcia

University of Campinas, Campinas, Brazil
marciaanaf@uol.com.br, luharris@fec.unicamp.br

Abstract. The cognitive-theoretical foundation referring to teach drawing as a way of thinking, as well as the construction of the environment by means of drawing using transforming geometries and the formal and para-formal computational process, creating unusual geometries through generative design processes and methodologies, can be seen as some of the main possibilities in exploring dynamic experimental structures for an Adaptive Architecture. This article presents the development of a model for articulated facades, inspired by Hoberman's Tessellates, and his Adaptive Building Initiative (ABI) project to develop facades models that respond in real time to environmental changes. In addition, we describe an experiment based on the retractable structures, inspired by Hoberman's work and experimentations. Solutions for responsive facades can offer more flexible architectural solutions providing better use of natural light and contributing to saving energy. Using Rhinoceros and the Grasshopper for modeling and test the responsiveness, the parametric model was created to simulate geometric panels of hexagonal grids that would open and close in reaction to translational motion effects, regulating the amount of light that reaches the building.

Keywords: Parametric architecture · Hoberman's Tessellates · Adaptive Building Initiative (ABI) · Articulated facades · Complex geometries · Retractable structures · Retractable polyhedra

1 Introduction

The aim of this article is to present and discuss explorations related to dynamic geometric structures by using models and simulations applicable to architectural elements, based on the work and experimentations by Chuck Hoberman. The explorations we present here are related to the author's teaching practices and strategies - searching for different strategies to approach the use of dynamic geometries. The article is structured in two main sections – we first outline specific aspects of Hoberman's approach, and secondly, present the development of a model for articulated facades, inspired by Hoberman's *Tessellates,* and his *Adaptive Building Initiative* (ABI), that respond in real time to environmental changes. We also describe an experiment based on the retractable structures, inspired by Hoberman's work and experimentations [1, 2]. Solutions

© Springer-Verlag Berlin Heidelberg 2015
G. Celani et al. (Eds.): CAAD Futures 2015, CCIS 527, pp. 563–581, 2015.
DOI: 10.1007/978-3-662-47386-3_31

for responsive facades can offer more flexible architectural solutions providing better use of natural light and contributing to saving energy. By using *Rhinoceros* and *the Grasshopper* for modeling and testing responsiveness, the parametric model was created to simulate geometric panels of hexagonal grids that would open and close in reaction to translational motion effects, regulating the amount of light that reaches a building.

1.1 The Creative Process of Chuck Hoberman

"Just imagine what can be, that isn't there yet. That's the first step of inventing." [3].

Chuck Hoberman

The so-called *kinetic architecture* or, as Hoberman named '*transformable design*', point one instigating direction in the investigation related to design processes, methodologies, and strategies in architecture, design and related fields. The complexity present in his works express the contemporaneity of projects in which concepts such as adaptation, transformation, mobility, and interaction take shape, based on principles of spherical trigonometry and mechanisms scissors. Hoberman Associates [4] is specialized in product design, structures, and environments that change size and shape. Hoberman believes that a fast changing world needs a design with an adaptive and interactive approach.

In an interview with high school students in May 1996, promoted by a program of Lemelson Center's Innovative Lives [5], Hoberman said that his geometric speculations started from studies of folds on slips of paper. He said that he was making folds until he could turn the paper strip into a complicated way that could unfold and open with just a twist or pull. In this experimental exploration, the initial structure completely changed in shape and turned to another object only by being folded in a different way. At this point Hoberman realized that, with just a piece of paper that has been folded, amazing and unexpected geometries can emerge. From this experiment, he developed the *split object* – a form that grows by itself, is not just something that moves, but that changes completely in size and shape.

Exploring folding as a creative procedure led Hoberman to develop folds and complex connectors with plastic and metal. The researcher was deeply exploring the idea of designing structure that could transform and grow, just as in nature. Since the beginning of his career, Hoberman was interested in exploring the possibilities of changing a figure into another using specific procedures, initially, geometric figures such as triangles, circles, stars, and a set of basic forms combining the pieces using articulated connectors similar to the scissors. Using these sorts of connectors, one can easily open and close the resultant structures. Concerning his production as a whole, some of his structures are composed of simple geometric shapes such as triangles and trusses. Other structures are formed by more complex shapes, such as polyhedral and icosidodecahedron, as examples. In order to build his structures, the researcher had to deepen his mathematical knowledge and use computers, reaching the point of developing his own graphics program.

In 1990, he founded the "Hoberman Associates" with the goal of creating objects with the same characteristics of living organisms. He described the structure he was developing as mathematics that could be seen as something beautiful, combining transformation and motion. In his words [3], he is trying to do "something that combines Mathematics and Art."

All through Hoberman's career, technological developments, such as CAD/CAM, contributed to his evolution in the exploration of principles of geometric transformations. He wrote custom codes for CAD drawings in Auto LISP, which were essential for the resolution of complex mathematical and geometric calculations necessary to control and test the design and mechanics of each component of the structures. At one point, Hoberman began manufacturing these mechanisms on a small scale using the first 3D printing technologies on a large scale computerized numerical control (CNC) to customize each of their splitting element structures, instead of using foundry tooling. In 2008, he became associated with Buro Happold [6] becoming a founding partner of the *Adaptive Building Initiative* (ABI) and began focusing on the design of adaptable structures for facades (Fig. 1), which correspond in real time to the physical and spatial needs of the environment. Hoberman and his associates believe in an adaptive and interactive design that can meet the needs arising from the rapid changes currently taking place in the world. In parallel to its partnership with ABI [7], Hoberman continued to develop structures based on principles governing Hoberman Associates, among them, the playfulness exhibited in his works. The sculpture "Hoberman Morph" (Fig. 2) represents a new exploration of the operating principles of the 'Transformable Design'. With this work, Hoberman introduces a new sculptural concept in which the geometrical forms are transformed into other forms. This implies a complete metamorphosis of the object, which undergoes a complete change from its shape and appearance. The sculptural elements are rotated in synchronous mode, thus creating a smooth transformation from the cube to the sphere.

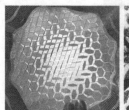   

Fig. 1. City of Justice/Madrid [8]   **Fig. 2.** *Hoberman Morph* [9]

Just as the "Hoberman Sphere", the "Hoberman Morph" was also exhibited at the *Liberty Science Center*. The exhibition *Archaelogy of the Digital* (2013) was the first of a series to display the work of the pioneers in the use of computers as a tool in architecture [10]. In this first exhibition, curated by Greg Lynn, Hoberman's work was included alongside Frank Gehry, Peter Eisenman and Shoei Yoh. Folding structures are structures in which structure and mechanism are identical. Hoberman works with principles and techniques that are used in order to enhance mechanical and structural functions. The "Hoberman Sphere" (Fig. 3) was first designed in 1991 and production later began in 1995. It is considered by many a product icon of contemporary design. The sphere belongs to the MoMA (Museum of Modern Art) collection [11]. In 1998, this project received the Parent's Choice Gold Award. It can be considered a trademark of Hoberman Associates. His story is in its use of toys for children, through facilities, and even on TV. The original Hoberman Sphere was first installed in 1992 at the Liberty Science Center atrium (Fig. 4) and was reinstalled in 2007 in the lobby of the museum. Nowadays, his folding structure can be found in several countries, among them: Japan, Germany, Estonia, South Korea, and Chile [12]. In Estonia (Fig. 5) you can interact with the structure – people arrive with their bikes and take the elevator, causing it to expand and contract. In one of his most recent projects, in partnership with Buro Happold, Hoberman was involved in a program to launch a satellite. As part of the process, they worked in the design of a capsule that protects the satellite structure during the launch

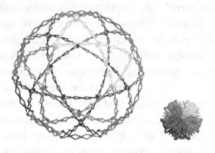

Fig. 3. *Hoberman Sphere* [4] (Source: personal archive)

Fig. 4. *Original Hoberman Sphere* (Source: personal archive)

Fig. 5. Tartu, Estônia/2011/AHHAA *Science Centre* [13]

2   The Geometry of Transformation: Kinetic Architecture and Beyond

The concept of kinetics in architecture is related to its own origins and the evolution of human beings living in nomadic civilizations that moved constantly in search of food [14]. This dynamic led to the development of shelters that could be easily assembled and disassembled. The concept of removable and portable elements is present nowadays as the basilar principia of the field of study named "kinetics". The term "kinetic architecture" was introduced by William Zuk and Roger H. Clark in the early seventies when dynamic spatial design problems were explored in mechanical systems [15]. New materials and construction techniques were developing all along in human history, enabling conceiving projects in design and architecture with structural freedom providing portability, flexibility, and movement [16]. The evolution of kinetic architecture is intrinsically linked to advances in the geometry of transformations, which enables the design and construction of more complex kinetic systems. Related to research in kinetics, biomimetics is the science of analyzing behavior of biological mechanisms found in nature. Kinetic architecture is based on certain biological principles like dynamism and adaptability, which exist in all living organisms. Its application to structures allows a constant flexibility and formal adaptation in response to different spatial or functional needs. The use of kinetic architecture based structures favors the construction of adaptive environments and potentially appropriate to local needs [17]. Another related field, "mobile architecture," has developed in three phases, according to Vassão (2002) [18]. Buckminster Fuller and Chuck Hoberman's works were considered by the researcher as key elements in the development of a mobile architecture, not conceptually, but which had an important role in the development of the first stage, which indicates the evolution of the technique. Studies were further developed during the 90's by Chuck Hoberman and the Kinetic Design Group based at MIT (Massachusetts Institute of Technology) who followed Fuller's predilection for the technical

Fig. 6. Metallic model on a wooden base with Rails for offset shafts expansion movement controlled by Automation [19].

Fig. 7. Expanding Geodesic Dome/New Jersey/Liberty State Park, 1991 [12].

and mechanical aspects of the geometrical structures that could be suitable for a mobile architecture. New developments in digital fabrication and rapid prototyping facilitate deep investigations and experiments concerning the behavior of these systems and mechanisms (Figs. 6 and 7).

3   Experimentations: Understanding the Scissors' Mechanism, Modular Units and Movement Structures

The Hoberman Sphere is called a "Unfolding Structure" or it is a split structure that contracts and expands. This is not the case of the tent for military use (Fig. 8) that was designed and built to be easily and quickly assembled and disassembled, then the patent name is 'Rapidly Deployable Shelters'.

Fig. 8.   Rapidly Deployable Shelter, 2006. Johnson Outdoors Eureka Brand [12]

There is a significant difference between unfolding and deployable structures, because of the fact that a structure is not folding implies being an ephemeral and temporary structure such as the Expanding Video Screen (Fig. 9) which was designed for U2'S *360* show tour. This structure followed the band on their presentations for about three years, and was easily transported to be assembled and disassembled quickly in several countries.

Fig. 9.   Expanding Video Screen (U2), 2009 [12]

Deployable structures are characterized by their ability to adapt their shape to the external conditions. The mobile theater (Fig. 10) of Emilio Pérez Piñero (27.08.1935 to 07.08.1972) was built in Spain in the 1960s [20]. It is a landmark for the scissor-hinge c structural mechanisms, because this structure was to motivate many architects and engineers in the development of these mechanisms. Their findings and projects continue to be a strong reference to the convertible structures. In 2012, The exhibition 'Emilio Pérez Piñero was inaugurated in Spain: Futuristic architecture en España' in honor of the 40th anniversary of his death and in 2013, the 1st International Congress on Architecture and Engineering Transformable was held in Seville, in which Felix Escrig's book, "Modular, Ligero, Transformable, Un paseo por la ligera architecture," was released and which is considered a reference in the use of scissor mechanisms.

Fig. 10. Mobile theater

Chuck Hoberman is a significant name with his angulated scissor-like element. He designed various deployable spatial scissor-hinge structural mechanisms like Iris Dome at the MOMA. There is some similarity of this book with the cover of the Plaza de Toros (1971), both open and close like a diaphragm (Figs. 11 and 12).

Fig. 11. Iris Dome (1994)

Fig. 12. Plaza de Toros, Projeto Experimental de Emílio Pérez Piñero [21]

In fact Hoberman often cite the influence of the geodesic domes of Buckminster Fuller (Fig. 13) and the structures and mechanisms scissor developed by Emilio Pérez Piñero, Sergio Pellegrino and Felix Escrig [22].

Fig. 13. "Dômes Pliants" Structures de Necklace Domes [23]

3.1   Geometric Construction

Simple expandable structures based on the concept of pantographic elements, i.e. straight bars connected through scissor hinges have been known for a long time. More sophisticated expandable or deployable structures have been developed in recent years. Many of these solutions are based on the so called angulated pantographic element [24].

In the project the authors were involved, to study the curvature of the scissor mechanisms, various modular units were made, each consisting of three elements: two subunits and a connector (push-button).

These modules complement the investigations and experiments on the retractable structures that the researchers were running previously. Repetition and the connection of the various modular units generate symmetry systems and subsystems with distinct characteristics. Connected to the investigations and experimentations, a series of workshops were prepared. For the workshops the researcher prepared kits with several modular units. These activities were part of a Ph.D. research in progress and aim to expand the possibilities of combinations of geometric units designed by the researchers that are:

Symmetrical Bars

- The connection point is centralized for each subunit (bar);
- The modular units connected together generate an articulated system without curvature, with constant and linear motion (Fig. 14).

Fig. 14. Expansion and contraction motion (Source: Maurício Oliveira)

Uneven Bars

– The connection point is not centered for each subunit. In this case, there are two possibilities:

(a) modular units interconnected generate an articulated system that presents variations in its curvature (Fig. 15) according to their deployment (expansion and contraction motion);

(b) modular units interconnected that generate an articulated system, but subject symmetry by reflection resulting in a linear deployment system (Fig. 16).

Fig. 15. Curvature deployment system [9]

Fig. 16. Linear deployment system [9]

Angular Bars

– Subunit that has an angle that is calculated for each case, as it is conditional on some parameters such as the number of divisions circumference, the radius value of the circle and the opening and closing;

– The modular units connected together generate an articulated system that has a constant curvature in its development (Fig. 17).

The systems, subsystems and present connections in expanding polygons, also present in retractable polyhedral, facilitated and complemented these geometrical studies related to symmetry. The construction of the retractable structures contributes to a better understanding of the principles present in the Kinetic Architecture [25].

Fig. 17. Linear deployment system [9]

Assembling robust bodies connected by movable connectors, allows great changes in form and structure. It can be applied in several fields, such as building shelters and emergency structures, solar panels and antennas space, stand assembly (displays) and also in the manufacture of instruments for minimally invasive surgery. The structural concepts in general are associated with the movement of Structural Engineering, but have other functions. The mathematical principles of these structures are fundamental to the development of innovative projects including the geometric and kinematic analysis and can be seen as an extension of the mechanisms theory [26].

The movement of the bar allows changes in shape. The structure varies according to the number of bars and the number of connectors among them. With Gruebler's equation, it is possible to calculate the degrees of freedom (DOF) of these bars. From this point on, the bars will be called links and connectors will be called joints to suit the nomenclature used in the equation for calculating the DOF, where N is the number of links (including the link basis) and P represents the number of joints, which are the pivot connectors among links.

Degree of freedom of a mechanical system is the number of independent parameters that define its configuration. The calculation of Degrees of freedom is equal for a tong linkage and a closed tong linkage:

$$DOF = 3 \times (N-1) - 2P$$

There is a difference between the calculation of the number of pivots (P) for tong linkage and closed linkage.

(a) Number of pivots for a tong linkage

$$P = 3N/2 - 2$$

(b) Number of pivots for a closed tong linkage

$$P = 3N/2$$

Retractable Cuboctahedron. The Cuboctahedron is an Archimedean polyhedra formed by regular polygons with six of its square faces and the other eight triangular (Fig. 18). Because of its properties is called Vector Equilibrium, as the name implies, it is a polyhedron composed of vectors that remain in balance.

8 triangles × 3 edges = 24 edges

Gruebler's equation was applied in calculating the amount of parts used to build the Retractable Cuboctahedron (Fig. 19).

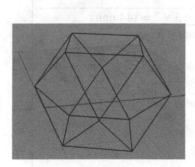

Fig. 18. Cuboctahedron

Fig. 19. Cuboctahedron retractable

The central section of the cuboctahedron is a regular hexagon. To construct a retractable polyhedron, each edge is divided in three equal portions (Fig. 20) where each part is two modular units forming a set of six units (Table 1).

Fig. 20. Top

To calculate the required number of pivots to each of the edges of the retractable polyhedron, the formula $P = 3N/2 - 2$, used in the case of tong linkage, was applied.

$$\text{If } N = 6; \text{then } P = 18/2 - 2 = 9 - 2 = 7$$

That is, these seven screws are in common, these are used among the pivots units (links). The other four are to secure the unit in the structural node. In total there are 11 Pivots × 24 edges = 264 Pivots.

Table 1. Modules and pivots

8 triangular faces	8 faces × 3 edges = 24 edges
Module	1 module = 2 units
24 edges de 3 modules	24 × 3 × 2 = 144 units
Unit	1 unit = 3 holes
	1 edge = 11 pivots

The angle of each unit (Fig. 21) was obtained by dividing the circle by the number of edges.

$$6 \text{ edges } \times 3 = 18 \text{ edges}$$

If $360°$: 18 edges $= 20°$; then supplement of $20° = 160°$

From the circumferences of rotation (Figs. 22, 23 and 24) a retractable cuboctahedron can be created.

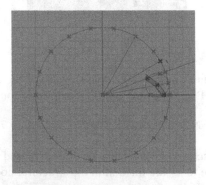

Fig. 21. Angle of unit

Applications and Experiences. One of the objectives of this research is the dissemination of knowledge and the Ignis Project[1] is an offshoot of the results obtained from the construction of the retractable polyhedra. Sangiorgi explains that *"Expandable length Retractable Cuboctahedron* (Fig. 25) *restricts the movement of gyro pressure causing the rotation frequency increase to increased stiffness gyroscopic."*

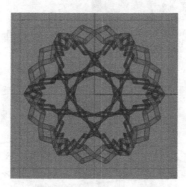

Fig. 22. Top: Grasshopper and Rhinoceros (Source: Maurício Oliveira)

Fig. 23. Perspective (Source: Maurício Oliveira)

---

[1] Diego Sangiorgi is a biologist, researcher and is responsible for the project. He says that after 8 years of research and experiments has developed an unprecedented arrangement. He was surprised to see the retractables polyhedrons that are being developed in this doctoral research, considered that this was the key to put in practice your own project. Thus was developed the retractable Cuboctahedron, known as "Vector Equilibrium". His research is based on Biomimetics observation of nature process, and the use of its standards as a measure in the structures and processes.

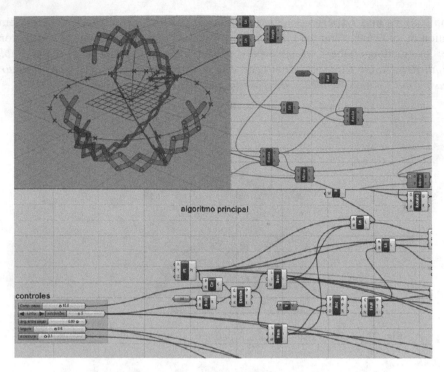

Fig. 24. Rotation (Source: Maurício Oliveira)

Fig. 25. Construction of the retractable structures

4 Exploring Dynamic Geometries Using Models and Simulations Applied to Architectural Elements

The case studies selected by the authors for the development of experimental dynamic structures include two highlights of Chuck Hoberman trajectory. One of them is the work Hoberman began to develop together with the ABI (Adaptive Building Initiative) and the other is the *Hoberman Sphere*, 'trademark' of Hoberman Associates [4] that we presented and discussed in the introduction of the present article. For the experimentation related to Shape Grammars, the researchers used Rhinoceros and the plug-in Grasshopper, that allows the simulation of parametric surfaces and structures. The resultant 'Smart surface' is the result of an interactive process that allows a constant flexibility and adaptation in response to different environmental and spatial needs [27]. This study is aimed at teaching and was presented as a proposal for innovation for the study of creativity in dissertation "The creative dimension of drawing as generative process" [27].

Mainly inspired by Hoberman's Tessellates, the project 'Tessellates' is a 'Smart Surface' [7] composed of a set of repetitions, generating an array of offsets visual effects similar to a kaleidoscope – a framed screen with a perforation pattern which can continuously change and evolve, creating a dynamic architectural element that regulates the entry of sunlight and thus controls the brightness, the ventilation and the air flow, and privacy. It is designed for walls, glass and glazing systems and partitions being a versatile and multifunctional facade. Several stacked panels can be constructed by various materials such as metals and plastics. As these layers move and overlap, the result is a visual kaleidoscope for display of alignment patterns that differ after forming a thin light diffusion matrix.

Adaptive Fritting (Figs. 26 and 27) is a motorized panel prototype that allows constant evaluation of standards of transparency and external visibility. Consists of a glass panel with pattern of paper that recombines brightness locks with different aesthetic results [19].

Fig. 26. *Adaptative Fritting* [19]   **Fig. 27.** *Adaptative Fritting* (Detail) [19]

The objective of this study is to obtain the desired structural configuration for creating smart adaptive surfaces [19], seeking a better use of natural light and contribute to the field of Kinetic Architecture, or for the understanding of the principles of a responsive architecture. The term "Responsive architecture" was coined by Nicholas Negroponte in the mid-seventies when spatial design problems were beginning to be explored through digital technologies [28].

The Grasshopper is a Rhinoceros plug-in that allows exploring dynamic geometric solutions for digital simulation models. Using the Grasshopper is possible to control various transformations and movements, enabling numerous simulations aimed at better formal and spatial adaptation of the architectural structure to the environment. It allows to generate dynamic arrays using the rotation and translation functions. For the researchers experimental projects, Grasshopper was used to simulate the effects obtained by the translational movement of the panels with the hexagonal surfaces. The parametric model designed to generate the simulation of "tessellates" came from the construction of three 'layers' having each one the same thickness. The resultant responsive facade structure is a system composed of *n* variables, which can be combined with each other and at the same time can be the result of other combinations, so the resultant behavior is subject to unpredictability (Fig. 28).

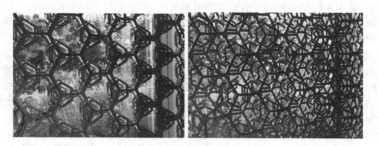

Fig. 28. Simons Center of Geometry & Physics – Transforming Façade (Source: ADAPTIVE Architecture: 2006–2010)

To study the translational sliding panels, the following variables were established:

(1) *Creation of Hexagrid (hexagonal base matrix):*

Variable 1: Measure the side of the external hexagon;
Variable 2: hexagons count by lines;
Variable 3: hexagons count by columns;
Variable 4: Distance between the hexagons (external and internal) that is measured on the side of the inner hexagon (given by the Offset value).

(2) *Construction of the volumetric surface:*

Variable 5: thickness of the layers;
Variable 6: Distance between the layers, interweaving of layers;
Variable 7: Displacement of parallel layers together.

The hierarchical combination of the variables presented here, allow simultaneous combinations generating system complexity. For Terzidis (2006) *Complexity* [29] is the term used to indicate the extent of the description of the system or the amount of time needed to create a system. The images generated are the result of numerous combinations of these variables. The resulting structures (Fig. 10) are from the simulation made with three layers moving on the same track (line). Two of the layers have the hexagons with the same dimensions and an additional one was altered, having different dimensions. During the experimental study was observed that, changing a variable amplifies the effect (Figs. 29, 30 and 31) for the understanding of visual permeability of these surfaces.

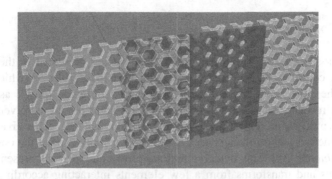

Fig. 29. Simulation (Source: Márcia Anaf)

Fig. 30. Top view of the effects obtained: different granulations and opacity (Source: Márcia Anaf)

Fig. 31. Effects of granulation (Source: Márcia Anaf)

Adaptive buildings can adapt their shape and function in real time to environmental changes [30]. The panels can be used as shutters, its operation can be manual or motorized.

5   Final Considerations

According Vassão (2010) [31], the parameterized design presented in the form of a diagram is a conscious generative process – a system of rules in which you can manipulate the rules themselves. Refers to the idea of game (*play*), as the space branches and reconfigures itself. As a reflection resultant for the involvement in the experimental process presented here, it can be said that the generative design of complex geometries and resultant spaces of great complexity express the contemporary *rhizomatic thinking* [32]. This dynamic and adaptive complexity is present in nature, which emerges and transforms from a few elements interacting according to simple rules or *parameters*.

In this article, the geometry of Chuck Hoberman is presented as a basis for the development of experimental structures – both physical dynamics and digital. Hoberman observes the principles existing in nature and employs them in geometry transformations. Experimenting with articulated structures that expand and contract, changing their sizes without changing their configurations are characteristic of his creative process. The versatility of his work resembles nature, with few rules that can generate such a huge variety of results.

References

1. Hoberman, C.: Mechanical invention through computation: mechanism basics. In: MIT Class 6.S080 (AUS) (2013)
2. Hoberman, C.: Mechanical invention through computation: expanding structures 2D. In: MIT Class 6.S080 (AUS) (2013)
3. Lemelson Center. http://invention.smithsonian.org/centerpieces/ilives/hoberman1.html
4. Hoberman Associates-Transformable Design. www.hoberman.com
5. Lemelson Center. http://invention.si.edu/chuck-hoberman-innovative-lives-presentation-1996
6. Buro Happold Engineering. www.burohappold.com
7. Adaptive Building Initiative. www.adaptivebuildings.com/
8. Adaptive Building Initiative. www.adaptivebuildings.com/city-of-justice.html
9. Hoberman Associates-Transformable Design. www.hoberman.com/news/hoberman-premieres-hoberman-morph.html
10. Archaeology of the Digital. www.cca.qc.ca/en/exhibitions/1964-archaeology-of-the-digital
11. Museum of Modern Art. www.moma.org/collection/object.php?object_id=132506
12. Hoberman Associates-Transformable Design. www.hoberman.com/portfolio.php
13. Science Centre AHHAA. www.ahhaa.ee/en/ahhaa_tartu
14. Barbosa, L.L.: Design sem fronteiras: a relação entre o nomadismo e a sustentabilidade. Tese de Doutorado. Orientadora: Maria Cecília Loschiavo dos Santos. Faculdade de Arquitetura e Urbanismo da Universidade de São Paulo (FAUUSP) (2008)

15. Zuk, W., Clark, R.H.: Kinetic Architecture. Van Nostrand Reinhold Company, New York (1970)
16. Barbosa, L.L.: Design sem Fronteiras: A Relação entre o Nomadismo e a Sustentabilidade. São Paulo: EDUSP/FAPESP (2012)
17. Kronenburg, R.: Flexible: Architecture that Responds to Change. Laurence King, London (2007)
18. Vassão, C.A.: Arquitetura Móvel: propostas que colocaram o sedentarismo em questão. Dissertação de Mestrado. Orientador: Prof. Doutor Carlos Roberto Zibel Costa. Faculdade de Arquitetura e Urbanismo da Universidade de São Paulo (FAUUSP) (2002)
19. Barbosa, L.L.: O design transformável através das criações da Hoberman Associates. In: 9° Seminário Internacional NUTAU 2012. BRICS e a Habitação Coletiva Sustentável. NUTAU, São Paulo (2012)
20. Rocha, D.C.: Desenvolvimento de estruturas articuláveis de madeira. Dissertação de Mestrado. Orientador: Ana Lucia Nogueira de Camargo Harris. Faculdade de Engenharia Civil, Arquitetura e Urbanismo da Universidade Estadual de Campinas (UNICAMP) (2010)
21. Fundación Emilio Pérez Piñero. www.perezpinero.org
22. Chuck Hoberman-Transformable: Building structures that change themselves - AAG 2012 - organized by RFR-HD. https://vimeo.com/51749695
23. Snyder, R.: Buckminster Fuller: Scénario Pour One Autobiographie. Éditions Images Modernes, Paris (2004)
24. Jensen, F., Pellegrino, S.: Expandable "Blob" Structures. J. Int. Assoc. Shell Spat. Struct. (IASS) 46(3), 151–158 (2005)
25. Anaf, M., Harris, A.L.N.C.: Transformable design: an approach between mathematics and arts. In: Geometria's 2014 Proceedings (2014)
26. You, Z., Chen, Y.: Motion Structures: Deployable Structural Assemblies of Mechanisms. Spon Press, New York (2011). Hardcover
27. Anaf, M.: A dimensão criativa do Desenho como processo gerativo. Dissertação de Mestrado. Orientador: Prof. Doutor Caio Adorno Vassão. Universidade Fernando Pessoa (UFP) (2012)
28. Negroponte, N.: Soft Architecture Machines. MIT Press, Cambridge (1975)
29. Terzidis, K.: Algorithmic Architecture. Architectural Press, Oxford (2006)
30. Hoberman, C., Schwitter, C.: Adaptive structures: building for performance and sustainability. Design Intelligence. Trends, Strategies, Research for Design Professionals. DesignIntelligence. N.p., 11 August 2008.www.di.net/articles/adaptive-structures-building-for-performance-and-sustainability/
31. Vassão, C.A.: Metadesign, ferramentas, estratégias e ética para a complexidade. Blucher, São Paulo (2010)
32. Morin, E.: Introdução ao pensamento complexo. Sulina, Porto Alegre (2007)

Material Computability of Indeterminate Plaster Behavior

Aslı Aydın[1(✉)] and Mine Özkar[2]

[1] Istanbul Bilgi University, Istanbul, Turkey
asliaydin87@gmail.com
[2] Istanbul Technical University, Istanbul, Turkey
ozkar@itu.edu.tr

Abstract. In this study, we revisit the concepts of abstraction and materialization with regards to the theoretical framework of new materialism. Underlining the changing relationship between design through abstraction (DtA) and design through materialization (DtM) in design history, we propose an integration of the two towards achieving design emergence. Additional to a theoretical framework, we provide a showcase through material experiments of plaster and abstractions in the form of shape computation. We discuss results as parameters for future digital implementations and potentials for design practice and education.

Keywords: Shape computation · New materialism

1 Introduction

In common architectural practice, material expressions come posterior to the designing of the form. While materials actualize design, because material research is in itself a separate field of inquiry, most practice treats them as unchangeable phenomena upon which to apply the form. Designers' digital design and fabrication tools reinforce form production mostly independent of material behavior and properties. In recent alternative approaches, both abstraction and materialization can be valued equally as to reciprocally impact each other in the creation of form.

Form is created as much by the designers' abstractions of the design problem as by the dynamics of the material(s). This is consistent with what DeLanda coins as *new materialism*, an approach to matter to draw abstraction and materialization together. This Deleuzian-ism follows that matter has itself the potentials of taking form [1].

Two methods are introduced to develop a perspective into evaluating existing design approaches in practice through design history. These are design through abstraction (from here on referred to as DtA) and design through materialization (from here on referred to as DtM). In DtA, the designer takes the reality, abstracts one or more aspects of it and works with these data in the search of creativity. The study considers any medium of design that only relates partially to the real existence of a design as abstraction – drawings, diagrams, models, hand sketches or CAD models, etc. Designers use these abstractions as representations to substitute reality. In DtM, the designer does not break ties with the physical reality of design and works with physical matter in search of creativity. The designer can work in real time and space once there are no limitations to reality; no suppositions,

© Springer-Verlag Berlin Heidelberg 2015
G. Celani et al. (Eds.): CAAD Futures 2015, CCIS 527, pp. 582–599, 2015.
DOI: 10.1007/978-3-662-47386-3_32

symbolizations, or conceptualizations. This fosters creativity beyond giving static shapes to materials. Usually processes separate the two methods. We argue for a conjunct design process where either method does not have priority over the other. Rather, both can feed from each in search of creativity and emergence.

A simple design process is devised to put the framework above to test. Two physical models are setup. In both models, the molds to cast the plaster are rigid in the x and y-axes and flexible in the z-axis. This is to allow for forms to emerge when the designer introduces probes. The movement of probes under the elastic mold differentiates the two physical model sets: (1) one uses static probes; (2) the other one uses dynamic probes. While experimenting with plaster to understand material properties that affect the becoming of form, its computational manipulation is sought via visual schemas [2].

Designers communicate in abstractions, mostly visually, drawings of their ideas to support creative processes. Stiny and Gips' [3] shape computation approach formalizes the designer's design process computationally without overlooking the visual aspect involved in the process. Shape computation theory aims to bring out the emergence of new shapes through execution of visual rules defined by the designer and visual schemas [4] as generalizations of rules. Schemas are valued in this work, as they do not aim to determine final shapes but they talk about the processes that create them and the potentials of becoming in shapes. Their less specific character allows designers to explore rule potentials for different becomings. Fittingly, the proposed process does not rely on static instances of designs but on duration and continuous flux in visual schemas where forms emerge from material behaviors with the designer's guidance and interpretation of material becoming towards use for future designs. As a result, DtA and DtM together foster the creative process of the designer.

2   A Philosophical Approach to Form and Matter

Form and matter in reality does not presuppose any hierarchy; they exist together. Reality is not static; it is a duration that is dynamic. Therefore, matter and form each constitutes a dynamic becoming where each influences the other. Any emphasis on matter and form in reality raises questions about the validity of abstractions. However, abstractions are necessary in solving scientific problems and as well as constructing a building. Then, it is crucial to investigate how appropriate abstractions are derived from materiality, which is closely linked to how one relates herself/himself to reality.

Bergson [5] defines two ways of knowing something: either by moving around the object or by entering into it. The former depends on the point of the observer and relies on the symbols, analysis and concepts that s/he puts forth to describe it. The latter, on the other hand, relies on intuition. Inexpressibility renders it to cross any ready concepts and abstractions to search for the uniqueness and essentiality in the object. The object then is not in a static state. There is a continuous flux and mobility in its becoming, which necessitates the dimension of duration in observation.

These abstractions and materializations have an implication for design professions different than for science. Designers seek creativity and emergence in their designs; they do not solely aim to explain reality. The synchrony of abstractions and materializations can provide the novelty a designer looks for in design.

We adopt a Deleuzian approach to form and matter that is described by Delanda [6] as *new materialism*, which defies static understanding of objects and considers them dynamic entities that are in continuous becoming in time. Becoming tendencies of objects are the result of the innate morphogenetic potentials of matter as well as the interior and exterior forces.

Deleuze's concepts of multiplicities, line of flight and singularities contextualize how new materialism can be interpreted in design.

Multiplicities explain dynamic processes and morphogenesis. They are spaces of infinite possibilities of becoming [7]. The theory of multiplicities is inspired by the Riemannian concept of n-dimensional surfaces or spaces rendered by two properties: the changeable number of dimensions and the absence of extrinsic higher dimensions to define and situate things in space [8]. Multiplicities as such are free of structural interdependence.

Line of flight is a concept much relevant to the designer's situation in the new materialistic approach. It is sort of a delirium [9], an open flux of possibilities before form emerges [10]. It is often interpreted as the leap or the creative moment.

Singularities are the inflection points or turning points that change the behavior of a system [11].

Bringing all these three concepts, it is possible to construct a role for the designer in the new materialist perspective. The role of the designer is to define any process of becoming form of matter when everything is possible. In the becoming of form, what changes the nature of the multiplicity is the singularity that is defined by either the designer or the material properties.

Morphogenetic interpretations of Deleuze's work are parallel to how Turing [12] studies morphogenesis by introducing morphogens as form generators. Morphogens differentiate form of organisms when they are diffused through a tissue. They lead the system to reach a state of instability. When the system is instable, irregularities tend to grow. Morphogens act similar to singularities of Deleuze; they are both form generators.

Within the framework our study, morphogenesis can be described as the differentiation of form of matter in relation to the properties that the matter embodies. It is observed physically as a phenomenon and then abstracted as close to reality as possible for an objective investigation.

The space of the morphogenesis in our study is crucial to set up, since it defines the constructs of the geometry of observations. Deleuze differentiates space as striated and smooth. In striated space points are the core of the geometry, all other geometries are derivatives of these point constraints. It belongs to the coordinate system of Euclidean geometry. A geometry defined in this space is consequently static. Vectors and trajectories, on the other hand, construct smooth space. Infinitely many points can be derived from it. Smooth space is essentially non-Euclidean and it does not aim to conceptualize space with projections of it on a coordinate system. We benefit from the definition of smooth space while constructing our experiments.

Our study aims to understand form and matter together. Surface, being the mediator between the two, is chosen as the object of focus. Variations and changes in the form of matter can be explored through its surface. Cache [13] provides a reference to our study with his investigations of formation with regards to the Deleuzian idea of vectors and singularities. He utilizes vectors as forces that change the landform in topography and singularities as a collection of points defined on a curve. He suggests via diagrams that there are two types of singularities that occur on curves: extrinsic and intrinsic singularities. While the extrinsic singularities are observable minima and maxima points, which are tangent to the curve at the top and at the bottom, the intrinsic singularities are the inflection points of the curve. These inflection points have no curvature; they do not suggest any top or bottom. Hence, they are the points where everything is possible. There are infinitely many possibilities of becoming of form when curve reaches an inflection point.

3   Modes of Designing – Abstraction and Materialization

Focillon [14] poses a problem of architecture regarding the reduction of materiality of architecture to solely scaled models and drawings. He states the danger in separating them. His emphasis is still true for some architectural practice today. It is important to signify methods of designing in order to do propose an alternative come back to the practice.

Within the framework of the previously discussed philosophical perspective, our study identifies two methods of designing: design through abstraction and design through materialization.

In design through abstraction (from here on referred to as DtA), the designer does not design in real space and time of the subject but takes one or more features of it and works on these features in another medium in the search of creativity. From Bergson's moving around the object perspective, any design process that involves analysis, symbols and concepts falls into this category. Therefore, the study considers any medium of design that relates partially to the real existence of a design as abstraction – drawings, diagrams, models, hand sketches or CAD models, etc.

In design through materialization (from here on referred to as DtM), the designer does not migrate the physical reality of design to another medium but rather works with the physical matter in search of creativity. Designing takes place in the real time and space of the matter and with the matter itself. The models of DtM are different than that of DtA; they are not representation. Once there are no specializations or limitations to reality, meaning there are no suppositions, symbolizations and conceptualizations in design process, the designer can work in real time and space. The designer can enter into the object and work with matters in their becoming of forms while occupying duration in reality as well.

The conception of duration in DtA is different than in DtM. Apart from dynamic, kinetic or interactive designs, abstractions do not occupy duration in real time and space. Duration in materialization, however, refers to the relationship of the designer with the design in their becoming of physical form and not the sensual or emotional interactions of people with these designs after they are built.

We go over the design history from a design methods perspective to understand the relationship between DtA and DtM and how the importance given to one or the other has had changed in time. It is possible to divide the chronology to five periods with regard to readings from Pérez-Gomez [15], Adamson [16] and Kolarevic [17]. Although their perspectives differ, the time periods overlap. Figure 1 shows these time periods as well as the proposed relationship which will be explained below.

Until the 15th century, building practice mostly depends on the DtM. Architects are referred to as master builders [17]. Only abstractions inseparable from constructions are architects' templates [15], which are not accurate drawings but geometrical and proportional rules that made construction possible [18].

During the Renaissance, between 15th and 18th centuries, the complexity of building construction gives birth to the use of orthogonal drawings and the recently discovered perspective [15].

In the 19th century, the introduction of descriptive geometry allows for a systematic reduction of three-dimensional objects to two-dimensions [15]. The separation of roles of the architect, engineer and contractor on one hand, drawings becoming legal documents between actors on the other, simultaneously disconnect DtA and DtM completely [17]. The Arts and Crafts Movement stands out in this period to revive crafts [16], *i.e.* DtM. Then, from the beginning of 20th century till 1960's, the estrangement of DtA and DtM is elaborated through the modernist discourse [15]. The increasing complexity of building design and construction necessitates further specialization of professions, leaving only the abstract mode of designing to the architect. The Zeitgeist of modernism yields to the designer's loss of control over built materiality [17].

After 1960's, with the introduction of computers to the design industry, the relationship between DtA and DtM takes a deceiving disposition. The two approaches observed in this period are (1) that DtA and DtM are connected yet discrete phases, and (2) that the border between DtA and DtM has dissolved. The first approach exalts the advancement of CAD/CAM technologies and the linear phasing of design and construction. Although the CAD/CAM integration creates a link between abstraction and materiality, it does not promise a material based design inquiry. The materials' potential of becoming is not sought after; instead materials take on the digital forms created by the designers. The second approach, on the other hand, inquires into materials for design creativity and aims to use the emergent potentials in materials. Designers take into consideration the material behavior while designing and execute material experiments to understand how the end products look like. Yet they neglect the becoming of form as something to calculate or design with.

At the turn of the new century, craftsmanship is redefined with the integration of DtA and DtM. Designers use emerging new technologies and build their own tools to design and construct with. The immediacy to making and having the scientific tools and knowledge defines the craftsmanship of emerging designers of the new century. Different from the second approach explained above, we focus on how the form emerges under material behavior and use this visual knowledge as something to design with. We aim to understand how the mode of design through computable abstraction can be tuned so that it can adjust itself to materialization, overcoming the problem of representing reality and becoming the reality itself.

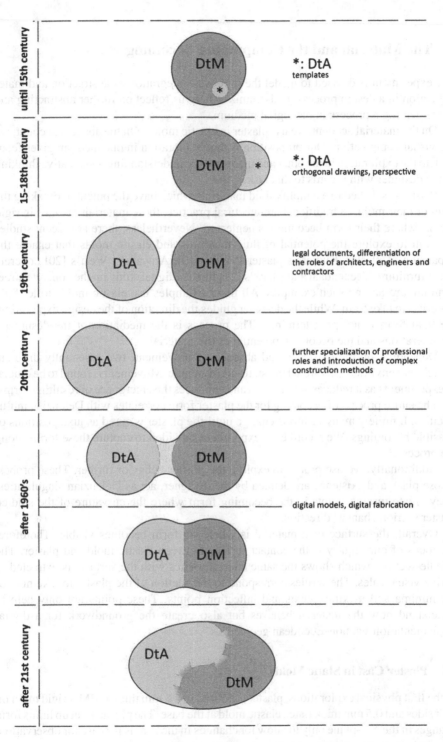

Fig. 1. Timeline of the changing relationship between DtA and DtM with their proposed integration after 21st century

4   The Material and the Computable Becoming

Our experiment is devised to model the proposed integration of abstraction and materialization in a design process. It also aims to help us reflect on further abstracting and implementing a process in the digital medium.

On the material account, we use plaster in elastic molds. On the abstract account, we use visual computation. Our proposition is that exploration in one medium gives feedback to the exploration in the other and increases the understanding and creative thinking of the designer with regards to that task.

Plaster is selected to exemplify fluid materials which have the potential of taking the form of their mold. In traditional architectural practice, these materials are cast in rigid molds, where their form becoming is neglected. Nevertheless, there are recent studies that aim to explore the potential of fluid materials and elastic molds that enable the expansion of plaster. Kudless's plaster P-Wall [19], Araya and West's [20] concrete street furniture, Veenendaal and Block's [21] further digital study on the concrete street furniture are among such examples. All these examples use elastic molds to let fluid materials to take form. While the designer guides the direction of the design exploration, the final form is not predetermined. The process is the mediation of the designer's considerations and the becoming potential of the material.

Depending on the existence and absence of movement, two essentially different experiment environments are set up: static and dynamic. Movement is found to be crucial in experiments as it reduces anticipation and enhances the emergence of resulting forms.

The entire process of becoming for the plaster form correlates with Deleuzian multiplicities. Infinitely many of forms emerge until the plaster is cured as juxtapositions of possible becomings. We record each experiment on video to capture these forms along the process.

Additionally, we use probes to explore the plaster behavior further. These probes, whose place and existence are defined by the designer, act as Deleuzian singularities. They create turning points in the becoming form where the curvature of the studied plaster section changes direction.

Overall, the surface of a material is where its form becomes visible. Therefore, the focus of our inquiry is the contact surface between elastic mold and plaster. The middle section, which shows the same characteristics with the surface, is extracted to derive visual rules. These rules correspond to the section of the plaster to take note of the minima and maxima points and inflection points. These points not only help to understand how the material behaves but also create the groundwork for a digital implementation via non-Euclidean geometries.

4.1   Plaster Cast in Static Molds

In the first physical explorations, plaster is poured in a 5 mm thick PMMA rigid mold on four sides and 0.5 mm thick Latex elastic mold at the base. The physical set up limits form changes in the XY-plane only to allow for changes in the Z-axis for ease for observation.

The fluid plaster in contact with the elastic base takes form according to forces acting on it. To specify further characteristics of plaster behavior, probes made from rigid PMMA are used in order to limit movement of the elastic mold (Fig. 2). Exploration of the plaster taking form encompasses the duration between it's being poured and its curing (Fig. 3).

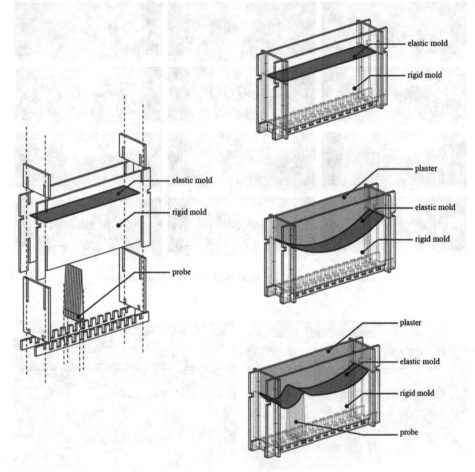

Fig. 2. Diagram of the assembly of mold for the physical model with static probes (on the left), form in becoming when plaster is poured in the mold (on the right)

After curing, we examined the sections of the plaster to derive visual schemas (Fig. 4). Weight algebras are introduced to represent the material properties as part of these visual schemas.

We avoid defining too specific shape rules to escape deterministic results. Instead, we define labels and weights to represent the features and forces that allow shapes to emerge. Labels specify where the probes are placed along the elastic mold (Fig. 5). Weights specify the actual weight of the plaster as a force that is exerted on the elastic base (Fig. 6). Although it is known that weight is distributed along the whole section, the locations of the weights indicate centers of mass where curve changes direction

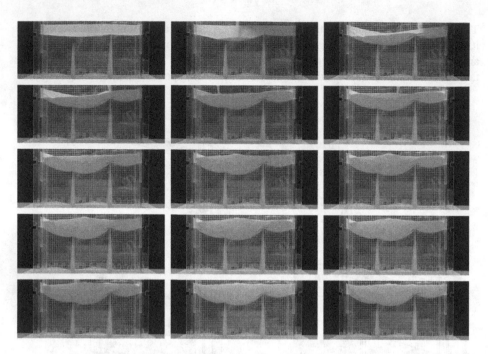

Fig. 3. Duration of physical exploration in static molds

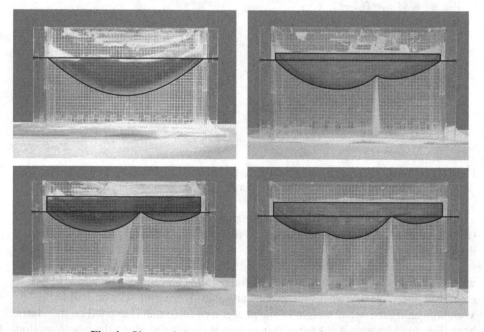

Fig. 4. Observed changes in the sections for four experiments

between probes or probes and section ends. While defining a visual rule for the placement of weights an abstract weight function is assigned to them. The function for the weight of the plaster is affected by two parameters: 1) quantity of the plaster, 2) viscosity of the plaster. Defining the weights is directly related to the probes. Sections also change based on the place and number of probes as seen in Fig. 4, although both of the above mentioned parameters are kept unchanged. Probes play a role in how weight is distributed.

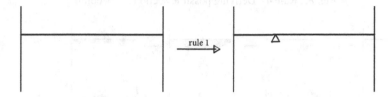

Fig. 5. Rule 1 - Insertion of probe label

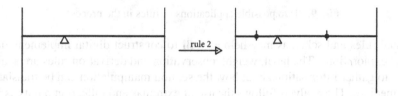

Fig. 6. Rule 2 - Indicator of material weight

An observation rule is defined that renders the changing area when the plaster is poured in the mold until it is cured (Fig. 7). A derivation rule indicates the possible sections that emerge and juxtapose when plaster is taking form, *i.e.* possible stops in the duration of becoming (Fig. 8). The derivation rule shows that there are infinitely many sections that the designer can observe and choose from while pouring the plaster in the mold by stopping to pour more material. The process of applying the rules is shown as a continuous visual computation in Fig. 9.

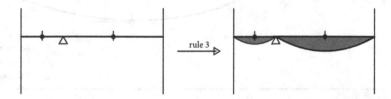

Fig. 7. Rule 3 - Changing section according to applied forces when plaster is poured

These rules are abstractions of real material behavior. As designing is primarily visual, these rules and schemas help designers interpret what they observe in material becoming and use them in their designs. Once s/he can understand material becoming via visual computation, s/he may continue with these abstractions.

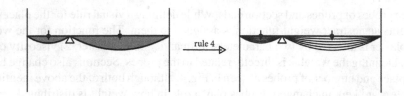

Fig. 8. Rule 4 - Deriving possible sections in becoming

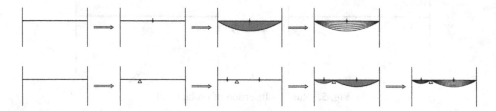

Fig. 9. Two possible applications of rules in the process

Visual rules and schemas may help as well to construct digital implementation of material explorations. The label, weight, observation and derivation rules are analyzed in order to gather information about how the section manipulation can be translated to digital medium. The analysis follows the use of extremas and inflection points as introduced by Cache (1995). As observed in non-Euclidean geometry, variations on the surface can be explained through curvature. It is seen in the section that there emerge extrema points, where the curve changes direction. Labels create maximum extremas and weights create minimum extremas. There also occur second order emergence along the section, which are the inflection points. Inflection points are zero curvature points where the curvature of a curve, in this case of the surface, changes direction (Fig. 10).

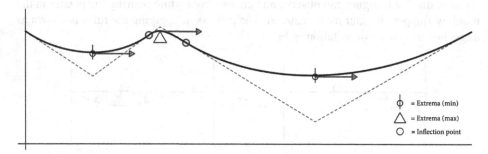

Fig. 10. Analysis of the section for digital implementation

In a digital implementation, labels and weights indicate the parameters. While labels show the placement of restrictions, weights include the location of the center of mass along with a function of mass and viscosity. The digital model should also follow the limits of labels as maximum extremas and weights as minimum extremas. An initial digital section containing these information is open to digital becoming, whose duration

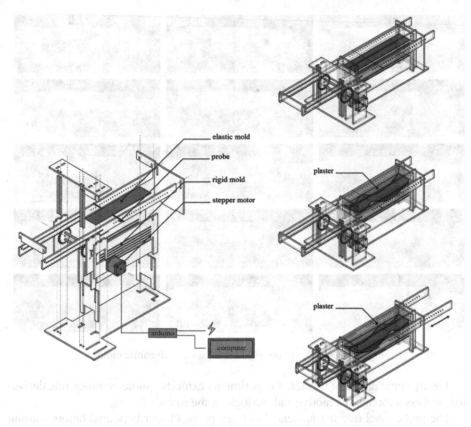

Fig. 11. The assembly of the dynamic mold (on the left), and the becoming of form when plaster is poured and probe is moved

can be documented in relation to the observation rule. Possible stoppages in the duration create possible sections, which can be selected by the designer as in the derivation rule.

4.2 Plaster Cast in Dynamic Molds

In the second set of physical explorations, mold setup is similar to the first explorations: while 5 mm thick PMMA rigid mold confines plaster on all sides, 0.5 mm thick Latex elastic mold enables plaster to take form at the base. However, the probe construction is more complex due to required movement. Ø2 mm metal rods replace PMMA probes. The probes are moved by a stepper motor that is connected to a computer via Arduino Uno board and simple script controls the movement of the motor (Fig. 11). Motor moves the probe in an interval back and forth and the interval is diminished at certain laps until zero. Duration from the initial movement until probe reaches a static position is correlated with the time it takes the plaster to cure so that the cured plaster is not forced beyond it can endure without losing its chemical property. Observation shows that seven-minute interval is appropriate to reach such state. In this setup, exploration of the probe along with the plaster taking form encompasses the duration between its being poured and its curing (Fig. 12).

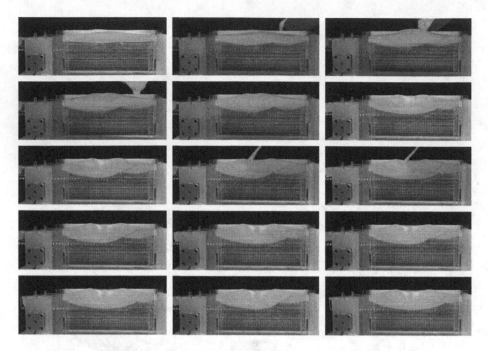

Fig. 12. Duration of physical exploration in dynamic molds

The dynamic nature of this set of experiments exhibits a more complex rule derivation process although the motive and the logic is the same.

The probe label rule is fragmented to three parts. Plaster is poured before starting the movement of the probe. Consequently, the first part of the probe label rule follows the same principle as the static probe label rule: it signifies where the probe rests before the plaster is poured (Fig. 13). The second part of the probe label rule shows the pouring of the plaster while initiating the probe movement (Fig. 14).

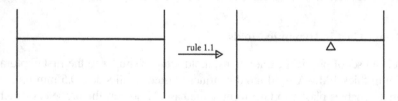

Fig. 13. Rule 1.1 - Insertion of initial probe label

The back and forth movement of probe yields in a rendered line on the section. Thirty-nine pairs of video snapshots are processed to find the rendered line. Each pair is selected to show the movement interval of the probe. The rendered areas of the sections, shown in gray, are juxtaposed to visualize the total movement of the probe and the final section of the plaster is marked with red color (Fig. 15a). It is seen in the visual that the final section is not in the center of the darkest gray area. Figure 15b shows the last twelve

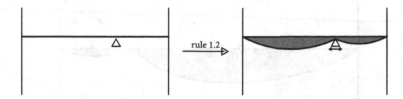

Fig. 14. Rule 1.2 - Pouring plaster while initiating movement of probe

pairs which affect the emergence of the final section. It is concluded that the movement of the probe affects the final section only after the curing process of the plaster starts.

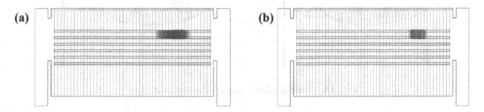

Fig. 15. (a) Juxtaposition of rendered sections, (b) Juxtaposition of twelve relevant pairs that affect the formation of the final plaster section

The third part of the probe label rule is derived from the observation of the pairs. The probe label stretches into a line, which affect the final section (Fig. 16).

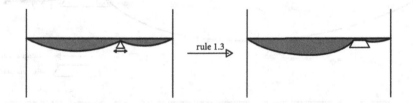

Fig. 16. Rule 1.3 - Signifying probe label that affects the final form of the plaster section

Weight rule for dynamic mold necessitates further exploration than static experiment. As mentioned above, weight label signifies actual weight force that is exerted by plaster on the elastic mold and it goes through the center of the mass. It is seen in the dynamic experiment that the center of mass does not coincide with the midpoint between section ends and the probe (as oppose to static experiment). The weights move closer to the probe (Fig. 17). We might have an intuition about weights, however, their exact location cannot be determined without a physical experiment. Consequently, weight rule is defined after curing as seen in Fig. 18.

Signifying an observation rule for rendered section and possible becoming sections in duration is almost impossible due to infinite number of possibilities resulting from

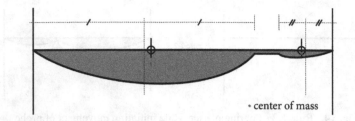

Fig. 17. The location of center of masses move towards probe label

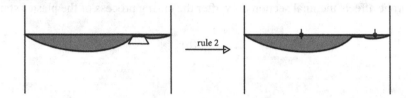

Fig. 18. Rule 2 - Indicator of material weight

Fig. 19. Process of application of rules

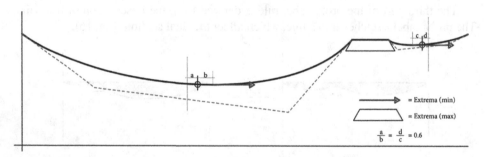

Fig. 20. Analysis of the section for digital implementation

movement, which cannot be reduced to one single snapshot. The final cured section is only one of them. The process of applying the derived rules is shown as a continuous visual computation (Fig. 19).

Abstractions, that are visual rules and schemas, are analyzed to put forth the constructs of a possible digital implementation. Similar to static molds, the analysis principles are Cache's (1995) extrema points and curvature plays an important role. Maximum extrema points occur due to probe label and draw a linear curve in probe interval. Minimum extrema points do not coincide with the weight as it happens in static molds, they move towards probes (Fig. 20). Nonetheless, a proportional similarity is found between both sides of the probe. In the analysis, symbols *a* and *d* signify the distances between weights and midpoints. Symbols b and c signify the distances between weights and minimum extrema points. The proportion a/b and d/c are found to be equivalent.

Another significant deviation from static experiments is that four instead of three control points make a curve between section ends and probe, which means the curvature is not symmetrical along the minimum extrema axis.

5 Conclusion

The design culture today invests significant value to abstraction in the design process, separating it from materialization. However, materialization plays an important role in design, just as abstraction, since designing cannot do away with reality and existence. Accordingly, we have sought to open to debate the material aspect of the design process and, with reference to an overview of its philosophical, historical and designerly tracks, proposed an integration of abstraction and materialization in design processes in a feedback loop. Our experiments to test an instance of this integration have been successful in conveying that:

- The integration of DtA and DtM provide a better understanding of abstraction with regard to materialization and vice versa. Without casting plaster in elastic molds, any rule to define plaster form would be only visual and it would be contemplating without evidence. Without defining visual rules, any material experiment would lack the understanding of the properties and behavior of the material that makes the particular form emerge. Designing with materials would be a tacit work that could only take place via physical experiments.
- Fluid materials (plaster in this case) are suitable for understanding the emergence in the process of designing, since their form when cast in elastic molds cannot be foreseen without actually working with them. The material study can be further extended to include concrete as well as other materials with strong tendencies to embody intrinsic properties which would lead to aid the creativity of the designer via emergence.
- Visual computation is instrumental not only for abstract designing processes but also for understanding how materials behave. They help designers interpret what they see in their experiments and design with what they learn from these.

6 Discussion

The proposed integration of materialization and abstraction in design processes has various implications for both design education and design practice.

In design education, the externalization of material becoming by way of visual schemas may strengthen the communication between students and instructors. Paying attention to both materialization and abstraction simultaneously may provide an opportunity to more effectively integrate structured material studies into the design education curriculum. This will in turn encourage the students to bridge reality and abstraction.

In design practice, materialization is an important component of the design process just as much as abstraction has been. Its externalization via visual schemas may help designers to use and explore materials in more informed, sensible and controlled ways.

Research into materials is an extensive subject. In further studies, similar materialization and abstraction processes can be explored to extend the material library and their visual schemas beyond plaster (and fluid materials).

Currently, physics engines such as *Kangaroo Physics* for *Grasshopper* in *Rhinoceros* provide opportunities to simulate principles from section analyses created for digital implementations. They capture some material complexity and emergence but not all. In our experiments, changing the amount and viscosity of material compositions as well as the speed and the motion decay times of probes constitute a material complexity that in return yields to emergence in the material form. Such concurrent materializations and abstractions require materially informed digital design environments that feed from ongoing material experiments and visual computations.

Acknowledgements. The study is the extended and revised version of a part of Aslı Aydın's master's thesis titled "Material Computability of Becoming Forms." The thesis was supervised by Mine Özkar and submitted to Graduate School of Science, Engineering and Technology at Istanbul Technical University in April 2014. The research is partially funded by Istanbul Technical University.

References

1. DeLanda, M.: Deleuze and the use of genetic algorithm in architecture. http://youtu.be/50-d_J0hKz0 (2009). Accessed 7 April 2013
2. Stiny, G.: What rule(s) should i use?. In: L. March (ed.), Nexus Netw. J. **13**(1), 15–47 (2011)
3. Stiny, G., Gips, J.: Shape grammars and the generative specification of painting and sculpture. In: Petrocelli, O.R. (ed.) The Best Computer Papers of 1971, pp. 125–135. Auerbach, Philadelphia (1972)
4. Stiny, G.: Shape Grammars, Part II, in ACM SIGGRAPH 2009 Courses, pp. 99–172. ACM, New York (2009)
5. Bergson, H.: An Introduction to Metaphysics (Hulme, T.E., trans.). G.P. Putnam's sons, New York and London (1912)
6. Dolphijn, R., Tuin, I.: New Materialism: Interviews and Cartographies. Open Humanities Press (2012)
7. DeLanda, M.: Intensive Science and Virtual Philosophy. Continuum, London, New York (2002)
8. Plotnitsky, A.: Bernhard riemann. In: Johns, G., Roffe, J. (eds.) Deleuze's Philosophical Lineage, pp. 190–208. Edinburgh University Press, Edinburgh (2009)
9. Deleuze, G., Parnet, C.: Dialogues. Flammarion, Paris (1987). Translated by Tomlinson, H., Habberjam, B. Dialogues, Athlone, London, Reissued with supplementary material (2002). Dialogues II, Continuum, London (1977)
10. Ballantyne, A.: Who?, in Deleuze and Guattari for Architects. Routledge, London, New York (2007)
11. Deleuze, G.: Logique du sens, Paris, Editions du Minuit, translated by Lester, M., Stivale, C. (1990). Logic of Sense, edited by Boundas, C.V. Columbia University Press, New York (1969)

12. Turing, A.M.: The chemical basis of morphogenesis. Philos. Trans. R. Soc. Lond. B Biol. Sci. **237**(641), 37–72 (1952)
13. Cache, B.: Earth Moves: The Furnishing of Territories. The MIT Press, Massachusetts, Cambridge (1995)
14. Focillon, H.: The Life of Forms in Art, 2nd edn. George Wittenborn Inc., New York (1948)
15. Pérez-Gómez, A.: Questions of representation: the poetic origin of architecture. In: Frascari, M., Hale, J., Starkey, B. (eds.) From Models to Drawings, pp. 11–22. Routledge, New York, London (2007)
16. Adamson, G.: The Craft Reader. Berg, Oxford, New York (2010)
17. Kolarevic, B.: Information master builders. In: Kolarevic, B. (ed.) Architecture in the Digital Age Design and Manufacturing. Spon Press, New York, London (2003)
18. Turnbull, D.: Talk, templates and tradition: how the masons built chartes cathedral without plans. In: Turnbull, D. (ed.) Masons, Tricksters and Cartographies. Routledge, London (2000)
19. Kudless, A.: Bodies in formation: the material evolution of flexible formworks. In: Borden, G.P., Meredith, M. (eds.) Matter: Material processes in architectural production. Routledge, New York (2012)
20. Araya, R., West, M.: Flat sheet fabric moulds for double curvature precast concrete elements. In: Ohr, J. et al. (eds.) Proceedings of the 2nd International Conference on Flexible Formwork, Bath, UK, pp. 38–45 (2012)
21. Veenendaal, D., Block, P.: Computational form-finding of fabric formworks: an overview and discussion. In: Ohr, J. et al. (eds.), Proceedings of the 2nd International Conference on Flexible Formwork, Bath, UK, pp. 368–378 (2012)

A Design Tool for Generic Multipurpose Chair Design

Sara Garcia[✉] and Luís Romão

University of Lisbon, Lisbon, Portugal
{sgarcia,lromao}@fa.ulisboa.pt

Abstract. Product classes share the same basic abstract layout, despite their great diversity. The present paper intends to (de)code the variety of types embedded in the class of multipurpose chairs. The contribution of this research is the development of a generative design tool, to be used at the conceptual chair design stage. A framework of five stages is proposed: (1) sample definition, considering chairs with a large diversity of types; (2) analysis of the syntax and semantics of the class through ontological classification; (3) development of a generic shape grammar, innovatively applied to product design; (4) implementation of a digital tool, that provides an interface to manipulate the chair components visualized in a 3D digital model; and (5) user evaluation of the program, in order to draw conclusions on the usability and usefulness of the tool and to collect inputs for further developments.

Keywords: Multipurpose chairs · Ontology · Generic shape grammars · Generative design tool · User experience

1 Introduction

Product classes share the same basic abstract layout, despite their great diversity. The present study expects to contribute to the study of form, through the mathematical codification of the variety of shapes and types inherent to one product class. The overall goal is to develop a generative design tool, based on a rule-based and parametric description, in order to support the designer at the early conceptual design stage of a chair. The intention is to join the best aspects of the machine and of the human performances in a design process, not to mimic or replace the designer.

The product class chosen for the present study was the multipurpose chair, due to its importance in product design history and practice, and its diversity of shapes, topologies, materials, and meanings.

1.1 Background and Significance

Type and style are both concepts used to classify a group of objects. The first one is general and context-independent and the second one is specific to historical background. A type describes a group of objects that share similar functions or morphologies (e.g.:

© Springer-Verlag Berlin Heidelberg 2015
G. Celani et al. (Eds.): CAAD Futures 2015, CCIS 527, pp. 600–619, 2015.
DOI: 10.1007/978-3-662-47386-3_33

armchair type). A style is indicates a set of qualities typical of a person (e.g.: Hepplewhite style), place (e.g.: Scandinavian style), or period (e.g.: Queen Anne style).

Both type and style issues are addressed by shape grammars. Shape grammars are a method of parametric and ruled-based description and generation of shapes. Relevant work on shape grammars in chair design is oriented to capture specific historical styles, as the Hepplewhite [1] and Thonet [2] backrest areas style.

General grammars are assumed to generate a language of one product class; as demonstrated in the examples of coffeemakers [3], motorcycles [4], and office chairs [5]. The underlying procedure is to break down the product into functional systems and subsystems of components, along with its interrelations and main shape parameters. General grammars can be customized to generate specific grammars, through rule selections and parameter value choices (e.g.: Braun coffeemakers and Harley-Davidson motorcycles). General grammars assume the goal of supporting early conceptual stages of design.

Despite the aim of reproducing a large class of products on the market, General grammars do not have the aim of achieving a high degree of completeness. This particular intention is assumed in Generic grammars [6]; these are ontology-based grammars that reproduce context-independent, generic design patterns. In theory they can achieve a broader range of completeness, although in practice they do not describe an entire class, as it is unfeasible to perceive every possible solution and every design variable. This paper's aim is to bring these generic guidelines into a multipurpose chair grammar, in an attempt to generate a large diversity of chair types. Although generic grammars can also be customized to achieve specific design languages, this issue will not be considered in this paper.

1.2 Method

The method followed a framework (Fig. 1) with five main stages: (1) *sample*, (2) *ontology*, (3) *shape grammar*, (4) *digital tool*, and (5) *evaluation*. These stages correspond to each sections of this paper and will be further detailed.

(1) *Sample*. The sampling process provided the definition of the population – the multipurpose chair class, and the study population – classic modern chairs. A representative sample of 26 chairs was selected, in order to ensure a large diversity of types.

(2) *Ontology*. In an iterative process with the sample definition, and considering textual sources, an ontological classification of the selected product family was developed. It provided a common language and a precise definition of the syntax and semantics of the shape, transversal to all chairs of the sample.

(3) *Shape grammar*. Based on the language proposed in the last stage, a shape grammar for multipurpose chair design was developed. The generative procedure is to successively add components of the chair, with its parameters constrained to variable ranges.

(4) *Digital tool*. The digital tool is an informal implementation of the shape grammar. It consists of an interface where the user can add/delete components and edit shape parameters, while visualizing the effects on a 3D digital model.

(5) *Evaluation*. The digital tool was evaluated by design students, in a computer-aided design class exercise. This exploratory usability test was oriented to evaluate the usability of the interface and the role of the prototype at the conception stage of a chair design process.

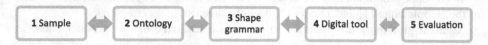

Fig. 1. Tool development workflow.

2   Population and Sample

2.1   Population

The population is defined according to a set of justified criteria, enumerated below. Starting from a partially sampled population (as many of the individuals are unknown), the criteria gradually led to a clearly defined study population.

(1) *Chair*. The chair presents a population with structural and formal multiplicity. Nonetheless, there are similar characteristics they all must have to belong to this product class, and those are expressed in the following definition: object whose function is to support the human body in a sitting position: the thighs are supported on a raised surface (seat), and the torso by an upright surface (back). Type of seat for individual usage and easily movable (glass and concrete chairs are excluded).

(2) *Multipurpose chairs*. This particular type of chair is versatile, being able to adapt to various spaces, uses, users and situations. They are also known as dining chairs, as they are expected to be used with a table. Office chairs, lounge chairs, easy chairs, lawn chairs, rocking chairs, children chairs, among others, are excluded.

(3) *No moving parts*. No folding, swiveling, reclining, or rolling chairs.

(4) *No upholstery*. No chairs with padded cover, except in slip seat pads. This criterion avoids hidden parts that disturb the process of geometry analysis. In chairs with a woven cover (weave, cane or textile), extra information is needed besides the 3D models available on the manufacturer's site (as they do not show hidden parts).

(5) *Minimum decoration*. Chairs with simple and functional shapes. This criterion excludes chairs with strictly ornamental components.

(6) *Modern chair classics*. Design classics industrially produced from 1850 to the present, including Portuguese classics. This criterion ensures recognized quality, easy access to information, and a large variety of materials and production methods (that largely evolved during this period), with their reflections on shape. For the present research, modern classics are the ones included in the referenced design collections [7–11].

(7) *Chairs with bilateral symmetry*. This criterion's purpose is to simplify the generation process, as one needs to encode only half of the chair.

2.2 Sample

The sample selection criteria reflect the similarities and differences in the population. As such, each element of the sample fulfils the criteria described in the population, and there is at least one element representing one type of chair. The sampling method used was theoretical sampling [12]. There were two sampling stages, considering two methods of data collection. The process went through the selection of the first sample group (A), the analysis of the emerging data (ontology), and the selection of a new sample group (B).

Group A - Technology breakthroughs. The selection was based on judgment sampling technique, considering the existing knowledge to include representative individuals. The criterion was to pick chairs that introduced a relevant technological breakthrough, according to the sources mentioned in Table 1.

Group B - Ontology gaps. An ontology was developed based on group A and other individuals of the population. From the analysis of the relevant characteristics, the choice of the individuals of group B was made in order to ensure that at least one individual of the sample represented one of the characteristics.

The sample size is 26 elements. Despite the effort to cover all types, there are still missing ones, such as the pedestal 5-star chair. Also, the ontology excludes some types from the population, such as the one-legged cantilever (e.g.: Model B5 of Stefan Wewerka [10]), or the Kreuzshwinger chair (invented by Till Behrens [10]).

Table 1. Sample elements. Sources: [7–11]

ID	Chair name	Designer	Manufacturer	Date	Criteria
A1	No. 14	Thonet	Thonet	1860	Bentwood frame [7]
A2	S33	Mart Stam	Thonet	1926	Cantilever chair [9]
A3	Zig Zag	Gerrit Rietveld	Cassina	1934	2nd Wood cantilever chair [7]
A4	Landi	Hans Coray	Vitra	1934	Shell in hard material [7]
A5	LCW/DCW	Eames	Herman Miller	1945	Moulded plywood in compound curves [7]
A6	DAX	Eames	Herman Miller	1948	Shell in fiberglass-reinforced plastic [7]
A7	DKR	Eames	Herman Miller	1951	Shell in wire mesh [7]
A8	Tulip	Eero Saarinen	Knoll	1956	"Wineglass" pedestal base [7]
A9	Supperleggera	Gio Ponti	Cassina	1957	Super-lightweight chair [7]
A10	Polyprop	Robin Day	Hille	1963	Polypropylene shell [8]
A11	Bofinger	Helmut Bätzner	Bofinger	1965	Monobloc plastic chair [7]
A12	Universale	Joe Colombo	Kartell	1967	Adult-sized injection-moulded chair [8]
A13	Panton	Verner Panton	Vitra	1968	Monobloc cantilever chair [7]
B14	Ant	Arne Jacobsen	Fritz Hansen	1952	3-Legged chair [7]
B15	Bellevue	André Bloc	Unknown	1951	Connection Seat & Front Leg [7]
B16	S	Tom Dixon	Cappellini	1991	Cantilever with round base [8]
B17	Y (Wishbone)	Hans Wegner	Carl Hansen	1950	Spindle back [9]
B18	Spaghetti	G. Belotti	Alias	1960	H-stretcher [10]
B19	Ply	Jasper Morrison	Vitra	1988	Open-back [7]
B20	Gonçalo	Gonçalo Santos	Arcalo	1940	Connection Arms & Rear leg [11]
B21	Magic	Ross Lovegrove	Fasem	1997	Reverse cantilever [10]
B22	RCP2	Jane Atfield	Made of Waste	1992	Double legged [10]
B23	Antelope	Ernest Race	Race Furniture	1950	Connection Arms & Back upright [8]
B24	MAA	George Nelson	Herman Miller	1958	Pedestal 4-star base [9]
B25	PK9	Poul Kjaerholm	Fritz Hansen	1960	Pedestal 3-star base [9]
B26	Chair One	K. Grcic	Herman Miller	2003	X Back [8]

3   Multipurpose Chair Ontology

Ontology systems are knowledge representation models that define a set of entities within a domain, and the relations between those entities. The ontology formalism was borrowed from philosophy and brought to computational systems by Tom Gruber [13] in order to provide a common vocabulary to enable knowledge sharing.

The domain of the ontology developed within this study is multipurpose chairs. The goal was to define a grammar of concepts that could support a grammar of shapes (described later). The ontology formalizes a taxonomic description of the components of the chair, its properties and relations. The ontology can also provide a quantification of qualitative knowledge, by giving minimum and maximum values of chair dimensions (e.g.: seat height range of multipurpose chairs).

In order to minimize the ambiguity of meaning, a detailed description of each component was developed, based on different sources. These sources were the afore-mentioned study population and literature on antique and modern furniture and wood-working subjects. Despite the effort to respect the woodworking terms, some new terminology was introduced, due to some terms being missing (usually related to some new types of chairs, such as the cantilever), and to the multiplicity of terms used for each chair part.

The terms in the discussed ontology were represented by a list of axiomatic defini-tions, by a diagram that shows their relations, and by schematic illustrations of their archetypes (Figs. 2 and 3). Each class is represented by a name and an acronym. The ontology is organized into two main classes: *Chair Parts* and *Chair Types*.

3.1   Chair Parts

This main class *Parts* (Fig. 2) is divided into three hierarchical levels.

(1)   The first level has two main classes: *Frame* and *Support*. The *Frame* is defined as the structure or skeleton that supports the seat and the back surfaces above the ground. The *Support* contemplates the nonstructural panels seat and back, that support a person's thighs and back while seated. This level is not represented in Fig. 2.

(2)   The next level contains six sets of parts: *Back, Seat, Legs, Leg Stretchers, Leg Base* and *Arms*. *Leg Stretchers* and *Leg Base* could be considered a subclass of *Legs*. Each group of parts is defined by its specific function and location in the whole of the chair, in a nearly planar surface.

(3)   Each set of parts contains the parts themselves, detailed at the last level of the hierarchy. Each part acronym is composed by the acronym of the set it belongs to, followed by the acronym of its location within the part (front, rear, side, cross, longitudinal, X, top, upright) or the technical name (splat). All chairs of the sample have bilateral symmetry, so there is no need to mention the location on the left or on the right side.

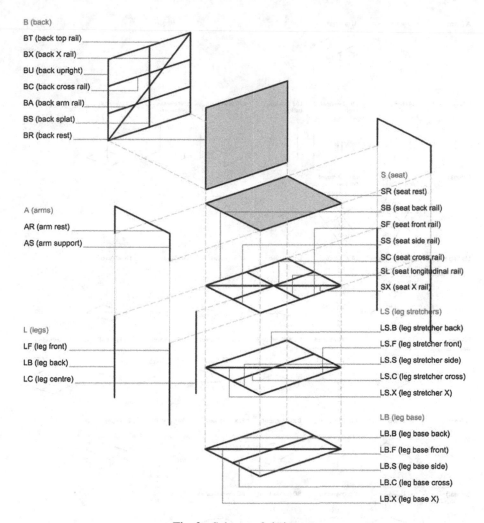

Fig. 2. Schema of chair parts

3.2   Chair Types

As types are related to groups of chair parts, the first two hierarchical levels of *Types* are identical to the ones of *Parts*. There are six kinds of classification (Fig. 3): (1) *number* of pieces, (2) *location* within the whole, (3) *topology shape* - resulting shape of the interrelation between parts, (4) *inner shape*, (5) *outer shape*, and (6) *connection,* when two or more parts are merged in one piece (this category is not represented in the schema). The classification of each group can combine two or more kinds. In some cases, there is a direct correspondence between types and parts; for example, the type *3-legged front* is a chair with two front legs and one back leg. Only the main types are represented; stylistic considerations are not contemplated, due to the generic abstraction level employed.

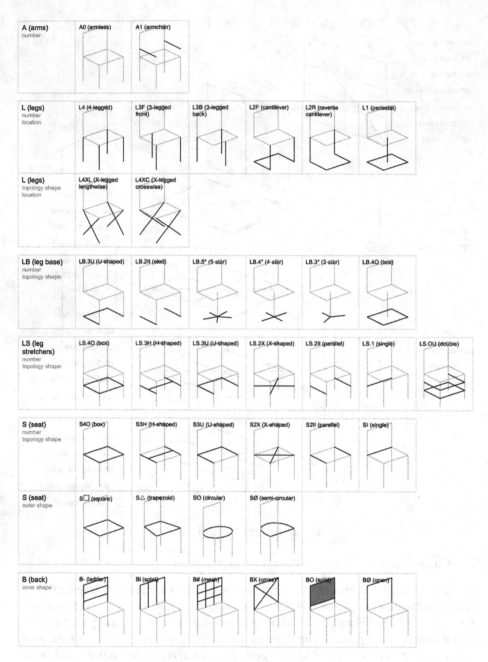

Fig. 3. Schema of chair types

4 Multipurpose Chair Shape Grammar

The shape grammar formalism was introduced by Stiny and Gips [14]. It is a method for describing and generating solutions through a process based on rules of the type *if/ then*. The design process consists of the application of rules one by one to an initial shape, until a final solution is reached.

A shape grammar was developed, in the scope of this study, with the intention of generating products of a specific class, and to include a wide number of types within the class. The proprieties of this shape grammar are defined in the following categories:

(1) The grammar design method combined both analytic and synthetic ones. First, an analytic grammar [15] was developed to describe a specific style (or design language) and to generate new designs within that style. Rules were then modified to create a set of existing styles (chairs of the sample). Secondly, new rules were formulated by vocabularies of shapes and their spatial relations (logic combinations of design elements), and rule parameters from methodologies or conventions used by designers (anthropometric guidelines). This approach of generating original designs from scratch is the one of synthetic grammars [16]. While with an analytic approach the designs originate the rules, with a synthetic approach the rules generate the designs.

(2) This is a set grammar [17], as does not consider emergence.

(3) The algebras [18] used in this grammar are U12, U22, V02, and W12. Algebras U12 represent lines, U12 planes, V02 labeled points and W12 line weights. This is a 3D shape grammar, although rules are represented in a 2D axonometric projection.

(4) This is a parametric grammar [19], as rules are represented by general schemas of shapes – flexible geometries ruled by constraints and variables that hence directly control the form.

(5) This is a generic grammar [6]. This kind of grammar is ontology-based (although it may not be explicit), as the amount of knowledge requires a need of classification and organization. This is an innovative application in product design.

(6) Concerning the rule order, the grammar is nondeterministic [20], as multiple designs can be generated in some step of the derivation, through a choice of what rule to apply.

(7) The rules used are from addition and substitution types [21]. An addition rule adds a shape to a design. A substitution (or condensed) rule combines both subtraction and addition rules (erasing and adding a shape from a design).

4.1 Corpus

The corpus of the grammar is composed by the 26 chairs in the sample. Chairs are represented by two main entities - the frame is represented by lines (and arcs), and the seat and back support elements by planes (Fig. 4). The information was extracted from pictures, 2D drawings and 3D models in a non-rigorous way. This is a raw simplification, as it does not show some slight angles and curves. At the moment, only one type of curve is represented - circular arcs. These planar curves are used to round the corners emerging from two lines with the same endpoints. The related parameter is the radius of the arc that joins the lines. Surfaces are planar.

Fig. 4. Corpus of the grammar

4.2   Initial Shape

The initial shape (Fig. 5) represents the nearly vertical back plane, the nearly horizontal seat plane, and the box underneath where the legs are placed. The box is parameterized according to the range values given by anthropometric standards – seat height (S_h), seat width (S_w), seat depth (S_d), backrest height (B_h), seat angle (S_a) and back angle (B_a). It is also assumed that all shapes have a bilateral symmetry, given by the vertical plane parallel to YZ at the middle of the chair's width.

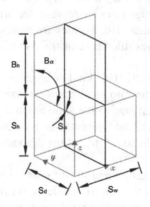

Fig. 5.   Initial shape of the grammar

4.3   Rules and Derivations

The grammar follows a bottom-up methodology, where 3D shapes (that represent the elements of the chair), are systematically added step-by-step until the final solution is reached. The elements and their categorization into sets and subsets are directly related to the ontology of the parts. There are five sets of rules: (1) *stage*, (2) *frame*, (3) *support*, and (4) *termination*. (1) *Stage* rules allow one to choose between stages 2, 3 or

4. (2) The *frame* set contains the following subsets: *Legs, Leg Base, Leg Stretchers, Seat Rails, Arms, and Black Slats*. Each subset contains the rules that correspond to parts of the chair, as described in the ontology. (3) The *support* contains the seat and the back parts. (4) The *termination* rule ends the design by erasing the initial shape. The grammar has a total of 50 rules.

The grammar flow diagram in Fig. 6 shows the rule application sequence. The vertices represent the sets of rules and the edges the possible sequences of operations. It is a mixed graph (some edges are directed and some are undirected), because there is not a fixed order of rule application. The grammar allows the user some choice about the sequence in which he applies the rules (e.g.: from the *initial shape* one can choose to design the *frame* or the *support*). Still, there are rules that can only be applied in a mandatory sequence (e.g.: one can only introduce the *Leg Stretchers* if the *Legs* are already placed).

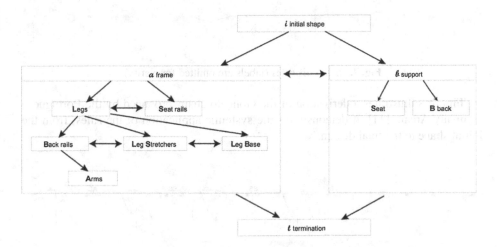

Fig. 6. Grammar flow diagram

Each rule is described with: (1) the rule name and acronym; (2) the graphic labeled description (the left-hand side – LHS – and the right-hand side – RHS); and (3) the algebra description (variables and its range of variation). As mentioned, some rules are not used in the generation process of any chair of the corpus. They were created by logic induction of another rule (e.g.: if there is one rule where the back leg is connected to the front seat rail, so, analogously, another rule can connect the front leg with the back seat rail, as illustrated in the last two rules of Fig. 7).

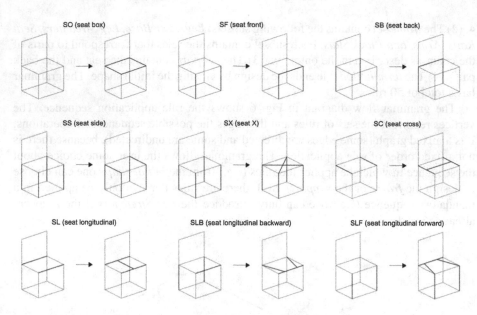

Fig. 7. Seat rails rules (labels are omitted for clarity)

Figure 8 illustrates a derivation of the Gonçalo chair, produced by the Portuguese company Arcalo [11]. It demonstrates the systemic application of the rules, from the initial shape to the final design.

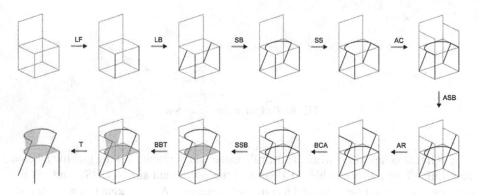

Fig. 8. Derivation of the Gonçalo chair (labels are omitted for clarity)

4.4 New Designs

Besides generating the 26 chairs of the corpus, the grammar creates new solutions (Fig. 9). As this tool is intended to be used at the conceptual stage of the design process, mistakes are to be expected. In the creative process, not every intermediate solution is comfortable, nor stable (e.g.: solution 1), nor complete (e.g.: solution 2), or in a more extreme case, can fit the human body at all (e.g.: solution 4). Naturally, the grammar cannot generate all existing multipurpose chairs; nevertheless, one can expect it to produce a broad range of exemplifying variants.

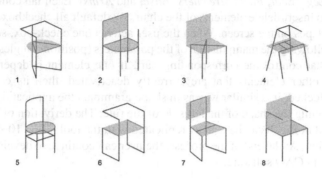

Fig. 9. New designs

5 The ChairDNA Digital Tool

A tool was developed as an informal implementation of the multipurpose chair shape grammar in a digital environment. The system is an interpretation of the shape grammar tool. Check-boxes correspond to rules; and sliders to rule parameters. The parts of the chair (and their geometric properties) are the common feature independently represented in the ontology, the grammar and the tool.

The purpose of the generative tool is to be used by designers other than its developer. In order to be tested by novice designers, the system needed to have a simple and clear interface [22], in an environment closer to the typical digital tools that designers use nowadays. Furthermore, it allows a quicker exploration of the solution space (combining parameterization and topology variations), and the debugging and improvement of the grammar. Moreover, while with the shape grammar the user can only add shapes, with the digital tool the user can add and delete shapes, by activating/deactivating check-boxes. The system thus allows bottom-up (adding elements to the initial shape) and top-down approaches (removing elements from a design – a generated chair of the sample or a random chair). Unlike the grammar, only the current shape is displayed graphically in the tool.

The digital tool name is provisionally called "ChairDNA", as an allusion the genetic code – of the chair. Two agents interact with the tool – the developer, who edits the programming language; and the user, who manipulates the graphical user interface (GUI) along with CAD software.

The programming language used was Racket (a dialect of Lisp), that supports multi-paradigm programming, and is a free open source software. The package Rosetta was used due to its portability, which allows interaction with diverse CAD softwares and programming languages [23]. The code consists of one main function with global variables and sub-functions to draw each element of the chair. The interface was programmed with the library racket/gui.

The tool is available in the format of an interface (GUI) for the manipulation of the parameters, which control a 3D model in AutoCAD or Rhinoceros (Fig. 10). The interface is divided into tabs that correspond to initial shape (*Guides*) and to the sets of parts of the chair (*Legs, Seat, Back, Stretchers, Base,* and *Arms*). Each tab contains several check-boxes to insert/delete elements of the chair. By default all checkboxes are off, so there are no shapes on the screen. When the user actives one check-box, several slides are revealed, allowing the manipulation of the parameters (positions, angles, radius, and dimensions) that control the corresponding part. If one element is dependent on the placement of other elements that are currently deactivated, then its corresponding checkbox is blocked, in a similar way as in shape grammars the application of one rule depends on finding the shape of the left side of the rule. The derivation of the Gonçalo chair presented in Fig. 8 can be exactly replicated with the tool – Fig. 10 shows a state of that derivation. At the end of the process, the user can continue to develop the model independently in CAD software.

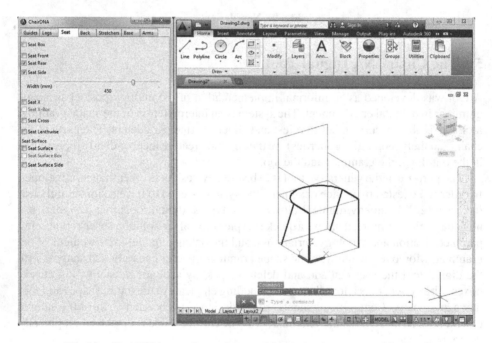

Fig. 10. ChairDNA snapshot: one step of the derivation presented in Fig. 8

6   Evaluation of ChairDNA

The application ChairDNA was evaluated through usability testing with potential end users of the tool at the conception chair design stage, within an intermediate design class. The main aims of this experiment were to:

(1) Evaluate the program ChairDNA as an auxiliary chair design tool. The products of the generation process of the students, from the initial concept to the final solution,

afforded an understanding of the role of the system in the implementation and exploration of design solutions.
(2) Evaluate the interface of ChairDNA. The goal was to evaluate the user experience of the program with intermediate design students and to gain useful inputs for further developments of the prototype.
(3) Evaluate the degree of completeness of the system, by measuring the accuracy of the program in reproducing students' intentions, in order to test the limits of the tool.

6.1 Method

The task proposed to the students was to initially formalize one initial concept or inspiration, and to then develop that idea in order to reach a final solution to be presented as a 3D digital model and a 3D printed 1/8 scale model. Students were invited to use the program ChairDNA. The experiment took place in four sessions of about one and a half hours each, plus one extra task of answering an online questionnaire. Sessions are described below:

(1) *Presentation and demonstration of ChairDNA.* The evaluator presented to the class an overview of the project, a brief introduction and demonstration of the program ChairDNA, and a description of the briefing of the task.
(2) *Installation and first experiments with ChairDNA.* The participants installed the program ChairDNA and had their first contact with the software. After watching a second demonstration of the program, the subjects carried out their first experiments.
(3) *Experimenting and designing with ChairDNA.* The participants used the program in a preliminary and exploratory approach. The evaluation method used was observation – recording methods were carried out by the observer (photographs and notes) and by the participants (screen capture). Notes were taken on students' difficulties with the program, the observer suggestions to solve the problems, and software bugs. Screen capture was performed by screen recording or screenshots, capturing both experimental and final generation processes.
(4) *Students presentations.* Students individually presented their work to the class, and at the end answered a brief interview of ten questions, regarding their design process, the tools used, the printing process and hypothetical materials of the final solution, and suggestions for the ChairDNA program.
(5) *Questionnaires.* Afterwards students answered an online questionnaire, with closed and open ended questions, by which they reported their experience with the program.

6.2 Population

The population of this experiment was composed of nineteen (19) design students from a 3rd year class of the Faculty of Architecture of the University of Lisbon. This experiment was part of the program of the computer-aided design discipline "Parametric

Modeling and Digital Prototyping in Design". All subjects already had previous experience in chair design, accomplished by two academic projects. In the 1st year they
designed mutations of the chairs Red and Blue and Zig Zag, from Gerrit Rietveld, and
in the 2nd year they designed and prototyped a chair from scratch. The students' previous
experience with CAD software consisted mainly of AutoCAD.

6.3   Results and Discussion

6.3.1   Design Tools

The design tools main results are presented in Fig. 11. Most students used the ChairDNA
program (79 %), but, of the ones using the tool, only a few used it exclusively (11 %).
All participants that did not use ChairDNA used the AutoCAD program (one student
also used AutoLISP) to build their model. Students that used ChairDNA used AutoCAD
as the backend software for visualization, justifying their choice as being due to having
previous experience with that software over Rhinoceros 3D. The CAD software they
used after ChairDNA was again AutoCAD, and one student also used 3ds Max.

The reason mentioned by students for not using ChairDNA (21 %) was because it
was not feasible to perform the initial concept, either because the type of chair was not
supported by the system (lounge chairs) or because most part of the solution could not
be implemented.

The adjustments students performed in the 3D model in CAD software after using
ChairDNA revealed the limitations of the program (Fig. 11). Those were mainly related
with construction errors: deficient joints (31 %), too low seat surface height (31 %), and
back surface extrusion error (17 %). Minor changes had to do with the absence of some
variables: back rails section angle (9 %), seat surface radius (4 %), back cross arm radius
(4 %), and legs taper angle (4 %).

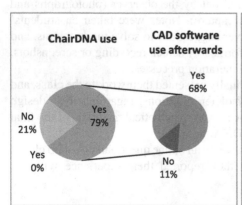
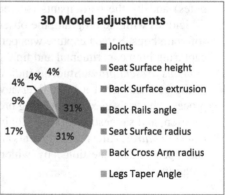

Fig. 11. Design tools main results

6.3.2   Design Process

Students were asked to formalize an initial concept or inspiration for the project development. Most students chose their own academic projects from past years (1st and 2nd years of the Design course) or chairs from well-known designers. There were only three exceptions: one student chose a chair from an unknown designer, one presented a written concept, and one student did not provide any concept.

The main results of the design process are presented in Fig. 12. The majority of the students did not strictly reproduce the initial concept (63 %). In the group of those that accurately replicated the initial concept (31 %), are included all the subjects that did not use the ChairDNA program (21 %), and few subjects that used (not exclusively) the program (11 %).

Of the ones that did not implement the initial concept (Fig. 12), the major reason was a combination of both ChairDNA limitations and exploration of solutions within the program (54 %). The exploration of the solution space was the main standalone factor for 38 % of the students. Few invoked the program limitations as the only reason for changing their initial idea (8 %).

There were limitations of ChairDNA that students reported but did not correct afterwards in CAD software, specifically the introduction of new variables (stretchers angle, armrest angle, leg radius, among others).

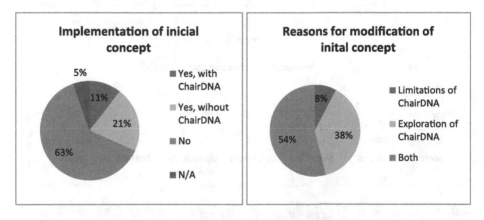

Fig. 12. Design process main results.

6.3.3   Design Solutions

Students had two options in what concerns to the printers and technologies available at the Faculty Lab (Fig. 13). Most of them chose the Fused Deposition Modeling (FDM) technique (74 %) among the 3D Printing (3DP) technology of ZCorp (26 %), as the first was the cheapest. 3D printing brought its own limitations (Fig. 13). Almost half of the students had to modify their digital model due to print constraints (47 %), mostly to increase thickness (42 %) and in one case to connect the components (5 %).

Students were asked about the materials they had envisioned for the real solution of the chair (Fig. 13). Participants gave generic classifications of materials. The materials mentioned for the frame were metal (12), wood (3) and both (2). The seat and back materials mentioned were wood (10), upholstery (3), both aforementioned (1), metal (2) and leather (1). Two students did not have an idea of the materials to use.

Thirteen prototypes produced with the help of ChairDNA (from the fifteen printed) are presented in Fig. 13. Two models are not shown as they broke during or after printing.

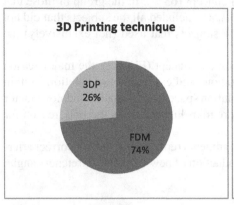

3D Printing technique

3DP 26%

FDM 74%

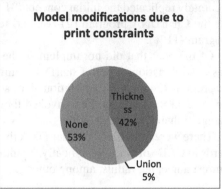

Model modifications due to print constraints

Thickness 42%

None 53%

Union 5%

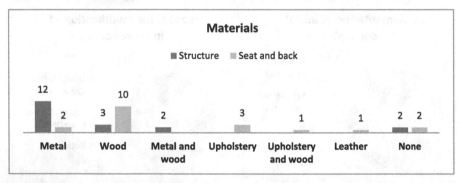

Materials

■ Structure   ■ Seat and back

12 2   3 10   2   3   1   1   2 2

Metal   Wood   Metal and wood   Upholstery   Upholstery and wood   Leather   None

Fig. 13. Design solutions main results

6.3.4   ChairDNA Outcomes

Students gave some suggestions on improvements of the ChairDNA program. The majority of them proposed the introduction of a save command (25 %), in order to save parameters and to not start from scratch in every new session. An important outcome was the need of making joints between components (24 %), which was one of the main adjustments students made in their 3D models after using ChairDNA. Many participants suggested the inclusion of numeric input along with the sliders (18 %), as sliders are slow and imprecise. Others mentioned system crashes as a major difficulty. Other suggestions concerned the insertion of new variables (curves and taper angles) and other types of chairs (lounge chairs) (Fig. 14).

Suggestions over ChairDNA

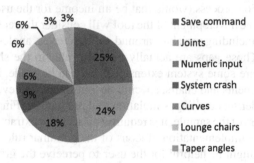

- Save command
- Joints
- Numeric input
- System crash
- Curves
- Lounge chairs
- Taper angles

Fig. 14. ChairDNA outcomes main results

7   Conclusions and Future Work

This paper described a framework for the development of a generative tool for the concept design of multipurpose chairs, able to reproduce a wide scope of different generic types. The prototype ChairDNA allows the user to create a chair by successively adding in its components and by manipulating its variables in an interface, while visualizing the result in real time as a 3D model. The five stages of the process for the development of the tool can be summarized as the phases of analysis (sample and ontology stages), generation (shape grammar and digital tool stages) and evaluation. The process was iterative but, although all stages are deeply interrelated, the transitions are not automated.

(1) *Analysis*. This phase comprehended the stages of the selection of a sample of 26 multipurpose chairs and its analysis through ontological classification. The main goal of reproducing a large variety of types was achieved, although it is still (and always will be?) incomplete. We noticed that many Parts have similar configurations, such as the *Leg Base*, *Leg Stretchers*, *Seat Rails*, and *Back Rails*.

Future work will concern the extension of the sample and the ontology, using both analysis and combinatory methods. Other classifications will concern connections between parts, planar elements, and the main shape of elements. It may become necessary to expand the population to chairs of well-known designers or producers. Beyond the ontology of parts and types one can also consider materials, functions, and generation process.

(2) *Generation.* This phase contemplated the stages of the development of a generic shape grammar and its informal implementation in the format of a digital tool. The rules of the grammar had a direct correspondence to the parts described in the ontology. The generation process considered the legs and the seat as the primary parts and the other parts were placed afterwards through links and connections of the first ones. The transition of the shape grammar into the digital tool was quite direct, as the grammar does not support emergence. The process allowed the merging of some rules. Discussion could be made around the possible simplification of rules (e.g.: *Seat Rails, Leg Stretchers* and *Leg Base* could turn into one rule of *Leg Connections*), that would allow a more unrestrained generation process (would that be an income for the user?).

Further work on the development of the tool will consider the reported insights from the user experience, including variables around solids, curves, angles, joints, and duplicated components. Those gaps are actually missing rules in the shape grammar. On another hand, there are some system extensions that can be made, in order to include other types of components and chairs, specific design styles, and even to get into other design stages, considering detailing, simulation and production. Finally, for the system to reproduce the chairs of the sample, it is required an accurate extraction of the variables from 3D models. The implementation of icons of the grammar rules and derivations in the GUI of the tool might be helpful for the user to perceive the grammar system, and to aid his decision making process.

(3) *Evaluation.* The program was evaluated in terms of usability and usefulness. Students from a design class developed an initial concept previously formalized, and presented one final solution in the form of a 3D model and a 1/8 scale model.

Overall, the results validate the interface design and encourage future improvements. The program had a good receptivity (most of the students used the program) and was easy to learn. As a design tool, the results showed that most of the students used ChairDNA as an exploration tool that, more than the limitations of the system, was the main driver of change of their initial ideas. The degree of completeness of the program is encouraging; although none of the participants was able to reproduce the initial concept with only the ChairDNA, the limitations concerned mostly the absence of the variables of the components and not the components themselves.

The experiment with the design students had a significant meaning to perceive the usefulness of the tool in a design process, and to gain important inputs to further work in debugging and improving the system. New usability tests will be made with other user targets (advanced design students and young Portuguese designers). The evaluation will consider a more controlled experience and the evaluation of the design solutions.

Acknowledgements. The authors would like to thank the students that participated in the evaluation of the tool, and to Mário Barros and António Leitão for their contributions to the tool development. This paper is part of a PhD research supported by the FCT (Fundação para a Ciência e Tecnologia) grant SFRH/BD/77927/2011, and by CIAUD (Centro de Investigação em Arquitectura Urbanismo e Design).

References

1. Knight, T.: The generation of hepplewhite-style chair-back designs. Environ. Plan. B Plan. Des. **7**, 227–238 (1980)
2. Barros, M., Duarte, J., Chaparro, B.: Thonet chair design grammar: a step towards the mass customization of furniture. In: Proceedings of the 14th International Conference on Computer Aided Architectural Design Futures, CAAD Futures 2011, Des Together, pp. 181–200 (2011)
3. Agarwal, M., Cagan, J.: A blend of different tastes: the language of coffeemakers. Environ. Plan. B Plan. Des. **25**, 205–226 (1998)
4. Pugliese, M., Cagan, J.: Capturing a rebel: modeling the Harley-Davidson brand through a motorcycle shape grammar. Res. Eng. Des. **13**, 139–156 (2002)
5. Hsiao, S.-W., Chen, C.-H.: A semantic and shape grammar based approach for product design. Des. Stud. **18**, 275–296 (1997)
6. Beirão, J.N., Duarte, J.P., Stouffs, R.: Creating specific grammars with generic grammars: towards flexible urban design. Nexus Netw. J. **13**, 73–111 (2011)
7. Vitra Design Museum: 100 Masterpieces from the vitra design museum collection. Vitra Design Museum (2013)
8. Design Museum: Fifty Chairs That Changed the World. Design Museum, London (2010)
9. Sibthorp, F., Quin, S.: Chairs: 20th-Century Classics. New Holland, London (2012)
10. Fiell, C., Fiell, P.: 1000 Chairs, 25th edn. Taschen, Köln (2005)
11. Parra, P.: Cadeiras de Design Nacional: 250 Anos a Sentar Portugal. Turismo do Alentejo - ERT, Évora (2013)
12. Marshall, M.N.: Sampling for qualitative research. Fam. Pract. **13**, 522–526 (1996)
13. Gruber, T.: A translation approach to portable ontology specifications. Knowl. Acquis. **5**, 199–220 (1993)
14. Stiny, G., Gips, J.: Shape grammars and the generative specification of painting and sculpture. In: Proceedings of IFIP Congress 1971 (1972)
15. Stiny, G., Mitchell, W.: The palladian gramar. Environ. Plan. B Plan. Des. **5**, 5–18 (1978)
16. Stiny, G.: Kindergarten grammars: designing with frobel's building gifts. Environ. Plan. B Plan. Des. **7**, 409–462 (1980)
17. Stiny, G.: Spatial relations and grammars. Environ. Plan. B Plan. Des. **9**, 113–114 (1982)
18. Stiny, G.: Weights Environ. Plan. B Plan. Des. **19**, 413–430 (1992)
19. Stiny, G.: Introduction to shape and shape grammars. Environ. Plan. B Plan. Des. **7**, 343–351 (1980)
20. Knight, T.: Shape grammars: six types. Environ. Plan. B Plan. Des. **26**, 15–31 (1999)
21. Knight, T.: Transformations of De Stijl art: the paintings of Georges Vantongerloo and Fritz Glarner. Environ. Plan. B Plan. Des. **16**, 51–98 (1989)
22. Chase, S.: Generative design tools for novice designers: issues for selection. Autom. Constr. **14**, 689–698 (2005)
23. Lopes, J., Leitão, A.: Portable generative design for CAD applications. In: ACADIA 11: Integration Through Computation, Calgary, Canada, pp. 196–203 (2011)

Author Index

Printed in the United States
By Bookmasters